ISBN: 9781313381673

Published by:
HardPress Publishing
8345 NW 66TH ST #2561
MIAMI FL 33166-2626

Email: info@hardpress.net
Web: http://www.hardpress.net

OLIN
F
74
D4
S54
1895
v.1

CORNELL UNIVERSITY
LIBRARIES
ITHACA, N. Y. 14583

JOHN M. OLIN
LIBRARY

George Sheldon

1636—POCUMTUCK—1886

A

HISTORY

OF

DEERFIELD,

MASSACHUSETTS:

THE TIMES WHEN AND THE PEOPLE BY WHOM IT WAS
SETTLED, UNSETTLED AND RESETTLED:

WITH A SPECIAL STUDY OF THE

INDIAN WARS

IN THE

CONNECTICUT VALLEY.

WITH GENEALOGIES.

BY

GEORGE SHELDON.

VOL. I.

DEERFIELD, MASS.: 1895.

Entered according to act of Congress, in the year 1895, by
GEORGE SHELDON,
In the Office of the Librarian of Congress, at Washington.

GREENFIELD, MASS:
PRESS OF E. A. HALL & CO.,
1895.

PREFACE.

In the first edition of this work, the Narrative closed with the Revolution, and the Genealogies contained only those families settled here before that date. The History is now continued to nearer the present time, but with less fullness. Failing health has prevented the necessary labor to continue the Genealogies in a satisfactory manner. Dependence has been had in that department upon such material as those interested in their own families have furnished in response to public solicitations. This will explain the presence or absence of particular families living here since the Revolution.

It is more than a quarter of a century since the work of collecting the facts given in these pages was begun. The time given to it would make many solid years. Had it not been a labor of love, it had ceased long ago. Setting forth the difficulties in the way, would give nothing new to the historical student and nothing of interest to the indifferent; so explanation is needless. I wish, however, to emphasize one of the *delights* attending these labors; this has been the uniform kindness and spirit of helpfulness shown by those having charge of the public records and books which I have had occasion to consult. To one and all of these I would tender my hearty thanks, but alas! many have passed the bounds of sight or sound. To name these men and women would be but to catalogue the officials at the State House, the Historical societies and great Libraries in Boston, Cambridge and Springfield; the Registers of Deeds and of Probate in the Counties of Essex, Middlesex, Norfolk, Suffolk, and the three River Counties, and also as well, the Town Clerks of Deerfield and the surrounding towns, who have held these offices during the last twenty-five years. Nor would I forget in my thanks the owners of the hundreds of garrets, closets and trunks which I have ransacked at will, or those kind friends who have given personal aid or sent corrections and additions to the first edition. While my limits forbid giving the names of all these, I must make a few exceptions to the silence. Without the free use of the manuscript Archives in the office of the Secretary of State, this work could not have been written. What is given in relation to the Captives of Feb. 29th, 1704, who remained in Canada, is mostly owing to the untiring researches of Miss C. Alice Baker among the manuscript Archives of Canada. The Massachusetts Historical Society has freely opened to me rich stores to be found nowhere else, and Dr. Samuel A. Green has been quick to give notice of any Deerfield items coming under his keen eyes.

In the earlier generations of New England genealogy, of course constant use has been made of the stupendous work of Savage; in the later generations unstinted aid was given by Rodney R. Field, James M. Crafts and William O. Taylor.

I wish here to associate the name of the lamented Martha G. Pratt with the first issue of this work, and that of Jennie M. Arms with the present. To their untiring zeal and patient helpfulness I am indebted. Finally, to the Pocumtuck Valley Memorial Association, under whose wing this child of my labor is now clothed in a more enduring garment, my heartiest and most grateful thanks are due and given.

My aim has been to write as far as may be from original sources of information; where this was possible I have taken nobody's say for it. The amount of manuscript matter available has been found to be surprisingly large. Old letters, diaries, records, &c., are coming to light every year, giving the later student that advantage over all others. If, in the light of these, I be found in some cases to have readjusted old facts, and thereby drawn new conclusions; if I be found to differ in some other points from accepted authorities, it is hoped good reasons for it have been given.

A careful study of the Indian relics found in our valley led to a deep interest in the people they represent, and I have been astonished at the amount of material found relating to the history of the Pocumtuck Indians. They were rarely mentioned by contemporaneous historians, and the Pocumtuck Confederacy seems to have been wholly unknown to them. The history here given has been chiefly culled from the records of the United Colonies, and the Documentary History of New York; tradition has been followed only when it harmonized with, or supplemented ascertained facts.

Particular attention has been given to the times of Philip's War, and I do not know where else can be found a more full and connected account of its events in the Connecticut Valley. Queen Anne's War, and other contests with the French and Indians have also been fully treated. As a matter of special interest, French official documents have been carefully searched for the underlying cause of particular raids on our frontiers; and the motive and the result are often given together. The real object of these incursions was never military conquest; the motive, when not purely for plunder, was always for political or religious effect.

As my treatment of the two myths connected with this region—the alleged appearance of Gen. Goffe as the deliverer of Hadley, and the romance of the Bell of St. Regis, may be found in other publications, they are very lightly touched upon in this work.

Deerfield, January, 1895. G. S.

TABLE OF CONTENTS.

CHAPTER I.
                                    Page.
Dedham Grant—Lady Armina—Apostle Eliot—Natick Indians—Indian Deeds—Town Street Laid Out. 1–22

CHAPTER II.
Topography—Local Names—Streams—Population—Graveyards. . 23–34

CHAPTER III.
First Settlement—Biographical Sketches. 35–48

CHAPTER IV.
Pocumtuck Indians—The Pocumtuck Confederacy—Agriculture—Indian Statescraft—War with Uncas—War with the Mohawks. . 49–70

CHAPTER V.
The Pocumtucks as Subjects of Massachusetts—Indian Relics—Indian Wars—Mohawk Raids—Indian Barns. 71–80

CHAPTER VI.
Philip's War—Character of Philip—Brookfield Burned—Fight at Wequamps—First Attack on Deerfield—Northfield Destroyed—Second Attack on Deerfield—Bloody Brook Massacre—Attack on Hadley—Attack on Springfield—Goffe the Regicide—Philip in the Winter of 1675-6—Philip at Squakheag—Attack on Northampton—Confederate Indians at Squakheag—Mrs. Mary Rowlandson—Canonchet—Indian Correspondence—Turners Falls Fight—Wells's Narrative—Atherton's Story—Attack on Hatfield—Mohawks in Philip's War. 81–178

CHAPTER VII.
Attempted Settlement in 1677—Wait and Jennings' Letters. . . 179–188

CHAPTER VIII.
Permanent Settlement—Ministry—Meetinghouses—Town Meeting—Town Officers—Revolution of 1688—Wapping 1685-90—Greenfield 1685-90. 189–219

CHAPTER IX.
King William's War—Attacks on Deerfield 1693; 1694; 1695; 1696. . 220–264

TABLE OF CONTENTS.   vii

CHAPTER X.

Common Field Fences—Stock—Mills—Roads—School Rates—Houses—
Home Industries—An Evening at Home. 265–282

CHAPTER XI.

Queen Anne's War—Capture of Deerfield Feb. 29th, 1704—Deerfield as
a Military Post—Redemption of the Captives—Stories of the Captives—Abigail Nims—Eunice Williams—Petty's Letter—Attack on
Deerfield 1709—Wright's Scout—Baker's Scout—Wood Land—John
Arms, a Captive. 283–384

CHAPTER XII.

Interval of Unquiet Peace—Clouds on the Eastern Frontier—French Intrigue. 385–392

CHAPTER XIII.

Father Rasle's War—Conference at Albany 1723—Conference at Boston
—Rev. Mr. Willard Killed—Fort Dummer—Indian Allies—Attack
in North Meadows—Connecticut Indians—Death of Father Rasle
—Scouting—Attack at Green River. 393–453

CHAPTER XIV.

Rev. John Williams and the Meetinghouse of 1729—The Bell—Death of
Mr. Williams—Slaves—Mr. Williams's Library—Rev. Jonathan
Ashley Settled—Town Clock—New Steeple—Shingling the Meetinghouse—Seating the Meetinghouse. 454–486

CHAPTER XV.

Agrarian Regulations—Proprietors of Pocumtuck—Grant of 1712—
Huntstown Line—Green River Laid Out—Shelburne Laid Out—
Turnip Yard—Conway Laid Out—Inner Commons. . . 487–511

CHAPTER XVI.

Land Grants—Fort Dummer—Corse's Journal—Indian Conference at
Deerfield—Conference at Fort Dummer—The Last Indian. . 512–528

CHAPTER XVII.

Old French War—Mr. Ashley's View of it—Cost of Living—Indian
Depredations on the North—Fort Massachusetts Captured—The
Bars Fight—Luce Bijah. 529–553

CHAPTER XVIII.

Raimbault, or St. Blein—Sergt. Hawks Escorts him to Canada—A Romantic Story—Sergt. Hawks's Journal—Capt. Melville's Scout—
Capt. Hobbs's Fight—Trouble Above Northfield—Fort Massachusetts Attacked. 554–569

TABLE OF CONTENTS.

CHAPTER XIX.

Municipal Affairs — Sequestered Land—Greenfield Set Off—Judicial Affairs—Mills—Hard Times—Deer—The Fleet—Sugar Loaf People—Conway Set Off—Shelburne Set Off—Roads—Prices of Labor and Produce. 570–593

CHAPTER XX.

Homesteads on the Old Street—Farm Lands. 594–627

CHAPTER XXI.

The Last French War—Young Washington—Frontier Forts—Capture of Mrs. Johnson—Attack at Charlemont—Attack on Hinsdale's Fort—Death of Braddock—Fort Edward—Bloody Morning Scout—Battle of Lake George—Death of Col. Williams—Attack at Greenfield—More Forts at Deerfield—Colrain Forts—Massacre at Fort William Henry—Alarm in Connecticut Valley—Abercrombie Defeated—Louisburg Captured—Wolfe and Montcalm—Destruction of St. Francis—Pitt and Amherst—Merriman's Journal—Downfall of Canada—Quaker and Puritan—A Real Estate Transaction—The Indian Question. 628–672

ERRATA AND ADDITIONS.

Read at the bottom of page 91, "Stephen Greenleaf wounded Aug. 25, 1675."
Sewell's Diary.

Page 172. Twelfth line from bottom, for *Samuel*, read Daniel.

Page 301. Note, "March, 1703-4, about midnight, the French and Indians set upon Deerfield, burnt 17 houses, killed above 50 persons, Captivated upwards of 90, amongst wch Mr Williams y^r minister." *Observable Providences*—from the Journal of Rev. John Pike, of Dover, Me., 1682-1709.

Page 602. Third line from top, for *Bradford* read Baker.

Page 623. Nineteenth line from bottom, for 1866 read 1686.

HISTORY OF DEERFIELD.

CHAPTER I.

DEDHAM GRANT AND INDIAN DEEDS.

"The Renowned Noble Lady Armina," amid the luxuries of her ancestral hall in old Lincolnshire, meditating upon the lost condition of the heathen in the New World, putting up her prayers and sending her gold across the seas for their redemption, represents a deeply seated sentiment of her time. It was her aim, that the occupancy of New England should result not only in the accumulation of earthly riches by the adventurers, but should redound to the glory of God in a large harvest of souls through the conversion of its barbarian inhabitants. Capt. George Weymouth, a historian of the times, active in promoting the settlement of our shores, testifies that the main end of all these undertakings was to plant the gospel in these dark regions of America.

The sagacious Capt. John Smith, warrior and trader, tired with his rough experience in Virginia, and looking to the settlement of new colonies as fields for profitable commerce, declares that he is "not so simple to thinke that any other motiue than wealth will euer erect there a commonweale," but hopes that "gaine will make them affect that which Religion, Charity, and the Common Good cannot," and he shrewdly urges the grasping Prince Charles to send settlers to this coast, pointing out a way in which he could serve both God and mammon at the same time. "Nothing," he says, "could be more agreeable to God than to seeke to conuert these poore Saluages to know Christ and humanitie, whose labours there with discresion will triple requite thy charge and paines." In the closing paragraph of this message Capt. Smith struck a theme which caught the popular ear, and sent hosts of adventurers across the wide waters, seeking the gold of another Mexico or Peru.

As to the result, had the two elements here indicated been left undisturbed, save by each other, it is idle to speculate. With the Mayflower, came ideas and purposes, before which all the others were dwarfed and subordinated. It was these that,—

> "Conquered wood and savage, frost and flame,
> And made us what we are."

With the missionary spirit of the Lady Armina, however, the Pocumtuck Valley is directly and intimately connected.

Her bounty expended in behalf of the Natick Indians, in a great degree determined the time and manner of the settlement of Deerfield.

The apostle Eliot, being filled with zeal for the conversion of the natives, learned their language and devoted himself to their instruction in Christian doctrines. Very soon he perceived that his teaching could have little effect so long as the Indians continued their national manner of living—that they must be civilized before they could be Christianized. He therefore bent his energies to the task of collecting the roving savages into permanent settlements, where he could instruct them in the "arts of civilitie," and where their children could be taught in schools. Eliot's first attempt to form an Indian town was at Nonantum Hill, in Newton. This proved a failure, mainly, as he thought, on account of its proximity to Boston; finding, like most missionaries, the example of a so-called Christian community unfavorable to making proselytes from heathenism to Christianity. About this time the General Court encouraged Mr. Eliot to continue his labors, and at his motion passed laws recognizing, in a manner, the Indian title in the land, and placing the natives in many respects on an equal footing with the colonists.

For a second trial, Eliot pitched upon Natick, sixteen miles west of Boston, where in 1651 the General Court set apart two thousand acres for an Indian plantation, and the £20 per annum, given by the Lady Armina, was placed at his disposal. Here the "Praying Indians" were collected, civil government established, and a church organized. The tract thus occupied proved to be territory belonging to Dedham, and for twelve years there was much trouble and litigation between the inhabitants of that town and the settlers at Natick. Both parties repeatedly appealed to the judicial and legislative authorities for redress. At length, on the first of May, 1662, the General Court decided,—

"That for a finale issue of the controuersy betweene the towne of Dedhame & some particular inhabitants of sd towne & the Indians, the Court at Naticke having considered the pleas & evidences presented by both partes, and finding that although the legall right of Dedham thereto cannot in justice be denyed, yet such haue binn the encouragement of the Indians in their improvements thereof, the w^{ch}, added to their native right, wch cannot, in strict justice, be vtterly extinct, doe therefore order, that the Indians be not dispossessed of such land as they at present are possessed of there, but that the same, wth convenient accommodations for wood & timber, & highwayes thereto, be set out & bounded by Mr. Thomas Danforth, Mr. Wm. Parkes, Mr. Ephraim Child, Mr. Edw. Jackson, or any three of them, who are hereby appointed a Committee to execute this order, and that the damages thereby susteined by Dedham, together wth the charges expended in suite about the same, be also considered & determined by sd Committee & such allowance made them out of Naticke, lands or others yet lying in common, as they shall judge equal, & apoint making report to this Court the matter of charge, that so the Court may determine where to lay the same or any part thereof. Y^e returne of ye Committee to remajne on file. May, 1663."

A report from this Committee was acted upon June 2, 1663, and,—

"For a finale issue of the case betweene Dedham & Natick, the Court judgeth meete to graunt Dedham eight thousand acres of land in any convenient place or places, not exceeding two, where it cann be found free from former graunts, provided Dedham accept this offer."

The terms being satisfactory to that town, the Court appointed, Oct., 1663, Ens. John Everard and Jona. Danforth to "lay out the same according to the graunt." Having secured a grant, the question was considered at a town meeting in Dedham, Jan. 1, 1663-4, "whether to sell their graunt," or "be at any further charge about seeking out land to take satisfaction in." By a vote of the town, the matter was "left over in the hands of the Selectmen." Under this action Henry Dwight was sent to explore the "Chestnut Country." On his return he reported good land, but hard to bring under cultivation. The location of the "chestnut country" is unknown, but as only "9 shilling were allowed for himself and horse" for the trip, it could not have been far away. At another meeting, "after lecture," Sep. 21, 1664, John Fairbanks reported having heard, through Goodman Prescott of

Lancaster, of a suitable tract near that town, Fairbanks and Lieut. Joshua Fisher were directed to go to Sudbury, and after consulting Ens. Noyes about the matter, to "proceed to Lancaster and to the place, and view the same, or to return, as they judge best." The view was had, and Nov. 6th, a report was made that the tract was already "so entered upon by several farms that it is altogether incapable of supply to us." In the meanwhile the Selectmen had not been idle. At the same meeting where the above report was made, they announced that,—

"Haueing heard of a considerable Tract of good Land that might be answerable to the Town's expectation, about 12 or 14 miles from Hadley, and not vnderstanding of any other place to be founde worth acceptance, thinke it meet, in the behalfe of the Towne to provide that that 8000 Acres may be chosen and layed out to sattisfie that grant ther, wth all conueanient speed, before any other Grantee enter upon it and p^{r}uent vs, and to that end doe nominate apoint empower and entrust Lieft Fisher, Tymo: Dwight, Ensign Fisher, Edw: Richards, Antho: Fisher, Serg^t Ellice, Serg^t Fuller, & Isaac Bullard, or any 4 of them whereof Lieft: Fisher is to be one to repayer to the place mentioned, and vpon view by the concurrance of the major pt of the 4 that shall attend that seruice to make choice and laye out the Land above mentioned according as to their best discretion shall be best for the Towne and proportionable to the grant of the Court in that case made, and we promise to each of these 4 men one hundreth Acres of Land in full satisfaction for thier paynes to be indifferently layed out to them, out of the grante aforesaid onely to Lieft Fisher for the vse of his Arte we in the behalfe of the Towne, promise such other sattisfaction as shall be judged equall, or in case the Town shall rather chuse to paye all these 4 men in other paym^t then in Land, then we engage equall & just satisfaction according to the nature & charge of the worke."

This action was satisfactory to the town; the same board was reelected at the next meeting, and on the,—

"2—11—64 [Jan. 2, 1664-5.] Vpon the Question whether the Towne would proceed and laye out the 8000 Acres Granted by the Court in sattisfaction for the Land posessed at Naticke by the Indians wthin our Towne at that place forementioned neere Hadly, they answer by voate affirmatiuely.

Further it is by voate declared that they doe leaue the further manageinge of the whole case about layeing out the Land aboue said to the selectmen this daye to be chosen who are entrusted and empowered to act therein in behalfe of the Towne according to their best discretion.

March 5, 1664-5. In order to the accomplishm^t and settling the case concerning the grante of the 8000 acres due to the Towne, the care, trust and power whereof was left to the selectmen in p^{r}sent, being it is this daye agreed to tender to Lieft: Fisher as artist in that worke and as one of the Committee for effecting the Layeing out the said grante in the place proposed to be about 12 or 14 miles more or lesse from Hadley 150 acres of Land, and Tenn shillings in countrey payem^t for euery daye he shall measure and to each of the other 3 persons being of the persons formerly named 150 acres, and liberty is giuen them to laye those their grants together by some one side or end of that tract indifferently takeing vpland and meadowe in proportion to the proportion of each sort of such Land in the whole tract.

March 20, 1664–5. Vpon further consideration of effecting the layeing out the 8000 Acres aboue mentioned, Lieft Fisher declaring his disaceptance of w^t was aboue tendered him in satisfaction for his paynes therein as artist, and his peremptory demaund being 300 acres, it is consented vnto provided he allso drawe for the Towne true and sufficient platt of that tract and Edw: Richards, Antho: Fisher Junio^r, and Tymo: Dwight, accept of the payem^t formerly tendered, vizt 150 achers to each of them, all to be layed out as is aboue exp^{r}ssed, or in case Tymo: Dwight shall be any way hindered that he cannot attend that seruice, then he promise to furnish Serg^t Richard Ellice wth a horse fitt for that occasion, who accept thereof and promise to vndertake the worke instead of the said Tymothie and they promise to vndertake the Journey for this end the daye after Election daye at Boston next ensueing, or the second daye of the weeke next following the daye aforesaid at furthest.

May 22, 1665, [the Selectmen] Assemb: in the morning to receaue the returne of the Comittee deputed to lay out the 8000 Acres of Land for the Towne.

The Comittee aforesaid doe enforme that they haue layed out all the grante of 8000 acres aforesaid, in land as they Judg conueanient in quallitie and scituation, for the accomadacion of a plantation and being by their estemation, about 10 miles distant from Hadly, the more particular description where of they shall giue account of at some other conueanient time."

On the 11th of October a plan of the grant was laid before the General Court, with the following report:—

"This tract of land, conteyning eight thousand acres, being layd out according to this plott given in to Court & remayning on file, beginning att A. & so running to L. by the ffoote of a mountejne south & by west two miles forty sixe rod; from L to K, along the same mounteine fiue miles forty rods south & by east two degrees easterly; From K to I upon a streight ljne two miles & a halff west halff a point southerly; From H to I, up on a streight line south, halfe a point easterly, fower miles; ffrom G to H, southwest fowr degrees, westerly three hundred & sixty two rod; ffrom E [F?] to G, S. S. east three degrees southerly, one hundred sixty rod; from E to F south three degrees southerly, eighty eight rod: from D to E southwest one hundred and eight rod: from C to D south east eighty rod; ffrom B to C south and by west three degrees westerly, five hundred & eighty rod; from A to B west north west two degrees westerly, one mile twenty rod. This tract of land is lajd out at a place called Pecumptick, to answer the grant of the honored Generall Court made to Dedham for lands at Natick, which the Indians are setled vpon by the Courts order, it lyinge northward from Hadley about tenn or twelue miles. Layd out as abouesajd May, 1665,   By me,   JOSHUA FISHER.

The Court allows & approoues of this returne, provided they make a towne of it, to majntejne the ordinances of Christ there once wthin five yeares, & that it interfere not wth Maj^r Genll Dennison & Hadley grant."

The Colonial Government having thus taken two thousand acres from Dedham for the benefit of the Natick Indians, and given in exchange eight thousand acres belonging to the Pocumtuck Indians, the town of Dedham now took steps to buy the same of the native owners. June 4, 1666, a committee was authorized to "employ the Worshful Col. Pynchon, to buy the Indian title *in* the 8000 acres." Pynchon was a fur trader of Springfield, well acquainted with the Pocumtucks, and had before been employed in a like service by Northampton and Hadley:—

"Whereas it apeere that some Indians are like to clayme a Title in the foresaid [ ] which in equitie would be cleered, the selectmen vnderstanding that the worpfull [ ] John Pinchion is acquainted wth those Indians so claymeing it is therefore, or [ ] that Ensi: Danll: Fisher, and Elea: Lusher be desired, and are heereby deputed and empowered to treat with the said Capt Pinchion, and empower him to contract wth those said Indians for the buyeing out of all thier Right or clayme in the p^{r}mises and allso with any other Indians that may haue a true Right made apeere there and what shall be so concluded the Towne shall be engaged to make good.

Dec. 27, 1665. Vpon treaty wth Tymothie Dwight in refference to furthering the erecting a plantation at pocomptucke according to the condicion of the Generall Court, he tender, that on condicion that a plantation be there effectually settled as aforesaid, if the Towne will paye him five pounds for his Journey, charges and seruice there, 2£ being in money and 3£ in Corne and Cattell he will laye down and resigne all his clayme to the Land engaged to him ther by his former agreem^t wth the select men.

And vpon the like treaty with Lieft Fisher, he allso vpon the same condicion with Tymothie Dwight, tender that if the Towne will paye him Tenn pounds for all his charge and seruice in refference to Pocompticke he will likewise release his clayme to the 300 acres, engaged to him provided the Tenn pounds be payed 4£ in money and six pounds in Corne and Cattell this is tendered upon condicion that the agreem^t to effect it as aboue said be at the next ensueing Genrall Towne meeting and the worke thereof be set in a meet waye for proceeding therein.

Jan. 22, 1665–6. At a Generall meeting of the Towne for the further consideration of the settling a plantation at pocumpatuck.

ACTION TO SECURE TITLE.

It is by generall voate concluded that each propriators Lands there shall paye Annually towards the mayntenance of an orthodoxe ministry there 2ˢ for each Cow Common that he shall keepe in his own hand whether he shall be liueing there or at Dedham and all others that holde any pt of the 8000 acres in proprietie vpon any other account besides kowe Commons shall paye proportionable except such Lands as shall be layed out for the accomadacion of teaching Church officers there.

And it is allso further concluded that if any propriator of Lands or interests ther doe tender his Rights at the price that shall be by generall voate set and no buyer doe so accept it then the persons Inhabiting there shall take his Rights at that price or discharge him of the aforesaid payem^t to the ministery.

It is allso further agreed and concluded that each propriator shall lay down his kow Common Rights there at that price that by the majo^r pt of proprieties shall be agreed vpon."

The proprietors at this time were mostly Dedham men who had no intention of removing to the new settlement, and this vote would naturally work hardship to settlers, if it did not stop emigration entirely, and so the grant would be forfeited. It does not appear to have been enforced:—

"June 27, 1666. Haueing vnderstood that the worp^{full} Capt Pincheon vpon treaty wth the Indians about the purchase of the Indian Title *in* the 8000 acres layed out for this Town at Pocumpatucke and haue made a contract with them accordingly and that he aduised the Town of Dedham to make entery therevpon, this p^{s}sent summer which, vpon consideration we conceaue may be of good vse thereby to take posession, doe accordingly order deput and empower Lieft Fisher, Ensigne Fisher and Tymothy Dwight to take care thereof that such an enterey be made and such posession be taken in the behalfe and to the vse of the Towne in due season as in thier discretion may be most effectuall and safe for the ensureing our Title."

Early in the year 1667, the Selectmen sent John Gay, Robert Ware and Nathaniel Fisher to take further observations of their far off possessions. On the 6th of June the town,—

"After consideration of the case respecting Pocompticke and the Information brought by those bretheren lately vpon the place, by deputation of the Selectmen doe desire and depute them, by themselues or some of themselues, as they shall thinke meete to make reporte to the Inhabitants of the Towne in publike the next Lecture day after Lecture for the sattisfaction of the Towne in generall and for their consideration in refference to the future.

Allso that the Towne be made acquainted with the disbursm^{ts} of the Worp^{full} Capt Pinchion in purchasing the Indians Right at Pocompticke at the request of the selectmen in the behalfe of the Towne who haue declared that he haue allready layed out about 40£

and is yet in prosecution of compleating that worke, and by word and writing haue exp^rssed his desire to be reimbursed, the payem^t he desire is money, wheat and porke, and we would desire the Town to remember and gratifie his paynes."

The following deed was probably produced as evidence of the purchase and claim:—

These presents Testifie That Chauk alias Chaque ye Sachem of Pacomtuck for good and valuable Considerations him there vnto moving, hath Given granted Bargained & sold, & by these presents doth (for himself and his brother Wapahoale) fully clearly & absolutely give grant Bargain & sell vnto Capt John Pynchon of Springfield for ye vse & behoofe of Major Eleazer Lusher & Ensign Daniel ffisher & other English of Dedham their associates & successors & to them & their heires for ever Certaine persels of Land at Pacomtuck on ye further side or vpper side or North side of Pacomtuck river, that is to say beginning a little above where Pukcommeagon river runs into Pacomtuck river and so a little way vp Puckommeag river & then leaving Puckcomeagon river runs off to ye hill Sunsick westward: All ye land from ye hill Sunsick on westward, downe ye River Pacomtuck eastward below Nayyocossick to Pochewee, neare ye Mouth of Puckcomeagon river, wch persells of Land are called Nayyocossick, Tomholissick, Masquomcossick, vssowwack Wusqviawwag & so to Sunsick hill, or by what ever other Names ye sd Land is or may be called: All ye aforedescribed Tract of Land, being called by several names as aforesd viz. Nayyocossick Tomholissick Masquomcossick vssowwack Wusqviwawag & Sunsick, or by what ever names it maybe called, Togither wth the Trees, waters, meadows, woods, Brooke, vpland, stone, proffits, comoditys & advantages thereoff & there vnto belonging or in any wise appertaining, the aforesd Major Eleazer Lusher & Ensign Danl ffisher of Dedham, theire Associates & successors, & their Heires are to Have Hold & Injoy & that forever, only the sd Chauk alias Chaque doth reserve Liberty of fishing for ye Indians in ye Rivers or waters & free Liberty to hunt Deere or other Wild creatures & to gather Walnuts chestnuts and other nuts things &c on ye commons: And the sd Chaque doth hereby covenant & promise to & wth ye sd Maj Eleazer Lusher & Danl ffisher, That he will saue ye sd Major Lusher & Danl ffisher, theire Associates & theire Heires & assignes, Harmless of & from all manner of Claimes of any person or persons Lawfully claiming any right Title or Interest in any of ye sd lands hereby Sold or in any part or parsell thereof & will Defend the same from any molestation or Incumbrance by Indians otherwise than as before reserved, In witness whereoff the sd Chaqve hath herevnto set his hand this 24th ffebr 1666–7   The marke of ⊓ CHAQVE

In presence of
      Jo^n Pynchon Ju^r:
Weqvanock an Indian witness his V marke, who helped ye Sachem in making ye Bargaine

The day aforementioned Chaqve acknowledged this Instrum^t to be his act & Deed
 Before me   JOHN PYNCHON, Asist

COW COMMONS.

[June 12, 1667.] "Vpon further consideration of takeing posession at the 8000 Acres, at pocomptatucke, and the further satisfaction to be brought to the Towne in refference to the Capacitie of the place to be a plantation, and other considerations of that nature, it is at p^rsent by voate resolued to call some other meet persons to Joyne with the Committee already deputed to take posession of the said place, & to take further viewe of what may concerne the same, and make returne to the selectmen   The persons nowe deputed as abouesaide
John Gaye Senr, Nath Coalburn Senr, Tho: Fuller, W^m: Averey, Robt: Ware Nath: Fisher"

Oct. 2, 1667, a rate was laid to raise funds for settling with Pynchon, payable in "specie, one fourth to be abated if payed in money." This rate amounted to £115-4-8. Sixty eight persons were assessed; among these were—

Maj^r Genll Leaverett	£ 3—8—8
Mr Joh: Allen	4—9—8
Lieft Josh: Fisher	10—6—0
Tymo: Dwight	10-18—5

I doubt if this tax was ever collected.

On a Country Rate at Dedham, at this time, ninety-two names were on the list, so it appears twenty-four proprietors had already sold out their rights at Pocumtuck.

Down to this date the meetings for action about the grant had been *town* meetings, as each voter in town held certain rights there; but so soon as taxes began to be imposed the shares rapidly changed owners, often falling into the hands of speculators, and all subsequent action was at *Proprietors'* meetings.

No one, however, was allowed to sell without the approval of the Proprietors. By a vote Aug. 26, 1668, "Left Fisher had leave to sell to John Stebbins of Northampton, his rights at paucomtucke, or a part of them." Similar votes were common.

In 1659 a large proportion of the territory of Dedham was held by the inhabitants in common. That year a plan was adopted for dividing this land, or any other they might acquire among the individuals. The apportionment was based partly on the tax list and partly on the number of cattle running on the commons. Each separate tract was divided into 522 shares, or "common rights," of which, under a somewhat arbitrary rule, each proprietor was to have his proper proportion. These shares were called "cow commons."

The "8000 acres Grant" at Pocumtuck was thus held by Dedham people in proportion to the "cow commons" owned at home. For many years the land here was bought and sold by the "cow commons." Fractions were reckoned by "sheep or goat commons," five of which equalled one "cow common."

Oct. 28, 1667, Pynchon bought of Rev. John Allen six cow commons and two sheep commons. Two days later Governor Leverett, for "6£ current money of N. E., and Several barrels of Tar" sold Pynchon all his "right and title to lands at a place usually called Pocumtuck, being part of the 8000 acres, * * * * 150 acres which I bought of Anthony Fisher of Dorchester, one part whereof being meadows containing 38 acres more or less, is already laid out between land of Lieut. Joshua Fisher, north & land Timothy Dwight South. * * * More, all the right and title belonging to 6 cow commons & 2 sheep commons, also my right and interest to 6 cow commons which I lately bought of James Draper of Dedham, 5 of them being his proper share—the other one he bought of Wm. Mackenney, who had it of Thomas Jordan, all of Dedham." Pynchon had previously bought of Joshua Fisher 16 cow commons and was now one of the largest owners in the grant.

Dec. 27, 1667. The Selectmen, having the general oversight of the Dedham Grant, suggested :—

"That the Towne may consider that the time p^{r}fixt by the Generall Court for the planting a Towne at Pocompticke doe shorten and it wer good to resolue what the Towne will doe in that respect and that if it be intended to emproue it according to the grante that then it might be put into some way conduceing thereto."

In the summer of 1667 Pynchon concluded his purchases of the Indians at Pocumtuck, obtaining three more deeds, one of which is lost, the others may be found below. It has been found impossible so far to locate the tracts conveyed by the Pynchon deeds. "Tomholissick" was covered by two of them. From the fact that they were witnessed by two young children of Pynchon it is evident that they were drawn and executed at Springfield, and it is more than probable that they were written from ill understood descriptions, or rude maps made by the Indians for Mr. Pynchon, and that the grantees themselves had little knowledge of what they were buying. There appear to be discrepancies and contradictions in description and point of compass, which could hardly occur had the writer of the deeds been on the ground. It is probable that as the Indian tongue becomes better understood, the names of the various tracts will assist in fixing their location, for every place name is descriptive of the locality to which it is applied :—

These presents Testifie that Milkeanaway alias Masseamet (ye Indian, owner of certaine Lands at Pacumtuck) Hath Demised Granted Bargained & sold vnto John Pynchon of Springfield for ye vse & behoofe of Major Eleazer Lusher & Daniell ffisher of Dedham & their associates & by these presents Doth demise Grant Bargain & sell vnto ye sd Maojor Eleazer Lusher Daniell Fisher & theire Associates & to theire heirs & assigns forever, All & singular the sd Milkeanaway alias Masseamet, his Lands at Pacumtuck on ye south or Southeast side of Pacumtuck River, wch lands are called Pojassick weqvunckcaug, ManePacossick & Southward to ye hills Pemamachuwatunch, or by whatever other names the sd lands are called, even all ye land from Mantahelant (wch wuttawolunncksin Sold to Mr. Pynchon) vp to Scowockcuck & so off to Qvinetticot River to Mattampawsh to ye Land Mr. Pynchon bought of Wuttawolunncksin togithir wth all ye woods Trees waters wet meadows profits & comoditys whatsoever to ye sd Land belonging, or any wise appertaining, only ye sd Indian reserves to himselfe Liberty for fishing, otherwise all the sd Tract of land the aforesd Major Eleazer Lusher, Danl ffisher & theire associates & their heires and assignes, are to haue hold & Injoy & that forever: both ye profits and appurtenances therevnto belonging: And the sd Masseamet alias Milkeanaway doth hereby covent & promise to save ye sd Major Lusher & Danl ffisher & theire Associates harmless from all manner of claime of any person Lawfully claiming any interest or right in any of ye Land hereby sold. In witness whereoff the sd Masseamet alias Milkenaway hath herevnto set his hand & seale this 13th of June 1667.

The marke of
MASSEAMET { Seal. }
Alias MILKENAWAY

Subscribed Sealed & dlid in ye presence off William Warriner John Pynchon Junr Amy Pynchon

June ye 13th 1667 Masseamet alias Milkeanaway did owne & acknowledge this writing to be his act & Deed, resigneing vp & releasing all his right Title & interest in ye lands abovesd .

Before me:
JOHN PVNCHON Asist

These presents testifie that Ahimunquat alias Mequinnichall of Pacomtuck Hath Demised Granted Bargained & Sold, And by these presents doth Demise Grant Bargain & sell vnto Major Eleazer Lusher & Daniell ffisher of Dedham their Associates & theire heires & assigns for ever. All the sd Ahimunquat, alias Mequinnitchall his lands at Pacomtuck, both on ye South or Southeast side of Pocomtuck River called weshatchowmesit & on ye North or Norwest side of ye sd River, called Tomholisick: the sd parcelles of Land called Tomholisick & weshatchowmesit from ye brooke downe ye River vp to Sunsick & bounded by ye Land wch Masseamet hath already sold, or by whatever other Names y^u sd Lands are called even all ye Land belonging to ye sd Ahimunquat alias Mequinitchall & to his Brother Kunckkeasacod togith^r wth all Tree waters profits & Comoditys whatsoever to ye sd Land belonging or anyways appertaining: The aforesd Major Eleazer Lusher Danl ffisher & theire Associates & theire heires & assigns are to haue hold & injoy & that for ever, wth all ye profits & appurtenances thereunto belonging. And ye sd Ahimunquat alias Mequinnitchall doth hereby covenant & promise to save ye sd Major Eleazer Lusher Danl ffisher theire Associates & theire heires harmless from all manner of claime of any person or persons lawfully claiming any right or interest in any of ye Land hereby Sold In witness whereoff the sd Ahimunquat alias Mequinnitchall hath herevnto Set his hand & seal, this 22 of July 1667.

The marke of AHIMUNQUAT **X**
Alias Mequinnitchall

Subscribed Sealed & dlid in ye presence off Amy Pynchon John Pynchon Jr

The marke of Grin ɯ neachchue Brother to Mequinnitchall, who Received pt of ye Pay, *viz.* 20. fadam: & approved of the Sale of ye Land: Mequinnitchall, alias Ahimunquat, did owne & acknowledge this writing abovesd, to be his act & deed, this present 22th of July 1667   Before me   JOHN PYNCHON, Asist

Another deed, perhaps the first given, and probably from Wuttawolunskin, has not yet been found.

By these deeds it appears that a few of the Pocumtucks were alive to claim and sell these lands. The tribe had been nearly all destroyed by Mohawks some years before; and where "Chauk, Sachem of Pocomtuck," obtained his title and authority, does not appear. He is not heard of before or after this transaction; nor are the names of the other grantors to be found elsewhere. These Indians were probably hangers on about the settlements on the river below. Chauk may have been put in authority by the English, pursuant to a policy to be noted hereafter.

About this time events were transpiring at Pocumtuck which called for immediate action. With the energy of a born pioneer, Samuel Hinsdale had actually taken possession, and his plowshare had already turned up the virgin soil. Born about 1642, he with his father, Robert Hinsdale of Dedham, removed in youth to Medford, married at seventeen, and soon after becoming of age, joined the settlers at Hadley. He invested largely in the Dedham grant, and becoming impatient with the delay in settling, he made a bold strike for a home, where he could place his young family. He must be considered the first settler here, and his son Mehuman was the first white man born on the territory:—

"May 18, 1669. Samuell Hinsdell of Hadley in the Countie of Hampshir haucing purchased some propriety in Pocumptucke in the Land Granted and layd out to the Inhabitants of Dedham, and made emprouem^t by ploughing Lande there, came this daye to the selcct men, and gaue account of the reasons of his so doeing, and demaunded the layeing out of the Rights he had so purchased of one of the Inhabitants of Dedham that he might settle himselfe vpon it and proceed in emprouem^t thereof for his owne supplye, or if it could not be yet layed out, that then some smale parcell of vpland might be granted and layed out to build an house vpon.

To which we answer, that we see not cause to forbid him seing himselfe is content to beare the ventur of the place wher he make emprouem^r, but it not being in our power to doe what he demaunde herein we thinke meet to doe what in vs lyes, to moue the propriators to promote, the layeing out each Inhabitants Right ther, and to that end that the Lotts may be p^{r}pard and drawen, that some better rule may be had for euery propriator to knowe where about his owne Interrest lyes and that in the first optunitie."

Sept. 24, 1669, four acres at Dedham were granted Lieut. Fisher "to pay him for his last journey to Paucumptucke," and another lot was soon after granted Sergeant Fuller for the same service. Probably as a result of the conference of the Selectmen with Samuel Hinsdale these men had been sent to Pocumtuck to note the progress of events and report plans for action. They doubtless brought back three more Indian deeds from Pynchon, for, Sept. 24, 1669, Maj. Eleazer Lusher reports them to be in his possession:—

[At a meeting of the Selectmen Sept. 24, 1669.] "Elea: Lusher this day p^{r}sent seuerall Deeds of Sale from the Indians propriators at Paucomticke procured by Capt John Pinchon Esqr allso giueing account of the state of that affayre, respecting the Towne and allso enforming that the said m^r Pinchion expect his payem^t in money at the next session of the Generall Court in october of which payem^t he giues an account how it arise, where vpon it is agreed to call a generall meeteing of the propriators for further resolution heerein the 4 day of the next weeke being 29 instant, at 9 in the morning"

Sept. 29, 1669. At a generall meeting of the propriators of land at Pawcomptucke called together to order payem^t to Capt Pincheon for the purchase of the Indians rights there

It is by voate agreed that a new Rate for that payem^t shall be forthwith drawen by the Select men, assessing each propriato^r ther at so much vpon each Cowe Common there, to be payed in money, as may pay the 96£ 10^s due vpon account to Capt Pinchion or as neere that just summe as it may conueaniently be cast vp.

The Rate for the payem^t of Capt Pincheon 96£–10^s for the pur-

DEDHAM GRANT AND INDIAN DEEDS.

chase of the Indian Rights at Pawcomptucke is this daye made to be forthwith Leauied in money by the Constable euery Cow Common being asessed at 3ˢ, 4ᵈ, which is 10ˢ short of what is nowe due, and some Rights yet to be purchased is afterward to be payed for in this Rate the Lands granted to particular persons, called the Farmes is Rated at 54 Cow Commons, the number of acres in those grants vpon account coming to so much, allwayes to be vnderstood, that those Lands are in the same capacitie in allowance of Land for high wayes and the like occasions as other Lands there doe, this Rate is to be leauied of the seuerall Grantees named, or thier heyers, Administratoʳˢ, Executoʳˢ or assignes.

	£ s d			£ s d
mʳ Joh. Allin	2 8 8		Joh: Dwight	2 0 8
Eldʳ Joh. Hunting	1 10 0		The Church Lott	1 6 8
Elea. Lusher	1 10 8		Ensign Chickering	2 19 4
Deac Hen Chickering	1 8 8		Hen. Phillips	1 10 0
Deac. Nath Aldus	0 16 8		Lieft Josh: Fisher	2 0 0
Antho: Fisher Sen	1 6 4		Jonath. Farbanke Senʳ	1 6 8
Joh: Kingsbery Senʳ	1 14 0		Pet: Woodward Senʳ	1 14 0
Joh: Luson	1 3 4		Josep: Kingsbery	1 11 4
Joh: Haward	1 6 8		Wm: Bullard	0 17 4
Joh. Eaton	1 8 0		Antho. Hubert	0 10 0
Rich: Euered	1 14 0		Joh: Mason	0 15 4
Nath Coleburn	1 17 4		Ralp: Daye	0 18 0
Robt Mason	0 10 0		Hen: Wilson	1 2 0
Joh: Gaye	1 18 0		Joh. Bacon	1 5 4
Hen: Smyth	0 10 0		Edw: Hawes	1 0 8
Ens. Dan: Fisher	1 8 0		Josh: Kent	0 14 0
Geo: Farbanke	1 6 0		Rich: Ellice	0 16 8
Sergᵗ Averey	1 0 8		Robt. Onion	0 10 0
Edw: Richards	2 1 4		Tymo Dwight	1 12 0
Lamb: Genery	1 0 0		Josep: Ellice	0 13 4
Christo: Smyth	1 10 8		Ralp: Freman	0 10 0
Nath: Whiteing	1 10 0		Joh: Rice	0 7 4
Theo: Fraery	1 3 4		Dan: Pond	0 14 8
Joh: Farbanke	0 18 0		Hen: Wight	1 4 0
Sam: Judson	1 16 8		Cornell: Fisher	0 16 8
Tho: Hering	1 0 0		Jonath: Farbanke Junʳ	0 12 8
Rich: Wheeler	1 8 0		Jam: Fales	0 10 0
Joh. Farington.	1 10 8		Joh: Houghton	0 10 0
Joh. Aldus	0 19 4		Jam: Draper	0 16 8
Tho: Fuller	1 10 8		Jam: Thorpe	0 10 0
Tho: Payne	1 0 0		Isaac Bullard	0 18 0
Robt: Ware	1 3 4		Ben: Bullard	0 6 8
Antho: Fisher Jun	1 1 4		Sam: Fisher	0 6 8
Thwa: Strickland	0 13 4		Joh. Newton	0 0 8
Robt: Fuller	1 3 4		Tho: Wight Senʳ	0 2 0
Tho. Metcalfe	0 10 0		Nath Bullard	0 2 0
Michaell Metcalfe	1 4 8		Tho: Fisher	0 0 8
Nath Fisher	1 0 0		Farme Lands	
Tho: Battely	1 5 4		Lieft Fisher	3 12 0
Tho: Jordan	0 15 4		Edw: Richards	1 16 0
Joh. Guilde	0 17 4		Tymo: Dwight	1 16 0
Andr: Duein	0 16 8		Antho: Fisher	1 16 0
Samll. Milles	0 16 8			"

"Jan. 1, 1669–70, the Selectmen proposed to the town whether Robt Hinsdell shall be accepted to be a purchaser of Lande at Paucomptucke or not."

[At a General Meeting Jany. 3, 1669–70.] "It is by voate, ordered that the answer to the question concerning Robert Hinsdell be delayed for p^rsent

The question being put whether it be not conueanient that the propriato^{rs} at Pawcomptuck should drawe Lotts in the first opportunitie that it might be better knowen wher each mans propriety will lye—it is by voat declared that the select men this day to be chosen are desired to apoint, and publish som conueanient time for the propriato^{rs} there to meet and order therein according as they see cause

"March 18, 1669-70. In order to the effecting of what was by the last Gen^{ll} Towne meeteing left to the select men to take care of respecting Pawcomptucke, it is according agreed that the 10th day of the 3 month next is appointed for the propriato^{rs} in that place to meete by 9, of the Clocke in the forenoone at the house of Lieft Fisher in Dedham"

"10:3:70: [May 10, 1670.] Assemb: according to former apointm^t for the consideration of draweing Lotts and settling proprieties at Pawcomptucke

Mr Allin pasto^r, Eld^r John Hunting, Lieft. Fisher, Joh: Haward, Joh: Gaye, Edw: Richards, Serg^t Fuller, Tymo: Dwight, Tho: Payne, Mich: Metcalfe, Elea: Lusher

The 23 daye of this Instant 3 month is apointed for a meeteing of the propriato^{rs} at Pawcumptucke for the furthering the aboue said motion, and its ordered that notice be giuen accordingly to the persons concerned, the meeteing to be at the meeting house in Dedham about 7, in the morning"

"23.3:70 Assemb: according to the apointm^t aboue written the propriato^{rs} by Grant or purchase the men heere vnder named

Joh: Pincheon Esqr, Mr Allin pasto^r, Lieft: Fisher, Ensi: Fisher, Joh: Haward, Joh: Gaye, Edw. Richards, Ensi: Phillips, Joh: Fuller, Mary: Buncker p^rsent by Elea: Lusher, Joh. Stebbin p^rsent by Sam: Hinsdell, Elea: Lusher, Serg^t Averey, Serg^t Fuller, Nath: Coleburn, Tymo: Dwight, Joh: Farington, Robt. Ware, Isaac: Bullard, Tho: Payne, Pet: Woodward Junr, Sam: Hinsdell, Mich. Metcalfe, Joh: Baker

It is agreed that an Artiste be procured vpon as moderat tearmes as may be that may laye out the Lotts at Pawcomptucke to each propriato^r according to thier Lawefull interest in each sort of Land that is to be deuided and drawe and returne to the Towne a true platt of what he shall doe therein

Ensi Hen. Phillips, Ensi. Dan: Fisher, and Elea: Lusher or any 2. of them are deputed to procure an Artist for the worke aboue saide

Mr Peter Tilton, Lieft Sam. Smyth, and Cornet Wm Allice are desired and deputed to direct, the Artist aboue mentioned in the worke aboue saide, who are also further deputed, and empowered to order the scituation of the Towne for the most conueaniencie as in thier discretion shall apeere best the whole Tract, and the quallitie of each sort of Land, and other accomadacions considered, and apointing the high wayes layeing out, and a place for the Meeting house, Church officers Lott or Lotts, and what euer else may be giuen them, in further instructions, and to proportion each seuerall sorte of Land ther according to the quallitie thereof that equitie may be attended to each propriato^r according to their proportion in every sort of Land deuideable

It is allso agreed that no man shall laye out more then 20 Cow Common rights together in one place

Joh. Pincheon Esqr. is intreated, and empowered, at all his best opportunities to take his time to visit the Committee, and Artist aboue mention and to giue them such aduice in that worke comitted to them, as he shall Judge most conduceable to the good of the plantation who allso is empowered to voate with the rest of the Committee when he shall be p^rsent:

Ensi: Daniell Fisher is allso deputed to Joyne with the Committee before named—any 3 of which Committee, haue power to proceed in the worke

The Committee before named, are allso empowered to viewe and make tryall of the layeing out of the Lands, allready layed out vpon grante commonly called the Farme Lands, whether they be truely layd out according to thier grants, and to rectifie, what mistakes they shall finde therein

It is further agreed to proceed to drawe Lotts, and p^rpare accordingly, and that in euery deuision of Lands of all sorts (except house Lotts) the length of the Lotts shall runne easterly and westerly, and the begining of layeing out Lotts in particular shall allwayes be on the northerly side, and make an end on the southerly side, and so proceede according to that rule each propriato^r. to holde that order of succession thoroughout

The names of the p^rsent propriato^rs with the number of Common Rights, and number of Lotts in succession as they wer drawn

No of lots as drawn.			Mens names.	No Cow Commons.	No Sheep Commons.	No of lots.
18	16	20				
39	29	26	Capt Pynchon	54	4	3
		20	Mr John Allin	16	0	1
		37	Left Fisher	6	1	1
		28	Ensi: Fisher	13	0	1
		38	Joh: Haward	8	0	1
		24	Joh: Gay	11	2	1
			Edw: Richards			
		16	Deacn: Chickering	8	3	1
16	16	16				
2	4	5	Ensi: Phillips	48	0	3
		9	Sarg^t: Fuller	20	0	1
		1	Jnh: ffarrington	18	2	1
		25	Isaac: Bullard	11	1	1
		19	Joh: Bacon	7	3	1
		21	Tho: Payne	6	0	1
		8	Robt: Ware and Nath: Fisher (ye first 8)	15	0	1
20	20	20				
7	10	22	Pet: Woodward Jr	60	0	3
		27	Tho: Mason	13	1	1
		33	Joh: Baker	13	2	1
		3	Nath: Colborn	11	1	1
		31	Sarg^t Auery	13	1	1
		32	Mary Haward	11	0	1
		6	Joh: Fuller	9	3½	1
		23	Elea: Lusher	9	1	1
		15	Mrs Buncker	17	3	1

TOWN STREET LAID OUT. 17

16	14	16				
14	30	34	Sam: Hinsdell	46	3½	3
		36	Joh: Stebbin	20	0	1
		12	Sam: Daniels	12	0	1
		17	Tymo: Dwight	12	0	1
		13	Rob: Hinsdell	8	0	1
		18	Church Lott	8	0	1
			Tho: Metcalfe			
		35	Joh: Hubbert	3	0	1
		11	Samson ffrary	9	3	1
			Total	515	35	39

Observe that to prevent mistakes that the figures in the first collm in the margⁿ showeth the succession of place as by the drawing of lotts they are layd out and the uppermost figures in those 3 [4?] men that have each of them 3 Lotts, show how many cow commons each of their lotts contain and furder note that whereas Robt Ware and Fisher drew together that Nathaniel Fisher is to have 8 cow commons laid out first in that number in the 8 place and Robert Ware to have 7 laid out adjoyning to him and so in each division and that the 2 collum showeth the names of propriety: the 3. the number of Cow Commons: the 4 of Sheep Commons: the 5 in how many divisions each mans land ought to be laid in each division."

During the summer of 1670 the committee chosen for that purpose went to Pocumtuck, laid out the town street and the highways; set out two divisions of land most suitable for tillage, and located in each the rights of the several proprietors, according to the draft above, and in the spring following made a full report, as follows:—

"May 16, 1671. Agreed by the Committee chosen by the proprietors of land at Pacomptuck for the settlement of the scituation of the Town Plott equalicing lands laying out Highways &c &c by their mutual assent and consent.

1 That for the situation of the Town Plott it shall be on that tract of land beginning [at] the Southerly end of it att a little brook called Eagle Brook & so extend Northerly to the banke or falling ridge of land at Samson Frary's celer & so to run from the banke or ridg of land fronting on the meadow Land Westerlie to the mountain Easterlie

2 That there shall be a highway for the common street laid out six rod in breadth about the middle of the tract of land above expressed begining on that side towards Eagle Brook and so to run Northerlie throughout the said tract; on both sides wharon the house lots shall be laid out: one teare of lot fronting on the said common Street Easterlie and another teare of Lotts fronting on the said Street Westerlie: the measure of the house lots to begin on the west range of Lotts att the North end:

3. That there be three highways laid out one at each end of the Towne which shall be each way three rod in breadth running Easterlie to the mountaine or woods and Westerlie leading in to the meadows: Also there shall be another highway running from the

middle of the towne three rod in bredth Easterlie into the woods or mountains: and Westerlie it shall run into the meadows; leaving it to be laid out in the most convenient place as may best acomodate the meadows and the fesibleness of the passage into the same: att the reare of John Stebbins Lot it runs four rod on the banke then to runn through the meadow to the river.

4. That as to the more higher sort of Lands called Intervale or plowland we order that [there] shall be two divisions made of the same out of both which all the proprietors shall [receive] their proportion: the first division which we judge best for the qualitie of Land begining Northerlie att the river called pacumptuck fronting Westerlie on the pine hill [and the] land called meadow or mowing land runniug Easterlie to the mountaine and extending Southerlie to the Town Plott: then to begin againe on the South side of the towne at Eagle Brook and so being fronted by the meadow Westerlie to runn till it come [to a ridg] of falling land and there to terminate and end the which running Easterlie to the [woods] or mountaine.

A 2d division to begin att the aforesaid ridg of land where the other ended and [so to run] Westerlie over the river by a ridg of high land which divides between the [intervale] and mowing land there till it comes to the hills or woods and so all the proprietors to have their lotts run through on both sides of the river from the mountains Westerlie [to the] mountaine and swamp Easterlie till the high land on the West side be runn out—the remainder to take their lotts on the East side of the river in the rest of the Intervale land till it be runn out to the wood land.

5 That there shall be a highway two rods in bredth which shall runn through both the divisions above mentioned both Southerlie and Northerlie; the highway running Northerlie to runn to pacomtuck rIver and so out into the woods [so that each] proprietor may come to his land which highway is left to be laid out for place as conveniency the best advantage may suite.

6 That there shall be a highway 2 rod in bredth running through the meadow lying on the East side of the river from one end to another—Northerlie and Southerlie [so] every man may come to his land.

7 That all the proprietors take up a proportion proportionable in the meadow Lands lying over the west side of the river and that there be a highway 2 rod in bredth run throughout the said meadow in the most convenient place as may best advantage the said [Land and] that every man may come att his land:

Whereas Samll Hinsdell, desiring to Injoy a percell of Land on which [at] present he is resident and saith it was granted him by the town of De[dham] and understanding by Capt. Pynchon (who was then present when it was [asked] for) that he thinks it was indeed so and finding the piece said to be inconsiderable for qualitie and quantity being about 3 or 4 acres and he abating as much in the 2d of his devisions of plow land; the said tract not also prejudicing any man's lott or lotts; we judg he may Injoy the said percell of land considering his expense on the same; and no damage is done either to the Comons [or] any particular proprietor.

HOME LOTS LOCATED.

That from the way running through the meddow on the est side [of the] river at the northelie end there shall be a way left of 2 rod in bredth leading to the river westerlie that there may be a passage to the same from the land lying opposite on the west side of the river.

A list of the houselots drawn by the Committee this 14:3:71: [May 14, 1671.]

	Lots	Commons	Acres	Roods	Rods
Robt Ware, Nat'l Fisher	1	15	00	5	¼	7½
Eleazer Lusher, Gent	2	9	1	3	—	39¾
Timothy Dwight's farm	3					
John Allin, Gent	4	16	0	5	½	24
John Hubbard	5	3	0	1	—	9½
Tim° Dwight	6	12	0	4	—	38
Anthony Fisher, Jr.	7					
Ensign Phillips	8	16	0	5	½	24
Samll Hensdell	9	16	0	5	½	24
Peter Wooderd	10	20	0	7	—	10
Samson Frary	11	9	3	3	¼	22½
Capt Pynchon	12	16	4	5	¾	29¼
John Stebbins	13	20	0	7	—	10
Capt Pynchon	14	18	0	6	¼	17
John Fuller	15	9	3½	3	¼	28
Peter Wooderd	16	20	0	7	—	10½
Mary Hayward	17	11	0	3	¾	21½
John ffarrington	18	18	2	6	½	0
Ed Richards farm	19					
Church Lott	21	8	0	2	¾	12
Leift Fishers farm						
Seargt Avery	22	13	1	4	½	25¾
Thomas Mason	23	13	1	4	½	25¾
John Bacon	24	7	3	2	½	29½
Seargt Thomas Fuller	25	20	0	7	—	10
Samll Daniell	26	12	0	4	—	38
Deacon Chicerins	27	8	3	2	¾	12
John Haward	28	8	0	2	¾	12
Peter Wooderd	29	20	0	7	—	10
Isaac Bullard	30	11	1	3	¾	33
Rob Hensdell	31	8	0	2	¾	12
Natl Coleborne	32	11	1	3	¾	33
Ensine Phillips	33	16	0	5	½	24
Left Fisher	34	6	1	[2	—	33]
Samll Hinsdell	35	16	0	5	½	24
Samll Hinsdell	36	14	3½	5	—	30½
Mrs Bunker	37	17	3	6	—	34½
Ensigne Phillips	38	16	0	5	½	24
John Baker	39	13	2	4	½	38
John Gaye	40	11	2	3	¾	24½
Ensign Daniel Fisher	41	13	0	4	½	[14½]
Thomas Paine	42	6	0	2	—	19
Capt Pynchon	43	20	0	7	—	10
[Total,		515	35]			,,

The town plot laid out by this committee in 1671 is that of to-day. The highways are essentially unchanged. Many of the lines now bounding the meadow lots are those laid out under the "artist" employed by these men. Many of the house lots are changed by bargain and sale to a more convenient size, while others remain the same.

The wilderness was now waiting for redemption, and the foundations to be laid for the settlement of Pocumtuck. The ground, as I have said, had already been broken by the plow of Samuel Hinsdale, the pioneer. The Pocumtuck Indians had been swept off by the Mohawks a few years before, under circumstances to be related, and few, if any, were now residents here. Those living under the shelter of the white settlements below, who claimed to be the owners of the Valley, had been fairly paid for their lands. Though it is true they did not understand the full import of the transaction, they were nevertheless ready and glad to obtain the Englishman's wares, at the same time retaining all that was of any use to them, the right of hunting, fishing and gathering wild fruits.

The price paid may seem trifling; but this matter must be viewed from the standpoint of the men of Dedham at that date. Assuming that the £136 10s voted to be raised to repay Mr. Pynchon represents the entire cost for the purchase, and allowing a reasonable percentage for expenses, it will appear that the price paid was about four pence per acre. Little enough this seems. But in 1665 two of the "farms" containing 450 acres, some of it the choicest meadow land at Pocumtuck, was offered at Dedham, for "6 pence per acre, 2-5 in corn and 3-5 in cattle," with no buyers. If this be a criterion of value, Dedham paid generously for the land, especially as she had already given one acre at home for four in this far-off region; and the Pocumtuck Indians were really deprived of nothing which, under the circumstances, could be of any value to them.

Dedham had hardly taken possession of her new estate before Hatfield complained of encroachment. In May, 1672, she petitioned the General Court for redress, claiming that the grant as laid out, extended one and three-quarters of a mile over her north line. The Court appointed Peter Tilton, William Clarke and Samuel Smith, a committee to "regulate and settle," the disputed line. Sept. 20th these gentlemen viewed the premises, and on the 9th of October reported to the Court that they had,—

"Ordered that Hatfield bounds northerly shall extend to a little brooke commonly called, by the English, Sugar Loafe Brook, at the comon place of passage ouer, where there is two trees marked, a little white oake on the west side of the way, and a great white oake on the east side of sajd way; and so to runne by the sajd line east to the Great Riuer, and on the west ljne from sajd riuer two miles into the woods.

Also the sajd Committee have determined that the Proprietors of Pocomtuck for and in consideration of the land taken out of their measure to acomodate Hatfield, they shall receiue it as followeth, vizt: on the north side of Pocumtuck Riuer, from the mouth of the ryver called Greene Riuer, a ljne to runne due east one mile, and west one mile, and north three-quarters of a mile; the whole tract of land to be two miles in length and three-quarters of a mile in breath, and for the remajnder to begin at Pocomtock Riuer, at the end of there propritjes, and to rune on an east ljne to the Great Riuer, and to extend in a south lyne two miles."

This return was approved by the Court, Oct. 11, 1672. The north line of Pocumtuck as thus established in 1672 is the present north bound of the town—the famous "8000 acre line," for the maintenance of which so many hard battles with Greenfield have been successfully fought by the patriotic descendants of the original settlers. The addition at the north was doubtless covered by the deeds already given. That at Great River on the east was included in the following :—

THESE PRESENTS TESTIFIE, That Mashalisk (the old woman, Mother of Wuttawwalunckstn) doth hereby Bargaine sell & allienate a Tract of Land in ye Southerly side of Pacomtuck River & so lying all along by Qvinetticot River side doune to ye Lower Point of ye Hill called Weqvomps & by ye English Sugarloafe hill: all ye Tract of Land between ye greate River Quinetticot on ye east & ye ledge of Mountaines on ye west, & on ye Northward fro Pacomtuck River Mouth, Mantehelant downe southward to Weqvomps & to ye very Point of land where ye hills come to ye greate River called Tawwat or Tawwat [—] Togither wth all ye Islands in ye greate River, called Mattampash, Allinnack, or Allinnackcooke, Taukkanackcoss, or by whatever other names they may be called, all ye whole sd Tract of Land Mantehelant Mattampash downe to Tawwat or Tawwattuck & so by ye ledge of Mountaines lie fro greate River westward.

The sd Mashalisk Doth sell all to John Pynchon of Springfield to him his heires & assignes forever, ffor & in Consideration of a debt of ten large Bevers & other debts of Wuttawoluncksin her sons wch shee acknowledges her self engaged for ye Payment off to John Pynchon aforesd: for the said Just and due Debts & moreover for & in consideration of sixty fada of wampum. 2. cotes some cotton & Severall other small things all wch ye sd Mashalisk acknowledge to haue Rec'd & to be therwth fully satisfied & contented, Doe fully clearly & absolutely give Grant Bargaine & sell vnto John Pynchon of Springfield aforesd, hereby giving granting & resigning up to him all my right Title & interest in ye aforesd land: To HAVE &

to HOLD all the sd land to yᵉ only proper vse & Behoofe of him yᵉ sd John Pynchon his heires & assigns for ever, wᵗʰ all yᵉ profits advantages & comoditys thereoff & therevnto belonging whatsoever, & that for ever: And yᵉ sd Meshalisk doth hereby covenant & promise too & wᵗʰ yᵉ sd John Pynchon, that shee will yᵉ sd Pynchon save harmless of & from all manner of claimes right title & interest of any other person whatsoever vnto yᵉ sd Land hereby sold & will defend yᵉ same from all or any Molestation or Incumbrance of Indians right to all or any part thereof: & as having full right & lawfull Power thus to doe, Doth in witness thereoff here vnto affix her hand & seale this 26th day of August 1672

                                        Mash ⋈shalisk
                                            her marke
This being done & also delid   (Seal)
in the Presence off
John Holtum
Isaac Morgan
     The marke of
Ackki ⋈[unbariet?]an Indian witness
          her kinsman

The name of the Indian witness is probably the same given in John Pynchon's accountbook as *Ackambowet*.

CHAPTER II.

TOPOGRAPHY, LOCAL NAMES, GRAVEYARDS.

Pocumtuck of two hundred years ago lay upon the west bank of the *Quinnehtuk*—*i. e.* long, tidal river*—with a shore line of twenty-five miles in length. Its north and west lines were each thirteen miles long; its average width below the great bend at *Peskeompskut*, was about nine miles. This territory, containing about one hundred and thirty-seven square miles, was bounded by the present towns of Northfield, Bernardston, Leyden, and Colrain on the north; by Montague, Whately, and Williamsburg on the south; on the east the Connecticut separated it from Northfield, Erving, Montague and Sunderland; west lay Goshen, Ashfield, Buckland and Charlemont. From this old township, Greenfield, including Gill, was set off in 1753, Conway in 1767, Shelburne in 1768; and fragments have gone to Whately and Ashfield, leaving only about thirty-six square miles, bounded by Greenfield and Montague north, Whately and Conway south, Montague and Sunderland east, Shelburne and Conway west—which is the Deerfield of to-day. The population of the old territory is given below:—

	1704	1765	1776	1790	1800	1810	1830	1850	1870	1880
Deerfield	300	737	836	1330	1350	1570	2003	2421	3632	3543
Greenfield		368	735	1498	1256	1165	1540	2580	3589	3903
Conway			897	2092	2013	1784	1563	1531	1460	1760
Shelburne			575	1183	1089	961	995	1239	1582	1621
Gill					644	762	864	754	653	733
	300	1105	3043	6103	6352	6242	6965	8525	10916	11560

The topography of the town is quite peculiar. Along the bank of the Connecticut river runs a strip of meadow, about a quarter of a mile wide, extending the whole length of the town. From this rises to the west a range of highlands, from one to two miles wide, including Wequamps on the south line, and Peskeompskut, attaining about midway at Po-

---

*In 1725, The Abenakis called it the "Gownitigou, otherwise Long River."

cumtuck Rock, an elevation of 750 feet. This is called East Mountain. From the foot of this range a plain or valley spreads westward, from one to two miles in width. On this, the Dedham Grant was laid out, and here are situated the "Old Street," the villages of Wapping, Mill, Bars, Bloody Brook and Mill River. Still to the west, the surface rises in swelling hills, one above another, to the western bounds, reaching at " Arthur's Seat," near the Shelburne line, a height of 1000 feet. These are the " Sunsick Hills " of the Indians, the West Mountain of to-day, and may be considered foothills of Hoosac Mountain. These hills are nearly bare of forest and afford the best of grazing land, while a few good farms are found in the valleys among them. Through the Sunsick Hills the Pocumtuck river has worn a deep, rocky bed, over which it hurries to the valley, entering it from the west, near the center of the Dedham Grant. From the point where the Pocumtuck debouches from the hills, the valley to the north has been scooped out by the action of its waters to the depth of one hundred feet, forming the remarkable basin known as the Pocumtuck Valley. The *Pocommegon*, or Green river entering from the north, assisted in this work of excavation. The valley is surrounded by a deeply indented bluff, the top of which marks the original level. From the top of the bluff on the south the plain broadens, stretching away to the Whately line. On the north it extends to the Leyden hills. According to a theory of Agassiz, at no very remote geological period, this plain was the bed of the Connecticut river, which, pouring its waters around the south point of Wequamps, left the large " pot hole " still to be seen there, as an evidence of its passage.

About the center of the Pocumtuck valley, and abutting against the East Mountain, lies a plateau one mile long and half as wide, surrounded on three sides by the meadows, above which it is elevated some twenty feet. In the middle of this plateau rises Meetinghouse hill, a table of fifty acres, occupying its entire width, and rising about twenty feet above the rest. Here is the natural center of the town. Here was the meetinghouse, the graveyard, the training field and fort. Running over this hill, and across the plateau to the north and south, the "Town Platt" was laid out in 1671, and here is "Old Street" of to-day.

TOWN STREET AND NORTH MEADOWS. 25

On a smaller plateau, similarly situated at the south end of the valley, lies the village of Wapping. Clinging to the face of the bluff, the village of Cheapside straggles across the northern extremity of the valley. Aside from these localities and Pine Hill, the whole valley is subject to inundation by the overflow of the Pocumtuck.

A minute description of the town will be convenient for reference and will save much repetition. Local names will be given freely, especially when descriptive or personal. The affixed figures indicate the year in which the older names are first met with. To some these names and dates may have no significance, while others will find in them landmarks of ownership, or the key to historic events. The view will be by sections, which agree substantially with the old school districts. The time is 1884:—

No. 1. *Old Street*, 1671. This contains one hundred and seven dwellings, two meetinghouses, Town hall, Memorial Hall, Dickinson Academy and Library, schoolhouse, postoffice, two depots, hotel, Grange Hall, three stores, shoe shop, blacksmith shop, livery stable, grist and lumber mill, pickle factory and two graveyards. From the Old Street as a starting point, Memorial Lane leads eastward to the depots and over East Mountain to Great River and Pine Nook. To the west Hitchcock's Lane—the new Academy Lane—leads to the old graveyard, the meadows, and across the Pocumtuck by a ford to Wisdom.

North Meadows, lies on the north and west of the Street. Some of its subdivisions are Plain Swamp, Pine Hill, 1671; Little Plain, 1686; Pine Hill Plain, 1701; Tim's Kiln, 1735; Poag's Hole, 1735; Neck, 1675; White Swamp, 1701; Great Meadows, 1688; Little Meadows, 1688; Harrow Meadow, 1701; Pine Hill Island, 1671; Field's Island, 1735; Great Pasture, 1725; Meadow Pasture, John Broughton's Hill, 1701. Some of the ponds scattered about the meadows are: Broughton's 1693; Beaman's, 1728; and Belding's, 1755. Frary's bridge is named in 1703.

The most notable feature in this tract is Pine Hill, near its center. This is about forty feet high, and covers thirty acres. It is doubtless a remnant of the original plain, preserved from denudation by a ledge of rock at its west base; in shape, an oblong square, rounded and scalloped at the ends, its contour is as symmetrical as many of the western mounds. The top is occupied by two level terraces running lengthwise.

South Meadows, 1671, lies south of the Street, with Eagle Brook Plain, 1690; Log Meadow, 1701; Beaver Dam, 1735; Wells's Pasture, 1701; Harrow Meadow, 1701; and Second Division Hill, 1671. This hill marks the south bound of the First Division of plow land, 1671. Beyond this is Second Division Plain, 1671; New Field, 1729; and Indian Orchard.

On the bluff east of the valley, ranging from south to north, are Fort Hill, 1688; Martin's Hill, 1688; Burying Ground Hill, 1801, now occupied as its name indicates; Woodchuck Hill and a Second Fort Hill, 1710.

No. 2. *Cheapside*, 1689. From the north end of Old Street a road skirting North Meadows on the east leads across the Pocumtuck to Cheapside, which occupies the territory between that river, Sheldon's brook, and Greenfield line. Here are one hundred and forty-seven dwellings, two schoolhouses, extensive machine shops, two stores, Hoyt's Meadow, 1805; Fort Hill, 1755; Town Swamp, 1750; West Meadow, 1755; Judith's Point, 1755; Clesson's Swamp, 1710; Petty's Plain, 1714; and Behind Noon, 1805. Three railroad bridges and four highway bridges are partly or wholly in Cheapside —two over the Connecticut, three over the Pocumtuck and two over Green river.

No. 3. *Wisdom*. This is bounded east and south by the Pocumtuck river, north by Cheapside, and reaches west to Shelburne line. It has sixty dwellings, two schoolhouses, meetinghouse, postoffice, depot, wagon shop, cider mill, two slaughter houses and six graveyards. Here lie Carter's land, 1693; Little Hope, Old Fort, 1686; Old River, Harrow Meadow Point, 1766; Grass Hollow, New Fort Meadow, 1686; The Nook, Belding's Grant, 1688; Amsden's Hill, 1735; Field's Hill, Martin's Hill, 1717; Indian Hill, Round Hill, Long Swamp, Old World, Arthur's Seat, Hawks's Grant, Wolf Lot, House Lot, and Blakely Hollow.

No. 4. *Hoosac*, lies across the Pocumtuck to the south of Wisdom, with nine dwellings.

No. 5. *Mill River*, is still southward, occupying the southeast corner of the town. It has thirty dwellings, schoolhouse, saw and grist mill, Sawmill Plain, 1747; Brooks's Hollow, Weller's Hill, Bear's Hole, Indian Hill, Long Hill West Division, 1688; and a graveyard.

No. 6. *Wapping*, 1687, one mile south of Old Street is the Plumbtree Plain of 1684. It has twenty-three dwellings and a schoolhouse.

No. 7. *The Mill*, 1795, is one mile west of Wapping, with nine dwellings, blacksmith shop, machine shop, saw and grist mill. Here are Indian Bridge, 1694; Gifford's Bridge, Stebbins Meadow, 1692; Sutlieff's Island, 1712; Locke's Island, 1773; Locke's Mill, 1783; Stebbins Island, 1735; Island Brook, 1767; and Stillwater Bridge, which leads over the Pocumtuck river to Wisdom.

No. 8. *The Bars*, 1675, adjoins on the south, with nine dwellings, Indian Hole, Squaw Hill, 1746; Bars Long Hill, 1685; Boggy Meadow, 1686. One schoolhouse accommodates both Mill and Bars.

No. 9. *Turnip Yard*,* 1753, lies two miles southeast of Wapping, with nineteen dwellings and schoolhouse.

No. 10. *Sugar Loaf*—the old town sheepwalk of 1753—lies southeast of Turnip Yard, between Wequamps, 1672, and the Connecticut, south to Whately line, with twelve dwellings, sawmill and graveyard. From here a bridge leads across the Connecticut to Sunderland.

No. 11. *Pine Nook*, 1709, or *Grindstone Hill*, is next north of Sugar Loaf, extending three miles up the Connecticut. It has twenty-four dwellings, schoolhouse, two graveyards, Will's Hill, and Devil's Hollow, 1800. Whitmore's Ferry leads thence to Sunderland.

No. 12. *Great River*, 1686, lies still northward, extending on the river three miles to the town bounds, Cheapside and Old Street lying on the west. Here are twenty-six dwellings, schoolhouse, cider mill, one graveyard, Clesson's Ferry to Montague, 1830; Martin's Meadow, 1686; Sheldon's Fields, 1768. At the latter place the Boston and Troy Railroad has established a freight yard, with extensive buildings and depot. The Indian name of this section was Mantahelek.

No. 13. *Bloody Brook*, 1675, is three and one-half miles south of the Street by Wapping Long Hill road, and extends

---

* The namby-pamby name of Hill Side has recently been applied to this district in accordance with a taste which would reduce to insipid sameness every original and suggestive local name.

southward to Whately line. Half a mile north of this line is a small triangular common. From this point Sugar Loaf Street runs across Sugar Loaf Plain, 1700, by the south point of Wequamps, to Sunderland Bridge; Depot Street west to Mill river; Conway street northwest to Conway, and the Northampton road south. Another road from the Old Street reaches Bloody Brook by Bars Long Hill. This is the old Hatfield road, down which Lothrop led his men to slaughter in 1675. It is the dividing line between Long Hill East, and Long Hill West, divisions of woodland in 1688. On the streets and roads named are one hundred and forty-eight dwellings, three meetinghouses, two schoolhouses, six stores, pocketbook manufactory, wagon shop, blacksmith shop, grist and sawmill, two hotels, livery stable, postoffice, two graveyards, and the monument to the "Flower of Essex."

Elevations—East Mountain is made up of two ranges parallel to the Connecticut river, about eleven miles long. The easterly one, of trap, is called Rocky Mountain. Its northern end, opposite the falls at Peskeompskut, rises boldly four or five hundred feet. The sides are generally precipitous and often bare of vegetation, more particularly the west slope. Its highest rise is at Hosmer's Peak, directly east of Pocumtuck Rock, whence it rapidly falls off to Turnip Yard and there disappears under the west range. At Cheapside there is a remarkable gorge, where the Pocumtuck river has cut a passage through the hill from crown to base, about two hundred and fifty feet in depth. Not far above this gorge on the north side is Sachems Head, with its Bears Den, and farther on, Poets Seat, places of much resort, from which are extensive and picturesque views of the Connecticut and Pocumtuck Valleys.

The west range of East Mountain, of red sandstone, is called the Pocumtuck range. It springs abruptly from the plain at Whately line to the height of five hundred feet, forming the noted "Weqvamps, called by the white men, Sugar Loaf" in 1672. From Wequamps, on which is a house for the accommodation of visitors, the prospect is charming, extending down the valley beyond Holyoke and Mount Tom. Northward, over Beaver Neck, is North Sugar Loaf, of equal height. Rising still northward, the range culminates at Pocumtuck Rock, 750 feet above the valley. The view from this point can rarely be surpassed in quiet beauty. "It is not excelled," said John Quincy Adams, "by anything I have ever seen, not excepting the Bay of Naples." Northward from "The Rock" the range gradually falls off, disappearing at length under the trap range in Greenfield.

The peculiar form of East Mountain, which suggests two strands of an enormous cable, did not escape the notice of the Indians, who called it Pemawachuatuck, *i. c.*, at the twisted mountain.

The origin of these two ranges is as different as their material—if our authorities are reliable. The geologist tells us that the trap range was forced up between the old and new sandstone by internal action. The Pocumtuck range, according to Indian tradition, is only the petrified body of a huge beaver, which used to disport itself here in a pond of corresponding dimensions. This animal, by continued depredations on the shores, had offended Hobomok, who at length determined to kill it. Accordingly, armed with the trunk of an enormous oak, he waded into the water and attacked the monster. After a desperate contest, the beaver was dispatched by a blow across his neck with the ponderous cudgel. The carcass sank to the bottom of the pond and turned to stone. Should any skeptic doubt the truth of this tradition he is referred to the beaver itself. Wequamps is the head, north of which the bent neck shows where fell the fatal stroke; North Sugar Loaf, the shoulders, rising to Pocumtuck Rock the back, whence it tapers off to the tail at Cheapside. All this is now as plainly to be seen by an observer from the West Mountain as it was the day this big beaver pond was drained off.

The hills west of the Dedham Grant belong to the Hoosac range and rise in gradual swells to the summit, twenty-five miles away, and twenty-four hundred feet high. The highest elevation attained in Deerfield is one thousand feet, at Arthur's Seat. This point is not difficult of access, and the view from it is extensive and grand. It is the peer of Kunckquadchu, 1664; while Pocumtuck Rock and Wequamps are dwarfed between them.

Streams.—The Connecticut River—the Quinnehtuk of the natives—runs the whole length of the old township, with a shore line, as already stated, of twenty-five miles. Its general course is southerly, but at the southeast corner of Gill, where it receives Miller's river from the east, it turns sharply to the northwest for a mile; continuing a westerly course of two miles to the Narrows, it again turns abruptly to the northward, and after a mile of rapids, plunges over a rocky precipice at Peskeompskut—now Turners Falls. About 1796 a dam was built here; and a canal, constructed for the benefit of river navigation, was opened Oct. 29, 1800. In 1866 a new dam was built, about forty feet high and one thousand feet long. It is in two parts, one end of each resting upon a rocky island near the middle of the river. This dam was made to utilize the power for manufacturing purposes on both sides of the river.

The large body of water and the height of the fall; the historic associations; the pre-historic revelations from the sandstone hard by, make this by far the most interesting cataract in New England. A few rods below, where Fall river enters from the north, the river bends to the west, and sweeping in a semi-circle for three miles, it receives the Pocumtuck from the south; and a mile eastward, the brook Papacomtuckquash, *i. e.*, little Pocumtuck, from Montague. Here it resumes its southward course.

Pocumtuck River, 1665, rises on the east slope of the Green Mountains in Vermont. Entering Massachusetts near the mouth of Hoosac Tunnel, and taking a southeasterly course, it forms the boundary line between Rowe, Charlemont and Shelburne on the left, and Monroe, Florida, Buckland, and Conway on the right, and for two miles, between Conway and Deerfield. From the falls in Shelburne the river descends rapidly and has worn out a rocky bed through the Sunsick Hills from two to four hundred feet in depth. The canyon is so narrow and its sides so precipitous that in time of high water it is impassable to man. In the course of ages its foot has receded from the original outlet, forming a level reach about a mile in length, called,—

Stillwater.—Here the weary stream, after its impetuous rush from the mountain, dallies for a quiet rest, in the dim seclusion; and Dryads and Naiads take it in charge to prepare it for a dignified progress across the sunlit North Meadows. The seething waters are soothed until every dash and ripple vanishes and every sound is silenced; the dancing foam is brushed away and the dark emerald surface lies like burnished glass. The nymphs then deck it with fringed garments of summer green, or autumn robes of purple and gold, which trail down on either side of its ample bosom, and leave it to glide out on its destined way. From the foot of the rapids to this outlet the water appears absolutely still—a perfect mirror, reflecting the forest trees which crown the rocky heights on either shore. Stillwater is a favorite resort for lovers of the romantic, and of each other. A row to the head of the reach reveals scenes of enchanting beauty which become grand and solemn, as one seems to be penetrating through the deepening shadows, the very heart of the mountain.

Pocommeagon, 1667; or *Green River*, 1672—rises in Southern Vermont, crosses Leyden, Greenfield and Cheapside, to the Pocumtuck, affording in its course power for many small manufacturing establishments.

Mill River, 1661, comes from the hills of Conway. Soon after crossing the town line at Mill river there is a fall, where a mill was built in 1693. Draining Long Hill West Division, it receives Bloody Brook near Whately line, and running due south, reaches the Connecticut in Hatfield. Hadley's first corn mill was built on this stream in 1661.

Fall River, from Windham county, Vermont, comes down through Bernardston, between Greenfield and Gill, entering the Connecticut a few rods below Peskeompskut, furnishing power for many small works.

To aid in the description of events occurring on the old territory of the town a concise notice of its principal brooks will be given:—

Mill Brook, 1726, rises about Frizzell's Hill in Leyden, crosses the southeast part of Bernardston, flows southerly five miles in Greenfield, and enters Green river at Nash's Mills.

McCard's [originally McHard's] *Brook*, a branch of Mill Book, also comes from Leyden. Another branch, *Ash Swamp Brook*, 1745, draining the Great Swamp at the eastward, enters near its mouth.

Glen Brook, from the famous Leyden Glen, supplies the Greenfield aqueduct and enters Green river one mile below the Leyden line.

Guy's Brook, another tributary of Green river, running

westerly through Greenfield village, drains the low lands east of it, and is utilized for the purpose of sewerage.

From the west slope of Shelburne the most considerable streams are *Wells's Brook*, which on reaching Greenfield receives *Jenny's Brook* from the south; *Hinsdale's Brook*, rising in Colrain and flowing southeasterly through Shelburne and Greenfield; *Allen's Brook* from the south, and *Stewart's Brook* from the north which are its branches. All this water finds its way to Green river in Greenfield.

From its southern slopes, Shelburne sends several brooks to the Pocumtuck—*Sluice Brook*, 1762, from Bald Mountain; *Dragon Brook*, with *Great Brook* and *Hawks's Brook* from Brimstone Hill, as branches; and *Shingle Brook*, from Shingle Hill, near the east line.

Conway, or Deerfield South West, abounds in streams. *South River*, 1763; and *Bear's River*, from Ashfield, cross the town northeasterly to the Pocumtuck; the former furnishing well improved mill power. The latter is noted for its deep channel. Near its mouth it is spanned by a railroad bridge, one hundred and forty-five feet above its bed.

From the southern slopes of Conway run *Avery's Brook* and *Sink Pot Brook*, which unite to form *West Brook*. *Popular Brook* is a branch of the latter. *Roaring Brook*, 1766, running through Sanderson's Glen, famous for its picturesqueness, absorbs *North Hollow Branch*. The water of all these streams enters Mill river in Whately,

In the opposite corner of the old township is Gill. There we find, running across the town to the southeast, *Woodward's Brook*, 1735, the outlet of Otter Pond. Its main branches are *Dry Brook*, 1734, on the left, and *Beaver Brook*, on the right. *Ashuela Brook*, 1743, and *Beaver Run*, lie to the northeast, and all fall into the Connecticut.

On the territory of the present town the larger streams have been noticed. Of the small ones, only those having established names will be described. *Eagle Brook*, 1670, comes down East Mountain by the side of the Pine Nook road, reaching the Pocumtuck at the south end of the Old Street. It was called *Sawmill Brook* in 1714, and *Bijah's Brook* as early as 1750. The north fork of this brook, running through Northam's Grant, is called in 1735, *Northam's Holm Brook*.

Plain Swamp Brook, rising under Meetinghouse Hill, runs parallel to the Cheapside road through Plain Swamp to the Pocumtuck at Cheapside. *Tan Yard Brook*, 1792, from Fort Hill; *Roaring Brook*, 1758—its name spoiled by the Connecticut River Railroad—and *Wateringtrough Brook*, are its tributaries from the east. *Taylor's Mill Brook*, rising in Pole Swamp, east of the Street, reaches the Pocumtuck a few rods above Cheapside bridge. *Hearthstone Brook*, 1687, from the south, between the two East Mountain ranges, enters the Pocumtuck near its mouth.

Running from the east slope of the Pocumtuck range to the Connecticut, are *Mill Brook*, 1715; *Peppermint Brook, Rail Brook*, 1710, or *Parsons Mill Brook*, 1720, in Pine Nook, and two miles below, *Roaring Brook*, 1699.

South of Wequamps, is the brook "called by the Indians *Weekioannuck*," 1672, and *Sugar Loaf Brook*, in 1700; heading in the low lands west of North Sugar Loaf, it enters the Connecticut near the Whately line. Another sluggish stream rises north of the above, comes down east of Bloody Brook village and parallel to it for half its length, when it crosses the street to the west. At this point stands the monument commemorating the fall of Capt. Lothrop and the "Flower of Essex," in 1675. On that tragic day this stream was baptized *Bloody Brook*. Continuing southerly it falls into Mill river, near the Whately line. *Wilkey's Brook*, a branch of the above, heads about Bear's Hole and drains the flat lands south of it. *Wash Brook*, from the east, 1750, is another branch.

Second Division Brook, 1688, rising near the head of Bloody Brook, runs in an opposite direction through the low lands of Long Hill East Division, Boggy Meadow, and Indian Orchard, into Second Division, where it was once dammed by beavers. Joined here by *Beaver Dam Brook*, it turns westward and reaches the Pocumtuck through Log Meadow. It was the outlet to the beaver pond and the boundary between First and Second Divisions of plow land in 1671. *Barnard's Brook*, 1695, drains the swamp under Bars Long Hill. It is crossed by Indian Bridge, near the Bars and Mill schoolhouse. *Stebbins's Brook*, 1779, rises near Grange Hall and runs west. *Broughton's Pond Brook*, or *Frary's Brook*, as it is sometimes called, forms the outlet of that pond westerly. The three last named enter directly into the Pocumtuck.

Wisdom is well watered. *Sheldon's Brook*, 1743, comes down through Little Hope. To the south lie *Carter's Land Brook*, 1780; *Jones's Brook*, *Hawks's Brook*, *Hoyt's Mill Brook*, 1795; *Amsden's Hill Brook*, all running eastward to the Pocumtuck. *Turkey Bin Brook*, 1795, draining Round Swamp, and *Lanfair's Brook*, Long Swamp, both run south to the same river.

The brooks for which names have been found are a small minority of those scattered in every part of the old township.

CHAPTER III.

FIRST SETTLEMENT.

When our ancestors planted themselves at Pocumtuck it became the northwest frontier settlement of New England. The wilderness stretched to Canada on the north, and to Albany on the west: Lancaster and Brookfield were the nearest towns on the east. On the river below were Springfield, settled by William Pynchon in 1635, Northampton, settled in 1654, and Hadley in 1659. At Warranoco, [Westfield] a trading post had been established in 1640, as a commercial rival to Springfield.

From the first contact of the whites with the natives of the valley, traffic in furs was a lucrative business. Pynchon, located at Springfield, was near the source of supply and found great profit in the business. The Connecticut towns, being in a measure cut off from the up river Indians, sought to checkmate Pynchon by a counter move. In 1640, Fenwick, agent of the Connecticut patentees, granted Gov. Edward Hopkins and William Whiting of Hartford, one thousand acres at Warranoco. The grantees at once built a fort there and established a trading post. That region was a favorite haunt for beaver, and a brisk trade with the natives soon sprang up. Massachusetts, which had derived quite an income from a tax on furs, could not quietly see so large a trade diverted to Connecticut. She set up a claim that the fort was on her territory, and ran an ex-parte line to prove it. Fenwick resisted the claim; but the Commissioners of the United Colonies decided in favor of Massachusetts. Warranoco was annexed to Springfield and was taxed two pence for each skin of beaver, otter, moose or bear obtained of the Indians. Soon after 1649 the post was abandoned. Before 1660 a company under the lead of Roger Billings, made an unsuccessful attempt to renew the settlement, under a grant from Massachusetts. A permanent colony was established there about 1660.

For more than thirty years friendly relations had existed between the English and Indians, to their mutual benefit, and no fears were now entertained of Indian hostilities. Under these conditions and with these surroundings, our fathers had decided to plant a colony at Pocumtuck. As we have seen, the pioneer, Samuel Hinsdell, had broken ground here in the spring of 1669, or possibly the fall before. The town had been surveyed and the land divided in 1671. It has often been stated by historians, and generally believed, that Deerfield was settled by a colony from Dedham, and that the list of proprietors of the eight thousand acre grant found on the town records is a list of the actual settlers. It is a remarkable fact, however, that not a single Dedham man became a permanent resident of Pocumtuck.

Samuel Hinsdell was soon followed by Samson Frary. A family tradition places Godfrey Nims here, as third settler, before 1671, but other evidence of this has not been found. Landless men, learning of the fertile, alluvial soil of this valley, where broad acres could be bought for a trifle, soon turned their faces toward this land of promise. Many rights in the Grant had been sold to speculators years before, but the question now being of settlement, picked men only were allowed a foothold on the new El Dorado. Although the house lots, and the best meadow land were held in severalty, real estate there was sold to such men only as were approved by Dedham. Entries like the following make part of the town record:—

"Dec. 4, 1671. Joh Plimpton is allowed to purchase Land of John Bacon at Pawcumptucke prouided that the said John Plimpton doe settle there vpon in his owne person

Dec. 4, 1671. Mr Tho: Weld of Roxbery came this daye with his brother Daniell Weld of Meadfield, moueing the select men to grant his said brother libertie to purchase Lande at Paucomptuke. this request was not granted"

"Feb. 16, 1671–2. Lieft. Fisher is alowed libertie to sell, 6 cowe Common Rights and one sheepe Common Right at Paucumptuck to Nathaneell Suttlife of Medfield"

These were acts of deliberation, and not mere formalities.

The grounds of objection to Mr. Weld, or what measures were taken to remove them, do not appear; but the next year he was an emigrant to Pocumtuck. An examination of the records of Dedham shows that the municipal affairs of the new plantation were for years exclusively under the control of the mother town. As the inconvenience of this arrangement became manifest, measures were taken to bring the ruling powers nearer home.

Samuel Hinsdell was sent to confer with the mother town in the winter of 1672–3.

"Feb. 3, 1672–3. The inhabitanc at pocomtick by Sam Hisdel desire that a company of meet persons: thier about be chosen: and invested with all such poure nesesary: for the well ordering of the afires: of that place, this being taken in to consideration: the fiue men vnder named are chosen to be the commity: Mr Petter Tilton Liut Sam Smith Liut Alice good Willard Sam Hinsdel"

"March 7, 1673. [Genera lmeeting.] SamH insdell in the behalfe of the inhabitanc of pecomtick: and the propriators: thier present thier request that the Towne of Dedham would consider thier case and the dificaltyes that are vpon them by reasone of thier remoatnes: from the plac whear the poure of ordring of prudentiall do reside: and to do something: that may: further thier setlement:

In Answer thier vnto: the Towne haue chosen thier trusty and wellbeloued and much esteemed freind: m^r Peter Tilton Liut Sam Smith: Liut Alice Richard Wilard: and Sam Hinsdel to be a comity for that place: and haue betrusted and impoured them accordingly: as first to alow of sutable inhabitanc by: purchis or other wise secondly: to order thier herding: cattel and regolating: swine: 3 to make orders about fence: 4ly: that this commity: and the inhabitanc thier with the aduice of the Elders of the 2 neighboring: churches: shall haue liberty to procure: an orthodox Minester to dispenc the word of god amogst them."

These neighboring churches were at Hadley and Hatfield. Hinsdell—who was made constable for Pocumtuck at this time—on his return made a report of the above proceedings to his fellow adventurers. Whatever they might have expected of the mother town, this action was unsatisfactory, and they resolved to cut loose from the authority of Dedham and set up an independent government. Samuel Hinsdell was again sent through the wilderness to the Bay; this time with an appeal to a higher power. The following action of the General Court at its session of May 7, 1673, shows the issue of this enterprise:—

In ans^r to the peticon of the inhabitants of Paucumptucke, Samuell Hindsdale, Sampson Frary, &c the Court judgeth it meete to allow the peticoners the liberty of a touneship, and doe therefore grant them such an addition of land to the eight thousand acres formerly granted there to Dedham, as that the whole be to the content of seven miles square, provided that an able & orthodox minister wthin three yeares be settled among them, and that a farme of two hundred & fifty acres of land be layd out for the countrys vse; and doe further appointt & impower Lef^t Wm Allys, Th^{os} Meakins, Sen & Sergent Isaack Graues, wth Lef^t Samuel Smith, Mr Peeter Tylton, & Samuel Hindsdell, to be a Committee, and any fower of them to act in all respects to lay out ye said farme in a convenient place to admit inhabitants, grant lands, & order all their prudentiall affaires till they shall be in a capacity, by meet persons from among themselues, to manage their owne affaires, & that the committee be advised wth about settling of a minister there.—[*Mass. Records*, IV, Part II, 558.]

In default of any subsequent action to that end, this "Liberty of a touneship" may well be taken as an Act of Incorporation of the town. In this act there is no provision obliging the settlers to seek "the aduice of the Elders of the 2 neighboring churches" in procuring a minister; which proviso in the Dedham order, may have been obnoxious to these sturdy independents, and caused their bold push for territorial and ecclesiastical liberty. It is probable, moreover, that influence from a *third* "neighboring church" had already practically disposed of the question of the minister. Samuel Mather, a nephew of Eleazer Mather, ten years minister at Northampton, was called to provide for the spiritual wants of the new town. He seems to have been paid about thirty-seven pounds a year. There is, however, no evidence that a church was formed at this time, or that Mather was regularly "settled." We find John Pynchon paid taxes for his support from December, 1673, until the settlement was broken up in 1675. A meetinghouse was built before August 1675.

The territory of Pocumtuck, as laid out under the above grant, is almost identical with that now occupied by the towns of Deerfield, Greenfield and Gill. The farm of two hundred and fifty acres for the "countrys vse" was laid out in the north part of the additional grant. "Country Farms," in Greenfield, probably indicates its location. More will be found on this subject later.

The prudential affairs of the incipient town were nominally under the control of the committee of six before named, but practically in the hands of those most interested. This appears from the following record of two meetings recovered from a collection of old papers in Connecticut. It is the earliest known record of action by the plantation, and will be given in full:—

Nouember 7th, 1673:

At a meeting apoynted by the Comitee ffor the plantation of pacomtucke of the Inhabitants, and proprietors of the Lands there:

These following particulars proposed by the Comittie at the said meeting to the Inhabitants and proprietors there ffor their consideration:

1. Whether it be not best and most conducable to the weal & Settlement of the plantation ffor the proprietors to laye downe all their wood lands now in propryetie to common—As also all those lands they recaued ffrom the Countrye, in leiw of what they parted with to Hatfeild.

This proposision was voted in the affirmative in both the parts And ffurther the said Inhabitants and proprietors, doe by these presents, ffor themselues and their successours, ratifie, confirm, and establish, the above proposision, *viz*: to laye downe all their woodlands now in proprietye to common,—As also all those lands they receaued from the Countrye in lieu of what they parted with to Hatfield provided withall, the said proprietors reserve to themselues and successours, a Comon right in the aforesaid lands and in all other lands belonging to the said plantation that are yet undivided according to the maner of other plantations:

2d. That all public Charges respecting the ministers sallerye or maintenance bee leuied and raised on lands for the present till the said towne be in a capasitye to manage their own affairs and may see cause to alter or some other way be agreed on by the Comittee.

This was voted in the affirmative by the proprietors

3d. Whether there should be a speedye course taken that those of the proprietors who want land of their measure which should have binn truely laid out to them be satisfied, to preuent future trouble.

This was voted in the affirmative, provided every person wanting his proportion, shall euince it by testimonye to the Comittee by the 29th of September next ensuing:

The Marck of

Richard Weler:—	Robert Hinsdell	Nathaniel Sutly :—
John Plympton	Samuel Hinsdell	John ffarrington
Joshua Carter:—	Experience Hinsdell	Thomas Hastings
Samson Frary	John Barnard	ffrancis Barnard
Quintin Stockwell	John: Weler	Samuel Daniel
Joseph Gillet	Samuel Herenton:	James Tufts
Barnabus Hinsdell	John: Hinsdell	
John Allin	Ephraim Hinsdell	
Daniel Weld	Moses: Crafts:	

The settlers here at this time were those who held their lands by virtue of being original Dedham grantees, or their legal successors, or men who had been induced to settle here by grants of land from the Proprietors. Other portions of the Grant had been, as we have seen, set out to individual owners. The undivided and ungranted remainder, which included Cheapside and Great River—the territory given the Proprietors "in liew of what they parted with to Hatfield"—was the land now held "in propryetie" by the present Proprietors. The "Inhabitants" included all actual settlers; and to the "Inhabitants," it will be noted, the seven mile square grant was made in May, 1673. By the record of the meeting above, it is seen that the interest of the "Proprietors" was merged with the larger grant of the "Inhabitants." All became joint owners, and they were the body hereafter known as the "Proprietors," while the "Inhabitants" of the future, included these and all new comers. The organization of the Proprietors was kept up more than a hundred years, and until all this land was disposed of. The individual interest in this large estate was according to the number of cow commons held by each at the time of the consolidation. Their Record books, full and complete, are preserved in the Archives of the Pocumtuck Valley Memorial Association.

This change in the tenure of land was an important one. Desirable lands were released which could be offered to new settlers. Liberal offers brought many adventurers to the place; a public house became necessary, and Moses Crafts applied for authority to keep one. Sept. 27, 1674, the Court at Northampton issued him a license "to keep an ordinary at Paucumtuck, and sell wines and strong waters for one year, provided he keep good order in his house."

SECOND MEETING.

Novemb^r 17, 1674. It is ordered by the Committee, that whereas according to a former order by the said Comittee, there having binn a list of land by the proprietors of Deerfeild presented which are wanting of their true measure, and their being at present some objection aboute some considerable error in that last measure &c, that therefore, there shall be 14 dayes, time allowed in which any proprietor or proprietors of the towne aforesaid, haue libertye to try or make triall of any part or parcells of the lands afore measured where they are the most jealous of mistakes, and if there be no considerable errors found, then the Committee to conclude the Testimony of the fformer measurers to be valid, in the particular parcells that are wanting, provided they giue notice to Robert Hinsdell, when they measure, to go with them The Committee haue appointed Joshua Carter and Jno Allen to measure any lands as aforesaid & to be paid by the whole in some small piece of land

The Committe with the proprietors have granted unto Mr. Saml Mather & his heirs forever within the township of Deerfeild an allotment to the quantitie of a sixteen Common alotment viz 48 akers viz that eight common lott that was the church lott of Dedham and an eight common lott more in the most convenient place provided he be resident in said town foure years ffrom the time of his ffirst dwelling here.

The Committee with the proprietors aforesaid haue granted to Richard Weller and his heirs foreuer: twenty akers of land part of which lying in two percells he desires known to the proprietors & the rest as conveniently for place as may be, provided he be a resident for his dwelling ffoure yeares ffrom the time of his first settlement with his familye. Also they have granted to him a hoame lott.

The Comittee with the proprietors aboues[d] have granted and giuen to Sergt plimpton and his heirs forever within the township of Deerfield a hoame lott allsoe a twelue common lott viz 36 akers of land in the most convenient place as may be, provided he be a resident for his dwelling there 4 years ffrom the time of his first settlement there—

The Committee, with the proprietors, doe Confirm the exchange of land between Leeft Clarke & themselves & Saml Hinsdell, & have granted to Leeft Clarke a house lott where he now hath accepted of

The Towne have granted with the Committee to Zebediah Williams a house lott of 4 akers as conveniently for place, as may be provided he dwell on the same for ffoure yeares.

On the back of this folio page is endorsed "Noumb[r] 1674, M[r] Mathers Grant, Rich Wellers Grant plimpton &c transcribed." If, as it appears in the last item of the above record, the "towne" took the initiatory steps in the grant to Zebediah Williams, it is the earliest action of the settlers as a *town*, yet discovered.

In the above paper, and from this time forward, our plantation was called Deerfield. By what authority, or for what reason, is left to conjecture. Springfield was doubtless named from Springfield in England, the home of Wm Pynchon its founder; Brookfield, says tradition, from its streams; Hadley and Hatfield were also named from towns in England; Southfield (now Suffield), Westfield and Northfield, from location in respect to the older settlements; Greenfield from Green river. An abundance of deer in this locality may have suggested Deerfield.

The settlers found the meadows clear of trees, except the elms and maples, which fringed the sinuous Pocumtuck, or were mirrored in the quiet ponds which they embowered. Here the natives had cultivated their corn, beans, squashes, pumpkins and tobacco. Frequent burnings had kept the woodlands clear of underbrush, to the detriment of timber trees, which were not abundant, except in swamps and wet ravines. It was not difficult to traverse the forests on horseback, and tours of observation and discovery were generally made by mounted men. Soon after the permanent settlement and for many years, the woods were protected from depredations, and the cutting of timber regulated by the authority of the town.

Along the town Street, houses were built upon the most available spots nearly its whole length. Some lots can now be identified as those drawn by the occupants in the original draft; others, less certainly, by subsequent ownership; incidental data give still less assurance in other cases. The description hereafter given, however, may be regarded as substantially correct. The growth of the colony was rapid. Samuel Hinsdell, the pioneer, built a house in 1669. Samson Frary followed the next year. In 1673 at least twenty families were on the ground.

The road from Hatfield came through Bars, Mill, and South Meadows, entering the Street from the southwest, on land long since washed away by the Pocumtuck. The Town Street of 1671 was not the comparatively dry and level thoroughfare of to-day. Going either north or south from Meetinghouse Hill, which was by no means the smooth area now represented by our "Common," the road plunged abruptly into a quagmire, crossed by a "corduroy" causeway. Remains of that on the northern side were dug up from a depth of ten feet, about 1870. Some seventy-five rods beyond this place a steep rise was met, while still northerly thirty rods, the road again fell off into a swamp, trending eastward from the Sheldon lot. This swamp, says a family tradition, remained a mass of tangled alders for eighty years after the settlement. By the same authority the timbers of the barn now standing on the Sheldon lot were cut on the margin of this swamp before 1730. Each of these depressions crossing the street marked the site of a former bed of the Pocumtuck river.

On three sides of the village lay the open meadows, spreading two miles north, two miles south, and about one mile to the west. Beyond this narrow circuit the unbroken forest stretched away to Canada on the north, to Lancaster on the east and the Hudson on the west. The nearest settlement was Hatfield, on the south, through which was kept up communication with the civilized world.

The hardy yeomanry, some of them born in England, and well on in years, all seeking a permanent home in the New

World, appear to have lived here in quiet contentment. Peace and plenty smiled upon the adventurers. The rich alluvial bottoms were easy of cultivation. The virgin soil yielded abundant crops of wheat, peas, rye, Indian corn, beans and flax. The men became skilled in woodcraft. Game abounded in the forests, while the waters teemed with the choicest fish. Their flocks and herds had increased rapidly and the Common Field had been inclosed with a substantial fence to protect the crops from the stock which roamed on the surrounding hills. A minister of their own choice was going in and out before them, and the young colony seemed established on a foundation of peace and prosperity. The dark cloud looming in the distance was unobserved or unheeded. The settlers had lived on the most familiar terms with the Indians and had no doubt of the fidelity of their dusky friends. The tormenting fear of their treachery, which afterwards so harrassed their children, found no place with the pioneers. When news of the outbreak in far off Plymouth reached them in the summer of 1675, it brought no disquiet to them. This trusting people could not conceive the horrors of an Indian war, and none dreamed that the besom of destruction, which was to sweep them from the face of the earth, was already poised in the air above them.

Biographical Notes on the men here before Philip's War, with location of their home lots, so far as ascertained. The numbers refer to the original draft. [See *ante*, page 19.]

Allen, John, son of Samuel of Windsor, Conn., was of the same stock as Ethan Allen. He married in 1669, Mary, daughter of William Hannum, of Northampton, and was killed with Capt. Lothrop at Bloody Brook, Sept. 18, 1675. He left three children who settled in Connecticut, where descendants are numerous.

Barnard, Francis, born in England in 1647, was an early settler at Hartford, whence he removed with the founders of Hadley in 1659. A genuine frontiersman, he pushed on to Pocumtuck with the first wave of emigration. The returning tide left him at Hadley, where he died in 1698. He married in 1664, Hannah Marvin. In 1677 he married widow Frances Dickinson. He had six children, from whom the

Connecticut valley Barnards are descended. An unmarried son, John, was killed with Lothrop.

Barsham, Philip, was of Hatfield in 1672. He was killed with Lothrop, leaving a widow—Sarah—and children. Nothing more concerning him has been found.

Bartholomew, William, was a carpenter, from Roxbury. He married in 1663, Mary Johnson; settled on house lot No. 10, the Col. Joseph Stebbins lot. He had five children. Surviving Philip's war, he retired to Braintree; but did not forget his old home, and in 1677 was one of the petitioners for aid in a resettlement. In 1685 he sold his home lot to Daniel Belding, and removed to Branford, Connecticut.

Carter, Joshua, late from England. He lived on that part of No. 36, occupied by the late William Sheldon. He married in 1663, Mary, daughter of Zechariah Field; was killed with Lothrop, leaving three children, who settled in Connecticut.

Crafts, Moses, son of Griffin of Roxbury, born in 1641. He married in 1667, Rebecca, daughter of Peter Gardner, and had, in 1674, at least three children. Sept. 29th of that year he was licensed by the Court at Northampton to "keep an ordinary." He retired to Hatfield on the breaking up of the plantation, thence to Branford, Conn., and in 1683 he settled in Wethersfield, where he was living in 1702.

Daniels, Samuel, son of Robert of Watertown, was an original Dedham proprietor and drew house lot No. 36—the Orlando Ware place—which he occupied. The lot was owned in 1704 by John Catlin. Daniels returned towards the Bay, and his subsequent history is unknown.

Farrington, John, from Dedham, settled on No. 18, the lot now owned by C. A. Stebbins. He married in 1649, Mary Bullard; returned to Dedham, where he died in 1676. His descendants are numerous in Eastern Massachusetts.

Field, Zechariah, son of Zechariah of England, Dorchester and Hatfield, born in 1645. He married in 1670, Mary Webb, and died here in 1674, leaving three children, who removed to Connecticut, and afterwards to Northfield.

Frary, Samson, son of John of Medfield, was of Hatfield in 1668, and here in 1670, the second known settler. He married in 1660, Mary Daniels, of Medfield. The last of his five children was born in 1675. He returned at the Permanent

Settlement, and with his wife perished when Deerfield was sacked by Hertel de Rouville, Feb. 29, 1704.

Gillett, Joseph, son of Jonathan of Dorchester and Windsor, born in 1641. He married in 1664, Elizabeth, daughter of John Hawks of Hadley, and settled on lot No. 32—the Dr. Willard lot—which his heirs sold in 1684, to Samuel Carter. He fell with Lothrop, leaving seven children, who settled about Windsor and Simsbury, where they left posterity.

Harrington, Samuel, here in 1673. Antecedents unknown; wounded in the attack, Sept. 12, 1675; married in 1677, the widow of Nathaniel Sutlieffe; was of Hatfield, 1679, and not found later.

Hawks, John, son of John of Hadley, occupied 16 cow commons of Col. Pynchon's land here in the summer of 1675. He was active through Philip's war; was in the Falls fight; and one of the brave men from Hadley who went to the succor of Hatfield, when attacked by Indians May 30, 1676, when he was wounded. He married in 1667, Martha Baldwin, with whom he lived ten years. He became a permanent settler in 1683, and married in 1696, Alice, widow of Samuel Allis. She was killed Feb. 29, 1704, when all his children and grandchildren of the name were lost. In his old age he removed to Waterbury, Conn., to live with his only surviving child, who had married Jonathan Scott of that town.

Hinsdell, Robert, born about 1617; one of the founders of the church at Dedham, in 1638, and of that at Medfield, in 1650; was a member of the Ancient and Honorable Artillery Company; removed to Hadley in 1672, and was here the next year with five stalwart sons and one married daughter. His second wife, Elizabeth, widow of John Hawks of Hadley, he married in 1672. He fell at Bloody Brook with three of his sons.

Hinsdell, Barnabas, son of Robert, born in 1639; lived on No. 9—the Ralph Williams lot—was of Hatfield in 1666, where he married Sarah Taylor. He fell with Lothrop, leaving five children, who retired to Connecticut.

Hinsdell, Samuel, son of Robert, born about 1642; of Hadley in 1666, and, as has been stated, the first settler here; was one of the most prominent men until his death at Bloody Brook. He married in 1660, Mehitable Johnson. Their son Mehuman was the first white man born in the town. He left six or seven other children, from whom the Hinsdales of Deerfield and Greenfield were descended.

Hinsdell, Experience, son of Robert, born in 1646; married at Hatfield in 1672, Mary, daughter of John Hawks, and at once brought his bride here, where two or three daughters were born. He was one of the guides for Capt. Turner on his march to Peskeompskut, May 18, 1676, and was lost in that expedition.

Hinsdell, John, son of Robert, born in 1648. Little is known of him save that he was a settler in 1673 and was lost with Lothrop, leaving a family, of which nothing certain has been found.

Hinsdell, Ephraim, son of Robert, born in 1650. He of all the sons survived Philip's war. He settled in Hatfield, where he married in 1676, Mehitable, daughter of John Plympton, and died in 1681.

Mather, Samuel, son of Timothy of Dorchester, born in 1651; graduated at Harvard in 1671; was minister here in December, 1673, and may have been earlier; was nephew to Increase, and cousin to Cotton Mather, the famous Boston ministers. Despairing of a permanent colony here, in 1680, he settled in Branford, Conn., and afterwards in Windsor, where he died in 1728. A volume of his printed sermons is in Memorial Hall.

Nims, Godfrey, bought home lot No. 35, in 1674, but I do not find him living here until the Permanent Settlement.

Plympton, John, of Dedham, 1642, removed to Medfield, and thence here before 1673. Escaping the dangers of Philip's war, he returned in 1677, when the war was supposed to be over, to rebuild his house. Sept. 19 he was taken captive by a band of barbarous marauders under Ashpelon, carried to Canada, where he was burned at the stake. He was called "Old Sergeant Plympton," and was doubtless born in England. He married Jane Dummer, by whom he had thirteen children. His son John was a soldier under Capt. Moseley in Philip's war; another son, Jonathan, fell at Bloody Brook.

Plympton, Peter, son of John, born in 1652; married Mary Munden; was in Moseley's company in Philip's war; came back at the resettlement, but removed to Marlboro about 1700, where he died in 1717.

Smead, William, son of widow Judith of Dorchester, born before 1640 married in 1658, Elizabeth, daughter of Thomas Lawrence of Hingham; was of Northampton, 1660. In 1674 he bought house lot No. 25 of Thomas Fuller, an original proprietor, where he built a house—perhaps the one now [1886] standing there—and where he died before 1704. He had ten children, and was probably the ancestor of all of the name in the country. His oldest son, William, born in 1661, was killed with Lothrop. His widow and three daughters were killed in the assault of Feb. 29, 1704.

Smith, Martin, probably from New Jersey; returned at the Permanent Settlement, was captured in 1693, by Indians, and remained a prisoner in Canada until 1698, when he returned to find his wife, Sarah, under a sentence of death for murdering her illegitimate babe. She was hanged at Springfield, Aug. 25, 1698. Her pastor, Rev. John Williams, preached a sermon there on the occasion, which was printed. Martin perished in the assault of 1704.

Stebbins, John, son of John of Northampton, born in 1647; was in the Lothrop massacre, and is the only man known to have escaped unhurt. The second day after, he enlisted under the gallant Capt. Samuel Moseley, and served with him until the close of the war. He remained a few years in the vicinity of Boston, working at the trade of a carpenter. Here he married Dorothy, daughter of John Alexander, a Scotsman, but returned at the Permanent Settlement. In 1704, himself, his wife and five children were captured and taken to Canada. Three of the younger children never came back. He lived on No. 35, and died in 1724.

Stockwell, Quintin, from Dedham, 1672, settled on No. 31— now the Orthodox parsonage—had wife, Abigail, and at least two children, before 1677. Like Sergeant Plympton, supposing hostilities had ceased, he came with him to rebuild in 1677, and shared his captivity, but not his horrible fate. He returned from Canada and wrote an interesting account of his experience, known as " Stockwell's Narrative."

Sutlieffe, Nathaniel, from Medfield, bought in 1672, lot No. 43 at the north end—the Asa Stebbins lot—and doubtless settled there. He married in 1665, Hannah, daughter of Old Sergeant Plympton; was killed with Capt. Turner, May 19,

1676, leaving a widow and three children, who settled in Durham, Connecticut.

Tufts, James, son of Peter of Charlestown, lived on the lot drawn by Mrs. Bunker, No. 37—now [1886] held by Mrs. Catharine E. B. Allen—and the site of Mrs. Hannah Beaman's schoolhouse in 1695; was killed with Lothrop. If he had a family, nothing is known of it.

Weld, Daniel, came from Medfield, 1672 or 3, where he was the first church recorder; married in 1664, Mary, daughter of Robert Hinsdell, and had five children. He was called "Mr.," and may have been a Ruling Elder before the advent of Mr. Mather. He lived on lot No. 23—now owned by Elisha Wells.

Weller, Richard, successively of Windsor, Farmington, Northampton, and of Pocumtuck in 1673. He married in 1640, Anna Wilson, and in 1662, Elizabeth Curtis. Of his six grown up children, the youngest, Thomas, born in 1653, was killed with Lothrop. He returned to Deerfield on the Permanent Settlement, where he died about 1690.

Weller, John, son of Richard, born in 1645. He married in 1670, Mary, daughter of Alexander Alvord, of Northampton. They had three children in 1675. He returned at the resettlement, and about 1686 the family removed to Connecticut.

Williams, Zebediah, sold out his land in Northampton, in 1674. He was here in 1675, and was one of the teamsters killed with Lothrop. His widow, Mary, daughter of Wm. Miller, married Godfrey Nims.

CHAPTER IV.

THE POCUMTUCK INDIANS.

Midway between the plantations of Pilgrim and Puritan on the seacoast, and the Dutch settlements on the upper Hudson, lay a region scarcely mentioned by the early writers of New England history, in which lived a people of whom the information they give is still more scanty. It is only here and there, as one pores over the musty records of the period, that a glimpse of this territory, or its occupants, appears through the primeval haze. Yet, on concentrating these feeble gleams on the speculum of patient scrutiny, at length there stands out in bold relief a powerful confederation of savages, occupying or dominating the great valley of the Connecticut river and its tributaries, from Brattleboro to Hartford.

Frontenac, governor of Canada, called them the Socoquis or River Indians; but this power may well be called the Pocumtuck Confederacy, for the Pocumtucks were the leading tribe and her chieftains the acknowledged head of its warlike expeditions.

The subordinate clans or allies of this confederacy were the *Naunawtuks*—as they were called by William Pynchon in 1648—situated on both sides of the river at Hadley and Northampton; the *Agawams*, in Springfield, Suffield and Enfield; the *Warranokes*, on the Westfield river and its branches; the *Podunks*, about Windsor; and the *Tunxis*, on the Farmington river. On the north were the *Squakheags*, occupying the Paquayag valley, and jointly with the Pocumtucks, the territory of Northfield, Vernon and Hinsdale. There is reason to think that the Squakheags were a fugitive band, settled here under the protection of the Pocumtucks—probably a fragment of the *Mahicans* on the Hudson, driven off by the *Mohawks*, about 1610. They were called Souquakes by the Dutch. The Pocumtucks proper were located in the Deerfield river valley, and were thickly settled on both sides of the Connecticut and the Deerfield about their confluence.

As the Pocumtucks rarely appear in history, save in their wars with other tribes, a brief view of the latter will aid us to a better estimate of the former. The period is about 1633.

I. The *Narragansets*, occupying what is now the State of Rhode Island, was the largest tribe in New England. Estimates of their numbers range wildly from two to five thousand warriors. Their chief Sachem was *Canonicus;* but *Miantonomo*, his nephew, was the ruling spirit of the nation.

II. The *Wampanoags*, or *Pokanokets*, were located east of the Narragansets, about Buzzard's Bay, and toward Cape Cod. The "Good old *Massasoit*" was at the head of this tribe. He was succeeded by *Wamsutta*, his son, who, dying in 1661, left his brother, *Pometacon*—better known as King Philip—chief Sachem.

III. West of the Narragansets, and having their chief seat about the Mystic river, and extending along the coast to the Niantic, lived the warlike *Pequots*. Their head Sachem was *Wapegwooit*. According to a tradition among them at this time, the tribe fought their way to the coast from the northwest. They were then holding as conquered territory, the Connecticut valley as far up as Windsor, and had subdued and held tributary, the *Niantics*, the Block Island Indians, and other clans as far westward as New Haven, and also some upon Long Island.

IV. The *Mohegans*, living north of the Pequots, were an offshoot of the latter. *Uncas*, their chief, was of the royal blood, his mother, *Meekumump*, being aunt to Wapegwooit, and he heir apparent to the sachemship of the Pequots, through the female line. At this period *Uncas* had but a scanty following. Events to be narrated show how he obtained a power which, for more than forty years, was a leading element in the affairs of New England. For half of that time *Uncas* may almost be considered the arbiter of its destiny.

V. Previous to 1633, there is reason to believe, the clans living on the Connecticut below Hartford had been in a confederacy under Sachem *Altarbaenhoot*, whose power had been broken by the Pequots. His son and successor, who had at this time no land nor followers, was *Sequasson*.

VI. The *Mahicans*, then in a broken condition, lived on the Hudson, below Albany. This tribe has often been confounded with the Mohegans, but I have failed to discover even the most distant connection. The Mahicans held friendly relations with the Pocumtucks and were at times allied with them in their wars against the Mohawks and the Mohegans.

VII. The *Nipmucks*, were scattered in small clans over the central part of Massachusetts and the northeast part of Connecticut. The *Quabaugs*, at Brookfield, were claimed as subjects by both *Uncas* and the Pokanokets, but they were finally absorbed by the Nipmucks.

VIII. The *Mohawks*, located on the river of that name, west of Albany, were one of the Five Nations. They were the most warlike of all the tribes enumerated. Brave, enterprising and rapacious, with all the power of the Five Nations to back them in an emergency, they were feared, hated and courted, alike by English, French and natives.

For estimating the population of the Pocumtucks at any given time a few slender data only are found.

In 1658 a fine was imposed by the Commissioners of the United Colonies upon certain allied tribes for damages done at Niantic. In the distribution of the amount, the Pocumtucks were assessed the same as the Narragansets. The lowest estimate of the population of the Narragansets met with, is that of Gookin—probably the best authority in the matter—who places it at 5000 souls as late as 1674. Again, in the winter of 1637-8, on account of the interruption of agricultural pursuits by the Pequot war in Connecticut the summer before, the English there were suffering for bread. The General Court, foreseeing that a supply could be obtained only of the Indians up the river, passed an order, Feb. 9th, that "Noe man in this River, nor Agawam shall goe vpp River amonge the Indians, or at home at their houses, to trade for corne," under a penalty of 5 shillings per bushel. This was on the ground that "if euery man be at liberty to trucke with the Indians vppon the River, where the supply of Corne in all likelyhood is to bee had to furnish our necessities, the market of Corne amonge the Indians may be greatly advanced, to the prejudice of these plantations." To prevent this corner in corn, March 9th, a contract was made with William Pynchon, the founder of Springfield, to deliver

500 bushels of corn at Windsor and Hartford at 5 shillings per bushel. For all above 500 bushels he might charge two pence more. Payment was to be made in wampum, three pieces for a penny, or in merchantable beaver, at ten shillings a pound. It was provided, however, that if Pynchon was obliged to pay the Indians more than "sixe sixes of wampum a pecke," then his price might be increased in proportion. A sort of non-importation act was also passed, for the benefit of Mr. Pynchon in this transaction. It was to the effect that no more than 4 shillings a bushel should be paid to Indians who brought their own corn down to sell, under a penalty of five shillings per bushel.

Corn was not found at Agawam, Warranoco, or Naunawtuk, and Pynchon or his agents, with generous bags of wampum, pushed up through the wilderness to Pocumtuck. This was only eighteen years after the Mayflower dropped her anchor in Plymouth Bay. The Pocumtucks had plenty of food to sell, and it must have been a busy and exciting day when Pynchon came among them to buy 500 bushels of corn, bringing twelve thousand strings of wampum to put in circulation there. Doubtless files of women, with baskets on their backs, were soon seen threading the narrow pathways to the river; for in a short time a fleet of fifty canoes, freighted with Indian corn, was on its way down the Connecticut to relieve the impending famine in the settlements below.

This great commercial event in the history of the Pocumtucks must have taught them to recognize the advantage of a market among the English. It may have been a reason for their long continued peaceful attitude towards the strange intruders. This large store of surplus grain, at that time of the year, tends to show that the Pocumtucks were an agricultural people, industrious and provident. By its sale they show knowledge of the law of trade and a readiness to better themselves by its operation. It is also strong evidence of a large population at Pocumtuck—which is the main point under consideration. Furthermore, in 1652, the Pocumtucks were ranked by the Dutch at New York as among the "*Great Indians,*" that is, the large tribes. From *existing evidence*, there is proof of a dense population, or of long continued residence. Concurring testimony to habitation is found on all the bluffs about the meadows and on every spot on their surface which rises above the spring floods. The practiced eye discovers similar marks all along the banks of the Connecticut, and particularly about the mouth of the Pocumtuck river, and at the falls of Peskeompskut. If these dwelling places were occupied contemporaneously they indicate a population so dense that the estimate of the Commissioners in 1658 should not excite surprise.

This region was well adapted to savage life. The meadows produced abundant crops of their staples, corn, pumpkins, squash and beans. The streams and ponds teemed with fish and water-fowl. Nuts and berries abounded. Beaver, otter, fisher, mink and muskrat were plenty and easily secured. The bear, deer and raccoon, on the hills, fell victims to the arts or prowess of the natives. "Silk Grass" and Indian hemp, for their lines and nets, grew freely about their wigwams; surviving patches of the latter still indicate their haunts. What more could the man of nature ask?

The soil appears to have been held in fee simple by petty chieftains, heads of families or clans, in tracts with well defined bounds. No evidence is found of feudal tenure, or of feudal service to the chief Sachem. Women's rights were so far recognized at Pocumtuck, that the right of squaws to own land, as well as to cultivate it, was fully acknowledged. At least four Pocumtuck women sold real estate to the English. *Mashalisk*, by two deeds, conveyed large tracts in Deerfield and Sunderland. Deeds of land in Northfield were signed by *Asogoa*, daughter of *Sowanaett*, deceased; by *Nenepownam*, with her husband, *Pammook*, and by *Pompatakemo*, with her father, *Mashepetott*.

It is known that nine deeds were made of territory at Pocumtuck proper, although not one foot of land was sold until after the great disaster of 1664, to be related hereafter.

In 1614, Adrian Block discovered the Connecticut, which he named Fresh river. He was from Holland, and in 1633, the Dutch sent a party up the river, who bought a tract of land at Hartford, and there erected the first house ever built in the valley. The land was obtained of *Wapegwooit*, the Pequot Sachem, who then held it by conquest. The conquered chief *Altarbaenhoot*, was forced to consent to the bargain. All parties, however, agreed that this purchase should be strictly neutral ground.

While the Dutch were making a foothold at Hartford, a party from Plymouth built a trading house above them, at Windsor, and within three years English colonies were established at Hartford, Windsor, Wethersfield and Springfield. Peace on the neutral ground was of short duration. War broke out between the Dutch and Pequots. Wapegwooit was treacherously slain, and *Uncas* laid claim to the Sachemdom of the Pequots. The bulk of the tribe, however, adhered to *Sassacus*, the son of their murdered chieftain, and he became its head. Proud, ambitious, cruel and aggressive, the new Sachem soon became the terror of both colonist and native. War was declared against him by the English, and in May, 1637, his principal fort was stormed and a large number of his men killed. Sassacus, with a few followers, fled to the Mohawks, but only to meet death at their hands. Scattered bands were hunted down and killed or captured, and in a few weeks the proud Pequot nation became extinct. The miserable few who escaped death, forbidden to use the tribal name, were divided between the Mohegans and the Narragansets, a yearly tribute being exacted from each individual.

How far the Pocumtucks became involved in the war which resulted in the extermination of the Pequots is not known. That they were implicated to some extent, is proved by the fact, that in September, 1637, a tribute of one and a quarter fathoms of wampum per man was assessed upon them by the English, toward paying the expenses of the war. The victorious Capt. Mason was sent to collect this, and it was doubtless paid with alacrity. The next year the Pocumtucks sent a present of beaver to Gov. Winthrop, on hearing a report that the English were about to make war upon them. The Governor told them they had nothing to fear if they had not wronged the English, and a treaty of peace was concluded between the Pocumtucks and the English, which was not broken by that generation which had witnessed the fate of the Pequots.

In 1638, a tripartite treaty was made by the colony of Connecticut, the Narragansets and the Mohegans. The Indians agreed, by its terms, that no appeal to arms was to be made by either tribe, in any quarrel between themselves or against other tribes, without first referring the case to the arbitration of the English, whose decision was to be binding. This treaty, the colonists made a poor pretense of enforcing, and the tribes appealed to it only as it suited their purposes. But, as it ultimately appeared, its consequences were important and far reaching.

Not long after, a conspiracy was planned by Miantonomo to cut off all the English settlers. In this project the Pocumtucks appear to have been involved, but the plot was discovered in August, 1642, and nothing came of it.

In August, 1643, Massachusetts, Plymouth, Connecticut and New Haven, "For comon Safety and Peace" formed a confederacy under the title of "The United Colonies of New England." Its affairs were managed by a Congress of two Commissioners from each colony. All power of dealing with the Indians, in peace or war, was delegated to this body; an act of wisdom if not of necessity, for the English were soon involved in the quarrels between Uncas and Miantonomo.

In 1643 Miantonomo, after several attempts to assassinate Uncas, regardless of the tripartite treaty, invaded the Mohegan country with an army of 1000 men. After Miantonomo had declined the challenge of Uncas to settle the condition of both tribes by a personal combat, a battle followed, in which the Narragansets were routed, and their chieftain captured. Miantonomo disdained to ask for his life of Uncas, but the most strenuous efforts were made by his tribe for his ransom; and an appeal was made to the Commissioners in his behalf. They could not interfere to save him, for by the terms of the tripartite treaty the English were bound to favor the invaded tribe. By their consent, Miantonomo was executed by Uncas, after a short captivity. Fierce war thenceforth raged between the Narragansets and the Mohegans. To all remonstrances from the Commissioners the Narragansets replied: "We must avenge the death of our Prince." At length Uncas was so hard pressed that English soldiers were sent to his defense, and the colonies were fully committed on the side of the Mohegans by declaring war against their enemy. The latter soon sued for peace, which was concluded Aug. 27, 1645, on an agreement to pay the English 2000 fathom of wampum, and send to Boston four children of their chiefs, as hostages.

Quiet was hardly restored in the South before trouble arose up the river among the Pocumtucks. An Indian arrested for burning a tar camp near Windsor, was forcibly rescued from the officers by *Chickwallop*, Sachem of the Naunawtuks. The commissioners at once sent messengers to demand the culprit. Not finding him at Naunawtuk, they proceeded to Warranoco, where the Indians were insolent, "vauntinge themselves in their armes, bows and arrowes, hatchets, swords, some with their guns ready charged, before, and in the presence of the English messengers, they primed and cocked them, ready to give fire, and told them that if they should offer to carry away any man thence, the Indians were resolved to fight, and if they should stay but one night at the English tradinge house, near all the country would come in to rescue any such Indian seized." The messengers returned without the offender.

In this state of affairs the Commissioners made proclamation, that in case any tribe refused to deliver up criminals taking refuge among them, an English force should be sent to make reprisals, and that the captives thus taken should be held as slaves, unless the fugitives be delivered up. This vigorous measure brought the Pocumtucks to terms. *Noynetachee*, a Sachem of Warranoco, went before the Commissioners, where he "denied" some things charged and "excused some part." He said no harm was intended to the English, and that "8 fathom of wampum" had been tendered in settlement. So harmony was temporarily restored.

Upon the murder of Wapegwooit, Sassacus, as we have seen, succeeded him, and claimed rulership over the tribes subdued by his father. Among the nominal chieftains of those tribes remaining in exile was *Sequasson*. When the Pequots were scattered, and Sassacus slain, he had emerged from obscurity, gathered a small following, and hoped to regain the power which Wapegwooit had wrested from his father, Altarbaenhoot. Upon the rise of Uncas under the protection of the English, who put under him the greater part of the Pequot captives, the hopes of Sequasson were blasted. He became the deadly enemy of the favorite, and plotted to ruin or kill him. Leave was given Uncas to retaliate, and Sequasson was driven again into exile, taking refuge at Warranoco. Here in the spring of 1646 he engaged one of his followers, named *Watchebrok*, whom he had before hired to kill an Indian Sachem, to murder either Mr. Hopkins, Mr. Haynes, the Connecticut Commissioners, or Mr. Whiting, a magistrate of Hartford. Sequasson said to him: "I am almost ruined, and the English at Hartford are the cause of it." He gave Watchebrok three girdles of wampum, in hand, and promised a "great reward" when the deed should be done. The murderer was then to flee to the Mohawks, giving out on the way that he had been hired by Uncas to "do the work for so much wampum. That would set the English against Uncas, and then he, the said Sequasson, should rise again." Watchebrok grew timid, and confessed the plot; upon which Jonathan Gilbert was sent to Warranoco to demand that Sequasson should come before the Commissioners to answer the charge. He was promised safe conduct, both ways, whatever the result of the examination should be. He refused to appear, and fled to Pocumtuck. The Commissioners were determined to take Sequasson by force, and at their request Uncas gladly undertook the service. He could thus serve the English and revenge himself on his old enemy at the same time. With a party of Mohegan warriors, he marched to Pocumtuck, and captured Sequasson, by a night surprise, and took him to Hartford. The charge against him not being fully proved, Sequasson was released, but he remained in exile until 1650, when at the intercession of the Mohawks and the Pocumtucks, he was allowed to return home.

Upon the execution of Miantonomo, *Pessacus*, his brother, became chief Sachem of the Narragansets. Finding that the Mohegans, backed by the English, were more than a match for him, he in 1647, made overtures to the Mohawks and Pocumtucks for assistance against Uncas. The latter tribe, who could not forgive Uncas for invading their territory and carrying off Sequasson, willingly consented. A grand-campaign was planned for the next year, in which the power of the Mohegan chief was to be forever broken. The Narragansets were to make their attack July 5th or 6th, 1648, and their allies, as soon as the corn was ripe, were to join in the war. The reason for this singular arrangement of the campaign does not appear, further than the "Narragansetts were to begin the war." The rendezvous for the allies was at Pocumtuck, and in July and August, reports reached the English that a thousand warriors were in arms there for the expedition. The Commissioners met early in September, and at once sent the State interpreter, Thomas Stanton, to learn the facts. He found the Pocumtuck Valley swarming with armed men who had been busy in making preparations for the march, and building "a very large and a stronge fort," while waiting for the Mohawks. Stanton found "one thousand warriors at Pocumtuck, 300 or more having guns, powder and bullets." Assembling the Sachems, he represented to them the danger of these proceedings. He told them that the English were a just as well as warlike people; that they were bound by treaty to defend Uncas against the Narragansets, and however much they wished to keep peace with the Pocumtucks, they were equally bound to defend them against any allies of the Narragansets. He probably reminded them of the fate of the Pequots when they incurred the hostility of the English ten years before.

Upon the representations of Stanton, and news that the French, or Eastern, Indians had attacked the Mohawks and killed two of their Sachems, the chiefs decided to give up the expedition. Uncas, who had easily repulsed the Narragansets, exultantly attributed this failure of the allies to their fear of him, for he had "*dared* the Mohawks, threatening, if they came, to set his ground, with gobbets of their flesh." He felt himself a powerful chief, and it would seem that Pessacus shared this view, for the next year, instead of attacking him in open war, he attempted to assassinate his hated enemy.

In 1650 the Narragansets were brought to terms by a threat of the Commissioners to invade and lay waste their country, and a few months of quiet followed. In 1652, a scheme was on foot between the Dutch of New York, and the New England Indians, for a secret rising to cut off the English and the Mohegans. Guns, ammunition, cloth and wampum, were sent from New York to the "Great Indian" tribes, to engage them in the plot. Among these "Great Indians" were the Pocumtucks. The result of the application is not known, as the plot was discovered in season to frustrate it.

In 1654 the Pocumtucks were again on the war path. *Ninigret*—Sachem of the Niantics—had engaged them to assist in the invasion of Long Island. On reaching Fisher's Island they were told that the Long Island Indians were under the protection of the English; when they at once turned the prows of their canoes homeward. A small party of young braves, however, separating from the main body, went on a raid against the *Potatucks*, carrying off some captives and considerable plunder. In relation to this affair, the Commissioners, in Sept., 1654, write to,—

"*Weerewomaag*, the Pecomtock Sachem, and the rest of the Sachems there, that the Commissioners are Informed, that though Ninegrett by Misinformation drew downe the Pecumtack Sachems and Indians, as farr as fishers Island, to Invade and make warr vpon the long Islanders, yett, when they vnderstood that the said long Islanders were frinds to the English * * * they desisted from their Enterprise and peacably Returned home, which the Commissioners accept as an euidence of theire respect, and shall not concent that the said Pocumptocks shallbee anyways desturbed or impressed by the Indians in Amity or Couenant with the English."

In regard to the unauthorized raid on the Potatucks, they urge that the captives and goods be returned, that the peace of the country be thereby better settled.

In 1655 or 6 the *Podunks*, a Pocumtuck clan near Hartford, were broken up and driven off by Uncas, contrary to the orders of the English authorities. To avenge this act, the Pocumtucks marched in force against the Mohegans, defeated Uncas in battle, killing and capturing many of his men. Uncas, pretending final submission to the Pocumtucks, sued for peace through the English. Connecticut sent messengers, with men and wampum, from Uncas to the Pocumtucks; but the latter were in no mood for peace. *Wonopequen*, one of the Sachems, abused one of the messsengers, "throwing an oxe horne and the wampum att him, charging his men to kill his horses," and tried to strike another with a gun. An arrangement for peace was finally made and the Pocumtucks gave up their Mohegan captives. This half peace was of short duration. On their return, the Connecticut embassy was again assaulted by Wonopequen, and one of Uncas's envoys taken away by force. Having accomplished his object, the treacherous Uncas at once made a hostile march against the Naunawtuks. The Commissioners, fearing lest they might become involved in a war with the Pocumtucks through the acts of their troublesome ally, called him to account for this breach of faith. But the Mohegan Sachem was a difficult subject to deal with, under the existing circumstances. He had great force of character. He was brave, fearless, and daring to rashness; fond of war and turbulent in peace; haughty, imperious, and often cruel to those under him; artful and faithless in dealing with the natives, he was hated by them as a traitor to his race. His ambition and avarice, as well as his gratitude for protection, held him ever loyal to the English.* He was insolent and aggressive to the tribes around him and engaged in war regardless of opposing numbers, believing that the maintenance of his power was so essential to the colonists that they would come to his help in case of disaster. He judged correctly in this, but the Commissioners were often placed in embarrassing circumstances, and say they feared he might "draw on mischievous effects above his power to issue:" and so it proved.

In May, 1657, *Massepetoat*, Chief Sachem of the Pocumtucks, having engaged the Mohawks, the Narragansets and Tunxis Indians as allies, determined on a war of extermination against the Mohegans. With a show of respect to the English, he sent to the General Court of Massachusetts to ask their consent to make war upon Uncas. His agents, *Wetowasnati* and *Wiscoqunc*, two Pocumtuck Sachems, are told that the Court does not understand the ground of the quarrel, and they are advised to refer the matter to the next meeting of the Commissioners. This advice had no effect, unless to restrain the Mohawks, who did not join the expedition. The Pocumtucks, with the other allied clans, made the proposed inroad. In August, 1657, they met the Mohegans and defeated them with great slaughter. Uncas was driven to his fort on the Niantic, where he was besieged. In his extremity he was relieved by a party of English, sent by the magistrates of Connecticut. The Commissioners of the United Colonies, at their meeting in September following, disowned this measure of Connecticut and ordered the whites to return home. By this double policy Uncas was saved and war with the Pocumtucks averted. Uncas was now ordered

---

*Parkman, in his "Discovery of the Great West," does great injustice to the Mohegans. He says LaSalle met with a band of Abenaki and Mohegan refugees in Illinois, who "after dancing round Puritan scalps in New England had been driven off in Philip's war." This is a serious mistake. The Mohegans were the firm and trusted friends of the English and active in their service from the opening to the close of Philip's war, and, as we shall see, contributed not a little to its successful issue.

to let the Podunks return home, and the Pocumtucks were notified of this order, and told that the Commissioners "expect they will forbear all hostility against Uncas until their next meeting," at which time the contending parties are urged to appear and submit their grievances to the Commissioners for a settlement. The Pocumtucks declined. They were an independent people and preferred to settle their quarrels in their own fashion. In the spring of 1658, Wonopequen led a small war party into the Mohegan country. By strategy, a company of the enemy in canoes, were enticed on shore, where they were set upon by the invaders, who killed several and took others captive. On their return a lawless element in the party made an assault on a farm house in Wethersfield, carrying off some corn and two children of *Chawquat*, a friendly Indian. Connecticut sent messengers to Pocumtuck to recover the plunder and captives, but "the Indians Returned nothing but Scoffs and Jeers."

Aug. 2d, 1658, the General Court of Connecticut wrote the Commissioners complaining of this, and other "affronts of the Pocumtuck Indians." The Commissioners are in session at Boston, whence they reply, Sept. 18:—

"We shall lett the Pocumtuck Sachems vnderstand how ill we Resent these injurious passages * * * our desire is and Endeauour shalbee that the English * * * may not suffer any Injuries or affronts from the Indians * * * whereby their pride and insolancy may bee encreased, or the honor of the English Impared * * * or suffer that to be done that might giue them Just cause to thinke wee are either afraid of them, or seeke a quarrel with them."

In pursuance of this policy, on the same day a message was sent to the Sachems at Pocumtuck, in which complaint is made of the conduct of Wonopequen in 1656, when the envoys went to Warranoco to treat for Uncas; and of the late outrage at Wethersfield. "Chawquatt," they say, "a peaceable Indian, liveing neare the English, and hath not bine engaged in any ware, or quarrells this twenty yeares, hath two of his Children taken violently away and kept Captive at Pocumtucke." Also, that "they fight within theire towns, and yards, which they cannot suffer." They ask "the minds of the Sachems heerin, how farr they will owne and approue the same expecting that if they Intend to keep Frindship still with vs they will take care to Render due Satisfaction."

What reply was made to this message does not appear. Certainly hostilities continued between the Pocumtucks and Uncas in the summer of 1659, and the danger of a general Indian war became imminent.

Sept. 3d, 1659, the Commissioners, then in session at Hartford, sent the following to the Pocumtucks by Samuel Marshfield of Springfield, as interpreter:—

Vpon seuerall complaints from diuers English of injuries done by the Pocumtucke Indians and their Confederates; a message was sent to the Pocumtuck Sachems as followeth;

Imp^r: Wheras there hath bine long peace & frindshipp between all the English and the said Sachems; which wee are willing and desirous should bee continued yett of late seuerall complaints haue bin brought to vs of Injuries and affronts offered to severall of our people by the said Sachems or some of theire men; and that without any provocation or cause giuen by the English; as wee are enformed; which wee cannot beare;

2. That in theire warrs and quarrells amongst themselues, they presse soe neare; and sometimes into the houses of the English, as to theire great disturbance and which tends directly to the breach of peace betwixt vs and them; if not speedily preuented;

3. That therefore the Commissioners are willing and desirous, to speake with the said Sachems; or some of them deputed by the Rest; both concerning the former Injuries complained of; and that some meet agreement may bee made and declared, how the English in all parts may bee secured from losse or disturbance by any of the said Sachems, theire men or adherents whiles they are prosecuting theire warrs with others; that soe that peace and frindship may bee continued between the English and them as in former times;

4. That if any of them Intend to giue the Commissioners a meeting heer, that it bee as soone as may bee; and by thursday night next, att the furthest; and whereas wee haue occation to speake with seuerall Sachems and other Indians; wee doe therefore desire and expect that all acts of hostilitie bee suspended and forborne on all sides during the siting of the Commissioners: the like Injunction, wee haue laid vpon Uncas and his party that soe the Pocumtucke Sachems or messengers may come and Return in safety;

Hartford Septem: 3: 1659
Subscribed by all the Commissioners

The ensuing message was likewise sent to Uncas:—

1. The Commissioners haue bin Informed of seuerall Injuries and affrontes done to some English by the Pocumtucke and Narragansett Indian whiles they were in the procecution of theire warr against him which quarrells haue been occationed by his want of attendence to the councell of the English:

2. The Commissioners haue sent to the Pocumtuck Sachems and the Indians att Tunksis whom they expect heer by wensday or thursday next and if hee see cause to take that opportunitie to sat-

isfy the Commissioners conforming his proseedings and Improve their enterest for makeing his peace; The Commissioners are willing to attend the same;

3. That we haue giuen charge to the Pocumtucke and Tunksis or other Indians to forbeare all acts of hostilitie towards him or his people during the siting of the Commissioners and doe expect and require of him that hee cause all his people to forbeare all hostile acts towards said Pocumticke Tunksis and other Indians; while the Commissioners shall continew att hartford; and while said Indians shalbee applying themselues to the commissioners

Hartford the 3: of September 1659
Subscribed by all the Commissioners

The result of this mission is told by John Pynchon in a letter received at Hartford, Sept. 7th or 8th, 1659:—

Much Honored Gentlemen,

The messengers sent according to youer desires to the Pocumtucke Sachems being returned; I shall briefly giue youer worshipes an account of the Successe of the Journey; Coming to Pocumtucke; hee that was Interpreter declared youer message to the Sachems there, according to his seuerall Instructions; and whoe to the first thing redily returned this answare; that it was all theire desires that peace and friendship betwixt themselues and the English should continew; and whereas in the message sent to them, there is mension of wronges and Injuries done by them to the English: They answered; first; that knew of none; and if any were done; it was not by the allowance of the Sachems; for they had charged theire men to doe noe wrong to any English or their Cattle:

2condly if it were made out to them; that any of theire men had done the wrong, they would make Satisfaction to the English Soe fare they would bee from countenancing any, in offending the English and what more to say to it they knew not:

to the second thinge that in the warrs they presse to neare the English &c; they say that as frinds, they come to the English for victualls, and charge theire people to carry it friendly; but if that the English Sachems will say they doe not alow of it; and will prescribe another way or Course for them to take if it bee reasonable they will attend it;

3d. To the desire of the Commissioners to speake with them: they say they can not come to Hartford; neither doe they know any engagement that lyes on them to come to the meetings of the English Sachems; and they doe not send for the English Sachems, to theire meetings; The Reasons why they can not come to the Commissioners, are two, first, because they haue a great meeting amongst themselues three daies hence, and must attend that; it being all one with the Commissioners meeting. 2condly they are in confederacye with many others, as with the Souquakes, and Mohawks and others, and can doe nothing without them;

Lastly, to the desire of the Commissioners, that all acts of hostilitie may sease during theire setting; they are not in a capacitie to attend to it;

1st because they haue sent out seauen or eight men to lye in waite for some of Vncas his men but two daies before; they being now gone can not be called in

2d if they could; yett it is not possible for them to giue notice to the Indians of the Duch Riuer, and others whoe are ingaged with them, and are dayly sending out some vpon the Designe;

To the third particulare, that some agreement may bee made how the English may bee secured; they desire the English Sachems to conclude what is best and fitt to bee attended by them; and they are resolued to attend it when it is declared to them; if it be that which shalbee found Reasonable; this is the sume of what they say to the messengers sent to them; and all along hold out a Resolution of liuing in peace with the English; and say they will not be the first to breake the peace; They are resolued not to bee beginers of any breach with the English; and will yeild to the English in anythinge but in making peace with Vncas; and that they would not haue the English to perswade them to it; for they can not haue peace with *him;* I am bould to p^rsent this Relation of theire answare, as I Scribed it from the Interpretor's mouth because William Edwards whoe accompany him is in hast; hee may possibly Relate somewhat more but his hastning giues mee time oneley to Relate the *maine* and sume of all; not haue else att present, I take my leaue,

And Subscrib youer Worships seruant,

JOHN PINCHON;

It was my desire that the messengers and Interpretor Samuell Marshfield would haue written the Pocumtucke Sachems answare to youer Message, with his owne hand; onely because hee being a slow Scribe, could not soe soone effect it, Neither could I perswade him to it; but I haue caused him to Read ouer what I haue writ, and to Subscribe his hand to the truth of it

Youer Worships Servant to Comaund
SAMUEL MARSHFIELD

This diplomatic as well as manly reply of the Pocumtucks was barely received by the Commissioners before a complaint was made to them by John Webb and others, inhabitants of Northampton, that,—

Two Duchmen, one Irishman, and one ffrenchman, stole away seuen mares and other cattle which they missed, and hauing driuen them away to Pocumtucke the last Lords day, they desired the Sachem to pursue the said thieues, and to apprehend them; and to bring back the mares, &c, for which they promised the Sachems fifty shillings for eury mare, if they brought backe the mares, as also the men; and the sd Sachem Wonopequen, vndertaking the same; and sending word to Northampton men to come and Receiue theire Mares; Wherevpon John Webb and others of Northampton, goeing for the said Mares, which they saw in the Indians possession as alsoe for the men; the said Wonopequen Refused to deliuer them according to agreement; and Required great sums of wampum; coates shirts liquors &c. Saying hee had bought them of the Indians that fetched them back and that eury mare was worth twenty pounds.

The Commissioners saw that prompt and decisive measures could no longer be delayed without incurring the contempt of the natives. The young Pocumtucks, of late, had been growing bold and insolent. Daily contact with the settlers at Springfield and Northampton, had disabused them of that superstitious fear which formerly clothed the English with supernatural power. The conciliatory, if not vacillating, course of the Commissioners was beginning to be considered as arising from fear, and some of the hot headed braves were ready for war. The chiefs, too, were getting restive under the continual interference of the whites in their tribal quarrels, and by their support of the treacherous Uncas. It shows a clear insight, by the Councilors, of the certain consequences of a war with the English, and the firm hold of the Sachems on their subjects, when a peaceful reply was returned to the following message:—

Instructions for Thomas Stanton and the company sent with him to the Pocomptuck Sachems the 10th of September, 1659:

Imp^r: You are to lett them know that wee Received theire answare but in seuerall particulares are unsatisfyed, as first as that they say they desire to keep peace yett haue comitted seuerall outrages against the English and pretended excuses not to come and answare for them; or giue satisfaction;

In their answare that they know noe wronge done to the English; they will not take notice of it: had they come they might haue heard proved—(as the Comissioners have done)—much Injury and an Intollerable affront put vpon Mr. Brewster during theire seige of Vncas ffort which was done by some of theire companie for which the Comissioners doe expect and Require Satisfaction of the Pocomtucke Sachem being the chiefe Captaine in that warr:

You shall Require the Pocomtucke Sachem to deliuer vnto you the Mares cattle and four men which they agreed to fetch in; yett after they sent for the men of Northhampton to Receiue them; they denied to lett them haue them according to their agreement and haue put them to great charge for which alsoe we expect they should giue them Satisfaction by abatement of what was promised;

You shall assure them the Comissioners will not bee baffeled by them but if they will not forthwith deliuer the mares and men and cattle; if you are sure they haue any in theire hands the Comissioners are resolued to Recouer them in such a way as will not bee pleasing to them if they desire peace as they pretend; if you Recouer the mares and Cattle they are to bee Returned to the owners the men you are to convey to Mr. Pinchon to bee sent to Boston Jayle; if you cannot obtaine what is expected you are to sertify the Gou^r of Conecticott and Capt: Pinchon speedily therof;

lastly if they continew there; wee expect and Require them to forbeare drawing neare in Armed companies to the English Townes or houses; that vpon noe pretences whatsoeuer they Invade or afront any English person, or house; that they neither trouble nor molest any Indian liuing in an English family; nor such peacable Indians that plant vpon land hired of the English; except they take them in actuall hostillitie; that they hinder not nor jnjury nor detaine any Indian sent with letters by the English or trauelling with them as guids or attending on them

Hartford the 10th of September 1659.

Stanton had hardly left town before Mr. Brewster appeared at Hartford with a particular bill of damage to his premises about three years before, at the time Uncas was besieged by the allies in his fort at Niantic. The Commissioners awarded him 40 fathoms of wampum, 10 to be paid by the Tunxis Indians; 15 by the Narragansets; and 15 by the Pocumtucks, and declared that "if said Indians shall refuse to pay; the Commissioners will take care that the most convenient means shalbe vsed." Mr. Pynchon was desired to send the bill to the Pocumtucks, with a demand from the Commissioners for its payment, and it was at once dispatched after Stanton to Pocumtuck.

At the same session the Commissioners also took peremptory action in regard to offenses by the Nipmucks at Quabague, the Niantics under Ninigret, and a remnant of the Pequots under Robin. One of the latter was imprisoned at Hartford for going with Uncas to war against the Pocumtucks. Measures were taken to secure the newly returned Podunks against the claims of other Indians, or of the rapacious English. The decided action of the Commissioners and their impartial dealings with the other tribes had a salutary effect on the Pocumtucks. Stanton returned Sept. 14, with a written message from these Indians in reply to the manifesto of the Commissioners. This document was evidently penned by Stanton at the dictation of the Chief Sachem. In its style, the figurative language usually put into the mouth of the Indian speaker is notably absent. The paper is remarkable for a clear, dispassionate and comprehensive view of the trouble between the parties, and a simple but politic answer to all charges against the Pocumtucks. It shows in the chief a mind well grounded in ethics, and able to deal with hard facts in a logical as well as diplomatic manner. He addresses the "English Sachems" as his equals, and in no spirit of servility. Although he openly expresses his disinclination for war, he gives no evidence that he fears its consequences. This document is given in full:—

The old league of ffriendship betwixt the English and our selues; wee are resolued to keep; wee cannot charge the English of doeing vs any wronge though our people haue mett with some particulare abuses; but wee know they are not countenanced by the Gours for soe doeing; alsoe some of our men that are younge and follish may haue done some particulare wrong to some English; this should not breake the league betwixt vs and the English seeing wee doe not countenance our men for soe doing: As for Mr Brewsters house wee had Information that two of our emimies were gotten in there; and that they did furnish Vncas with Guns and powder and shott; as Mr Thompson did as the two weomen did Relate to vs when they came out of the ffort to vs; these two men shott att vs from the other side of the Riuer; wherevpon our young men went ouer; and not finding them concluded they were received into the house

The goods that were taken in an Indian sacke was not the Englishes but our enimies which was left there Reveiled to vs by Wawequas wife; And as for any wrong done to any of the English it is not done with a sett purpose to breake with the English; Neither for time to come will wee come with our armies neare the English houses neither will we meddle with any Indian that lives as a servant vnto the English; nor any that plant on theire ground they hauiug markes wherby wee may know them; as a white cloth in theire locke or giueing theire Names wherby wee may know they are such Mohegans that fight not;

As for the busines of the Mares you may haue them—what was said against vs about them was out of mistake for they vnderstood not vs nor wee them—as it is vsuall for the English to speake much to vs that come—though they vnderstand little, what goods of the English that was stollen out of Mr Brewster's house was Returned againe with a Reprofe to My *men* for that attempt and miscarriage of theirs in acting without My *priuitie;* like madd men; and therfore, as a year since at nianticke; when som damage was done to some wheat by our men's trampleing vpon it; wee made satisfaction to the full of the Englishes demaunds; soe shall wee doe for the future when wee are giuen to vnderstand what is Just to bee done by us; and alsoe for any wrong done to Mr Brewster; but for the present wee are Ignorant; Wee desire the English Sachems not to perswade vs to a peace with Vncas although hee promeseth much hee will performe nothinge; wee haue experience of his falcenes; alsoe wee desire that if any Messengers bee sent to vs from the English they may bee such as are not lyares and tale carryers but sober men; and such as wee can vnderstand;

From Pocomtucke   pr. me Thomas Stanton
Sep 12, 1659.

With this dignified State paper the recorded correspondence with the Pocumtucks closed, and nothing is known of any subsequent wars between the Pocumtucks and the Mohegans. For a few years nothing relating to the history of the Pocumtucks is discovered. They next appear as aggressors of the Mohawks.

In 1663 the Pocumtucks are found allied with the Pennekooks and the Abenakis of the east, and with the Wappingers and Mahicans of the Hudson river. Events unknown to me having broken the friendship between the Pocumtucks and the Mohawks, the former, with their new allies, now invaded the country of the Mohawks with such success as to weaken and humble that tribe. The Dutch at Albany, to whom the Mohawks had been a bulwark against the French in Canada, at once took measures to end this war against their allies. In May, 1664, a party of Mohawks, with a deputation of Dutchmen, was sent over the mountain to meet the eastern tribes, probably at Pocumtuck. With the help of some of the English a treaty of peace was arranged, and the embassy returned to report its terms for the acceptance of the Mohawks. It appears that these were satisfactory, for on the 21st of June, 1664, Saheda, a "Mohawk prince," with a suitable retinue, left Albany for "Fort Pocomthetuck," (*sic*) bearing presents for the ratification of the treaty and a ransom for their friends who had been taken captive.

The pride of the Pocumtucks had now reached that pitch which goeth before a fall. In their arrogance they not only refused to ratify the treaty of peace, but basely murdered the ambassador and his suite in cold blood. This offense, not less rank among savage than among civilized peoples, called for the direst vengeance. Events were conspiring to this end. In September of the same year, the Province of New York was surrendered by the Dutch to the English. Sept. 24th a treaty of "peace and accommodation" between the new powers and the Mohawks was signed at Albany. The Mohawks were keen diplomates, and after a night's reflection, they proposed new articles, which were accepted by the English and incorporated in the treaty, on the 25th.

By these new articles the English agree to make peace for the Mohawks with the Mahicans and other Hudson river tribes which had been in league with the Pocumtucks against them in the campaign of 1663. They also agree not to assist the Pennekooks, the Abenakis, or the Pocumtucks; and further, in case the Mohawks "be beaten by the three nations above mentioned, they may receive accommodation from the English."

Having thus shrewdly freed themselves from enemies near home, having secured the neutrality of the English, and made sure of a place of retreat in case of disaster, they sent an embassy to treat for peace with the French in Canada. The field being thus cleared for action, the Mohawks mustered a powerful force and marched to avenge the murder of Prince Saheda.

Local tradition has preserved an account of this inroad on the Pocumtucks. The principal stronghold of the tribe was on a bluff, about half a mile northeast of the common in Old Deerfield, which is still called Fort Hill. On the approach of the enemy, the Pocumtucks gathered in this fort, upon which the Mohawks made a furious assault. They were repelled and driven off by the stout defenders. They retired from the contest, but this may have been only a stratagem to draw their foes into the open field. Their retreat was through Plain Swamp and across the North Meadows towards Pine Hill. Here the Mohawks rallied, and a hot engagement followed. The pursuers were broken and in turn driven back to their fort, which, after a bloody struggle, was stormed and taken, and its inmates all slaughtered, by the now doubly enraged Mohawks.

After burning the fort and wigwams, and laying waste the cornfields of the Pocumtucks, the victors swept northward, and the Squakheags were soon involved in the common ruin. Turning thence to the eastward, the Pennekooks and the Abenakis felt in turn the fury of the avengers, until blood enough had been shed to appease the manes of the murdered ambassador. So thoroughly was the work of the Mohawks done, that when, in 1665, the English from Dedham laid out the "8000 acre grant" at Pocumtuck, there was not a syllable in their report, or in the debates thereon in town meeting at Dedham, to indicate that a single wigwam or a single human being was found on this scene of desolation. Their forts and dwellings had become ashes fertilizing the rank weeds over their sites, and sad silence brooded over their bleaching bones, or grass grown graves.

Thus fell the head of the powerful Pocumtuck Confederacy. In one fatal day their chieftains and warriors, in their pride and strength were laid in the dust. A feeble remnant, renouncing their independence, sought the protection of the

English in the towns on the river below. Three original deeds, now in Memorial hall, testify that within three years the deserted lands at Pocumtuck were sold to men of Dedham. The enervated remains of the Pocumtuck Confederation—rebelling against English domination—appeared for a few months in Philip's war. At its close the few miserable survivors stole away towards the setting sun and were forever lost to sight. Never after do we find in recorded history, a single page relating to the unfortunate Pocumtucks.

CHAPTER V.

POCUMTUCKS AS SUBJECTS OF MASSACHUSETTS; INDIAN RELICS.

The remnant of the Pocumtuck Confederacy, adopting in part the English costume, had gathered about the English, in the valley towns, had given them their allegiance, and were held amenable to the English government, thus bartering their native freedom for protection against the avenging Mohawks. Here they lived a vagabond life, eking out, as they could, a miserable existence on the outskirts of civilization, the all controlling sentiment being fear of the incensed foe. In consequence of this they could neither hunt nor fish in their old haunts, nor anywhere except near the towns. So hampered, their stock of venison or beaver, with which to traffic for English comforts, was small, and the baskets and birch brooms made by the squaws, ill supplied their place. Much inconvenience and annoyance was experienced by the whites from the intrusions and petty depredations of their dusky dependents. Troubles often arose which the magistrates were invoked to settle. The savages were held to the same strict observance of the laws as their Christian neighbors, and the penalties for their transgression equally enforced against both—in theory at least. A few specimens are given from the court records:

In 1665, *Nenawan* was fined "40s or 20 fathom," for breaking into Praisever Turner's mill. In 1667 Quequelett was "whipt 20 lashes" for helping Godfrey Nims and Benoni Stebbins "about running away to Canada." Indians were fined "40s" for a "breach of the Sabbath, in traveling two and fro," at Springfield. For "bringing apples from Windsor, and firing a gun," on Sunday, a fine was imposed on a party at Warranoco. Sachem *Umpachala*, and Wattawolunksin of Pocumtuck were fined for drunkenness.

On the other hand, Samuel Marshfield was obliged to give up land seized under a mortgage which he had extorted from the Indians "when in a straight." Sachem *Wallump* obtained redress for damages to his corn, by English cattle. The courts were also appealed to in settling disputed questions amongst the Indians themselves. Alliquot and Wallump complained that Amoakesson had sold land to Lieut. Cooper that belonged to them, and settlement was made by compromise. Enough was retained by the Lieutenant, who was also a surgeon, to pay him for "looking after the bones of Whalehwaet."

The Indians were very fond of liquors, and in spite of stringent laws against its sale they were generally supplied by unscrupulous traders. They were quarrelsome under its influence, and maimed or killed one another in their drunken brawls. Heavy fines were imposed upon the illicit dealers, but still the trade went on. The price of a gallon of rum was four fathoms of black wampum, or a beaver skin; and six quarts were given for "a great beaver."

After a few years' trial it was seen that this attempt to govern these children of the woods by the white man's laws had proved a failure, and representations to that effect were made to the General Court. A committee of that body made a report detailing the condition of affairs and recommending that the natives be "placed directly under the control of some principal Indian or Indians, to be appointed and declared Sachem or chief, or head of them," the said Sachems to be held responsible for their misdeeds. According to this plan Sachems were appointed by English authorities. Little is known of the results of this measure save that soon after, these new officials were selling large tracts of land to the English, and pocketing the proceeds. It is probable that "Chauk, Sachem of Pocomtuck," under whose deed we hold our landed heritage, was one of these convenient dignitaries. All the deeds of land at Pocumtuck, from the Indians, were made and executed at Springfield, and no one has yet been found ingenious enough to define their exact location or bounds, with the single exception of the deed from Mashalisk. *She* was of one of the "old families." Her estate lay on both sides of the Connecticut, and she may have escaped in the Mohawk invasion by being on the east side of the river. The fear of the fugitive Pocumtucks for the Mohawks was well founded, for these had not abated one jot of their enmity, and their scouting parties continued to harrass and kill them at every opportunity. This matter was a source of much concern to the English. The Pocumtucks were now their subjects, and English faith was plighted to protect them.

After vain remonstrance and negotiations by local officials, an appeal was made to the General Court. The petition was referred to a committee of which John Pynchon was chairman. After a hearing he reported the necessity of stringent measures, saying that it was "necessary that they be told that these actings of theirs look as if they intended to pick a quarrel with us, they being expressly against the promise of those in our hands, whom we secured against the violence of the Indians, and sent home with manifestations of love and friendship," and that these actions are "contrary to the agreement made with our Indians last year * * * that then your people would not meddle with any Indians that wore English cloaks, or that had their hair cut short," and that these things "are not to be borne." The General Court accepted the report and sent a long letter to the Mohawks detailing grievances and concluding "we never yet did any wrong to you or any of yours, neither will wee take any from you, but shall right our people according to justice; yett we are desirous to continue all amicable correspondence with you, if the fault be not in yourselues, by offering insolencjes to our people, which wee may not beare or suffer." This firm language had considerable effect. Two or three years later £20 were sent by the Mohawks to indemnify English owners for animals slaughtered in their raids. £3-10s were allowed for an Indian servant killed at Northampton. It does not appear that any losses by the Indians were considered in this settlement. But after this the River Indians were somewhat relieved from the incursions of the Mohawks, and more at liberty to resume their native mode of life. It was soon found, however, that they had lost their self respect and their spirit of self reliance, and had retained their acquired habits of shiftlessness and dependence. When on the verge of starvation they occasionally assisted the English in "laying stone wall" or doing farm work in the field.

The end came with Philip's war. The change in the condition of affairs in the valley for ten years before the war, was gradual, but the savages were surely disappearing in consequence of their environments—the weaker race before the stronger. The same causes, with like results, have attended the march of civilization across the continent. The Indian cannot endure before the vices and the restraints of the white man. The story of frontier life was the same here as everywhere. The legislation of the colonies aimed at a strict preservation of the rights of the natives, and these laws were no dead letter; yet the natives were crowded at every turn. The actual contact was on the fringe of the settlements, where the unscrupulous pioneer sold the natives rum, and cheated them when drunk. To prove these abuses before a magistrate when sober, was difficult, and the reparation tardy and unsatisfactory, when a case was made out. To these wrongs add the fines, imprisonments and lashings caused by their own misdeeds, and it would seem that their cup of misery was full. When the emissaries of Philip came among them, assuring them that the time had come when the English should be swept from the land, and as an earnest of good times coming, distributing freely, wampum, garments, and other spoil already taken from the English, it was inevitable that the remembrance of their abuse, their sufferings and their poverty, should come uppermost in their minds; that they should consider this the golden opportunity for revenge on the English; that they should join the artful Wampanoag in a war of extermination. They could not be expected to see that this act could only hasten their impending doom.

RELICS OF THE DEPARTED RACE.

Dwelling Places.—The most constant and most unmistakable evidence of habitation is the presence of fire stones. Before contact with the whites the natives used for culinary purposes vessels of wood, bark, clay or stone. To seethe their food these were supplied with cold water, into which heated stones were put, one after another, until the object was accomplished. In this region large sized gravel stones were used for that purpose. A considerable number of these found together and bearing the peculiar marks of fire and water, surely indicates a place of abode. I have found as many as a bushel in one pile, but on arable land they have usually been scattered by cultivation. Piles of stone chippings, with occasionally an unfinished weapon, or worn out tool, point out definitely the homes of their artisans, and attest their fancy in the choice of material, as to color or quality. If enough of the fire stones and chips are found to indicate a village, certain other features may be predicted with confidence, and generally found, unless the face of the country is essentially changed. These are an easily cultivated planting field, a properly sloping promontory for store houses, a burial place and a defensible post. If the village was a permanent one, what may be called the sweat box was another usual, and perhaps constant, accompaniment to a settlement. This was an excavation in the ground used by the medicine man for steaming his patients, by means of a blanket, hot stones and a decoction of potent herbs. One of these I discovered on Pine Hill; and another at Sheldon's Field, while excavations for the Canal railroad were in progress. In connection with the indications of abode named, fragments of weapons and utensils can always be found. With these proofs about him the close observer can say with confidence, here dwelt the red man; here stood his fort, here lay his cornfield, and standing on a selected spot he can add, underneath my feet lie his moldering remains.

On village sites, and scattered over the haunts of the Indians, are found on the surface, or turned up by the plow and spade, or discovered in their graves, a great variety of weapons, utensils, ensigns, ornaments and other articles. Each of the species named below has been found in this town and is represented in Memorial Hall: Axes, spear and arrow points, knives, tomahawk heads, arrow straitners, hammers, drills, gouges, chisels, bark peelers, rubbing stones, fleshers, skin dressers, hoes, corn mills, pestles, spinning bobs, stone "beeswax," ear ornaments, gorgets, amulets, pendants, totems, ceremonial ensigns—as maces or banner stones—pipes, aukooks and fragments of clay pottery. In graves are found, besides these, beads, shell ornaments, wampum, burnt and unburnt vessels of clay, and bone awls. All the above, not otherwise noted, are of stone. The aukooks were made of soapstone and varied in size from half a pint to twelve quarts. They were quite common, but the nearest known quarry of this material is thirty miles away. The clay pottery was rudely ornamented with conventional lines and dots, although quite elaborate specimens are occasionally found. These vessels, being of a frail character, are never found entire, except in graves, and are very rare in New England. Less than half a dozen are known to me from that region. Yet to be noticed is another interesting article, of which there are about three or four hundred specimens in Memorial Hall. They are of stone, usually roundish or oval disks, varying in size from four ounces to fifty pounds. The *characteristic* artificial mark is one or more corresponding pits, or depressions, on the opposite sides. A few triangular and quadrangular prisms have three or four pits; one irregular, oval specimen contains fifty pits. These articles are not found at random, wherever Indians have lived, like other relics, but only in particular localities. This collection was mostly gathered within the compass of a mile from the Hall, and rarely from a greater distance than two miles away. If a collection has been made from any other place in New England I am not aware of it. These stones have been found in particular localities in New Jersey, Western New York and Ohio. There has been much speculation about these relics, but no satisfactory name or use has yet been assigned them. Theories that they are hammers, nut crackers, or club heads, are at once dissipated by an examination of this collection. They must not be confounded with "chunke-stones," to which they bear but slight resemblance. It may be, that they were used in some Indian game played only at national gatherings, like that held here by the Pocumtuck Confederacy, Sept. 10, 1659; but this is purely conjecture. They may be relics of a race which preceded the Pocumtucks. A Japanese visitor to the Hall had seen something of the kind in a museum at home, said there to have been connected with ancient religious observances.

"*Indian Barns*," as the English called them, were excavations in the earth for storing provisions. In studying Indian occupation, for the history of Northfield, my attention was attracted to certain peculiar appearances, uniformly called by tradition either "deer traps," or "wigwam places." A slight examination showed that tradition was at fault, and that an explanation must be sought for in other directions. Some months later, on reading Hubbard's account of the discovery of some "underground barns" at Peskeompskut in 1676, I surmised that the clue to the mysterious "wigwam places" had been found, and determined upon an investigation. Engaging two trusty friends our party started at daylight on a summer's morning, armed with pick and spade, to make a private examination of some "wigwam places," just over the Vermont line, on the farm of Elijah E. Belding, which had been shown to me by the owner. Two hours' work proved beyond a doubt the correctness of my conjectures. We had struck a group of thirty-three Indian granaries, lying within a space of 90 x 45 feet. Each showed a basin-like depression from six to fifteen inches in depth. Those examined were about four and a half feet deep. One was found to have been lined with clay. In others acorn shells, fragments of wood, bark and broken stone were found. On communicating this discovery to Hon. John M. Stebbins of Springfield, he called to mind certain peculiar depressions in a pasture on his father's farm in Hinsdale, N. H. We examined these in company, and found they also were the remains of Indian granaries. Many others were afterwards discovered in various parts of Northfield. These barns varied in size, being from four to twelve feet deep, and from three to twenty feet in diameter. They were usually placed in groups, being thus more easily protected from wild animals by a stockade, and, for obvious reasons, always on a watershed.

In Deerfield several storehouses have been discovered, sometimes through traditions of "wigwam places," but generally through knowledge gained by experience at Northfield. Frederick Hawks informed me that a group of "wigwam places" was plainly to be seen on his father's farm in Wisdom. On visiting the spot it was found that they were destroyed in building the Hoosac Tunnel railroad. My attention was called by Mrs. Nancy Campbell to certain "Indian lookouts" on Pine Hill. These proved to be barns of considerable size. South of the road from Bars Long Hill to Mill River the barns were common. Three large ones were found on the farm of Isaac Wing, which have since been nearly filled by cultivation. On the banks of the ravine southwesterly of Mr. Wing's house, and about Bear's Hole, several of a large size are still to be seen. On the south side of the ravine three others have been filled up within a few years by Joseph N. Fuller, in leveling his land for the plow. None of these interesting remains have been found about the Street, Wapping or Great River, all having been destroyed by cultivation of the soil.

Indian Graves.—Two distinct modes of burial prevailed here, as shown by the position of the body in the grave. Whether this be an indication that two tribes, with different customs, lived here at the same time—or successively—or whether it be a distinguishing mark of rank, or sex, cannot be determined by the evidence at hand. In one case the body was placed erect, facing the east, the knees drawn up to the chin and clasped by the arms. In the other it was curled up, like a sleeping dog, and laid on the right side, the face turned to the east. A single instance of a third mode has recently come to light. On an elevated sandy plain, at the head of a beautiful valley opening north from the falls at Peskeompskut, a burial place was disturbed by workmen repairing the highway in 1881. The spot was on the farm of T. M. Stoughton, and the ground was at once examined by Mr. Stoughton and his son William, mainly in a search for relics. They found twelve graves, about two feet below the surface. The bodies had been extended and radiated from a center, head outwards, the feet resting on a circle five or six feet in diameter. Small fragments only of the bones remained, but enough to show the position of the bodies. Many stone weapons were disinterred and a number of smooth stones of unknown use. All these bore the marks of fire, from the effects of which many of them had been broken into fragments. They had evidently been cast into the fire while whole, and not as fragments.

Graves have been found singly or in groups in all parts of the town. On the side hill west of Old Fort, it was common, fifty years ago, to turn up Indian skulls while plowing without disturbing any other bones. At the foot of Bars Long Hill, just where the meadow fence crossed the road, and the *bars* were placed which gave the village its name, many skeletons were exposed in plowing down a bank, and weapons and implements were found in abundance. One of these skeletons was described to me by Henry Mather who saw it, as being of monstrous size—"the head as big as a peck basket, with double teeth all round." Mather, who was about six feet tall, made the comparison, and says the thigh bones were about three inches longer than his own. The skeleton was examined by Dr. Stephen W. Williams, who said the owner must have been nearly eight feet high. In all the cases noted in this paragraph, the bodies had been placed in a sitting posture, facing the east. In those that follow they were laid on the right side, as above described.

On the home lot of the writer, about twenty graves have been examined. In some the bones were entire and sound; in others scarcely a scrap was left. In several graves was a quantity of what appeared like fine blue sandy clay. In one grave there was found what appeared to be the remains of a basket made of thick, rough bark, filled with earth having the blue, clayey appearance. In another, that of a child, was a stone figure, about four inches long, perhaps representing a fish or serpent. With another child was found abundant remains of birch bark wrappings. A grave discovered in 1866, in which the skeleton was well preserved, was rich in relics. There was a vessel of burnt clay, rudely ornamented, which is a great rarity in New England. There were also shell pendants for the ears, thin disks of shell about one inch in diameter perforated through the center, and some fifty pieces of white peag or wampum. These were all of Indian manufacture. Other articles, evidently procured from the whites, were about five hundred small glass beads, red, white and green—mostly the latter—much corroded by age; six red beads, half an inch in diameter, handsomely inlaid with stripes of blue and white. A bodkin or awl of bone was also found. These graves were uniformly about three feet deep, situated near together on a promontory overlooking the Meadows. About seventy rods to the northwest of this, on John Broughton's Hill, skeletons were found more than fifty years ago. There, surface relics, also, have been very abundant. A few rods north of Indian Bridge, the remains of a woman, who was apparently buried with a child in her arms, were uncovered by Lemuel Childs, about 1840. The bones were mostly sound, and the skull of the child was quite perfect. In a grave discovered on Petty's Plain in 1884, were found a pipe, trinkets of copper, and the metal foundation of an epaulet. Many other Indian graves have been found in different parts of the town, but the mode of burial has not been ascertained. Hardly a year passes without the discovery here of isolated graves. There was an Indian burying place west of the "Old Street burying ground." The place was used as a gravel pit, and has long ago been carried away, and the bones scattered, or used for repairing the highway. Beads of the larger kind described above were found here, also another kind which were faceted. The latter were precisely like specimens recently received from S. L. Frey of Palatine Bridge, N. Y., who took them from a refuse heap of the Iroquois. Graves have been opened at Farmington, Ct., and in the burial places of the Podunks, where the position of the body corresponded exactly with that of those described as lying on the side here. I am not aware that this position has been noticed elsewhere.

These notes are offered as a contribution to a more complete history of the Connecticut Valley Indians.

CHAPTER VI.

PHILIP'S WAR.

The war of 1675-6, will always be known as "Philip's war;" but, rather because it was instigated by the Pokanoket Sachem, than that it was carried on under his orders. The fears of the colonists, indeed, made Philip the omnipresent arch fiend who planned each cunning ambush, ordered each bloody massacre, and directed every incendiary torch; the foremost in every attack, the most daring of his race. The evidence now before us fails to sustain these assumptions. We have no proof that Philip was ever in a single action in the colony, or that he was the leader of more than a small clan. He never held rank as commander-in-chief of the allied forces. In the spring of 1676, the Pocumtuck Sachems at Squeakheag threatened to take his head to the English as a peace offering; and at Wachusett, Sagamore Sam and other Nipmuck chiefs contemptuously ignored Philip, and overruled his more sagacious plans respecting the ransom of captives.

Philip should rather be ranked with the Seer or the Politician. He may have exceeded his fellows in political foresight, but he failed in that equipment of genius and that moral honesty necessary to inspire respect as a leader and to secure a loyal following. In his character we miss every element of greatness, and find him essentially narrow and mean. He was artful and his principal weapon was treachery. He was cruel, and a Sagamore of his own tribe accused him of cowardice, deserting him on that account. Volunteers from his own clan, hunted him in his extremity from swamp to thicket. Members of his own household betrayed his hiding places; and finally he fell by the avenging bullet of one of his own tribe, whose brother he had wantonly murdered; his body was vilely insulted and barbarously mutilated by his own countrymen.

From first to last Philip showed lack of state-craft, lack of military skill, lack of the essential elements of leadership; and his low cunning, ambition and desire for revenge, and his success as an agitator, were but poor substitutes. In six weeks after the first blow was struck at Swansea, he was driven from his country and his tribe scattered. With about forty or fifty followers he escaped up the valley of the Blackstone and took refuge among the Nipmucks at Wennimisset, arriving there the day after their retreat from the attack on Brookfield, in which, it is often said, he took part.

The relations of the English and Nipmucks had been nominally friendly from the first. But the two races had no common sympathies and had never mingled as equals. The industrial possibilities of the savage had been much increased by contact with civilization. With English weapons and implements, game was more easily procured, wigwams and canoes more easily made, and land more profitably cultivated. The barter of fur, venison and corn, for blankets and articles of metal, was of great advantage to the Indians, but the restraint put upon them when they gave their allegiance to the English was irksome. It was galling to these children of nature to be hedged in by forms and subjected to rules. The contempt of the whites made them conscious of being an inferior race, and they responded with envy and hatred.

Fearing an outbreak at Mount Hope, the Governor of Massachusetts, on the 13th of June, 1675, sent two messengers to compose the troubles, if possible. On the same day an embassy was sent to the Nipmucks, at Wennimisset, near Brookfield. Here, after three days' negotiation, the Sachems and rulers signed an agreement not to favor Philip or break the peace. It is probable the wise old men made this treaty in good faith, but that they were unable to restrain the young braves, whose discontent, with the natural love of war and desire for plunder, led them on regardless of consequences.

When news of the outbreak at Swansea reached Uncas, he at once sent six messengers to Boston offering his services in the war, while he made the same offer in person to the authorities of Connecticut. His envoys reached Boston, July 9th, and about the 11th Governor Leverett sent Ephraim Curtice of Sudbury,* who had an Indian trading post at Quin-

---

*Ancestor of our distinguished Statesman, George W. Curtis.

sigamug, to escort them through the Nipmuck country, as their nearest way home. Curtice had also a charge to find out the temper of the Nipmucks towards the English. At Natick he was joined by three friendly Indians. On reaching the Indian fort at Okomakomesset he heard news that would have stopped a less resolute man. It was that Matoonas, Sachem of Pakachaug and a dependent of Philip, was ranging the country with fifty men accoutered for war; that this party had already robbed his own house at Quinsigamug, and some of his goods were shown him to prove it. He was assured of certain death if he met Matoonas, or any of the Nipmucks. Curtice, however, pushed on to Marlboro, where he was furnished with an escort of ten troopers and one more Indian. Leaving Marlboro the party passed through the Indian towns of Hassanamisco, Munchaug, Chabanagonkamug, Manamexit, Senexit, and near to Wabaquasset, where the Mohegans considered themselves safe. These towns were all deserted. Curtice had traversed the very heart of the Nipmuck country without seeing a single Indian. He afterwards found them collected at Wennimisset, in a strong position, on an island of four acres, formed by the Menameseek river and the Wennimisset brook, and encompassed by a deep morass.* Though met by abuse and threats of death, Curtice at length reached the island by the only practicable pass. Here he had a conference with the Sachems Mattamuck or Mawtamp, Konkawasco, Willemather, Ushutugun or Sagamore Sam, Kekond, and "twelve Grandees." The chief Sachem was Mattamuck. The conference was friendly, the Indians representing that they had fled from their home for fear of the English, but, says Curtice, "I left them well appeased." He made a report of this expedition at Boston, July 16, 1675.

Within two or three days Curtice was again dispatched to Wennimisset with a letter from the Governor and Council to the Nipmuck Sachems, containing assurances of their good will. The envoy was well received and had a satisfactory conference with Sagamore Sam, Willemather, Apequanas or Sagamore John, and Kekond, to whom the letter was read, "which they seemed to accept of very well," and promised that some of the chiefs would go to Boston to speak with the

---

*For a description of this Camp see Temple's History of Brookfield.

Great Sachem in four or five days. When Curtice inquired why he met such abuse when last there, he was answered that Black James, the Constable of Chabanagonkamug, had told them "the English would kill them all because they were not praying Indians." Whether this was Black James's way of making converts, or a blind on the part of the wily Nipmucks, may never be known; but it is certain that at that very moment, though unknown to Curtice, an emissary of Philip was in their camp, distributing spoils taken from the English. On the 24th, Curtice again reported in Boston.

July 26th, Oneko, oldest son of Uncas, with two younger brothers and fifty Mohegan warriors, reached Boston and reported for duty. The younger brothers were kept as hostages and the rest hurried off towards Pocasset, the seat of war. On reaching Rehoboth they heard of the escape of Philip from Pocasset Neck, and joined a party of men from adjoining towns, who were about to follow his trail. Philip was overtaken by this force, thirty of his men were killed and much plunder taken. The next day the Mohegans joined Capt. Daniel Henchman, who was also in pursuit of the fugitives. But they were not again overtaken, and the chase ended at Wabaquasset.

HUTCHINSON AMBUSHED AND BROOKFIELD BURNED.

The Governor and Council, having no news from the chiefs at Wennimisset according to promise, and not being satisfied of the good faith of the Indians there, on the 28th of July, appointed Capt. Edward Hutchinson, a Commissioner, to go and find out the real condition of affairs among them. He was to demand that Matoonas and his band, and any other hostile Indians there, should be given up. Curtice went as guide, and Capt. Thomas Wheeler, with twenty troopers, as escort. The party reached Brookfield at noon, on the first day of August. Curtice was now sent a third time, with one companion, to Wennimisset, which lay about eight miles northwest, to arrange for a meeting with Capt. Hutchinson. As in previous visits, he found the old men disposed (or pretending to be) for peace, while the young men were insolent and full of the spirit of war. At length an agreement was made that the Indians should meet the Commissioner the next morning, on a plain near the head of

Wickabaug pond about three miles from Brookfield, to negotiate a treaty of peace and amity. Accordingly, Monday, Aug. 2d, Hutchinson, not without some misgivings, with his whole party, including Joseph and Sampson, sons of old Robin Petuhanit, and George Menicho, three Natick Indians, and John Ayers, William Prichard and Richard Coy, three of the leading men of Brookfield, marched to the appointed place. Not an Indian was there to meet them.

After consultation, and upon the representations of the Brookfield men, who strongly endorsed the integrity of the Indians, but against the remonstrance of the Naticks, Capt. Hutchinson continued his march four or five miles farther towards the Nipmuck camp, until he reached a narrow defile where the treacherous Indians lay in ambush. While advancing in single file, with a deep morass on one side and steep hill on the other, they were fired upon. The Brookfield men paid for their confidence with their lives. Five other men were killed and five wounded—Capt. Hutchinson and two others mortally, and Capt. Wheeler dangerously. Menicho was captured. The survivors fought their way out as best they could, and being guided in a by-way by Joseph and Sampson the Naticks, found their way back to the town.

The alarmed inhabitants hurriedly gathered into John Ayers's tavern, the largest and strongest house in the village. Hasty attempts were made to fortify this with such logs as they could find for the outside, and feather beds hung over the windows and on the walls, inside. In the panic the garrison was scantily provided with provisions and other necessaries for so large a number. Fourteen men and fifty women and children of the inhabitants were crowded together there.

In about two hours the savages arrived. After pillaging and burning the deserted houses, they made a furious attack on the tavern, "sending their shot amongst us like hail through the walls, and shouting as though they would swallow us up alive." The command had devolved upon Simon Davis of Concord, who, with his twenty-six men, made a brave defense. Many ingenious attempts were made to burn the house, and it was twice set on fire. "Wild fire in cotton, and linen rags with brimstone in them," were tied to arrows, set on fire and shot upon the roof. All these efforts were continued, and successfully resisted, until the night of

Aug. 4th, when a final attempt was to be made to burn the building. So intent were the savages on this project that their guard was relaxed, and the air was so filled with yells of fiendish exultation at the prospect of the bloody feast so soon in store for them, that Maj. Simon Willard, with ninety-four men, rode within gunshot of the garrison before they were discovered. The Indians soon raised the siege, and before daybreak they set fire to the meetinghouse, which they had fortified for their own protection, and disappeared into the wilderness.

This rescue was seasonable. The besieged could hardly have withstood the assault about to be made. In the morning it was found that two formidable inventions for firing the house were nearly completed. A barrel with a pole stuck through holes in each head for an axletree formed the front; to the projecting ends of this axletree long poles were fastened; to these more long poles were spliced, one after another, running back like thills to a wagon, till they extended about fourteen rods. Under each splice a pair of the settlers' cart wheels had been placed. A platform over the barrel was piled high with combustibles. These poles could be spliced to any extent, and the machine pushed against the house in the darkness with impunity. Plenty of fire arrows were found, with which to ignite the combustibles at the proper moment. These operations had been retarded by a shower, but the ultimate success of the scheme, if left uninterrupted, can hardly be doubtful. The assailants were about five hundred, while the strength and the ammunition of the brave defenders, now reduced to twenty men, were alike nearly exhausted. A horrible death stared them in the face. At the beginning of the siege twenty-six fighting men, with fifty women and children, were crowded into the house with five wounded men to care for, to which four more were soon added. At its close this number was lessened by one—Curtice sent out for aid—and by five men killed or wounded; and increased by the birth of two pairs of twins.

What imagination can compass the manifold wretchedness of the besieged during those three sultry August days? The stifling fumes of the burning gunpowder in the shut up rooms, aggravating the sufferings and hastening the death of the wounded—the incessant strain of watching the burning arrows and avoiding the flying bullets—the horrid yells of the savages—the birth of the children in this pandemonium —with the growing consciousness that the end was nigh, in a horrible death!

The attack on Brookfield by the Nipmucks put a new aspect on the affairs of New England. For the first time a general rising of the Indians was seriously feared. Troops were at once put in motion from the east and west towards the scene of the disaster. Capt. Thomas Lothrop of Beverly and Capt. Richard Beers of Watertown joined Maj. Willard there with full companies, Aug. 7th.

Maj. Pynchon heard the news at Springfield, from some travelers, Aug. 4th. In great alarm he posted a messenger that night to Hartford, asking aid to secure Springfield and succor Brookfield. The War Council met at Hartford at one o'clock in the morning, Aug. 5th, and dispatched Capt. Thomas Watts, with forty dragoons and thirty Indians to Pynchon, "for the securitie of those towns, and to pass to Quabaug, if there be reason;" and on the 6th the Council raised two hundred and thirty dragoons, to be ready to march at an hour's notice. Aug. 7th, Maj. Pynchon, having satisfied himself of the fidelity of the River Indians, joining to the Connecticut forces, Lieut. William Cooper, with twenty-seven dragoons and ten Indians, sent the whole to Brookfield, where they formed a junction with Maj. Willard's command, the same day. Aug. 8th, the whole force, now about three hundred and fifty men, marched to Wennimisset, but the Indians were not to be found. The river troops searched the woods ten miles farther north, but found no trace of the enemy. Maj. Willard, fearing they had moved westward towards the river towns, decided to send a force thither.

Wednesday, Aug. 4th, before word had reached Boston of the outbreak at Brookfield, Capt. Samuel Moseley was dispatched with supplies to Capt. Henchman and orders to join him in the pursuit of Philip. On the 7th, however, he met Henchman on his return from Wabaquasset, and the united forces marched to Mendon, and thence to Marlboro. Here they parted, on the 8th; Henchman went to Boston for further orders, while Moseley pushed on with both companies for the new seat of war, reporting to Maj. Willard at Brookfield, Aug. 9th. He found Lothrop and Beers under marching orders for the Connecticut river. Taking Moseley's surgeon, William Locke, Lothrop moved off for Hadley, and Watts for Springfield. Word of the latter's arrival reached Hartford on the evening of the 10th. The Council met at 10 p. m., and sent their Marshal to visit their Indians, "to enquire after their welfare," to see that "they receive no affront from the English," to thank them for their fidelity, and "give everyone of them a dram." Besides these Indians who went up with Watts, Attawamhood had led thirty Mohegans to Springfield the day before. Watts and the Indians remained under the direction of Pynchon. Lothrop, after a short delay at Hadley to rest and refit his men, took the woods again for Brookfield.

Aug. 14, Maj. Willard directed another expedition to the north and west. Lothrop, Beers and Moseley marched together as far as Wennimisset. The first two, destined for Hadley, moved westward. Moseley went some eight miles farther north and then returned to Brookfield. The next day he was sent against a party of hostiles above Chelmsford, and reached Lancaster, en route, at 7 o'clock p. m., whence he sent dispatches to the Governor.

Pynchon, the commander on the river, feeling the responsibility too heavy for him, sent to the Council at Hartford, Aug. 12th, that he "was alone and wanted advice." Maj. John Talcott, with an escort of ten dragoons, was sent to his assistance, with a recommendation to Pynchon to send an agent to Albany, "if it be safe," to secure the aid of the Mohawks, if the enemy went that way. Thus early did these astute men foresee the policy of Philip. Gov. Andros was at Albany when Pynchon's messenger arrived, and at once engaged the Mohawks not to join the war, or entertain the hostiles. Aug. 24th he wrote Pynchon to that effect.

Headquarters were established at Hadley, a town well situated for a defensible post. Pynchon's forces had been active from the first in scouring the woods in search of the enemy. The Indians living near Hatfield and Northampton had volunteered in the same service. Attawamhood soon discovered that they "made fools of the English," and plainly told Pynchon that nothing could be accomplished while they were with the English in any pursuit; that by their shouts they gave notice to the enemy of the approach of the English, that they "might look to themselves."

On the arrival of Lothrop and Beers at Hadley, about the 16th, the whole force took the field for an extended scout. Capt. Watts went up on the west side of the Connecticut and the Bay troops on the east. Watts returned to Hadley, Aug. 22d, leaving ten of his men in the garrison at Deerfield, and twenty men were sent to secure Northfield. Lothrop and Beers ranged northward, and eastward again to Brookfield. On the 23d they were both back at Hadley, and doubtless Maj. Willard went with them, to consult with Maj. Pynchon. During all this marching and countermarching not a single hostile Indian was seen. The only visible result was the burning of seventy deserted wigwams; but the whereabouts of the enemy was unknown. In the following letter to the Council at Hartford Pynchon sums up the state of affairs:—

Spr. Aug. 22: 75.

Capt. John Allyn. Sr, In ye night a Post was sent me from Hadley, that o^r forces are returned; Capt. Wats thither, and the Bay forces to Qvabaug. Nothing done but about 50 Wigwams they found empty wch they haue burnt. They write from Hadley they expect nothing but ye enymy to insult & fall vpon ye remote Townes; that they are in great feares; a guard of 20 left at Squakheak is too week: some of yor soldiers left at Pocomtuck, Capt. Wats speaks of calling off, wch trobles y^m g^rtly: Suspect o^r Indians y^t went out to be fearefull or false or both: say y^t ye sheepe at Squakeake are driven away sence ye soldiers were there: suspect ye enymy to be betweene Hadley & Sqvakeak, at Paqvayag, about 10 miles from ye Gr^t River —I am sending to Capt. Wats to stay wth his forces there: I would gladly you would allow it & give further order about it; as y^t they make no discovery for ye enemy at ye place forenamed. The Indians you formerly writ off comeing in to Vncas it must be seriously considered whether none that are murderers of ye English be among them & such must be deliv^rd vp. I pray God direct you & vs & be o^r salvation. Comunicate advice & concill as you may judge needfull. They much desire ye p^rsence of some principall man at Hadley to direct, as need req^{rs}, & to expidite affairs. You^{rs} in ye L'd Jesus   JOHN PYNCHON.

Momonto thinks ye Indian enymy may be in a swamp called Momattanick about 3 mile off Paqvayag, between Hadly and Sqvakeak: it is a pitty but they should disrested; & yor Indians will be ye most likely to doe something. I pray give further orders about Capt. Wats & if Mag^{or} Talcot might be wth y^m I hope it w'ld turne to good.

[Directed,] These For Mr. John Allyn, at Hartford. Hast, Post Hast.

Escaping the pursuit of Henchman and Oneko, Philip, as we have seen, with about forty followers, reached the swamp near Wennimisset, on the 5th of August, taking refuge with the hostile Nipmucks. If he became their leader his first act was to infect them with the fear which had winged his flight from Pocasset Neck. Whoever led, the whole crew hurried away to hiding places, probably in great swamps lying in the eastern part of Franklin county. In a retrograde movement of this character Philip doubtless showed skill and activity as a leader, for he was a cautious and cunning man. When the provision plundered at Brookfield was exhausted the enemy drove off sheep from the Northfield commons. Their spies, no doubt, watched every movement of the English, that they might be able to strike the most effective blow.

FIGHT AT WEQUAMPS.

Aug. 24, 1675, a Council of War was convened at Hadley to investigate the conduct of a motley collection of Pocumtucks. Naunawtucks and vagabond stranger Indians, occupying a fort on the west bank of the Connecticut river between Northampton and Hadley. Grave suspicions were entertained of their fidelity. On the first alarm they professed friendship and gave up their arms. When Capt. Watts came up a few days later they offered their aid against any hostile Indians, and their guns were returned to them for this service. Abundant evidence was given to the Council of friendly feeling and intercourse between these Indians and the Nipmucks, and after hearing the objections of the Indians it was decided to demand their arms again. The Sachem who was present said on leaving that he would bring in his own, and try to persuade the rest to do the same. A messenger was sent to the fort in the afternoon, who was put off with evasive answers. When he went again in the evening, according to appointment, he was rudely insulted. Lothrop now determined to take their arms by force, and sent orders to the forces at Northampton to march at midnight quietly up near the fort, while he and Beers would cross the river above and come down upon it. According to this plan the two detachments met at the fort about daylight. The occupants had fled, leaving nothing but the dead body of an old Sachem who was killed for refusing to join in their flight to the enemy. Probably he was one of the ready-made Sachems, forced upon them by the English; if so he paid for his gratitude with his life.

Sending home a part of his force to guard the towns, Lothrop, with Beers and about one hundred men, made a rapid pursuit on the trail towards Deerfield. "Intending to parley with them," no precautions were taken against a surprise. No one seems to have dreamed that the Indians would presume to meet them with arms. On the other hand, the Indians were ready for war; they expected this pursuit, and prepared for it. Loaded with all their worldly goods, encumbered with their women and children, it was evident they must soon be overtaken. A favorable place was selected near the "Pocumtuck path," about eighty rods south of Wequamps, and here they lay in ambush, awaiting their pursuers. So little had the English learned by the experience of Capt. Hutchinson, at Brookfield, that they marched heedlessly into the trap. Their first notice of danger was the discharge of some forty muskets upon their ranks from the swamp on their right. Part of the English rushed down into the thicket, where a sharp fight from behind cover, Indian fashion, was kept up for three hours, when the Indians fled. Lothrop lost six men on the ground, one of whom "was shot in the back by our own men," and three others died of their wounds. They were Azariah Dickinson of Hadley, Samuel Mason of Northampton, Richard Fellows and James Levens of Hatfield, John Plumer of Newbury, Edward Jackson of Cambridge, Joseph Persons of Lynn, Matthew Scales of Rowley and William Cluff of Charlestown. John Parke of Watertown—afterwards of Newton—was shot in the elbow.* A squaw captured within two weeks said that the Indians lost twenty-six men in the action. Puckquahow, an active Nipmuck of Wennimisset, and in the Hutchinson ambush, was in this fight. He probably instigated the revolt and planned the ambush, so fatal to the English.

---

*In a petition to the General Court, March 15, 1677, Parke says he was "under the chirurgeon's hand about half a year"—that the shot so shattered the elbow that the bones came out. He was allowed, for loss of time, doctor's bill and "vituals" £9. Twenty-five years later he was allowed £2 10 s. per annum.

This was the first armed conflict between Englishmen and Indians in the Connecticut valley, and it gave a new meaning to the onset at Brookfield. It was now seen that a general war of races had begun, which must result in the extermination of one or the other.

The Council of Connecticut was opposed to the policy of disarming the Indians in the fort at Hatfield, and on the 25th of August, while the fight at Wequamps was still going on, was engaged in preparing a letter of remonstrance to Maj. Pynchon. Later in the day, the fact of the fight being known, George Graves, with twenty dragoons, was dispatched to Northampton. The next day the Council ordered the Hartford county dragoons to be in readiness to march on an hour's notice, and appointed a fast for "each County for all their towns the 4th day of the weeke monthly, till farther order, to begin in New Haven county Septr the first next."

Aug. 27th, the Council had word that the Wabaquasset Indians had captured "about 111 of Philip's men, women & children." They were probably on their way to join Philip in the Nipmuck country. On the 28th, the Council, still adhering to the policy of trusting the neighboring Indians, wrote to Pynchon advising him not to disarm those about Springfield. Aug. 31st Talcott was again sent up to advise with Pynchon, and Maj. Robert Treat, with a regiment of dragoons, marched for Northampton; but he was recalled the next day, by an alarm near Hartford.

Deerfield had at this time about one hundred and twenty-five inhabitants, with twenty-five or thirty men. The houses were scattered nearly the whole length of the present street. Three of these, as a measure of precaution, had been fortified with palisades. The ten men left by Capt. Watts were still here. No direct evidence has been found as to the situation of these forts, as they were called; but it would be safe to assume that one was on Meetinghouse Hill, at the house of Quintin Stockwell, where the minister boarded. The Catlin lot, where Sergeant Plympton then lived, was probably the south one, and the north fort may have been on the home lot of Mrs. C. E. B. Allen, then owned by James Tuffts.

I have said that the outbreak at Swansea caused no uneasiness among the settlers here. The affair at Brookfield created sufficient anxiety and alarm to induce precautionary measures. The last attack was at their very doors, and the horrors of an Indian war, still very little comprehended, had now become a reality to them. Doubtless the English looked upon the savages as a weak and cowardly race, to be easily subdued; and at this time we find no trace of fear on their part. Their only anxiety seems to have been to find the enemy, having no doubt about the result of the meeting. It was at a terrible cost that wisdom in this respect was acquired.

FIRST ATTACK ON DEERFIELD.

After the swamp fight of Aug. 25th, we get no trace of the Nipmucks, the Wampanoags, or the Pocumtucks, until Sept. 1st, when the latter made an attack on our town. On the morning of that day about sixty of them were lurking in the woods, watching a favorable opportunity for an attack. They were discovered by James Eggleston, a soldier of Windsor, while out looking for his horse. He was shot down, and the alarm being thus given, the inhabitants fled to the shelter of the forts, which all reached in safety. The Indians rushed on, as if to carry all before them; but the stockades, with a dozen men in each, were easily defended, and after losing two of their men, the assailants discreetly retired out of gunshot. The English were too few prudently to engage in the field with the unknown numbers pitted against them, and they had the mortification of seeing the despised Indians burning their buildings and destroying with fiendish glee their hard earned estate. The leader in this attack is unknown. Menowniett, a Connecticut Indian, is the only one of the party known by name. He was also in the swamp fight, Aug. 25th.

The news of this first attack on any town in the Connecticut valley, caused great consternation in the towns below. It reached Hadley while the inhabitants were assembled in the meetinghouse observing a fast, and Mather says they "were driven from the holy service they were attending by a most sudden and violent alarm, which routed them the whole day after." This brief allusion of the historian to the alarm at Hadley on hearing of the assault on Deerfield, is the slender foundation on which was built the elaborate account, that has gone into accepted history,* of a furious attack on Hadley that day, when the town was only saved from destruction by the appearance and valor of Gen. Goffe, one of the Regicides. A careful study of all the authorities leads to the conclusion that this whole romantic tale is a pure myth. A full *expose* of this story by the writer may be found in the New England Historical and Genealogical Register, Oct., 1874. Also see Beach's Indian Miscellany, 461, and History and Proceedings of the Pocumtuck Valley Memorial Association, I, 202.

NORTHFIELD SURPRISED.

Thursday, Sept. 2d, a party of Nipmucks under Sagamore Sam and One Eyed John, surprised a party at work in Great Meadow, and killed eight men. The women and children, on the alarm, fled to a small stockaded enclosure, which was defended by the surviving men. But the inmates, like their friends at Deerfield the day before, saw the enemy wasting and burning everything beyond the range of their muskets.

Meanwhile the Northfield people had not been forgotten at headquarters. The news of the attack on Deerfield raised fears at Hadley for the safety of that exposed town, and measures were at once taken for its succor. Sept. 2d was spent in preparation. Richard Montague, the baker, was "impressed" to make bread. William Markham, with cart and oxen, was "impressed" to transport ammunition, and the settlers' horses were taken to mount the soldiers. On the morning of the 3d, Capt. Beers, with thirty-six mounted men, marched for the beleaguered town, " with supplies, both of men and provision, to secure the small garrison there." Beers encamped for the night three or four miles south of the village. The besieged fort had, we may be sure, been carefully guarded by the Indians to prevent any information of the disaster reaching the English. But the movements of Beers the next morning are inexplicable except on the theory that he had some inkling of Indians being about the town, and that he pushed on his dismounted soldiers, intending to raise the siege by a surprise; supposing, perhaps, that

---

*See Hutchinson's Hist. Mass., I. 201; Stiles's Judges, 108; Hoyt's Antiquarian Researches, 135; Judd's Hadley, 145, 214; Holmes's Annals, I. 272; Palfrey's New England, II. 507, III. 164.

he had only the small party that beset Deerfield to deal with. Neither Philip nor the Nipmucks had been heard of since they left Wennimisset, and Beers had not yet learned that it is always the unexpected which happens in Indian warfare. The men of those days seem to have been very slow to discover this.

On the morning of the 4th, leaving his horses in camp with a small guard, Beers continued his march towards Northfield. Forgetful of the surprise of Hutchinson at Brookfield, and of his own at Wequamps, apparently neither vanguard nor flankers were thrown out, and the company was led directly into an ambuscade at the north end of Beers Plain, "when they were set upon by many hundreds of the Indians out of the Bushes by the Swampside." After the first shock, Beers rallied his shattered force and retreated, fighting bravely, to a hill on the right of his line of march, since called Beers Mountain, where he fell. Hubbard says he "was known to fight valiantly to the very last." Savage believes that he made a nuncupative will, after he was wounded. If these statements are well founded it would appear that some of his company must have remained with him to the last, and then escaped. He was buried where he fell. The spot is known, but unmarked. [See Temple and Sheldon's History of Northfield.]

A partial list of those slain Sept. 2d, are: Sergt. Samuel Wright, Ebenezer and Jonathan James of Northfield; Ebenezer Parsons and Nathaniel Curtice of Northampton; John Peck of Hadley, Thomas Scott and Benjamin Dunwich, residence unknown. Samuel Wright, Jr., was severely wounded. Those killed on the 4th were: Capt. Richard Beers of Watertown, Benjamin Crackbon of Dorchester, Ephraim Childe of Roxbury, John Getchell of Marblehead, Jeremiah Morrell of Boston, Joseph Dickinson and William Marcum of Hadley, John Genery of Dedham, George Lickens, Thomas Cornish, James Mullard, John Wilson, Elisha Woodward, and "8 others of whom there is no account." One of these was from Taunton. John Harrington of Watertown, and Robert Pepper of Roxbury were wounded, and the latter captured. There is a tradition that several of the above were taken alive and put to death by torture. Thirteen of the party reached Hadley that evening with news of the disaster.

The alarm which recalled Maj. Treat to Hartford, Sept. 1st, had small foundation. Sept. 2d, Treat was appointed Commander-in-Chief of the Connecticut forces in the field, with orders to lead his command through Westfield to Northampton, and thence where most needed; and to send home all the men now in the up river service except the twenty-nine in the garrisons at Westfield, Hatfield, and Deerfield. On the 3d, Treat, with a strong force, including at least ninety dragoons, began his march. He reached Northampton on the 4th, and during the night learned the fate of Beers. The same news reached Hartford on the 5th, and at once the Council gave orders that one hundred Mohegans and Pequots should follow Treat; and the next day twenty dragoons under Joseph Wardsworth were sent to Westfield, and twenty under John Grant to Springfield, to guard those towns.

TREAT'S MARCH TO NORTHFIELD.

Sunday morning, Sept. 6th, Treat crossed the river to Hadley with above one hundred men, and took the route to Northfield. He probably spent the night on the site of Beers's encampment, and reached the beleaguered stockade on the morning of the 6th. It must have been a joyful occasion to the inmates, who had been shut up four days, with death staring them in the face every hour. Not an Indian was seen on the march, or on reaching Northfield. They had doubtless watched the motions of the English and fled to their hiding place on the advance of Treat. Learning that the bodies of those slain Sept. 2d were still lying on the meadows where they fell, Treat detailed a party to bury them. That of Sergeant Wright, commander of the little garrison, naturally received the first attention. It was carried up the bank and placed in the first grave ever opened in the present village cemetery.

The following tradition, taken by the writer in 1876 from the lips of Mrs. Polly Holton of Northfield, who died in 1879 at the age of ninety-eight, is not found elsewhere; but without doubt it refers to the events of Sept. 2-6, 1675, and is reliable. Sergt. Wright was great-great-grandfather to Mrs. Holton; his son, Samuel, Jr., her great-grandfather, who was sorely wounded the same day, lived until his daughter, her grandmother, was thirty years old; Mrs. Holton was twelve at the death of the latter; so she had the story only second hand from one who took part in the affair. The story, which came out in a conversation about the old cemetery, was this: "The first one buried there was a man by the name of Wright, from Northampton. He was killed by Indians. He was not found for several days. He was found in the meadow in a decaying condition. He was carried up the bluff and buried just as he was, in the present burying ground." This tradition preserves an interesting fact, and explains several otherwise obscure contemporaneous statements.

The grave of Sergt. Wright was hardly filled before the sad duties of the party were rudely interrupted. A party of Indians fired upon them from the bushes, where they had been skulking. No one was hurt, although Maj. Treat was struck by a spent ball. Duty to the living now superseded care for the dead, and the rest of the bodies were left where they fell.

In the upward march, says Hubbard, Treat's men "were much daunted to see the heads of Capt. Beers's soldiers upon poles by the wayside * * * One (if no more) was found with a chain hooked into his under jaw, and so hung up on the bow of a tree, ('tis feared he was hung up alive) by which means they thought to daunt and discourage any that might come to their relief and alsoe to terrifie those that should be spectators with the beholding so sad an object, insomuch that Maj. Treat and his company * * * were solemnly affected with that doleful sight, which made them the more haste to bring down the garrison." On reaching the stockade these disheartened soldiers met about one hundred men, women and children, faint and weary with watching, whose nerves had been stretched to their utmost tension for four days, and each party had its tales of horror for the other. Add to this the sickening sight of the decomposing bodies in the meadow, and it would seem little was wanting to create a panic. More than enough was furnished by the appearance of the enemy, the attack on the burial party, and the narrow escape of the commander. It is no wonder that Maj. Treat "concluded forthwith to bring off the garrison; so they came away the same night leaving the cattle there, and the dead bodies unburied." The panic had reached a crisis. The danger was magnified. Treat feared to wait the slow moving ox teams, by which the most valuable effects of the settlers might have been saved, or even to drive off the neat stock, so necessary to the owners, and so easily moved. Everything was left behind but their horses. Not a ray of historic light has been shed on this night retreat. We may assume that each trooper took one of the rescued party behind him, and all stole silently away into the darkness. We are left to imagine the long cavalcade, a line of strange, black looking spectres, threading its way the livelong night through the gloomy woods, and the panic stricken riders, peering fearfully right and left into the thickets, or crowding together in terror at the hoot of the owl or bark of fox or wolf, sure that each was the war-whoop of a pursuing foe. They were only reassured when met by a strong reinforcement under Capt. Samuel Appleton, who had just arrived from the Bay. Appleton tried to induce Treat to turn back and "see if they could make any spoil upon the enemy;" but Treat could not be persuaded. The demoralized soldiers of Treat seemed to infect all classes at Hadley with despondency and gloom. Maj. Pynchon, writing about this time, says:—

"And when we go out after the Indians they doe so sculk in swamps we cannot find y^m & yet do waylay o^r people to there destruction. Burne y^r houses as lately they have destroyed a small village at Wussquakeak from whence formerly ye Maquas drove these Indians."

The danger of ranging the woods at random was now realized. A council of war was held on the 8th, when it was decided to give up operations in the field and only garrison the towns. To that end Pynchon sent Capt. Appleton with his company to Deerfield—probably about the 10th. Maj. Treat reported the action of this council at Hartford on the 9th, and all the Connecticut forces were ordered home except sixteen at Westfield under Ens. John Miles, and fifteen at Springfield under Lieut. John Standly. This policy of inaction was not satisfactory to the Connecticut Council, and the next day, Sept. 10th, they wrote the Commissioners for the United Colonies recommending active aggression. The Commissioners took the same view, and Sept. 16th voted to raise one thousand men for that service. For operation in the valley, Massachusetts and Connecticut troops should be employed, with Maj. Pynchon as Commander-in-Chief; the Connecticut Council being authorized to appoint a Connecticut man to "be second in command," Maj. Treat was appointed.

After two days' consideration, bolder counsels had prevailed at Hadley, and a vigorous campaign was agreed upon. At the request of Pynchon, on the 11th, Treat, with a large force of Connecticut soldiers, was again sent up the river by the Council.

SECOND ATTACK ON DEERFIELD.

This town was now the frontier, and from its peculiar location was much exposed and difficult to defend. From the hills on the east and west every movement in the valley could be seen by Indian spies. Not a messenger could come or go, not a party enter the meadow to secure their crops, not a movement between the forts by the soldiers, without the lurking enemy being fully apprised of it.

Observing on the morning of Sunday, Sept. 12th, that the soldiers as well as settlers had collected in the Stockwell fort for public worship, the Indians took advantage of this circumstance, and an ambush was laid in the swamp just north of Meetinghouse Hill, to intercept the north garrison on its return. Accordingly, as twenty-two men were passing over the causeway, they were fired upon from the swamp. All, however, retreated to Stockwell's in safety, except Samuel Harrington, who was wounded by a shot in the neck. Turning now to the north, the Indians captured Nathaniel Cornbury, who had been left as a sentinel, and was trying to reach his comrades. He was never afterwards heard from. Capt. Appleton soon rallied his men and drove the assailants from the village, but not until the north fort had been plundered and set on fire, and much of the settlers' stock killed or stolen. As Appleton had not force enough to guard the forts and engage in offensive operations outside, the Indians still insultingly hung round the outskirts and burned two more houses. The stolen horses were loaded with beef, pork, wheat, corn and other spoils and driven to their rendezvous at Pine Hill. The attacking force was doubtless the Pocumtucks, recruited from other tribes. No estimate of their numbers has been found, but as there were probably from seventy-five to one hundred men in the forts, the force opposed must have been a large one. An express was sent at once to Northampton. Red tape and a storm prevented action that night, but the next night a party of volunteers, with a few from Hadley, and "some of Lothrop's men," came up to the relief of our town. On the morning of Tuesday, the 14th, the united forces, under Appleton, marched to Pine Hill. Spies had doubtless reported the arrival of reinforcements, and the Indians had all fled.

Capt. Moseley, who was to play an important part in succeeding events, arrived at headquarters at Hadley on the night of the 14th, and was at once sent to this town. Maj. Treat, with the Connecticut forces, reached Northampton on the 15th, on which date the Council ordered Capt. John Mason to join him with a strong force of Mohegans. The concentration of so many men in the valley made it necessary to lay in a large stock of provision at headquarters. At this time wheat was the staple crop at Deerfield, used not only at the table, but as a circulating medium in barter, and in payment of debts and taxes. Maj. Pynchon owned a large estate here, and he with others had a great quantity of wheat in the straw, "about 3000 bushels was supposed to be there standing in stacks," says Hubbard. This had been spared by the Indians in the expectation that it would soon be their own. About the 15th Pynchon sent orders to have a part of this thrashed and put in bags, and to impress teams and drivers for its transportation. Capt. Lothrop was sent up with his company from Hadley to convoy the train to headquarters. He reached here without molestation, probably on the 17th of September.

BLOODY BROOK MASSACRE.

We now turn one of the darkest pages in the history of our town. Early in the morning of Sept. 18, 1675—a day memorable in our annals—"that most fatal day, the saddest that ever befel New England," Capt. Lothrop, "with his choice company of young men, the very flower of the County of Essex," followed by a slowly moving train of carts, marched proudly down the old Town Street, two miles across South Meadows, up Bars Long Hill, to the heavily wooded plain stretching away to Hatfield meadows. The carts were loaded with bags of wheat, upon which were a few feather beds and some light household stuff. These things may have been taken by Joshua Carter for his widowed sister, Sarah Field, planning an asylum for herself and helpless babes in her father's house in Northampton. But no evidence appears at this time of any intent to abandon the settlement. Southward along the narrow Pocumtuck Path, through the primeval woods, moved Lothrop and his men—brave, fearless, foolish. Confident in their numbers, scorning danger, not even a van-guard or flanker was thrown out.

Meanwhile the whole hostile force was lying like serpents in the way; but unlike the more chivalric of these reptiles, their fangs will be felt before a warning is given. The probable leaders were Mattamuck, Sagamore Sam, Matoonas and One Eyed John, of the Nipmucks; Anawan, Penchason, and Tatason, of the Wampanoags, and Sangumachu of the remnant of the Pocumtucks. There is no evidence that Philip was present, and the probabilities are against it.

Keen eyes had seen the preparation for Lothrop's march; swift feet had carried the news to the chieftains below, who at this moment were giving their last orders to their warriors lying in the ambush at Bloody Brook, into which Lothrop was marching in fatal security. From the top of Long Hill the path lay through the dense forest for a mile and a half, when it approached on the left a narrow, swampy thicket, trending southward, through which crept sluggishly a nameless brook. Skirting this swamp another mile, a point was reached where it narrowed and turned to the right. Here the path crossed it diagonally, leaving the marsh on the right. The soldiers crossed the brook and halted, while the teams should slowly drag their heavy loads through the mire; "many of them," says Mather, "having been so foolish and secure as to put their arms in the carts and step aside to gather grapes, which proved dear and deadly grapes to *them*." Meanwhile the silent morass on either flank was covered with grim warriors prone upon the ground, their tawny bodies indistinguishable from the slime in which they crawled, or their scarlet plumes and crimson paint from the glowing tints of the dying year on leaf and vine. Eagerly but breathless and still, they waited the signal. The critical moment had come. The fierce war-whoop rang in the ears of the astonished English:—

> "When swarming forth from out their vine-clad hive
> The infernal hornets came,
> And sting on sting made all the copse alive
> With darts and wounds and flame."

The men of Pocumtuck sank, the Flower of Essex withered before it, and the nameless stream was baptized in blood.

> "Then groans, and silent all; but now the bronk,
> That from the forest glides,
> Swells with a crimson flood, and angry look
> And bloody are its sides.
>
> O what rich currents gave
> Their ruby tincture to the carpet green
> And bade for aye the wave
> Be Sanguinetto for our Thrasimene."*

Moseley, who with about sixty men had gone out from Deerfield to range the woods in another direction, "hearing the reports which the guns gave of this battel, came up with a handful of men though too late." He arrived on the scene about ten o'clock in the morning, and found the savages plundering the carts and stripping the dead. They had ripped open the bags of grain and the feather beds, and scattered the contents in the bloody mire. This disorganized mass was quickly driven from their prey. Among the slain lay Robert Dutch of Ipswich, who, says Hubbard his pastor, had "been sorely wounded by a Bullet that rased his skull, and then mauled by the Indian Hatchets, and left for dead by the Salvages, and stript by them of all but his skin, yet when Mosely came near, he came towards the English to their no small amazement."

Among these "Salvages" were many of Eliot's "Praying Indians." They could speak English, and were acquainted with many of the colonists. Some of them recognized the leader of the rescuers, and exulting in their success, with confidence in their numbers, dared him to the combat, shouting "Come, Mosely! Come! You seek Indians; you want Indians; here's Indians enough for you!" Although the enemy were ten to one, the gallant Captain at once charged upon them. Keeping his force in a compact body he swept through and through the swarming legions, cutting down all within

---

*William Everett's poem at the Bi-centennial Celebration on the spot.

reach of his fire. In this manner he fought them for five or six hours, defying all attempts of the enemy to surround him, or to reach his wounded; but he was not able to drive them from the ground, and their rich harvest of plunder. His Lieutenants, Perez Savage of Boston and John Pickering of Salem, greatly distinguished themselves in the action, "being sometimes called to lead the Company in the Front," says Hubbard, "while Capt. Mosely took a little Breath, who was almost melted, laboring, commanding, and leading his men through the Midst of the Enemy." Exhausted by these heroic efforts, Moseley was about to retire from the unequal contest, when, "just in the nick of time," welcome relief appeared. During the morning of this day, Maj. Treat left Northampton with one hundred Connecticut soldiers and sixty Mohegans under Attawamhood, second son of Uncas, for Northfield, at or near which place he had planned to establish headquarters for the Connecticut forces. Somewhere on the march he heard the firing, and hurried to the scene of conflict, where he joined Moseley. The savages were driven westward through the woods and swamps until darkness put a stop to the chase. The united forces then marched to Pocumtuck, carrying their wounded and leaving the dead where they fell. Mather says, "This was a black and fatal day, wherein there was eight persons made widows, and six and twenty children made orphans, all in one little Plantation." That little plantation was Pocumtuck; and these were the heavy tidings which the sad, worn out soldiers brought to our stricken inhabitants.

Of seventeen men of Pocumtuck who went out in the morning as teamsters, not one returned to tell the tale. The torturing anxiety and sickening fear, crowding the hearts of the distracted women the live-long day, now only gave place to the awful certainty of the worst. Their husbands, fathers, brothers, were slain, and the last offices of love denied. Their mangled bodies now lay uncared for in the dark morass at Bloody Brook. The curtain shrouding the valley of the Pocumtuck, and hiding the pitiful distress of that terrible night, has never been lifted; and what imagination will dare an attempt to depict the agonizing scenes behind it!

On the morning of Sunday, Sept. 19, Treat and Moseley marched forth to bury their dead comrades on the field where they fell. A spot was selected twenty-five rods southerly from the fatal morass. Scouts were sent out, sentinels stationed to prevent a surprise, and the melancholy duties of the day began. Parties were detailed to gather the dead, and workmen to prepare a common grave. Tenderly the mangled bodies of the victims were borne to the spot, and slowly and reverentially they were laid in the bosom of mother earth.

When the stark forms of these patriot dead, this "choice company of young men, the very Flower of the County of Essex," had been placed side by side with the hardy yeomen of the valley, "the principal inhabitants of Pocumtuck," to sleep for aye in this western wilderness, far from the sounding sea they loved so well,—when the work of the workmen was done, and all that was mortal hid forever in the earth, "sixty-four persons in one dreadful grave,"—when the whole command were collected about the spot, leaning with bowed heads upon clinched firelocks, their manly forms convulsed by suppressed sobs,—while the dusky braves of Uncas stood aloof with sad but curious interest,—what rite or requiem was heard? Was the stillness broken, and the solemn Sunday service concluded by the voice of Pastor Mather or Chaplain Whiting? Did they entreat with piteous supplications to the Most High, that the sacrifice of these young lives might be enough? That the Divine vengeance might here be stayed? That the Sword of the Lord might henceforth prevail against the Serpent of the Wilderness? That the widows and orphans in the little plantation hard by might be gathered under His wings? Did officers and men here vow to avenge their slaughtered countrymen? Were the echoes aroused by a wailing war-whoop from the Mohegans, or a last volley fired over the soldiers' grave?

We question in vain. Those who could have answered died and left no sign. But we may be sure all nature was in sympathy; that the pitying pines sighed and moaned, as they stretched out their protecting arms above the spot; that the conscious brook crept softly over its broken banks to lap the sanguine stain; that the birds sang sweetly on the swaying vine; that the crimson leaves fell lightly on the bare, brown earth, and the soft September sun struggled to send bright beams to fleck the swelling mound. So we leave its tenants behind the dim mists of two centuries, to the "Resurrection at the last Day, to receive their Crowns among the Rest of the Martyrs, that have laid down and ventured their Lives, as a Testimony to the Truth of their Religion as well as Love to their Country."

Lothrop had traversed his line of march one or two days before and saw no enemy. He did see, and as a military officer was bound to note, its dangerous passes. One was at the place where he was ambushed Aug. 25th. Had this lesson been lost upon him? Onward two miles he crossed the morass where he fell. Had he no premonitions, born of the Beers tragedy at Northfield? Still another two miles and the track fell off, by a long descent to the Bars, on a narrow spur, from the wooded ravines on either side of which, a thousand men could pour their shot unseen. Had he no vision of the death of Hutchinson and the men of Brookfield? How could any commander have been better prepared to secure his line of march, or have profited so little by his opportunities. Lothrop was doubtless brave; reckless, he must have been. These two qualities in action, are simply foolhardiness; and Lothrop must be held responsible for the young lives entrusted to his care. Perhaps his scouts, if he had any out, had not discovered traces of the force lately come over the river. Perhaps he relied on the movements of Moseley and Treat to keep the Indians quiet. Probably, he despised the race and underrated their prowess. A vigilant vanguard would have roused the ambush in time for Lothrop to prepare for fight; or, if the odds were too great, for a retreat, with small loss, save the inevitable sacrifice of the train. But once in the toils, no other result but the one we deplore was possible. The soldiers were massed on the south and west of the swamp. The head of the convoy, some twenty rods in length, was struggling through the mire. From the front and the right flank of the troops, and from the left flank of the train, deliberate aim could be taken by the enemy. The commander, and doubtless a large part of his company, fell at the first fire. The survivors, instantly surrounded, twenty to one, were shot down in detail. Had the brave Moseley, with all his fighting qualities, allowed himself to be thus ensnared, nothing could have saved him from the same fate.

Hubbard criticises Capt. Lothrop and condemns him "for taking up a wrong notion which he was always arguing for," that the best way of meeting the enemy was to fight them "in their own way, by skulking behind trees, and taking aim at single persons * * * not considering the great disadvantage a small company would have in dealing that way with a greater multitude; for, if five have to deal with one, they may surround him, and every one to take his aim at him, while he can level at but one of his enemies at a time." Hubbard probably voiced the popular sentiment, when he says of the slain, "Their dear relatives at home mourning for them, like Rachel for her children, and would not be comforted, not only because they were not, but because they were so miserably lost. Had he ordered his men to march in a body, as some of his fellow commanders advised, either backward or forward, in reason they had not lost a quarter of the number that fell that day * * * The gallant Mosely marched through and through that great body of Indians, and yet came off with little or no loss in comparison with the other."

The writer makes no distinction in his argument, between the surprise of Lothrop, and the open attack of Moseley. Nor has he a word of condemnation for the real cause of the disaster. This seems the more strange as in the course of the whole war, with the exception of the attack on the Narraganset fort, and the retreat from Turners Falls, scarcely a life was lost save by surprisal.

Accounts vary as to the number slain. Hoyt says "The whole loss, including teamsters, was ninety * * * only seven or eight escaped." Hubbard says, Lothrop had "about eighty men * * * not above seven or eight escaping," and again that "seventy-three men were cut off." A dispatch received by the Governor and Council at Boston, Sept. 22d, reported "above forty of Lothrop's men, with himself were slain * * * also others that belonged to the carriages, so that the next day they buried sixty-four men in all." Rev. John Cotton wrote from Boston, Sept. 23d, that "Lothrop had about forty-six men * * * Capt. Lothrop slaine and all his men only two, and eighteen men of Deerfield slaine also." Sewell, in his diary writes, "Capt. Lothrop and sixty-four men" were killed. A letter to London of Dec. 28th, re-

THE LOSS AT BLOODY BROOK. 107

lates "the loss of Capt. Lothrop of Beverly and about sixty men." Cotton Mather makes the loss "above threescore." Increase Mather, "above sixty buried in one dreadful grave." Rev. John Russell, who made up a "List of men slain in Hampshire County," some months after, says, "ye 18 Sept. 71 men slaine;" but he "cannot get the names of all;" and gives the names of but sixty-one. In this list of sixty-one are seventeen of our townsmen. Judd considers Russell the best authority, and thinks "some of the teamsters may have been buried in the towns below."

Weighing all the evidence obtainable, the conclusion is reached that the loss was Lothrop and forty-three men; Deerfield seventeen and Moseley three—"sixty-four men in all."

As it must seem presumptuous to differ so widely from such excellent authorities as Judd, Hoyt and Russell—especially the latter—some of the considerations are given which lead to that decision. There is no contradiction, and but a trifling discrepancy, among the six contemporary authorities cited. The numbers given are, "sixty-four," "about sixty-three;" "Lothrop and sixty-four;" "Lothrop and about sixty;" "above threescore;" "above sixty." It is impossible to reconcile their statements with that of Hubbard; but a suggestion will be offered as a possible explanation. The names of sixty-five men who served under Lothrop in the valley are known. The historian may have found a roll of Lothrop's men and added to them the men of Deerfield, to make his "eighty men;" and supposing Lothrop's whole force was with him, and only "seven or eight escaped," made his statement accordingly.

Judd's suggestion to account for the discrepancy seems inconsistent with the spirit of the times, and may be dismissed on its improbability.

Hoyt followed Hubbard, whom he often quotes, but evidently misunderstood him, and adds the seventeen Deerfield men to the total of the latter, making ninety-seven engaged, of whom "only seven escaped," leaving his "90 slain."

Had Russell, then living at Hadley, made up his list at the time of the event, his conclusions would be beyond question. But he did not do this. So much is evident from the fact that the list is not complete. Who were the ten men whose names he "cannot get"? Is it supposable that Moseley or his men did not know the names of their dead or wounded comrades? Nor can it be believed that a complete list of Lothrop's loss could not have been made, when the names can now be given of twenty-five survivors of his company, who were then at Hadley or Northampton. The Boston dispatch was doubtless sent by those who buried the sixty-four men. This is the best authority. It is not possible that from seven to twenty-six bodies were left unburied where they fell. Maj. Treat was on the field in force, and there was no occasion for such haste as this would indicate. There is no reason for supposing that any man, unless it were Moseley's three, fell more than forty to sixty rods, at farthest, from the place of burial.

The following, with one addition, is Russell's list of the slain, arranged alphabetically, with residence added, so far as ascertained :—

LOTHROP'S COMPANY.

Capt. Thomas Laythrop, Beverly.
Sergt. Thomas Smith Newbury.
Sergt. Samuel Stevens, "
Alexander Thomas, Salem.
Ally Solomon, Lynn.
Allyn John, Deerfield.
Balch Joseph, Beverly.
Barnard John, Deerfield.
Barsham Philip, "
Bayley Thomas, Weymouth.
Bennet John, Manchester?
Buckley Thomas, Salem.
Button Daniel, Newberry.
Carter Joshua, Deerfield.
Clarke Adam, Salem.
Cole George, Lynn.
Crumpton Samuel, Salem.
Dodge Josiah, Beverly.
Duy William, Salem.
Farah Ephraim, "
Friende Francis, Salem.
Furnell Benj., Lynn.
Gillet Joseph, Deerfield.
Harriman John, Rowley.
Hinsdell Barnabas, Deerfield.
Hinsdell John, "
Hinsdell Robert, "
Hinsdell Samuel, "
Hobbs John, Ipswich.
Hobbs Thomas, "
Homes Robert, Newbury.
Hudson Samuel, Marlboro.
Kilbourne Jacob, Rowley.
Kimball Caleb, Ipswich.
Kinge Joseph, Salem.
Lambert Richard, "
Littlehall John, Haverhill.
Maninge Thomas, Ipswich.
Marshall Eliakim, Boston.
Mentor Thomas, Ipswich.
Merritt John, Manchester.
Mudge James, Malden.
Osver Abel, Salem.
*Pitman Mark, Marblehead.
Plum John, "
Plympton Jonathan, Deerfield.
Roper Benjamin, Dorchester.
Ropes George, Salem.
Sawier Ezekiel, "
Smeade William, Deerfield.
Stevens Samuel, Ipswich.
Trask Edward, Beverly.
Tuffts James, Deerfield.
Warmen Steven, Lynn.
Waynwritt Jacob, Ipswich.
Weller Thomas, Deerfield.
Whiteridge Samuel, Ipswich.
Williams Zebediah, Deerfield.
Wilson Robert, Salem.
Woodbury Peter, Beverly.
Two [One] unknown. [61.]

---

*Pitman is now placed in this list for the first time, on evidence furnished by Bodge from John Hull's account book.

THE SURVIVORS AT BLOODY BROOK.

Wounded.

Bodwell Henry, Newbury.
Dutch Robert, Ipswich.

Toppan John, Newbury.
Very Thomas, Marblehead.

MOSELEY'S COMPANY.

Killed.

Barron Peter, Watertown.
Oates, John.

One unknown. [3.]

Wounded.

Russ Richard, Weymouth.
Stevens John, Newbury.

And about six others.

John Stebbins of Deerfield, ancestor of all the tribe here, is the only man who is known to have escaped unhurt.*

Bodwell, a man of great strength, was shot in the left arm at the first fire. With his clubbed musket in his right hand, he fought his way through the swarming horde and escaped to Hatfield. Toppan, disabled by a shot in the shoulder, crept into the bed of the brook and drew the weeds on the bank over him as well as he could. He heard the Indians stepping over him, but was not discovered. Dutch has been previously noticed. In a petition to the Council three years later, Russ says he "received a shot in the bottom of his

---

*The evidence of his escape is found in the following petition from the Massachusetts Archives, Vol. 69, p. 208.

To the much Honoured counsel now sitting in Boston, the Humble petition of John Stebbens (of muddy River), Most Humbly sheweth, your pore petitioner, hath bene a souldier, in the service of the countrey (about a year & halfe) & was under the comand of captain Lathrope & with him when he and his company were destroyed, & under the comand of captain mosley the Greatest part of the time he was out, I was never forced or pressed into the service, but volentarily gave my selfe frely to the wars of the Lord, & my country—and now of late your petitioner, hath followed in these parts his caling of A carpenter, sometimes in one towne, & sometimes in another, about 5 months I have wrought in cambridg vilage, & after my worke there was finished, & removed to muddy River to doe worke there promised, the constable of the villiage, by order of the militia, came & pressed me for a garison souldier for Hadley, I went not out of the Viliage to avoid the prese, for I heard nothing of the prese, but my worke there was finished, and my selfe removed more a weke before, as may be made appear, your pore petitioner hath bene warned to appear before the commitee of militia, at the viliage, for not attending that service, & by them assigned to pay fower pounds where vpon your pore petitioner, doth look upon himselfe much wronged & put to much trouble by being illegally pressed by the constable of another towne, & it hath bene the loss of much time & greatly to the damage of your petitioner—my humble request therefore to your honours is, thay you would be pleased to put an issue to the mater, or that you would be pleased to appoint a time for the hereing of the case, and that parsons concerned may have notice thereof. I cast my selfe downe at your Honours foot, and shall quietly sit downe satisfied with your Honours determination, & granting the request of your pore petitioner, he shall be farther engaged & incoredged in your service, & shall not cease to pray for your Honours hapiness.

July 4th 1678 The Council on hearing of this Case declare that they judge it meet to discharge the said Stebbins from ye said fine & his surety also.

belly, the bullet carrying in with it the ring of his Bandolier, where he hath borne it with payne, until about six weeks ago it was cut out by the Dutch Chyrurgeon, for which, tho very poore, he gave forty shillings."

The number of Indians in this surprise is estimated at from five hundred to twelve hundred. Moseley, who had at least all the opportunity he desired, judged them to be one thousand. This force was made up of perhaps six or seven hundred Nipmucks, and from seventy-five to one hundred of Philip's Wampanoags, who had crossed the Connecticut river three or four days before, and the Pocumtuck clans, who may have increased to one hundred and twenty-five or one hundred and fifty before this time.

The loss of the Indians was reported at ninety-six. This statement, and that of twenty-six being killed in the Wequamps fight, must be taken with a large allowance. The Indian loss in any conflict is rarely known. " In all battles the Indians endeavor to conceal their loss, and in effecting this they sometimes expose themselves more than in combat with the enemy. When one falls his nearest comrade crawls under cover of brush or trees, and fixing a *tump line* to the dead body, cautiously drags it to the rear," and dead bodies have been seen sliding along the ground with no apparent cause.

On the 19th, while our forces were yet at Bloody Brook, our afflicted settlement had a narrow escape. The Indians, on being driven from their prey by Treat and Moseley, retreated over Mill River plain, crossed the Pocumtuck below Stillwater, and continued along the Wisdom meadows. When opposite the town, the next morning, they threatened an attack. The commander of the garrison—probably Capt. Appleton—made a show of defiance, and they withdrew. Their spies having been called in, the weakness of the garrison had not been discovered. Had it been otherwise, the burial party returning from Bloody Brook would probably have had to repeat here the sad duties of the morning. Hubbard says of this affair that their success on the 18th " so emboldened the enemy that they durst soon after adventure upon considerable Towns, though well garrisoned with Soldiers, and gave them Occasion of most insolently braving the Garrison at Dearfield the next Day, hanging up the Garments of the

English in Sight of the Soldiers, yet on the other Side of the River. However it pleased God, who is always wont to remember his People in their low Estate, to put such a Restraint upon them, that when they passed very near the garrison House at Dearfield (wherein were not left above twenty-seven Soldiers,) their Captain used this Stratagem: to cause his Trumpet to sound, as if he had another Troop near by to be called together, they turned another Way and made no Attempt upon the House where that small Number was, which if they had done with any ordinary Resolution, so small a Handful of Men could hardly have withstood the Force of so many hundreds as were there gathered together."

These garments were doubtless taken from the bodies of their victims at Bloody Brook.

When the enemy struck the line of communication between Deerfield and headquarters at Hadley, fourteen miles away, it was a death blow to the former. Two of the four companies sent from the Bay to protect the towns in the Valley had been cut to pieces. Deerfield had lost her ablest defenders. Pynchon, realizing the danger of attempting to hold this settlement any longer, against the successful hordes around it, as was usual with him when in a strait, sent to Hartford for advice. Sept. 21st, the Council of War forwarded him their "sense about quitting the Pocumtuck garrison." We can only infer the tenor of their advice from the fact that the town was abandoned soon after. The inhabitants were scattered in the towns below; the savages destroyed at will the fruits of their labor, and the Pocumtuck Valley was restored to the wilderness.

ATTACKS ON HATFIELD AND SPRINGFIELD.

The Council of War at Hartford had decided to regain Northfield and establish there headquarters for Connecticut troops and a center for offensive operations. Treat, as we have seen, had left Northampton for that place on the 18th. On the 19th the forces from New Haven county, under Lieut. Thomas Munson, and the dragoons from Fairfield county, under Ens. Steven Burret, then at Hartford, were dispatched to join Maj. Treat "at or near" Northfield. The events of the 18th so changed the face of affairs that this scheme was given up. Brookfield, Northfield, Swampfield and Deerfield were now in ashes. The frontier had been crowded down to Hatfield and Hadley, and it was evident that the remaining towns could only be saved by vigorous measures.

Sept. 21st, the Council of War at Hartford received a message from the Commissioners, then at Boston, that they had agreed to raise one thousand men, to be "every way fitted with armes and ammunition, to be in readiness to march at an hour's warning, whereof 500 to be dragoons or troopers, with long armes." Pynchon was appointed Commander-in-Chief and the Council was authorized to name a Connecticut man as second in command. Maj. Treat was selected. These officers were allowed to call out as many soldiers as they judged best, and add as many Indians as they might find useful. The Council was desired to assist and advise Pynchon from time to time. Pynchon received his commission Sept. 22d. With it came orders to employ all forces called out, in field operations. No soldiers were allowed to garrison the towns. This direction had been issued Sept. 16th, before the strength of the enemy was known, and with the belief that they would never dare to make any open attack. Though against his judgment, Pynchon, in obedience to his orders, set about plans for gathering the scattered commands and massing a force large enough to sweep the valley of the enemy.

Meanwhile the woods were full of skulking Indians, watching opportunity for spoil. Sept. 26th, Pynchon's farm-house, barns and crops, on the west side of the river at Springfield, were burned. On the 28th Praisever Turner and Uzackaby Shackspeer were killed at Northampton.

Connecticut was prompt in getting out her troops. There was more delay at the Bay. Secretary Rawson wrote, Sept. 30th, "The slaughter in your parts has much damped many spirits for the war. Some men escape away from the press and others hide away after they are impressed." The same cause had "much damped" the spirits of those here. All industry was paralyzed; the crops lay ungathered in the meadows; scouting and posting were alike distasteful and dangerous. A good account of the condition of affairs here is found in the following extract from a letter by Pynchon to Gov. Leverett, of Sept. 30th:—

"We are indeavoring to discover ye enemy, dayly send out scouts, but little is effected. We sometimes discover a few Indians, & sometimes fires, but not the body of y^m, and have no Indian friends here (altho we have sent to Hartford for some) to help us. * * * Our English are somewhat awk and fearful in scouting out and espying though we do ye best we can. We find ye Indians have their scouts out. 2 days ago 2 Englishmen at Northampton, having gone out in ye morning to cut wood, and but a little from ye house, were both shot down Dead, having 2 bullets apiece shot into each of their bodies. The Indians cut off their scalps, took their arms, and were gone in a trice: though the English run presently thither, at ye report of ye guns, but could see nothing but ye footing of 2 Indians.

Last night our scouts, who went out in the night to discover at Pacomtuck, about Midnight, being within 4 Myles of Pocomtuck, met 2 Indian scouts coming down this way to the towns, but it being darke they were both one upon another within 2 or 3 rods, before either discovered ye other, which made both p^{ts} Run, & nothing else done. Ours also last night, that I sent on this side of ye river, towards Squakheak, when they were gone about 7 or 8 miles, one of y^m fell ill, & were forced to return.

We are waiting for an opportunity to fall upon ye Indians, if the Lord please to grant it us.

Capt. Appleton is a man y^t is desirous to doe something in this day of distress: being very sensible of ye Cause & people of God at stake: & is much to be comended & Incouraged & upon y^t acct to be preferred before many y^t dare not jeopard there Lives in ye high Places of ye field."

The discouraged Pynchon soon after sends in his resignation as Commander-in-chief.

Gent my sad state of affairs will necesitate yor discharging me, & truly I am as full of troble & overwhelmed with it y^t I cannot act busyness I beseech you doe not expose me to those Temptations wch will overbeare me. If y^o do not discharge me.

I would not willingly sin ag^t God not offend y^o & I Intreat y^u to ease me of my [Trust?]

On the 4th day of October, with many misgivings, but in accordance with the Commissioners' strict orders, Pynchon led all the soldiers from Springfield to headquarters at Hadley, to join the army collecting there. This was to move out before daylight the next morning, on a grand expedition, which was to clear the valley of the foe. But the Sachems, who were well aware of Pynchon's intentions, had other views and different plans. Their late successes had made them confident that the valley would soon be cleared of the English, and Springfield, the most isolated town, was next marked for destruction. The Wampanoags and the Pocumtuck clans, with recruits from the Nipmucks, were now gathered in a hiding place about six miles from that town, watching an opportunity.

The Springfield Indians had lived, for forty years, on the most friendly terms with the settlers. Since the war broke out they had sent a war party against the hostiles at Wennimisset. Wequogan, their Sachem, had given hostages for their fidelity and their professions of friendship were renewed this very day, before Pynchon marched away. The Springfield people trusted them fully, knowing they had no cause for complaint. The natural ferocity of the savages, however, had been so aroused by the success of their countrymen, and their fear of the English so much diminished, that they were now only waiting for the most effective moment for a revolt. The orders of the Commissioners were well known and the coveted opportunity was now close at hand. The soldiers would soon be too far away to be recalled; the defenseless town could be surprised, and these treacherous cowards could ply the incendiary torch and murderous tomahawk among their life-long neighbors in safety. The attack was to be made the next morning. On the evening of Oct. 4th, Toto, a friendly Indian, revealed the plot at Windsor. Swift messengers were instantly posted to Maj. Treat at Westfield, and to the doomed town. Aroused by the midnight courier, the frightened people fled to the shelter of their palisaded houses, prepared as they could for defense, and dispatched a post to Pynchon at Hadley. The night passed in quiet, and many believed the alarm to be a false one. Early the next morning Lieut. Thomas Cooper, a resident of Springfield, taking Thomas Miller, rode out towards the Indian fort to find out the facts. About forty rods beyond the village they were fired upon from the bushes. Miller was killed, and Cooper mortally wounded, but able to regain the town. The Indians, who had probably been waiting for the men to disperse about their work in the field, when the women and children would be an easy prey, now raised the hideous war-whoop and rushed to attack the town. Had no warning been given it would doubtless have been utterly destroyed and most of the inhabitants butchered. As it was, the stockades were easily defended, but the Springfield people had the same mortifying experience endured by those of Brookfield, Northfield and Deerfield in helplessly seeing the devastation in every direction beyond the range of their guns. Besides Cooper and Miller, Pentecost, wife of John Mathews, was killed. Edward Pringrydays, Nathaniel Brown, Richard Waite and one or two others were wounded —the two former mortally.

About 11 o'clock Treat with his forces reached the west bank of the Connecticut. Five daring men, at great risk, took a boat over to them, but Treat could not cross in the face of the enemy who held the river bank until succor came from the north. The post sent to Hadley from Springfield repeated Toto's story, that five hundred Indians lay in wait at their fort at Long Hill to destroy Springfield. Pynchon, Appleton and Sill, at once marched with one hundred and ninety men for her relief. The Indians, "about 2 or 3 of the clock, signified their sense of their approach by their whoops and watchwords, and were presently gone." The condition of affairs on the arrival of the English is best told in the following letter to Rev. John Russell, at Hadley:—

Springfield Oct. 5—75

Reverend S^r

The L^d will haue vs ly in ye dust before him: we y^t were full are emptyed. But it is ye L^d & blessed be his holy name: we came to a Lamentable & woefull sight. The Towne in flames, not a house or barne standing except old Good^n Branches, till we came to my house & then Mr Glovers, John Hitchcock's & Good^n Stewart, burnt downe wth Barns corn and all they had: a few standing ab^t ye meeting house & then fr^m Merricks downward, all burnt to 2 Garrison houses at ye Lower end of ye Towne. My Grist Mill & Corn mill Burnt downe: wth some other houses & Barns I had let out to Tenants; all Mr Glovers library Burnt, wth all his Corne, so y^t he none to live on, as well as myself, & Many more: y^t haue not for subsistance they tell me: 32 houses & ye Barns belonging to y^m, are Burnt & all ye Livelyhood of ye owners, & what more may meete wth ye same stroaks, ye L^d only knows.

Many more had there estates Burnt in these houses: So y^t I beleeve 40 famylys are utterly destitute of Subsistence: ye L^d shew mercy to vs. I see not how it is Possible for vs to live here this winter, & If so the sooner we were holpen off, ye Better. S^r I Pray acquaint our Honored Govr wth this dispensation of God. I know not how to write, neither can I be able to attend any Publike service. The L^d in mercy speake to my heart, & to all our hearts is ye Reall desire of

y^{ors} to serve you,
JONH PYNCHON.

P. S. I pray send down by ye Post my doblet cote linnen &c I left there & Pap^{re}.

This letter Russell sent to Governor Leverett, who wrote a letter of consolation to Pynchon, Oct. 9. This is in cipher and some of it illegible:—

Major Pinchon, by yours to Mr Russell from Springfield 5 instant. We [heard] the Lord [answering] the prayers of his people by terrible things [indeed]. To receive the intelligences thereof with a still spirit is very difficult: Yet the great undertaker and teacher of his people knows [how] to teach [us] to [profit by evil] and we shall find it matter of acknowledgement to his praise when he will take any course to do us good who is faithful that hath said all things shall worke together for good to them that love and fear him of which number I hope through grace we will be found.

Sir if it be true what is sayd, that the old Sachem Wequogan, in whom so much confidence was put was an actor and incourager in this burning, I doubt not but you see how [failing] confidences are in such who cannot be truer than whom they serve and whether there hath been all that done to have secured those Indians that might have been is to some a [question]: But the will of the Lord is done and therefore to reflect upon anything that might have been before is but for caution for hereafter and not to add affliction by blaming you or any for what was not done. May we be [sincerely] humbled and refined and [abhor] ourselves in dust and ashes. The same almighty God that hath bereved can restore the like we are bereaved of and will [   ] give that that is better.

Sir, by the Councils order to Capt Appleton sent by Leftenant Upham you will see [theyr] readiness to gratify you and give in what as they can to you yet not doubting that by Counsell and otherways you will be assisting to the utmost unto him and the whole service in those parts: Hadley wants some countenance and encouragement and direction for theyr fortification which I think they have in a good forwardness for theyr security. I desire [you] as you have opportunity to be assisting them therein. You intimate as if Springfield were not like to be tenable if so it will be a more awful stroke that hath such a consequence as to breake up a [church] and town which we must leave to the Lord directing you upon the place."

He says Lieut. Upham with thirty men, and Corporal Poole with thirty-five at Quabaug, are ordered to reinforce the army in the Valley, and that it is left to him and Capt. Appleton, to decide whether to keep a garrison at Quabaug, or to desert the place. He concludes:—

"If you could [attain] to be with the General Court this session, it may be of great use to the publique and not disservice to yourselfe. * * * I commend you to the Lord and with mine [and wives] kinde respects sympathizing with you and your dear wife in your affliction and remain Sir

Your humble ser[vant] J. L.

Boston 9. 5. 75.

Oct. 8, Pynchon wrote Gov. Leverett repeating the story of the disaster. He says he had "Called off all the Soldiers that were in Springfield leaving none to secure the Town ye Commissioners order was so strict." That night "word was sent to me that 500 Indians were about Springfield intending to destroy it."—Early in the morning he marched down with about two hundred soldiers, when he arrived he found "All in flames about 30 dwelling houses burnt & 24 or 25 barns— My Corn Mill, Sawmill & other Buildings * * * Generally Mens hay & Corne is burnt & many men whose houses stand, had their goods burnt in other houses w^h they had caryed y^m too * * * Leift Cooper & 2 more slayne & 4 persons wounded 2 of wch are Doubtful of their Recovery." He sent out scouts, but "couldnt find which way they are gon, their Tracts being many ways * * * A considerable Tract upwards"—He says he cannot take the field with the army. His presence is necessary at home as the people are discouraged and threatened to "Leave ye Place"—he "needs Orders about it." Desertion, he says, would encourage "o^r Insolent Enemy * * * & make way for giving up all ye Towns above." To hold it needs many soldiers and "how to have bread for want of a mill is difficult * * * Solders complaining already * * * although we have flesh enough * * * No Mills will drive many Inhab away *. * * For my owne particular it were far better for me to goe away than bee here where I have not anything lift I mean noe corn neither Indian or English & noe meanes to keep one beaste here, nor can I have Relief in this Toune because soe many are destitute."

"Sir I am not capable of holding any Comand being more & more unfit & almost confounded in my understanding, the Ld direct y^r Pitch on a meeter person than ever I was: According to Liberty from ye Councill I shall devolve all upon Capt Appleton unless Maj Treat return againe *. * * All these Touns ought to be Garrisoned." He reminds the governor that he had advised this before, and that, had he been left to act for himself, this disaster might have been prevented.

The news of his discharge and the appointment of Capt. Appleton to succeed him was received by the anxious Pynchon on the 10th. On the 12th he wrote Leverett "I am very thankful for my dismission & discharge from y^t trust wch I had noe ability to manage," that he will "cast in his mite & help Appleton & the cause and interest of God & the people." He again remonstrates against the orders for exclusive field work, leaving the towns defenseless; and hopes the orders will be less "strict" and more be left to the discretion of Capt. Appleton. He once more reminds the governor that "Springfield was destroyed for this reason" but "it is ye Lds owne doeing & oh y^t we may bless his name." Having finally exonerated the Commissioners at the expense of the Lord, he continues: "Many are Plucking up. I dont know what will be the Issue * * * Mr. Glover, if he can, will goe to the Bay before winter." Although deserted by the minister, Pynchon says he shall stay "to encourage the People" for if he should go to Court "all would fale here."

Pynchon was a wise magistrate, a prudent counselor, an enterprising, honorable and successful man of business. He was influential and useful in Connecticut as well as Massachusetts. But he had no genius for war. He failed in the essential faculty of prompt decision in emergency, and he was too easily discouraged by adversity.

The Commission to Appleton ran as follows: It was dispatched to Pynchon by Lieut. Upham, Oct. 8th:—

Capt Appleton. The Council have seriously considered the earnest desires of Maj. Pinchon & the great affliction upon him and his family* & have at last consented to his request to dismiss him from the Chiefe command over the army in those parts, and have thought meete upon mature thoughts, to commit the chiefe Command unto yourselfe being parsuaded that God hath endowed you with a spirit and ability to manage that affayre: & for the Better inabling you to yor employ we have sent the Council's orders enclosed to Maj Pinchon to bee given you; & we refer you to the Instructions given him for yor direction, ordering you from time to time to give us advice of all occurances & if you need any further orders & instructions they shall be given you as ye matter shall require. So Committing you to the Lord, desiring his presence with you and blessing upon you, wee remain:

Boston 4th of October 1675.   Your friends and Servants
Capt Samuel Appleton Commander in Chiefe at the head quarters at Hadley.

Oct. 9, Gov. Leverett wrote Appleton referring to the action of the Council,—

---

*What "affliction" was upon Pynchon at this date is not known. As the Commission was not sent until Oct. 8, when the fate of Springfield was known, this clause may have been inserted in the official draft.

"Whereby they commit the care and conduct of all the military forces from us and Connecticut unto yourselfe * * * You are to take notis that while the [seat] of the war is kept in the Colony you are to have the chiefe command and [neither] you nor Major Treat with Connecticut forces are to be drawn off but by the Commissioners or the concurence of counsels there. If you both draw into another Colony Major Treat is to have the command in chiefe and if there should be any orders [inferior] to the Colony of Connecticut men you are [fairly] to entreat them and let them see that it is a breach of the agreement by the Commissioners a copy whereof I herewith remit unto you. I doubt not but the Lord will direct you with that wisdom [how?] to carry it towards Major Treat * * * I desire you will be careful of giving advice and incouragment to Hadley respecting theyr fortifications for theyr better security and so of the whole there was [former] order to Leftenant Upham to march with 30 men and Corporal Poole from Quabaug with 35 men to fill up your companies and to send off any that may be [disenabled] by sickness:"

It had been a question whether or not to desert Brookfield, Pynchon thought a garrison there necessary to keep up a line of communication with Boston. The authorities at Boston took a different view, but the governor, in this letter, leaves the matter discretionary with Pynchon and Appleton, only stipulating that supplies to support the people there must be sent from the Connecticut valley, Brookfield being about a " 3d of the way from you. * * * If there should be a necessity of deserting Springfield as Major Pinchon intimates it will be very awful but the conclusion thereof must be left with you on the place." The fact of the forces being so much scattered still troubles Leverett, although he has now put the whole matter into the hand of the local officers. In a marginal note, he says, "one thing more I leave to your consideration that your forces lying on both sides the river that provision be made for transport one to the other [with] securitie from the enemy['s] shot. They have horse boats built as stanchions and with planke they may secure the men." I do not know that this shrewd suggestion ever bore fruit.

By the same post as the above Leverett writes Mr. Russell at Hadley:—
"Reverend Sir
By yours of the 4 and 5 with your other of the day after * * * together by the enclosed from Major Pinchon namely of the dreadful and terrible stroke of God upon us at Springfield and that in a[nswer] to prayers and [   ] solemn humiliation of Churches and people of God as it shows the greatness of our provocations * * * for the Lord carries it as being angry with our prayers."

After speculating upon the cause and the effect of God's anger, and the remedy, he comes down to tangible affairs to consider a complaint of Mr. Russell in regard to "those intricacies" in the orders "respecting several in command." He says "By the ultimate conclusion that comes by Leftenant Upham you will find the knot tyed: and the command placed upon Captain Appleton which must be without exception being according to the conclusion of the Commissioners. Nor is Major Treat to be commanded of but by the Commissioners or the concurrence of the counsels there on the place and should ther be motion contrary upon any pretence it may be of sadder consequence than the present stroke." He says he has written to Pynchon and Appleton about "your fortifications," and concludes—"thus with kind respects to you *and all friends with you.** I commend you to the Lord and remain sir your ser[vant.]"

The correspondence given above discloses the facts, elsewhere hinted at, that there had been considerable friction between the officers of the Massachusetts and those of the Connecticut forces, and that it became necessary for the Commissioners of the United Colonies to take the matter in hand. The Connecticut soldiers were made a part of the army of the confederacy, and so put beyond the control of the Connecticut authorities.

Oct. 12, Appleton marched from Springfield and "came that night to Hadley near 30 mile." On his arrival he wrote the governor in regard to his appointment to the command which is against his own wish and judgment; wishing an abler man may be put in his place. He begs for orders which will leave the matter of garrisoning the towns with the commanders; reminds him that the loss at Springfield was for lack of such discretionary power. He says there were "33 houses and 25 barns burnt and about 15 houses left unburnt on the Town Platt; * * * that on the west side of the river and the outskirts of the east side are about 60 houses standing and much corn in & about them."

In the attack of Oct. 5, Wequogan, the Springfield Sachem, "was ring-leader in word and deed," and Puckquahow, the Nipmuck, who was with the Naunawtuks when they revolt-

---

*Probably an obscure allusion to the Regicides, Goffe and Whalley, whom Leverett knew were then harbored at Mr. Russell's.

ed, and with them in the swamp fight, was doubtless the one who shouted that he "was one y^t burnt Quaboag, & now would make them like to it." The assailants were about forty Springfield Indians and two or three hundred of the allies. Their retreat was so skillfully ordered as to leave no clue to their movements, so that Pynchon, who "sent out scouts y^t night & ye next day, discovered none, nor satisfie ourselues wch way they are gon." This outbreak, and the retreat, were doubtless planned by Philip. The treacherous professions of friendship, renewed to lull suspicion only the day before the attack, and the tactics of the retreat, were in accordance with his character and methods.

From Springfield Philip led his clan and a part of the Pocumtucks to the Narragansets, full of a plan for involving that tribe in the war.

On the 7th a party of Indians were discovered at Glastonbury. An alarm was raised and Maj. Treat was ordered home with sixty men. Provision was made in the towns for the security of the women and children. Large parties of men were ordered to go out together to harvest the corn, and remove all grain to safe places. To stimulate the Mohegans, a liberal bounty was offered them for hostile scalps or prisoners.

On the same day the Connecticut Council of War wrote to the Massachusetts Council "That it is high time for New England to stir up all their strength, and make war their trade * * * to suppress the enemy before they grow too much for us." They are earnest for an army to take and keep the field, and want five hundred more soldiers sent from the Bay to the valley, where they should be joined by the forces from Connecticut. Unless this is done, they shall be obliged to withdraw their men to secure the towns at home; and in particular Hartford, where the Councilors are, and where the General Court is to meet on the 14th.

Appleton's Commission was received Oct. 10th. The new commander at once found himself in a strait between his duty to obey the strict orders of the Commissioners, to keep his army in the field; and the moral certainty that if he did the defenseless towns would be destroyed. This he could not permit, and on the 12th, when he marched to Hadley, he left Capt. Sill, with sixty men, to protect Springfield, "choosing," he says in a letter to Gov. Leverett of that date, "rather to adventure hazeard to myselfe than to the publike." Here speaks the man of decision and the true patriot.

On reaching headquarters at Hadley, Appleton began at once sending out scouting parties, which continued for several days to seek out the hiding places of the enemy. At this time Capt. Moseley was at Hatfield; Capt. Seely, with sixty Connecticut men, at Northampton; Capt. Jonathan Poole, with Lieut. Upham and sixty men, who had arrived from Boston and Brookfield about the 10th, were at Hadley. There was no further attempt to resettle Brookfield. On the 15th, Appleton, with his whole force—except Seely from Connecticut, who refused to obey orders—marched out towards Northfield, where, it was believed, the main body of the Indians were collected. He had gone but about two miles when a post reached him with news that a scout of four men, sent by Moseley to Pocumtuck, had returned and reported great numbers of the enemy there: that they found "the rails weadged up and made very fast about two miles from the town," either to "trapan the skoutes * * * or else to faight us there if wee goe in pursuith of them." Moseley, writing Oct. 16th, to the Governor, tells the same story, and adds "but I intend to bourne all their railes up, please God to grant me life and health." This fence was at the Bars, the entrance to the common field by the Hatfield road.

The commander at once changed his course and crossed the river to Hatfield. Leaving there after sunset, he attempted a night expedition to Pocumtuck. After marching a few miles he saw the flash and heard the report of a gun, and the vanguard heard the shouts of Indians. It was evident that their march had been discovered. A council of officers was held, most of whom, especially Capt. Moseley, advised returning to secure the defenseless towns. This was rather against the will of Appleton, but the army finally returned to their quarters in the night.

On the evening of the 16th an urgent call for help came from Northampton, "and while these messengers are speaking," writes Appleton,—

"Capt. Mosely informs, y^t ye enemy is this evening discovered wthin a mile of Hatfield, and that he verily expects to be assaulted too morrow; wch I am so sensible of y^t I account it my duty presently to repair thither, now, at 10 or 11 of the clock in the night. Some of the forces having already crossed the river."

About twenty men were left to guard Hadley. Appleton writes, the next morning, " We have wearied o^{r}s wth a tedious night and morning's march, without making any discovery of the enemy." Moseley writes, the same day,—

"Wee are tould by an Indian, that was taken att Springfield, y^t they intend to sett upon these 3 townes in one Day. The Body of them y^t waits this exploite to Doe, is about 600 Indians, and further wee are informed, that they are makinge a forte some sixty miles above this place, up in the woods * * * I make no question that the Enemys will make an tempt within a shorte space of time upon these towns * * * I expect them every hour, at night as well as day, for they have fired upon my sentinels at night."

Maj. Appleton is cramped for want of men, and laments the absence of Maj. Treat and the Connecticut forces, which prevents his taking the field with any effect. At this very time, however, Connecticut is having a great scare, and messengers are even now on their way to Appleton for help. A plot has been reported for a general rising of all the Connecticut Indians. Gov. Andros has written that "five or six thousand Indyans engaged together * * * designed this light moone, to attack Hartford itself and some other places this way, as farre as Greenwich." Active measures were at once taken to "remove their best goods, and their corn, what they can of it, with their wives and children," to the larger towns which were to be fortified, and troops were raised for their defense. There is good reason to believe this report was founded on fact, and that only seasonable notice and prompt action saved the Connecticut towns from the fate of Springfield.

Roger Williams, in a letter from Providence to Gov. Leverett, dated Oct. 11, 1675, says that "since ye dolefull Newes from Springfield, here it is said y^t Phillip with a strong Body of many hundreth cut throats steeres this way." He gives an account of an interview with "the young Prince," Canonchet, in which he tries to neutralize the influence of Philip, and told him if he were false to his engagements he would be pursued with a winter's war. He writes, "I am requested by our Capt. Fennor to give you notice y^t at his farme in ye woods he had it from a Native, y^t Phillip's great Designe is (among all other possible advantages and Treacheries) to drawe C. Mosely & other your forces (by training & drilling & seeming flights) into such places as are full of long grasse, flags Sedge &c, & then inviron them round with Fire, Smoke, & Bullets. Some say No wise Souldjer will be so catcht."

ATTACK ON HATFIELD.

The blow predicted by Moseley now falls upon Hatfield, and some of the tactics indicated in Williams's letter are to be employed. Oct. 19th, about noon, fires were discovered in the woods towards Wequamps, and Moseley sent a mounted scout of ten men to reconnoiter and find out what it meant. Two miles from the town the party fell into a trap set by the Indians, and baited with the fires above. Six were killed, three taken prisoners, and one, an Indian, escaped back to Hatfield. The garrison of the town consisted of the companies of Moseley and Poole; the latter, with Lieut. Upham and sixty men having arrived at Hadley from the Bay about the 10th. On the alarm Maj. Appleton with his company crossed the river from Hadley and took post at the south end of the town. Moseley was placed in the center and Poole at the north end. About four o'clock, "seven or eight hundred of the enemy came upon the town in all quarters * * but they were so well entertained on all hands where they attempted to break in upon the town that they found it too hot for them," and after a contest of two hours were driven off with considerable loss. Maj. Treat, who had a genius for appearing in the right place at the right time, came up from Northampton with sixty men, in season to give the finishing blow. The loss of the English was, Thomas Meekins and Nathaniel Collins of Hatfield, Richard Stone, John Pocock, Samuel Clark, Abraham Quidington, John Petts, William Olverton and Thomas Warner, of Moseley's scouts—Warner and two others being taken prisoners.

At the town Sergt. Freegrace Norton fell mortally wounded, while fighting by the side of Maj. Appleton. The lattter lost a lock of hair by an Indian bullet. "A few barns and other buildings were burnt."

The savages moved into the west woods with their prisoners. One of these was barbarously murdered on the 21st, after being grievously tormented for the amusement of the savages. "They burnt his nails & put his feet to scald against the fire & drove a stake through one of his feet to pin him to the ground." The Sachems, knowing Appleton was seeking their main body to attack it, hoped through the device of the fires in the woods to draw his army into an ambuscade and there cripple or destroy it. when the town would be an easy prey. The Indians, like the English, differed as to the best method of conducting the war. The policy advocated by the young warriors was to cut off the soldiers; this done, the inhabitants would be at their mercy. Their method had been adopted, but they had succeeded only when able to surprise their enemy. Not the smallest defended post had been carried. Being defeated in their great attempt on Hatfield they were discouraged, and the counsels of the old men, to break up into small bodies, hover about the settlements, kill, pillage or burn, as chance gave opportunity, were now heeded. It was seen that however great their numbers, they were no match for the English in open combat, and rarely or never, was so large a force again seen together in the field. The Nipmucks gradually drew off to their own country. The Pocumtucks sent a party of thirty to their old allies, the Mahicans, on the Hoosick river; and here the remainder of them—after harassing the frontier some ten days longer—joined them about Nov. 7th, and were made welcome.

A few days after the Hatfield affair, an attempt was made on Northampton; but on the approach of the ubiquitous Maj. Treat, the assailants fled, after burning four or five houses and a few barns. On the 27th, Pynchon and five or six Springfield men were ambushed on their return from Westfield, where they had been looking for ore. John Dumbleton of Springfield, William and John, sons of William Brooks, an early settler of Deerfield, were shot down, while the rest escaped. At another time one Granger was wounded, and several houses and barns were burned at Westfield. Oct. 29th a party of Northampton farmers who had gone into the meadows to gather some crops were fired upon, and Thomas Salmon, Joseph Baker and his son Joseph, were killed. The Indians then made an attempt to burn Northampton mill, but a guard stationed there beat them off. The next day the frightened cattle came running out of the woods into Hatfield, thus giving notice of the presence there of a party of the enemy. A company was sent out, but their tracks only were discovered. On the 31st, Appleton crossed the river and scoured the woods for ten or twelve miles round without success. Nov. 4th a large force ranged toward Deerfield. The search was continued for a few days longer, but no trace of a present enemy was discovered. The Indians had left for Hoosick river. Appleton, believing they had returned to their old haunts eastward, prepared to follow Capt. Sill, who had already been ordered to Hassenimisset.

Garrisons were established in the valley towns; thirty-nine men under Pynchon, at Springfield; twenty-nine at Westfield, under Capt. Aaron Cooke; twenty-six at Northampton, under Lieut. Wm. Clark; thirty-six at Hatfield, under Lieut. Wm. Allis; and thirty remained at Hadley, under Capt. Poole.

Nov. 16th, Maj. Treat led home the Connecticut forces. A few days later Maj. Appleton appointed a Council of War, made up of Capt. Poole, Lieut. David Wilton of Northampton, Dea. Peter Tilton of Hadley, Sergt. Isaac Graves of Hatfield, with the commissioned officers of these three towns—Poole to be President, and presumably Commander-in-Chief.

About Nov. 20th, Appleton and Moseley, with all the soldiers not in the garrisons, marched for the Nipmuck country. The Nipmucks, on their return home, had begun depredations on their frontiers; and early in November Capt. Henchman had been sent against them. Meeting some reverses, he was reinforced by Capt. Sill and other troops. The Indians soon after disappeared, probably going to the region about Northfield and Vernon, where their non-combatants had before taken refuge. A large quantity of corn was destroyed in the Nipmuck country, which was a serious blow to the enemy, and before spring they were reduced to the verge of starvation. Appleton, on his arrival, finding all quiet in the interior, continued his march to Boston, and joined the expedition against the Narragansets, Dec. 10th, as the commander of the Massachusetts forces.

Philip, as before noted, left this region for Narraganset, after the burning of Springfield. The Indians seen at Glastonbury, on the 7th, were probably part of his force. Philip reached his destination about Oct. 10th, loaded with spoils from the English. From the first outbreak the young Narragansets had been forward to join in the war. The invasion of their country and the treaty of peace forced upon them, July 15th, by Hutchinson, Moseley and others, "with a Sword in their Hands," could not be forgiven. On the first hostile movements of the English, Philip had sent all the women and children of his tribe to the Narragansets for protection. One provision of the treaty was that all subjects of Philip should be given up. The fact that the Narragansets were an independent nation was ignored, and the treaty was signed while the Sachems were virtually looking into the muzzles of the English muskets. One of the strongest unwritten statutes of the Indian was the law of hospitality. This they were called upon ruthlessly to violate. When the pressure was withdrawn, the great hearted Canonchet asserted his manhood, and declared boldly that he "would not give up a Wampanoag, nor the paring of a Wampanoag's nail," and otherwise little regard seems to have been paid to the treaty.

The successful Philip found in Canonchet an instrument by which he could gain time, and surely involve the Narragansets in the war. It is easy to believe that it was by his instigation that Canonchet negotiated the treaty of Oct. 18th, at Boston. If this was a deliberate act of treachery, as generally accounted, it is the only dishonorable act recorded against Canonchet. From what we know of the character of the two men, may we not presume that the impulsive Canonchet was deceived in some way by the artful Philip? Especially as the high minded Narraganset, shortly after his return, sent back word to Boston that the treaty must be considered null and void. It could not be enforced without the co-operation of Philip. By its terms the Narragansets engaged to deliver up within ten days all hostile Indians among them, including the followers of Philip, of Weetemo, and the Pocumtucks. There was no intention on the part of Philip of allowing this clause to take effect. It was only a blind to allay suspicion awhile longer. Philip's hand is plainly seen in this transaction. Exactly the same tactics were employed successfully by him at Springfield two weeks before. Not unlikely he expected, before the ten days were out, to be on his way to Pocumtuck, with a strong war party of Narragansets. If so, he failed in this, but he had surely involved that fated tribe in the war.

Nov. 2d the Commissioners, now assured of the hostile disposition of the Narragansets, formally declared war against them, and raised one thousand soldiers to prosecute it. Dec. 19th the stronghold of the tribe was stormed and hundreds of them slain. The remainder were scattered in the wilderness, their wigwams burned, their winter store of provisions destroyed. Many were killed or captured by ranging parties of the English, and others perished by cold and hunger. The warriors who escaped, fled northward to the Nipmucks, and their avenging blows were soon felt on the English frontiers. The loss of the English in the attack on the fort was eighty killed and about one hundred and forty wounded.

The prudent Philip, in the meantime, to secure himself from the rising storm, had left the Narragansets and joined the Pocumtucks at the Hoosick river, where we shall soon follow him.

After Nov. 10th no Indians were seen in the Connecticut valley. The route to Boston by the Bay Path was shut up by the Nipmucks, and the only communication with the government was by means of the soldiers in the Narraganset war. Through these the results of the rupture with that powerful tribe became known, and the inhabitants of the river towns lived in constant fear of an attack. Citizens and soldiers were alike busy in fortifying houses and building stockades about the towns, and fearful were the forebodings of the coming spring. Events leading to the next hostile attempt in this valley will now be briefly sketched.

PHILIP IN THE WINTER OF 1675-6.

There is very little *direct* information as to the movements of Philip during the fall and winter of 1675-6. By carefully collating all accessible contemporaneous accounts, the conclusions given below seem to be well sustained. Better evidence on some points would be more satisfactory.

When Philip joined the Pocumtucks, who were with the Mahicans west of the Hoosick mountains, he had a purpose besides that before mentioned. Knowing that the Mahicans and other Hudson River Indians had formerly been confederates of the Pocumtucks in their wars with the Mohegans, he hoped, the tribes being now together, the alliance might be renewed, and so a new force enlisted in the war. Philip met a friendly reception and such measure of success as to secure at least a supply of ammunition, and not unlikely a promise of co-operation. In December the hostile clans from the east established winter quarters in the valleys of Manchester and Sunderland, Vermont, not far from the head waters of the Pocumtuck. Sancumachu, the Pocumtuck Sachem, was in command. Philip was reported ill, but probably he was on a secret expedition to Canada. On his recovery, or return, the wily chieftain undertook the delicate task of reconciling the Pocumtucks and the Mohawks for the purpose of uniting them against a common enemy. We have seen that previous to the rupture twelve years before, these tribes had been allies in fighting the Mohegans. Philip so far succeeded in his plan that the Mohawks were willing to join the hostile forces in warring against Uncas, but they would not consent to fight the English.

Sancumachu, with about four hundred Pocumtucks and Wampanoags, had in the meantime, prudently taken post farther eastward. Young recruits, ready for blood and plunder, flocked to the headquarters, from the Mohawks, Scatakooks, Mahicans, and others, until about the middle of January, fully fifteen hundred warriors were in arms. Soon after this they were joined by five or six hundred French Indians, from Canada. This army was ostentatiously paraded "in two ranks" for the inspection of the two English scouts who were captured at Hatfield, Oct. 19th. The captives were then released and sent to Albany, to report what they had seen. These men counted twenty-one hundred warriors, generally armed with good firearms. They said that Philip, whose "own men were not above a hundred," was with another party of four hundred; but "he had little esteem or authority among them." About this time Sagamore Sam visited the camp, and here the campaign for the spring was planned. This, as it appears in the light of subsequent events, was that the confederates here should rendezvous at Northfield, and from there swoop down upon the defenseless towns in the valley, while the Nipmucks and Narragansets were ravaging the frontiers of the Bay towns, and so preventing aid being sent to the river. In the valley thus cleared of the English, headquarters were to be established, the non-combatants collected, the fields planted with indian corn and a winter's stock of fish laid up from the abundance of the streams. They would be under the protection of the French, who were to come from Canada and settle among them. It was now indeed "full sea with Philip his affairs." He might well feel confident that in the coming campaign the traitorous Mohegans would be annihilated and the hated white men driven from the valley. To make the event more sure, the subtle Sachem sought to embroil the Mohawks with the English, as well as with the Mohegans. To that end he caused some Mohawks to be killed and accused the English of being the murderers. This foul artifice was his fatal mistake. It cost him all he had gained during the winter, and changed all his future life. One of the Mohawks left for dead, revived and reached his home. When the truth became known, the enraged Mohawks fell upon the Eastern Indians, killed and captured many of them, and the great hostile army was scattered. Philip, with the Pocumtucks and his few disheartened followers, fled over the Green Mountains and reached Northfield the last week in February.

As has been said, after the destruction of their fort in December, the scattered Narragansets joined the Nipmucks. The general rendezvous of the combined forces was at Wenimisset. From thence war parties carried the musket and torch all along the frontiers of the Bay towns, with death and destruction in their train. Lancaster was surprised, Feb. 10th, 1675-6. About fifty people were killed or captured. Among the latter was Mrs. Mary Rowlandson, wife of the minister, and their three children, Sarah, the youngest, five years old, being grievously wounded. The captives were taken to Wenimisset, where some of them were barbarously murdered. At this place, Feb. 18th, Sarah died of her wounds, and was buried the next day. By an erroneous but commonly accepted tradition, this child died and was buried on a mountain in Warwick, which in consequence was named for her, Mount Grace. But Grace is not Sarah, and Warwick is many miles from Wenimisset.

Information of the gathering at Wenimisset was given to the English by Mary Shepherd, a girl of fifteen, captured at Concord, Feb. 12th, who escaped on a horse taken at Lancaster, and made her way through the woods to the settlements. An expedition was at once planned against the place. Three foot companies under Captains Turner, Moseley and Gillam, and Capt. Whipple with a troop of horse, all under Maj. Savage, reached Quabaug, March 2d, where they met Maj. Treat, with three or four companies from Connecticut. The next day, leaving Turner to establish a garrison at Quabaug, the rest of the command marched against Wenimisset. Scouts from the Indians had doubtless reported the movements of their enemy, and the whole body, some two thousand men, women and children, made a hasty retreat northward. The fugitives reached the Paquayag river in the present town of Orange, March 3d, and before night on the 5th, had all crossed the river on rafts. They reached Squakheag in safety on the 7th. On the 9th they crossed the Connecticut river and joined Philip and the forces which had recently come over the Green Mountains from the Hoosick valley.

Maj. Savage, finding no Indians at Wenimisset, pursued on their trail, but deceived by the "lapwing stratagem" of their rear guard, he was kept on a false scent for two or three days, and only reached the Paquayag on the 6th, in time to see the smoking ruins of the Indian camp on the north shore. No attempt was made to cross the river, or pursue the enemy any farther. This retreat was skillfully planned and conducted.

Foreseeing the danger to which the river towns would now be exposed, Savage at once took up his march for Hadley. Capt. Turner, leaving a garrison at Quabaug, took his command to Northampton. Maj. Treat, with two Connecticut companies, reached the same town the 13th, "in the evening." Capt. Moseley, with two companies, was stationed at Hatfield. As we shall see, these movements were made none too quickly.

ATTACK ON NORTHAMPTON.

Soon after the arrival of Philip at Squakheag, scouts were sent out to discover the condition of the settlements below. About the first of March, John Gilbert, a boy of seventeen, was captured, carried to Squakheag and closely examined. It does not appear from what place he was taken.

No other depredations hereabouts at this period are recorded, except at Westfield, where March 9th, "five bushels of meal were stolen" and "a man wounded," two houses and a barn burned. About the same time, Moses Cook, a resident, and Clement Bates of Hingham, a soldier of Capt. Lothrop's company, were killed while out on a scout, probably in search of the depredators. This affair occurred the same day on which the mass of Indians from Wenimisset formed a junction with Philip, at Squakheag.

Two or three days later, doubtless on the return of the scouts, with reports that no Bay troops had come to the valley, a force was organized against Northampton, with the evident expectation of finding it an easy prey. On the morning of March 14th they made an assault on the sleeping town. The defensive works—a single line of palisades, erected during the winter—were quickly broken through in three places. Through the gaps thus made the horde crept in, and at daylight began the work of destruction. The assailants, ignorant of the newly arrived forces, had no fear of the small garrison, and no doubt of the speedy destruction of the town. Surprised by the appearance of the soldiers of Treat and Turner, they fell back, but in the attempt to scatter, in accordance with their usual tactics, they found themselves in a pound. A panic followed. They rushed pell-mell for the three narrow breaks in the palisades, where they were exposed to the fire of the English while crowding through. Getting out proved more dangerous than getting in. This lesson was not forgotten. The Indians never again attempted that method of attack, and these slight works proved a real defense.

Maj. Savage writing from Northampton, March 16th, gives the following brief report of this affair:—

On the 14th just aboute breake of ye day the enemy fiercely assaulted Northampton in three places at once and forced within the lines or palisades and burnt five houses and five barns and killed four men and one woman and wounded six men more.

Ten buildings had been fired before the garrison was fairly aroused. Robert Bartlett, Thomas Holton, Mary Earle, of the inhabitants; James McRennal of Turner's company, and Increase Whelstone, another soldier, were killed, and six other men wounded.

Driven from Northampton, the Indians at once made for Hatfield. Here another surprise awaited them. The gallant Moseley was on the alert, and they were easily repulsed. Grievously disappointed at the result of the expedition, from which so much had been confidently expected, the Indians were loth to return without one more effort, and an attempt was made for a night surprise of Northampton. About two o'clock on the morning of the 16th the sentinels discovered them approaching the town from opposite directions. On the alarm being given they disappeared. The main body, with a number of horses, sheep and other plunder, retreated to Squakheag; but small parties remained hovering about, waylaying the English, as chances occurred. Several men were killed and others wounded in the towns about Hartford. Rev. John Russell, writing from headquarters, March 16th, to Governor Leverett, giving a detailed account of the attack on Northampton, says the assailants were "near 2000 as judged," which Judd calls a "strange delusion," and says, "there may have been 3 or 400." An average of these numbers would probably be an underestimate. Philip was not present and the leaders are not named, but doubtless Canonchet, and Sancumachu the Pocumtuck Sachem were prominent. Mr. Russell, in the letter above referred to, writes:—

Although the Lord has granted us an interval of quietness this winter, yet since ye coming on of ye spring, the war here is renewed, and like to be continued with more strength and violence here, than in any other part, while we remain. For as we had intelligence by the captive who is returned, (commonly called speckled Tom,) Philip intended with his whole force to come upon these towns, and taking them, to make his planting place and fort this year at Deerfield * * * Here also, above Deerfield a few miles, is the great place of their fishing, w^h must be expected to afford them their prouision for the yeere. So that the swarm of them being here, and like to continue here, we must look to feele their utmost rage, except the Lord be pleased to break their power. My desire is, that we may be willing to do or suffer, live or dy; remain, or be driven out from our habitations, as the Lord God would have us, & as may be conducible to the glory of his name, and the publike weale of his people.

The Massachusetts Council at this time had very imperfect information of the numbers or movements of the enemy, apparently supposing them to be all in one body. In a letter from their Secretary to Maj. Savage, of March 14th, which crossed that of Russell on the way, he is told that "the 150 troops and dragoons" which had been ordered to join him "are retarded by the appearance of the enemy on our frontier towns yesterday;" that they had been "ordered to march o Groton and Lancaster;" that they would not be sent to the river unless the enemy are heard of there. This letter was not received until March 26th—doubtless delayed by the danger of posting.

The depredations in Connecticut continuing, the Council of War ordered extraordinary precautions against surprise. In each town the night watch was directed to call up the inhabitants every morning "an hower at least before day," who were to arm and stand upon guard at their assigned posts "until sunne be half an hower high," when the "warders are to take their places * * * Two scouts from each end of every town" are to be sent out on horseback to spend the day in scouring the woods.

In Massachusetts the alarm seems to have been almost a panic. The activity and success of the enemy against the frontier towns of the Bay, was such that the Council thought it necessary, not only to detain the troops under orders for the Connecticut valley, but also to withdraw those already there; and on the 20th of March another letter was sent Maj. Savage with "*advice*," which was equivalent to a command, "to desert all the towns" but Springfield and Hadley, and concentrate their strength there. "The lesser towns," they say, "must gather to the greater * * * To remain in such a scattered state is to expose lives and estates to the merciless cruelty of the enemy, and is no less than tempting divine providence;" that unless they come together and well fortify the large towns, "*all* will be lost * * * the enemy being so many in *these* parts that our army must remove from thence * * * We cannot spare them or supply them with ammunition." Maj. Savage was instructed to act in accordance with these views. Had this plan been adopted, the dissensions among the miscellaneous clans at Squakheag and Pocumtuck would have been healed and the whole become a unit. Philip would have been again in the ascendant, with every encouragement to prosecute the war with vigor and confidence. The order was not obeyed.

The new year opened gloomily for the colonists. The first Sunday in 1676, March 26th, by the old calendar, was a day of disaster. Had the present mode of communication existed, the devotions of Maj. Savage would have been interrupted by news of the raid on Windsor, and the burning of Simsbury, Connecticut; of the destruction of Capt. Pierce and sixty men on Patucket river; the desolation by fire of the greater part of Marlboro, and of the attack on the people at Longmeadow; all of which occurred that day. In addition, an express arrived that day from Boston with the discouraging Council letters of March 14th and 20th before referred to, "advising" Savage to concentrate the inhabitants, and march his troops to the Bay.

From contemporary accounts of the last mentioned attack, we learn that "8 Indians assaulted 16 or 18 men beside women and children, as they were going to meeting," from Longmeadow to Springfield, on horseback. The rear of the cavalcade was surprised, John Keep "and a maid" were killed, and two men wounded at the first fire. Sarah, the wife of John Keep, and another woman, each with an infant in her arms, were seized by the savages in the confusion, and at once hurried into the woods. The escort, after depositing the rest of the women and children in a place of safety, returned to the scene of the disaster. Maj. Pynchon at once sent out a party in pursuit. These were joined the next morning by sixteen men, sent by Savage from Hadley, " who found their Track and soon after discovered them; who, seeing our men approach, took the two poor Infants, and in the Sight both of their mothers, and our Men, tossed them up in the Air, and dashed their Brains out against the Rocks, and with their Hatchets knokt down the Women, and forthwith fled. The Place being exceeding rocky, and a Swamp just by, our Horse could not follow, and on foot were not able to overtake them." Mrs. Keep died; the other woman recovered. The conduct of the escort was characterized by the Council, " as a matter of great shame, humbling to us," and it was ridiculed in the following couplet:—

> Seven Indians, and one without a Gun,
> Caused Capt. Nixon, and 40 men to run.

These Indians were doubtless part of those living at Longmeadow before the outbreak of Oct. 5th, and the assailed party were old neighbors. The survivor of the wounded women said she "knew every particular person of those eight Indians." They talked very freely with the women and told them they should be taken to Deerfield, where the Nashua captives were. The women were treated very kindly until the pursuers came up. Much information was obtained from the woman as to the resources, plans and forces of the enemy. They did not want for powder. They were supplied by "Jerrard, and Jacob, two Dutchmen who had lived with Maj. Pynchon, but now lived at Fort Albany, and two Dutchmen more." These men had recently "brought four bushel on horseback from Albany, and had gone for a new supply two days before." They were "very inquisitive as to the number of our men," and informed very freely of their own. They had "3000 Indians at Deerfield and 300 at Squakheag, and had built 300 wigwams above Deerfield." About the 20th, "Capt. Tom, of Natick, and the rest of them Indians with him was come to Deerfield, and that they do intend to make that their headquarters." The "Mohawks had killed some of their men, but peace had been made again." They also told her that some Frenchmen had been among them, who "persuaded them not to burn and destroy the houses, but to make what slaughter they could of the people, because they intend to come and inhabit them;" and that preparations were being made to "fall on the towns shortly."

At this date all the Connecticut soldiers, both Indian and English, had been withdrawn from Hampshire county. On the 25th, Maj. Treat had been directed to lead an expedition against the Narragansets. The events of the 26th, however, caused serious alarm at Hartford, and he was recalled on the 27th, to guard the settlements about that place.

In this crisis, overtures looking to a peace were made by both colonies, to the enemy. On the 28th, a small party of friendly Indians under Towcanchasson, bearing a flag of truce, were sent from Hartford by order of the Council, to the Indians at the northward, with proposals for exchanging prisoners, and an offer to treat for peace with any Sachem who may desire it. Whatever the motive of this mission, from fear, policy or humanity, it bore some fruit, as we shall see.

March 28th, Maj. Savage writes the Massachusetts Council, "I shall do my best endeavours to discover the enemy by sending forth scouts according as you desire, but have no Indians to go forth with our scouts, but only those six that came out with us [Naticks, who came as guides] who are unacquainted with the woods;" that the Connecticut Indians "would not be persuaded" to remain. Scouting was a dangerous service; our men had not yet learned the wiles of the natives; children of the woods only could match them. The letter concludes with an account of the Longmeadow affair. By the same courier the authorities of Northampton write the Council, asking a garrison of fifty men for that town, engaging to furnish pay and rations.

During the next ten days, confusion, indecision and fear ruled all round; in the camp of the clans up the river, as well as in the counsels of the English. Savage had orders to find the enemy and attack them, and he had tried in vain to arrange with Connecticut, an expedition against the hordes about Pocumtuck, as he did not dare to move against them without the co-operation of Maj. Treat. Connecticut feared to leave her towns unguarded, and hesitated. Massachusetts authorities considered it imprudent to leave Savage longer in the valley, while the Bay towns were being constantly ravaged. The Indians were successful at every point. Lancaster, Concord, Medfield, Weymouth, Groton, Billerica, Chelmsford, Marlboro, Wrentham, Bridgewater, Hingham, Scituate, Sudbury, Haverhill, had successively felt their fury. The alarm of the Council was well founded. Had the savages been united, or well led, all would indeed "have been lost." Communication was slow and uncertain; the real condition of affairs was ill understood, in the valley, at the Bay, or by the Indians up the river. The "advice" to Maj. Savage had raised such a storm of indignant protest in Connecticut, as well as in the doomed towns, that the plan of consolidation was not executed, and the settlers were spared that great loss and humiliation. This, however, was yet in the future, and did not lighten the clouds and gloom which shrouded them at the departure of the troops on which they had relied for defense. On the 7th of April, Savage, under peremptory orders, without even giving notice to the Connecticut authorities, with four companies, under Moseley, Whipple, Gilman and Drinker, marched towards the Bay. Capt. William Turner of Boston was left at headquarters, to command in the valley. He had in garrison at Hadley, fifty-one men; at Hatfield, under Sergt. Robert Bardwell,* forty-five men; at Northampton, under Sergt. Ezra Fogg, forty-six men. Sergt. Roger Prosser, with nine men, was sent to Springfield, to increase a force already there. These soldiers

---

*Recently from London and ancestor of all of the name in the country.

were only to do garrison duty, and guard the inhabitants while at their labors. Directly on the news reaching Hartford of Savage's march eastward, all the forces in the field under Maj. Treat were disbanded, and thenceforth a strictly defensive policy prevailed in the Connecticut valley. The soldiers, however, were ordered to be in readiness to take the field at an hour's notice.

THE CONFEDERATES AT SQUAKHEAG.

Meanwhile, up the river, shifting about on the territory of Squakheag and Pocumtuck, were gathered the great body of hostile Indians—at a low estimate more than three thousand souls. They were of different tribes and clans, each under its own chieftain. There was no "Commander-in-Chief," nor is the assumption that Philip ever did hold or professed to hold that office, warranted by facts. He was far-seeing, politic, subtle and crafty; but lacked personal magnetism and prowess. He failed to command the respect of the warriors or show the qualities of a leader in war. He sowed the wind, but could not reap, nor bind the whirlwind.

Full sketches of the notables now gathered on our soil, with descriptions of the daily life of their followers would be replete with interest. Scant material for this is to be found, but from what is available, brief notes on some of the former, and faint glimpses of the latter will be given.

Philip, on being driven eastward by the Mohawks as before related, made his way with small following over the Green Mountains, reaching the Connecticut river the latter part of February. Gathered about him now were the chief men of his tribe; his uncle and chief counsellor, Unkompoin; his cousin, Penchason, and Tatason, war Sachems of note. Philip's brother-in-law, the powerful Tuspaquin, husband to his sister Amey, probably met him here. Anawan, his chief captain, who had obtained renown in the wars under Massasoit, and who remained faithful to his son until the last. With Anawan were his two sons, one of whom fired the first shot in this war, and fell with Philip, Aug. 12th, 1676. Here also was a princess of the Wampanoags, a sister of Philip; and wise and wary Awashonks, the powerful squaw Sachem of Sogkonate, with all her braves, led by Peter Awashonks, her son and chief captain, afterwards faithless to Philip, but a faithful soldier under Capt. Church. But perhaps the most noted figure at the court of Philip was the unfortunate Nanumpum, better known as Weetamoo. She was doubly sister-in-law to Philip, having married Wamsutta, his brother, while Philip's wife was Wotonekanuske, her younger sister. At her marriage, Weetamoo was squaw Sachem of Pocasset, and was "counted as Potent a Prince as any round about her, and had as much Corn, Land, and Men." Not long after her marriage, Weetamoo complained to the Plymouth authorities that her husband, and his father, Massasoit, were selling her land. Getting no relief from English law she made it over to trustees, under Indian rules. Wamsutta died soon after under a suspicion of being poisoned by the whites. Philip had artfully fomented this suspicion, healed the quarrel about the land, and after much wavering, the "Queen of Pocasset" joined him in the war with three hundred warriors. For a second husband Weetamoo had married Petananuet, who at this juncture proved a traitor to his wife and Queen, and joined the English. The indignant Weetamoo at once repudiated the nuptial bond, and in December or January following took for a third consort, Quinnapin, thus allying herself to a royal family of the Narragansets. To this tribe she had fled when driven from Pocasset. Quinnapin, who was with her at Squakheag, was nephew of Miantonomo, and cousin to Canonchet, the head war chief of his tribe. Quinnapin had declared he would "fight it out to the last, rather than submit to the whites." With him were his brothers, Ashamaton, and Sunkeesunasuck, both Sachems, and a one-eyed brother, without any command. A fourth brother had fallen in the "great swamp fight," Dec. 19th, 1675. Among the war Sachems Quinnapin ranked next to Canonchet.

Canonchet, also called *Nannuntcmo*, son of Miantonomo, was the hereditary chief of the Narraganset nation. With him were about twelve hundred warriors, with their Sachems. Canonchet, like all savage potentates, was fond of show. When presiding over a council he dressed in a style befitting his rank. He wore a brilliant silver-laced coat, a richly embroidered mantle of wampum over his shoulders, the ends hanging down in front; his buckskin leggins were gaily fringed with tufts of hair and feathers, and a heavy stripe of wampum work ran from his waist to his moccasins; the latter were handsomely figured with beads and quills. Over all he wore a gorgeously adorned scarlet blanket, sweeping the ground as he walked. In person, he was tall and commanding, with the well-knit frame of an athlete: "A very proper man, of goodly Stature, and great Courage of mind as well as Strength of Body." Around his council fire were gathered many of the notables of the tribe. Pessacus—also called Sucsusquench, Coousquench, Peticus, and Canonicus the Second—a brother of Miantonomo, and for twenty years regent, during the minority of Canonchet, now chief councillor and ruler; the fiery Quinnapin and his sons; old Pomham, a "mighty man of valor," "one of the most valiant Sachems," on whose death it was said "the glory of the nation has sunk with him forever." With him was his comely son, and a grandson already a noted captain; Potucke, "the great Indian counsellor," of "wonderful subtlety;" the treacherous Stonewall John, "one of the most distinguished Narraganset captains," "an active and ingenious fellow, who had learned the mason's trade, & was of great use in building their forts," who boasted before the swamp fight, Dec. 19th, that the English *durst not* fight them; and Wennaquabin, and Necopeake, Sachems of lesser note. Canonchet was a young man and he represented the temper of those forward for the war. He had declared he would never submit to the English. He was looked upon as the real leader in the war, and the young braves from other clans and adventurers from distant tribes flocked to his standard. During the season occasional bands of Nipmucks were also here, led by Mawtamp of Quabaug, Sagamore John of Lancaster, Capt. Tom of Natick, Old Matoonas and others. Here were the apostate Christians from the towns of Praying Indians, established by Eliot—"*Preying* Indians," Hezekiah Usher called them. They were under Wattasacompanum, whom Eliot called his "chief assistant, * * * a grave and pious man, of the chief sachems blood of the Nipmuck country." These renegades affected the costume of the English, and may have been seen on horseback, "with hats, white neckcloths, and sashes about their waists, and ribbons upon their shoulders." These pious lambs proved the worst wolves of the whole bloody crew. One of them for an ornament wore "a string about his neck, strung with Christian fingers." Here was Sancumachu, the

THE PRAYING INDIANS. 141

Pocumtuck Sachem, with the survivors of the Pocumtuck confederation, and what volunteers he could muster from the Mahicans, or other western tribes during the winter. He came with Philip, heading about three hundred warriors. From this force most of the scouts to our frontiers were doubtless selected. Megunneway, an Abenaki, was in the Falls fight, and it is probable that other Eastern Indians had joined the hostiles.

Philip, in his state dress, was not eclipsed by the popular Narraganset chieftain. His mantle, a belt nine inches in width, gorgeously wrought with beads and wampum in figures of beasts, birds and flowers, hung from his neck to his feet. Another belt, equally fine, circled his head, the ends, adorned with pendant flags, hanging down his back. All of these had an edging of rare red hair, obtained in the Mohawk country. His buskins "were set thick with beads, in pleasant wild works." Elegantly carved powder horns, filled with glazed powder, hung upon each arm. A richly adorned red blanket, trailing behind him, covered the whole.

Neither the costume nor occupation of the unfortunate Wotonekanuske, his queen, has been ascertained, but those of her sister, Weetamoo, may well represent the mode, at the court of King Philip.

The marriage of the Queen of Pocasset to Quinnapin, was doubtless for reasons of state, rather than from affection or romance, for the latter had already two wives. The honeymoon had been spent in a dangerous retreat to the Nipmuck country, before the victorious English. Weetamoo took at least one waiting maid along with her, and after the attack on Lancaster, Quinnapin presented her with another in the person of Mrs. Mary Rowlandson, the minister's wife, whom he bought from one of his men, by whom she was captured. From this new servant we get many glimpses of Indian life and character. She says of her mistress:—

> A severe and proud dame she was, bestowing every day in dressing herself, near as much time as any of the gentry of the land. Powdering her hair and painting her face, going with her necklaces, with jewels in her ears and bracelets upon her hands. When she had dressed herself her work was to make girdles of wampum and beads. At great dances she wore a kersey coat, covered with girdles of wampum from the loins upward. Her arms, from her elbows to her hands, were covered with bracelets. There were handfuls of neck-

laces about her neck, and several sorts of jewels in her ears. She had fine red stockings and white shoes, her hair powdered and her face painted red, that was always before, black.

On similar occasions Quinnapin "was dressed in his Holland shirt, with great stockings; his garters hung round with shillings, and had girdles of wampum on his head and shoulders." This coin, doubtless the Pine Tree money of Massachusetts colony, was hung so thick as to jingle when the wearer moved. Each of the wives of Quinnapin kept up a separate establishment. One was old, the second young, with two children. Weetamoo had at least as many. Early in April one of Weetamoo's children died. It was buried the next day, and "for some time after a company came every morning and evening to mourn and howl" with the sorrowing mother.

Wotonekanuske had also with her at least two children, a boy of eight or nine, and a young pappoose attended by a nurse maid. One day the latter demanded of Mrs. Rowlandson a piece of her apron "to make a flap" for this royal scion of the Wampanoags. Mrs. Rowlandson refused. Weetamoo ordered compliance, and a furious war of words followed. Her white servant still refusing, the fond aunt rushed at her with a club, to enforce her command, when the captive was glad to escape by giving up her whole apron.

The future of this infant is unknown, but the horrible fate of Wotonekanuske and her boy, by an act disgraceful to civilization, is blazoned on the rolls of infamy. They were captured Aug. 1st and sent from the free, cool shade of a New England forest to pine and perish under the lash of a taskmaster, beneath the burning sun of the tropics. They were sold into West Indian slavery! No savage had yet mastered the art of a torture equal to this.

The condition of Mrs. Rowlandson among the Indians seems peculiar. She appears in a measure to have been master of her own time and did many odd jobs of needlework out of her mistress's family, for which she received pay. At Philip's request she made a shirt for his unfortunate son, for which he gave her a shilling. With this she bought a piece of horse flesh. For making the same lad a cap she was invited to dine at the royal table. Although often on the verge of starvation, if she was detected in getting food from others, she was punished for having disgraced her master by begging. The Indians were well provided with dry goods, needles, &c. Mrs. Rowlandson knit stockings for Weetamoo, and for a warrior, she ravelled out a pair that was too big, and knit them to fit. For making a shirt for her sannap, one squaw gave her a piece of beef; and another a quart of peas for knitting stockings. Upon this rare stock of provisions Mrs. Rowlandson made a feast. " I boiled my beef and peas together," she says, "and invited my master and mistress to dinner; but the proud gossip, because I served them both in one dish, would eat nothing, except one bit which he gave her on the point of his knife." An Indian gave her a knife for making a shirt for himself and an unborn child. When Quinnapin saw the knife he asked her for it. She gave it to him, and was glad she had "anything they would accept of and be pleased with." For a shirt made for a pappoose, the mother gave her a dinner of broth thickened with powdered bark. Again she made a shift for a squaw, who replaced her lost apron, and she got a hat and silk handkerchief for knitting three pairs of stockings. After the Sudbury fight she made a shirt for Quinnapin's pappoose from a Holland laced pillow beer, part of the plunder.

On the arrival of the confederate tribes at Squakheag, the plan of the campaign agreed upon in January seemed feasible. The towns about the Bay were being ravaged daily, and the valley was defenceless. Two problems presented themselves to the Indians, the solution of which was necessary to success; the first, to stave off starvation until the fishing season; the other, a much more difficult one, to get a supply of ammunition. For the latter purpose a party of Pocumtucks and Nipmucks was at once dispatched to Canada, with captives taken at Lancaster, to be exchanged for powder. A plan was discussed of sending a like expedition to Albany; but the arrival of the Dutch traders [see ante, page 136] made this unnecessary. The small stock of provisions they had been able to carry with them had been exhausted, and they were now existing from hand to mouth. Light foraging parties had been sent out on the English frontiers by Sancumachu, and one party brought in from Westfield five bushels of meal. Another captured John Gilbert and Edward Stebbins, two Springfield lads, by whom they learned that no Bay troops had come to the valley. Within two days after the arrival of Canonchet a council met and a decision was made to attack Northampton at once. Canonchet had not forgotten the taunt of Roger Williams, the October before, while dissuading him from joining Philip, that "the Indians were so cowardly that they had not taken one poor fort from us, in all the country." An opportunity now offered for a practical reply. Runners were sent through the camps giving notice. The night of March 11th was spent in a war dance by the braves, and by the squaws in preparing such food as could be obtained for the march. On the 12th, a strong force set out down the river, fully expecting to return loaded with plunder and prisoners. The result of the attack has been given, [ante, page 132.] Although the cattle, sheep and horses secured were a great relief to the hungry multitude, the main object of the movement was not accomplished.

This repulse and the discovery that the valley towns were well defended, changed the whole aspect of affairs at Squakheag. Philip, whose headquarters had been on the west side of the river, scented danger, and on the 16th moved northward, and crossed to the east side. On the 20th, Capt. Tom, with five hundred Nipmucks, took post at Pocumtuck to guard their frontier. The Pocumtucks were especially disappointed. They had been fully assured that their old home was about to be restored to them. Their discontent was increased by news that the expedition to Canada for powder had failed. It had been attacked by Mohawks and two of the Pocumtucks killed. This loss was charged directly upon Philip; the cause of Mohawk hostility being well known to them. They saw in the failure of these plans, their own ruin, and accused Philip of inciting them into a war for which they had no just ground, simply to gratify his own personal hatred.

Meanwhile the daily struggle for existence went on. "Many times in the morning," says Mrs. Rowlandson, "the generality of them would eat up all they had * * * and yett I did not see one man woman or child die with hunger, though many times they would eat that that a hog would hardly touch. They would pick up old bones, and if they were full of maggots, would heat them to "drive them out, then boil them, and drink the liquor." The softer part of the bones were pounded in mortars and eaten. "They would eat horses guts and ears * * * dogs, skunks, rattlesnakes, yea, the very bark of trees." But their chief reliance was ground nuts, and other roots dug from the earth as the frost came out. Had not the winter of 1675-6 been one of remarkable mildness—the ground then opening in February—it seems impossible that these hordes could have survived it. Mrs. Rowlandson being exhausted one day, an Indian gave her a spoonful of samp, and "as much as she would, of the water in which he was boiling a dried horse's foot." With this treat her "spirits came again." For one day's travel, five grains of corn was all the food allowed her. On the occasion of her invitation to dine with Philip, she says: "I went, and he gave me a pancake about as big as two fingers, it was made of parched wheat, beaten and fried in bear's grease." With this niggardly hospitality the royal banquet closed—an exhibition of the meanness of Philip, or the leanness of his larder.

The responsibility of the campaign rested on Canonchet. One problem had been solved. The Dutch would supply powder in barter for furs. On the failure at Northampton he saw that the non-combatants must be permanently located here, and provision made for their support. His plan, which he laid before the Sachems in council, was to make this region the general rendezvous, and place of refuge for the old men, women and children, with a party of his own men, who were on good terms with the Mohawks, for a guard. Nowhere else, he might well say, could provision for the summer and stores for the winter be so easily procured. The river at Peskeompskut would afford abundance of shad and salmon in their season. The broad meadows at Pocumtuck and Squakheag would yield a supply of corn, beans and squashes. Berries and nuts would abound on the hills. The ponds would soon be covered with wild fowl, and here were the favorite haunts of the deer, raccoon and beaver. The only lack was seed for planting. Canonchet said there was corn enough in the barns of the Narraganset country, and called for volunteers to go and get a supply. This being a service of great danger, with little chance for glory, no one came forward until the chief declared he would go himself, and then only thirty offered to accompany him. With this little band Canonchet left the valley and took his way toward the Narraganset Bay. It seems he reached his goal in safety, and dispatched his escort with the precious seed, while he lingered to meet the main body of his army, which was to follow and join him. On the 2d of April, while in camp with six or seven men on the bank of the Pawtucket, he was surprised and captured by a party of English under Captains Avery and Dennison, and Indians led by Oneko and others. The first Englishman who addressed Canonchet was Robert Stanton, twenty-one years old, son of Thomas Stanton, the interpreter, who began to question him. Canonchet, looking scornfully upon him, said, "You much child, no understand matters of war; let your chief come, him will I answer," and no more would he say. He was taken to Stonington and executed the next day. No man ever carried himself more nobly than this captive chieftain. He was offered his life on condition he would "send an old counsellor of his to make a motion towards submission," but he refused. When told he was to die, he replied, "I like it well. I shall die before my heart is soft, or I have spoken anything unworthy of myself;" but "killing me will not end the war, for I have 2000 men who will revenge my death." Being taunted with his boast that he "would not give up a Wampanoag, or the paring of a Wampanoag's nail," and that he "would burn the English in their houses," he only answered, "Others were as forward for the war as myself. I desire to hear no more about it." The only favor he asked, was that the indignities of torture might not be inflicted, and that his executioner might be Oneko, son of Uncas, whom he acknowledged as a fellow prince. These requests were granted. He was executed by Oneko, as Miantonomo, his father, had been by Uncas. His head was sent to Hartford, the receipt of which was noted April 8th. [Conn. Rec., II, 432.] Mistaken accounts give the date of the capture as April 9th.

Thus fell a man who should be ranked first of all New England Indians in the qualities which go to make up a patriot, nobleman and warrior. His death "was a matter of rejoicing to all the Colonies." He was called the "Ringleader of almost all this mischief, and great incendiary betwixt us and the Narragansets," and as "the son of Miantonomi, and heir of all his pride and insolence, as well as his malice against the English * * * a most perfideous villain." With all the vituperation, the only charge brought against his honor was a violation of the October treaty at Boston. This treaty was in accordance with the treacherous policy of Philip, and made at his solicitation, Canonchet being unfortunately under his influence at that time. But let us remember the fact, which his detractors overlooked, that very soon after he returned home he sent notice to Boston that the treaty was to be considered null and void.

Meanwhile, awaiting the return of Canonchet, the struggle for existence continued at Squakheag and few hostile movements were made. Scouts watched their own frontier and hovered about that of the enemy. The English, however, being thoroughly alarmed and on the alert, gave few opportunities for spoil. An occasional success cheered them. Early in April a party, doubtless Pocumtucks, being on the high lands overlooking Hadley, saw workmen with a guard go out into the meadows. Creeping towards the scene of labor the scout patiently waited events. They soon saw the vigilance of the whites relax, and their own opportunity for action. Deacon Richard Goodman, one of the workmen, left the guard to examine his boundary fence, and three of the guard climbed the hill to view the prospect. All came within range of the scouts' guns, and all fell. Thomas Reed was captured. He was brought to headquarters and closely questioned, but the plans of the English being in utter confusion, as we have seen, no information of value could be obtained from him.

About this time another element of discord was introduced into the camp. Towcanchasson, with another Indian messenger, bearing a flag of truce, arrived from Hartford with the following message:—

These are to signify unto all or any of those Indians whoe are now at war with the English, that the Councill of Conecticott, haueing not wronged nor injured them in the least so as to cause them to take up armes against us, but being called according to covenant to assist our confederates of Massachusetts and Plimouth, haue taken sundry Indians captiues, and some are deliuered to vs ; therefore we haue thought meet to declare to the s^d Indians that we are willing to tender them an exchang of captives, for such English as they have in their hands; and that upon the return of o^{rs} to Hadley where we will meet them, theirs shall be set at liberty to come to them. We also do tender, that if the s^d Indians doe desire any treaty with vs, and make appeare that they haue been wronged by any of the English, we shall endeavour to haue that wrong rectifyed, and heare any propositions they haue to make vnto us; and if any of the Sachems desire to treat with vs, they shall have liberty to com to vs and goe away without any molestation, sending word when and where before hand. And they may know that we are men of peace and willing to farther peace with all o^r neighbours.

Dated in Hartford, March 28. 1676.
P^r order of the Councill,
J. A. Sec^{r}y.

These to be convayed by Towcanchasson.

This overture was well received by the Pocumtucks and Nipmucks, who had no real cause for war. They were tired of the hardships it involved, and indignant against Philip, who enticed them into it. It was different with the Narragansets. Their homes were desolate, their people slain and their vengeful natures forbade thoughts of peace. At any rate no action could be had until the return of their chieftain, Canonchet.

The departure of Maj. Savage from Hadley, April 7th, was reported by scouts at once, and caused great exultation, dampening all thoughts of peace, and greatly strengthening the war feeling. It now appeared that their friends at the east had carried out their part in the programme of the campaign. The troops had been forced to return home, and if all united, the valley towns must soon be in their hands, with all their corn and cattle. The occupation of the peacemaker was gone.

Within a day or two, however, came the sickening news that their valiant leader, their anchor of hope, the noble Canonchet, had fallen. The blow was a stunning one. Consternation took the place of confidence, and confusion and discord reigned. The Pocumtucks at once deserted the cause and threatened to seek a peace, with the head of Philip as an offering. On the 10th that prudent sachem moved towards safer quarters in the fastnesses of the Wachusett mountain. Within a week news of another disaster reached the camp. Forty men, including several counsellors and sachems, had been killed near the place where Canonchet was taken.

The care of the disorganized multitude now fell upon Pessacus. Measures were taken for defense here, and a fort projected at a *cowass* some forty miles up the river, as a retreat, in case of need. Three forts were built for defense against invasion, on the ground now occupied. Scouting parties were sent to skulk about the towns below, to keep them in a constant state of alarm, and on the defensive. Cattle and horses from their pasture grounds added to the provisions in the camps. Though generally successful in their raids, the last week of April one party reported a disastrous issue. While on the bank of the Connecticut river, near Springfield, they were surprised and fired upon by the enemy. Three of them were mortally wounded, but plunging at once into the water, their scalps were saved. The peace party had again become a power, and increased with every reverse. Towcanchasson was still here, and it was urged upon Pessacus to attempt a treaty with the enemy. The Narragansets were in no mood for peace, but the wily Sachem, whose object was to gain time until the winter's stock of fish was laid up and the planting season over, saw here an opportunity to ensure delay. To that end he dispatched Tiawakesson, his own official "messenger," with Towcanchasson and suite, bearing an ambiguous message in writing to the Connecticut Council. In a short time Tiawakesson came back with the following message in reply:—

To Pessicus, Wequaquat, Wanchequit, Sunggumache, and the rest of the Indian Sachems up the River about Suckquackheage, these:—
You may hereby be informed, that we have received your writing, brought by o[r] two messengers, and by Pessicus his messenger, and in it we find no answer to what we propownded, and therefore once again we haue sent these lines to you, to inform you that, as we sayd before, we are men of peace, and if they will deliver unto us the English captives that are with them, either for money or for captiues of yours in o[r] hands, to be returned to them, wee shall accept of it so farr: and if they will attend a meeting at Hadley, within these eight days, if the Sachems will com thither bringing the captives with them as a signe of theire reall desire of peace, we shall appoynt some to meet them there, and to treat them upon tearmes of peace; and they shall haue safe conduct both in comeing and while they stay; and they shall have free liberty to depart, if we doe not agree to tearmes of peace. But to this we doe desire their speedy answer, to be brought to Hadly, within five dayes; and if one or two men come with the Sachems answer to this and come without armes, with a white cloath vpon a pole, they will receiue no damage, and their answer will be speadily handed down to vs. They know we never use to breake our promise to Indians, and doe keep peace with all o[r] own Indians, though some fewe are kept in a comfortable

house, put there by theire own free will as pawnes for the rest, till the wars be ended, and are well used, as friends not as prisoners.

Dated in Hartford,
May 1st, 1676.

P^r order of the Councill of Conecticott,
Signed, John Allyn, Secret^{r}y.

It was evident to Pessacus, by the tenor of both the communications from the English, that the principal object of these overtures was to get the prisoners from his hands; that their continuance in his camp would embarrass hostile movements, and he had no intention of giving up this advantage. So no response was made to the invitation for a meeting at Hadley. And as the spring advanced, and the hardships of the confederates diminished, there was less and less desire for peace. Changeful as children, the fickle savage was elated, or cast down, by the events of the hour.

As warm weather came on food was more and more readily procured. The springing herbage not only furnished food in itself, but revealed the esculent root beneath. When the ponds opened, water fowl became common, and as the shad and salmon appeared in their annual migration, abundance followed the long winter of starvation. Mrs. Rowlandson says, after being for weeks almost famished: "I was never again satisfied; though it sometimes fell out that I had got enough and did eat till I could eat no more, yet I was as unsatisfied as when I began." Feasting and gorging brought content to the Indians and everything wore a more hopeful aspect. Every week brought news of successes by their friends at the East, and the enemy shut up in the towns below seemed to be at their mercy when the time for action should come. The peace party had disappeared.

While crowds were catching and drying fish to store their barns with a winter's stock, others were engaged in preparing the ground for planting at Pocumtuck and Squakheag; and by the middle of May a wide area had been planted. English scouts reported three hundred acres in corn at the former place. Indian scouts reported to the Sachems no reinforcements to the English force, but, on the contrary, that part of the garrisons had been withdrawn from the towns; that the settlers were neglecting their fields from fear, and that no laborers left the stockades without a guard. Week by week the confederates grew more and more secure. The

FATAL FEAST AT PESKEOMPSKUT.

Sachems about the camp fires talked over the plans for the summer, assured of an easy success in driving the whites from the valley. The escaped captive, Reed, reported them "as secure and scornful, boasting the great things they had done, and will do," annihilating in their war dances many an imaginary foe.

Their principal camp was at the head of the rapids on the right bank of the river at Peskeompskut; another was at some distance above it; a third, nearly opposite on the left bank, while a fourth was on Smead's Island, a short distance below; and still another at Cheapside guarded the ford of the Pocumtuck river. Beside these, every fishing place on the Connecticut as high up as the Ashuelot had its camp.

Quiet and plenty had lulled the Indians into a sense of security. The escape of the English captives, Gilbert, Stebbins and Reed, in consequence of their relaxed vigilance, brought no premonitions of danger. The English and the Mohawks, like themselves, they reasoned, must attend to their planting. May 12th, Pessacus, learning that the Hatfield people had turned their stock into the north meadows to feed, promptly sent a party to secure the prize; and that very night seventy or eighty head were brought off. A part were left in the common field at Pocumtuck, and the fence repaired to keep them in, others taken to the camps for slaughter, and the cows brought to headquarters for their milk, where the English captive women were made to milk them. Beef now became as plenty as fish. But the end was drawing near.

On the night of May 18th a grand feast was held at Peskeompskut. Sachems and warriors, women and children, alike gorged themselves on the choice salmon from the river, and fresh beef and new milk from the Hatfield raid. Late in the night, perhaps to secure a further supply, a party went out in canoes to spear salmon by torchlight. A shower unfortunately extinguished the torches, and the fishermen went ashore to mingle again in the frolic and festivity. This lasted until near morning. At its close, without posting a single sentinel, the whole party, stuffed to repletion, and lulled by the monotone of the falling waters, fell into a profound slumber. From this criminal security and stupid torpor, warrior and people were rudely aroused. The foe were even now at their very door.

TURNERS FALLS FIGHT.

On the recall of Major Savage, as before stated, garrisons had been left in the valley towns at their request and their offer to pay the expense of the same. This proved a heavy burden to the harassed settlers, and as the weeks wore on, a feeling grew up, that, as all field operations were forbidden, they themselves could defend the stockades, and a smaller force of soldiers guard them in their labors. About the first of May a petition was sent to the General Court to the effect, that, if one-half of the garrisons be supported by the Colony, no objection would be offered to the withdrawal of the other half. This change was made, and the returning troops were doubtless the escort to the provisions which Turner had been ordered to send to the rendezvous at Quabaug.

The inhabitants were not deceived by the quiet of the Indians. Aware of their numbers and occupation, they knew that when planting and fishing were over, and the trees in full leaf, the whole valley would be alive with them. The boldness of the enemy in settling so near, and their successful raids on the frontiers, had at length aroused more indignation than fear. Left to their own resources by the government, their inherent manhood rebelled against the fact that a horde of the despised race was insolently domineering over them. Their pride was aroused. The panic of the early spring gave way to an urgent desire for offensive action. The following letter represents this feeling to the General Court:—

Hadly Apr. 29. 1676.

It is strange to see how much spirit (more than formerly) appears in o^r men to be out against the enemy. A great part of the inhabitants here, would o^r committees of militia but permitt would be going forth. They are dayly moving for it, and would fane have liberty to be going forth this night. The enemy is now come so near us, that we count we might goe forth in the evening, and come upon them in the darknesse of the same night. We understand from Hartford some inclination to allow some volunteers to come from there up hither. Should that be, I doubt not but many of o^{rs} would joyne with them. It is the generall voyce of the people here y^t now is the time to distresse the enemy, and that could we drive them from thair fishing, and keepe out though but lesser parties against them, famine would subdue them. All o^r late intelligence gives us cause to hope that the Mohawks do still retaine their old friendship to us, & enmity against our enemies. Some proofe of it they have of late, in those they slew higher up this River. Two of whom, as the Indian messengers relate, were of o^r known Indians, and one a Quaboag Indian. And further proof its thought, they would soone give, were the obstructions (y^t some English have or may put in their way) removed, and the remembrance of the ancient amity and good turns between them, and these colonies, renewed by some letters, & if it might be, by some English messenger. We would not tho' out of so good an end as love and zeal for the weale publique, that we should be transported beyond o^r line. We crave pardon for o^r reaching so far, and wth many prayers, so desire to beseech the father of mercies & God of all Counsell to direct you in the right way, and so praying we remain,

Sir, Your Worships most Humble & devoted Serv'ts.

JOHN RUSSELL.
WILL TURNER.
DAVID WILTON.
SAMUELL SMITH.
JOHN LYMAN.
ISAACK GRAVES.
JOHN KING.
DANIELLE WARNARE.

The same day on which this letter was written, another of similar import was sent the Connecticut Council also giving notice of the arrival of Towcanchasson from Squakheag, with Tiawakesson, the messenger of Pessacus. The Council are cautioned against giving full credit to the stories they tell, as "they doe (especially he that belongs to these parts,) labor to represent the enemies state as much to their advantage as may be, whether agreeing with truth or not." Tiawakesson and his party arrived at Hartford the next day, and on the 1st of May were sent away with the message already given, [see ante, page 149,] and orders issued for raising one hundred soldiers, who were to leave Hartford on the 8th for Hadley, the place and time appointed for the meeting with the Sachems. A letter was also sent to Mr. Russell, in reply to his of the 29th, giving the substance of the message sent by Tiawakesson, and asking that any answer to it being received, should be posted to Hartford, at the same time cautioning them against making any hostile movements while the English captives remained in the hands of the Indians, "whom they will in such case be likely to destroy."

The eight allotted days passed and no tidings from Pessacus, and so no Connecticut troops came to Hadley. "The spirit to be out against the enemy" grew stronger day by day, and when the great loss of stock from Hatfield meadows was known, that spirit was shared by the commander.

May 15th Thomas Reed, the escaped captive, came into headquarters and gave a full account of the unwarlike condition of affairs up the river. All now agreed that the time had come for a trial of arms; and that day Mr. Russell, who seems to have been their mouthpiece, wrote the Connecticut Council giving an account of the raid on Hatfield meadows and the news brought by Reed, concluding:—

> This being the state of things, we think the Lord calls us to make some trial of what may be done against them suddenly, without further delay and therefore the concurring resolution of men here seems to be to go out against them to-morrow night so as to be with them, the Lord assisting, before break of day. We need guidance and help from heaven. We humbly beg your prayers, advice, and help if it may be. And therewith committing you to the guidance and blessing of the Most High, remain
> Your worship's in all humble service
> JOHN RUSSELL.

To this was appended:—

> Altho this man speaks of their number as he judgeth yet they may be many more, for we perceive their number varies, and they are going and coming, so that there is no trust to his guess.
> WILLIAM TURNER.
> JOHN LYMAN.
> ISAAC GRAVES.

The resolution "to go out against them to-morrow night," the 16th, was not carried out. But after waiting for two days the result of the appeal to Connecticut for help, on the 18th, a force of about one hundred and forty-one men was gathered at Hatfield for an expedition against their enemy at Peskeompskut. It was made up very nearly as follows: From the garrisons of Hadley, Hatfield and Northampton, thirty-four; from those at Springfield and Westfield, twenty-two, under Lieut. Josiah Fay, of Boston. The rest were volunteers. From Hadley, twenty-five, and Hatfield twelve, under Sergeants John Dickinson and Joseph Kellogg; twenty-two from Northampton, under Ensign John Lyman; twenty-three from Springfield and three from Westfield, under Capt. Samuel Holyoke. Of these, nineteen at least had been, or became, citizens of this town. Rev. Hope Atherton of Hatfield, "who was a courageous man and willing to expose himself for the public good," was the Chaplain; Benjamin Waite and Experience Hinsdell were guides. The whole was under Captain William Turner of Boston. Each man was furnished with provision for three meals. Nearly all were mounted, but there were a few footmen. After sunset, Thursday, May 18th, this little army set out on a memorable march—memorable for its material, for its good and bad fortune, and for the results achieved. After fervent prayer by the chaplain, and a tearful God-speed from their friends, the cavalcade passed out from Hatfield street with high hopes and determined hearts. Crossing the meadows to the north, vowing vengeance for the stolen cattle, they wended their way slowly up the Pocumtuck path. Tall Wequamps loomed up before them like a pillar of cloud against the dim northern sky. They followed the exact route which had led Beers and Lothrop into an ambush nine months before. Thoughtful eyes peered into the fatal swamp as they passed. Over the Weequioannuck and through the hushed woods as darkness was closing down, to Bloody Brook. Guided by Hinsdell, the troops floundered through the black morass, which drank the blood of his father and three brothers, eight months before; they passed with bated breath and clinched fire-lock, the mound under which slept Lothrop and his three score men. As they left this gloomy spot, and marched up the road, down which the heedless Lothrop had led his men into the fatal snare, the stoutest must have quailed at the uncertainty beyond. Was their own leader wise? Did he consider the danger? Did not they all know that if Towcanchasson was treacherous or any swift-footed friend of Pessacus had revealed to him their plans, that they were marching to sure destruction? Was it prudent to neglect precautions against surprise? What if the information of Reed should prove incorrect? Burdened with thoughts like these, the command made its way to Pocumtuck, guarding with closed ranks against the gaping cellars of our ruined village. More than one of these men, by toil and frugality, had here built their homes and gathered their families. As they passed the desolate hearthstones, what but faith in the Most High could raise their sinking hearts? Onward across North Meadows, where one of the guides, Benjamin Waite, was later to end his eventful life in the brave attempt to rescue the captives of 1704, and where the boy hero of this expedition, famous later as Capt. Jonathan Wells, tried vainly to temper his rash zeal. Over the Pocumtuck river, at the mouth of Sheldon's brook, to avoid the ford guarded by the Indian fort, and up the steep side hill to Petty's Plain. Even with this precaution, the wading of the horses was heard, and the Indian sentinel gave the alarm. With lighted torches a party examined the crossing place, but finding no tracks, concluded that the noise was made by moose crossing the river. So narrowly did the party escape discovery. Following the Indian trail at the foot of Shelburne hills, the adventurers entered the mysterious and unexplored wilderness stretching away to Canada. Full of boding fancies, they marched on under the gloomy arches of a primeval forest, the darkness made more intense by the glare of lightning, and the silence occasionally broken by a peal of thunder, the bark of the startled wolf, or raccoon, the ghostly flitting of the wondering owl. What wonder if these brave men and boys, superstitious as they were, and worn by fatigue and excitement, lost their self-possession a few hours later. Marching two miles northward, then crossing Green river at the mouth of Ash-swamp brook to the eastward, skirting the great swamp, Turner reached the plateau south of Mount Adams, before the break of day, tired and drenched by a shower, which fortunately drove in the fishermen. [See ante, page 151.]

Leaving his horses under a small guard, Turner led his men through Fall river, up a steep ascent, and came out on a slope* in the rear of the Indian camp. He had reached his objective point undiscovered. Silence like that of death brooded over the encampment by the river, save for the sullen roar of the cataract beyond. With ears strained to catch any note of alarm, the English waited impatiently the laggard light, and with the dawn, stole silently down among the sleeping foe; even putting their guns into the wigwams undiscovered. At a given signal the crash of a hundred shots aroused the stupefied sleepers. Many were killed at the first fire. The astonished survivors, supposing their old enemy

---

* Now the farm of T. M. Stoughton.

to be upon them, cried out "Mohawks! Mohawks!" rushed to the river, and jumped pell-mell into the canoes which lay along the shore. Many pushed off without paddles; in other cases the paddlers were shot, and falling overboard, upset the canoe; many in the confusion plunged into the torrent, attempting to escape by swimming. Nearly all of these were swept over the cataract and drowned. Others, hiding about the banks of the river, were hunted out and cut down, "Captain Holyoke killing five, young and old, with his own Hands from under a bank." A very slight resistance was made, and but one of the assailants wounded; another "was killed in the action by his friends, who, taking him for an Indian as he came out of a wigwam shot him dead." The wigwams were burned, and the camp dismantled. Says a letter writer of the day:—

We there destroyed all their ammunition and provision, which we think they can hardly be so soon or easily recruited with as possibly they may be with men. We likewise here demolish't Two Forges they had to mend their arms; took away all their Materials and Tools, and threw two great Piggs of Lead (intended for Making of Bullets) into the River.

There were skilled mechanics among the Indians, doubtless renegade disciples of Eliot.

The disasters of the English which followed their success is attributed to various causes. "The want of health of Capt. Turner, unable to manage his charge any longer," being "enfeebled by sickness before he set out," but "some say they wanted powder, which forced them to retire as fast as they could by Cap. Turner's order." The real cause was, that there was too long a delay on the scene of conflict, which gave the Indians from the other camps time to gather about them. When that condition of affairs was observed, the English, it would seem, drew off towards their horses in considerable disorder. A party of about twenty who had gone a little distance up the river to fire at some canoes that were seen coming over, were left behind, and they were obliged to fight their way to their horses, and were surrounded while mounting. One of this number, Jonathan Wells, a boy of sixteen, after being wounded, managed to escape and make his way up to Capt. Turner, whom he begged to go back to the relief of his party in the rear, or halt until they came up. Turner replied, "Better save some, than lose all," and pushed on. About this time, one of the released English captives reported that Philip with a thousand men was at hand. This created a panic amongst the exhausted men, and the retreat became a rout. The guides differed as to the safest route, each crying out, "If you would save your lives follow me," and the command was in a measure broken up, each fragment taking its own course. A party following guide Hinsdell into a swamp on the left flank were all lost. Turner received a fatal shot as he was crossing Green river near "Nash's Mills." Capt. Holyoke, on whom the command now devolved, labored bravely to restore order, and if he "had not played the Man at a more than ordinary rate, sometimes in the Front, sometimes on the Flank and Rear, and at all Times encouraging the Soldiers, it might have proved a fatal Business to the Assailants. The said Capt. Holioke's horse was shot down under him, and himself ready to be assaulted by many Indians just coming upon him, but discharging Pistols upon one or two of them, whom he presently dispatched, and another Friend coming up to his Rescue, he was saved, and so carried off the Soldiers without further loss." The line of retreat being through a dense forest, the fleet Indians had the advantage of the mounted fugitives. They hung like a moving cloud on flank and rear, shooting as opportunity offered, and even followed across North Meadows and through the Town Street to the Bars. On mustering the force at Hatfield, forty-five men—nearly one-third of the command — were missing, and two mortally wounded; two came in that night, two Sunday and two more on Monday. The total loss was Captain Turner, Sergt. John Dickinson and Guide Hinsdell with thirty-nine men.

List of men in the Falls Fight under Captain William Turner, May 19th, 1676; made up from all available sources, but chiefly from the Mass. M. S. Archives. Absolute knowledge might require slight changes. Those marked thus *, were killed; those thus †, were wounded.

Allis, William,* Hatfield.
Alexander, Nathaniel, Northampton.
Alvard, Thomas, Northampton.
Arms, William, Hatfield.
Ashdown, John,* Weymouth.
Atherton, Hope, Hatfield.
Ball, Samuel, Springfield.

Baker, Timothy, Northampton.
Barber, John, Springfield.
Bardwell, Robert, Hatfield.
Bedortha, Samuel, Springfield.
Beers, Elnathan, Watertown.
Belcher, John, Braintree.
Belding, Samuel, Hatfield.

CAPTAIN TURNER'S SOLDIERS.

Belding, Stephen, Hatfield.
Bennet, James,* Northampton.
Bennitt, John, Windham.
Boltwood, Samuel, Hadley.
Bradshaw, John, Medford.
Buckley, George.*
Burton, Jacob,* Topsfield.
Bushrod, Peter.
Chamberlain, Benjamin, Concord.
Chamberlain, Joseph, Concord.
Chapin, Japhet, Springfield.
Chase, John, Newbery.
Church, John,* Hadley.
Clapp, Preserved, Northampton.
Clark, William, Northampton.
Colby, John, Almsbury.
Colby, Samuel, Almsbury.
Colefax, John,* Hatfield.
Coleman, Noah, Hadley.
Crow, Samuel,* Hadley.
Crowfoot, Joseph, Springfield.
Cunnaball, John, Boston.
Dickinson, John,* Hadley.
Dickinson, Nathaniel, Hadley.
Drew. William, Hadley.
Dunkin, Jabez,* Worcester.
Ebon, George.†
Edwards, Benjamin, Northampton.
Elgar, Thomas,* Hadley.
Field, Samuel, Hatfield.
Flanders, John, Salisbury.
Foot, Nathaniel, Hatfield.
Foster, John.*
Fowler, Joseph,* Ipswich.
Fuller, Joseph, Newton.
Gillett, Samuel,* Hatfield.
Gerrin, Peter.*
Gleason, Isaac, Springfield.
Griffin, Joseph, Roxbury.
Grover, Simon, Boston.
Hadlock, John,* Concord.
Harrington, Robert, Springfield.
Harrison, Isaac,* Hadley.
Harwood, James.
Hawks, Eleazer, Hadley.
Hawks, John, Hadley.
Hindsdell, Experience,* Hadley.
Hitchcock, John, Springfield.
Hitchcock, Luke, Springfield.
Hodgman, Edward,* Springfield.
Hoit, David, Hadley.
Howard, William,* Salem.
Hughs, George,* Springfield.
Hunt, Samuel, Billerica.
Ingram, John, Hadley.
Jones, Abell, Northampton.
Jones, John,† Cambridge. (?)
Jones, Roger, Boston.
Jones, Samuel,* Yarmouth.
Keet, Franc[is], Northampton.
Kellogg, Joseph, Hadley.
King, John, Northampton.
King, Medad,* Northampton.(?)
Langbury, John,* (Came up with Capt. Lothrop; served later under Moseley.)
Lee, John, Westfield.
Leeds, Joseph, Dorchester.
Leonard, Josiah, Springfield.
Lyman, John, Northampton.
Lyon, Thomas.*
Man, Josiah,* Boston. (?)
Mattoon, Philip, Hadley.
Merry, Cornelius, Northampton.
Miller, John,* Northampton.
Miller, Thomas, Springfield.
Montague, Peter, Hadley.
Morgan, Isaac, Springfield.
Morgan, Jonathan, Springfield.
Munn, James, Colchester.
Munn, John, Colchester.
Newbery, Tryal, Malden.
Nims, Godfrey, Northampton.
Old, Robert, Springfield.
Pearse, Nathaniel, Woburn.
Pike, Joseph,* Charlestown.
Poole, Benjamin,* Weymouth.
Pratt, John, Malden.
Pressey, John, Almsbury.
Preston, John, Hadley.
Price, Robert, Northampton.
Pumrey, Caleb, Northampton.
Pumrey, Medad, Northampton.
Ransford, Samuel.*
Read, Thomas, Westford.
Roberts, Thomas.*
Rogers, Henry, Springfield.
Ropes, Ephraim,* Dedham (?)
Ruggles, George.*
Salter, John, Charlestown.
Scott, John.
Scott, William, Hatfield.
Selden, Joseph, Hadley.
Simms, John.*
Smead, William, Northampton.
Smith, John, Hadley.
Smith, Richard.
Stebbins, Benoni, Northampton.
Stebbins, Samuel, Springfield.
Stebbins, Thomas, Springfield.
Stephenson, James, Springfield.
Sutlief, Nathaniel,* ‡ Hadley.
Sykes, Nathaniel, Springfield. (?)
Tay or Toy, Isaiah, Boston.
Taylor, John.*
Taylor, Jonathan, Springfield.
Thomas, Benjamin, Springfield.
Turner, Capt. William,* Boston.
Tyley, Samuel.
Veazy, Samuel,* Braintree.
Waite, Benjamin, Hatfield.

---

‡ Judd speaks of a tradition in the Sutlief family that Nathaniel was burned at the stake.

Walker, John.*
Warriner, Joseph, Hadley.
Watson, John,* Cambridge. (?)
Webb, John, Northampton.
Webb, Richard, Northampton.
Weller, Eleazer, Westfield.
Weller, Thomas, Westfield.

Wells, Jonathan,† Hadley.
Wells, Thomas, Hadley.
White, Henry, Hadley.
Whitterage, John,* Salem.
Worthington, William.
Wright, James, Northampton.

Killed 41.   Wounded 3.

Nine veterans of this company were living in 1735, Nathaniel Alexander, Samuel Belden, John Bradshaw, John Chase, Joseph Fuller, Samuel Hunt, James Munn, Jonathan Wells. In 1734 Samuel Hunt petitioned the General Court for a grant of land to the survivors and heirs of those engaged in the "Falls Fight." In 1736 a grant was made them six miles square, to be located on the north bounds of Deerfield. Of the 145 men known to be in the fight only 97 claimants appeared when the tract was laid out in 1736. Two more appeared, and in 1741 an additional grant was made of the Gore lying between the former one and "Boston town, No. 2," [Colrain] on the west. The whole was called Falls Fight Town, Fall Fight Township, Fall Town, and on securing a Town Charter in 1762, Bernardston. Among the few affidavits made to sustain claims, found in the Massachusetts MS. Archives, is one from John Chase, in which he states that he and Samuel Colby were in the fight and helped to bury Capt. Turner. A grave which was probably that of Capt. Turner has been discovered within a few years on the bluff westerly of where he fell.

George Ebon, who was wounded in his head, was a soldier at Westfield, August, 1676.

Although successful, this expedition into an almost unexplored wilderness against unknown numbers, was rash in the extreme. Had the march been discovered, another and similar tragedy would doubtless have been added to those of Beers and Lothrop. By good fortune, however, the object of its design was accomplished. The people proved prophets.

No intelligent estimate can be made of the number of Indians engaged in this affair, and contemporary accounts differ widely as to their loss. Captive Indian women said that four hundred were killed, including seventy Wampanoags. If this be true, the latter must have been women and children. We know that there was no distinction of age or sex in the slaughter. Other Indians said "the number of slain and drowned was three hundred and upward that we are able to give an account of, and probably many more, for all the Indians that had confederated in this war were got together in these parts, and we could not tell their numbers. We miss many that might be lost" there. Another said that about sixty warriors were killed of the Pocumtucks, Nipmucks and Narragansets, including three or four Sachems and some of their best fighting men; but that many who went over the falls got on shore below. Wennaquabin, a Narraganset Sachem, who was there, said that he "lost his gun and swam over the river to save his life." Necopeak, of the same tribe, said that he "ran away by reason the shot came as thick as rain; * * * that he saw Capt. Turner, and that he was shot in the thigh, and that he knew that it was him for the said Turner said that was his name." Both these Indians were executed with Quinnapin at Newport, R. I., August 26th, 1676. The Pocumtucks suffered severely, and their power was broken forever. From this time and place, they pass into oblivion. Here was written in bloody characters the final page in their history as a tribe or nation. A miserable remnant was absorbed by the Mahicans or the Cahnawagas.

Lying before me is a manuscript from which some vandal has cut the signature, but clearly in the handwriting of Steen, son of Rev. John Williams, dated "Springfield, L. M., [Long Meadow,] Feb. 1, 1731-2." The substance of this was published by Rev. John Taylor, in an appendix to the "Redeemed Captive," in 1793; but as it is intimately connected with our narrative, it seems fitting to give the entire paper in this place. Mr. Taylor prefaces the story by saying it was "the substance of an attested copy of the account, taken from his own mouth." At the date of this manuscript, Mr. Wells, the hero in fact and name, was living in Deerfield, where he died January 3d, 1738-9. To this paper will be added some statements connected with it, from other manuscript in the same handwriting, together with a tradition elucidating one point in the story.

ESCAPE OF JONATHAN WELLS.

I shall give an account of the remarkable providences of God towards Jonathan Wells Esq then aged 16 years and 2 or 3 months who was in the action [at the Falls Fight, May 19th]. He was with the 20 men y^t were obliged to fight wth the enemy to recover their horses; after he mounted his horse a little while, (being then in the rear of ye company) he was fir'd at by three Indians who were very near him; one bullet pass'd so near him as to brush his hair another struck his horse behind a third struck his thigh in a place which before had been broken by a cart wheel & never set but the bones lap'd & so grew together so y^t altho one end of it had been struck and the bone shatter'd by ye bullet yet the bone was not wholly loss'd in ye place where it had knit. Upon receving his wound he was in danger of falling from his horse, but catching hold of ye horse's maine he recovered himself. The Indians perceving they had wound'd him, ran up very near to him, but he kept ye Ind^s back by presenting his gun to y^m once or twice, & when they stoped to charge he got rid of them & got up to some of ye company. [In this fight for life, as appears by another scrap of our manuscript, he stopped and took up behind him Stephen Belding, a boy companion of sixteen years, who thus escaped]. Capt. Turner, to whom he represented ye difficulties of ye men in ye rear & urg'd y^t he either turn back to y^r relief, or tarry a little till they all come up & so go off in a body; but ye captain replid he had 'better save some, than lose all,' and quickly ye army were divided into several parties, one pilot crying out, 'if you love your lives follow me;' another y^t was acquanted wth ye woods cry'd 'if you love your lives follow me.' Wells fell into the rear again and took wth a small company y^t separated from others y^t run upon a parcel of Indians near a swamp & was most of y^m killed. They then separated again & had about ten men left with him, and his horse failing considerably by reason of his wound, & himself spent wth bleeding, he was left with one John Jones, a wounded man likewise. He had now got about 2 miles from ye place where y^y did ye exploit in, & now y^y had left ye track of ye company & were left both by ye indians y^t persued y^m & by their own men that should have tarried with y^m These two men were unacquainted wth ye woods, & without anny track or path. J. W. had a gun & J. J. a sword. J. J. represented ye badness of his wounds, & made his companion think they were certainly mortall, and therefore when y^y separated in order to find the path, J. W. was glad to leave him, lest he sh^d be a clog or hindrance to him. Mr. W. grew faint, & once when ye indians prest him, he was near fainting away, but by eating a nutmeg, (which his grandmother gave him as he was going out) he was reviv'd. After traveling a while he came upon Green river, and follow'd it up to ye place call'd ye Country farms, & pass'd over Green river, & attempted to go up ye mountain, but as he assend'd the hill he fainted & fell from his horse; but after a little he came to himself & found y^t his horse's bridle hung upon his hand & his horse was standing by him. He tyed his horse and laid down again. At length he grew so weak y^t he c^d not get upon his horse, & conclud'd he must dye there himself, & so pitying his horse he dismiss'd him, never thinking to take any provision from him, altho he had three meals of provision behind him. Ab^t noon this, & at ab^t sun an hour high at n^t, being disturbed by ye flies, he stop'd ye touch hole of his gun & struck fire, & set ye woods on fire;

but there being much rubbish, he had like to have been burnt up by it, not being able to get out of y⁰ way; but by scraping away yᵉ leaves, &c., he was wᵗʰ much difficulty preserved from burning; his hands and hair were much burnt, notwithstanding all yᵗ he cᵈ do. He then made a fire of some wood yᵗ lay in his reach & lay down by it. Now new fears arose: He concluded yᵗ his fire would direct the indians where to come to find him, & being so weak he cᵈ not stand or go, concluded he must then be killed by yᵉ indians; he flung away his powder horn one way and his bullet pouch another, yᵗ yʸ might not have yᵐ, reserving a little horn of powder yᵗ he might have one shot before yʸ killed him; but wⁿ yᵉ fire spread considerably, he expected yʸ wᵈ be as like to look in one place as another, & again took courage & took some tow & stopd into his wound, & bound it up with his hand kerchief & neckcloth, & so securely laid him down to sleep; and when asleep, he dreamt yᵗ his grandfather came to him & told him he was lost, but yᵗ he must go down yᵗ river till he came to yᵉ end of yᵉ mountain & then turn away upon yᵉ plain, (he was now abᵗ 12 miles from Deerfield) & yᵗ was yᵉ way home. When he awoke in the morning, (having been refresht by his sleep & his bleeding being stopd), he found he had some strength, & found yᵗ wᵗʰ yᵉ help of his gun for a staff he cᵈ go after a fashion; when yᵉ sun arose he found himself lost, (tho before he thot yᵉ direction in yᵉ dream was quite wrong), but upon considering yᵉ rising of yᵉ sun, &c., he resolved to go according to yᵉ direction of yᵉ dream, (he had now got 6 miles further from home than yᵉ place was where they did their exploit upon yᵉ enemy) & picking up his powder horn & bullets he girt up himself & set forward down yᶜ river & found yᵗ at length he came to yᵉ end of yᵉ mountain & to a plain (as in his dream, which before he knew nothing of, for he was never above yᵉ place called Hatfield Clay Gully before this expedition, & when he went up 'twas nᵗ, as before observd, & he was now many miles from any place where yᵉ army came).

He travelled upon yᵉ plain till he came to a foot path wᶜʰ led up to yᵉ road he went out in, where he cᵈ see yᵉ tracks of yᵉ horses. He travelled by leaning upon his gun as a staff, & so he came down to Dᵈ river, but did not know how to get over. He met wᵗʰ much difficulty, for yᵉ stream carᵈ his lame leg acrost yᵉ other leg; but at length by putting the muzzell of his gun into yᵉ water, (for he was loth to wet the lock), he got over, but filled the muzzell of his gun with gravel & sand. Being much spent when he got up yᵉ bank, he laid down under a walnut bush & fell asleep, and wⁿ he awoke an indian was coming over the river in a cano to him coming ashore to him—near—his distress was great; he could not run from his enemy & was quite incapacitated from fighting, (his gun being full of sand & gravel), but he presented his gun, and when the indian discovered him, he jumped out of his cano, (leaving his own gun wᶜʰ was in yᵉ head of yᵉ cano), & made his escape & went & told yᵉ indians yᵗ yᵉ English army was come again for he had seen one of yᵉ scouts. Mr. W., suspecting the indians wᵈ come to search for him, went away into a swamp (yᵗ was hard by) and finding two great trees yᵗ had been left by yᵉ flood lying at a little distance from each other & covered over wᵗʰ rubbish, he crept in betwixt them & within a little while heard a running to & fro in ye swamp, but saw nothing; within a little while all was still, and he ventured to proceed on his journey.

(The indians afterwards gave out that a Narragansett indian was going up the river after eals, that he saw ye track of a man in ye path y^t went up ye bank & was going to see, & saw a man on ye bank & jumped out of ye canoo, & went & told ye indians ye English army were coming again; y^t he had seen one of ye scouts; upon w^h y^y went to ye place, but not seeing anything, y^y concluded he was afrightd groundlessly, for ye Narragansetts, y^y s^d, were no better than squaws, &c., and so y^y made no strict search).

A digression from the narrative, but not to be skipped.

The Indian story in the parenthesis above appears to be an attempt to cover up the humiliating fact of their being outwitted by a crippled boy. It is not improbable that Wells told the story as written, with the double purpose of annoying the Indians on a sensitive point, and of concealing the artifice for future emergencies. No one brought up on Cooper's novels could for a moment believe that Wells escaped in the manner described, and from the writer's boyhood, this part of the story has thrown a shadow of doubt over the whole account of this romantic experience. Any one closely observing a pile of drift wood *in situ*, will see how difficult it must be for the most careful hand to remove any part of it without leaving unmistakable evidence of the disturbance. And the trail of the hobbling boy, from the track "in ye path y^t went up ye bank" to the great trees and rubbish "left by ye flood" in the swamp, must have been patent to the most casual eye, let alone an Indian on the trail of an enemy. A more interesting and romantic story of border warfare in real life is rarely met with. Carefully trace the events as modestly, naively told, with no whining and no complaint. Note the hero's bravery and coolness when attacked; his knightly courtesy in stopping in his flight to rescue Belding; his thoughtfulness for those behind, and judgment in pleading with Capt. Turner to keep his command in a body; his humanity in releasing his horse; his resignation when lying down to die; his forethought in putting out of the reach of the foe his powder horn and bullets; his courage in preparing for "one more shot;" his expedient for lighting a fire to keep off the insects; his self-possession in building a fire to lie down by, after his narrow escape from being burned to death; his clear-headedness when "lost" or "turned round" in the morning;

A YOUTHFUL LEATHERSTOCKING.

his persistent care for his gun and ammunition ; his ingenuity in saving himself when in the very jaws of the enemy; his fortitude under the discouragements by the way, and his expedients for overcoming them ; his reverence and care for the dead at Bloody Brook. Here stand, clearly revealed, traits of the noblest character, in a lad ripened to self-reliance by the exigencies of frontier life. It is with great satisfaction that the writer is able to dissipate the faint shadow resting upon the narrative.

The key to this remarkable escape is found in a tradition handed down in the family, and given me by Rodney B. Field of Guilford, Vt. By this it appears that the "two great trees y^t had been left by ye flood a little distance from each other and covered over with brush," were lying, one end on the river bank, with the other projecting into, and supported by the water. Wading along to the nearest tree, ducking his head under its trunk, and standing erect between the two, with head above water, Wells was securely hidden and no trace of his footsteps was left. This was a device which might well baffle his pursuers and was worthy of Leatherstocking himself. The real danger,—that which could not have been foreseen,—appeared when the Indians in their "running to & fro" stopped for a moment on this cover. Under their weight it sank, forcing the poor boy's head under water, so that several times he was nearly drowned.

Narrative continued:—

In Deerfield Meadows he found some horses' bones, from which he got away some small matter; found two rotted beans in ye meadows where ye indians had thrashed y^r beans, & two blew birds' eggs, wch was all ye provision he had till he got home. He got up to Df^d town plat before dark, Saturday, but ye town was burned before & no inhabitants, so he kept along. His method of travelling was to go a little ways & then lye down to rest, & was wont to fall asleep, but in ye n^t twice he mistook himself when he awoke, & went back again till coming to some remarkable places, he was convinced of his mistake & so turned ab^t again, & at length he took this method, to lay ye muzzell of his gun towards his course, but losing so much, he was discouraged & laid himself down once & again, expecting to dye; but after some recruit was encouraged to set forward again, but meeting wth these difficulties he spent ye whole n^t in getting to muddy brook (or, as some call it, bloody brook); here he buried a man's head in ye path, y^t was drawn out of ye grave by some vermin, wth clefts of wood, &c., and upon ye road to H'f'd was (like Samson after the slaughter of ye Philistines) distressd for want of drink, & many times ready to faint, yet got no water till he came to Clay Gully, but divers times he was refresht by holding his head over candlewood knots y^t were on fire, ye woods being then on fire on ye plains, & got to Hatfield between meetings on Sabbath day.

He lay lame under Dr. Locke for some time, & was under Mrs. Allen & Mr. Buckley four years & 2 months (in all) & never had anything allowd him for time or smart, tho y^y p^d ye surgeon; he lay at one time half a year in one spot on a bed, without being turned once, or once taken out; often dispared of his life; all his skin came off his back by lying in one posture.

The Indians have given the account following to Jonathan Wells, Esq., viz.: That the Monday after the fight, 8 Englishmen that were lost came to them and offered to submitt themselves to them, if they would not put them to death, but whether they promised them quarter or not, they took them, and burnt them; the method of Burning them was to cover them with thatch and put fire to it, and set them a running; and when one coat of thatch was burnt up, they would put on another, & the Barbarous creatures that have given this account of their inhumanity, have in a scoffing manner added, that the Englishmen would cry out as they were burning, "Oh dear! oh dear!" The indians themselves account it very unmanly to moan or make ado under the torments and cruelties of their enemies who put them to Death.

On another paper Mr. Williams refers "to an account of the wonderful providence of God towards the Rev. Mr. Hope Atherton, who was likewise in the expedition. He was unhorsed, lost & left & would have surrendered himself to the indians, but they would not receive him but ran from him. He got over the Great River and got safe into Hadley. This account was drawn up by himself, and signed by himself, but the account would be too long to insert in this extract, &c."

When Mr. Williams wrote the above meagre abstract, the original MS. was in his possession. A copy of this follows:—

MR. ATHERTON'S STORY.
[Read after his sermon, Sunday, May 28, 1676.]

Hope Atherton desires this congregation and all people that shall hear of the Lord's dealings with him to praise and give thanks to God for a series of remarkable deliverances wrought for him. The passages of divine providence (being considered together) make up a complete temporal salvation. I have passed through the Valley of the Shadow of Death, and both the *rod* and *staff* of God delivered me. A particular relation of extreme sufferings that I have undergone, & signal escapes that the Lord hath made way for, I make openly, that glory may be given to him for his works that have been wonderful in themselves and marvelous in mine eyes; & will be so in the eyes of all whose hearts are prepared to believe what I shall relate. On the morning (May 19, 1676) that followed the night in which I went out against the enemy with others, I was in eminent danger through an instrument of death: a gun was discharged against me at a small distance, the Lord diverted the bullet so that no harm was done me. When I was separated from the army, none pursued after me, as if God had given the heathen a charge, saying, let him alone he shall have his life for a prey. The night following I wandered up and down among the dwelling places of our enemies; but none of them espied me. Sleep fell upon their eyes, and slumbering upon their eyelids. Their dogs moved not their tongues. The next day I was encompassed with enemies, unto whom I tendered myself a captive. The Providence of God seemed to require me so to do. No way appeared to escape, and I had been a long time without food. They accepted not the tender which I made, when I spake, they answered not, when I moved toward them they moved away from me. I expected they would have laid hands upon me, but they did not. Understanding that this seems strange and incredible unto some, I have considered whether I was not deceived; and after consideration of all things I cannot find sufficient grounds to alter my thoughts. If any have reason to judge otherwise than myself, who am less than the least in the kingdom of God, I desire them to intimate what their reason is. When I have mused, that which hath cast my thoughts according to the report I first made, is, that it tends to the glory of God, in no small measure; if it were so as I believe it was, that I was encompassed with cruel and unmerciful enemies; & they were restrained by the hand of God from doing the least injury to me. This evidenceth that the Most High ruleth in the Kingdom of men, & doeth whatever pleaseth him amongst them. Enemies cannot do what they will, but are subservient to over-ruling providence of God. God always can and sometimes doth set bounds unto the wrath of man. On the same day, which was the last day of the week, not long before the sun did set, I declared with submission that I would go to the Indian habitations. I spoke such language as I thought they understood. Accordingly I endeavored; but God, whose thoughts were higher than my thoughts, prevented me; by his good providence I was carried beside the path I intended to walk in & brought to the sides of the great river, which was a good guide unto me. The most observable passage of providence was on the Sabbath day morning. Having entered upon a plain, I saw two or three spies, who I (at first) thought they had a glance upon me. Wherefore I turned aside and lay down. They climbed up into a tree to spie. Then my soul secretly begged of God, that he would put it into their hearts to go away. I waited patiently and it was not long ere they went away. Then I took that course which I thought best according to the wisdom that God had given me.

Two things I must not pass over that are matter of thanks-giving unto God: the first is, that when my strength was far spent, I passed through deep waters and they overflowed me not, according to those gracious words of Isa. 43, 2; the second is, that I subsisted the space of three days & part of a fourth without ordinary food. I thought upon those words "Man liveth not by bread alone, but by every word that proceedeth out of the mouth of the Lord." I think not to too much to say, that should you & I be silent & not set forth the praises of God thro' Jesus Christ, that the stones and beams of our houses would sing hallelujah. I am not conscious to myself that I have exceeded in speech. If I have spoken beyond what is convenient, I know it not. I leave these lines as an orphan, and shall rejoice to hear that it finds foster Father's & Mother's. However it fare amongst men, yet if it find acceptance with God thro' Christ Jesus, I shall have cause to be abundantly satisfied. God's providence hath been so wonderful towards me, not because I have more wisdom than others (Danl 2, 30) nor because I am more righteous than others; but because it so pleased God. H. A.

Hatfield, May 24th, 1676.

This interesting narrative has been long lost and sought for. At length it has been discovered, and can now be traced directly back to the hands of the author. Mr. Atherton never recovered from the effects of his terrible experience, and died June 4th, 1677. His only surviving son, Joseph, settled in Deerfield. The paper was loaned by him to Lieut. Timothy Childs, and was seen in his hands by Ebenezer Grant, who, by leave of Atherton, sent it to Rev. Stephen Williams, who was then preparing his valuable "Appendix" to the "Redeemed Captive." Mr. Williams made a copy of this, and doubtless sent back the original to the owner, according to the conditions of the loan. Who among the Athertons has the *original?*

In 1781, Mr. Williams sends his copy to Pres. Ezra Stiles; and in 1857, Dr. Henry R., son of Ezra Stiles, sends it to Sylvester Judd, and J. R. Trumbull of Northampton has recently found it in the Judd collection of MSS. Mr. Trumbull has kindly sent me a *verbatim* copy, which it seems fitting to print, with the accompanying letter. The story of Jonathan Wells confirms the correctness of Atherton's narrative.

Extract from a letter (dated June 8th, 1781,) of Stephen Williams, to President Styles:—

"In looking over my papers I found a copy of a paper left by the Rev. Hope Atherton, the first minister of Hatfield, who was ordained May 10th, 1670. This Mr. Atherton went out with the forces (commanded by Capt. Turner, captain of the garrison soldiers, and Capt. Holyoke of the county militia) against the Indians at the falls above Deerfield, in May, 1676. In the fight, upon their retreat, Mr. Atherton was unhorsed and separated from the company, wandered in the woods some days and then got into Hadley,* which is on the east side of Connecticut River. But the fight was on the west side. Mr. Atherton gave account that he had offered to surrender himself to the enemy, but they would not receive him. Many people were

---

* This conclusion does not seem warranted by the text.

not willing to give credit to his account, suggesting that he was beside himself. This occasioned him to publish to his congregation and leave in writing the account I enclose to you. I had the paper from which this is copied, from his only son, with whom it was left. The account is doubtless true, for Jonathan Wells, Esq., who was in the fight and lived afterward at Deerfield and was intimately acquainted with the Indians after the war, did himself inform *me* that the *Indians* told *him* that after the fall fight, that a little man with a black coat and without any hat, came toward them, but they were afraid and ran from him, thinking it was the Englishman's God, etc., etc."

The "deep waters" above mentioned were probably the Deerfield river, which he *must* have crossed. Atherton was on the Hatfield side Saturday night; the spies he saw, Sunday morning, would naturally be on the west side. Why should he *cross* the river that was such a "good guide unto" him and would lead him directly home to Hatfield?

After the Falls Fight the English frontiers were carefully covered by guards and scouts under the direction of the Committee of the Militia. A scouting party of which John Hawks was one, reported seeing in the evening of May 22d, Indian fires at the site of the Falls Fight and at the camp on the opposite side of the river. A large force appeared to be there. They had probably been observed by the scouts from the summit of Rocky Mountain at Poets Seat. No Indians, however, were seen about our towns until they came in force.

Attack on Hatfield. May 30th, the enemy appeared at Hatfield with seven hundred warriors and drove the inhabitants within the stockades. Remembering their experience at Northampton, no attempt was made to penetrate the lines; but spreading themselves about they pillaged and burned houses and barns and slaughtered cattle at their will, the inhabitants not daring to sally from their shelter. This condition of affairs being seen at Hadley, twenty-five resolute men crossed the Connecticut in a single boat to their aid. When nearly over they were discovered by the Indians, who, in a futile attempt to prevent a landing, wounded one of the men in the boat.

The Hadley men gallantly fought their way towards the town through the one hundred and fifty Indians who had been attracted by the firing, but were so hard pressed that five were shot down near the fort, and none would have escaped had not Hatfield men sallied out to their succor. The

Indians fought desperately and exposed themselves unusually in this encounter, and lost twenty-five men. As more reinforcements might be expected from adjoining towns, an ambush was laid on the Northampton road, and another party watched the Hadley crossing.

A post had been sent to Hartford, on the return of Capt. Holyoke to Springfield, asking for help, and on the 22d, Capt. Benjamin Newbury was sent up with eighty men, most of whom were now posted at Northampton. On hearing the alarm, Newbury went to the relief of Hatfield, three miles distant. Avoiding the road where the ambush lay, "fearing it beforehand," says the captain, he crossed the Connecticut, marched to Hadley, and attempted to follow the twenty-five volunteers; "but," he says, the enemy "lay so thick about ye landing we could not get to Hatfield." This prudent detour of several miles, and putting a wide river between his men and the enemy, seems better calculated to secure their own safety than to afford relief to beleaguered Hatfield. It is gratifying, however, to note that something had been learned of the tactics of the Indians, even though nothing had been devised to meet them. The Indians at their leisure withdrew up the river, driving all the Hatfield sheep. They had burned twelve houses and barns, destroyed much property, and killed five men, viz: Jobanna Smith of Farmington, Richard Hall of Middletown, John Smith of Hadley—ancestor of the famous Oliver Smith—and two of Capt. Swain's garrison soldiers, whose names are not known, and wounded three—John Stow and Richard Orvis of Connecticut and John Hawks of Hadley. Hawks and Smith had both been in the fight at Turners Falls.

One incident of the day, preserved by tradition, is given as a picture of Indian warfare: Soon after the Hadley men got ashore, a Pocumtuck Indian discovered an old acquaintance behind a tree near him in the person of John Hawks, and hailed him. The recognition was mutual, and each calling the other by name dared him to come out from his cover and fight it out, meanwhile watching his chance for an advantage over his adversary. The Pocumtuck knew that his chances were the best. At any moment he might expect some of the gathering Indians to appear in the rear or on the flank of Hawks's position, forcing him from his cover, and giving an opportunity to shoot or capture him. For this, he could afford to wait. In a short time these expectations seemed about to be realized. Hawks suddenly exposed his person and leveled his gun, as if to repel an attack in another direction. Deceived by this feint, the Pocumtuck sprang from his tree to rush up and capture his ex-friend, as soon as his gun was discharged. Quick as thought Hawks wheeled, and before the Indian could raise his gun or reach his cover gave him a fatal shot. The whole transaction was over in a second or two. The reasoning of Hawks as to his peculiar exposure had been the same as that of his antagonist, and his ready wit suggested the scheme, by which, trusting to steady nerve and quick eye, he might be saved. Hawks was wounded later in the fight, and "lay a wounded man 12 weeks." He and his brother Eleazer were in the Falls Fight on the 19th and both became settlers of this town.

The following extract from a letter by Capt. Benjamin Newbury to Capt. John Allyn at Hartford, is the only account of the event to which it refers that I have met:—

"Sir, on Thursday morning y^r was Alarum at Hadly, his man was shott at goeing to ye mill, and pr'sently after foure men more being sent foreth as a scout to discover, were also shott at by seaven or eight indians and narrowly escaped. The Indians made sevoral shotts at ye mill, but throow God's goodness none was hurt. We being sent [for?] drew all over & together with sevoral of ye town went foreth to ye mill. Saw many tracks and also where ye indians Lay ye Ambushments as we judged, but could not finde ye Indians so as to make anything of it. Some s^d they saw some, but so kept of that we could not come at them. We found where they had newly kild nine horses young and old, and to be feard have driven away sevoral cattle y^t could not be found. I much doubght y^r some effictual course be not taken, much Loss of cattle if ,not of men will soon be in these parts. Our being hear as garrison cannot pr'serue ye cattle, neither can we pursue after to relieve them but with great hazard." [This letter was dated] "Northampton, May 26th, '76."

CLOSE OF PHILIP'S WAR.

Soon after the party which left Squakheag with Philip, April 10th, had reached Wachusett, negotiations for the redemption of the English captives were opened by Gov. Leverett. These resulted in the recovery of several, among whom was Mrs. Rowlandson, who reached Boston May 3d. Philip bitterly opposed the policy of giving up the captives, or of any friendly intercourse with the English, and would have killed their messengers had not Sagamore Sam prevented. The far-sighted Wampanoag feared that this intercourse with the English would end in breaking up the Confederacy, in bringing the war to a close, and in his own destruction. Powerless to prevent it, Philip, with his usual duplicity, sent an evasive letter about the prisoners, pretending a desire for peace, and asking that in the meantime the Indians might not be disturbed in planting on the Nipmuck lands. To give opportunity for this, and gain time until the foliage was dense enough for shelter, was the object of this movement. The letter was also signed by three Nipmucks, and two Narraganset Sachems. One of the former, Sagamore Sam, was really in favor of peace, and would have given up all the captives to obtain it; and to procure those in this valley, he left Wachusett about the middle of May. Events before narrated frustrated his plans, and he returned only to find his wife a prisoner, a raid having been made on his own tribe in his absence. The correspondence of Gov. Leverett with the Indians was kept up several weeks, and a few more captives were redeemed. Meanwhile, with the expectation of peace, part of the English force in the field had been dismissed, and little was done in the prosecution of the war. The General Court becoming satisfied of Philip's real object, wrote to Connecticut on the 26th of May, "We finde the Indians heereabouts doe but dally, & intend not peace, therefore concurr wth you in a vigorous prosecution of them;" that five hundred horse and foot would be on the march towards Wachusett by the first of June, and ask that a "proportionable" force be sent from Connecticut to meet them. On the 5th of June, the Massachusetts troops, under the command of Capt. Samuel Henchman, marched westward from Concord. Within a day or two he surprised a camp of Nipmucks and killed or captured thirty-six, among them the families of Sagamore Sam and other leaders. Henchman reached Marlboro on the 9th and Hadley on the 14th.

Maj. John Talcott, sent by Connecticut to join Henchman in an attack on the enemy about Wachusett, left Norwich June 2d and reached Quabaug the 7th, having killed or captured seventy-three Indians on the way. Two of these, taken near Quabaug, "reported 500 fighting men at Pocumtuck." Not meeting Henchman, nor daring to venture an attack on the fastnesses of Wachusett alone, Talcott pushed on to Hadley, which he reached on the 8th. His force was two hundred and fifty mounted English and two hundred Indians, the latter principally Mohegans under Oneko. The death of Joshua, another son of Uncas, prevented a much larger force of Mohegans from taking the field. Talcott established his headquarters at Northampton, and sent to Hartford for ammunition and other supplies. These were forwarded by Capt. George Dennison, who arrived at Northampton with his company June 10th at midnight. About five hundred and fifty men were now collected at headquarters, and there was great rejoicing among the inhabitants. This joy would have been ten fold greater, could they have foreseen the events of the next two days. Henchman was daily expected, when the whole army would push on up to Pocumtuck.

The slow movements of Henchman from the east were doubtless known to the Indians up the river, while they were ignorant of the march of Talcott and Dennison; and to forestall the arrival of Henchman, Hadley was beset on the 12th by a force of seven hundred warriors.* A strong party was posted at the north end to intercept any English going to the north meadows, or coming from Hatfield; the rest lay at the south end for a similar purpose, and both waited events. The latter party was first discovered. Three men who left the stockade in the morning, contrary to orders, fell among them and were killed. On the alarm, Capt. Jeremiah Swaine, who had succeeded Turner in command, sent out a force against the enemy. While so engaged at the south end, the Indians at the north end rushed from their covert to overrun that part of the town. To their surprise they found the stockades lined with soldiers and Indians, and soon fell back in disorder. They had fired a barn at the outset and got possession of a house. While plundering this on their retreat, it was struck by a missile from a small cannon which sent them tumbling out in great terror. They were pursued northward for two miles, and a few of them killed. This was their last attempt in the valley during the war.

The junction of Capt. Henchman with Talcott at Hadley, June 14th, formed an army of more than one thousand men.

---

*This is the occasion assigned by Gen. Hoyt and Dr. Holland for the mythical appearance of the regicide Goffe in the character of the Guardian Angel of Hadley.

The example of aggressive warfare which the inhabitants had set when forced to self-protection, had been recognized in the counsels of Massachusetts and Connecticut as the true policy, and this force was sent to carry it out. On the morning of the 16th the army moved up the valley, Henchman on the east side of the river and Talcott on the west. No Indians were found at Pocumtuck, and both divisions reached Peskeompskut at night, drenched by a heavy rain. A cold, northeast rain storm had set in, which continued all the 17th and the night following. Much of their provision and ammunition was spoiled, and the main body forced to return on the 18th. Scouts ranged the woods to the west and north, but no enemy were found. One party discovered the body of Capt. Turner, and saw charred stakes where they thought English prisoners had been tortured. About the 20th Major Talcott marched home; and Henchman moved towards the Bay two or three days later. Capt. Swaine, again left in command in the valley, sent a scout of thirty men northward on the 28th, who destroyed a stockaded fort, thirty canoes, and a large quantity of provisions stored in underground barns, and burned one hundred wigwams on Smead's Island.

Not an Indian had been seen in the valley since June 12th. After Turner's attack they had retired up the river, probably to the place provided by Pessacus for such an emergency. They sallied thence to attack Hadley on the 12th. Surprised to find the Connecticut forces there, especially the Mohegans, and disheartened by their repulse, this party returned to their headquarters only to find their camp sacked and fifty of their women and children lying dead amidst the ruins. Their worst fears were now realized. The dreaded Mohawk was upon them. No part of the Connecticut Valley was now tenable. Capt. Henchman, reporting his observations to the Council, June 30th, says:—

Our scouts brought intelligence that all the Indians were in a continual motion, some towards Narraganset, others towards Watchuset, shifting gradually, and taking up each others quarters, and lay not above a night in a Place. The twenty-seven scouts brought in two squaws a boy and a girl, giving account of five slain. Yesterday, they brought in an old fellow, brother to a Sachem, six squaws and children, having killed five men and wounded others, if not killed them, as they supposed by the blood found in the way, and a hat shot through. These and the other inform that Philip and the

THE END DRAWING NEAR. 175

Narragansets were gone several days before to their own places. Philip's purpose being to do what mischief he could to the English.

This vivid picture of the disorganized condition of the Wampanoags and Narragansets, might well apply also to the Nipmucks and Pocumtucks. The former were drifting towards Maine and Canada, while the latter scattered westward, seeking refuge with their old allies, the Mahicans. Caspechy, or Cogepeison, of Springfield, with a small party ventured to Albany, and pretending peace had been made, tried to procure a supply of powder. They were secured by Gov. Andros, but he refused to give them up at the demand of Connecticut.

Fears were now entertained that the Indians who fled to the Hudson would return with recruits. Scouts, therefore, ranged the woods, and guards watched over the laborers in the fields. July 11th, Mr. Russell wrote to the Connecticut Council for more soldiers while "inning the corn;" but it being time of harvest there, also, none could be spared. The grain was secured in safety, and no Indians appeared in the valley until July 19th, when some hundreds were seen near Westfield, going westward. They were pursued by the garrison, and took a southwest course, as if to cross the Hudson at Esopus, "to avoyd the Mohawks." August 11th, another party of two hundred crossed the Connecticut on a raft at Chicopee, and were discovered near Westfield the 12th. The soldiers there fired upon them and recovered a stolen horse. Major Talcott pursued them, and on the 15th overtook them at Hoosatonic river, where he killed or captured fifty-five. By taking this route through the settlements, the fugitives showed more fear of the Mohawks, who were ranging the northern woods, than of the English, who had but a feeble force in the valley.

The condition of things here is well shown in a letter from Pynchon to Gov. Leverett, extracts from which are given below. The news of Philip's death, three days before, had not reached the valley, and Pynchon supposed he had fled westward with those fugitives who crossed the Connecticut the day before.

[SPRINGFIELD, August 15, 1676.]

"When I was at Hartford my cousin Allyn Rec'd a letter f^r Capt. Nichols, governor Andros his Secratary, who writes y^t y^u North Indians y^t came in to them they had Secured by putting y^m under ye watch of .4. Nations of Indians. And he hopes it will not be thought y^t their Govern^t doth Harbor o^r Enemy, inasmuch as we doe accept of such as come to us: But surely it is ye worst of Indians y^t are gone thither, o^r Indians who most Treacherously ruined this Town & some of y^m y^t we know murdered o^r people wthout any provocation, & I suppose Philip is now gone wth y^t Company: So y^t I suppose it may be necessary that Gov. Andros be again sent to to d^{lv} vp ye Murderers, as we drd vp .2. Murderers in Lovelace, his tyme wch fled to Springfield fr^m their Justice. I hope no answer wil be taken short of this for if some the chief of y^m were apprehended & sent to vs all ye rest would be quiet & not till then.

Severall Indians are come in at Norwich & as I hear; they say y^t ye Bay Army killed *Quanapin*, & *Jvmps* or *Allumps* is dead, his wife & children having come in to Norwich: I desire to hear whether *Canonicus* came in ther to Treate & what is become of those Indians [sic] came in? but I am so Troublesome & will not longer detaine you. I Pray g^d give y^o ease & Mitigate y^r Paine & illness * * *

P. S. If it be thought meete & y^o send order for ye releaving of one halfe of ye Soldiers here in Garrison at Springfield, I shall doe it vpon intimation. Possibly it may be meete to leave 18 or 20 till Indian harvest be over for there will be most hazard of sculking Indians about vs."

All fugitives were sheltered by Gov. Andros, and none were ever given up to the New England authorities. The Massachusetts Council passed an order August 12th—the very day on which Philip fell—directing Capt. Swaine to collect the garrison soldiers from all the valley towns and "march to Deerfield, Squakheag, and the places thereabout, and destroy all the growing corn, and then march homeward." The corn here was cut down on the 22d. While so engaged, six Indians were seen on the other side of the Pocumtuck, who discharged their guns in the air. Swaine called to them to come over the river. They did not come, but "hallooing, other Indians answered, and shot off a gun down the river." Not understanding their intentions, and "fearing they might ensnare them," the night coming on, Swaine marched away. This may have been a lingering band of Pocumtucks, who saw with the falling corn their last hope vanish, and were ready to surrender. Their presence, however, was alarming, and Major Pynchon wrote a vigorous letter to the Bay on the 24th, remonstrating against the withdrawal of the soldiers. The Council reply the 28th, that if Connecticut will send a force against the fugitives collecting on the Hudson, Swaine may join them with all his command. The Connecticut Council sent to Gov. Andros on the 19th, asking leave for such an expedition. Andros declined, saying *he* would take care to restrain them. He also refused a demand to deliver up six of the ringleaders, two Pocumtuck and four Nipmuck Sachems, known to be near the Hudson. These refugees were finally incorporated with the Mahicans, and became known as the Scatakooks.

Menowniet, a captive Indian, said "the Indians hid a great many guns about Pocumtuck," and described the place. On the 23d, Lieut. Thomas Hollister, with ten men to escort the prisoner, came up to recover them. The result is not known. On the first of September, the war being considered at an end, Capt. Swaine and all his men were discharged.

THE MOHAWKS IN PHILIP'S WAR.

Judd says that the stories of Mohawk attacks on the hostile Indians were false; and Drake seems to give them little credence. The reported facts lead me to an opposite conclusion. The contemporary correspondence on the war, and its early historians, often allude to stories of Mohawk hostilities. A careful collation and comparison of these notes with undisputed facts, tends strongly to prove their truth, and gives the key to many otherwise unexplained events. Continual aggressive acts of the Mohawks are clearly shown in the spring and summer of 1676. They drove Philip and the Pocumtucks from the Hoosick river in February. They cut off the messengers sent from Squakheag to Canada with prisoners to exchange for powder, in March. The cry of "Mohawks! Mohawks!" when surprised by Turner, May 19th, shows the allies felt they had more reason to expect an attack from that enemy than from the English. The attack on their camp June 12th, noted by Mather and Hubbard, is proved by the letter of Andros, July 5th. The Mohawks having made several forays on our west frontiers in June without discovering any Indians, suspected peace had been made, and complained that the English had closed the war without notifying them. Some knowledge of the correspondence between the belligerents, already given, had probably reached them, and explanation was necessary.

July 8th, the Connecticut Council of War sent the Mohawks word through Gov. Andros that they may "be fully assured that we have made no peace with the Indians, neither is there at present anything amongst us looking that way." Then follows a detailed account of the offensive operations of the troops and plans for the future, with the request that they also "would speedily prosecute them in those northern parts above Suckquackheag and farther up the river, eastward from the river, about Wachuset." They also advise about a sign to distinguish them from the enemy, and think some "yellow cloath may be best." They point out the haunts of the enemy and suggest definite arrangements for the conduct of the Mohawks when approaching the English frontiers with war parties. This style of correspondence would hardly be held with a neutral or indifferent power.

The Council ordered that Major Talcott and Capt. Mason "advise with Uncas concerning the sending a present up to the Mohawks, and what may be a suitable present." The messenger, sent by Andros July 5th, said that the Mohawks had killed one hundred and forty of the enemy, and on the day of his departure three hundred Mohawk warriors moved this way in search of the enemy. The route of the fugitives flying westward in July and August, shows their fear of the old enemy. Other reasons and authorities might be given, but may it not be seen from the above that the Mohawks were an important factor in Philip's war?

Many of the soldiers who came here during Philip's war remained as settlers at its close, and gave a character to the population of this valley. At least seven of those on Turner's roll of April 7th, and twelve who served under him later, became residents of Deerfield. To these men, the families of Arms, Bardwell, Barrett, Field, Hawks, Hoyt, Mattoon, Wells and others may look for their ancestry. Of others on the same rolls of honor whose namesakes came among us we find the names of Alexander, Atherton, Belden, Chapin, Clapp, Clark, Clesson, Conable, Hinsdale, Hunt, Kellogg, King, Lyman, Miller, Morgan, Munn, Nims, Pomroy, Price, Scott, Selden, Smead, Smith, Stebbins, Sutlief, Taylor and Wait.

CHAPTER VII.

ATTEMPTED SETTLEMENT OF 1677.

The men of Pocumtuck who had escaped the storms of Philip's war, scattered in the towns below, anxiously awaited an opportunity of returning to cultivate their lands and gather their families under roof-trees of their own. A short time after the death of Philip, the hopeful Quintin Stockwell began to build a house on the Willard lot, his old home; but this was soon in ashes. In the spring of 1677, this persevering man, with a few other bold adventurers, again returned to Pocumtuck. Here they planted their fields in quiet and proceeded to build houses. They were cheerful, hopeful and helpful to each other. A house was put up for Sergt. John Plympton " 18 feet long." Of his six children, one had died in peace; one slept at Bloody Brook, and four were settled in homes of their own. This small house was large enough for the sergeant and his "old wife Jane." Stockwell hoped his third attempt would provide a shelter for his wife and babe before the winter set in. John Root, thirty-one years old, had married the widow of Samuel Hinsdale, a victim at Bloody Brook. He thus became the protector of a helpless flock, for whom he was making ready a home on the Russell lot, the spot where they were born. Benoni Stebbins, cheerily working to secure a dwelling place for his bride, the widow of James Bennett,—who was lost with Capt. Turner—was probably engaged on the Samuel Wells lot, where his house was burned and he killed Feb. 29th, 1704. Philip Mattoon, another young man, was about to pitch his tent here. July 31st, 1677, he made a bargain with John Pynchon, by which he could secure a home for his bride, and Sept. 10th, he married Sarah, daughter of John Hawks of Hadley. The attempt at settlement failing, Mattoon came here later, and here died in 1696. This contract, the oldest met with, is given as illustrating in several points the condition of business affairs among the pioneers. It is found in John Pynchon's account book.

July 21, 1677. Let out to Philip Mattoon my 18 cow commons and 4 sheep commons at Pocumtuck, all the intervale land belonging to s^d commons, (excepting the home lot which is already disposed of) according as it is laid out in several divisions, towards the upper end of Pocumtuck Meadows, for 11 years from the first of March next, to pay all rates, taxes and charges, make & leave good fences, to build on the land a good dwelling house, strong, substantial & well built, & compleatly finished, 30 ft long, 20 ft wide & 10 ft stud. Also a barn at least 48 ft long, 24 ft wide & 14 ft stud, well braced, all pts to be strong, substantial & workmanlike, & to compleate & finish the same before the end of the term, & then leave & deliver up all in good repair. He is also to pay thirty shillings a year for nine years, £3 the tenth, and £4 the last year. He is to have the use of two cows between the ages of four and seven years, & return two of like ages.

Other men may have been here, but the only other person known was Samuel, son of Philip Russell, a lad of eight years.

Two years and a day had passed since the blow fell at Bloody Brook, which "made 8 persons widows and 26 children fatherless in this Plantation." It was the soft evening twilight of Sept. 19th, 1677. The labors of the day were ended. The tired workmen were awkwardly preparing their suppers about their camp fire, chatting hopefully perhaps of the future, when this service should be more deftly performed by their helpmates, when they were rudely interrupted and amazed by the whistling of bullets, the crash of musketry, the wild war-whoop and furious rush of a band of savages who seemed springing from the ground all around them. Stockwell rushed down the hill into the swamp. He was seen, pursued and fired upon. He "slumped and fell down" in the mire. One of the pursuers thinking he was wounded came up to tomahawk him. Stockwell kept him at bay with an empty pistol. The Indian told him they "had destroyed all Hatfield and the woods were full of Indians," but assured him of safety if he would yield. Whereupon, Stockwell surrendered. Plympton, Stebbins, Root and Russell also fell into their hands. Root was soon killed, and after an ineffectual attempt to take the frightened horses of the settlers, the captives were led away into the woods on East Mountain. There, to their astonishment, and with mingled feelings of joy and sadness, they found seventeen Hatfield people, likewise captives. Here Samuel Russell met several of his playmates and learned that his mother and little brother had been murdered at home, and the doleful tale of that morning's work of horror was told.

About eleven o'clock, this same party had surprised a few men who were raising a house at the north end of Hatfield, and shot three men from the frame; they then attacked and burned several houses outside the palisades and killed or captured most of their occupants, and hurried off in triumph.

The killed were Isaac Graves and his brother John; John Atchison, John Cooper, Elizabeth Russell and son Stephen; Hannah Coleman and her babe Bethiah; Sarah Kellogg and her baby boy; Mary Belding, and Elizabeth Wells, daughter of John. Her mother and another child were wounded, as were Sarah Dickinson and a child of John Coleman, but they all escaped. The captured were Obadiah Dickinson and child; Martha, wife of Benjamin Waite, with their children, Mary, six years old, Martha, four, and Sarah, two; Mary, wife of Samuel Foote, their children, Nathaniel, and Mary, three; Sarah Coleman, four, with another child of John Coleman; Hannah, wife of Stephen Jennings, with two of her children by Samuel Gillett, between three and six years old; Samuel Kellogg, eight, Abigail Allis, six, and Abigail Bartholomew of Deerfield, five.

The assailants were a party of twenty-six Indians from Canada, under Ashpelon; one was a Narraganset, the others Pocumtucks. With the captives they retreated hurriedly up the river. On reaching this vicinity, the smoke of their camp fires may have betrayed the settlers, and another prize was easily secured.

The captives were bound, and the march to far-off Canada began. They were the first party of whites ever taken on the sad journey, so often traveled in years to come. In scattered order they traversed the woods northward, the captors imitating the voices of beasts and birds that they should not lose one another, or be discovered by the English, if followed. They halted for the night near the mouth of Hearthstone brook, and at daybreak crossed Connecticut river at Sheldon's rocks. From this place ten men were sent back to the town, who returned with about ten horses loaded with corn and other provisions. Here they marked on trees, as was their custom, the number of killed and captured. Continuing their march, they crossed the river again at Peskeompskut and camped for the night a few miles above. Here the captives were "staked down," and told the Indian law was to do this for nine successive nights. They were "spread out on their backs," the arms and legs stretched out and fastened to the ground with stakes, and a cord tied about the neck, so that they "could stir noways." Stockwell says, "the first night of staking down, being much tired, I slept as comfortable as ever." On the 21st, the party crossed the river to Northfield. Here they stopped awhile, but when their scouts reported English soldiers in pursuit, they went over the river again and scattered on the west side.

These soldiers were a party sent up from Hartford under Capt. Thomas Watts, Lieut. John Mawdsley and Ensign John Wyatt, with John Hawks and some others of the Hampshire men who joined. This party returned after going forty miles above Hadley, without finding the marauders.

Ashpelon's party went up the river perhaps as far as Putney, Vt., and crossed to the east side, where they were "quite out of all fear of the English but in great fear of the Mohawks." Here they built a long wigwam and had a great dance, preparatory to burning some of the captives. Ashpelon and others opposing, this ceremony was given up. From here, a small party went to Hadley; they were discovered near the mill, and captured or gave themselves up. They declared they came to make arrangements for the redemption of the captives, which is not unlikely. They were released after an agreement to meet the English on a certain plain in Hadley, on Sunday, Oct. 14th. To attend this meeting, Major Treat came up from Hartford with forty men "to lend his advice and grant assistance in defending the plantations, and the persons as shall be appointed to treat, in the best way and manner as they can. That all due endeavours be used for the redemption of the captives, by paying a sume of money or other goods; probably a quantity of liquors may not be amiss to mention in the tender." All this preparation was thrown away. Not an Indian appeared. The reasons will be seen.

When Ashpelon left Canada, a party of Nipmucks were in

company. Somewhere on the route they parted from him, apparently fixing on Nashua ponds as a rendezvous. The same day on which Ashpelon struck Hatfield, the Nipmucks reached the place where Wonalonset, with eight men and some fifty women lived. He was a Pennacook Sachem, who had been neutral through Philip's War. Partly by persuasion and partly by force, he was induced to remove to Canada, and the whole party moved towards Lancaster. Meanwhile, Ashpelon sent messengers to notify the Nipmucks to come to him on the Connecticut. With these went Benoni Stebbins. On the return of the party, Stebbins escaped about Oct. 2d, from a point near Templeton and reached Hadley on the 4th. As a consequence of this act, the English prisoners were all in danger of torture, and it was only through the kindness and policy of Ashpelon that this fate was averted. A short time before, the Indians taken and released at Hadley had returned; and the question of the meeting at Hadley, for which they had arranged, was under discussion. The captives urged it, Ashpelon was in favor of it, and it was proposed to send Wonalonset as agent. The Nipmuck Sachems were opposed to the policy. "They were willing to meet the English, indeed, but only to fall upon them and fight them and take them." The peace policy being overruled, Ashpelon advised the captives "not to speak a word more to further that matter, for mischief would come of it."

About October 20th the whole party moved towards Canada. Samuel Russell and little Mary Foote were killed by the way; the rest straggled into French or Indian towns about the first of January. Soon after, old Sergt. Plympton was burnt to death at the stake.

Since the opening of Philip's war, in Hampshire County alone two hundred and seven persons had been killed and forty wounded.

WAITE AND JENNINGS'S EXPEDITION.

When Capt. Watts returned from the pursuit northward with no tidings of the captives, it was generally thought that the Mohawks were the guilty ones, as a small party of that tribe were at Hatfield the day before; and Benjamin Waite, whose whole family was swept away, determined to seek them westward. He traversed the wilderness over the Hoosac Mountain, but found no trace of the marauders. At Albany he became satisfied that the Mohawks were innocent. Returning with letters for Pynchon from Capt. Salisbury, commander at Albany, he reached Springfield Oct. 4th. Without a day's delay he pushed on to Boston, bearing a petition from Hatfield asking authority and aid for an expedition to Canada. The petition was granted, and on the 12th Waite was appointed agent. The very day Waite left the valley for Boston, Benoni Stebbins came in, and Pynchon at once dispatched a post to Capt. Salisbury, urging him to incite the Mohawks to pursue Ashpelon's party, "their old enemy and ours," with a promise of reward for the service. "Ben. Waite," he says, "is gone home before the Intelligence came to me. He talked of goeing to Canada before, and I suppose will rather be Forward to it now, than Backward." Pynchon judged the indomitable man rightly. He would never pause until he found his hapless family. With this object, neither distance, climate nor foe had terrors for him. Stephen Jennings, a like-minded man, also bereaved of wife and children, now joined Waite in this knightly quest.

With letters for the authorities in Albany and Canada, the men set out from Hatfield October 24th, and reached Albany the 30th. Here in an interview with Salisbury they were coldly received, and directed to wait upon him again. The impatient men, however, pushed on to Schenectady to procure an Indian guide. Here the old jealousy of New England appeared, and upon the most stupid pretext they were arrested and sent back to Albany, and finally to New York, for an examination before Gov. Brockholds. Through this vexatious hindrance, while every hour seemed a day, it was not until Dec. 10th, that these harassed men were able to resume their journey. Six weeks of precious time had been given to smooth the ruffled dignity of Commander Salisbury.

Now, with a Mohawk for a guide, the adventurers turned their faces toward a northern winter and an unknown wilderness. The Indian left them on reaching Lake George, and with no clue but a rough chart which he drew for them on a piece of birch bark, these men of tender hearts and iron will pushed forward on their chivalrous errand. At the lake they found an old bark canoe, which the Mohawk had patched up;

this they dragged over the snow, or paddled through the icy waves of the lake, as necessity compelled. Were they cold or hungry, the thought that their wives and little ones might be freezing or starving urged them forward. With the birch bark chart in hand, they toiled day after day over the dreary wastes, until on New Year's day they reached the foot of Lake Champlain. Following the river Sorel, they passed the French outpost at Shambly, and soon after Jennings was rewarded by finding his wife—a meeting to be imagined only. It was not long before the surviving captives were found, all in the hands of the Indians, save a few who had been pawned to Frenchmen for liquor. In a few days the travelers set out for Quebec, one hundred miles down the St. Lawrence. They were kindly received by Governor Frontenac, and by his help the ransom of thé whole party was effected by the payment of £200.

On the 22d of January, before Waite could have returned from Quebec, his wife gave birth to a child, who was named *Canada*. Fifty days later a girl was born to Jennings, and named *Captivity*.

Slowly the long Canada winter wore away, and on the 2d of May the whole party left Sorel and joyfully turned their faces homeward. An escort of French soldiers was sent by Frontenac as far as Albany, where they arrived on the 22d. From Albany, letters were posted to Hatfield. These letters, which are given below, gave the first news of the captives since the escape of Benoni Stebbins, and caused great rejoicing, mingled with sorrow for the fate of those who came not back.

ALBANY, May 22, 1678.

LOVING WIFE:—Hauing now opportunity to remember my kind loue to the and our child and the rest of our freinds, though wee met with greate afflictions and trouble since I see thee last, yet now here is opportunity of joy and thanksgiving to God, that wee are now pretty well, and in a hopeful way to see the faces of one another before we take our finall farewell of this present world, likewise God hath raised us freinds amongst our enemies, and there is but 3 of us dead of all those that were taken away—Sergt. Plympton, Samuel Russell, Samuel Foot's daughter. So I conclude, being in hast, and rest your most affectionate husband till death makes separation,

QUINTIN STOCKEWELL.

From ALBANY, May 23, 1678.

TO MY LOVING FRIENDS & KINDRED AT HATFIELD:—These few

lines are to let you understand that we are arrived at Albany now with the captives, and we now stand in need of assistance, with my charges is very greate and heavy; and therefore any that hath any love to our condition, let it moove them to come and help us in this straight. There is 3 of ye captives that are murdered—old Goodman Plympton, Samuel Foot's daughter, Samuel Russell. All the rest are alive and well now with me at Albany, namely, Obadiah Dickenson and his child, Mary Foote and her child, Hannah Gennings and 3 children, Abigail Ellice, Abigail Bartholomew, Goodman Coleman's children, Samuel Kellogg, my wife and four children and Quintin Stockwell.* I pray you hasten the matter, for it requireth greate hast. Stay not for ye Sabbath, nor shoeing of horses. We shall endeavour to meete you at Canterhook, it may be at Houseatonock. We must come very softly because of our wives and children. I pray you, hasten them, stay not night nor day, for ye matter requireth great hast. Bring provisions with you for us.

Your loving kinsman,
BENJAMIN WAITE.

At Albany, written from myne owne hand. As I have bin affected to yours, all that were fatherless, be affected to me now, and hasten ye matter and stay not, and ease me of my charges. You shall not need to be afraid of any enemies.

These letters, warm from the heart, reached the heart of the whole colony. They were copied by John Partridge, who, in company with John Plympton, son of the tortured captive, carried the copies to Medfield. Rev. Mr. Wilson at once sent them to the Governor at Boston with the following letter:—

Worshipful S^r
humbly presenting my humblest Servic to yor wor^{ps} keeping with these letters Copy^d out and newly brought fr^m Hadly by one John Partridge and not understanding of any Couriers to the Bay besydes: I have written out of these two Copys word for word as I take it & make bold to send it to your Worship:
y^t so you might be enformed of the Mercy of God in ye return of these Captives so far as ye two letters set Down. John Partridge and John Plimpton come in this night & none with y^m but a young mayde so y^t I suppose yor Worsh^p will have ye very first view of ye News in Boston being very crasy am unfit to enlarge & y^t I might not trouble your Worsh^p further

With my humble Servecs presented to you^r most virtuous Lady humbly reste

Your Worsh^s most humble
Servant   John Wilson

Medfield, May 29–78

A fast had been appointed for June 6th. The Governor received the letters May 29th, and the next day sent copies

---

* There is 2 or 3 frenchmen Embassadors coming to go to Boston. This sentence was erased. These men may have been stopped by Pynchon in the valley.

of Waite's letter to all the churches, to be read from the pulpit on that occasion, with a recommendation that a contribution for the benefit of the captives be taken up in every congregation. "And the ministers are desired to stir up the people thereunto. For quickening this work we do hereby remit a copy of Benjamin Waite's letter to be read publickly." This touching appeal of Waite was generously responded to,* and many an offering dropped on the altar of charity that day was sanctified by tears. Who shall say that the gratitude engendered in the hearts of Benjamin and Martha Waite by the outpouring of that day was not nursed in the hearts of their descendants, until it bore fruit in that act of *Oliver Smith*, from whence flows the broad stream of charity which to-day blesses, and shall forever bless, the widow and fatherless in this valley!

"They remained in Albany five days," says Judd, "and on Monday, May 27th, walked twenty-two miles to Kinderhook, where they met men and horses from Hatfield." With the tired women, and, besides the two babes, twelve children under eight, the statement that they walked to Kinderhook, seems improbable. Did not Waite procure horses at Albany? and was not this expense, "charges" from which he sought "relief" by meeting horses from Hatfield? Judd continues, "They rode through the woods to Westfield, and soon all reached Hatfield in safety. The day of their arrival was one of the most joyful days that Hatfield ever knew."

The attempt to resettle the town in 1677 was not a rash, unconsidered affair, but fully in accord with public opinion and State policy. The catastrophe here did not change that policy, but it incited to greater caution.

October 22d, 1677, the General Court ordered the towns to "endeavour the new moddelling the scittuation of their houses, so as to be more compact, and liue nearer together for their better defense;" and a committee was appointed for Hampshire:—

"To ord^r and contrive the same * * * and as a further provisions for the security of those townes, it is ordered, that a garrison be stated at Deerefield, and for effecting the same, it is ordered that the inhabitants of that place doe repayre thither this winter, (if the com-

---

* In the church at Dorchester " £8 5s 6d in money " was contributed " after ye evening exersiz."

itee doe judge it safe) and provide for the settling thereof in the spring, which shallbe in a compact way, as ordered by the comittee, and this winter, stuff for fortiffication to be prouided, ready to be sett up there in the spring, viz, in March or Aprill ; at which time twenty soudjers shall be sent up by the Gouner & council to that place as they shall see cause, whose worke & care shallbe, to preserue & secure that place, & those adjoining there from the Indyans.

At the same date, six soldiers were ordered to Hatfield, to be under Lieut. Allis, and employed in the winter time in getting out timber for the fortifications at Hatfield and Deerfield. Maj. Pynchon was directed to treat with Connecticut about joining "in keeping the garrison at Deareffield." The six soldiers were sent to Hatfield, but no evidence is found that anything was done *here* during the winter of 1677–8. The "Comittee" probably did "not judge it safe."

CHAPTER VIII.

PERMANENT SETTLEMENT.

The settlers driven away in 1675 still called themselves "inhabitants," and at no time gave up their intention of returning as a community to their old homes. In addition to the inevitable delay, a new trouble had come upon them, the danger of losing their beloved minister. The condition of affairs is fully shown in the following petition:—

To the honoured Generall Court of the Matachusetts Bay now seting in Boston ye 8th 3, '78 : Rigt Worshipfull :

We the small Remnant that are left of Dearfield's poor inhabitants (that desolate place) hauing mett with a smile from your Honors the last General Court, by the merciful tender you made unto us of garison men for our assistance, we are therby Incouraged & Imboldened (under great hopes of acceptance) to prostrate ourselves at yor Worship's feett in this o^r sorrowful complaints & fervent desires.

We doe veryly hope that your thoughts are soe upon us & our condition, that it will be little better than superfluous to tell you ; that our estates are wasted, that we find it hard work to Live in this Iron age, & to Come to the years end with Comfort ; to tell you that our housen have been Rifled & then burnt, our flocks and heards Consumed, the ablest of our Inhabitants killed ; y^t our Plantation has become a wildernesse, a dwelling for owls and a pasture for flocks, & we that are left are separated into several townes. Also our Reverand & esteemed minister, Mr. Samuel Mather, hath been Invited from us, & great danger ther is of o^r loosing of him ; all which speaks us a people in a very miserable condition, & unlest you will be pleased to take us (out of your fatherlike pitty) and Cherish us in yor Bosomes, we are like Suddainly to breathe out o^r Last Breath. Right Honoured, the Committie appointed to manage o^r affairs for us, the Rev. Mr. Mather, who hath not yet quitt forsaken us, and we the Remaining Inhabitants, Joyntly doe desire that we might returne and plant that place again. Yet we would earnestly begg (may it stand with the pleasure of Infinite Goodness) that we may Repossess the said plantation with great Advantage Both for the advancing the cause and kingdome of Jesus, and for o^r own saftie & comfort than ever we have heretofore.

You may be pleased to know that the very principle & best of the land ; the best for soile ; the best for situation ; as lying in ye centre & midle of the town : & as to quantity, nere half, belongs unto eight or 9 proprietors each and every of which, are never like to come to a settlement amongst us, which we have formerly found grevious & doe Judge for the future will be found intollerable if not altered. O^r minister, Mr. Mather, (that is still waiting to see what alteration may be made), & we ourselves are much discouraged as judging the Plantation will be spoiled if thes proprietors may not be begged, or will not be bought up on very easy terms outt of their Right. O^r designe (the Lord permitting & yor Worships helping) is to go when such a number of Inhabitants as (we hope) may be able to afford matter for a church; we have it from ye Rev. Mr. Mather, that if the place was free from that Incumberments, he could find a sufficient number of men, pious & discreet, that would enter Into ye plantation with him to build up a church in the place; Butt as long as the maine of the plantation Lies in men's hands that can't improve it themselves, neither are ever like to putt such tenants on to it as shall be likly to advance the good of ye place in Civill or sacred Respects; he, ourselves, and all others that think of going to it, are much discouraged. We would therefore humb^{le} beg of this Generall Court that some expedient way might be found out to Remove that impediment that is so great a Lett & hindrance to the plantation's growth & ye planters' outward happiness—pittie it is, that a plantation soe circumstanced should lie desolate.

All Judicious men that have any acquaintance with it, Count It as Rich a tract of land as any upon the river; they Judge it sufficient to entertain & maintain as great number of Inhabitants as most of the upland townes, alsoe were it well peopled it would be as a bulwark to the other townes; also it would be a great disheartening to the enemie, & veryly (not to make to bold with your worship's patience) It would mightily Incourage and Raise the hearts of us the Inhabitants, yor poor & Impoverished servants. Thus begging yor pardon for o^r boldnesse, waiting for the Result of yor Judicious mind, and again earnestly beging, humbly Intreating, with greatest importunity, that something may be done to remove the fore said Impediments; and for the building the plantation Before this court be ended.

Soe we rest, praying yor honors' happinesse; and subscribing ourselves with the Committe Consenting, and subscribing yor devoted and humble servants this 30th of Ap'l, '78.

MOSES CRAFTS,	
RICHARD WELLARD,	in the name
WILLIAM SMEDE,	of the rest.
WILLIAM BARTH'MEW,	
WILLIAM ALLIS,	
THOMAS MEEKINS,	The hands
SAMUEL SMITH,	of y^e
PETER TILLTON,	Committee.

Oct. 1678. In ans^r to the petition of the remayning inhabitants of Deerefield, the court judgeth it meete to referr the peticoners to the proprietors for the attayning of their interest, so farr as they shall judge necessary, leaving ye matter wth the Comittee to regulat ; improvements & charges to be levyed thereupon, as they shall judge legall & meete, for the encouraging the rebuilding of that plantation.

At the same session the soldiers at Hatfield were ordered home. In May, 1679, the General Court directed that no town should be resettled except by the consent of a committee appointed by the Council, or county court having jurisdiction in the premises. Such committee are to be "at the charge of the people intending to settle." It is made their duty to order "in what form, way & maner such towne shallbe settled & erected, wherein they are required to haue a principal respect to neerness and conveniency of habitation for security against enemyes, & more comfort for Xtian comunion and enjoyment of God's worship & education of children in schools & civility." A fine of £100 was the penalty for disobedience of this order. Under this act, upon the petition of some of the proprietors, the county court, March 30th, 1680, appointed "Lieutt. William Clerk, Mr. Peter Tilton, Lieutt. Philip Smith, Medad Pumry and Jno. Allice, all of which, or any three of them, Lieutt. William Clerk, or Mr. Tilton being one, to be a Comity for ye work," of resettling this town. Nothing further appears to have been done at this time. Mr. Mather, after declining repeated invitations, became at length discouraged, and in 1680 accepted a call to Brainford, Conn.

In addition to the land troubles indicated in the petition of 1678, the uncertain condition of the Indian affairs was another cause of delay in a resettlement. The Indians had been expelled but not subdued. They had never, as a body submitted in form to the English. Individuals had returned to their old haunts, and others were seeking conditions on which they might follow. With such, the county court was authorized in May, 1680, to make definite arrangements. Although no treaty of peace was made with any of the hostile tribes, Philip's War really closed with the capture of Anawon by Church, August, 1676. For several years, however, there was a general distrust, and apprehension of danger to isolated settlements. The attitude of the Mohawks was not well understood. Their incursions, invited in 1676, continued after the war closed. Friendly Indians were harassed, and some depredations made on the stock of the settlers. These things had in a measure been winked at by the authorities, in consideration of the importance of keeping peace with this powerful tribe. At length, when these "insolencyes & outrages" could no longer be endured, Maj. Pynchon was sent to demand redress. He left Springfield for Albany Oct. 13th, 1680, with a suitable retinue. A meeting was held there, Nov. 9th, in the presence of Capt. Brockholds, the commander. The Mohawks were very diplomatic. They said they had acted only against supposed enemies of the English, pretending that they did not know the war had closed. On the 19th [?] another meeting was held, at which the old treaty was renewed: and no further trouble was anticipated or felt, at the hands of the Mohawks.

As soon as the news of this treaty was received, a meeting of the Proprietors of Pocumtuck was warned to be held at Northampton, Dec. 12th, 1680, and measures were at once taken to forward the reoccupation of their lands. The men named by the county court, May 30th, 1680, to have charge of this work, will hereafter be designated as the "Committee," simply; and the owners of the 8000 acres, who took the title of the "Proprietors of Pocumtuck, alias Deerfield," will be called the "Proprietors." These bodies acted independently, meeting together, or separately, as was most convenient. Neither at first had a book for records. At Proprietors' meetings, propositions to be acted upon were generally made in writing. If adopted, each slip of paper was laid before the Committee, and its approval or veto was endorsed thereon. The slips were then taken by those whom they concerned. Such of these votes as could be collected at a subsequent period, were transcribed, some of them many years after the event; and the Town Record for this period is thus made up. It was done without a full sense of the importance of chronological order, or consecutive action. Indeed, many of the votes are without date, and a large portion was doubtless entirely lost. Hence, our earlier records are imperfect, obscure, and liable to mislead one as to the order of events. Sources of information beside the Town Record for this period, are General Court Records of Massachusetts and Connecticut, County Court Records, and the manuscript archives of the State.

The actual date of the permanent reoccupation of the

SETTLERS WHO COME TO STAY.

town cannot be fixed with certainty. The spring of 1682 is assumed to be the time of the arrival of those named hereafter as first " Permanent Settlers." The evidence leading to this conclusion will be found below in the course of the narrative.

A meeting of the Committee and Proprietors to promote the settling of Deerfield, was held at Northampton, Dec. 12th, 1680. The only action known, was "granting to Thomas Hastings seven cow commons, likewise to David Hoite six cow commons, and to Samuel Field, six cow commons, all which grants of land is thus to be understood, [that is] they are to haue Lieft. Allis's land that was granted to him there, divided amongst them three, and the rest to make up their grants or quantity [of land] in some other convenient place." [Lieut. Wm. Allis had died September, 1678.] Martin Smith had six acres added to a former grant of six acres.

Some doubt seems to have arisen as to the authority of the Committee, for in May, 1681, their appointment was confirmed by the General Court.

March 6th, 1681-2. The Committee and Proprietors decide that one condition of the grants shall be the occupancy by the grantee personally, for four years.

March 30th, 1682, grants were made of seven cow commons each, to Samuel Davis and Joshua Pomeroy, to lie on the north side of Deerfield river, below the mouth of Green river; and home lots of four acres each, to Davis, Pomeroy, Lieut. Clark, Samuel Field, David Hoite and Martin Smith.

The petitioners of 1678, getting no relief from the General Court, appealed to the owners of the land. They seemed to have been favorably received, and by some or all of them every tenth acre was given into a common stock, to be used in promoting the settlement.

May 22d, 1682, " Richard Weller & other inhabitants of Deerfield," sent a petition to the General Court the import of which, as judged by the reply, was, that this provision might be made to cover the estate of deceased owners. The answer to the petition was:—

> The Court not being sattisfied that they may give away other proprietjes wthout their consent, yet being desirous to doe what may promote the setling sajd plantation, doe commend it to the rest of the proprietors to follow the good example of those that haue given vp

euery tenth acre, or otheruise, as they shall see cause, it being a very probable way to gaine more vsefull inhabitants for planting & setling sajd place ; and as for the orphants, whose right & propriety[s] are not to be made voyd by this Court, but rather secured for them, or that which maybe as good for them, the Court judgeth it meet that they choose their guardians, who may act for them, referring to those orphants lands as such guardians judg best for securing the orphants estate wth respect to the furthering, promoting the planting, & speedy setling of sajd plantation ; and for such children as are not capable of choosing guardians, the County Court for Hampshire are to make supply in appointing guardians who may act for them accordingly : and this order of Court to be their warrant in so doing, and security to such guardians hauing allowanc & approbation of the County Court therein.

The action under this terse and lucid order was probably satisfactory, as nothing more is heard on the subject to which it relates.

Quintin Stockwell presented to the Committee a bill of ten pounds, "due from the former inhabitants of Deerfield for boarding Mr. Mather;" and the Committee "desired ye now inhabitants to give him some land in satisfaction for ye debt." Agents were chosen by the inhabitants, who agreed with Stockwell for twenty acres on Green river, "bounded northerly on ye hill on ye north side of ye Brook y^t comes out of ye great ash swamp; easterly upon ye hill on ye east side of Green river and westerly on the west swamp & so to run southerly to make up ye quantity of twenty acres."

For this land Stockwell gave a receipt, November 24th, 1684. He was then living at Suffield, Conn.

January 6th, 1684-5. The Committee allowed the above grant. At the same meeting, the Committee ordered John Hawks, Thomas Wells and Joshua Pomeroy to

"measure men's allotments at Deerfield and to bring in an account of what land is wanting in every man's allotment which being done these three men with Joseph Barnard and Jona. Wells joyning them shall haue full power to look out land where it may be found in any of ye common land and to lay out to such as want land as neere as they can to each man's want; * * * and in order to satisfaction they are to cast lots where to begin and which shall be the first 2d and 3d percells, and where to begin each percell."

The lots, as we have seen, had been drawn at Dedham. They were laid out by measuring the width only of each lot in the several divisions, according to the number of cow commons owned by each party. The area of these lots often fell short of the amount to which the owner was entitled. Hence, this deficiency was called "wanting land." At Boggy Meadow, two hundred and twenty-four acres, on the east side of the Bars road, were granted for wanting land—usually three acres for one—to Thomas Hunt, Henry White, Jona. Church, Samuel Carter, William Smead and Joseph Gillett. Some of the lots ran from the meadow fence ninety-two rods south, to Long hill. West of the road, grants were made to Thomas Hurst, the heirs of Nathaniel Sutlief, and Ephraim Hinsdell. John Sheldon had the island near Red rocks, called eight acres. Daniel Belding, forty acres at Wisdom, still known as "Belding's grant;" Samuel Northam, twelve acres on East Mountain, "at or near the head of the first swamp or brook lying against the middle of the town platt." This was in lieu of seven acres want, in the meadow. Whether the "Northam's Grant" of to-day covers the seprecise acres is not certain.

For keeping up a meadow gate at Wapping, Ephraim Beers had twenty acres joining Northam. For various reasons, John Evans had eight acres at the mouth of Hearthstone brook; John Broughton, a lot in the "Elbow at New forte;" John Sheldon and William Smead, eight acres each "on the Fort Hill, which lies at the east end of the meadow land, over Eagle Brook and without the meadow fence."

Godfrey Nims, for five acres want, had fourteen acres "at the south end of the commonly called Martins Meadow: that to be his south line: to run in length from the Grate river to the Grate hill & so take his breadth northerly." At the same place grants amounting to about one hundred and thirty-five acres were made to Henry White, Rev. John Russell, Joseph Barnard, Jona. Church and Simon Beaman.

Ensign Thomas Wells had "40 acres of land by the Grate river; beginning at the south end of that little meadow and below the meadow commonly called Martins Meadows to run in length from the Grate river to the Grate hill; the south end of s^d little meadow to be his south line to run in bredth northerly." At the same place, northerly in succession, grants were made to the heirs of Barnabas Hinsdell, Moses Crafts, and John Evans, amounting to about 110 acres. These two localities have not been exactly identified. Martin Smith had twelve acres on the great river in 1680. This not being easy of access for cultivation, it was exchanged for a lot of the same area on the hill above New Fort, not far from "Martins Falls." It is not improbable that he lived on "Martins Hill." Smaller lots, usually joining lands of the grantee, were given to John Catlin, Simon Beaman, Henry White, John Weller, John Broughton, Timothy Nash, Thomas Wells, Edward Allen, John Allen, James Brown, John Williams and others.

"For the frame of a house, formerly Barnabas Hensdells, which was bought of the administrator, by the former inhabitants of Deerfield," his heirs had twenty acres below Martins Meadow. Hinsdale was killed with Lothrop, and this frame must have escaped destruction in Philip's War.

Feb. 5th, 1686-7, at a meeting of the inhabitants, Lieut. Thomas Wells, Henry White and Thomas French, were made choice of to measure the common fence and to lay out to every proprietor his due proportion. The list below is given because it contains the names of all who owned land in the Common Field with the amount of fence set to each on the basis of "two Rhods to ye common, or eleven foot to y^t acre."

	rds	ft	in		rds	ft	in
Allison, Thos	13	11		Hensdell, Bar'bas	21	26	
Allen, Jn's [heirs]	32			Hensdell, Jn	15		
Allyn, Mr Dan'l	32			Hensdell, Sam,l	36		
Barnard, Joseph	32			Hoyt, David	2	11	
Barrett, Benj	14			Hunt, Thos	18	3	3
Beaman, Simon	40			Hurst, Thomas	19		
Belding, Daniol	13	11		Nash, Timothy	6	11	
Brooks, Wm	6	5	6	Nims, Godfrey	27	11	
Broughton, Jn gates & highway	7			Northam, Sm'l Middle gate & highway	15		
Broughton, Th's	12	5	6	Plympton, Jn	2	11	
Brown, James	13	11		Plympton, P'tr	6		
Carter, Joshua	42	5		Price, Robert	2	5	
Catlin, John	33			Pynchon, Maj J	43	8	6
Church, Jona	13	11		Root, John	7		
Evans, John	24			Root, Thomas	7		
Field, Zechariah	25	11		Root, Hez & Jacob	12		
Frary, Samson	9	13	3	Russell, Mr Jn	36		
French, Thos	10	7		Seldon, Joseph	23		
Gillett, Joseph	19	4	6	Seldon, Thomas	6		
Hastings, Benj	16			Severance, Jn	2	11	
Hawks, Eleaz'r gate going out of the meadow to Hatfield & the highway both being ten rods new fence.	10			Sheldon, Isaac	36		
				Smead, Wm	26	11	
				Smith, Martin	10		
				Stebbins, Benoni	69		
				Stoddard, Sol'm	44		
				Sutlief, Nath'l	14	16	2
Hawks, John	15	11		Weld, Daniel	16		

ADVENT OF JOHN WILLIAMS. 197

	rds	ft	in		rds	ft	in
Weller, John	12			Wells, Lt Thos	50		
Weller, Rich'd	5	9		White, Henry	35		
Wells, Jona	21			Williams, Mr John	13	5	6
Eagle B Gate & Highway				Town fence	20		

The Ministry. Public law and public policy alike required any company of men engaged in settling a new plantation, to procure at once a sound and learned minister for their spiritual guide. Mr. Mather, the first minister, as before stated, became discouraged by the delay in resettling Pocumtuck, and left his charge in 1680. It is not quite certain who took his place. Probably Samuel, son of Rev. John Russell, officiated for awhile. He was a graduate of Harvard in 1681 and teacher of the Hopkins School in Hadley, 1682-3. He certainly became a land-holder here about the time of the resettlement. Savage thinks he was here several years.

Samuel Russell married about 1683-4, and succeeded Mr. Mather at Brainford in 1687. It is not unlikely that it was at Russell's suggestion, that Joshua Pomroy and Joseph Barnard were sent to Ipswich in search of a minister, where, Feb. 21st, 1684, they called upon Noadiah Russell, with an invitation to be a candidate. Noadiah was a classmate of Samuel Russell, and was at this time engaged in teaching school and studying astronomy. He published an almanac the same year. He declined the call, and in 1687 settled in Middletown, Conn.

In May or June, 1686, John, son of Samuel Williams of Roxbury, came to the waiting field, and it soon became evident that he had come to stay. He was born Dec. 10th, 1664; was a graduate of Harvard in 1683. This young man, whose piety and misfortunes, far more than his talents, have made his name a household word all over the land, then began here his life work, which was finished in 1729. September 21st, 1686,—

"The Inhabitants of Deerfield to Incourage Mr. John Williams to settle amongst them to dispenc the blessed word of Truth unto them, have made propositions unto him as followeth :"

"That they will give him 16 cowcommons of meadow land with a homelott that lieth on the Meetinghous hill.

That they will build him a hous : 42 foot long, 20 foot wide, with a lentoo of the back side of the house & finish sd house : to fence his home lott, and within 2 yeares after this agrement, to build him a barn, and to break up his plowing land.

ffor yearly salary to give him 60 pounds a year for the first, and 4 or 5 years after this agrement, to add to his sallary and make it eighty pounds."

"Att a meeting of the Inhabitants of Deerfield, Dec.: 17,: 1686, there was granted to Mr John Williams a certaine peice of land lying within the meadow fence : beginning att Joseph Selden's North line and so runs to Deerfield river North or North east : the owners of the comon fence, maintaining it as it is now att the day of the grant.

Jan. 5, 1686, the Comitty approves and ratifies the above sd propositions, on the Condition Mr. Williams settle among them.

As attest Medad Pomroy, by ord^r of the Comitty."

This real estate was afterwards "made sure to him and his heirs forever." The salary was to be paid "in wheat, peas, indian corn and pork, in equal proportion, at ye prices stated: viz.: wheat at 3 shillings 3 pence p^r bushel; peas at 2 shillings 6 pence p^r bushel; indian corn at 2 shillings p^r bushel; fatted pork at 2 pence half penny p^r pound." In 1711 he was paid £63 in money.

The salary of Mr. Russell, who had been twenty-eight years minister at Hadley, was then about £80, in grain at the same prices. Mr. Williams married July 21, 1687, Eunice, daughter of the Rev. Eleazer Mather of Northampton, and continued "to dispenc the blessed word of Truth" as the spiritual guide of the people. Oct. 17th, 1688, a church was formed, and he was formally ordained as their minister for life.

The connection of the young minister with the pastors of the two neighboring churches was intimate, and continued harmonious. His cousin and classmate at college, William Williams, was settled in the ministry at Hatfield. In the events of their settlement and marriage the Hatfield Williams was a year in advance of John. Both were sons-in-law of the Northampton ministers, John of Eleazer Mather, and William, of Mather's successor, Solomon Stoddard. Both had large families, and each educated three sons for the ministry. William preached at the ordination of two of John's sons, and a son of William at the funeral of a third. Later, a new link bound the ministry of Hatfield and Deerfield, when a daughter of William married Jonathan Ashley, the successor of John Williams. Some of the consequences of this intimacy will be seen hereafter.

During the land grant mania the minister was not forgotten, but, Dec. 13th, 1687,—

"'There was granted Mr. John Williams 20 acres of land upon the Green river and a home lot; provided he pay rates for it this year and so forward:"

Probably he found it difficult to meet the conditions, as no income could be derived from it during the war; at any rate, he gave up the grant. By a vote of the town Dec. 23d, 1689, the salary of Mr. Williams was "for this present year 1689 seventy pounds." No other action for an increase in salary appears on record, unless it be the following vote:—

Dec. 29, 1693, at the desire of ye Rev. Mr Jno Williams it was agreed upon and voted by ye town, y^t s^d Mr Jno Williams shall have ye use of ye Towne home lot y^t lies next his own home lot during his stay and continuance in ye work of ye ministry here in Deerf^d and shall carry on ye work of ye ministry himself: s^d Mr Jno Williams to make and maintain all ye fence belonging to s^d lot; and not to break up any part of s^d lot

It was difficult, if not impossible, for our impoverished people to pay the county, town and minister's taxes. In common with his people, Mr. Williams endured the calamities and hardships incident to a frontier town. His small stipend was often in arrears.

He had a large family, ten children having been born down to 1702. Of these, seven survived, the oldest being thirteen years old. Notwithstanding his straitened circumstances, the tender-hearted, self-denying minister made the following declaration, which was presented to the town, March 3d, 1701-2, and ordered to be recorded. It stands to his credit on the records to-day, in strong contrast with records to follow:

for ye prevention of any future trouble about my sallery I doe freely acquit ye Town of Deerfield from all dues upon ye account of Rates from my first Settlement to ye Rate of this present year 1701-2 and desire it may be entered upon Record; more over be it known to Suruiuers y^t ye time when my yearly Salery doth Begin is about ye midle of June: JOHN WILLIAMS.

In a letter to Gov. Dudley the following October, Mr. Williams writes:—

"When the country abated them, their rates formerly, i was yet moued from certain knowledge of their pouerty & distress to abate them of my salary for several years together, tho they never asked it of me, & now their children must either suffer from want of clothing, or the country consider them & i abate them what they are to pay me; i neuer found the people unwilling to do when they had ability; yea they haue often done aboue their ability."

This pathetic statement presents a touching picture of the character and condition of pastor and people. The only outside help received by either before 1704, so far as appears, was a grant of ten pounds by the General Court in the successive years of 1696 and 1697.

Sequestered Land. "Dec. 17th, 1686, The Inhabitants voted that a piece of Land lying on ye meeting hous hill by estimation 4 acres be it more or less as also 2 percells of Land lying one on the east side and the other on the west side of the mouth of the Green river by estimation thirty acre be they more or less shall be and is sequestered for the ministry in Deerfield forever :"

The Green river lands are still held by trustees for the benefit of the "First Congregational Parish of Deerfield," to which they come by descent and are secured by legal enactment. The four-acre lot was the "church officers lot" of the original draft. It is the "Town home lot" voted Mr. Williams in 1692, and is the lot south of Hitchcock's Lane, and includes the homestead of Robert Childs. In 1760, by leave of the General Court, all this lot, except the part south of the training field, and in front of the Ephraim Williams homestead, was offered for sale "to accommodate tradesmen."

Meetinghouses. Every new Plantation was obliged by law to employ a minister, as a fundamental condition of its existence. Meetinghouses were only less essential, but more latitude was allowed in that direction. By the terms of the Dedham Grant, the grantees were obliged to settle a minister within five years, but they were not enjoined to build a meetinghouse; that was to follow as a matter of course. No prosperity, it was held, could be expected where this "Candle of the Lord" was wanting. If the meetinghouse was burned in the devastation of towns by the Indians, it was considered a mark of divine anger; and of mercy, when it escaped destruction.

No record has been found of the time and manner of building our first meetinghouse. In an examination of the account book of John Pynchon of Springfield, "The Worshipful Major Pynchon," of Philip's War, items are found which prove that a meetinghouse was built before the breaking up of the first settlement. It was probably a small, cheap affair, built of logs, put up by voluntary contributions, and not by a tax. It was erected before August, 1675.

MEETINGHOUSE HILL.

The following extract from the old account book is given partly as a curiosity from its age, partly for its historic value, but chiefly for its testimony on the subject in hand in naming meetinghouse hill:—

August 19, 1673, agreed with John Earle that he shall haue one of My Homelots at Pacomtuck, ye one next ye church Lot, being nere 6 acres, wch is 28 rod Broad, for wch Lot & fencing wch I haue made on it, viz., ye 28 rods of five raile fence; In lew of all, I am to haue of him & he hereby makes over to me, his meddow land ag^t Eagle Brooke over ye river, being nere about 8 acres, wch was ye 2d Devision of mowing Land belonging to ye Lot No 26, wch he purchased from Joshua Carter. This persell of meddow Land, being nere about 8 acres, as he gueses it, he absolutely sells to me wth y^t p^t of ye 15 rod of 5 raile fence belonging to it, on y^e *meeting house hill*, I allowing him beside ye homelot abovsd, more, 12s wch is due him & al^d as above; to this exchange & setl^{mt} I must have ye proportion of woodland belonging to ye 8 acrs I haue of him, & he is to haue the proportion of ye woodland belonging to ye 6 acrs he had of me wth all ye appurtenances to each of s^d persels belonging.

To this agreamt witness our hands Aug. 19, 1673.

JOHN PYNCHON.
JOHN EARLE.

It was agreed between vs y^t if James Osborne chalenged any interest in ye Homelot aboue s^d, Jo Earle hath; that Jo Earle shall let him have 2 acrs of it, or some few rods more, he paying ye due worth of it, & satisfying for what he had expended on it; provided s^d Osborne doe agree about it by Michelstide come 12 mo.

This fixes the fact of a *meetinghouse hill*. The following extract settles the question of a *meetinghouse*, and also shows further, that this people were building a house for their minister; another testimony to the prosperity and high character of the little colony:—

Rates at Pacomtucke, alias Deerfield, on my land there. Having disposed of some of my land there.

that wch I keepe is the farme lot acct^d 11 cow-commons, & that I had of Maj. Lusher, 9 commons, in all 20 commons.

And at ye hither end, my 18 cow commons & 4 sheep comons.

1st y 1674. The Minister's Rate on which I pay to Mr. Samuel Mather, Anno 1674, ending in Dec. 1674, is £03, 18s.

1675, 2d y. To Mr. Mather for ye y 1675, ending in Dec. 1675. They give me an acc^t of some commons being wantıng, y^t my Rate is £03, 11s.

To ye Rate to ye Minister's house this year they set me at £07, 01s.

To ye little house for a Meeting House that y^a Meet in & to make Highway this y 1675, I allowed £1.

If all the cow commons were taxed at the rate paid by Mr. Pynchon on his, the salary of Mr. Mather would be about fifty pounds, and the expense of building his house about ninety-seven pounds.

A second meetinghouse was probably built soon after the permanent settlement. The town voted March 11th, 1692-3, "that the meeting hous shall be new seated; that Deacon David Hoyt & Deacon Jn° Sheldon shall be 2 of y° persons to doe it and Ben° Stebins to be wth y^m in s^d work." From this time forward for one hundred and twenty-five years, "seating the meeting house" became a subject of frequent legislation and social agitation. The action of 1693 may have developed the fact that there was a lack of seats of high "dignity" for ambitious aspirants. That the delicate task of the seaters in this case was not executed without dissatisfaction, seems to appear in the next vote on the subject: "There shall be no Reference to former Seating in y° present Seating." But whatever the reason, a new meetinghouse was demanded, and provided, in the face of war and famine:—

Att a legal Town Meeting in Deerf^d Oct 30th 1694 Ensign John Sheldon Moderator

That there shall be a meeting house Built in deerfield upon the Town charge voted affirmatively:

That there shall be a committy chosen and impowered to agree with workmen to begin said building forthwith and carry it on fast as may be voted affirmatively

That ye meetinghouse shall be built ye bigness of Hatfield meeting house only ye height to be left to ye judgment and determination of ye committy voted affirmatively

That there shall be a Rate made of one hundred and forty pounds payable this present year in pork and indian corn in equal proportions for ye carrying on s^d building voted affirmatively

For ye carrying on s^d work there was chosen as a Committy Ltt David Hoyt Sergt John Hawks Henry White: Thomas ffrench: and Ens John Sheldon

That ye Committy above s^d shall have full power to Bargain with and let out unto particular persons ye severall persalls of work for the carrying on and completing s^d Building as ye falling hewing framing shingling clabording &c voted affirmatively

Att a legal Town Meeting in Deerf^d Novemb: 22 1695 Godfrey Nims was chosen Collector to collect and gather two rates y^t is to say a Town Rate and a Meeting house Rate both made in ye year 1694 which Rates he is to deliver being gathered to the Selectmen

The records of the town meetings above and that following are given in full:—

Jan 15th 1695-6.   Att a legal Town Meeting in Deerfield John Catlin Moderator

There being a place or plat of land agreed upon by ye Town whereon to set there meeting house now in building: ye Town have left it with ye committy chosen for to carrie on ye building of s^d house where about on s^d plat to set s^d house as also ye scituation of ye same   Voted affirmatively

That there shall be a Rate Granted to be paid in pork and indian corn att an equall proportion for defraying what charge shall be expended on s^d Meeting house between this time and this time twelve month (y^t is after ye first or present Rate is run out) which Rate is to be paid some time in ye month of January 1696-7   Voted affirmatively

That ye modell for ye seats in s^d meeting hous shall be after ye present modell of Hatfield Meeting House Seats only two short seats on each side of the house more   Voted affirmatively

That ye panels or boards of s^d seats shall be of pine boards and not wainscot   Voted affirmatively

The work went slowly on, but at length the edifice was so far completed that it could be occupied. There was no ceremony of dedication. It was not set apart exclusively for sacred purposes. The meetinghouse of early days was literally a house for meetings of all kinds. Town meetings were held in the meetinghouse here, until the "old meetinghouse" was pulled down in 1824. It was usually the place of storing the town stock of ammunition, and the town bier. If our new building was not consecrated, certain other proceedings were thought necessary before it should be used for divine worship. The "Seater" was called to do his work, that each citizen could listen to the "blessed word of Truth," as it fell from the lips of their beloved minister, from a proper and becoming position.

There were real aristocratic distinctions in this little democracy, and nowhere were they more apparent than in the meetings for religious exercises. No one seems to have doubted the fitness of this condition of society; how to rank individuals under it, was the disturbing element. "Age" was fixed by the calendar; "Estate" by the rate book; "Dignity" there was the rub! Few at this day can realize the social condition among the founders of New England. They were still bound by the fetters of custom and habit brought from motherland. Emancipation from its aristocratic practices came only with the slow growth of democratic ideas, and emancipation from kingly rule.

Rank was graded in every town from the minister, esquire, captain, selectman, down through the different stations in the nicest manner. The wife of a corporal must give way before the lady of a sergeant, but her compensation lay in being able to take precedence over the wife of the private soldier. The punctilios of these poor, ragged, half-starved, incipient republicans seem laughable enough in this irreverent age. But it has its sad, as well as comic element. How much heart-burning and jealousy was engendered. How much loss of self-respect. How much wasting of hard earnings to keep up appearances on Sunday and Lecture day. But can we afford to smile at these ways of our ancestors? Were they laid in an even scale, over against the folly and extravagance of our time; or the sterling integrity of their leading men to balance the character of ours, would not the latter surely kick the beam?

However we may regard this question of rank, it was real business with our worthy sires, of equal importance, it seems, with their personal security. This is shown at the town meeting held Oct. 31st, 1696, where the two subjects acted upon are treated with equal respect. Voted:—

Thatt all Train Souldiers belonging to the Town of Deerfield shall labor about their fort ye next Monday and Tuesday being y^u 2d and 3d days in November next ensuing for a generall way beginning att one certain place of ye fort and so going on Voted affirmatively

That there shall be five men chosen as seaters to seat y^t is to say to determine where every person to be seated shall sit in ye new meeting house Voted affirmatively

That Deacon Hoit Deacon Sheldon Mr Jno Catlin Edward Allen and Thomas French shall be ye seaters for ye seating of ye new meeting house Voted affirmatively

That ye Rules for seating of persons shall be age state and dignity Voted affirmatively

Three years later, the edifice is still unfinished.

Janu'ry 2 1698-9, voted, that jice and board be provided for y^u meeting house Galleries upon ye Town charge to be paid for in ye year 1699

Y^e Town confirmed ye first committy chosen for ye building of s^d meeting house to see s^d Galleries finished:

The next vote directed the galleries to be finished by the last day of December, 1700.

At length, after seven years' labor, the meetinghouse is

SEATING THE MEETINGHOUSE. 205

ready for occupancy in all parts. But the galleries have not been *dignified*. How this is to be done becomes the exciting topic. Naturally the task would be assigned to the two deacons and their associates, who had successfully solved the same problem in the "body." No; for this important matter a town meeting must be called, which every voter must attend under a penalty of five shillings. The record is given in full, as due such a grave matter:—

Oct. 2, 1701. Att a legall town meeting in Deerfield Oct 2d 1701 Lieutt Hoyt moderator

That Seaters shall be chosen to seat ye meeting house Voted affirmatively

That 5 men shall be chosen for s^d work was voted affirmatively

The persons chosen to seat ye meeting house were Capt Wells: Lieutt Hoyt: Ensign Sheldon: Sergt Eliezer Hawks and Thomas French:

As to estimation of Seats ye Town agreed and voted y^t ye fore seat in ye front Gallery shall be equall in dignity with ye 2d seat in ye Body of ye meeting house:

That ye fore seats in ye side Gallerys shall be equall in dignity with ye 4th seats in ye Body of ye meeting house :

That ye 2d seat in ye front Galery and ye hinde seat in ye front Galery shall be equall in dignity with ye 5th seat in ye Body of ye meeting house

That ye 2d seat in ye side Galerys shall be esteemed equall in dignity with ye 6th in ye Body of ye meeting House:

That ye hinde seat in ye side Galerys shall be esteemed the 7th seat in dignity and the 3d seat in ye front Galery ye 8th in dignity:

That ye Rules which ye seaters shall seat persons by shall be: age: estate: place and qualifications:

It will be observed that the four highest military officers in town are on the board of seaters. Two of them are deacons, to be sure, but in the records their ecclesiastical titles are sunk in the military. Is there any significance in this fact? Does it proclaim that all rebellion, by ambitious spirits whose yearnings for a high grade of seats may not be satisfied, shall be put down by the strong hand? Or does it simply imply, that, as these men had few social equals, they were thus delivered from temptation in their official action, and could safely rank themselves No. 1 without giving offence?

TOWN MEETINGS.

The first town officers on record were chosen at a meeting without date, but which appears to have been held December

16th, 1686. At this meeting Thomas Wells was chosen moderator :—

Wm Smead Joshua Pumry Jno Sheldon Benoni Stebbins Benj Hastings and Thomas French ware chosen Selectmen Townsmen or Overseers to continue in office until oth^s be chosen and they discharged according to law. Jonathan Wells was chosen commission^r to joyn wth ye Select^m to take lists for the County Rate and officiate in ye business according to law

That the Town and Ministers' Rattes shall be raised upon Lands heads & flocks att the same prices as hath been ye last year past. Voted in ye affirmative   *   *   *

Edward Allyn Thomas Broughton & Thomas Allison were chosen server^s for ye year ensuing.

Philip Mattoone Jonath Church & Robart Alexander were chosen Haywards for ye year ensuing   *   *   *

That ye Selectmen Townsmen or Overseers aboue named shall haue pow^r to order all ye prudentials of ye Town.

A "Town brand" was established, and all horses ordered "to be branded y^t wth on the left should^r." Grants of wanting land were made, and the whole action appears to have been that of an independent commonwealth. As a matter of form, the land grants were approved by the Committee. In point of fact, the authority of the Committee at this time was little more than nominal, and their meetings were held merely to ratify the action of the inhabitants. The last act of the Committee was December 20th, 1687, when "Joseph Barnard was, with the consent of the Town of Derefield, and the aprobation of the Comitte appointed Clark and Recorder, for the Towne of Deerefield, as atteste, Medad Pomry, by order of s^d Comitte."

Down to this time, the meetings and action had been of "the Inhabitants." After this the meetings were "town meetings." The voters collectively were called "the Town," and their action, that of "the Town;" and to this day, the term, "Town of Deerfield," has two distinct meanings recognized in law: One, a certain extent of territory bounded by fixed lines; the other, the legal voters, acting collectively, or by their chosen agent. A third meaning, more loosely applied, and used in this work, is the old village on the "Town Plat," laid out in 1671. This is still called "Old Deerfield," "Old Town," and "Town Street." Those living here were called "Town's people," and those scattered in the outlying districts, "farmers."

Town meetings seem to have been called on slight provocation, but the method of warning does not appear. At least sixty town meetings were held before 1704. Town officers were usually chosen in March, when the general business of the town was transacted; the time fixed for "opening the meadows," in September; and rates laid in December.

"The Town" acted on all matters pertaining to the welfare of the community: Divided the land, built fortifications, meetinghouses, schoolhouses, ferry boats, and pounds; hired the minister and schoolmaster; chose military officers; laid out highways and graveyards; levied rates, prescribed the "specie" in which it should be paid, and fixed its price; fixed the price of grain betwixt man and man, and the price of labor; looked carefully after the common field, the fences and the stock; fixed the time for opening and closing the meadows; regulated the building of mills, and settled the toll for grinding and sawing; rented the sequestered land; enforced attendance on divine worship and its own meetings. The civil officers chosen were Recorder, Townsmen, Commissioner of Assessment, Assessors, Collectors, Tithingmen, School Committee, Wardens, Seaters, Surveyors of Highways, Fence-viewers, Haywards, Hog ringers, Town measurers—of land—Town appraisers, Clerk of the market, Sealer of weights and measures, Sealer of leather, Packers, Surveyors of hemp and flax, Surveyors of wheat and flour, Surveyors of clapboards, Cullers of brick, Cullers of shingles, Cullers of lumber, Pound-keeper, and Treasurer; but the latter was not chosen until 1720. The Collector had charge of the "specie"—always pork or grain—in which rates were paid. Most financial transactions were by barter or settled by orders. In 1686, Deerfield was indicted for neglecting to choose Cullers of brick.

Among other transactions at the first "Town meeting" was laying out the wood lands. The list below contains the names of all the Proprietors of that date, with the number of Cow Commons held by each.

A list of the wood lots as they were Drawn April 20 1688. lying in two Divisions the first Division beginning at the Long Hill att ye left hand [of the highway and ending] att Hatfield bounds ye 2d Division beginning att s^d bounds on ye oth^r side of the highway and ending att ye long hill running east & west.

No. of Lots		No. of Commons	Width of Lot-Rods	No. of Lots		No. of Commons	Width of Lot-Rods
1	Nath¹¹ Sutlief	8½	12¾	26	Eleazer Hawks	10	15
2	Sam¹¹ Hinsdell	12	18	27	Jos Barnard	16	24
3	Tho Root	3½	5¼	28	Col Jnº Pynchon	19	28½
4	Joseph Seldon	13	19½	29	Benoni Stebbins	26	39
5	Wᵐ Smead	14	21	30	Jnº Hawks	13	19½
6	Jno Hinsdell	8	12	31	Eph Hinsdell	6	9
7	Tho Seldon	3	4½	32	Jnº Sheldon	18½	27¼
8	Tho Allison	10	15	33	Mʳ Sol Stoddard	22	33
9	Joshua Carter	13	19½	34	Wᵐ Brooks	4	6
10	Zach Field	13	19½	35	Robert Price	1	1½
11	James Brown	9	13½	36	Jos Gillet	9½	14¾
12	Richard Weller	6	9	37	Jnº Stebbins	8	12
13	Tho Hurst	4	6	38	Godfre Nims	14	21
14	Daniel Belding	10	15	39	Peter Plimton	3½	5¼
15	Jnº Broughton	7	10½	40	Tho Broughton	10	15
16	Benj Barret	10	15	41	Tho Hunt	13½	20¼
17	Mʳ Wᵐ Williams	16	24	42	Sam¹¹ Northam	12	18
18	Benj Hastings	16	24	43	Simon Beaman	12	18
19	Jnº Catlin	16	24	44	Samson Frary	20	30
20	Mʳ Jnº Russell	14	21	45	Henry White	18	27
21	Daniel Weld	8½	12¾	46	Edward Allen	5	7½
22	Ltt Thomas Wells	30	45	47	Jnº Evans	14	21
23	Mʳ John Williams	8	12	48	Tho French	10	15
24	Jonath Wells	16	24	49	Capt John Allis		
25	Jonath Church	3½	5¼	50	Timº Nash		

Here it must be noted that he yᵗ hath yᵉ first in yᵉ first Division hath also yᵉ first lot in yᵉ 2d division (which is according to yᵉ order of yʳ Comittee) so he that lies next yᵉ long hill in one of his divisions lies next or near Hatfield bounds in his other division All yᵉ lots ly in this order except Capt Jnº Allis & Timº Nashes who were afterwards ordered and yⁿ lie both divisions next hatfield bounds.

These divisions have been subsequently known as Long Hill East, and Long Hill West Divisions. There was recorded at the same time—

A List of Wood Lots on the Mountain, the first Lot beginning at Deerfield River Laying along by the River side :—

No. of Lots		No. of Commons	Breadth of Lot-Rods	No. of Lots		No. of Commons	Breadth of Lot-Rods
1	Godfre Nims	14	28	10	Siman Beamon	12	24
2	Thoˢ Hurst	4	8	11	Mʳ Jnº Russell	14	28
3	Samson Frary	20	40	12	Tho Broughton	10	20
4	Eph Hinsdell	6	12	13	Mʳ Sol Stoddard	22	44
5	Wᵐ Smead	14	28	14	Tho French	10	20
6	Tho Hunt	13½	27	15	Benj Barret	10	20
7	Ltt Thomas Wells	30	60	16	Sam¹¹ Hinsdell	12	24
8	Tho Selden	3	6	17	Jnº Hawks	13	26
9	Jos Selden	13	26	18	Daniel Belding	10	20

VILLAGE STATECRAFT.

No. of Lots	Name	No. of Commons	Breadth of Lot-Rods	No. of Lots	Name	No. of Commons	Breadth of Lot-Rods
19	James Brown	9	18	35	Henry White	18	36
20	Col Jnº Pynchon	19	38	36	Jnº Sheldon	18½	37
21	Jnº Broughton	7	14	37	Jnº Evans	14	28
22	Edward Allyn	5	10	38	Mr Wm Williams	16	32
23	Tho Allison	10	20	39	Elear Hawks	10	20
24	Jnº Hinsdell	8	16	40	Jonath Church	3½	7
25	Joseph Barnard	16	32	41	Jnº Stebbins	8	16
26	Jnº Catlin	16	32	42	Samll Northam	12	24
27	Benj Hastings	16	32	43	Mr Jnº Williams	8	16
28	Wm Brooks	4	8	44	Joshua Carter	13	26
29	Benoni Stebbins	26	52	45	Jos Gillett	9½	19
30	Jonath Wells	16	32	46	Rob Price	1	2
31	Petr Plimton	3½	7	47	Daniel Weld	8½	17
32	Zach Field	13	26	48	Nathll Sutlief	8½	17
33	Tho Root	3½	7	49	Capt Jnº Allis		
34	Richard Weller	6	12	50	Timº Nash		

The following are names of men not on the above list who are found on a meadow fence list, and must have been owners of land in the Meadows: John Allen's heirs, Mr. Daniel Allyn, Ephraim Beers, Joseph Bodman, Ebenezer Brooks, Barnabas Hinsdale's heirs, David Hoyt, Francis Keet, Hezekiah Root, John Severance, Isaac Sheldon, John Weller.

Thomas Howard was also a resident, as appears by an "ear mark" recorded to him on the town records, but he held no land. By this list it appears that two only of those originally drawing commons in 1671, were now owners—John Pynchon and Samson Frary,—and in but one case, that of John Stebbins, are descendants found holding the land. Further town action relating to wood lands, roads, meetinghouses, schools, rates, fences, meadows, &c., will appear under those respective heads.

THE REVOLUTION OF 1688.

It is only through information gleaned from the old State manuscript archives that the history of this period can be given. Since the last recorded meeting of April, 1688, great changes had taken place in the aspect of affairs. The shadow of Indian hostilities had fallen across the valley. A revolution had swept the arbitrary Andros from the Governor's chair, and a provisional government had been established. In these events our town had been prominent; but on her records not the slightest indication appears that anything unusual had occurred. The record of the following meeting is given as notable for what it does *not* contain or intimate:—

May 30th, 1689. Att a legal Town meeting in Deerfield Godfre Nims was chosen constable for the year ensuing until anoth^r be chosen & sworn,

Ltt Thomas Wells Mr John Catlin, Lieut Jonath Wells Sam^{ll} Northam & Jos Barnard were chosen Townsmen for the year ensuing until others be chosen.

Daniel Belding & Martin Smith were fence view^{rs} for the North of ye common fence for the year ensuing.

Joseph Goddard and Joseph Bodman were chosen fence view^{rs} for the South part of the common fence for the year ensuing. Jno Allyn Eliz^r Hawks & James Brown were chosen serveie^s for ye year ensuing

Tho. French Jno Stebbins & Sam^{ll} Cart^r were chosen Haywards for ye year ensuing

Jonath Churches Home lot being forfited the town renewed his grant of s^d Home lot provided he fulfil his former obligation and build a dwelling hous upon it within a twelve month from this 30th of May:

There was also granted to Robbart Alexander a hom-lot att Wapping or plumb tree playne (which lot was formerly given to Sam^{ll} Hastings but is now forfited to the Town) he ye s^d Alexander fulfilling ye obligations y^t Sam^{ll} Hastings was und^r as to fenc & also to build a dwelling upon it within one year after the grant and dwell upon s^d lot 3 years

Ebenez^r & Nath^{ll} Brooks had att ye same meeting ye grant of ye hom-lot renewed for one year they performing ye obligations as in ye form^r grant. There being formerly a bargain between William Brooks deceased and the Inhabitants of Deerfield concerning his ye s^d Brooks dwelling house whareby s^d house became ye Towns prop^r estate Mary Brooks widow of s^d Wm Brooks made application to the Town desiring y^t they would grant or give unto her s^d dwelling house she relinquishing that benefit of choyce of lots which he had in recompenc for s^d hous as may be seen in record of s^d bargain.

That the widdow Brooks shall have and Injoy s^d house as her own forever provided she take it away off from the Town Land or common street att or before the last day of November 1689 but if s^d house be not removed by the time prefixt then to return to the town according to first bargain voted in ye affirmative.

To those having the clue, the unsettled condition of the country might be discovered in the following action at a town meeting June 26th, 1689:—

Considering the circumstances that the Town is att present und^r that Selectmen cannot be chosen amongst us every way according to Law without greatly burthening p^{r}ticular p^{r}sons: the town have agreed y^t ye Selectment chosen in May shall stand in ye place and office and the town do bind y^{m}selvs to stand by y^m in s^d office and to obey all such acts and ord^{rs} as s^d Selectmen shall doe and put forth for the good and benefit of the Town provided such acts and ord^{rs} shall not be repugnant to the Laws of this Jurisdiction Voted in ye affirmative

Further action at this meeting will be given hereafter. A few words on the political condition of the colony at this time are necessary to the understanding of our annals.

On the vacation of the charter, Dudley was made royal Governor in 1686. He was succeeded the next year by Sir Edmund Andros, who was put at the head of all the New England colonies by the Catholic King James. Andros, being tyrannical and oppressive in his administration, aroused much opposition. He was of French extraction, and there was a strong undercurrent of feeling that he favored the Roman Catholics, and was intriguing to transfer these colonies to French dominion. He had been unpopular in New England during Philip's War. His Indian policy seemed to be adverse to their interests, and never more so than now. He was aware of this feeling, and at this date, he was making a progress through New England looking after his political interests, but ostensibly, "to prevent a second Indian war." He was at Hadley about October 15th, where he had a meeting with town officers, Committees of the Plantations, officers of the militia, &c. From Boston, he issued orders on the 1st of November, that ten companies of sixty men each be raised as "standing forces * * * for the defense of the country against the Indians, &c.," and sent out commissions for the officers. Pynchon was made a colonel, to command in the valley, and Aaron Cook, major. Thus he formed a standing army under his direct command. However, it failed him in his hour of need.

News reached Boston about April 12th, 1689, that the Prince of Orange had landed in England. On the 18th, Andros was seized by the people and imprisoned, with his principal adherents. The government was assumed by a Committee of Safety, which on the 2d of May issued a call for the towns to choose representatives to meet in Boston on the 9th. A few men only gathered on this short notice, and little was done besides appointing a fast on the 16th, and issuing another call for representatives of the people to meet on the 22d.

There is no record of any meeting here in response to this call. The people, however, were ripe for revolt, and the Selectmen stepped at once to the front, assuming the grave responsibility. A paper found in the manuscript archives of the State, tells a story of which there is no hint in the town records:—

Deerfield, May 17, 1689.

We the Town of Deerfield, complying with the desire of the present Counsell of Safety, to choose one among us as a representative to send down to signify our minds and concurance with the Counsell for establishing of the government, have chosen and deputed Lieutenant Thomas Wells, and signified to him our minds for the proceeding to the settlement of the government, as hath been signified to us, from the Honorable Counsell of Safety, and those other representatives.

JOHN SHELDON,
BENJ. HASTINGS,
BENONI STEBBINS,
THOMAS FRENCH,
} Selectmen.

All honor to these patriotic men who took this post of danger, especially Lieut. Wells, who held his commission—now to be seen in Memorial Hall—under the hand of Andros himself. A failure of the revolution meant for him, a court martial, and the penalty of treason, at the hands of the vindictive Governor, and punishment for all concerned. The names of the first two Selectmen do not appear on this certificate of election or appointment, but there is no evidence of a divided sentiment here, unless it is found in the fact that an entirely new board of Selectmen was chosen at a town meeting on the 30th. It is more likely, however, that that was part of the policy of the town. Even the prying eyes of Edward Randolph himself could find no treason in the record of this meeting, or in the diplomatic vote of June 26th, already given. Shrewd men were managing affairs here at this crisis. Another of the unrecorded transactions, found in the State Archives, shows the *real* object of the June meeting. Should the revolution fail, the following paper, like the Wells certificate, would be in safe hands. The representatives met on the 22d of May, and on the 24th chose Simon Bradstreet, then 86 years old, for Governor.

June 26, 1689,—To the Governor and Council of the Massachusetts Colony for the safety of the people and conservation of the peace : Right Honorable, in pursuance to an order bearing date June 14, for the nomination of Military officers, the town of Deerfield being convened according to the above s^d order, have made a full and free voat for nomination of Thomas Wells for lieutenant and David Hoyt for ensign bearer.   JOSEPH BARNARD, Clerk.

    Bradstreet held his office until May 14th, 1692, when Phipps, who was appointed by the King under the second charter, succeeded him.

    The second topic passed by in silence at the meeting of May 30th, 1689, was the Indian raid from Canada. Indians had occasionally visited the English settlements, and mingled to some extent with the inhabitants, and it was no remarkable thing, when on the evening of July 24th, 1688, fifteen Indians came to lodge at the house of Lieut. Thomas Wells. Part of them, it proved, belonged to a war party sent out from Canada, by Gov. De Nonville in time of peace. They had orders, it appears, to take no prisoners, with a promise of ten beavers for each scalp taken. Part of the story is told by Wells in an affidavit made Oct. 15th, 1688. A full account of the raid may be found in Temple & Sheldon's history of Northfield:—

    The examination of Thomas Wells, aged thirty-six years or thereabouts, taken Oct. 15, 1688,

    This examin^t sayth, that about the Latter end of July, there came by water to his house fifteen Indians, who after he had some discourse with, he understood that eight of them were formerly North Indians, but now livd neere Albany, & had been out with ye Maquas, & in their way home came to these parts to hunt. That four more were lykewise North Indians [in other depositions these 12 Indians are called Scaghooks] whom ye eight overtook a hunting; & that ye other three were part of eleven Indians, formerly North Indians, but now lived amongst ye ffrench, & came in pursuit of ye s^d eight Indians, whom together they overtook. That ye Capt or ye chiefe of ye s^d eleven Indians, was called Wahacoet, who not suffering his party to fall on ye eight Indians when they met them, eight of his company were displeased thereat & left him; & he and two others, were ye three that came with ye other twelve Indians to Deerfield. That all ye s^d 15 Indians staid one night at this examin^t's house; that ye next morning ye s^d eight Indians went by land from Deerfield intending for Hatfield, & desired ye s^d Wahacoet and ye other two Indians to go with them, wch he refused, but said he would come to them by & by. Soon after ye s^d four Indians likewise intending for Hatfield, by water, asked ye s^d Wahacoet and ye s^d two Indians, to goe with them, but he likewise refused, but sayd as before y^t he would come to them by & by. That soone after the s^d twelve Indians were gone, Wahacoet and the two Indians went away by water, and told this examin^t that he was going for Hatfield, & from thence to Boston. That ye next morning all ye s^d 8 Indians, and three of ye four Indians came again to Deerfield to this Examin^t's house, & finding that

Wahacoet & ye two others were gone, & not come to them att Hatfield, as they promised, one Camaghtroett who was Capt or chiefe of ye s^d eight Indians, told this exia^nt in ye Indian language, which he well understood, that ye s^d eleven Indians were Rogues, & that he feared they were gone to doe mischiefe; and that they would have done mischiefe at Northfield as they came down the River, had not they been in company with them; & that the said Wahacoet that told him that they were sent out by the French, & had orders to kill English, Indians, Dutch, & Maquas, and that he should bring noe English captives, but only their scalps; & advised the English Inhabitants to be Careful of themselves. That ab^t three Days after, this examinant heard that five Indians were killed, & others taken, at Spectacle Pond, neere Springfield; & ab^t three weeks after, that three men two women & a girl were murdered by Indiens at Northfield, wch this examin^t veryly believes was done by the s^d eleven Indians. & further sayth not. Sworne the 15 October 1688 before me

THOMAS WELLS   E RANDOLPH

The five Indians were killed July 27th. Pynchon at once sent posts to the towns above and below, scouts in search of the marauders, and a party to bury the slain. A few days later, strange Indians were seen about Northfield. Micah Mudge and others went out in search of them, and found them camped in the woods. Mudge found Wahacoet, and Cungowasco, with whom he was well acquainted, and others whom he knew to be "North Indians," formerly belonging to these parts. Mudge "told them that there was peace between the Kings of England and France, which Wahacoet replied he knew well enough and promised ye next morning to come in to Northfield, which they did not."

These motions of the Indians caused excitement and alarm in the river towns. August 6th, Pynchon left Springfield for Northfield with six men; he picked up twenty-four more on the way, arriving there on the 11th. After repairing the fort, and scouting a few days in the woods, Pynchon returned, leaving a small garrison at Northfield. No more Indians were seen, and the alarm subsided. The Indians summoned from Connecticut were sent home. This quiet was soon interrupted. Pynchon writes Aug. 16th, 1688:—

By post from Northfield, I hear the Indians have killed 5 persons there, and were at the upper end of the town when the messengers came away. Samuel Janes and Josiah Marshfield brought the news. Thomas Powell was sent post to Quaboag, Sam'l Thomas to Westfield, and Jonathan Morgan to Hartford, with the news.

The next day, Lieut. Colton with sixteen men from Springfield, Lieut. Taylor, with thirty-four men "from the upper Towns, with horses," went to Northfield. Pynchon sent to Connecticut for thirty or forty Indians, but as only ten came up they were dismissed.

The consternation at Brookfield was such that the town was about to be abandoned. On the 19th, Pynchon sent six men " to bring off such women as desired to come away," but with a command to the men for "their continuance there." August 21st, a small garrison was sent to Northfield, and about a week later, Sergt. Bigelow, with fifteen men, joined it and remained until Oct. 9th. Capt. Jonathan Bull, and fifty-one men, left Hartford November 9th, for Northfield, where they remained until after the imprisonment of Andros. This was one of the companies raised under his order of November 1st, and was sent by him to Northfield. He complained to the King of their desertion of his government; but Andros was then powerless for harm, and nothing came of it. By the same authority, and at the same time, Warham Mather was sent to Northfield as their minister for six months. Small garrisons were kept there through the summer of 1689, and probably during the following winter, but in the spring of 1690 Northfield was deserted a second time, and Deerfield again became the frontier town.

It seems that a few Indians still lingered in the valley, subject to the English, and in view of the late raid from Canada the General Court passed the following order:—

Mch 20, 1689, for the better settling the Inds belonging to Hampshire, John Pinchon, Esq., is requested and hereby empowered to dispose said Inds to such place or places for their abode as may prevent their being exposed to danger, & with such limitations & directions as may be least disquiet to the English, the Inds to have warning y^t they exceed not the limits appropriated y^m upon their uttermost peril.

Wapping—1685-90. Grants of home lots were not confined to the Town Plat. A street was early laid out at Plumbtree Playne,—as Wapping was called until 1689,—where, August 1685, home lots were granted to Benj. Barrett and James Brown; and soon after, to Thomas Broughton, Benjamin and Samuel Hastings, John and Benoni Stebbins, Benjamin and Jonathan Church, Joseph Bodman, Ebenezer and Nathaniel Brooks, Robert Alexander, Martin Smith, Ephraim Beers,

Joseph Gillett and Thomas Hurst. These grants were generally made on condition of being built upon within a year, and maintaining all abutting meadow fence. This little band consisted of young men, nearly all with wives and young children, seeking a permanent home in this fertile valley. Their social relations were intimate, being closely connected by blood or marriage. The Brookses were brothers, and Benoni Stebbins their brother-in-law. The Stebbinses were brothers, while John was brother-in-law to Alexander and Barrett, and the latter, brother-in-law to Benjamin Hastings. Barrett married a sister of Alexander; the Churches were probably brothers, and brothers-in-law to Samuel Hastings. The wives of Bodman and Gillett had brothers in the Town Street. This harmonious little community faced cheerfully the hardships of a new settlement. It was a time of peace, and no fears of the Indian disturbed their labors. That they were prosperous, and growing independent, with separate herds of cattle, is shown by the following vote, which is all the reference found as to their estate or financial condition:—

June 26 1689, att the desire of the people at Wapping: it is agreed y^t so long as s^d Wapping people keep and maintain a good and sufficient Bull among themselves and let him run att liberty on the common: y^a shall be freed from any charges in ye Town as to hiring or buying of bulls:

The rough hand of war soon after scattered this happy family. In 1690 Alexander and Jonathan Church fell in the service. Barrett and Benjamin Church died the same year. Broughton was slain and Smith captured in 1693. The latter, and Benoni Stebbins were killed, and John Stebbins captured, in 1704. Bodman, Brown, Beers, Gillet and Samuel Hastings, disappear from the scene. The Brookses, Benjamin Hastings and John Stebbins became permanent residents in the Town Street. It was many years before Wapping was again occupied as a dwelling place.

Green River—1686–90. While landless new comers were being provided for at Wapping, another colony was settling at Green river. The present Main street of Greenfield was selected as a site for the houses of those who had grants of meadow land on the river. The Town Measurers laid out twenty home lots, of four acres each. These were to be drawn by lot for actual settlers, except that William Brooks had "liberty to take his two lots together * * * at what place he should choose in s⁴ tract" in consideration of his giving "to yᵉ Inhabitants afors⁴ (in recopense for that benifit or priviledge) his dwelling hous yᵗ stands in the Town Street in Deerfield."

The numbering of the lots began at the west end, and they were drawn as follows. On the south side: No. 1, Ebenezer Wells; 2, David Hoyt; 3 and 4, selected by Brooks; 5, Edward Allen. This came up to Arms's corner. On the north side: No. 1, Samuel Smead; 2, the mill lot; 3, Joseph Goddard; 4, Robert Goddard; 5, John Severance; 6 Jeremiah Hull; 7, John Allen, which came about to Pond's block. No others were located at this time. Home lots were afterwards granted to Robert Poag, Nathaniel Cooke, Nathaniel Brooks, John Williams, Philip Mattoon and Samuel Beaman. How many of these men actually built on their lots cannot be told. The same cause which broke up Wapping also scattered this plantation. The heirs of David Hoyt sold his lot to Roger Newton in 1776. The first house built in Greenfield, so far as known, was that of Joshua Pomroy, referred to in the following vote:—

Feb. 5, 1686-7, There was granted to Joshua Pumry esteemed 7 acres be it more or less, lying on the back side of his now dwelling house bounded by the Green river [torn,] by yᵉ brow of the hill east, by a little brook west which peice of land s⁴ Joshua Pumry is to have in exchange with yᵉ Town for four acres of land formerly given him by the Town: lying on the plain called yᵉ little plain:

This gift was in 1682. He had probably lived on the Town Street, but followed, or led, the colony to Green river.

The land along Green river was doubtless clear of forest, as it was called "meadows" from the first. Its west bound was called "the swamp." Lots were granted here to all who have been named as having house lots except David Hoyt, (who had bought a grant of thirty-six acres, laid out to Sergeant Plympton,) John Severance, Nathaniel Cooke and Thomas Broughton. These lots contained twenty acres each, running from Green river to the west line of the town. Wm. Brooks's grant was to join Stockwell's, which he had bought. This may explain his right to two home lots. All grants on Green river were on condition of "paying part of the *Indian purchase money,*" paying yearly rates, and sometimes a personal occupation of three years. Unless Sachem Chaque's deed covered this territory there is no "Indian purchase" known.

On the destruction of Schenectady the settlers retired to the shelter of the fortifications at the Town Street, and not a single one occupied his lands permanently. The Goddards, Cooke, Poag and Beaman no longer appear. Wm. Brooks died in 1688, Hull in 1691, Broughton was killed in 1693, Severance went to Connecticut in 1702, John Allen, Hoyt and Mattoon fell in 1704. Wells retired to Hatfield; his children and those of the Allens, Severance and Nathaniel Brooks, subsequently occupied their fathers' lands. Edward Allen, Jr., lived, died and was buried on home lot No. 5, given to his father. On this lot was the old graveyard for the early dead of Greenfield. Here they rested in quiet until 1881, when, in order to lay out the cheapest highway to the railroad station, the mercenary vandalism of Greenfield obliterated every vestige of this God's acre.

No more efforts were made to settle at Green river, until after the peace of Ryswick, in 1697.

While settlements on either hand were being encouraged, the community at the Town Street was itself increasing in numbers and prosperity.

During the war, the most accessible fields were cultivated, with little care for proprietorship or lines. With a wider occupation, came a call for better defined ownership. A vote was passed March 16th, 1698-9,—

That all lands within ye meadow fence together with all wanting lands and homelots be measured by ye Town Measurers : and that all lands not yet Recorded to be Recorded by the Town Clerk in ye Town Book of Records : ye Town Clerk having first received an account of s^d unrecorded land from the Town Measurers.

The great staple was Indian corn. A failure in this crop was a public disaster, so the policy of public protection was adopted, as appears by the following vote:—

That every house holder shall kill 12 Black Birds apiece this summer or else what they shall want of s^d number shall pay pence apiece in the Town Rate : and for what they shall kill above s^d number they shall receive of the Town pence apiece untill the last of May next : and for what Black birds they shall kill from thence to ye middle of Sept a half a penny apiece : and whosoever shall kill crows this summer shall have four pence apiece peayd them by ye Town.

This policy was continued in effect, until within about fifty years.

March 3d, 1701, Voted y^t a Commity be chosen whose work it shall be to Methodize ye form and manner of Recording of ye meadow lands in all four of ye divisions : as also to determine to whom lands shall be recorded determining upon the following Rule y^t is to say to those y^t shall produce ye last legal deed of such and such lands : Capt Wells : Ensigne Jno Sheldon : and Benoni Moor were chosen as a Commity to doe ye work mentioned in ye next above written vote :

No such book of records has been discovered ; it may have been destroyed in the house of the Clerk, Feb. 29th, 1704.

CHAPTER IX.

KING WILLIAM'S WAR.

The success of the Prince of Orange brought on war with France, in which their colonies became involved, and Canada Indians under French guidance were soon ravaging our frontiers. Feb. 18th, Schenectady was surprised and burned by an army from Canada and the inhabitants massacred with a barbarity shocking to civilized warfare. Sixty were murdered, twenty-seven carried off to Canada, while the rest were driven half naked through the deep snow towards Albany. Twenty-five of these lost their feet by freezing.

When the news of this horrible affair reached Deerfield, a town meeting was at once called. This town was equally exposed to attack, being entirely without defensive works. The most energetic measures were at once taken to supply this neglect and meet the danger:—

Att a Leagall Town meeting Feb^r 26th 1689-90
That y^r shall be a good sufficient fortification made upon the meeting hous hill: it was voted in the affirmative
for the stating proportioning and dividing to every p^{r}son his part or proportion of fortification: for stating the height flankrs gates &c the Town have made choice of Mr Jno Catlin Jonath Wells Samuel Northam Benj Barret Thos French Henry White and Benoni Stebbins to act and doe in every part and particular as to ye p^{r}mises as y^a shall Judg for ye good benefit & safety of the Town: voted in ye affirmative
That ye fortifications shall be don & finished by ye 8th of March next emediately ensuing: voted affirmatively
Thatt all persons whose families cannot conveniently and comfortably be received into ye houses y^t are already upon ye meeting hous hill and shall be wthn the fortifications: such persons shall have habitations provided for y^m wthn s^d fortifications att the Town charg but any p^{r}son or p^{r}sons y^t shall provide habitations for y^{m}selves shall be exempt from ye charges afores^d: voted in the affirmative
That Sgt Jno Sheldon Benoni Stebbins & Edward Allyn shall have full pow^r to appoint where every persons hous or cellar shall stand w^t bigness y^a shall be: y^t is such houses or cellars as are to be built by ye town as afores^d: voted in the affirmative:

It was not known here that the horde which destroyed Schenectady had returned to Canada. The same party might fall upon this town at any time, and every nerve was strained to prepare for a visit. It was no trifling thing that the inhabitants of Deerfield undertook. The task they set themselves shows their self reliance. Under the direction of the Committee, an area large enough to shelter the whole population was to be enclosed with a palisado. For this, many hundred pieces of timber, twelve to fourteen feet long, must be cut, hewed on two sides, and hauled to the spot: a trench two or three feet deep, dug in the frozen earth. In this the palisades were to be set solid and each pinned to a horizontal rail running across near the top. Planks for the gates and flankers were to be sawed out, and set up. All this to be finished in *ten days*, though the whole force of men which could be mustered for this service, including the Greenfield and Wapping refugees, could not have exceeded sixty; and this force was doubtless weakened by the "great sickness" which proved so fatal in the Connecticut valley this year. We find no account of the exact size of this stockade.

"Scouts of 14 or 16 men to bee out by the week together for the discovery of the enemy," were sent away weekly by Pynchon, to cover the frontiers during the spring months. Their pay was guaranteed by the county court, "if y" General Court do not pay them." A garrison of sixty Connecticut men under Capt. Colton, was established here as being the most exposed point on the river. The alarm at Albany equaled that here, and an application was made to Massachusetts for aid in its defense. Gov. Bradstreet, in a reply dated June 24th, declined the request on the ground that Deerfield was as likely to be attacked as Albany. The failure of the expedition for the invasion of Canada this year left the frontiers in greater fear than before. Revenge was sure to follow, and extra precautions were taken to prevent a surprise by more vigilant watching and warding.

In addition to the labor, danger and loss, occasioned by the war, the town suffered severely this year from a malignant distemper, and several prominent men died. The following letter gives a sad picture of the afflicting visitation.

Peter Tilton writes Governor Bradstreet, August 23d, 1690:—

The righteous Lord is sorely visiting these frontier towns at present, with sickness by agues and fevers, of which many are sick and weak and many are carried to their graves. The arrows of mortalitie and death, are flying thick from town to town, & from family to family. A hundred persons sick at Deerfield, about forescore at Northampton, many at Hadley & Hatfield. The disease increases in the towns downward. Capt. [William] Lewis, and Capt. [John] Moseley, are dead.

1691. This year, Major Peter Schuyler led a party of Mohawks against the Canada Indians, and being kept on the defensive, no war parties molested our frontiers.

December 14th, town officers were chosen: Selectmen, Eleazer Hawks, Edward Allyn, Samson Frary, Godfrey Nims and Henry White. Sealers of weights and measures, and packers of pork, were now for the first time chosen, they becoming necessary on account of the large dealings with the commissary department.

In November about one hundred and fifty Indians came here from the Hudson, complicating affairs, and increasing the alarm. Concerning them, Pynchon wrote to Gov. Bradstreet:—

SPRINGFIELD Dec 2, 1691.

Hon'ble Sir

There being Several Indians lately come into these pts who have Setled y^{m}selves near Dearefeild, betweene it and Hatf^{ld}, I judge it most meete and acc^t it but Duty, to aquaint y^r Honor therewith and to crave advise & directions from y^r Hon. & Council concerning them, & what may be necessary for safety in this time of danger & hazzard of enemyes; having such loud cals both from heaven & earth to be awakened; whereby we have as much cause, if not more, to look out for approaching danger this winter then last, when it was thought needful to continue a garrison at Dearefeild. The Indians came into Dearefeild sometime in Nov * * * Yesterday I rec'd a letter from Capt Partrigg who writes the Indians y^t are come down are about 150 of y^m men, women, & children, & are Setled at Dearefeild under ye Side of ye Mountain Southerly from the Town, living in ye woods East of Wapping, about a mile of ye Town. The men Plying hunting & Leaving their Women & ch at home * * * They brought a written Pass Subscribed by ye Mayor of Albany, that they, behaving y^{m}selves orderly, ye English would carry it friendly to them; Mr Partrigg writes for ye general they have been quiet hithertoe, only one or 2 of y^m were high & Insolent towards a Lad at Dearefeild, taking Some of his fathers Corn & Pumpkins wthout leave; & one of y^m y^t came to Hatfield, upon one of our men req^{tlng} a Debt of him, ye Indian pulled out his knife. There are many of y^m y^t were o^r former Enymy Indians wch Setled at Albany til now.

I doubt whether difficultys many ways may not arise, or jars upon yt acct., wch may raise spts & be provocations to Some; ye rather bee I understand (tho have note certaine Legal knowledge) some of or people let ym have cider & rum, being so besotted with lucre of unrighteous gain & Insensible of God's anger on those accounts, & there owne danger, that it is to be feared thay expose ymselves & others—

Were ye Indians honest, as they pretend, they may be advantagious in scouting & giving notice of an enemie if approaching; yet also, being so Setled, they have opportunity of entertaining an Enemy & betraying ye Townes, if they should pve false; & we having noe assurance of ym. I propose what may be necessary & meete to be done, yt we may be in some way of defending orselves—whether a garrison at Dearefeild be not convenient, is wth yr Hons: to consider, & then the writing to Connecticut to afford men & assist therin, will be necessary; & whether also these scouts of 4 men a week allowed by ye General Court in this County * * * be not profitable to be continued: Sometimes I am thinking it convenient that 40 or 50, or 60 men out of these upper towns, be apointed to be in readyness & listed under a Capt & officers to command ym, might be very useful, who should abide at home til occasion & then move presently upon notice * * * If such a company in their Arms should only march once or twice this winter to Dearefield, ye very sight of them might awe these Inds, who will thereby see & know we are in a warlike Posture; a laishlike indiscretion may procure some smart blow (as it did at Scenectoke) which should stir us up to diligence & Prudence; or people minding there owne busnes, without Arms, or watches, requires yt some orders be given for rousing ym up, especially, considering ye talke is of yt the French coming down on us this winter—Doubtless there is this winter as much danger as ye last * * * I crav leave to propose one thing more, which * * * is to write to ye Mayor of Albany concerning these Indians; to gain a certaine knowledge what they are & ye occasion of there coming &c; which if you think convenent & ordere me to doe, I wil take care to send, if there can be Passing thether:

Onething I had almost sliped. Leiut Wells of Dearefeild, who would have been very useful & is much wanted for these affairs being dead, (a sad froune of God in this juncture of affairs) there wants a Lieut to be commissiond for Derefeild, which I think ought to be minded. If yt Company have not applied ymselves to the Gen Court, I shall mention either David Hoite, or Jonathan Wells, or one Shelden who dwels there, to be there Lieutenant. I pray consider how times call for a Settlement. They have only an Ensign now, & that is Hoite before named, & Shelden & Wells are Chief Sergants.

1692. January 1st, 1691-2, Pynchon writes again in great perplexity, asking advice. He says the Committee of the Militia have had several meetings, and many have been to see him, but he knows not what to do.

On the same day, Samuel Partridge and John King, senior, write in behalf of the Military Committee, on the same subject. They say:—

We have feares they may be unfaithfule & soe betray us to our Enemies if they come, as they are not under our command but goe & come at pleasure. It is said their is some among them of the Penicook Inds that might have a hand in the late mischiefe done at Cocheco & Samon Falls, [in 1690] & of those that did mischiefe at North^{ld}. Their numbers as nere as we can come at, are between 40 & 50 fighting men & women & children about 100.

We humbly propose * * * them sent back to Albany, or setled & put under limits & bounds that we may know their incomers & find out if they are our enemies.

They ask the governor that,—

Application may be made to Conniticot to send 100 men as she did last year, for Jany and Feb, that being the only time they can pass the rivers and lakes on the ice.

The Council write Pynchon January 8th, to keep a sharp lookout, to organize a company of fifty men as he suggested, to continue the four scouts, to send a message of inquiry to Albany, "and, if necessary, to have a garrison of 50 or 60 Conn. men, and in all things to use your best judgment." They write to Connecticut the same day asking for forces to be sent to Deerfield. These were sent as requested. Capt. Whiting and fifty men came up about February 1st to garrison the town.

Pursuant to his broad instructions, Pynchon drafted a proclamation, with which he sent Capt. Partridge to the Indians. This was read to them, article by article, they responding, in the same manner. This paper is given below, as illustrating the relations between the two races at this period.

When the natives sold land to the English, they usually reserved the privilege of hunting and fishing on the territory. Gov. Bradstreet seems to have recognized this general native right, but assumed the power to regulate its exercise on the ground of public exigency; to this action the Indians took no exceptions in their replies to Pynchon's directions.

Directions concerning y^e *Indians* lately come fro Albany & some proposals to be made known to them by Capt Saml Partrigg & such interpreter as he shall Improve:—

I. Altho yo^u ought to have made application to vs to have had liberty to sit downe in ovr towns, yet, having Passes from ye Mayor of Albany for hunting, &c, we shal for ye present overlook y^r seeming intruding vpon vs & allow yor abiding where you are this winter time, you behaving y^{r}selves Peaceably & orderly & carrying it wel to all o^r people ye time of y^r staying til spring, when you are to returne to Albany whence you came & wher you will be expected:

To wch their answer was:
1. They owne it should have bene so at their coming
2. They intend no il to ye English, but to carry it peaceably
3. They desire there sqvas may be safe under our protection, while they are hunting:

II. We doe particularly caution you to beware of strong drink, wch intoxicates men's braines, & makes y^m more disorderly than otherwise they would be, & to warne your *young men* in special least it occasion quarrels, wch are carefully by you & by vs to be preuented, wherefore we allow not o^r people to sel it, & you would doe well to aqvaint vs wth any wch does, that we may deale with y^m for their disorder: Their reply—

.1. Our young men & sqvas wil buy it for all y^t, & your English *wil* sel it.
.2. They are afraid inform of ye English that do it least they do y^m mischiefe, Yet gave such hints in privite as 'tis hoped wil put a stop to that wickedness.

III. We let you know we are now apprehensive of some approach of ye French & Indian enemy, & therefore intend to keep out scouts & to haue more strict wach & shortly to settle some more soldiers in Dearefield, wherefore none of you (who account yourselves our friends, whom we hope are so & desire to approue themselues accordingly) are to goe or wander from y^r present position, without order in writing from some one of ye Captains in these towns or ye Lieut of Dearefield, & not aboue five in a company when they goe out hunting: And if o^r scouts find you wth a greater Number, or without an order as aforesaid & laying downe your armes, then to be acco^ted as enemy Indians: Also not to come into any of o^r townes after sunset, to disturb ye watches, the day being sufficient—especially in this troublesome season—for y^r necessary occasions. Nor at noe time to be wth your Armes in o^r towns; all wch we expect your carefull & due observance off, & y^t you forthwith give notice fully & distinctly to all Indians at home & abroad, accordingly y^t peace & orderly living ye little time you stay here may be promoted & friendship encouraged:

Lastly, we expect that if you understand anything of any enymys approach, or have any inteligence thereof, y^t you forth^wth acquaint vs thereof, or with whatsoeuer you know that may be of use to us: Whereby you will approve yourselves to be, as you say, o^r friends & we shall be enabled thereby to render ye better acc^t of you to yor Masters at Albany. Given under my hand at Springfield: Jan. 18th 1691. JOHN PYNCHON.

To the 3d and last Article they say, they consent to it in every particular thereof, & shall accordingly endeavor to attend it, promising (so far as their promise is good), to make w^t discovery they can of an approaching enymy, & forthwith to inform ye English thereof. Their returns wer made Jan 21, 1691-2.

SAMUEL PATRIGG.

Pynchon organized two new militia companies in the towns below, to be ready to march on an alarm, and kept the four scouts constantly out towards Canada.

February 22d, Pynchon sent the Council a copy of his "Directions" to the Indians, with the endorsements of Capt. Partridge. He writes that he hears the Indians intend planting here in the spring, but hopes that they will go back to Albany, and says he shall write to the Mayor to call them home; that they appear friendly, but he is suspicious of them. Rumors had reached town that a great army of French and Indians had been seen on Lake Champlain, coming this way. Some of the inhabitants "meditated a remove," but on the arrival of the Connecticut soldiers, all were reassured, and united heartily with them in strengthening the fortifications.

On the breaking up of the ice in the Connecticut river, the danger of a winter's invasion was considered to be over, and the Connecticut men went home. Pynchon writes to the Council soon after, that he fears "the men at Deerfield will be unquiet in their stations there, unless your Honors think of some way for their security, or they should hear of some check upon the French."

For the military company here, Pynchon appointed as lieutenant, Jona. Wells, brother of the late Lieut. Thomas Wells. Hitherto the highest military officer in town was a lieutenant. Before the close of 1692, Wells was made captain, David Hoyt, lieutenant, and John Sheldon, ensign. Early in May, the town was again alarmed by the story of a great army coming over the lakes. The intended invasion, of which news had been received about the 1st of February, had been stopped, it would seem, by the breaking up of the ice. The party now marching this way were four or five hundred French and Indians, so one Mr. Trowbridge wrote, that might be expected here about the middle of May. The inhabitants were all gathered into the fort and preparations made to defend it to the last. The story of Trowbridge was soon confirmed. Some of the hunting Indians met some Albany Indians, who told them they had seen the track of the army, and that they would be "likely to be upon Deerfield the Saturday or Sabbath day," the 15th or 16th of May. The attack was not made. The foe rarely came when expected. Their visits were usually a surprise. About May 20th, a party of Indians arrived here from Albany, who were sent by the Mayor to call the hunters home—in anticipation of the inroad from Canada—and the town was relieved from the fear of their treachery. These messengers from Albany brought news about the French army, which explained its failure to attack Deerfield. An advance guard had encountered some Dutchmen, who captured six of them. The French commander, knowing that his march was thus discovered, and that a surprise was impossible, instead of marching against a town that was ready to receive him, turned to the eastward, and on the 10th of June attacked the town of Wells. Failing to surprise the garrison, this army of five hundred men, after three days' fighting, was beaten off by Capt. Converse with thirty resolute men. The approach of the enemy to Wells was discovered by the cattle running into town.

It was probably belated news of this army, that caused Pynchon to write, May 25th, "We have sure news that the Earl of Frontenac has collected a large force, with munitions of war at Montreal, for a descent on the settlements." No enemy, however, was seen in this vicinity for more than a year, but watch and ward were strictly kept, and all cultivation of land was at the imminent risk, of life.

Capt. Wells, who had been chosen representative to the General Court, was so much needed at home, that this roundabout way was taken to secure his release: Oct. 4th,—

The Town made choice of, appointed, & impowered, Joseph Barnard to wright to Capt. Partrigg in ye behalf of ye s^d Town, to labor wth ye Assembly, in ord^r to get Capt. Wells his release from serving as deputy.

This "labor" was in vain, for the name of Capt. Wells is found among the Deputies serving in 1692.

Dec. 26th, "Ens. Jno Sheldon, Ltt. David Hoyt, Sergt. Benoni Stebbins, Corp. Thomas French, & Simon Beaman, were chosen selectmen for the year ensuing." This vote shows the importance attached to military titles, and also, it may be, the judgment of the people that the most efficient administration of affairs, in this time of distress, could be secured by a union of military and civil power.

1693. The opening of this year found the settlers in a sad condition. For obvious reasons, their crops had decreased as danger from an enemy increased, and had been yielding less and less from year to year. The area planted in 1692 had been small, and the returns meagre. In addition to the difficulty in cultivating the land, armies of caterpillars had made havoc with the Indian corn; nevertheless garrison soldiers must be supported, and scouts constantly fitted out for service.

Municipal affairs were not neglected.

This year the colony was reorganized under the new charter, and in March the town voted that the "Town officers chosen Dec. 26th, are now chosen again; and confirmed; to stand and serve until others be chosen."

The following paper shows the real condition of affairs here at this time:—

Feb ye 8, 1692-3. To His Excellency, Sr Wm Phipps, Kn^t, Govr of ye Masachusets, with ye Hon^r Counsell & Assembly in ye Great & General Court convened in Boston:—

The Inhabitants of ye town of Dere^{fd}, in the County of Hampshire, Humbly petition this Hon^d Courts consideration of their present afflictive estate & condition as followeth: Hauing for a long time Been Much exercised, & at great expenses in purchasing & setling our place anew, & by reason of feares and Hazzard of the approaching of enemies, improving a great part of our time in Watchings, Wardings, & Scoutings & Making of fortifications, beside the inevitable losses & mishaps we now meet with in oure labors, both by ye hand of God, & the inconveniences of improving our lands or labors in these times of fears and hazzard as afors^d to any measure of advantage for support of our families and ye necessary expenses of our Town and church, and reliefe of such amongst us as we are bound in contience to relieve; whereby we have been exposed to many straits and are brought very low & in a likely way to come to extremity, so that it becomes a question amongst us, whether we have not a call to apply ourselves to this Honora^{ble} Court, for an order to depart ye place, we being already convinced that if we should let our whole accommodations to pay ye charge, and take no other rent, we should be gainers as at present things are circumstanced, besides ye more eminent hazzards we are in of ye excursions of ye enemy, being 13 mile distant northward from any other of ye towns in this County, and a little handful more in ye mouths of ye enemy afores^d being but about 50 men.

Upon the considerations afores^d, and many more too large here to number up, we humbly entreate that we may have such creedence from your Honors, and such helps and reliefe as our nesessities if not extreame difficulties call for: and being heartily wiling to serve ye King & Queen's majesties and your Honors as Good and Loyal and obedient subiects, and especially Christ and his interests in this place, satisfing ou^{r}selves in your speciall care and readynes to relieve such, (thinking with allowance to hold it here a Little longer,) places as are mostly exposed as afores^d, Humbly propose that we might haue a grant from your Honors out of their Maiesties treasury in this prouince, a suitable supply of amunition, we hauing no Town Stock; as also an abatement of those taxes that are now called for in ye year 92, and those yet to be called for, till such time, (if euer it be,) we may recouer our-selves from this low estate we are now in, yᵉ granting of wich will much oblige your poor ptitionrs, and for your Honors euer to pray.

DAVID HOYT, } In yᵉ
JNO. SHELDEN, } name of
SIMON BEAMAN, } yᵉ Town.

In answer to the Inhabitants of Deerfield this House doe judge it Meete and Requisite that a Committee be chosen out of the Towns Adjacent to be joined with some meet persons of Said Town of Deerfield, who shall manage that affair, and sett men to worke for the Repairing their fortifications for the Security of the said Town, and that something be allowed them for supply of Amunition, all wᶜʰ to be paid out of the Treasury of the province not exceeding the sume of ———— that the place may be mainetained and not deserted.

This action was timely; without it, it may be, the Town would have been abandoned by the disheartened inhabitants.

Feb. 19th, 1692-3, news reached Pynchon of the disastrous attack on the Mohawks by the French and Indians from Canada, which news he posted to Governor Phipps. By return post, Feb. 27th, he received orders for securing Deerfield; Capt. Cooke was joined with him in this commission. Pursuant to these orders on the 2d of March they went to Connecticut. March 6th, the General Court made arrangements for soldiers to be sent to Deerfield. Pynchon writes Mar. 8th:—

They Readyly granted men for Securing that Post: 40 or 50 men to garrison yᵉ upper Towns when they should be called for & 150 men more in readyness to march upon notice of need of them wᶜʰ in regard yᵉ French yᵗ assaulted yᵉ Maquas Forts are returned home & probably the spring or winter now breaking vp at Canida wil not allow yᵐ to stir again til about May: I did not insist to have yᵐ Presently Post away their men to Dearefield: also because though Connecticut wil furnish wᵗʰ yᵉ men & be at yᵉ charge of their wages, yet wil not of their Dyet (as they say) wᶜʰ Dearefield *I doubt* cannot furnish yᵐ wᵗʰ. Their corne last yeare being destroyed by yᵉ worms & Provisions will not be had wᵗʰout sending it frᵐ yᵉ next Townes, though Possibly some meate or few barrels of Pork (wᶜʰ are scarce) may be in Dearefield, yet they belong to particular persons who wil quickly transport yᵐ away (wᵗʰout yoʳ Excelᵉˢ order for stopping yᵐ wᶜʰ I concieve necessary) & then provision will be wanting for Soldiers Posted there.

Now is yᵉ season to secure meate there & pᵉvent charge afterwards & it wil be more easy bec: mens Rates there may be appointed to pay yᵉ owners of such Porke (If any be) provided yoʳ Excel give orders wᶜʰ I only suggest:

I feare I am to tedious & not being willing to offend yʳ Excellency shal forbeare further particularizing being assured youⁿ will from Hartford Gent Have al yᵗ is needful for me to add. As also an account concerning ye French y^t cume to ye Maquas Forts who are returned wth their Indians (among whom were 30 Eastern Indians) Having lost 25 french & ten Indians y^t were killed by Maj. Schuyler's Men & although ye French marched off wth 250 Maquas yet they are al recovered & got hom only y^t ye Maquas have there Forts or Wigwams burnt down   Please let me vnderstand whether you would have me hasten ye Posting those Soldiers from Connecticut to Dearefield & how they shal be provided for.   I will Indeavour exactly to attend order in hastning y^m for I am in Paine least my good husbandry in delaying y^m (to ease ye Country's charge) should prove of any dangerous consequence wch I shal be ready to Rec: check for & make amendment by hastning y^m vpon the least Information:

Propose next weeke to visit Dearefield to Incourage y^m & vnderstand their State when shal further consider w^t may be necessary & forward vigorous & careful scouting,

Yo^r Excel caution & direction as to ye readyness of ye Militia in this regn^t I accept with great thankfulness & al due acknowledgm^t of care for o^r p^eservation, Have been & am in attendence therunto & shal proceed according to my vtmost Indeavors, a greate want wth vs & y^t wch disheartens some soldiers is ye scantiness of Powder.

If yor Excellency would please to send ..2 or 3. barrels of Good Gun Powder & some Bal (wch I would Indeavor to secure preserve & husband to advantage) it would quicken & enliven Some Soldiers sp^ts.

Craving y^r Pardon wth ye tender & prostrating of al humble service
I am Yo^r Excellencys
Springfield   Faithful Servant
March 8th 1692   JOHN PYNCHON
        93

[Addressed]
For there Maties Service
To his Excellency Sr Wm Phips Kn^t
Capt Generall & Govr in Chief in &
over there Maties Province of ye Massachusets Bay
in Boston:

To be forwarded by y^e
Constables of Brookefield
Marlborow &c
for there Maties Service

Precaution and vigilance, however, did not prevent a severe blow from falling upon the town.

The story of the attack on the Wells and Broughton families is thus told by Rev. Stephen Williams, in his appendix to the "Redeemed Captive."

June, 1693, the Widow Hepzibah Wells and her three daughters were knocked on the head and scalped; two of them died, but the other lived: at the same time Thomas Broughton was killed, and his wife, great with child, and three of their children.

TRAGEDY AT THE NORTH END. 231

That is *all* that history has given of this tragedy. From a manuscript by the same Mr. Williams, recently rescued from a pile of rubbish, a more detailed account is gleaned. The paper, 3½x7½ inches, closely written, with erasures, and interlineations, and many abbreviations, is hard to decipher. It has been submitted to several of the best experts in the State, who have given willing aid; probably nothing can be added to the copy given below:—

y^y suspect^d mischief before Broughton & Wells family & Capt. Wells laid in wth Cutawak to find out w^t was doing & he suspect^d it but c^d get nothing. Several Indians trading liv^d ov^r the River at Carter's land, & June 6, 1693, [in ye beginning of ye evening—erased] ab^t midnight y^y came upon y^m & killed Thos Broughton & his wife & xdren 3, & scalp^d 3 of ye Widow Wells daughters (Dan^{ll} being asleep in ye chamber not hurt, & Nathl Kellogue jumped out of Mrs. Wells' chamber window & escap^d) 2 dyd of y^r wounds & ye 3d liv^d & one Holms lay in ye chamber at B & saw y^m & heard ye people plead for y^r lives; ye man plead^d if his own life might not be spar^d his xdren might, but y^y answer^d in indian, we dont care for ye xdren & will kill y^m all, & Holms lay still & escap^d. Mrs. Wells was from home wth a sick child & ventured there, & before ye people went wth her & (then she returned having hid her xdren).

The words in parenthesis are erased, and others interlined, which no expert has been able to make out with certainty, and the same is true of part of what follows in the narrative.

took care of ye xdren & then hid herself; no body * * * came 'till ye break of ye day.

Kellogue escaped by flinging down a beam, lying in ye chamber wh^n (?) ye indian run up & beat him back.

Some of ye indians came into ye Town in ye morning & ye English sent for ye young capt & chedaw, wh^m ye indians deliverd up & y^e [wound^d,?] Mary Wells accus^d chedaw & he trembling & quivering deny^d it. T. Broughton accus^d ye Young Capt, he deny^d it. T. Broughton liv^d a day or 2 & dyd. Ashpelon s^d y^t ye young woman did not ling [talk? this word is plain] as if she was fitt to give an evidence; she seem^d distracted. These 2 accus^d were car^d to Springf^d & putt into custody, but broke away y^r prison by ye help of some Dutchman as was tho^t—y^t came there to see y^m, & all the hunting indians drew off ab^t y^t time—'twas suspect^d y^t these y^t did ye mischief were some canada indians principally, but y^t some of ye hunting indians had join^d wth y^m, but y^t ye generality of ye trading indians were ignorant of it, & I remember w^t my indian mistress s^d to me ab^t it. [Probably while Williams was a captive in Canada.]

No attempt will be made to reconcile or explain the discrepancy in these two statements by the same author. Neither seems to be in accordance with the facts. Mrs. Wells was the widow of Lieut. Thomas. The daughters were Mary, aged twenty; Sarah, seventeen; and Hepzibah, seven. It does not appear elsewhere, that Mrs. Wells was injured. She married, in 1699, Daniel Belding, and was killed in 1704; Mary, who was then living unmarried with her mother, was also killed. Hepzibah married, about 1715, John Dickinson, and was grandmother to our "Uncle Sid." Sarah only was killed. Thomas Broughton was thirty-two years old. His wife was Hester Colton; her age, or the ages or names of their children, are unknown. The only other paper found relating to this affair is the following from the records of Connecticut, Oct. 4th, 1694:—

Upon the motion of Widow Wells of Dearefield that she might haue liberty to craue the charity of the good people of this colony for her reliefe of the great charge she hath bin at in curing the wounds of her children which they receiued by the Indians, this Court recomends to the congregations in Windsor, Hartford and Weathersfield and Farmington to be charitably helpful to the woman therin.

Mrs. Wells was a native of Windsor, and had doubtless returned to her old home for medical treatment for her children. In 1673, the year of her marriage, and again in 1676, the proud young dame had been fined by the County Court for "wearing silk." Now she was a licensed beggar.

It appears that a band of Scatacook Indians, after their winter's hunt, had camped about a mile northwest of the town, for the purpose of trade, bartering their furs for English productions. It is not unlikely that this was part of the same party which left here in the spring of 1692. The suspicion of Capt. Wells, indicated in the old manuscript, is the only evidence discovered of uneasiness at their presence. It appears that Ashpelon, so prominent in the raid of Sept. 19th, 1677, was of this party, and was advocate for the accused Chedaw. The murderers were doubtless Canada Indians, who were sheltered by the trading party; but apparently some of the young hunters came over the river to witness, and possibly to share, the exploit. Two were recognized by the victims. As the lips of all were to be sealed in death, there was no need of disguise. On being named in the morning, the young captain and Chedaw were sent for, and were delivered up to the officers. The plan of the assailants seems to have been to do their bloody work with tomahawk and scalping knife, without alarming the town. No firearms were used, nor any buildings set on fire. On the successful resistance and escape of Kellogue the Indians probably took the alarm, and fled in haste, leaving Daniel Wells asleep in his mother's house, and Holmes unharmed in the chamber at Broughton's.

We are left to imagine how the cry of "Indians! Indians!" woke the sleeping town, and how the people fled for their lives to the fort. It might well be supposed that an army of French and Indians was upon them, and that an ambuscade lay ready for any who should venture out from the lines. An attack might be expected at any moment, and active preparations were made for defense. All the power of Capt. Wells, however, could not keep the heroic widow Hepzibah Wells within the palisades after hearing the story of Kellogue. The great love which fills the heart of a mother, inspired her with courage to rush seemingly into the very jaws of death, in a forlorn hope of saving her children. At the earliest moment consistent with prudence, no doubt, Capt. Wells sent a party to the scene of slaughter and to her relief.

The news of the arrest of Chedaw and the young captain flew fast and far. It will be interesting to note its effect on the Indians. The Scatacooks, a tribe made up largely from Pocumtuck and Nipmuck refugees, located by New York authorities a few miles north of Albany, were now allied with the Mohawks, and under the protection of the New York government. Deputies from this tribe met the authorities of Albany in council, June 15th. Their address is worth preserving in connection with our history:—

We have been as if in great Darknesse or cloud for some time and now the light is come againe the Sun Shines.

We return o^r hearty thanks for the presevacion of o^r wives and children in o^r absence while wee were hunting in the winter. [Here the orator presented two beaver skins.]

Twenty years agoe wee were received as Children of this Government and have lived peaceably ever since under its protection. and seeing severall of o^r people are deteined Prisoners in New England upon Suspicion to have killed some of their People at Deerfield wee submit the whole matter to the judicious Consideration of his Excell: [Gave three.]

Our Governor is a great man: Wee pray that hee would take care o^r future preservacion & since the French are also Potent Let us have our Eyes open and bend all o^r Strength against them. [Gave four beavers.]

Meanwhile Gov. Fletcher on his route from New York to Albany, hearing of the murders and of the imprisonment, sent Maj. Wessells at once to Deerfield to make inquiries. Arriving at Albany, the governor gave audience to the Mohawks, June 21st. Rode, their chief orator, made a characteristic speech, giving a beaver at the close of each paragraph. He gives the Governor a new name, Cayenquiragoe, or lord of the swift arrow, and thanks him for his prompt action in behalf of the suspected Indians. He says:—

Before we knew o^r men were detayned by the people of New England you were so kind as to send an expresse thither for their releasement this is so particular a kindness and favor, that wee must return o^r thanks in an especial manner.

Fletcher made such investigation as he could, and what evidence he found in favor of the prisoners was sent to this colony. The strongest item was the affidavit of John Baptiste Van Eps, that he identified a war club found at the scene of the murders, as belonging to an Indian he well knew in Canada, while he had been a prisoner there.

Pynchon writes Gov. Phipps, June 28, 1693, that he has been too busy with public business to write sooner, but,—

According to my ability I have not been wanting to get an vnderstanding of ye state of affaires here in refference to ye Indians and Murder at Dearefield:

W^{ch} as my time allowed, I have made report of to his excellency (al wch I know you are fully aqvainted wth) at same time Major Wessells hasting his return, By reason of my dispatch of him & w^t was necessary to Govr Fletcher, I was enforced to [illegible] contract yet mind not anything material y^t I neglected. The 2 Indians one a Maqva & ye other an Albanian whom I verily supposed are Gilty in ye murder, are in safe Custody, I desire a sutable time & Gen^{tm} Commisioned be appointed for there Tryal &c which please to lay before his Excelency. The 3d Indian put into o^r Jaile before I came hom, Nothing appearing agst him But his saying he would kil .20.·English, evadenced by one single man who says ye Indian was in drink when he s^d it, wch was sometime before ye Commotion at Derf^{ld} & he minded it not til that Disturbance; He and others saying also, y^t this Ind: always caryed it wel: The Indian saying He knows not he ever spake such words, & if he did he was in Drink & was sorry for y^m: He is discharged & set at Liberty (the Gen^t y^t comitted him judging it best: Colonol Allyn & Capt. Stanly (who were here) also advising to it) and went away to Albany wth Major Wessels, & those 6 Indians (one a Maqva Capt) who came with Major Wessels, so y^t they wil see (though this Indian wel deserved Imprisonment yet) we are not desirous to pvt any neadlessly vpon there

Tryal. They would haue bene glad we would have discharged ye other .2. setting forth y^t good service ye Maqvs haue done, endeavoring to vindicate al there Indians, & there being in good termes wth ye English, saying they disclaime this murder & are not gilty But y^t it was done by ye French Maqvas: & therevnto they Improve ye sight of some woden Swords or Mauls y^t were found when o^r People were murdered wch had marks & signes on y^m, as evidences y^t al was done by ye French Inds. To wch we Replyd, Such things might be to collour there wickedness, & y^t ye Positive assersions of dying persons were so express as could not anticipate ye legal Tryal of those persons, from w^t they were charged wth. And so they left off; desiring we would deliberate & heare againe from Albany before proceeding to there Tryal. I told y^m o^r Govr was very cautious of giving any just provocation, wherewth they seemed wel satisfied, Telling vs ye Indians Including ye 5 Nations Hold firm there friendships wth al there Maties Subjects, Desyring we would (as they terme it) hold ye Cov^t fast.

Govr Fletcher Intends a Present of 5 or 600^l for ye 5 Nations to Ingage y^m to vigorous p^{secution} of ye War agst ye French & french Indians wch was to be d^{lvd} vpon Major Wessels return hom, who is a g^{rt} man wth ye Indians;

They tel me theres some p^{tys} of French Indians come over ye lake, reckne o^r Towns in much hazzard being so open &c: Say ye French are in g^{rt} want of provisions some of them lately come from Canida brought in 3 Scalps & more they expect dayly. If any further acc^t be to be had from Albany I suppose we shal have it nexte weeke or ye beginning of ye weeke after, for Major Wessels s^d they should send againe & desyred I would take care there Indians might come safely, for we have noe Indians left al being gon off vpon y^t disturbance here & there Corne neglected.

Before a reply is received to this Pynchon writes again by the post from Gov. Fletcher:—

Spr^d July 2d 1693

Excelent S^r

In ye Night past Receiving ye Packet here wth from Govr Fletcher for y^r Excclency By Mr. Schuyler ye Maqvas Son & .5. Maqva y^t come along wth him. The gent being weary & desiring me to sped away a Fresh Post as also Govr Fletcher desires ye Like I haue dispatched ye bearer [as?] wth Govr Fletcher Letter to y^r Excel so also w^t he wrote to me, his letter I have sent for y^r Excel pervsal wth al ye pap^{es} or Posts now Recd w^h may be of vse to me to have y^m returned as also ye letter againe I hope your Excel wil write so ful to Albany & to Govr Fletcher y^t I need not nor am I willing to presume to deliver any of my owne sentem^{ts}, matters are much clogged & made difficult & it is such a tender case y^t I Pray God to help & guide mee through it I shal Indeavor to attend your exact comands & directions not doubting but upon your ful consideration of al things you wil come to such a Resulte as may be Pleazing to God & for ye good of his People wch I heartily Pray for & am

Yo^r Excel humble Servt
John Pynchon.

> The Gent here Lt Schuyler
> requests ye Post may be wth al
> speed dispatch^d wth you Letter to
> Gov Fletcher before he returns for
> Yorke.
> To his Excellency Sr Wm Phips Kn^t.
> Capt Genl & Gov in Cheife in & over
> their Maties Province of y^e
> Massachusetts Bay &c
>   In Boston

Gov. Phipps to Gov. Fletcher:—

Sir I have before me yours of the 28th past relating to the murder perpetrated by some Indians at Deerfield the beginning of the same month together with the Examinations sent Inclosed of a French Prisoner and one Henry an Indian concerning a Canooe with some Enemy Indians therein discovered upon the Lake five or six Dayes after the doing of the mischief, and the reasons given to induce a suspicion that they might be the Actors thereof wch I Apprehend might obtain further were it not that ye accusacon and evidences are so direct and positive against ye persons taken up and in custody for that crime being well known unto their accusers and were lodged in or near the Town at the time, besides other circumstances concurring to strengthen the suspicions upon them I am very sensible of the difficulty of this Case, and the unhappy Consequences that may ensue thereon and shall meditate to proceed with circumspection in so momentous affaire. Yet as it concerns blood think all due inquisition ought to be made after the same I propose to defer a present Tryal if Probably Providence may make a fuller and more clear discovery of the matter.

S^r I am very studious that no just provocation be given or injury done to any of our friend Indians and shall be as ready to cause the same to be redressed when made to appear assuring myselfe Your Excellency will herein Concur that it is no less reasonable to expect satisfaction as the Law requires for any mischiefe done by them towards their Maj^ties Subjects when legally convicted thereof especially of so horrid a crime as murder and desire you would please to let the Indians understand there is no intention on our part to break with them but to continue firme to former agreements. I shall be glad to give your Exc^y satisfaction that no violence or injustice shall be offered to the Indians now in Custody or any others heartily desiring they may appear innocent (if so) And that yor Endeavours to hold them firm to their Maj^tys Interests may be succeeded

No Intelligences from Europe have arrived here for a considerable time past A ship or two belonging to this place are daily Expected If any thing occur for their Maj^ties Service I shall give you account thereof and Remain Sr Y^r Exc^ys humble Servant
  Boston July 4th 1693

July 2d, Fletcher met the chiefs of the Five Nations in council at Albany. He told them in an address, what he had done in behalf of the imprisoned Scatacooks. Two days later the orator of the confederate tribes responded:—

We are very thankful to you o^r Great brother Cayenquiragoe for the sending two expresses to New England about that accident at Deerfield and o^r people imprisoned there wee doubt not but in a short time it will be made appear that the Canada Indians have committed this murder And the Brethren of New England who are in Covenant with us must have patience till such cases can be found out We doubt not but that the Governo^r of New England is a man of that prudence & conduct who will not be soe hasty since it cannot be long undiscovered.

The same day, Fletcher had a conference with the Scatacooks. He commends them for joining the Five Nations in warring against Canada, advises them not to draw off all their men to go to hunting, thus leaving the women and children without protection; and tells them,—

There is another stupendous folly you are guilty of when your huntng is over you'll set down nere some place where in a few days you drink out what has cost you the labor of some month's & then come home beggars as you went, the evill consequence of this appeared lately unto you at Deerfield & I hope will caution you for the future but I must advise you that from henceforth you will bring all the effects of yor hunting into yor own country which by prudent managem^t will support you the rest of the year.

The Indians in reply thank him for his care over them, calling him that high tree under the branches of which their old men, women and children find shelter, when the warriors are absent, and promise to follow his directions. Thanking him for sending the messengers to New England on their behalf, they say:—

Wee assure you that wee are Innocent of the mischefe done at Deerfield & soe are likewise those prisoners that are there in Custody believe us o^r hearts are good and wee desire only to live und^r yor protection in peace & quietness.

Phipps writes again to Fletcher July 13th:—

In my Lett^r of the 4th past I omitted my awknowledgment of yor goodness & Generosity In the Comprehention by the late Renuall of the League with the Maquas therefore doe by these manifest my Thankfulness for the same on the part of their majesties subjects of the province Acknowledging myselfe obleidged at all times to Indeavo^r the utmost serviss for their majesties & their Subjects I assured your Excy that I was very Sensible of the difficulty of the Case Relating to the maquas charged with the murders perpetrated at Deerfeild and the Ill consequences that might Atend *any* wrong step therein—therefore haveing Advis^d with my Councill Intend to send meet Persons to wait on Yourself at new Yorke for your advice & direction and assistance towards their proceedings on a trety with the maquas concerning that Affaire soe as to bring the same to a good Isue & to manefest our own Good Likeing and firm Adhereance on our part unto the League Lately Renued with them & to make some proposals relating to our Indian Enemy at the Eastward In all which thes Gentlemen sent with the tender of my respects are to consult with yo^rself and Receive your Advice & direction wherein I Request yor Favor that a Right understanding may be had Between their Majesties Subjects of the province & the Maquas soe that noe Discontent Arise & yet that Justice may proceed In the triall of the persons accused of the murder.

Gov. Phipps to Pynchon July 26, 1693:—

I have communicated unto the Council your several Letters refering unto the two Indians in Custody within your County on suspition of being Actors in the murders perpetrated in Deerfield. As also what I have received from Govr Fletcher Mr V. Cortlandt and Col^o Bayard of the several Examinations and Evidences taken concerning that matter particularly the Deposition of one John Baptist Van Eps late prisoner in Canada of his knowledge of the marks and figures upon the clubs found at Deerfield and the persons that bear the same being of the Enemy Indians of Canada. The Council have likewise procured the Examinations and Evidences taken from the wounded people being chiefly what others report to have heard them say, and not directly from themselves, besides that it's much doubted whether they were of sound mind, and upon consederation of the whole, are of opinion, the Indians cannot be convicted by those Evidences, advising that they be dismissed if no further material evidence appear against them, which I accordingly order, and that care be taken that they may pass homeward without any violence being offered them, yourself directing to the most probable way for there Sucure passing, and send a copy of this my L^re to the Mayor of Albany for his better satisfaction in this matter.

It is of great concernment to the whole of there Maj^ties Interest in these Teritories that the English be in good termes with the Maquas &c at this Critical hour when they are so much Solicited to go over to the side of the Enemy & that no just provocations be given them for a Rupture. As all caution ought to be used that no muther escape Justice, so it being plainly evident before hand that these Indians cannot by this evidence be found guilty upon Tryal, its thought more advisable to dismiss them without and to avoid the inconvenience that may ensue there being longer detained which the Indians (not understanding the formalities of Law) may improve to disaffect them to the English Interest I am

Your Humble Sev^nt

Boston July 26, 1693
To the Honble John Pynchon Esqr

Gov. Phipps to Gov. Fletcher July 26, 1693:—

Sir
 In mine of the 13th current I intimated unto yor Exc^y that I intended to send some meet person to waite on yourr selfe at New York for your advice direction and assistance in order to a treaty with the Maquas relateing to some of that Nation taken into custody on suspicion of the murder committed at Deerfield and to Endeavour to bring that affaire unto a good Issue &c.

 Since which I have a Letter from Mr V Cortlandt and Col^o Bayard at Albany with the Deposition of one John Baptist Van Eps late prisoner in Canada relating to the marks and figures upon the clubs found at Deerfield, and advising upon the severall Examinations and Evidences relating to that murder have ordered Major Pynchon to dismiss the two Indians taken into custody and to direct for there safe passage home, withal to send a Copy of my Letter to him unto the Mayor of Albany for the better satisfying of the Indians.

Before Pynchon sent this letter he had written the one below to Gov. Phipps.

SPRINGFIELD July 29 1693.

May it please yor Excelency
 I have not yet had opportunity to aquaint yor Excel^y of ye 2. Indians being gon til now: wch first offers it selfe as followeth

The .2. Indians in Custody vpon ye acc^t of ye murder at Dearefield escaped out of Prison July 27, when in ye morning p^esently sent out about .20. men to search after & pursue y^m, some of whom finding their Tratts just a cross ye streete from ye Prison house followed y^m for nere half a mile finding they bare Northerly, but coming into the Bushes could no longer follow y^m & so returned tho ye Jaylor spent all ye day, & sent to ye next Townes &c The manner how they fitted for an escape is evident to be by some File or Files conveighed to y^m (as is supposed) by some Indians y^t might secretly & unknown (we having none here unless by stealth) put y^m in to y^m in ye Night, for it is very plaine & evident there chaines were cut by some sharpe thin file like a knife, or some thin steele chissell they being as smooth as may be where they are cut asunder & very narrow y^t it was very thin instrument, when by this meanes they had got y^mselves at Liberty in ye room they pulled out some stones & got to ye foundation & so crep out & are gon probably Irrecovably vnless sending to Albany may Recover y^m thence wch is submitted to y^r Excelency.

Jesuit Peter Millet, of Canada, from Onidye, where he is a prisoner, writes Father Dellius, at Albany, July 31st: An Indian from Canada reports that a party of Indians who had been out towards Boston had brought home nine scalps; that the leaders of the party are Sajatese and Onontaquiratt; that he believes "that the Maquas & River Indians who are put in prison at Pekamptekook are wrongfully accused."

At a meeting of the Five Nations at their Grand Council Fire at Onondaga, Aug. 17th, Kajarsanhondare, speaking with the dignity and conscious power befitting one representing eighty sachems, said:—

Tell our brother Cayenquiragoe if any mischief be done to any in covenant with us as in New England it must not be said upon hearing of our language presently the five nations have done it, nor upon so light occasions must we be imprisoned, it is always known by whom the mischeife is done.

At the date of Father Millet's letter, July 31st, the Indians, in whose behalf he testifies, were already at liberty, and they arrived in Albany the next day. They had broken from their prison, by the help, it was believed, of some Dutchmen from Albany.

July 27th, a party of Canada Indians killed seven people at Brookfield and captured others. They were traced northerly by Capt. Colton with a party from Springfield, who surprised them on the 30th, killed several and recovered the captives. On the 31st, Capt. Whitney and Capt. Wells left Deerfield to search the woods about the swamps of Warwick, "looking for those villains who did the mischief at Brookfield." They did not know that Colton had routed them the day before. The Brookfield captives were told by these Indians, that "Canada Indians had been at Deerfield a month since and had done mischief there, who presently returned after they had done the mischief at Deerfield and near all got safe home to Canada." They inquired about the Indians in prison at Springfield, and said they were innocent.

On this new alarm from Brookfield Capt. Partridge writes for "40 or 50 soldiers to constantly scout the woods for two months." Our fort was now in a defensible condition, and well garrisoned. All, however, could not remain within its shelter. At whatever risk, the crops must be secured or starvation stared them in the face. Small parties of the enemy were constantly hovering about the frontiers, watching chances for spoil. Oct. 12th, Mr. Williams, the minister, as afterwards appeared, had a narrow escape from a party lurking near Wequamps. Oct. 13th, Martin Smith, venturing to Wapping early in the morning, was seized by Indians and carried to Canada.

At a town meeting held Sept. 9th, 1693, it was voted,—

That y^r shall be a man sent to Boston on Town acc^t to act & doe for ye Town such business as shall be committed to him: that ye Town shall find money to bear his charges and pay for his time for his Journey &c.

The town appointed and empowered the selectmen to hire and agree wth either Capt Jonath Wells Ensign John Sheldon or Joseph Barnard to goe to Boston on ye business afore s^d

Some of this business is probably indicated in a paper from the Massachusetts archives, given below:—

An acc^t of the fortifications made in Deerfield by order of Warrant from Maj. John Pynchon; made in May, 1693; the mesure or whole Compass of the fort is two hundred and two rods: vallued by the Committee of the Militia and ye Selectmen: to be worth five shillings p^r rod in money

Deerfield   ⎧ Attest hereunto Jonathan Wells, Capt, in name of
Oct. 6,   ⎨ ye rest of the Com'tte of Militia. per Joseph Bar-
1693.   ⎩ nard in the name of the rest of the Selectmen.

We having intimation from Maj. Pynchon in s^d warrant, that it was an Order of Court concerning said fortification, that we should be allowed out of our County rates for s^d work, wee therefore present this account to ye Honorable Court.

The following petition was doubtless presented by the same messenger:—

To his Excellency, Sr William Phipps, Kn^t, Capt. Gener^l, & Govr in Chiefe, of ye Ma^{sts} Province of the Massachusetts Bay; & to ye Hon^{ed} Councell and Representatives convened In Generall Assembly—

The Humble Petition of ye Inhabitants of Deerfield, in ye County of Hampshire sheweth that ye s^d Town of Deerfield, being a frontier town, is liable unto, and of late hath been much Infested wth the Incursions of o^r Indian Enemies, to o^r great impovershment & prejudice—

That unless o^r distressed Condition, be Considered by this Hon^d Assembly and some Assistance afforded us, we must of nesesity forsake o^r habitations, and draw off to some Neighbouring towns—

We therefore, Humbly Acknowledging the Care & regard, hitherto afforded us by y^r Excelency: Doe pray that o^r part of the thirty thousand pound rate, remaining yet uncollected (by reason of o^r Inability to pay it,) may be remitted and ye s^d Town in future taxes, may be Exempted during the present distress; & that a Garrison of Eighteen or twenty sould^{rs} may reside wth us, for o^r defence & ye security of s^d County, and y^r Petitioners shall ever pray for y^r Hon^{rs}; and Subscribe ourselves y^r Honors most Humble & obliged serv^{ts}.

JNO. WILLIAMS.
JOSEPH BARNARD.

In ye name & behalf of ye Inhabitants of Dearf^d
Dearfield, Novemb^r
6th, 1693.

The petitioners were backed by Pynchon, who writes that the people are

"much impoverished by maintaining garrison men, and otherwise so many ways, that they are not able to subsist or maintain their families, rather choosing to draw off, if it were not that the Gov. & Council ordered them to abide, the attendance of which (though willing) yet are not able, unless enabled * * * till such peaceable times wherein they may attend their occasions, of which they are almost wholly obstructed at this day."

Both papers were favorably received.

Nov. 26, 1693, Tuesday. The Petition and acc^t of the Town of Deerfield for the garrisoning of that town by the order of his Excellency the Governor, containing a line of 202 rods being read. Ordered, that there be £40 allowed and paid s^d Town by discount on the public Assessment towards the charges of s^d Fortifications.

No colony tax was levied upon the town until after the close of the war.

1694. Voted in town meeting,—

March 5th, 1693-4, that the Selectmen shall have full pow^r * * * to make all such orders and by laws as y^a shall judge needful and necessary in ord^r to ye managem^t of the prudentialls of the Town: in w^{t}ever p^{r}ticul^{rs} y^a shall judg y^t Law doth not comprehend or reach ye full of s^d circumstances Voted affirmatively.

Under this action the following were the "Ord^s & Laws made by ye Selectmen":—

1 That all common fences shall be made up by the owners of such fences att or before the 7th of April next according to law

2 That Haywards or any oth^r y^t shall Lawfully Impound any hors kind cattle sheep or swine: shall have for Impounding as in the Law specified: before such hors cattle sheep or swine be released:

3 That all cattle or hors kind that shall be left in the meadow except fast teddered upon ye owners land: all such owners shall pay 3d p^r head to those y^t shall Impound y^m:

4 That all beside working cattle that shall be found baiting wthin the common fence shall be liable to be impounded:

5 That who so ever shall leave open any of ye common field gates or bars wthin ye time y^t ye selectmen shall order it to be inclosed such persons or ye overse^{rs} shall pay as a fine five shillings: one half to ye Town ye oth^r half to ye Inform^r:

6 That every man shall have a stake at the North end of his common fence: marked wth the first lett^r of his name: and for want of such stake or Stakes shall pay one shilling to ye fence viewer

Voted and passed by the Town
                         Attest   Tho French ⎫
                                        Jno Porter ⎬ Selectmen.
                                        Jona Wells ⎭

Passed and allowed by Justices sitting in quart^r sessions att Northampton March 6th 1693-4.

Attest   J^{No} P<small>YNCHON</small> Clerk.

The town officers for this year were chosen at this meeting. The next day they all went to Northampton to take the oath of office before the County Court, and get the by-laws confirmed. From that time until now the annual meeting for the choice of officers has been the first Monday in March.

The spring of 1694 opened gloomily upon the harassed settlers. As soon as the leaves were out no one felt safe for one moment outside the palisades. Each bush or tree was a covert, whence the deadly bullet, from an unseen foe, might at any moment issue. Under such conditions, but little could be effected in raising crops; but the summer passed, and no enemy appeared. Frontenac was engaged in a more profitable adventure. The eastern Indians had made a treaty of peace and alliance with the English in August, 1693. The polity of France required that this treaty should be broken, and French Jesuitism was successfully employed to that end. During the following winter, and in the spring, a French army was sent to join the Indians in an attack on the eastern settlements. Oyster River was surprised, and about one hundred inhabitants were killed or captured.

ATTACK ON THE TOWN, SEPT. 15TH, 1694.

On the return of the French army from the east, flushed with victory, and loaded with spoils, an expedition was fitted out against Deerfield, under Castreen. This was done with such dispatch and secrecy, that no news of it reached our frontiers. Eluding the scouts that were ranging the woods, Castreen arrived undiscovered, September 15th, and the town had a narrow escape from a complete surprise. He halted in the woods on the East Mountain, overlooking the town, evidently intending to make his attack at the north gate of the fort, which was in the street, in front of the present brick meetinghouse. Watching his opportunity, he came down the ravine in the rear of the William Sheldon home lot, to creep up the alder swamp, and enter the street where Philo Munn's shop stands. On emerging from the ravine, however, the party was discovered by Daniel, son of Joseph Severance, who lived on this lot. Daniel was shot, and the alarm thus given. Mrs. Hannah Beaman, the school dame, with her young flock, on the home lot next northward, started for the fort. It was a race for life; the dame with her charge up the street, the enemy up the parallel swamp on the east, to intercept them before they should reach the gate. Fear gave wings to the children; the fort was reached in safety, and the gate shut. But not a second too soon. The Indians were near enough to send a volley of bullets among the fugitives as they were crossing the causeway at the foot of Meetinghouse hill, and entering the fort gate. All, however, escaped unhurt. Meanwhile within the stockade all was activity without confusion. Capt. Wells had for years been training the inhabitants for just such an emergency. Each man snatched his loaded firelock from its hooks on the summer tree, the powder horn and bullet pouch from the mantle tree, and in less time than it takes to relate the fact, was on the way to the point of danger, ready to sally out if need be, to the rescue of the little ones, who, as we have seen, were in the same brief time safely received within the gate.

The heroic conduct of Capt. Converse and his little band, in defending Wells against a horde of the enemy two years before, had been on the lips of all New England, and doubtless inspired these men of Deerfield on this occasion. Castreen had led his army three hundred miles through the wilderness to surprise the town, butcher its inhabitants, burn their dwellings, and carry their scalps in triumph back to Canada. He failed of a surprise, found a resolute people ready to defend their wives and children, and was driven ignominiously back into the wilderness.

This repulse of the enemy gave the settlers fresh confidence in themselves. The panic of last year gave way to a feeling of ability to defend their homes, and the idea of giving them up to this cowardly foe was abandoned. They now felt that they were indeed permanent settlers, and, six weeks later, the town voted to build a new meetinghouse. The loss to the English in the assault was only two men wounded —John Beaman and Richard Lyman.

I have found no mention hitherto of Zebediah Williams being engaged in this affair; but the fact is established by the following paper from Massachusetts Archives, vol. 70, page 359:—

To ye Hono^rable Wm Stoughton Esqr L^tt Govr &c. & Counsell & Representatives Convened in Gen^ll Corte this Octr 13 1697

The Humble Petition of Zabadiah Williams who was a Sould^r in Derefield & Wounded by ye Enemy w^n they set upon Derefield Garrison Sept 16 1695 [1694?] & lay wounded 22 weekes for wch the Doct^r Requires four pounds beside w^t I am to pay other Chirurgions & my tyme & Expences wch hath already beene motioned to this Corte & Now againe I intreate my case may be considered & allowences Granted mee as yor Honor^s shall Judge meete & for you^r Hono^rs I shall Ever pray

ZABADIAH WILLIAMS.

Oct 20. Voted. In answer to ye aboues^d petition y^t he shall receiue fifteene pounds out of ye prouince Treasury: for full compensation

This sum was paid Williams Dec. 4th, 1697. In another petition Mch. 22d, 1697, Williams states that,—

In Sept last when ye enemy came upon a family in Deerfield, as he was running with others to relieve that family the enemy wound^d him on the arm in two places w^h wound has preuented his labor and occasions much pain & charge for more than three months, is but newly come of age having little to begin withall

Rev. John Williams attests the truth of these statements. Dec. 4th, 1697, Zebediah was allowed £15.

John Bement had sent in a petition as follows, in 1695:—

To ye Honble Leiut Govr & Council & to ye Representatives now Assembled, may it please yor Honors to releive a Pore Wounded Soldier who is in al respects Needy and wanting supply: His Pay for his Service being ordered to com fr^o Enfeild Constable who Pays nothing, renders him ye more needy, & cals for yor order to help him therin, but most especially for a due consideration of his wound he Rec^d on ye 15th of Septr last at Dearefeild, wch besides ye misery & Paine, hath disabled him fr^o Labor for now neere eight months & when I shal be able to get anything I know not, wherefore Pray yor compashons & speedy ordering of Just releife y^t I may not stay in Boston where it is too expensive for him y^t hath noe Money, But be at Liberty to returne wth yor Honors favorable orders & Due allowance, wch wil Thankfully Ingage him ever to Serve you as he is able, who is   Yo^r humble Servt

Boston June 5 1695   JOHN BEMENT.

John showed his wounds in the House, and June 8th, he was sent on his way rejoicing, with ten pounds in his pocket.

Dec. 12th, Gov. Stoughton writes Gov. Treat and the Connecticut Council, asking them "to relieve our Garrison at Deerfield by posting forty or fifty fresh men there sometime in Jany at the charge of ye Colony, to continue there for the space of six months following if occasion be."

1695. Jan. 3d, Connecticut in reply to Stoughton's letter of Dec. 12, that after "seriously considering" the matter, it is concluded to "send the Assistance of 32 men for the space of two months" or until the winter breaks up provided Massachusetts will furnish provision.

Jan. 12th Stoughton returns his thanks, but thinks they should send more men and provision them; they being as much interested in keeping the frontier as Massachusetts. But he writes Pynchon at the same time to provide for the Connecticut soldiers and discharge the garrison at Deerfield when they arrive. Soon after Lieut. Stephen Hollister with thirty-two men arrives here.

March 6th Connecticut sends word to Stoughton that she is willing to do her share in the work of defence and the General Court will consider the matter at its May session. This does not quite satisfy our authorities, who write March 16th to the Governor and Council of Connecticut giving thanks for their men and hope they will be continued. They say:—

"Our interests cannot be divided, It is a common Enemy we are engaged ag^t. and tho ye seat of War do^s prudentially lye nearer to our doors, yet it is ye over Turning & Exterpation of ye whole y^t is sought & Endeavoured, and if we be necessitated to give way and draw in you may not Expect to stand; It has been received a maxim in war y^t it is better to Engage ye Enemy at a distance than within our own borders."

A mutual commission is invited to determine the best way of "disresting of ye Enemy and what Quota of Men and Money" each should furnish.

After a service of ten weeks Lt. Hollister is recalled. Pynchon notifies Stoughton, who writes March 28th, to remonstrate. He urges the disrespect of such an order without notice, and the danger to Deerfield involved in it, and hopes the governor will "see cause to retrieve that unhapy mistake." Treat replies that it is not in his power, but that he will refer the matters in his late letters to the General Court in May.

May 6th Stoughton reminds Treat of this promise. He gives news from Canada that after planting is over the Indians may be expected on our frontiers.

May 21st Stoughton again urges Connecticut to send a garrison to Deerfield. June 1st, Connecticut declines, as they have need of all their men for their husbandry, and they hear Maj. Pynchon has furnished a garrison for Deerfield. "Upon news of any Assault coming upon them" they will "respond with all speed."

June 17th Stoughton sends a sharp reply. He is much pained "that Deerfield, a post of such consequence for the Security of yor Colony, is so much slighted by you." He gets no satisfaction from the reply.

July 3d. The authorities of Connecticut say it is impossible to send soldiers to garrison Deerfield; for Gov. Fletcher has called for their full quota of men "which they are considering how to raise."

No large parties were sent against our frontiers this year. The Mohawks had in a measure recovered from the disasters of 1693, and Frontenac found occupation for his soldiers in operations against them. Smaller bands of the enemy, however, hovered about the English towns, waylaying roads and fields, watching safe opportunities for attack. Their occasional success kept the settlers in a state of continual alarm. An impending disaster here was averted by a mere accident.

The Indians about Albany continued their friendly relations with our people, and still made this vicinity their hunting ground. A party of about twenty arrived here the first week in August. It was probably this party which on the morning of the 10th was surprised by a war party from Canada, near the mouth of the Ashuelot river. One of the hunters, whose arm was broken by a shot, escaped, swam the Connecticut and brought the news to Deerfield. Capt. Wells at once sent a post to Springfield for help. Pynchon, reporting the affair to Gov. Stoughton, August 12th, says:—

Capt. Wells writes in these words: 'August 10, 1695. Just now an Indian called Strawberry, his son, Hath made an escape from Nashawelot above Northfield. He is come in this evening much wounded; says this day, about 8 or 9 o'clock in the morning, the enemy made a shot on them and killed 8 or 9 of them; so many he reckons, he saw as good as dead. He says he saw many canoes; accounts the enemy to be 40 or 50 men, upon which Capt. Wells desires some assistance be speedily sent to them; which Capt. Patrigg enforces by his lines by the same post, which was writ in the night Aug. 11, saying the Relation of the wounded Indian was undoubtedly true.'

The messengers called Pynchon "out of bed an hour before day." He at once summoned Capt. Colton, who "had 24 troopers together by 8 o'clock well mounted and fixed." They left for the north "a little after the first Bell rang * * * for meeting, which I suppose you will reckon was speedy to fit out so many men so presently." Pynchon recommended Colton to march up the east side of the Connecticut, asking the men from the towns above to go up on the west side. He thought of sending a party to follow with supplies, that Colton might pursue the enemy, "although they had gone almost to Canada," but did not like to undertake it on his "own head without orders." He thinks "in all reason this has put a stop to ravaging Deerfield, or some other town, which it is supposed they intended," and that the danger is over, as the custom of the Indians is to return home after each exploit. They may have done so in this case, but if so another party was soon in the field.

Joseph Barnard killed at Indian Bridge. In the town records for this year may be read these two entries:—

March 1, 1694-5. Joseph Barnard was chosen Town Clerk for the year ensuing;—
Sept. 17, 1695. Thomas French was chosen Town Clerk.

No other clue to the surprisal at Indian Bridge is found on the town books. In an appendix to the "Redeemed Captive," Stephen Williams briefly notes this affair as occurring August 18th. Subsequent historians have accepted this date, which is doubtless a mistake, as the 18th was Sunday. Pynchon, whom I follow, is the better authority.

On the morning of August 21st, 1695, five men started together for mutual protection to go to mill, three miles away at Mill River. They were all on horseback, each with his gun across his saddle bow, and his bag of grain beneath him. By some subtle and mysterious influence, Capt. Wells, the commander of the town, had the night before been warned of impending danger from the Indians, and passed a sleepless and watchful night in consequence. On seeing the mill party riding down the street, he went out to stop them. He could give no substantial reason for his order. The bright morning sunshine may have weakened his nocturnal impressions, and seeing Mr. Barnard, whom "he thought to be a prudent man, he let them go on." The result is given below in the words of Stephen Williams.

Joseph Barnard, Henry White, Philip Mattoon, Godfrey Nims, going to mill came to the place ab^t y^u drain, & ye horses snuffing & being fright^d one of y^m cryd out, indians, indians, & y^y turned ab^t, & ye indians fir^d upon y^m & wound^d Mr. Barnard in left hand (one wrist broke to pieces), & one bullet in ye body, & his horse shot down, & then N[ims] took him up & his horse was shot down & then he was mounted behind M[attoon] & came of home.

Joseph Barnard lingered until September 6th, when he died. The stone marking his place of rest bears the earliest date of any in the old graveyard.

Pynchon writing to the Governor, gives a more particular account of this affair, and of subsequent events in connection.

The letters of Pynchon, hastily penned under the pressure of exciting news, with all their tedious details, are photographic pictures, showing the condition of the plantation at this trying period, albeit the shading *is* dark. No abstract, or narrative based upon their contents, can compare in value. The originals are in the Massachusetts archives.

SPRINGFIELD, Sept. 13, 1695.

Honble S^r:—

So little Travelling hath bene, y^t I haue not had opportunity to give y^r Honor such acc^t of affaires as might be needful, though I haue writ twice If not thrice, w^{cb} letters (after long stay) I suppose are wth you. By my last you would haue ye acc^t of about 8 Indians at Deerefield, this was on y^u 21st of Aug^t, who within a mile of ye garrison lay in waite close by ye Road, Hid & altogether vnseene, so y^t 5 men of Dearefeild coming out in ye Morning on Horses goeing to mil & wth Baggs under y^m, Had 7 or 8 guns discharged upon y^m, vnexpectedly, & seeing noebody till ye guns were shot of, wherein eminent gracious providence appeared that noe more mischeife was done to o^{rs}. For except Joseph Barnard, who was shot downe off his horse and sorely wounded, not one more hurt, whenas ours were surprised & ye Indians had time. For y^t our men, one of y^m his horse starting, threw him and stuned him for ye present, ye rest were Imployed in getting vp Jos Barnard, & setting him vpon his horse, so y^t ye Indians had opportunity, yet God suffered y^m not to be so hardy, as to run in vpon our men (Possibly bec one of ours kept a calling as If they had more) y^t ye men behind would come vp) whereby ours had also opportunity to set Jos B. vpon his horse, wth one to hold him on. The rest also mounted & made to ye Garrison; when p^{r}sently a shot was made on y^m, and killed ye horse dead y^t Jos B. was sat on, yet then againe they mounted him vpon another Horse, when another gun (tis supposed Jos B's owne gun wch the Indian had taken vp), was discharged vpon y^m, & this shot also light vpon Jos Barnard againe: Al wch notwithstanding, our men got off, & came al to ye garrison; though since Jos B. is dead, a Humbling providence, he being a very vseful & helpful man in ye place so much vnder discouragement, & will ye more find & feel ye want of him.

We were not wanting in persuing ye enemy. Dearefeild men, & a parcel of Nthampton men, y^t had bene vp ye River, being just come in, went out after y^m imediately, about 30 or 40 men in al (beside more y^t followed from Hatfield & Nth) who soone tooke their tracks Westward vp Dearefeild river, & followed y^m, tho lost y^m after a while, yet were so Intent vpon it that they found y^m againe & persued ye enymy 7 or 8 miles, till they could noe longer discover any tracks, & altho they Ranged westward & Northward & vp ye river to ye place where Capt. Colton found and broke 2 cannoes, yet could they not find or discover ye enymy who are skilful in hiding y^{m}selves in Swamps & Thickets.

Possibly these Inds. might draw off wholy, But if they did, yet others were about presently, & then were (& now are) in those q^{r}trs, & Dearefield people who are (in a sence in ye enemy's Mouth almost, & are often & so continualy Pecked at, (tho wonderfully preserved) being apprehensive of their danger & Hazzard, the Number of soldiers there (viz 24) being few to maintaine so large a fortification, when some must necessarily be Imployed in guarding ye Inhabitants who are in ye fields at worke & others vpon ye scout &c—wherein always some of ye Inhabitants are Improved. They addressed y^{m}selves to me for some Further addition & supply of men, w^h I cannot but think necessary & needful to secure ye Fort, & prevent their Surprisal, wch would be of woeful consequence If (for want of suficient strength there) the enemy should attayne it.

But having noe order from yourselfe, (tho I moved it,) to Place more men there, & knowing how hard it would be to find y^m here, we having more men out already than can wel be spared, I thought it advisable to move ye Gent at Hartford, & thervpon writ to Col. Allyn &c that they would be so kind as to send 40 men to range ye woods wel wth some of ours, w^h they readyly granted to ye Number of 30, under Lt. Holister, who haue been of good vse & incouragement to Dearefeild. But they Intending their stay about 3 weeks only. The people at Dearefield, thoughtful of their danger when they should draw off, Intimated ye same to me & that the Number of men for ye garrison might then be increased. So y^t I took occasion thereby againe to write to Hartford that 12 of their men might be left at Dearfield till Indian Harvest was in, tho' they called off ye rest presently; wch they haue Lovingly & readyly complied wth; ordering Lieut. Holister to leave 12 men wth a sergt, till ye 10th of October, who hath accordingly done it & is gon home ye beginning of this weeke, hauing drawn off al their soldiers But 12 left for about a month longer from this time, & I hope these wth ours, wil be suficient in al respect, if noe more of ye enemy appears then at present, & when Indian Harvest is in, & Busyness over, our 24 men may doe, probably, tho what may by y^t time be further discovered I know not. We know Indians are now lurking about, & are satisfied y^t some number of y^m are waiting to get some booty, for besides some seen at Northampton, as also at Hadley, there haue been some ab^t Spr^d; twice one hath bene seene, whether the same Indian or another cannot conclude. But upon any appearance we range al ye woods about, beside our dayly scouting out 4 men a day on Horses by Turnes, wch God may bless to awe ye enemy who cannot but perceive it, for these towns are dayly Infested by ye enymy; so it is not prudent to empty our towns of men [as we are] by so many at Dearefield & Brookfield, wch take 22 men from vs, whereof 30 are out of Spr^d & every day we look that some mischief or other wil be done, when to Relieve one another it may prove hazardous ye weakning ourselves, If ye enymy take notice therof and haue strength to manage any designe ag^st vs.

We desire to waite vpon God in ye due use of means for our safety, leaving ye success to him on whom our dependance is for Blessing & Preservation.

It is a troublesome time here, we having had 2 Alarmes lately, wch it is mercy prove nothing in reality. But the same, wth other disquiets, & exercises, refering to ye enymy & our own safety, take up my time & proves hard for me to do w^t belongs to me, wch I am desirous to be found in, & anxious for ye Publicke good, wherein I shall be glad of any good directions from y^r Honors, who am

Honble S^r
Your very Humble sev^t,
JOHN PYNCHON.

Postcript. An Indian from Wiyantemick come in to Hartford reports (as Col Allen writes me) that ye Mohawks Have done greate Spoile upon ye French at Canida. Killed & taken Captive about a hundred. If true it may something allay ye enymys motion but it wants Confirmation & seconding by some good hands. If y^o have occasion to write to Hartford may it not be of use to take notice of there sending men up (as above declared) to o^r assistance & Intemate y^r acceptance wch probably may tend to further there readyness another time when they find I have observed it to you & y^t y^o doe accept it to them wch is only hinted at by

Your Servt J. P.

[Superscription:]
These for the Honble Wm.
Stoughton his Maties Lieut. Govr
in Dorchester
For his Maties Service.

Stoughton follows Pynchon's suggestion and writes the Governor Sept. 15th, thanking him for "giving help in puruing the enemy & your Enforc^nt of the Garrison at Deerfield with twelvemen when Joseph Barnard was killed."

For his Maj^ties Service—To ye truly Honble Wm. Stoughton, Esq., his Maties Lieut. Gov. for his Province at ye Massachusetts Bay in Dorchester:— Post haste.

SPRINGFIELD, Sept. 30, 1695.

Honble S^r:—Not being awar of my Neighbors goeing so soone, I am prevented much (of enlarging) yet may not omit to give y^r Honor some acc^t of ye discouraged state of ye Inhabitants of Dearefeild—

They having discovered many stragling Indians since y^t sudden surprise when Jos Barnard Rec[d] his death wound, & now y[e] Relation of a Maqua come in there, (as he says from y[e] eastward where he hath been several years) startles y[m] very much, who says y[t] 600 French & Indians designe mischeife upon Albany (w[ch] he is going to advise y[m] off, They being (as he tells) out upon y[t] designe: & Intend to visit Dearefield in their way, w[ch] overbeares y[m] wth feares of some sudden onset vpon y[m], & makes y[m] shy of Leaving their Fort, or goeing out to gather in their Corne accounting they haue not strength enough. (They haue 24 soldiers out of this county in garrison there From Conecticot 12 more, w[h] y[y] yeilded to leave til 9th of October —In al 36.) But y[t] if they scatter about their busyness Shall hazzard y[e] Fort & endanger their Breaking vp, or abetting & incouraging of y[e] enymy, w[ch] would be of very ill Consequence to y[e] country, if any such thing should be; wherfore they sent to me for further assistance, & on y[e] 24th inst. by Post, they signifie that y[t] morning an Indian discovered himselfe on y[e] other side of their river ag[t] Carter's Land, and not far from their Fort, vpon w[ch] they sent out 15 men, who could find noe Indian or Indians, though some signes. Returning againe not long after, about Noone Two men Plainly saw another Indian or y[e] same, or about y[e] same Place, walking as if he designed to make y[m] see him. They at Dearefeild are jealous (as they wrote) least y[e] enemies' designe is to draw their men from y[e] Fort & so ensnare y[m] or come vpon y[e] Fort when they are out of it or weake in it and soe take it. Inasmuch as there scouts y[t] were out y[e] day before, saw tracks of 2 or 3 Indians & discovered where corne y[t] had been gathered was eaten by leaving y[e] cobs or gr[t] ends of at least 50 eares of corne & this in a corner of y[e] Neck towards Carter's land afore mentioned, or not far from it, w[ch] is a Bushy swampy Place. Hence Capt. Wells desired my speedy sending some more soldiers to their assistance, & to range about &c., whervpon I ordered Capt. Clap of Northampton, y[e] next to y[m], (Capt. Partridg being here at y[e] Sessions), to draw out 20 men of his Company y[e] most apt for service, to range y[e] woods and afford y[m] all y[e] assistance they were able, who accordingly went to Dearf[d] y[e] 25th of this instant Sept, & returned y[e] 27th, at Night, making little or noe discovery of y[e] enymy. But y[t] evening one of y[e] garrison soldiers y[t] was at Hatfield goeing vp to y[e] garrison, discovered two Indians about 2 miles on this side of Dearfield Fort, & shot at y[m] as he says &c. Capt. Clap, who hath bene at Dearefield, is very sensible of need of men to be sent vp to strengthen y[m], & to guard & scout about while they issue their harvest. Capt. Partridg also joyns wth him in writing y[t] I would send vp 20 for a fortnight or three weeks, w[ch] y[e] people much desire, fearing some sudden mischeife Thervpon I have ordered y[m] some men, w[ch] I suppose went vp or are this day gon, 8 from N. H., 4 from Hatfeild, & 4 from Hadly, y[e] next towns, in al 16 men added to their number of 36, to be there a week or ten days, whom I have directed to Capt. Wells for y[e] best improvement of y[m] for their saftie, & for y[e] Public advantage. I hope it will be acceptable to y[r] Honor. I am very sensible of y[e] Countrys charges. But if there should be any sudden surprise there, y[e] want of strength may abet y[e] enemy, Before we can send further aid, w[ch] vpon y[e] least notice of, I shall send to y[m] wth al y[e] strength y[e] county can afford if nere, & procure from

Hartford I hope more, could we haue any timely discovery of any enemy on y^m, wch ye good L^d prevent if it be his blessed wil & save his Pore people. I shal gladly Receive from y^r Honor Further & better directions & orders as you se meete & best, wch I shal as I am able readyly attend, & in meanetime desire to be found doeing my duty, begging y^r Prayers for God's guidance therein, & y^t I may act for ye best good of this Pore Wilderness People.

wth humble service I am s^r
y^r Honors Faithful Servt
JOHN PYNCHON.

At a town meeting, Sept. 1695, "it was then agreed and voted y^t Mr. Samuel Porter of Hadley should carry their present County Bills to get them passed at Boston and to receive the money or orders for ye same."

The vigilance of the inhabitants and the garrison with the activity of the scouts secured the town from further depredations this year.

The General Court declared that all Indians found within five miles easterly or twenty miles westerly of the Connecticut river should be considered enemies, and soon after a bounty was offered for Indians captured, or scalps of those killed; $50 for men, and $25 for women and children under fourteen years of age.

1696. From beginning to end this proved another troublesome year to the town. Fear and distress pervaded the household, danger and death lurked in every by-way about the fields. Only the least exposed ground could be planted, and the harvest was scanty. The Green River lands had not been wholly deserted by the owners, who had continued to cultivate them to some small extent. This was no longer possible, and all land at Green River was this year exempt from taxation. Notwithstanding the unsettled condition of business affairs it was considered necessary that every freeman of this little Commonwealth should punctually attend to his civil duties. March 2d, "It was agreed and voted y^t a penalty of one shilling shall be laid upon every legall voter not attending Town Meetings, provided they be legally warned therto." The building of the meetinghouse went on. A rate had been laid for that purpose in 1695, and in January of this year another was laid, both payable in "pork and indian corn in equal proportions." It was a seasonable relief when, in June, the General Court voted £10 for the support of the ministry here. The Court also provided a garrison; and scouting was continued on the frontiers. Although this dangerous service was performed with boldness and fidelity, sudden inroads of the enemy could not always be averted. Like a whirlwind they came and went, leaving destruction in their track.

Belding Family Surprisal. The following account of the attack is from the Stephen Williams manuscript:—

7^{ber} 16, 1696, John Smead & John Gillett being in the woods, looking or tracking Bees, were besett by a company of French Mohawks. J. G. was taken prisoner & J. S. escapd—the indians fearing a discovery by S. 16 of them hastend away toward the town, and three were left with J. G. It being lecture day the people were got out of ye meadows, that so y^y might attend ye lecture, so that ye enemy came as far as Mr. Danl Beldings house, that was within gun shot of ye fort. Mr. B. being belat^d a^{bt} his work was but just got home f^{rm} the Fiealds & left his cart (y^t was loaded wth corn) & went into ye house & left ye xren wth ye cart, & ye indians rushed upon them & took him prisoner & his son Nathl ag^d 22 years of age & his daughter Esther age 13 years & kill^d his wife & his sons Daniel & John & his daughter Thankful, & one of y^m took his son Saml from the cart, but he kick^d & scratch^d & bit, so that ye indian set him down & struck ye edge of his hatchet into ye side of his head; he twich^d twice or thrice to pull it out and so left him for dead [illegible] & as he came to himself he look^d up & saw y^m running f^{rm} him. Bled considerably & brains came out at ye wound & went in a maz^d condition towards ye Fort, til he came to ye little bridge where fell off & was carr^d to Mr. W^{ms} & was so bad as left for dead, but it pleas^d god his life was spar^d & his wound healed & he is yet living; he was once or twice account^d to be dying & once acct^d as dead, a day or two after his being wound^d

Abigail Belding another daughter was shot in ye arm as she was running to the fort, but it is generally tho't ye bullet y^t struck her came from ye Fort. Sarah Belding another of ye daughters, hid herself among some Tobacco in ye chamber & so escap^d.

The people in the fort (being then at the public worship) were alarmed & shot from the Fort & wound^d one of ye enemy in the fleshy part of the thigh. the indians fired at ye Fort and wound^d one Mr. W^{ms} [Zebediah] as he open^d ye gate. the enemy presently withdrew (were not one quarter of an hour in doing ye exploit) and were followed by some Brisk young men into the meadow, who came within 30 rods of them & fired at them & ye indians at them again without damage on either side. the indians kill^d some cattle that were feeding in ye meadows, & a boy that had the care of the cattle hid himself in the weeds & escap^d. the enemy went up Green River & came to their companions that they had left wth Gillett. John Smead came into the Town soon after Mr. Belding's family were well off. Y^e 1st night ye enemy lodg^d in a round hole near the river, above ye rock, at Nf^d st., where y^r fires were fresh, thence set away for Canada by yᵉ way of Otter Creek, leaving Connecticut river &c. When they came near Otter creek, they came upon some tracks of Albany indians that were going to Canada, (for in those times yᵉ indians from Albany were wont to go a-scalping, as they call it, to Canada) they sent out their scouts & were upon the lookout, and at length discovered yʳ smoak; and then they flung down their packs & painted themselves & tyᵈ their English captives to trees & left two men to guard them: & proceeded to yʳ business, & having dividᵈ themselves into two companies, they sett upon the secure company (wᶜʰ consistᵈ of six men) & killᵈ two of yᵐ, took two & 2 escapᵈ. Among yᵉ slain was one Uroen an indian known among yᵉ english (& suspectᵈ to be a bloody fellow & sometimes mischievous to yᵉ english). Of their own men one was woundᵈ in yᵉ fleshy part of the thigh (as one had been before at D'f'd). the prisoners were one a Scatocook indian & yᵉ other a young Albany Mohawk. When the skirmish was over, the English were brot up & so they proceedᵈ on their journey. Mr. B. asked the Scatacook Indian, (now his fellow prisoners) what he thought the enemy would do with them, who replyᵈ that they would not kill yᵉ english prisoners, but give some of them to yᵉ french & keep some of them themselves; but he expected to be burnt himself, but when they came to yᵉ lake, one rainy night, they made no fire, and some of them lodgᵈ under yʳ canoes, from whom this Scatacook made his escape having loosed himself by some means from his cords &c., and altho he was psuᵈ the enemy could not recover him &c. As to the young Albany Mohawk, he was kept alive, being of their own nation (the french mohawks went from yʳ nation over to Canada for yᵉ sak of yᵉ romish religion) Wⁿ Mr. B. & company came to the fort callᵈ Oso, the males were obliged to run the Gauntlet near it. Mr. B. being a very nimble or light footed man, received but few blows, save at first setting out, but the other men were much abusᵈ by clubs, firebrands, &c:

They arivᵈ at Canada 8ᵇᵉʳ 9. Now they found what the Scatacook indian had said, to be true, for the indians kept Mr. B. himself & his daughter with them, & gave J. G. & N. B. to the french. J. G. worked as a servᵗ to yᵉ Nuns at their Farm. N. B. worked for the Holy Sisters. On yᵉ 9ᵗʰ of July following, Mr. B. was sold to yᵉ french & lived as a servᵗ with the jesuits at the seminary; his business was to wait upon them & cutt wood, make fires & tend the garden &c. He accounted himself favorably dealt with. In yᵉ winter following Coˡˡ Abrᵐ Schyler with some others came to Canada & brought with them a copy of yᵉ Articles of peace between England and France & returnᵈ home wᵗʰ some Dutch Captives. In Aprill following Coˡˡ peter Schyler & Coˡˡ A. Schyler & the Dutch Domine, wᵗʰ some others, came to Canada & the French governor gave liberty to all captives, English & Dutch, to return home, yea alowed them to oblige all under 16 years of age to return wᵗʰ them, those above yᵗ age were to be at their liberty &c. These Dutch Gentlemen gatherᵈ up wᵗ captives both English & Dutch they could & returned june 8 & took Mr. B. and his xdren and Martin Smith with abᵗ 20 more English with them, & arrived at Albany in about 15 days, where yᵉ Dutch showed to him a great deal of kindness, offered to send him home directly to Deerfᵈ. Coˡˡ Schyler clothᵈ him & his xdren at the desire of his brother Mr. John Belding of Norwalk, who paid him for the clothes &c. after about three weeks' stay at Albany, Mr. B. & his children went down the River to N. York wnere his B^r had provided a place for his entertainment & from York he went in a vessill to Stamford & from there went to Norwalk to his friends & after some stay there, return^d to D'f'd. J. G. got home a little before him by the way of France & so to England, having received great kindness in England.

At Deerfield it was thought that the assailants of the Belding family were some pretended friendly Indians. This sentiment was voiced by Capt. Partridge, who wrote Oct. 6th, 1696, that "the Deerfield people are fearful concerning the pretended friendly Indians proving enemies, being worse than open enemies;" and he proposed sending them "over the sea, or near the sea coast on some island." This suspicion was natural enough under the circumstances; their fears were justified; the day before, Oct. 5th, a party of Albany Indians who were staying about Hatfield, had killed Richard Church of Hadley, while both parties were hunting in Hadley woods. Four of the Indians were arrested and tried for the murder. Two of them were convicted, and executed at Northampton, Oct. 23d, 1696. [For detailed account, see Judd's Hadley, 263-5.]

Oct. 6th, a party of Indians was discovered between Deerfield and Hatfield. Oct. 7th, a letter, signed by John Williams, Solomon Stoddard and Capt. Partridge, was sent to Hartford, "declaring their distressed condition by reason of the mischief done among them by the Indians, and their great and continuall fear of more mischief from their barbarous enemies, with an earnest desire that the Gen'll Assembly would grant them a speedy supply of fortie or fiftie men for their defence." There was another party of Indians hunting at Deerfield, and a repetition of the Hadley tragedy was feared. On the receipt of this paper by the General Court, it "having seriously considered the matter, and compassionating the condition of their distressed friends, and also apprehending that his Majesties interest and the security of his subjects was deeply concerned, and that their was a necessity of speedy relief, did order, that forthwith fortie men, two of them officers, be forthwith levied" and well fitted and furnished, to be put under Lieut. Stephen Hollister and "to march with all possible speed up to Dearfield, there to employ themselves for the defense and security" of the inhabitants.

Part of this employment may have been to put the defensive works in repair. There was need of it, and the town voted Oct. 31st,—

"Thatt all Train Soldiers belonging in the Town of Deerfield shall labor about their fort y⁶ next Monday & Tuesday being y⁶ 2d & 3d days in November next ensuing for a general way beginning att one certain place of y⁶ fort and so going on."

The only other business at this meeting related to their defense against the devil. It was upon securing for each a proper seat in the new meetinghouse.

At a meeting Dec. 11th, 1696, voted,

"Thatt upon consideration, y⁶ Joseph Brooks, his cattle were killed by y⁶ enemie he shall have his cattle y⁶ he has sence bought, y⁶ is to say, 3 cattle one horse, Rate free for y⁶ year." "There was granted to Eleizer Hawks twelve shillings, which was formerly granted to Godfrey Nims as constable to pay him and was lost by y⁶ burning of s⁶ Nims house."

The sad casualty to which reference is thus made, occurred Jan. 4th, 1694. A step-son of Nims, Jeremiah Hull, perished in the flames. The particulars of the affair are learned from the return of the jury of inquest.

The said Jeremiah Hull, being put to bed in a chamber with another child, after some time, Henry, said Godfrey Nims's son, a boy of about 10 years of age, went into the chamber with a light & by accident fired some flax or tow, which fired the house. S⁶ Henry brought down one child, & going up again to fetch s⁶ Jeremiah, the chamber was all aflame & before other help came, s⁶ Jeremiah was past recovery.

This house stood on the site of the present Nims house, and where another house was burned with three children in it, Feb. 29th, 1704.

1697. This year proved to be another of uncommon hardship. It became evident before the opening of spring, that the short grain crop of the year before would soon be exhausted; and an appeal was made to Connecticut for charitable aid. Feb. 18th, six of the leading ministers of that colony wrote Gov. Treat, asking help for "such as are, or are likely in a short time to be in distress." March 6th, the Governor and Council,—

having heard and considered their affecting lines, and bearing on their spirits a deep sense of their obligation to works of charity to such of God's people as stand in need, doe see cause to order that a brief be sent forth through the Colonie, and do hereby recommend it to all the reverend elders, to exhort * * * the several congregations to contribute as God has blessed them * * * suitable relief to their christian brethren in distress.

Agents were selected to receive and transport the contributions, and a day of fasting and prayer appointed "for Wednesday come seven night."

March 27th, the Massachusetts Council ordered the regimental commanders to visit the frontier towns, and after consulting with the principal persons, to order such repairs on the old fortifications, and the building of such new, as they judged necessary for protection. This was to be done at the expense of the respective towns.

Our town had already anticipated the action of this order. March 1st, the town voted,—

> Thatt there shall be 3 Mounts built to ye fort about ye Town: to be set where and built according to ye Appointment of ye Committy of militia for ye Town: The 3 fort great gates to be built new strong and substantial with conveniences for fastening both open & shut as also y^t ye whole fort shallbe repaired and maintained sufficient & substantiall att these 3 particulars: To be done on a Town charge: only y^t ye fort and gates are to be maintained on a Town charge but for a twelve-month after ye date herof.

This was for the emergency. Usually, individuals had special parts of this work assigned them in proportion to their ability.

The spring was backward, with little promise. The summer was cold and wet. There was frost every month, and the crops were smaller than ever. The danger of invasion was imminent. Parties of English and Indians from Connecticut ranged the woods to the north and east continually. About twenty-five men came up in April. In May the number was increased to sixty-four, under the command of Lieut. Peter Aspinwall; and quite as many continued here until the fall of the leaves in October. Our frontiers were so well guarded that the only depredation recorded for this year was the killing of Sergt. Samuel Field at Hatfield, June 24th. No particulars of this affair have been found.

> Sept. 15, Capt Jona Wells and Ensigne Jno Sheldon were made choice by ye Town to view & look over all those Town papers (together with ye Town Clerk) y^t were left lose & unrecorded by ye former Town Clerk and to judge what papers are needful to be recorded and ye present Town Clerk is hereby ordered to record them.

The result of this action was the preservation of much important information on the records.

1698. The winter of 1697-8 was long and severe. Gov. Walcott writes:—

In February and March the snow was very high and hard. There was a great cry for bread, the cattle famishing in the yards for want, the sickness very distressing and mortal. Those in health could hardly get fuel, tend the sick, and bury the dead. Many suffered for want of fire and tendence.

Though this was said of Connecticut, the condition of things here was essentially the same. No mode of relief appeared but in an appeal to the Most High, and the 23d of March was appointed a day of fasting and prayer, "considering the hand of God upon his people in great sickness and mortality, and the sharpness and long continuance of the winter season." No Connecticut troops were sent up to Deerfield this winter, but sixteen Massachusetts soldiers were in garrison here, and June 10th, by an act of General Court, 16 men were allowed to garrison Deerfield.

The Peace of Ryswick, signed Sept. 20th, 1697, was proclaimed in Boston in December following. It was not proclaimed in Quebec until Sept. 22d, 1698, and it did not release the settlers from fear of Indian hostilities; and the continued necessity of watching by night, warding and scouting by day, seriously interfered with every other occupation. Alarms were frequent, but no attack was made on Deerfield this year, the vigilance of the guards preventing a surprise.

Joe English, a friendly Indian captured in 1697, came into town and reported that he left Canada "with a party of Indians, with some French joined to the number of near 70, in the whole (from whom he made his escape) and that 16 of them are designed for Deerfield, the remainder to assault the Frontiers lying upon the Merimack." This news was expressed to Boston, and laid before the Council, at a meeting on Sunday, June 12th. The invaders were not after heard from, having probably turned back on Joe's escape. A dispatch was sent to the Governor of New York, asking him to prevent the Scatacook, or River Indians, from joining the Indian rebels in this Province.

On the 15th of July a party in Hatfield north meadows

were fired upon by four Indians; John Billings, aged twenty-four, and Nathaniel Dickinson, Jr., thirteen, were killed. The horse of Nathaniel Dickinson, Sen., was shot under him, and his son Samuel, and Charley —— were captured. A post reached here with the news after dark. It seems to have been known or suspected that the Indians had canoes somewhere on the Connecticut, and a party was at once organized under Benjamin Wright to march up the river and intercept them. The English reached the great bend, in Vernon, Vt., some twenty miles distant, before daylight. Securing their horses at a safe distance, they silently posted themselves on the west bank of the river. The only account of what followed is found in Cotton Mather's "Wars of the Lord," published a few months after. I give it in his own quaint words:—

They perceived the Indians in their canoos coming up the river, but on the other side of it, within a rod or two of the opposite shore; whereupon they so *shot* as to *hit* one of the Indians, and they all jumpt out of the canoos, and one of the boys with them. The wounded Salvage crawled unto the shoar; where his back being broken, he lay in great anguish, often endeavoring with his hatchet for to knock out his own brains, and tear open his own breast, but could not; and another Indian seeing the two boys getting one to another, design[d] em a shot, but his gun would not go off; whereupon he followed em with his hatchet for to have knock[d] em on the head; but just as he came at em, one of our men sent a *shot* into him that spoil[d] his enterprise: and so the boys getting together into one canoo, brought it over to the friends thus concerned for them. These good men seeing their exploit performed thus far; *two Indians* destroyed and *two children* delivered, they fell to *praising of God*; and one young man particularly kept thus expressing himself: *Surely 'tis God, and not we, that have wrought this deliverance!* But as we have sometimes been told, that even in the beating of a *pulse*, the dilating of the heart, by a *diastole* of delight, may be turned into a contracting of it, with a *systole* of sorrow: In the beating of a few *pulse*, after this, they sent five or six men with the canoo, to fetch the other which was lodged at an island not far off, that they might pursue the other Indians; when those two Indians having hid themselves in the high grass, unhappily shot a quick *death* unto the young man, whose expressions were but now recited. This hopeful man's brother-in-law was intending to have gone out upon this action; but the young man himselfe importuned his mother to let *him* go: which, because he was an *only son*, she denied; but then fearing she did not well to *withhold her son* from the service of the publick, she gave him leave saying: *See that you do now, and as you go along, resign, and give yourself unto the Lord; and I desire to resign you to him!* So he goes, and so he dies; and may *he* be the *last* that falls in a long and sad war with *Indian Salvages*.'

This brave and pious young man was Nathaniel Pomroy of Deerfield, then eighteen years old. He was not an "only son," but he *was* the last that fell in that war. No memorial marks the rude grave, where his comrades tearfully laid him to his long sleep beside the murmuring river; but let "*Pomroy Island,*" the spot where he fell, keep green the story of his sad fate to all coming generations.

It was thought at first that this party of Indians were from Scatacook, and by order of the Council Joseph Hawley and Joseph Parsons were sent to Albany to give a particular account of the affair. They were guarded by Benj. Wright, Wm. King, Benj. Stebbins, Jona. Taylor and Nath'l Gillet.

The following paper, found in the Massachusetts Archives, gives the names of the men in the "Pomroy pursuit:"—

To the Gentlemen appointed to grant Debenters, or others who may Be Concerned therein. These may Inform that the Persons y^t followed and waylaid the Indians: Redeemed ye Captives with the loss of one and in probability of two of our enemies, on the 14 [16th] of July, 1698, Are As follows: Benj. Wright, Corporal of the troop, Leader; Benj. Stibbins, Jonathan Taylor, troopers; Thomas Wells, Benoni More, Ebenezer Stebbins, Nath. Pumrey, Dragoons; Corporal gillit, Benj. King, Jonath Brooks, Saml (?) Root, Jos Petty, Jos Clesson, Henerey Dwit, Garrison Soldiers at Deerfield.

We are of opinion that the persons above mentioned ought to be well rewarded. The 3 first Newly come into Deerfield weary out of the woods, and upon hearing of the news from Hatfield, four of the town, with seven of the garrison joining with them, went away in the Night. Their Journey was difficult, their undertaking hazardous, The issue successfull, & we hope of good consequence. The ready spirit of the Soldiers to go out tho under pay already, we beleive will be taken notice of for incouragement. The time of their service may well be esteemed two dayes. They travelling all the Night Before and the first three the night after from deerfield to Northampton, where they did belong. They all found themselves horses And provisions.

Deerfield, Augs^t 26, 1698—A true account as attest Jona. Wells, Capt of the fort in D^{fld}
   & Comander of the garrison there.
                                                JOSEPH HAWLEY.
                                                SAMUEL PATRIGG.

Nov. 9th, 1698, Benj. Wright was allowed £3, the "six inhabitants," £2 each, and the garrison soldiers £1 each, by the General Court.

Aug. 13th, Earl Bellamont wrote a letter to Frontenac, Governor of Canada, complaining of the attack at Hatfield. The latter replies Sept. 21st, regretting it and says: "This obliges me to send a second order to these Indians to make them cease hostilities." The assailants were Pocumtucks, and some of them were known to the captive boys. Frontenac pretended they were Acadians, and that the attack was to avenge the imprisonment of some of these people in Boston. He had been willing that the Indians should harass our settlers until formal complaint was made. But Sept. 22d, the day after he wrote to Bellamont, peace was proclaimed at Quebec, by Frontenac; a year and a day after, the treaty was signed.

In April, 1698, Col. Schuyler and others went from Albany to Canada to gather and bring away the English captives. In June, Daniel Belding and his children, with Martin Smith, and about twenty other prisoners, left Canada by the way of the lakes for Albany, where they arrived after a journey of fifteen days. There Mr. Belding and his children were entertained and provided with clothing at the expense of his brother, John Belding of Norwalk, Connecticut. After recruiting three weeks, the Belding family went down the Hudson to New York, and by a vessel to Stamford, whence they walked to Norwalk, to visit their benefactor, after which they returned to Deerfield. Martin Smith was sent home from Albany. John Gillett reached home before the Beldings by the way of France and England.

Gillett's story is well told below by Col. Partridge:—

Wheras John Gillet who hath been a very active and willing sould^r within the County of Hampshire & Being on the 16th day of Sept 1696 out upon service & together wth some others was that day taken by the Enemy & suffering hardship was carried to Canada Captive & there Remayn^d till Sept^{er} Last & then was sent from thence Prison^r unto old ffrance & thence (by the later Articles of Peace) the s^d Gillet together with other Captives was Released & carried into England: Since his Arrivall there hath Lived & obtained pay for his Passage by the Charitie of some English Marche^{ts} there: & now being arrived here Destetute of Money or Cloaths for his P^{r}sent Reliefe Humbly propose it to y^r Hono^{ble} Gen^{ll} Cor^{te} to allow him something w^t this Cor^{te} judge meet for his P^{r}sent Reliefe

        SAMUEL PATRIGG—

June 17 1698—In the House of Representatives—Orderdered that there be allowed and paid out of the Publick Treasury the sum of six pounds to the above named John Gillet for the consideration above mentioned

        NATH^l BYFIELD.
         Speaker

By vote of the town, December 27th, 1698,—

CRIME AND FATE OF SARAH SMITH. 263

Daniel Belding & Martin Smith, being new returned out of captivity, their heads, together with w^t Ratable estate was on there hands at ye date of ye present meeting, were freed from Town charges y^o year 1688.

Among the prisoners sent home from Canada under the treaty was Martin Smith, who was taken in 1693. A sorrowful tragedy awaited him. His wife was in prison at Springfield, about to be tried for murder. Little is known of the Smiths, beyond what is found on the court records. Judd thinks they came from New Jersey. Martin received several grants of land here, among the first settlers. The first mention we find of his name is on the court record at Northampton: "May 31, 1674, Martin Smith, a resident of Pocumtuck, was fined 20 s for trying to kiss the wife of Jedediah Strong, on the street." Aug. 4th, 1694, Sarah Smith enters a complaint against John Evans of Deerfield, for "attempting to force an unclean act upon her." Two young soldiers of the night watch were witnesses of the act, which was at her house, "ten rods south of the south gate of the fort." I find no action under this complaint. In the assault of Feb. 29th, 1704, Martin Smith was "smothered in a seller," with the family of John Hawks, Jr. No children of Martin and Sarah Smith are known. The crime and fate of Sarah appear in the following record:—

At a meeting of the Council in Boston, Aug. 8, 1698—Upon information given by His Majesty's Justices in the County of Hampshire, that one Sarah Smith lies in prison for murdering her bastard child. * * * Ordered and appointed that a Court of Assize and General Gaol Delivery be held and kept at Springfield within said county of Hampshire by the Justices, upon Thursday, the eighteenth of the present month of August for the trial of said Sarah Smith.

Pursuant to this order three justices, Wait Winthrop, Elisha Cooke, and Samuel Sewall, escorted by a guard of twenty-six troopers, went up to Springfield and held a court. Sarah Smith was indicted by a grand jury of sixteen men, John Holyoke, foreman, and charged that,—

on Tuesday the eleventh day of January in the year of our Lord God one thousand six hundred and ninety-seven–8 betwixt the hours of one and five a clock afternoon of the same day at Deerfield * * * in the dwelling house of Daniel Wells * * * by the providence of God one female bastard child did bring forth alive * * * being led by the instigation of the devil, between the hours of one and seven a clock afternoon of the same day, withholding her natural affection, neglected and refused all necessary help to preserve the life of s^d child, and with intent to conceal her Lewdness the said child did strangle and smother.

She pleaded not guilty, was tried, and found guilty before a jury of twelve men, Joseph Parsons, foreman. Justice Winthrop pronounced the sentence, that she be hung the following Thursday, Aug. 25th. Her minister, Rev. John Williams, preached a sermon before her on the day of the execution, in accordance with the custom of the times.

Tradition concurring with known facts, fixes the place of the murder to be in the northeast room of the house now standing on the east side of the street on the second lot north of Memorial Lane, now owned by C. Alice Baker. By the same authority, in several generations, this house has been haunted. The last visible ghost disappeared about thirty years since.

CHAPTER X.

COMMON FIELD FENCES—STOCK—MILLS—ROADS—
SCHOOLS—RATES—HOUSES.

One of the earliest and most frequent subjects of legislation by the settlers was that of fencing the meadow lands. It was an affair of vital interest. These lands, as we have seen, were laid out in long, narrow strips; this, and the fact that they were subject to inundation, alike made it impossible to fence the lots separately. The stock was allowed to run at large on the East Mountain, and to protect the crops on the meadow a common fence was built as a prime necessity. Beginning at the "point of rocks," at Cheapside, it ran by the foot of the hills to the north end of the street, thence along the rear of the west home lots to South Meadow, along its north and east borders to Wapping, by the west end of Wapping home lots to Boggy Meadow, thence westerly, crossing the the Hatfield road at the Bars, and skirting Stebbins Meadow to the Pocumtuck River at Stillwater—an extent of about seven miles. Later the meadows at Cheapside and Wisdom were also enclosed, requiring about seven miles more of fence. This fence was laid out in "divisions," and two fence viewers were annually chosen to each division, whose duty it was to see that the fence was made secure, and that all orders concerning it were obeyed. In 1692 it was found necessary to extend the fence from the "point of rocks," along the bank, to the mouth of Deerfield River, "to prevent the cattle going over [the river] to Cheapside to damnify the corn and grass there. A committee was chosen to lay out to the proprietors of land at Cheapside their proportion of said fence, and the rest of s^d fence to be done by ye town."

All fences were ordered "to be made sufficient as against orderly cattle, so also against hoggs that be sufficiently ringed," but no prescribed material or mode of building is found at the period we are considering. This common fence was supported by the owners of land enclosed, in proportion to their interest. February, 1687, Thomas Wells, Henry White and Thomas French, were chosen a committee to apportion the fence and locate each man's share. They reported a list of fifty-seven owners, and the length set to each in rods, feet and inches. The shortest was to Francis Keet—ten feet three inches. The owners of home lots in the town were obliged to build one half of their rear fence, and those at Wapping the whole of it. A condition was made in all grants there, that the grantee should make all fence wherever the grant abutted on the common field.

Gates were set up on all roads leading into the meadows, except on the road leading from Hatfield into South Meadows, where there was a set of *bars*. The name of the village there testifies to that fact to this day. The first gate-keepers were John Broughton, at the north gate, Samuel Northam, the middle of the town, Jonathan Wells, at Eagle Brook, and Ephraim Beers at Wapping. Eleazer Hawks had care of the bars. Beers, in 1686, agreed to keep up forever, two rods of fence across the highway, including the Wapping gate, in consideration of a grant of twenty acres of land in Wisdom. When cow commons in the meadow fell short of measure, "wanting lands" were located elsewhere; but the rule was to assess the fence on the original number of commons. Votes like the following illustrate this practice. After granting sixteen acres to John and Benoni Stebbins, "for want of 8 acres of measure in the meadow, y^t is to say, in the whole 36 cow-com'ons (formerly John Stebbins' sen'r), ye s^d Jno. & Benony making com'on fence, & paying Rates for the whole 36 com'ons forever." In a similar case, William Smead was "to maintain com'on fence & pay Rates for his land as it now lies for, by com'ons, in the meadow."

The regulations about the fence were strict, and provision made to bring easily home to the offender any neglect in keeping his share secure. It was voted,—

"that any person whatsoever, concerned with any com'on fence * * * shall set up a stake with the two first letters of his name fairly written, at ye north end of every part * * * of ye com'on fence to be made up, on penalty of 12d a stake for every stake y^t ye viewers shall find wanting, & so from time to time, as often as they shall by y^m be found wanting."

A few years later, stones in place of stakes were ordered for this purpose.

The fall feeding, or "opening the meadows," was yearly a subject of legislation. The Common Field fence was "made intire," or closed, in the spring, and opened in the fall, at times fixed, first by the selectmen, and later in town meeting. The earliest action recorded was:—

April 4, 1692; whereas ye Selectmen have taken great care and paynes y^t all defects in ye common fence be repayered for the preservation of ye meadows now the Town does hereby order y^t all common fence y^t shall be found defective after ye 11th day of this instant: ye own^r of s^d fence shall pay as a fine to ye use of ye Town one shilling p^r rod for one day & so forward for every day till such defective fence shall be repayered

That all cattle baited upon other mens land without leave shall be liable to be pounded

That any persons baiting cows or young cattle upon ye meadows shall be liable to be pounded tho there be a keep^r wth y^m

That all hoggs shall be rung according to law: * * * the hog ringers shall have 6d p^r head for every hogg y^a ring.

That all horses and cattle found in ye meadow are liable to pay 12d p^r head: and for hogs 6d p^r head & for sheep 4d p^r head

That ye penalty for leaving creatures in the meadow wilfully shall be 3d p^r head

That pounding creatures shall be *present pay*

Similar regulations in even more stringent language were passed in December following, and repeated in some form every year.

March 3d, 1693-4, the by-laws already given were adopted by the town. A vote was passed,—

Sept 15 1697; that the time for opening the meadow or corn field shall be on Monday at night being the 4th day of October unless ye Townsmen having hereby power see cause to lengthen the time. That the selectmen now in being shall have pow^r to make sale of ye old Red Town Bull & dispose of ye money to ye Towns use.

Dec: 7: 1697 ye Town Bargained with Ens Jno Sheldon to maintain a gate at ye uper or South end of their meadows on ye highway at ye meadow fence: * * * to be made and set up by the first of April next.

Mch 7 1697–8 voted that if any person or persons shall leave open any of ye Meadow gates wilfully or carelessly within ye time of the meadow being inclosed: Such persons or their overseers shall be liable to pay 2s 6d for every such offence ye one half to ye informer ye other to ye Townsmen for ye use of ye Town.

By this arrangement the *bars* were discontinued, a nuisance abated, and doubtless a great strain on the morals of travelers removed. Sergt. John Hawks was accepted in place of Capt. Wells, to maintain the gate at Eagle Brook, and the fence was made into three divisions.

In 1699, the disputed question as to the rights of the public on highways was settled. The town voted "That all proprietors of land within y⁰ meadows or Com'on Field, shall have liberty to feed or mow such highways which their land shall abut upon, and no other person."

Lands were cultivated at Cheapside and Wisdom, and to protect the crops there, it was voted:—

Mch 1, 1700, yᵗ wᵗ cattle horse kind or any other creature soever usually impounded shall be found at liberty on y⁰ westerly or northerly side of Deerfield river within y⁰ township of Deerfield shall be liable to be impounded provided they be found there within y⁰ time of y⁰ enclosing of y⁰ common field.

That y⁰ meadows be Cleared by y⁰ Haywards by y⁰ eleventh of y⁰ instant March.

The bad effect of allowing stock to trample the land in the spring was then realized. In pursuance of this vote, the selectmen were charged with the duty of clearing the meadow of Hatfield horses by driving them into the Hatfield meadows. Voted: "That all y⁰ common fence * * * be kept up in good repair untill y⁰ towns next election meeting in next March so as to pass y⁰ fence viewers." This policy seems to have continued. The same vote was passed Sept. 15th, 1701; also, "That all swine of 16 inches or upward * * * found in y⁰ meadows or common field unringed shall be impounded and Ringed before released out of y⁰ pound y⁰ owners * * * to pay 6d a head for impounding 3d for ringing." Four divisions were made of the fence in 1702, and eight fence viewers chosen.

During this period the stock was branded or marked, and ran at large on the East Mountain; the milch cows under the care of a "cow-keeper," hired by the town. His wages were assessed on the owners of the cows. A bull to run at large, was furnished at the expense of the town. In 1686, the people at Wapping procured a separate bull to run with their own herd.

Saw and Grist Mills. For some years the settlers got out boards, slit-work, and plank in saw-pits. Logs were squared with the broad axe and taken to the pit, where the work was done by two men, the "top-sawyer," who guided the saw, and had the largest wages, and the "pit-man" whose place was under the log in the pit. About one hundred feet of boards was a day's work.

Grain was pounded in a mortar, or carried to Hatfield mill on horseback. This mill had no bolter; if flour was desired, the meal was sifted by hand, in a sieve, at home.

It is not known when the first sawmill was erected. One stood on Mill river as early as 1689, when the town authorized the selectmen to bargain with Capt. John Allis of Hatfield, to build a corn mill upon the same stream. Mr. Allis died in January, 1690–91, before his mill was finished. Feb. 3d, 1690–91, a committee was authorized to make a bargain with Joseph Parsons, Sen., of Northampton, on essentially the same terms granted Mr. Allis. The mill put up by Parsons stood on Mill river, "where the sawmill now stands," and where Mr. Phelps's sawmill stands to-day. It was probably finished before Dec. 20th, 1692, at which date the town granted Parsons as part of the bargain, a tract of land,—

Att the uper end of the meadow comonly called Stebbins meadow all that tract of land that lies between ye last lot y^t is now layd out and the comon fence; by estimation, 30 or 40 acres * * * bounded by the land of Maj^r John Pynchon northeast; by the comon fence southwest; by the Dearf^d river northwest, and by ye comon fence south east; s^d Joseph Parsons being to make comon fence for it, as shall be found by measure proportionally to what other men doe for their lands on the meadows; and to pay rates att present only for so much of it as is Improvable.

"Ten acres of upland," was also granted. By the contract, signed Dec. 29th, 1692, Parsons was—

To take for his tole for Grinding ye twelfth part of all grain except wheat and Barly Malt and only the fourteenth part of wheat and ye eighteenth part of Barly malt: and for provender the fourteenth part: * * * the mill to be set up and fit to grind att or before May 31, 1693, and to be kept in good Repair fit to doe ye towns work.

Should the mill be deserted, or destroyed, "except in case of extraordinary Providence as the Town being driven out by the enemie; * * * the remainders of said Mill as Irons, Stones," &c., were to revert to the town, unless Parsons rebuilt. If a place more for ye Towns Benefit to have a mill set there," be found, Parsons is to "have the first offer of s^d place. The town agree to furnish ye help of 6 cattle and two men to draw y^u millstones to ye place; s^d Joseph Parsons to call for them in a time y^t may be as little hindrance to their occasions as he can." These stones may have been procured from Mount Tom where Pynchon got millstones in 1666. The stone now lying in front of Memorial Hall was doubtless one of those set running by Parsons in 1693. Its dimensions agree exactly with those got out by Pynchon at Mount Tom. No further account of this mill appears; and it was probably destroyed by Indians during the war.

Aug. 3, 1699, Att a Meeting ye town, considering y^t they were in great want of a mill to Grind their Corn, made Choice of a Commity, viz Ens Jno Sheldon; Benony Moor and Thos. French whose work it was to view and consider of a place or places * * * for to erect a mill in as also to discourse with Mr. Joseph Parsons to see * * * whether he will Rebuild his mill upon the Sawmill Stream * * * in another place, or throw up his interest in a mill or mills at Deerfield.

Four weeks later Mr. Parsons was asking of the *Proprietors* "liberty to set a corn mill on Green river. Being considered, it was granted for ye space of a twelve month." If a mill was then built on Green river, it did not give satisfaction as it appears by a vote passed,—

March 11, 1700-1, That a Commity be chosen to discourse with Mr Joseph Parsons concerning the Corn mill built by him in Deerfield whether he will stand to his Bargin, either to maintain s^d mill in good Repair fit to doe ye towns Grinding or throw it up into ye towns hands.

The same committee above named, except Edward Allen in the place of French, were chosen to apply this "prod" to Parsons, and nothing more is heard of the mill for ten years. This topic will be resumed at a later period.

Roads. Among the duties assigned the committee which laid out the Dedham Grant in 1671, was that of "apoynting the highways and laying out." Their report shows that the town street was then located, from the middle and each extreme of which, roads three rods wide were laid to the mountain on the east, and meadows on the west. They also provided for roads two rods wide, running through each division of meadow, "so that every man may come to his land." These roads are essentially the same with those now in use.

The "Country highway" was the road to Hatfield through South Meadows, and up Bars Long Hill. Before 1687, there was a road leading southerly from the middle mountain road, in the rear of John Catlin's home lot, [now the Ware lot] almost exactly where the road to the Connecticut River railroad freight depot, and the sawmill, now runs, and so through the woods east of Wapping through Turnip Yard to Sunderland bridge.

March 16 1698–9, ye Committy Chosen to Consider ye mater (viz Lieutt David Hoyt: Ens Jno Sheldon and Edward Allyn,) made y^r Return to ye Town Clerk in y^s maner: viz: * * * that they had stated and settled ye middle heiway leading up to ye mountain to be eight rods wide at ye front on Town Street: and then at ye end of eighteen rods and a half from ye front upon s^d John Catlin's North line ye heiway comes to be Three Rods wide and so holdeth thurowout to ye Reer.

This is Memorial Lane.

March 3d, 1700-1, Capt. Jona. Wells, Sergt. John Hawks, and Daniel Belding, were chosen to look up a road from the south end of the town, along the west side of the East Mountain, "to the head of Muddy brook swamp," as also "to view ye way now began to be made from Wapping towards Hatfield to se where they shall be stated if found to be feasible: and make Return of w^t they find upon these accounts in writing to ye Town." No return of this commission has been found.

In 1690, a road was laid across the land of Thomas French in Little Meadow, to give access to the lands at Old Fort Meadow. In compensation, French was given the same quantity, to be taken in the rear of his home lot—worthless sidehill, for rich meadow land. But the road has been carried off by the river long ago, while the side-hill still holds the Orthodox parsonage lot to the East Mountain.

March 5, 1693–4, Henry White & Simon Beaman and Jos Barnard * * * are appoynted a Com'itty to examine the Antient Records and Acts of the form^r Com'itty with reference to hieways in Dearf^d Meadows: and accordingly State a hieway to the land on the west side [of the] riv^r Com'only Called Carter's Land.

Nothing appears to have been done respecting the road at this time.

March 3d, 1700-1, Godfrey Nims, Sergt. John Allyn and Corp. Thomas Wells were chosen to lay this road. They reported June 14th, 1701, that they have laid out ye hie way to Carters land in this manner: we begin to turn out of ye hie way y^t leads down into ye Neck in Samuel Carters lot on the northerly side of it next to Mr John Catlins land: and to Run down there untill it comes to ye River: and then to run along by ye river until it comes of Henry White's lot:

Here we find the origin of "White Swamp." The river at this point has largely encroached on the meadow, and nearly the whole of the lots named have been washed away, and added to the Carter's Land farm opposite, where George W. Jones had the benefit of it. The committee also reported:—

As to ye hie way to ye Green River lands we turn out of ye Country Road which is Easterly of the Green River Town plot, and to Run near upon a west line throw ye middle of s^d Town plot down to ye River, and Runs over ye River into Peter Evans his lot: then Runs northwards into Joseph Petty his lot and across his lot untill it comes to ye North side of and so in Joseph Pettys lot untill it comes up ye great hill westerly and then it Runs in Benony Moors lot until it comes to the foot path and then it runs in ye foot path to the uper end of Green River lands: the breadth to be one Rod and a half except in the part of it from the Country Road down to and so thorow ye Town plot afores^d.

This part was what is now the Main street of Greenfield. The "country road," I suppose, included the present High street, and led from Deerfield to Northfield. The "foot path" was the Indian road, which crossing the Pocumtuck at Stillwater, ran northerly through Wisdom and Greenfield Meadows, and up the hill at the right of Mrs. Eunice Williams's monument.

"Sarveyors of Roads" were chosen with the earliest town officers, and annually thereafter. Their duties were the same as those of to-day. Highway taxes could be paid at will in "specie" or labor, the latter "as he shall be warned thereto by the sarveigher." The price of labor on the road was fixed by the town and varied with the season and from year to year.

Schools. No town action regarding education is found until after the close of King William's War. The first schoolhouse was built, and a school master hired, in 1698. Before this, doubtless, schools had been kept by dames in private houses. It has been seen that Mrs. Beaman had a school in 1694. In 1698 the town established a school, and enforced attendance by hiring a master at the expense of all those having children of school age.

THE FIRST SCHOOLHOUSE.

Mch 7, 1698, It was agreed and voted y^t a school be *continued* in ye Town: That all heads of familes y^t have Children whether male or female, between ye ages of six and ten years, shall pay by the poll to s^d school whether y^n send such children to School or not

That a School house be built upon ye Town Charge in ye year 1698 ye dimensions of s^d house to be 21 foot long eighteen foot wide and seven foot betwixt joynts

That a Com'ity shall be chosen to look after ye building of said School House, and to hire a school master

That ye persons for a Com'ity y^t ye Town did choose and empower in ye carrying on ye school house aforesaid and in hiring a school master: were Mr. Jno. Catlin Benony Stebbins and William Armes:

Att a legal Town meeting in Deerfield, March 21, 1698, Capt Wells Moderator further relating to a school, it was y^n agreed y^t what children soever shall be sent to s^d school above ye age of ten years or under ye age of six years shall pay for according to ye time y^a shall improve s^d school; voted affirmatively

This meeting was a special one, and no other business was transacted. The schoolhouse was built and a school master engaged. Probably "Mr. John Richards," who was certainly a resident in 1699, and school master in 1701-2-3. Another meeting was held Dec. 27th, 1698, when it was voted,—

That there be a schooll maintained in ye Town of Deerfield

Att ye same meeting ye Town agreed and voted y^t from ye time of ye date hereoff, untill ye term of 20 years forwards be expired they will give twenty pounds towards ye maintaining of a Schooll in ye Town

This heavy tax, in the then exhausted condition of the town, shows the spirit of some controlling influence. In March, 1700, the school committee chosen were,—

Mr. Jn^u Catlin, Sergt Jno Hawks and Jno Stebins * * * whose work shall be to hire a meet person or persons to teach ye Towns Children to Read and write as also to repair ye Towns School house at their discretion which is to be repaired at ye Towns Charge; as also to proportion ye providing of firewood to ye Scholars:

In 1701, a change of policy is noticed, although no cause for it appears. The town,—

Unanimously voted to make null and void their former act of twenty pounds for twenty years towards a School and have voted to pay fifteen pounds in *pay* yearly for ye space of Seven years from ye day of y^s date hereof towards ye maintaining of a School in Deerfield:

The Com'ity chosen for looking after the concerns of ye afores^d, were Ensigne Jno. Sheldon, William Arms, Sergt. Eliezer Hawks.

Their duties were defined to be the same as those given above. The committee for 1702 were Benoni Stebbins, Godfrey Nims and Simon Beaman. In 1703, "Mr. Jno. Catlin: Dea. Hoyt: and Ebenezer Smead were chosen." They,—

Bargained with Mr Jno Richards to pay him for ye teaching of their Town children for ye year Twenty and five pounds in manner folowing: y^t is to say They have by Bargin liberty to pay him ye one 3d part of s^d sum in Barley and no more: ye other two 3ds in other grain y^t is to say in indian corn: peas: or Rye in any or all of them: oats wholly excepted: all these aforementioned to be good and merchantable;

The Town y^n voted y^t all children y^t is to say boys from four to eight: and Girls from 4 to six years old y^t live in ye Town plat shall pay their proportion of ten pounds for ye year ensuing whether they go to School or not:

This is the last record of any action on the subject of education until 1720, when the town had in a good degree recovered from its broken condition.

Rates, or Taxes. The first record of any rate was that raised Dec. 17th, 1687, when "Jonathan Wells was chosen Com'issioner to joyn wth ye Selectm^n to take lists for the Country rate and officiate in ye business according to Law. That the Town & Minist^r Ratte shall be raised upon Lands heads & flocks at the same prises as hath been ye last year past." It appears from the above, that this was not the first general tax; the previous impositions had doubtless been made under the direction of the Committee. Subsequent action of the town shows the "prises" (or valuation) to have been:—

Heads att 16 pounds; oxen 3 pounds, cows 2 pounds; 3 yr olds 2 pounds; 2 yearlings 1 pound ten; 1 year old 15 shillings; horses 3 pounds; 2 yr olds one pound ten; 1 year old 15 shillings; hoggs 10 shillings; sheep 5 shillings; lands 2 pounds per acre.

The "specia" in which the minister's rate was to be paid, was fixed at his settlement. For town rates, it was varied from time to time, probably as different crops were scanty or abundant. Rates were generally laid in December and for expenses already incurred.

In 1691-3, the town rate was paid in wheat and Indian corn in equal parts. In 1694, it was to be paid "one-half in indian corn at 2s a bushell, & one-half in fatted pork, at 2 pence half-penny a pound."

In 1695 the Green River lands were made "rate free," and in 1696, no tax was laid on "fat cattle and swine killed in ye town." No reason for this exemption appears.

In 1697, rates were to be paid in Indian corn at 2s; the next year in rye at 3s, barley 3s, Indian corn 3s, one-third each.

In 1699, the "Country Rate" was £5 for Deerfield. Swine were rated according to goodness: ten shillings for ye Best and so downward, when for market. "And wheras homelots were last year Apprized According to Industry, y^t now y^a shall not be so aprized." The "specia" was "Rye at 3s per bushel, and Indian corn at 2s per bushell."

The prices fixed "for grain between man and man shall be thes folowing, namely, viz Winter wheat at 4s per bushell: Sumer wheat at 3s 6d per bushell: Rye at 3s per bushell: Barley at 3s per bushell: peas at 3s per bushell: Indian Corn at 2s per bushell: and oats at 1s 6d per bushell:"

Dec. 16th, 1700, "Lieut David Hoyt: Sergt. Jno Allyn: and Benony Moor: were chosen aprizers," to appraise "all lands and stocks Rateable in Deerfield * * * according to ye best of their Judgment upon the Rates set and prescribed for Aprizal ye last year:" a few weeks later, March 3d, 1700-1, "Ens Jno Sheldon was Chosen Com'isioner for Assesments for ye year ensuing * * * Capt Jona Wells and Mr John Richards and Ens Jno. Sheldon were chosen Assessors for the Country Taxes." The special functions of these three boards does not clearly appear. Down to 1702, the valuation of taxable property had continued as it was in 1686. In January of that year, a new departure was made. The regular meeting for December, 1701, was held and money raised as usual. There is no record of this action, but it appears in the following votes:—

Jan. 27, 1701-2, The Town then unanimously agreed and voted, y^t notwithstanding their minister and Town Rates are already made yet y^t they will alter the former way of Rating, which was by ye Country law by way of income The town then also voted y^t heads shall be Rated at 24 pounds Estate * * * As to aprisall of lands ye town proceeded in this maner folowing viz. : That the Great meadow and pine hill plain that is from little meadow hill and Jno Broughton's hill to Deerfield River and also Cheapside; Tho Frenches lot in Harrow meadow; log meadow; and part of Stebbines meadow; that is to say from the northerly part of it unto James Browns south line shall all be set at 30 shillings an acre: * * * That Carters land: Newfort mowing land of ye 2d Division Capt Wellses pasture; from 2d Division hill to ye south line of Mr. Catlin's lot in 2d Division; with the Residue of Stebbinses meadow all to be set at eighteen shillings an acre; That ye Residue of harrow meadow and Eagle Brook plain from Capt Wellses pasture to 2d Division hill shall be set at fifteen shillings an acre:

That old fort meadow and little plain shall be set at ten shillings an acre:

That ye Residue of 2d Division, from ye South line of Mr. Catlins lot Southward shall be set at Six Shillings an acre; That Green River lands shall be set at five shillings an acre That ye Best homesteads shall be Aprized at Eight pounds and so to descend according to goodness to be aprized by ye Select men: Ens Jno Sheldon and Thomas French were chosen to joyn with the Select men in taking a list of all estate Rateable:

Cattle and horse kind to be aprised as in ye Country law; Yearling Cattle and horses to be Aprised at ten shillings: Two year old cattle and horses at twenty shillings: 3 year olds at thirty shillings.

The taxes for this year's charges were paid in "Rye at 3s, barley at 3s, corn at 2s and oats at 1s 6d, an equal proportion of each."

DWELLINGS; AND AN EVENING AT HOME.

The first houses of the settlers were doubtless of logs, one story high, "daubed" with clay. A common form was eighteen feet square, with seven feet stud, stone fire-places, with catted chimney, and a hip-roof covered with thatch. These structures generally gave way in a few years to large frame houses, covered with clo'boards and shingles, having fireplace and chimney of brick, which was laid in clay mortar, except the part above the roof, where lime was used. Of these houses, two styles prevailed; one represented by the "Old Indian House," the other, less elaborate, by the house now [in 1888] standing on the Smead lot. This house is thirty feet square, two stories, with pitch roof, facing the street westerly. It is covered with cloveboards, apparently the original, with no signs of paint. It has four windows in front, and five at each end. The front door, a little south of the center, opens directly into the south front room, which is sixteen by eighteen feet. On the north of this is the huge chimney, which rises through the ridge, and the north front room, twelve by thirteen feet. North of the chimney is a large, dark closet. East of it is the kitchen, eleven by twenty feet, south of which is the buttery. Stairs to cellar and chambers occupy the southeast corner. The space over the kitchen is unfinished. The southwest chamber is fifteen by fifteen, the northwest twelve by thirteen. Each story is seven and a half feet stud. The frame is of hewn timber, generally nine by fourteen inches. The plates are nine by sixteen; those at the ends in the upper story project twelve inches over the walls, supported by the side plates, and studs on the inner edge. The rafters are sawed, four by four inches, and supported by purlins which are framed into heavy beam rafters at the middle and each end of the roof. The whole building is of pine. There was no lath and plaster; the walls were made of matched boards. The ceiling was finished by planing the joists and underside of the floor above; the floors were double or of matched boards.

The "Old Indian House," built by John Sheldon about 1696, stood at the north end of the training field, facing the south. Its frame was largely of oak. It was twenty-one by forty-two feet, two stories, with a steep pitch roof. In front, the second story projected about two feet, the ends of the cross beams being supported by ornamental oak brackets, two of which are preserved in Memorial Hall. A lean-to thirteen and a half feet wide, ran the whole length of the north side, its roof being a continuation of that on the main building.

The ground floor was thus thirty-four and a half by forty-two feet. Near the centre rose the chimney, about ten feet square at the base, with fire-places on the sides and rear. South of it was the front entry, which, including the stairway, was eight by twelve feet. The lower floor was laid under the sill, which, projecting beyond the wall, formed a ledge around the bottom of the rooms, a tempting seat for the children. Stepping over the sill into the front entry, doors on either hand opened into the front rooms; stairs on the right led by two square landings, and two turns to the left, to a passage over the entry, from which at the right and left doors led to the chambers. In the rear of the chimney was a small, dark room, with stairs to the garret. Including the garret, there were five rooms in the main structure, each of them lighted by two windows with diamond panes set in lead.

The kitchen was in the central part of the lean-to, with windows in the rear; east of this was a bedroom, and west, the buttery and back entry.

The fire-place was a deep cavern, the jambs and back at

right angles to each other and the floor. Here, hanging on nails driven into a piece of wood built into the structure for the purpose, hung the branding-iron, the burning-iron, the pot-hook, the long-handled frying-pan, the iron peel or oven slice, the scooped fire-shovel with stout tongs standing by. In one end was the oven, its mouth flush with the back of the fire-place. In this nook, when the oven was not in use, stood a wooden bench, on which the children could sit and study the catechism and spelling book by firelight, or watch the stars through the square tower above their heads, the view interrupted only by the black, shiny lug-pole, and its great trammels; or in the season, its burden of hams and flitches of pork or venison, hanging to be cured in the smoke. The mantletree was a huge beam of oak, protected from the blaze only by the current of cold air constantly ascending.

The preparation of fuel was no light task, and "building a fire" was no misnomer. The foundation was a "back-log," two or three feet in diameter; in front of this the "fore-stick," considerably smaller, both lying on the ashes; on them lay the "top-stick," half as big as the back-log. All these were usually of green wood. In front of this pile was a stack of split wood, branches, chips and cobs, or, if cob-irons were present, the smaller wood was laid horizontally across these. The logs would last several days and be renewed when necessary, but the fire was not allowed to go out. Should this happen, the fire-pan was sent to a neighbor for coals, or the tin lantern with a candle for a light. In default of neighbors, the tinder-box, or flint-lock musket with a wad of tow, was used to evoke a spark. "Tending fire," meant renewing the lighter parts of the fuel; for this purpose, there was, in prudent families, a generous pile of dry cord-wood in the kitchen.

With these appliances, considerable warmth was felt in the room; the larger part of the heat, however, was lost up the chimney. Fresh air rushed in at every crack and cranny to supply this great draft; and although the windows were small, and the walls lined with brick, there was no lack of ventilation. In this condition of things, the high-backed settle in front of the blazing fire was a cozy seat. It was the place of honor for the heads of the family and distinguished guests. Sometimes the settle was placed permanently on one

FINISHING AND FURNISHING.   279

side of the fire-place, the seat hung on leather hinges, under which was the "pot-hole," where smaller pots, spiders, skillets and kettles were stored.

The fire-places in the front rooms were of the same pattern, but smaller than that in the kitchen. Fires were seldom built there except at weddings, funerals, or on state occasions. The furniture, for the most part home-made, rude and unpainted, was scanty—a few stools, benches and splint-bottomed chairs; a table or two, plain chests, rude low bedsteads, with home-made ticks, filled with straw or pine needles. The best room may have had a carved oak chest, brought from England, a tent or field bedstead, with green baize, or white dimity curtains, and generous feather bed. The stout tick for this, the snow-white sheets, the warm flannel blankets, and heavy woolen rugs, woven in checks of black red blue or white, were all the products of domestic wheel and loom. There were no carpets. The floors were sprinkled with fine white sand, which, on particular occasions, was brushed into fanciful patterns with a birch broom, or bundle of twigs. The style of painting floors called "marbling," hardly yet extinct, was a survival of this custom.

The finishing of the "Indian House" was more elaborate than that of the Smead house; but there was no lath and plaster, the ceiling being the same. The partitions and walls were of panel-work, with mouldings about the doors and windows. These mouldings were all cut by hand from solid wood. In some cases the oak summertree was smoothed and left bare, with a capital cut on the supporting posts; generally, hereabouts, it was covered with plain boards, it may be, in the best room, with panels. No finer lumber is found than that with which these old houses were finished.

Their massive frames, each stout tenon fitted to its shapely mortise by the try rule, whose foundations were laid by our sires so long ago that the unsubdued savage still roamed in the forest where its timbers were hewn, stand as firmly as when the master builder dismissed the tired neighbors, who had heaved up the huge beams and pinned the last rafter to its mate (for there were no ridge-poles) at the raising.

The ample kitchen was the centre of family life, social and industrial. Here around the rough table, seated on rude stools or benches, all partook of the plain and sometimes stinted fare. A glance at the family gathered here after nightfall of a winter's day, may prove of interest. After a supper of bean porridge, or hasty-pudding and milk, which all partake in common from a great pewter basin, or wooden bowl, with spoons of wood, horn or pewter; after a reverent reading of the Bible, and fervent supplication to the Most High, for care and guidance; after the watch was set on the tall mount, and the vigilant sentinel began pacing his lonely beat, the shutters were closed and barred, and with a sense of security, the occupations of the long winter evening began. Here was a picture of industry, enjoined alike by the law of the land and the stern necessities of the settlers. All were busy. Idleness was a crime. On the settle, or a low arm chair, in the most sheltered nook, sat the revered grandam—as a term of endearment called granny—in red woolen gown, and white linen cap, her gray hair and wrinkled face reflecting the bright firelight, the long stocking growing under her busy needles, while she watched the youngling of the flock, in the cradle by her side. The goodwife, in linsey woolsey short-gown and red petticoat, steps lightly back and forth in calf pumps, beside the great wheel, or poising gracefully on the right foot, the left hand extended with the roll or bat, while with a wheel-finger in the other she gives the wheel a few swift turns for a final twist to the long-drawn thread of wool or tow. The continuous buzz of the flax wheels, harmonizing with the spasmodic hum of the big wheel, shows that the girls are preparing a stock of linen against their wedding day. Less active, and more fitful, rattles the quill wheel, where the younger children are filling quills for the morrow's weaving.

Craftsmen are still scarce, and the yeoman must depend largely on his own skill and resources. The grandsire, and the goodman, his son, in blue woolen frocks, buckskin breeches, long stockings, and clouted brogans with pewter buckles, and the older boys, in shirts of brown tow, waistcoat and breeches of butternut-colored woolen homespun, surrounded by piles of white hickory shavings, are whittling out with keen Barlow jack-knives, implements for home use:—ox-bows and bow-pins, ax-helves, rakestales, forkstales, handles for spades and billhooks, wooden shovels, flail staff and swingle, swingling knives, or pokes and hog yokes for unruly cattle and swine. The more ingenious, perhaps, are fashioning buckets, or powdering tubs, or weaving skepes, baskets, or snow shoes. Some, it may be, sit astride the wooden shovel, shelling corn on its iron-shod edge, while others are pounding it into samp or hominy in the great wooden mortar.

There are no lamps or candles, but the red light from the burning pine knots on the hearth glows over all, repeating, in fantastic pantomime on the brown walls and closed shutters the varied activities around it. These are occasionally brought into a higher relief by the white flashes, as the boys throw handfuls of hickory shavings on to the fore-stick, or punch the back-log with the long iron-peel, while wishing they had "as many shillings as sparks go up chimney." Then, the smoke-stained joists and boards of the ceiling, with the twisted rings of pumpkin, strings of crimson peppers, and festoons of apple, drying on poles hung beneath; the men's hats, the crook-necked squashes, the skeins of thread and yarn hanging in bunches on the wainscot; the sheen of the pewter plates and basins, standing in rows on the shelves of the dresser; the trusty firelock, with powder horn, bandolier and bullet pouch, hanging on the summertree, and the bright brass warming pan behind the bedroom door—all stand revealed more clearly for an instant, showing the provident care for the comfort and safety of the household. Dimly seen in the corners of the room are baskets, in which are packed hands of flax from the barn, where, under the flax-brake, the swingling knife and coarse hackle, the shives, and swingling tow have been removed by the men; to-morrow the more deft manipulations of the women will prepare these bunches of fibre for the little wheel, and granny will card the tow into bats, to be spun into tow yarn on the big wheel. All quaff the sparkling cider, or foaming beer, from the briskly circulating pewter mug, which the last out of bed in the morning must replenish from the barrel in the cellar. But over all a grave earnestness prevails; there is little laughter or mirth, and no song, to cheer the tired workers. If stories are told, they are of Indian horrors, of ghosts, or of the fearful pranks of witches and wizards.

This was the age of superstition. Women were hung for witches in Old England and New, and witchcraft believed in everywhere. Every untoward event was imputed to supernatural causes. Did the butter or soap delay its coming, the churn and kettle were bewitched. Did the chimney refuse to draw, witches were blowing down the smoke. Did the loaded cart get stuck in the mud, invisible hands were holding it fast. Did the cow's milk grow scant, the imps had been sucking her. Did the sick child give an unusual cry, search was made for the witches' pins by which it was tormented. Were its sufferings relieved by death, glances were cast around to discover the malignant eye that doomed it. Tales of events like these, so fascinating and so fearful, sent the adults as well as children to bed with blood chilled, every sense alert with fear, ready to see a ghost in every slip of moonshine, and trace to malign origin every sound breaking the stillness,—the rattle of a shutter, the creaking of a door, the moan of the winds or the cries of the birds and beasts of the night. For more than a century later, the belief in witchcraft kept a strong hold on the popular mind, and must have had a marked influence on the character of the people.

For two or three evenings previous to Feb. 29th, 1704, a new topic of supernatural interest had been added to the usual stock. Ominous sounds had been heard in the night, and, says Rev. Solomon Stoddard, "the people were strangely amazed by a trampling noise round the fort, as if it were beset by Indians." The older men recalled similar omens before the outbreak of Philip's War, when from the clear sky came the sound of trampling horses, the roar of artillery, the rattle of small arms, and the beating of drums to the charge. [See Sewell's Journal Vol. 1, for noises heard in the air about 1672.] As these tales of fear, coupled with their own warning, were in everybody's mouth, what wonder if the hearts of the thoughtful sank within them; that they cowered with undefinable dread, as under the shadow of impending diaster; and asked each other with fear and trembling the meaning of this new and dire portent. They had not long to wait the answer.

CHAPTER XI.

QUEEN ANNE'S WAR—1702—1713.

The peace of Ryswick was of short duration. The harassed settlers of Deerfield had small chance to recover from their low condition, before the quarrels of European princes to establish a balance of power, brought fire and sword all along the frontiers of New England. Charles II. of Spain died Nov. 1, 1700, making over the throne by will to Philip of Anjou, a French Bourbon heir. The possession was resisted by Archduke Charles of Austria, in behalf of the House of Hapsburg, and the war of the Spanish Succession broke out.

Sept. 16, 1701, exiled James II. of England, died in France, where his son, the "Pretender," was at once proclaimed King of England, by the French monarch, Louis XIV. William III. of England, resenting this insult and threat, formed a strong alliance with Austria and other powers against France, but he died soon after, March 8, 1702. His successor, Queen Anne, declared war against France May 4, 1702, and for more than ten years Europe was convulsed to its center in a conflict to establish a balance of civil and ecclesiastical power. The scent of blood crossed the sea, and the English colonies soon felt the fury of Romish zeal and savage ferocity.

Joseph Dudley, with a commission from Queen Anne as Governor of Massachusetts, landed at Boston June 11, 1702, bringing news of the impending war. The same news had reached Canada at an earlier date, for only two weeks later, the inhabitants of Deerfield became aware of preparations for hostilities among the Indians, as appears by the following record:—

Att a legall Town meeting in Deerfield, June 26, 1702: Ens. Jno. Sheldon, moderator:
That ye Town fort shall forthwith be Righted vp   Voted affirmatively   That every man shall for ye present Right vp his proportion of ye fort y^t was last laid out to him   Voted affirmatively.

That all ye fort shall be Righted vp by Wednesday next at night vpon penalty of 3 shillings p^r Rod for every Rod y^n defective and after y^t one shilling per Rod per day so long as s^d fortification shall lie unrepaired: Voted afirm: That ye comisioned officers shall be ye men y^t shall Inspect and pass ye fort in General: Voted afirm

That a pitition be sent to ye Gouerner for help and Relief in our present distress occasion by a prospect of war: The Town left ye wording of s^d petition with Capt Jonath Wells and Mr Jno Richards together with ye selectmen: Voted afirmatively:

The action of the Council on the petition sent under this vote shows that the evident alarm here was not considered groundless:—

In the Council July 2d 1702.

Upon a representation made by the inhabitants of Deerfield in the County of Hampshire, the most westerly frontier of the Province, that a considerable part of the Line of Fortification about their Plantation is decayed and fal^n down, praying for some assistance in rebuilding and setting up the same, for that they are apprehensive of some evil designs forming by the Indians, an unwonted intercourse of Indians from other Plantations being observed.

Advised, That his Excellency do write to John Pynchon Esq Coll. of the Regiment of militia in that County, directing him forthwith to send his Lieut. Coll to Deerfield aforesaid to view the Palisado about that Town, and to stay there some short time, to put the Inhabitants upon the present repair of the said fortifications in all places where it is defective, and to cover them with a scout of ten men by turns out of the next towns whilst they are about the said work, and to assure them of an necessary support and to take the like order as to Brookfield saving the scout. The scout not to be paid. [Six soldiers were paid £65 for this service.]

On the peace of 1697, some of the settlers had left Meetinghouse Hill and located "some a mile and some two miles" away; now they were gathering again within the palisades.

Att a legall Town meeting in Deerfield Sept 11: 1702: Ens Jno Sheldon moderator The Town y^n agreed and voted y^t ye Comon field shall be opened on wednesday in ye morning being ye 30th day of y^s instant September 1702 There was also at ye same meeting a little piece of land Granted to Sergint Jno. Hawks to builde on in ye fort for his lifetime: which land is to be in ye middle hieway leading into ye meadow and on ye South East corner of Mr. Jno Williams his home lot adjoyning therevnto as it shall be laid to him by a Comitty:

The Comitty Chosen for s^d work were Capt Jonathan Wells Liett Dauid Hoyt and Sergeant Benony Stebins:

Town meetings for public business were often held at this period, and always under the lead of military officers.

"Dec^{mb} 24: 1702: Ens Jno Shelden moderator The Town y^n

VAUDREUIL SUCCEEDS CALLIERES.

agreed and voted y^t all timber or firewood y^t shall be only fal^n and not cut vp shall be forfeted at any time after it hath lain fal^n 3 months"—a provision, it seems, for getting a winter's stock of fuel with the least exposure to an enemy. There is no account of any hostilities about here at this time, but "John Santimore and Peter Boyloe, two Frenchmen, prisoners" of whom I learn nothing—they may have been spies— were taken from Deerfield to Boston by Stephen Belden and Samuel Allen, for which service they were paid by the Council, Jan. 17, 1702–3, £6, 10 s.

In May, 1703, Lord Cornbury, Governor of New York, sent word to Gov. Dudley, that, through his Mohawk spies he had learned that an expedition against Deerfield was fitting out in Canada. Similar information was sent here by Maj. Peter Schuyler not long after, and twenty soldiers, enlisted in the towns below, were stationed here as a garrison.

M. de Callieres, Governor of Canada, had already secured the neutrality of the Iroquois, and Dudley, in the same line of policy, met the sagamores of the Eastern Indians at Casco, June 30th, 1703. Here the old treaty was solemnly renewed. Both parties "added a great number of stones" to the piles called the "twin brothers," erected at a former treaty; volleys were fired by each. and the Indians sang and danced for joy. They declared "that as high as the sun was above the earth so far distant shall their design be of making the least breach between each other." The savages were doubtless honest in these expressions, but they had placed their destiny beyond their own control, and in six weeks were all in arms against the English. Before the arrival of Dudley the sagamores had sent to Canada for help to revenge on the English some fancied or real wrong. M. de Callieres died about that time and M. de Vaudreuil, Governor of Montreal, succeeded him. Vaudreuil eagerly responded to this appeal of the Abenakis, and sent Lieut. Beaubassin, with five hundred Indians and some French, to their aid. On his arrival Beaubassin was told of the new treaty of peace and of the satisfaction for their complaints, but he declared it was too late; they had been sent for, and came, to fight the English, and if the Abenakis refused to join them, themselves should be the first object of attack. This rupture "was not effected without protracted discussion," says French authority, but the savages at length succumbed to Beaubassin's threats. The army was divided, and at 9 o'clock a. m. of Aug. 10th, 1703, by concerted action, every English town on the coast was surprised.

The sending of this force to Maine was one of the earliest of Governor Vaudreuil's official acts, and to his ambition must be attributed the horrors of the Indian war that followed. He gleefully writes to France that Beaubassin "laid waste more than fifteen leagues of territory and took or killed more than 300 prisoners."

His conduct was not approved at home. Ponchartrain, the Minister of War, condemns this expedition. He says: " M. de Vaudreuil was wishing for it, in M. de Callieres' time, who would never consent to it, no more than I. I have a perfect knowledge that the English want only peace, aware that war is contrary to the interests of all the colonies. The French have always commenced hostilities in Canada." Fears were entertained in France that the English would in turn incite the Iroquois to attack Canada.

Vaudreuil had written the War Minister that he "considered it highly necessary to embroil the Indians of these parts and the English, otherwise the Abenakis, who are wavering, might * * * eventually be opposed to us," and that "the serious attack we have obliged them to make" was part of his plan. Again he speaks of "the absolute necessity we were under to embroil them with the English * * * The English and the Indians must be kept irreconcilable enemies * * * The Jesuits were watching the Indians * * * Father Rasle wrote that the Abenakis would take up the hatchet when I pleased."

The Iroquois, not understanding the cause of the outbreak, offered, says Vandreuil, "to act as mediators between the English and us." This did not meet the views of the governor, and this Christian office of the savages was declined by the American representative of " His Most Christian Majesty " of France.

After the return of Beaubassin six Indians were killed at Pigwacket by a party of English under Col. March.

The disapproval of the home government did not reach Vaudreuil in season to prevent his fitting out another expedition—this time against our devoted town. We shall see how closely this was connected with the events on the Maine coast, which have been noticed.

The condition of affairs here at this time is vividly pictured in the letter of our minister given below. No one was for a moment safe outside the palisades; but there was less risk, it was thought, in being out after dark than in the daytime, when every movement could be observed from the adjoining hills. It was found, however, that danger lurked under the shades of night, as well as in the glare of sunshine. The common field had been opened Oct. 1st; on the 8th two young men, probably after their milch cows feeding there, were surprised, captured and taken to Canada by Indians. The following account of the affair is found on a scrap of paper, in the handwriting of Stephen Williams:—

Zebediah Williams & John Nims went into ye meadow in ye evening to look after creatures, & wer ambushed by indians in ye ditch beyond Frary's bridge, who fir^d at y^m, but miss^d y^m, and took W. quick, & N ran to ye pond, & then return^d to y^m (fearing to be shot,) ye Indians [then?] woun^d cattle and went off. Y^e men were carried to Canada, where W. dyd, & N ran away in ye year 1705, wth joseph petty, Thos Baker and Martin Kellogue. My father escaped narrowly ye n^t before at Broughtons hill.

The alarm caused by news of hostilities in Maine was now increased ten fold. Military affairs in Connecticut were put into the hands of a Council of War, with authority to defend Hampshire county as well as their own borders. By the following paper it would appear that a garrison of sixteen men, probably from Connecticut, was continued here through the season:

An account of Billets of Sixteen Soldiers at the Garrison in Deerfield, from the 21st of October, 1703, to the sixth of December following, amounted to £6-3-5, having been examined by your Commissary General, was presented;

And it was paid to the order of Capt. Jona. Wells. The pay of Massachusetts garrison soldiers was five shillings per week, as established by order in Council, May 29th, 1703.

It had become a question whether our fortifications were strong enough to resist an attack, and a town meeting was called for Oct. 15th, 1703.

The Town at s^d meeting Considering there nesasaty of fortifing agreed & voted y^t a comitty should be chosen to ioyn with Colonell patrigg to consult agree & determin wheither to fortifi or no and if y^a agree to fortifie then in what manar place or places   The comitty to s^d work were: Capt Wells: lieut Hoyt: Ens Jno Sheldon: and Daniel Belden:

One result of the consultation ordered above appears in the following petition:—

To his Excellency, Joseph Dudley, Esq. Capt Genl & Govr over this Prouince of the Massachusets Bay & to ye Counsell & Representatives in Gen Corte assembled this 27 Oct. 1703.
The Town of Deerfield who lye much exposed to ye present enemy, wch obstructe them much in their occations, their Lives hanging in doubt everywhere w^n they goe out. Also they are now forced to rebuild their fortifications at much disadvantage to them, & it being 320 rod or upwards, will fall very heavy to do it all upon their own charge, were verry earnest with me w^n lately there, to plead with this Corte for some allowance towards the doing of it out of their publique Rates now to be collected there; as also, that they might be Quitted of Rates to ye publique for ye tyme being of this present warr, w^h is so destressing upon them.

SAML PARTRIDGE.

By the statement of Col. Partridge it is seen that 320 rods of palisading was required. Mr. Williams says 206 is required. In 1693 "the whole compass of the fort was 202 rods." Perhaps the present plan was to enclose with stockades the houses of Capt. Wells and Lieut. Hoyt, as places of refuge in sudden alarms—they were both well situated for that purpose, south and north of the main fort—and not unlikely to add flankers to the latter. There is no evidence of any works at Hoyt's, but when the shock came, the stockading of Wells's house proved the salvation of many.

The following modest, ingenuous and pathetic letter, gives a vivid picture of our settlement at this time. It was addressed:—

For his Excellency Joseph Dudley Esq her Majesties Govenor for the Prounce of Massachusetts Bay in N. E &c at his dwelling house In Roxb:
Deerf. October 21, 1703.
May it please your Excellency:
As i am bound in duty i would thankfully acknowledge your care and concernment for our safety in the seasonable provision to get the fortification made up, & in the care to have a supply of souldiers with us, so i am emboldened to lay before your Excellency our distress^d state & condition, knowing your forwardness to commiserate & incourage frontiers, that you may stir up your Councele & the Assembly to an encouraging of them, i would be far from showing any discontented complaint; an evil too common & frequent, to the dishonour of God, the scandal of religion, & the great exercise of them

that are in place of power: yet I would lay open our case before your Excellency as it is; we have been driven from our houses & home lots into the fort, (there are but 10 house lots in the fort). Some a mile some 2 miles, whereby we have suffered much loss, we have in the alarms several times been wholly taken off from any business, the whole town kept in, our children of 12 or 13 years and under we have been afraid to improve in the field for fear of the enemy, (our town plat & meadows all lay exposed to the view of an enemy if they come at any time on the mountains). we have been crowded togather into houses to the preventing of indoor affairs being carryed on to any advantage, & must be constrained to expend at least 50£ to make any comfortable provision of housing if we stay togather in cold weather: so that our losses are far more than would have paid our taxes; the people have been very ready & forward to pay their taxes, & know sensibly that the present curcumstances of the country call for & require great taxes, & would not in the least grumble, but i lay it before your Execellency, to move your Compassions of us: Strangers tell us they would not live where we do for twenty times as much as we do, the enemy having such an advantage of the river to come down upon us, several say they would freely leave all they have & go away were it not that it would be disobedience to authority & a discouraging their bretheren: The fronteir difficulties of a place so remote from others & so exposed as ours, are more than be known, if not felt. i am very sensible that if they have no ease as to their rates under these circumstances, the people must suffer very much; when the Country abated them their rates formerly, i was yet moved from certain knowledge of their poverty & distress, to abate them of my salary for several years togather, tho they never askt it of me; & now their children must either suffer for want of clothing, or the Country consider them, or i abate them what they are to pay me: i never found the people unwilling to do when they had the ability, yea they have often done above their ability; i would request your Execellency so far to commiserate, as to do what may be encouraging to persons to venture their all in the fronteirs, their charge will necessarily be trebled, if this place be deserted: i would humbly beg they may be considered in having something allowed them in making the fortification: we have mended it, it is in vain to mend & must make it all new, & fetch timber for 206 rod, 3 or 4 miles if we get oak: The sorrowful parents, & distres^d widow of the poor captives taken from us, request your Excellency to endeavour that there may be an exchange of prisoners to their release; i know i need not use arguments to move your Exc^{ys} pitty & compassion of them & endeavours to have them returned; the blessings of them y^t are ready to perish will surely come upon you, in endeavours of this kind: i pray God direct & every way assist & encourage your Excellency in the great work before you, in a day of so great exercise & trial as this is: my duty to yourself and Good Lady, with due respects to your Honorable family, requesting forgiveness for any failure in my writing as exercising your patience, begging prayers for me & mine, i rest your Excellency humble sevant, JOHN WILLIAMS:

[P. S. on the back.]

The people of the town earnestly requested me to draw something to present to your Excellency & the assembly in their behalf & desire this may be presented in their name both to yourself, Council & Representatives.

Your Excelancys humble servant.
[Mass. Archives, 113-350.]

This letter and the following from the Northampton minister, doubtless accompanied the petition of Partridge, and both were written for the same end. There seems to be a good deal of force in Stoddard's recommendation to train dogs to track the enemy, particularly in the suggestion that the men, being relieved from the danger of ambush, could follow the savages so much more effectively. A practical objection, however, may have existed in the difficulty of teaching the dogs to distinguish between the enemy, and the friendly Indians employed as scouts.

These letters are given entire, not only as presenting pictures of the sad condition of our town, but because they contain much of value from other points of view.

Rev. Solomon Stoddard to Gov. Dudley:—

Excellent S^r

The Town of Deerfield has suffered much formerly from the Indians: of late two of their young men are car. into Captivity: this makes great impression on the Spirits of the people & they are much discouraged. This puts it upon me to make two proposals to your Excellency—

The first is that they may be put in a way to Hunt the Inds. with dogs—Other methods that have been taken are found by experience to be chargable, hazzardous and insufficient: But if dogs were trained up to hunt Inds as th do Bears; we sh. quickly be senseble of a great advantage thereby. The dogs would be an extream terrour to the Inds; they not much afraid of us, they know they can take us—& leave us, if they can but get out of gun-shot, th count themselves in no great danger, however so many pursue them they are neither afraid of being discovered or pursued; But these dogs would be such a terrour to them, that after a little experience it w^d prevent their comming & men would live more safely in their houses & work more safely in the fields and woods: In case the Inds sh. come near the Towne the dogs w^d readely take their track & lead us to them: Sometimes we see the track of one or two Inds but cant follow it; the dogs would discover it and lead our men directly to their enemies; for want of w^h help we many times take a good deal of pains to little purpose—Besides if we had dogs fitted for that purpose our men might follow Inds w^h more safety, there would be [no?] hazzard of their being shot at out of the bushes, they would follow their dogs with an undaunted spirit, not fearing a surprise; & indeed the presence of dogs would very much facilitate their victory: the dogs would do a great deal of execution upon the enemy, & catch many an Ind that w^d be too light of foot for us.

If it should be thot by any that this way is impractible & that dogs would not [deavor?] to do what we expect from them, these two things may satisfy them, one is that in a time of war with Inds in Virginia, they did in this way prevail over them, though all attempts before they betook themselves to this method proved in vain; the other is that our Hunters give an account the dogs that are used to hunt Bears, mind no other track but the track of a Bear; from whence we may conclude, that if dogs were used to persue Indians they would mind nothing else.

If the Indians were as other people are, and did manage their warr fairly after the maner of other nations, it might be looked upon as inhuman to persue them in such a maner. But they are to be looked upon as theives and murderers, & they doe acts of hostility, without proclaiming war, they dont appear openly in the field to bid us battle, they use those cruelly that fall into their hands, they act like wolves, & are to be dealt withall as wolves.

There must be some charge in prosecuting this design, something must be expended for purchasing suitable dogs, & their maintenance, the men who spend their time in this service must be paid, but this will not rise in any proportion to the charge of maintaining a suitable number of garrison soldiers—I have taken advice with several of the principal persons among us & they looke upon this way as the most [favorable?] expedient in this case.

The other proposal is that the town of Deerfield may be freed from Country Rates during the time of the war; their circumstances doe call for commiseration: sometimes they are allarmed & called off from their businesse, sometimes they dare not goe into the fields & when they doe goe, they are fain to wait till they have a gard; they cant make improvement of their outlands, as other Towns doe, their houses are so crowded, sometimes with souldiers, that men and women can doe little businesse within doors, & their spirits are so taken up about their Dangers, that they haye little heart to undertake what is needful for advancing their estates: it seems to be a thing acceptable to God, that they should be considered & freed from Rates; Your Excellency will not take it amiss that I take my accustomed freedom & am so officious as to tender my advice before it is asked.

The Good Lord guide y^r Ex'cy & the Genrl Assembly; to do that w^h shall be servicable to this afflicted Country w^h is the hearty prayer of your humble servant. SOLO: STODDARD

Northampton Oct 22d 1703.

Since I wrote: the father of the two Captives [Godfrey Nims] belonging to Deerfield, has importunately desired me to write to y^r Ex'cy that you w^d endeavour the Redemption of his children—I request that if you have any opportunity, you w^d not be backward to such a work of mercy.

The Assembly record for Nov. 26th, 1703, contains the following:—

Considering the extraordinary impoverishing circumstances the

Town of Deerfield is under by Reason of the present War, Resolved, that the sum of Twenty Pounds·be allowed and paid out of the publick Treasury towards the support of the ministry in the said Town of Deerfield for the y^r cur^t.

The weeks dragged slowly on. The green robes of summer had been changed to garments of scarlet and gold, among which the painted and plumed warrior could lurk unseen; but the town was unmolested. The blasts of autumn had laid this gaudy screen, seared and dry, upon the ground, forming a russet carpet, which not even the soft moccasined foot of the Indian could traverse undiscovered. The snow of winter piled unusually deep, and the wooded wilderness, stretching two hundred miles between the settlement and Canada, seemed a safe barrier; and with each changing season the feeling of security grew stronger. The settlers breathed more freely and gradually resumed their wonted ways of life, believing that the warnings of invasion were founded on unreliable reports.

Among the interesting events of the winter were the successful attempts of two Deerfield maidens to secure "French and Indian captives." The affairs were settled by treaties of alliance, which were ratified by Pastor Williams. The victorious contracting parties were Abigail Stebbins with James Denieur—one of three Frenchmen from Canada living here —and Elizabeth Price, with "Andrew Stephens ye Indian," of whom nothing more is known, save that he was killed in the assault of Feb. 29th.

Another notable marriage was that of John, son of Ensign Sheldon, to Hannah Chapin. Their wedding journey was a winter's horseback trip from Springfield to the since historic "Old Indian House," the bride on a pillion behind the groom. What but the great love which binds a woman's heart to her husband could have induced her to leave her secure home in Springfield, to brave with him the dangers of this doomed frontier? Of the six persons married as above, five were, within a few weeks, swallowed up by death or captivity.

The guard of twenty men, allowed by the Council in May, 1703, were now here quartered among the inhabitants, two of them in the house of the minister. The winter wore away, even to the last day, and no enemy had been seen; the only alarm being the supernatural one, already noted. Mr. Williams, the pastor, did not share in the general feeling of security, and did not attempt to conceal his anxiety. He urged caution and vigilance, and above all, counseled the people to repentance of sin, and to walking in the ways of the righteous, that the wrath of God might be averted. He says:—

> I set apart a day of prayer, to ask of God, either to spare, and save us from the hands of our enemies, or prepare us to sanctify and honor him in what way soever he should come forth towards us * * * The places of Scripture from whence we were entertained were Gen. xxxii. 10. 11. *I am not worthy of the least of all the mercies, and of all the truth which thou hast shewed unto thy servants. Deliver me, I pray thee, from the hand of my brother, from the hand of Esau: For I fear him, lest he will come and smite me, and the mother with the children,* (in the forenoon.) And Gen. xxxii. 26, *And he said, let me go, for the day breaketh: And he said, I will not let thee go except thou bless me* (in the afternoon.) From which we were called upon to spread the causes of fear, relating to ourselves, or families, before God ; as also, how it becomes us, with an undeniable importunity, to be following God, with earnest prayers for his blessing, in every condition. And it is very observable, how God ordered our prayers, in a peculiar manner, to be going up to him: to prepare us, with a right Christian spirit, to undergo, and endure suffering trials.

His people had need of all the Christian faith and fortitude with which this devout man could inspire them, for the day of trial was come.

The tale of the assault on Deerfield, Feb. 29th, 1703-4, shall be told in the words of those who gave or felt the stroke, or were contemporary witnesses. No attention will be paid to any modern versions conflicting with these. The speculations are my own.

THE CAPTURE OF DEERFIELD, FEB. 29TH, 1703-4.

Governor de Vaudreuil writes to the war minister at Paris, Nov. 14th, 1703, that he should send a strong party against the English in the spring, "were it only to break up the measures the English might be adopting to induce the Abenaquis to conclude peace." And again, one year later, Nov. 17th, 1704,—

> We had the honor to report to you last year, my Lord, the reasons which had obliged us to embroil the English with the Abenakis, and the heavy blow which, with that view, we caused Sieur de Beaubassin to strike. Shortly after he had retired, the English having killed some of these Indians, they sent us word of it, and at the same time demanded assistance. This obliged us, my lord, to send thither Sieur de Rouville, an officer of the line, with nearly two hundred

men, who attacked a fort, in which, according to the report of all the prisoners, there were more than one hundred men under arms; they took more than one hundred and fifty prisoners, including men and women, and retreated, having lost only three men and some twenty wounded.

That the true motive of the expedition against Deerfield has been thus given, is shown by another letter from Vaudreuil to the Minister, Nov. 16th, 1704, in which he speaks of "the success of a party I sent this winter on the ice as far as the Boston government at the request of the Abenakis." Charlevoix, in his history of New France, tells the story of an attack by the English on the Abenakis, whose

chiefts called on M. Vaudreuil for aid, and he sent out during the winter 250 men commanded by the Sieur Hertel de Rouville * * * who, in his turn, surprised the English, killed a large number of them, and took 150 prisoners. He himself lost only three Frenchmen, and some savages.

In the letter of November 16th, quoted above, Vaudreuil commends de Rouville, and asks his promotion, complacently adding, "Sieur de Rouvilles party, My Lord, has accomplished everything that was expected of it; for independent of the capture of a fort, it showed the Abenakiss that they could truly rely on our promises; and this is what they told me at Montreal on the 13th of June, when they came to thank me."

Thus this representative of a Christian nation, sent an army through the wilderness, not to fight an English force, but to surprise and butcher the settlers of an English plantation three hundred miles away, merely to keep on good terms with a savage tribe, and gratify his own ambition. It was an act of hardly less than cold-blooded murder. De Rouville's command was made up of two hundred French, and one hundred and forty Indians, part French Mohawks, or "Macquas" of Caghnawaga—probably in civilized dress—and part Eastern Indians in native costume. The oft-told tale that the Indians for the love of their favorite valley, came back to punish the white intruders, is pure romance; for not a Pocumtuck or the son of a Pocumtuck appears on the scene. On the contrary, the Macquas were the hereditary enemies of the Pocumtucks.

The invaders were provided with moccasins and snow shoes, and brought an extra supply for the use of captives

Provisions were brought along on sleds, some of which were drawn by dogs, and each man carried a pack upon his back. Their food becoming exhausted, the whole force was scantily supported on game killed by the Indian hunters. When De Rouville reached this vicinity, the French were half starved, almost in a state of mutiny, and would doubtless have surrendered to the English at discretion had the attack on the town been unsuccessful.

The route of the invaders was probably up the Sorel river and Lake Champlain, and by French river over the Green Mountains, and down the Connecticut river. On reaching the mouth of West river, at the foot of Wantastiquat Mountain, the sleds and dogs were left with a small guard. The main body pushing rapidly on, reached Petty's Plain, February 28th, at night. Skirting the foot of West Mountain along the bluff overlooking North Meadows, a halt was made, probably near or on the farm now occupied by Lucius B. Wise, a mile and a half northwest from the fort. Here, sheltered by a low ridge from possible observation from the town, their packs were deposited, the war paint put on, and other preparations made for the assault. Creeping down the hill, and crossing the Pocumtuck on the ice near Red Rocks, spies were sent towards the fort, and the advance regulated by their reports. The following, published in 1726, is from Penhallow, who gives as his authority Rev. Solomon Stoddard, whose son John,—afterwards the famous Col. Stoddard,—was one of the two soldiers in the house of Mr. Williams that night.

PENHALLOW'S ACCOUNT OF THE ASSAULT.

Towards morning, being February 29th, the enemy sent scouts to discover the posture of the town, who observing the watch walking in the street, returned and put them to a stand; after awhile they sent again and were advised that all was still and quiet; upon which two hours before day, they attacked the fort, and by advantage of some drifts of snow, got over the walls. The whole body was above two hundred and fifty, under the command of Monsieur Arteil, who found the people fast asleep, and easily secured them. The most considerable part of the town thus fell into their hands. They left no garrison unattacked, excepting that of Capt. Wells; but at Benoni Stebbins they met with some repulse and lost several. Sixty English fell whereof many were stifled in a cellar, and a hundred were taken captive, who with melancholy countenance condoled each others misery, yet durst not express the anguish of their souls. That day and night were spent in plundering, burning and destroying. The next morning they withdrew to the woods.

The writer's mistake as to the time the enemy spent in town, which has been followed by other writers, is corrected in the next extract.

REV. JOHN WILLIAMS'S RELATION.

On Tuesday, the 29th of February, 1703–4, not long before the break of day, the enemy came in like a flood upon us; our watch being unfaithful, an evil, whose awful effects, in a surprisal of our fort, should bespeak all watchmen to avoid, as they would not bring charge of blood upon themselves. They came to my house in the beginning of the onset, and by their violent endeavors to break open doors and windows, with axes and hatchets, awakened me out of sleep; on which I leapt out of bed, and running towards the door perceived the enemy making their entrance into the house; I called to awaken two soldiers in the chamber, and returned to my bedside for my arms; the enemy immediately brake into the room, I judge to the number of twenty, with painted faces and hideous exclamations. I reached up my hands to the bed-tester for my pistol, uttering a short petition to God for everlasting mercies for me and mine, * * * expecting a present passage through the valley of the shadow of death. Taking down my pistol, I cocked it, and put it to the breast of the first Indian that came up; but my pistol missing fire, I was seized by 3 Indians who disarmed me, and bound me naked, as I was in my shirt, and so I stood for near the space of an hour; binding me, they told me they would carry me to Quebec. My pistol missing fire, was an occasion of my life being preserved. The judgment of God did not long slumber against one of the three which took me, who was a Captain; for by sun-rising he received a mortal shot from my next neighbor's house, [Benoni Stebbins] who opposed so great a number of French and Indians as *three hundred*, and yet were no more than seven men in an ungarrisoned house. * * * The enemy fell to rifling the house, entering in great numbers into every room. * * * The enemies who entered the house were all of them Indians and Macquas; insulting over me awhile, holding up hatchets over my head, threatening to burn all I had; but yet God, beyond expectation, made us in a great measure to be pitied; for tho some were so cruel and barbarous as to take and carry to the door two of my children and murder them, as also a Negro woman; yet they gave me liberty to put on my clothes, * * * gave liberty to my dear wife to dress herself and our children. About sun an hour high, we were all carried out of the house for a march, and saw many of the houses of my neighbors in flames, perceiving the whole fort, one house excepted, to be taken. * * * Upon my parting from the town, they fired my house and barn. We were carried over the river to the foot of the mountain, about a mile from my house, where we found a great number of our Christian neighbors, men, women and children, to the number of an hundred, nineteen of whom were afterwards murdered by the way and two starved to death near Cowass, in a time of great scarcity or famine, the savages underwent there. When we came to the foot of our mountain they took away our shoes, and gave us in the room of them Indian shoes to prepare us for our travel. * * * After this we went up the mountain, and saw the smoke of the fires in town, and beheld the awful desolations of Deerfield. And before we marched any farther they killed a sucking child of the English. There were slain by the enemy, of the inhabitants of our town, to the number of thirty-eight, beside nine of the neighboring towns.

Whilst we were there, the English beat out a company that remained in the town, and pursued them to the river, killing and wounding many of them; but the body of the army being alarmed, they repulsed those few English that pursued them. I am not able to give you an account of the number of the enemy slain, but I observed after this fight no great insulting mirth, as I expected; and saw many wounded persons, and for several days together they buried of their party, and one of chief note among the Macquas. The Governor of Canada told me, his army had that success with the loss of but eleven men, three Frenchmen, one of which was the lieutenant of the army, five Macquas and three Indians.

At Quebec Mr. Williams learned through "the soldiers both French and Indian, that they lost above forty, and many others wounded, among whom was the Ensign of the French."

WELLS AND WRIGHT'S STORY OF THE AFFAIR.

The next paper, copied from the original in the Massachusetts archives, is also by those who took part in the events of that day:—

To his Excellency the Governor, together with the Hon[d] Council & Representatives, met in the Great & General Assembly at Boston, May 31, 1704:—

The Humble Petition of Jonathan Wells & Ebenezer Wright, in behalfe of the Company who encountered the ffrench & Indians at Deerfield, ffeb. 29, 1703,

Showeth—ffirst, That we understanding the extremity of the poor people at Deerfield, made all possible haste to their reliefe, that we might deliver the Remnant that was left & doe spoil on the enemy.

2dly, That being joyned with a small number of the inhabitants and garrison souldiers, we forced the enemy out of town, leaving a great part of their plunder behinde them; & persuing them about a mile & an halfe did great execution upon them; we saw at the time many dead bodies, and we & others did afterwards see the manifest prints on the snow, where other dead bodies were drawn to a hole in the river.

3dly, That the enemy being reinforced by a great number of fresh men, we were overpowered & necessitated to run to the fort, & in our flight nine of the company were slain, & some others wounded, & some of us lost our upper garments which we had put off before in the pursuit.

4thly, That the action was over & the enemy withdrawn about fourscore Rods from the fort before any of our neighbors came into the fort.

Wherefore we doe Humbly suplicate this Hon[d] Assembly, that according to their wonted justice & bounty, they would consider the service we have done in preserving many lives & much estate & making a spoil on the enemy; the hazzard that we run, the losse we susteined, the afflicted condition of such as have lost near relations in this encounter & bestow upon us some proportionate recompense, that we & others may be incouraged on such occasions, to be forward and active to repell the enemy & rescue such as shall be in distress though with the utmost peril of our lives & Your Petitioners shall pray, &c.

JONATHAN WELLS.
EBENEZER WRIGHT.
In the name of the rest.

[Endorsed] In y[e] House of Representatives, Read 1st time June 2, 1704.

To the petition of Wells and Wright above, the two following lists of names were annexed. The only change made in copying, is an alphabetical arrangement of the first list and adding the name of Richard Biling, evidently omitted by accident. The mark :o: apparently indicates those killed on the meadow, in the pursuit.

A list of names of those that fought In the Dearfield Medow on the last of Febewarey, 1703-4:—

John Allice [Allis]
Samuel Ellice [Allis] :o:
Thomas Aluard garison soulder
John Armes
Samuell barnod
Thomas barnod
Serian [Sergeant Wm?] Beldin
[Richard Biling]
Robard Boltwhood :o:
Serian Samuell Boltwhood garison soulder :o:
Samuell Boltwhood : iur
James Bridgman
Joseph catlin :o:
Joseph church
Samuell church
Joseph Clesson garison soulder
Nathanell colman
Samuell crofoot
Eben'r Dickeson
Nathaniell Dickeson
Samuell Dickeson
Benjamin field garison soulder
Samuell field
Zacrye field
Samuell Foot (left no wife or children) :o: garison soulder
Samuell gillit
John graves
David hoit :o:
Thomas Hove
Jonathan ingriem :o:
John marsh
John matoone
John mountecu
John mun
primus, Negro
Thomas Russell garison soulder
Ebenezer seldin
Joseph siverance
John smeed
John smith
Joseph smith
Beniamin Stebings
Preservid strong
Serian Benj. wait :o:
John waite
Daniell warner
Ebenezer warner
John warner
Nathaniell warner :o:
Samuell warner
John wells
Capt Jonathan Wells
Jonathan wells [Jr.]
Thomas wells

Nathaniell white Joseph wright
Serjan Ebenezer wright Samuell wright [58]

June 8th, 1704, the General Assembly passed a resolve,—

That the Summ of five Pounds be paid to each of the widows of those Slain mentioned in the List annexed, being four in number. [Sergt. Boltwood, Joseph Catlin, David Hoyt and Sergt. Waite.]

And altho but one Scalp of Indians slain by them is Recovered, yet for their Encouragem^t, that the sum of Sixty Pounds be allowed and Paid to the Petitioners whose names are contained in the s^d list annexed as serving, as Scalp money, to be equally Divided amongst them. Together with all Plunder whereof they give account.

The second list accompanying the petition was the following:—

An Acount of what was lost by the souldeirs in that axshon at Dearfield:—

	£	s	d
John Allise, A coat,	1	10	00
Samuel Allise, o, gun & stript,			
Richard Biling, A coat,	3	18	
Robard Boltwhood, o, one iacket,		9	
Samuell boltwhood, a coat,	1	00	00
James bridgmon, a coat & gloves,	1	2	
Joseph Catlin, o, gun & stipt,			
Joseph church, coat & jacket,	1	10	
Samuell crofoot, pr shoose,		6	
Nathaniell dickeson, one hat & pair gloves,	2	7	
Samuell dickeson, a coat,		16	
Samuel foot, o, gun & stript,			
Samuel gilit, pr shoose,		6	
John graves, a coat, wascote & belt,	2		
David hoite, o, gun & stript,			
Thomas Hove, a coat,	1	1	
Jonathan ingrem, o, coat iacket & gun,	3		
John Mounticu, coat & neckeclothes,	1	3	
Ebenezer Seldin, coat & gloves,		16	
John smith, one coat & jacket,	1	6	0
Joseph smith, one coat & gloves,	1	8	0
Beniamin waite, o, stript,			
Daniell warner, coat & jacket,	2	3	00
Ebenezer warner, A coat,	3	9	00
Nathaniell Warner, o, A coat, iacket, gun & hat,	3	6	00
Nathaniell white, coat & hat,	1	6	0
Ebenezer wright, one pr new shooes & spurs		9	00
Sum total, [Sic]	33	5	00
More thirty four s,	1	14	
	34	19	00

The slain marked o

Sir, since 1 spak with you I have Resaued an account from dearfield of the loss of some cloaths in the fight at dearfield:

Thomas barnod 2 wascorts	01	02	00
Joseph siverance one hat		12	

please to ad it to the account.
This last taken by order of Capt. Wells—Ebenezer Wright.

This paper was directed "To cap preserved Clap, In Boston."

June 8th, the General Assembly—

Resolved, that the Losses of the Petitioners be made good, and Paid out of the Publick Treasury to such as sustained them according to their acco^t here with exhibited, amount^g to the sum of Thirty Four Pounds & Seventeen shillings.

The third paper contains an account of the "Plunder" referred to in the vote of the Assembly given above, those who secured it, and the amount for which it sold. The names of a few men appear on the list who were not in the fight on the meadow.

An account of w^t plunder was taken from the enemy on the last of Febewary, 1703–4: & sold by ye company

John wells one gun	01	09	0	Thom hovey A hatchet	00	02	0
more one bareill of gun	00	05	6	Sa^{ll} church A powder horn	00	01	2
Samuell barnod on^e gun	01	09	0	Nath^{ll} white A blancket	00	05	8
Thomas Russell on^e bareil and lock	01	03	0	Eben Seldin A baganet	00	04	6
				Sam^{ll} field A hatchet	00	02	0
John matone A piece of gun	00	14	0	Joseph brooks A gun	01	11	6
John wells 3 pieces of gun	00	07	0	Zacrye field in^d shoes	00	00	10
Thomas Barnod on^e hatchet	00	02	0	Nath^{ll} Colman gun case	00	00	6
hezeciah Root on^e blancket	00	09	0	primus negro glas botle	00	00	6
Thomas barnod on^e blancket	00	03	8	Richard biling [torn]	00	08	04
				John Wait A hatchet	0	02	07
Samuell Carter blancket	00	04	0	Zacrye field A squaline	0	01	07
Jonathan wells "	00	04	4	Sam^{ll} warner A squaline	0	02	10
Ebene Sarles on^e cap*	00	04	6	Nath^{ll} Colman A squaline	0	01	06
Jonathan wells "	00	06	0	Jona Wells A squaline	0	01	02
William belding "	00	02	0	Zacrye field A cap	0	02	10
Jonathan Wells "	00	03	0	Sam^{ll} wright A Knife	0	01	0
Ebenezer Wright on^e gun	01	15	0	Sam^{ll} warner "	0	01	03
Benia^n stebing on^e pistill	00	10	0	Zacrye field A pair of sno shoes	0	05	03
John graves on^e hatchett	00	01	6				
Joseph Smith on^e gun	02	00	6	Zacrye field A blancket	0	02	08
Ebene boltwhood on^e pistile	00	09	0	John graves A blancket	0	03	c
Sam^{ull} dickeson A hatchet	00	02	0	Thomas Wells A blancket	0	05	c
Natha^{ll} white A hatchet	00	02	0				
				Sum totall [Sic]	16	12	10

In 1736, when the General Court was granting land on the lightest provocation, Jonathan Wells and fifty-three others asked for a township in consideration of being in the Meadow Fight, and received a grant of 11,037 acres, joining Hatfield on the west.

The petitioners say:—

In the night following the 28th of Feb., 1703–4, we were alarmed with the Surprizeing news of the Destruction of Deerfield. * *

---

* The powder horn carried by Ebenezer Searls on this occasion is among the relics in Memorial Hall.

The garrison was taken with an army of three hundred & fifty of the French and Indian enemy, who soon satiated their Savage Nature and thirst in the barbarous murder of many of the Inhabitants, and had captivated the rest all except a few that had found means to escape to Capt. Wellses garrison, a little fortress distinct from that round the town and five or six men that defended one House More; the Other Buildings were Consumed in Flames, the Light of which gave Notice to the Towns below a long Time before we had News from the Distressed people, and it must ever have passed for criminal negligence for any that could Serve, to wait till Constrained, before they Repaired to the Releif of that people. Accordingly as many as could then man out, being a little above forty in number, hasted to their releif, who we found in the most Lamentable and pityous Circumstances, and when we entred at one gate the enemy fled out at the other, & being joyn^d with fifteen of Deerfield men, we pursued them with utmost Earnestness & Resolution, and in our Pursuit had the Success of killing many of them, and havieng pursued them about one Mile and a half, they came to a River Bank where was an ambuscade of a Numerous Company of the Enemy, fresh Hands, that had drawn off from the garrison before, who Rose up Fired upon us, and pursued us back; our breath being Spent, theirs in full Strength, the Battle was Sore against us. We retreated with caution, faceing & fireing, so that those that first failed might be defended; notwithstanding many were Slain and others wounded, whose Loss can never be made up, and the rest of us had very little Consideration for it.

This particular and graphic account of the pursuit and retreat is invaluable, as complementing that given by the same parties in their petition in 1704. It is also interesting as illustrating the tendency to exaggeration in tradition; showing how the story of the losses here had *grown* in thirty-two years. It is here stated that *nearly all* the inhabitants were killed or captured, and *all the buildings but two* were laid in ashes. Succeeding generations accepted these statements as facts, and they have since passed into current history. By means of newly discovered papers, a more correct story can now be told.

The following account of the tragedy is essentially different, but it bears internal evidence of being genuine; it is abundantly supported by collateral testimony, is consistent with subsequent action here, and must be considered final authority in the case. The manuscript containing it was found a short time ago amongst the papers of Fitz John Winthrop, Governor of Connecticut, 1698-1707. It was probably an official report, by an officer of the troop that came up on the alarm. It is carefully drawn up and must have been prepared on the spot. The manuscript is held by the Massachusetts Historical Society, which kindly submitted it to my inspection and use.

There are some errors in the table of losses. Mistakes not unlikely occurred in the identification of the naked and mangled bodies, especially those of young children, where the whole family was swept away; nor could it be certainly known at that time, who had perished in the burned houses.

AN ACCOUNT OF YE DESTRUCTION AT DEREFD, FEBR 29, 1703-4.

Upon ye day of ye date above s^d about 2 hours before day ye French & Indian Enemy made an attaque upon Derefield, entering ye Fort with Little discovery (though it is s^d ye watch shot of a gun & cryed Arm, wch verry few heard) imeadiately set upon breaking open doors & windows, took ye watch & others Captive & had y^{ir} men appointed to Lead y^m away, others improved in Rifleing houses of provissions, money, cloathing, drink, & packing up & sending away; the greatest part standing to their Arms, fireing houses, & killing all they could y^t made any resistance; alsoe killing cattle, hogs, sheep & sakeing & wasting all that came before y^m, Except some persons that Escaped in ye Crowds, some by Leaping out at windows & over ye fortifications. Some ran to Capt. Well[s] his Garrison, & some to Hatfield with Litle or no cloathing on, & barefooted, wch with ye bitterness of ye season caused y^m to come of wth frozen feete, & Lye Lame of y^m One house, viz, Benoni Stebbins, they attaqued Later than some others, y^t those in it were well awakened, being 7 men, besides woemen and children, who stood stoutly to y^{ir} Armes, firing upon ye Enemy & ye Enemy upon y^m, causing sev^{ll} of the Enemy to fall, of wch was one frentchman, a Gentile man to appearance. Y^e Enemy gave back, they strove to fire ye house, our men killed 3 or 4 Indians in their attempt, ye Enemy being numerous about ye house, powered much shot upon the house; ye walls being filled up with brick, ye force of ye shot was repelled, yet they killed sayd Stebbins, & wounded one man & one woeman, of wch ye survive^s made no discovery to ye Assailants, but with more than ordinary Couridge kept fireing, haveing powder & Ball sufficient in s^d house; ye Enemy betook y^{m}selves to the next house* & ye Meeting house, both of wch but about 8 rod distant, o^r men yet plyed their business & accepting of no q^r, though offered by ye Enemy, nor Capitulate, but by guns, giveing little or no Respite from ye tyme they began (say some of ye men in ye house shot 40 tymes, & had fair shots at ye Enemy all the while) about an hour before day till ye Sun about one hour & half high, at wch tyme they were almost spent; yet at the verry pintch, ready to yield o^r men from Hadley & Hatfield about 30 men, rushed in upon ye Enemy & made a shot upon them, at wch they Quitted their Assaileing ye house & ye Fort alsoe; the house at Libertie, woemen & children ran to Cap^n Wells his fort, the men wth ours still p'rsued the Enemy, all of them vigorously, causing

---

* The Old Indian House.

many of yᵉ Enemy to fall, yet being but about 40 men p'rsued to farr, imprudently, not altogether for want of conduct, for Capt. Wells, who had led them, called for a retreate, which they Litle mynded, yᵉ Enemy discoviring their numbeˢ haveing ambushmᵗˢ of men, caused oʳ men to give back, though to Late, being a Mile from yᵉ Fort; in yˡʳ drawing of & at yᵉ Fort Lost 11 of oʳ men, viz, Sergt Benj Waite, Sergt Samˡˡ Boltwood, & his son Robᵗ Boltwood, Samˡˡ Foot, Samˡˡ Alliss, Nathˡ Warner, Jonᵗʰ Ingram, Thomas Selding, David Hoite, Jos Ingersoll, & Jos Catlin, & after oʳ men recovered the Fort againe, the Enemy drew of, haveing at sᵈ house & in yᵉ ingagmᵗˢ (as is Judge by yᵉ best calculation we can come at) Lost about 50 men, & 12 or 15 wounded (as o'ur captive says) wᶜʰ they carried of, & is thought they will not see Canada againe (& sᵈ Captive escaped says) they, viz, the Enemy, went 6 mile that night; about midnight yᵉ same night were gathered of oʳ uper & Lowʳ Towns neer about 80 men wᶜʰ had thoughts with that numb'er to have Assaulted yᵉ Enemy that Night, but yᵉ snow being at Least 3 foot deep & impassable without snow shoes (wᶜʰ we had not a supply of) & doubtfull whether we could ataque yᵐ before day, being in a capacitie to follow yᵐ but in their path, they in a Capacitie to flank us on both sides, being fitted with snow shoes, & with treble oʳ Numbʳ, if not more, & some were much concerned for the Captives, Mr Wm's famyly Especially, whome yᵉ Enemy would kill, if we come on, & it was concluded we should too much Expose oʳ men. The next day by two of the Clock Coniticut men began to come in, & came by p'tis till within Night at wᶜʰ tyme we were Raised to 250 men in Derefᵈ, but the aforesᵈ Objections, & the weather verry Warme, & like to be so, (& so it was wᵗʰ Raine) we judge it impossible to travill, but as aforesᵈ to uttermost disadvantage, Especially wⁿ we came up to yᵐ to an attaque, (Providence put a bar in oʳ way) we Judge we should Expose o'rselves to yᵉ Loss of men and not be able, as the case was circumstanced, to offend the Enemy or Rescue oʳ Captives, which was yᵉ End we aimed at in all, therefore desisted, & haveing buried the dead, saved wᵗ we Could of Cattˡˡ, hogg, & sheep, & other Estate, out of yᵉ spoyles of yᵉ Remayneing Inhabitants, & some of oʳ N. H., Hadly & Hatfⁱᵈ men settled a Garrisson of 30 men or upwards, undʳ Capt Wells, & drew of to oʳ places; of yᵉ destruction of Derefˡᵈ see more over the Leafe.

On the same folio sheet with the foregoing report is the table on the following pages, giving the loss of life, liberty, and property, and also a list of remaining inhabitants. The figures in the property column probably represent pounds, current money of New England. All the persons referred to on this list are identified, except one child with Frary, and the servant girl of Beaman. The figures in brackets indicate corrections which have been made on the authority of the town records, or of Rev. Stephen Williams, who was one of the captives.

FITZ JOHN WINTHROP'S TABLE OF LOSSES.

	Captivitie or Burnt	Slaine	Alive at Home	Estate Lost
The Rev'nd Mr John Williams	7 [6] himself & 6 [5] children	3 Mrs Wms found dead 2d days journey of ye Enemy 2 children	1 at Hadly	300 house, Barn burnt & all in them.
Godfrey Nims	3 [4] wife & 2 [3] children	4 children	1 himself	250 house. Barn burnt & all in them.
Phillip Mattoone	0 [1 himself]	3 [2] himself wife & child [wife & child burned in a cellar. S Williams's M S]	0	50 Lost.
Benj Mun	0	0	3 himself wife & child	20 Lost
Samson Frary	1 wife	3 himself & 2 children	2 children	250 house. Barn burnt, Estate in it
Martin Kellogg	2 [5] himself & Son [4 children]	4 [1] children	1 wife	40 Lost
Benj Burt	2 himself & wife great with child [born Apr 14 1704]	0	0	20 Lost
David Alexand'r	1 [2] wife [and child]	2 [1] himself & child [himself]	0	20 Lost
Wid Coss [Elizabeth Corse]	2 herself & child	0	0	20 Lost
Mr Jno Catlin	2 children	2 himself & Son burnt in his house	1 Wife	250 house. Barn & all in ym burnt.
Jos Catlin	0	1 himself	2 Wife & child	20 Lost
Tho: French	7 himself wife & 5 children	1 child	3 himself & 2 sons at home	100 Lost
Dan'll Belding	1 wife	1 daughter.		150 house. burnt cattl, boggs, &c.
Eben'r Werner [Warner]	4 himself wife & 2 children	0		20 Lost
Sam'll Carter	5 [7] wife 4 [6] children	3 [1] children	1 himself	100 Lost Barn burnt & house Rified.
Eben'r Brooks	0	0	3 himself wife & children [Sic]	70 Lost house burnt.
Lt [David] Holte	7 himself wife & 5 children	0	2 children	50 Lost
Deacon [Ehs John] Shelding	3 children	2 wife & 1 child	2 himself & 1 child	100 Lost
Jno Shelding his Son	1 wife	0	1 himself	20 Lost
Mahuman Hinsdale	2 himself & wife	2 [1] children [& Josiah Rising?]	0	100 Lost
Jno Stebbins	7 himself wife & 5 children	0	0	100 house burnt & Estate in it
Denyon [Denienr] & wife & 2 Frenchmen	4	0	0	20 Lost
Simon Beaman	3 himself wife & Servant girl	0	0	100 house & all in it burnt catl killed
Nath'l Brooks	4 himself wife & 2 children	0	0	70 house burnt & Estate
Benoni Stebbins	0	1 himself	6 Wife & 5 children at home	300 houses & all goods Barn & catl burnt
David Holte jn'r	0	1 himself	2 wife & child she wounded	50 Lost
Joseph Pettee	2 himself & wife	0	1 child	50 Lost
[Footing]	70 [77]	33 [25]	32	2340

[Second Page]

Jno Allison	0	2 himself & wife	10 Lost
Tho Allison & mother of 84 yrs	2 Hatf'd persons	2 himself & Mother	10 Lost
Jno Marsh & Sarah Dickinson	2 himself & wife	0	5 Lost
Jos Pomery	1 himself	0	20 Lost
Jno Wilton		0	60
Sam'll Smeed		1 himself	50 house burnt
Jno Hawks ju'r	0	0	70 house burnt
Andr Stephens ye Indian	1 wife	0	20 Lost
Wid [Sarah] Hurst	7 herself & 6 children in captivitie	0	20 house burnt
Jno Hawks Sn'r	2 children	1 himself	50 house burnt
Jno Field	2 [8] wife & [2] child	1 himself	10 Lost
Robt Price	1 child	1 himself	50 house burnt
Mr John Ritchards	1 child	5 himself wife & 3 children	10 Lost
Jos Brooks	0	4 himself wife & 2 children	0
Capt [Jonathan] Wells	0	9 himself wife & 7 children	0
Eleaz'r Hawks	0	10 himself wife & 8 children	
Wm Arms	0	8 [7] himself wife & 6 [5] children	
Wm Belding	0	4 himself wife & 4 [2] children	0
Wid [Sarah] Williams	0	3 herself & 2 children	0
Wid [Sarah] Mattoone	0 [1 daughter]	7 herself & 6 children	0
Jno Smead	0	3 himself wife & child	0
Eben'r Smead	0	6 himself wife & 4 children	0
Michael Mitchall	0	6 himself wife & 4 children	0
Eben'r Severns [Severance]	0	7 himself wife & 5 children	0
Jno Aline	0	8 himself wife & 6 children	0
Edward Allne	1 child	7 himself wife & 5 children	0
Garrison Sould'rs sent up	5 captivitie	10 at home	
foregoing page	25 [27]	105 [104]	375
	70 [77]	32	2640
[Total]	95 [104]		
	20 [19]		
	38 [25]		
	58 [44]	137 [136]	3015

There is yet Left of ye Inhabitants 25 men & 27 are Killed & in Captivitie.

There is 17 houses with Barns to ym burnt within side and without the Fort.

There is yet houses standing within side ye Fort, 9 houses & without, 15 houses, of wch Capt. Wells is one of them, well fortified, in wch is the Garrison now kept.

The Woemen & children at home are come of to Northampton, Hadley & Hatfield, also the wounded men and one wounded woeman are in Hatf'd undr Doctor Hastings cure.

[This paper was indorsed.] "The destruction of Deerfield Feb 29, 1703-4."

[next pa

To the above list of captives must be added Joseph Alexander, John Burt, Abigail Brown, Mary Harris, Daniel Crowfoot, Frank, negro slave to Mr. Williams, killed the first night, and Samuel Hastings.

To the list of slain, Joseph Ingersol, Pathena, wife of Frank, Thomas Selden, and two, names unknown, of the seven from towns below who were killed on the meadows. Total of killed, 49; of captives, 111.

Papers in the Massachusetts Archives show that three men were wounded in the Meadow Fight, one, a prisoner, in mere wantonness. We learn that John Smead, after doing heroic service, received a bullet in his thigh. Thomas Wells, Joseph Clesson and John Arms certify that John Smead was in the fight and carried the bullet to his death, in 1720. In a petition to the General Court, May, 1743, his son John says of him:—

By the blessing of Providence on his Endeavors, 'tis thot he did as much or more Spoil on the Enemy as any man there, * * * slaying two of the Indian Enemy, which, it is likely, is more than any other person did, & which Experience shows, has been a rare thing amongst us.

The following certificate accompanied this petition:—

I was in Dearfield Meadow fight, * * * and I see the said Smead kill an indian, & some of the souldiers tock off this Indian's scalp & secured it, & I see the said John Smeed shoot at another Indian, which he gave a mortal wound, & ye Indian died in a short time at the place where he received y^e wound, or very near the place. EBENEZER WARNER.

Two hundred acres of land at Poquoig were granted the petitioner, Jan. 14th, 1743.

Samuel Church of Hadley, in a petition for aid, May, 1705, says:—

Haveing Rec^d a Wound in my Arme in y^e fight at Derefield feb^r 29 170$\frac{3}{4}$ In the healeing of s^d Wound I was disabled for to work & Labor for the space or tyme of twelve weeks & am weak in my Arm still Humbly Petition &c &c * * * it haveing been a great hinderence to me & Lose in my ocations and affairs

June 15th, two pounds were allowed him on this petition.

May 30th, 1705, Benjamin Church of Hadley, says:—

Haveing Rec^d a Wound in my Foot, in the fight at Derefeild Feb. 29, 1703–4. In the healeing of said wound, I was disabled for to work or labour, for the space, or tyme, of twenty-five weeks, & am weak in my foot still * * * I entreat I may be considered as aforesaid, & for your Excellency & Honors I shall Ever Pray.

Four pounds were allowed him, June 15th, by the Court.

John Bridgman of Northampton was captured, but escaped during the Meadow Fight. In a petition, May 22d, 1705, he says:—

Being at Dearfeild upon the 29 day of faber, 1703–4, at the time when it was destroyed, & there meet with considerable Loss in estat, & maime in his body, being in her Majesty's service & under pay:—

1ly I lost in goods, cloathing and money, to the value of five pounds eleven shillings & six pence.

2 I was taken by the Enimy, & when I was in there hands, they cut off the forefinger of my Right hand,

3 by which wound I Lost my time & was disenabled from work four months.

The items of loss were:—

Sadel, £1, 6s, 0d; leath^r breches, 15s; leather^r wescot, £1; gloves, 3s; leather^r wescot, 16s; neckcloth & handkerchief, 6s; stockings, 4s; shirt, 5s; powder & lead, 2s, 6d; money, 14s.

Seven pounds were allowed him, June 26th, 1705.

The several statements, already given, referring to the sentinel appointed to watch the town, and warn the sleeping inhabitants in case of danger, appear quite contradictory. But a tradition told me by Mrs. Sylvia Munn, when in her 88th year, may be interpreted to reconcile them all. She said she had "always heard," that while on his beat, towards morning, the wearied watchman heard from one of the houses, the soft voice of a woman, singing a lullaby to a sick child; that he stopped, and leaning against the window of the room where the child lay, listened to the soothing tones of the singer until he fell asleep. If this story be true, he was doubtless rudely aroused from his criminal slumber by the noise of the attack, and was the man referred to in the Winthrop paper as "ye watch who shot of a gun & cryed Arm, wch verry few heard." The alarm came too late, and they soon "took ye watch captive."

The following list of killed and captured, taken from the "Redeemed Captive," was made by Stephen Williams, one of the captives. I have added the age of each person, when it could be ascertained. Some slight corrections and additions have been placed in brackets.

Names of those who were slain in or near the Town:—

308   QUEEN ANNE'S WAR—1702—1713.

David Alexander		Henry Nims,	12
Thomas Carter,	4	Mary, ⎫ supposed to	5
John Catlin,	(?) 60	Mercy, ⎬ be burnt in	5
Jonathan Catlin		Meh'tble, ⎭ the cellar	7
Sarah Field, 10 months		Sarah Price,	(?) 53
Samson Frary,	(?) 64	Mercy Root,	15
John French, 4 weeks		Thos Shelden [Selden]	26
Alice Hawks,	(?) 50	Mrs [Hannah] Sheldon,	39
John Hawks, Jr,	30	Mercy Sheldon,	2
His wife, [Thankful]	26	Sam'l Smead's wife and two children	
Thankful Hawks,	2	[Mary Smead,	23
John Hawks,	7	Sarah Smead,	4
Martha Hawks,	4	William Smead,]	2
Samuel Hinsdale, 15 mos		Elizabeth Smead,	(?) 64
Joseph Ingersol,	28	Martin Smith,	(?) 50
Jonathan Kellogg,	5	Serg Benoni Stebbins,	51
Philip Matoon's wife & child		Andrew Stevens, [Indian]	
[Rebecca Mattoon, 24, and infant son]		Mary Wells,	30
Parthena, a negro, [servant to Rev John Williams]		John Williams, Jun,	6
		Jerusha Williams, 6 weeks	

SLAIN IN THE MEADOW.

Samuel Allis [Hatfield]	25	David Hoyt, Jun., [Deerfield]	24
Serg [Sam'l] Boltwood, [Hadley](?)	53	Jonathan Ingram, [Hadley]	27
Rob't Boltwood [Hadley]	21	Serg Benjamin Wait, [Hatfield]	(?) 54
Joseph Catlin [Deerfield]	(?) 23	Nathaniel Warner, [Hadley]	22
Samuel Foot [Hatfield]	(?) 26		

Taken Captive—Where is this Sign, †, against the Person's Name, it is to signify they were *killed* after they went out of town. And this mark, *, is to signify that they are *still absent* from their native country.

Mary Alexander,	36	*Elizabeth Corse, jun,	8
Mary Alexander, jun,	2	*Daniel Crowfoot,	3
Joseph Alexander, ran away the first night	23	*Abigail Denio,	17
		Sarah Dickinson,	(?) 24
*Sarah Allen,	16	Joseph Eastman,	20
Mary Allis,	22	Mary Field,	28
Thomas Baker,	21	John Field,	3
Simon Beaumont,	47	*Mary Field, jun,	6
Hannah Beaumont,	36	†Mary Frary,	(?) 64
†Hepzibah Belding,	54	Thomas French,	47
John Bridgman, ran away in the meadow	30	†Mary French,	40
		Thomas French, jun,	14
Nathaniel Brooks,	39	Mary French, jun,	17
†Mary Brooks,	(?) 40	*Freedom French,	11
*Mary Brooks, jun,	7	*Martha French,	8
*William Brooks,	6	*Abigail French,	6
Abigail Brown,	25	*Mary Harris,	(?) 9
Benjamin Burt,	23	*Samuel Hastings,	20
John Burt,	21	†Elizabeth Hawks,	6
Sarah Burt,	22	Mehuman Hinsdale,	31
†Hannah Carter,	29	Mary Hinsdale,	23
†Hannah Carter, jun, 7 mos		Jacob Hix, [Hickson] died at Cowass [He died on French river.]	
*Mercy Carter,	10		
*Samuel Carter,	12	Dea David Hoit, died at Cowass,	52
*John Carter,	8	Abigail Hoit,	44
Ebenezer Carter,	6	Jonathan Hoit,	15
†Marah Carter,	3	Sarah Hoit,	17
John Catlin,	17	†Ebenezer Hoit,	8
Ruth Catlin,	(?) 20	†Abigail Hoit, jun,	2
†Elizabeth Corse,	(?) 32	Elizabeth Hull,	15

AN INTERESTING TRADITION.

*Thomas Hurst,	12	*Josiah Riseing,	9
*Ebenezer Hurst,	10	Hannah Sheldon,	23
†Benjamin Hurst,	2	Ebenezer Sheldon,	12
Sarah Hurst,	(?)40	Remembrance Sheldon,	11
Elizabeth Hurst,	16	Mary Sheldon,	16
*Hannah Hurst,	8	John Stebbins,	56
Sarah Hurst, jun,	18	Dorothy Stebbins,	(?)42
Martin Kellogue,	45	John Stebbins, jun,	19
Martin Kellogue, jun,	17	Samuel Stebbins,	15
Joseph Kellogue,	12	*Ebenezer Stebbins,	9
*Joanna Kellogue,	11	*Joseph Stebbins,	4
Rebecca Kellogue,	8	*Thankful Stebbins,	12
John Marsh,	24	*Elizabeth Stevens,	20
Sarah Mutoon [Mattoon]	17	Ebenezer Warner,	27
†Philip Mutoon [Mattoon]	23	†Waitstill Warner,	24
†Frank, a negro, [slave to Mr. Williams.]		*Waitstill Warner, jun,	2
		Sarah Warner,	4
†Mehitable Nims,	36	Rev Mr Jn Williams,	39
Ebenezer Nims,	17	†Mrs Eunice Williams,	39
*Abigail Nims,	2	Samuel Williams,	15
Joseph Petty,	31	Stephen Williams,	10
Sarah Petty,	(?)31	*Eunice Williams, jun,	7
Lydia Pomroy,	20	Esther Williams,	13
Joshua Pomroy,	28	Warham Williams,	4
†Esther Pomroy,	(?)27	John Wilton,	(?)39
Samuel Price,	(?)18	Judah Wright,	26
*Jemima Richards,	(?)10		

Three Frenchmen who had lived in the town for some time, and came from Canada, were also taken.

The following letter from Mrs. Lucy D. Shearer of Colrain, a descendant of John Catlin, to the writer, giving an apparently authentic tradition, handed down in the Catlin family, should have a permanent record here. The "Frenchman" was doubtless the officer who fell in the attack on the house of Benoni Stebbins. The "uncle" was probably Jonathan Catlin, an older brother, who fell with his father, in the defense of their home. Mrs. Shearer was born in 1804.

COLERAINE, Nov. 1, 1875.

Mr. Sheldon:

' DEAR SIR,—John Catlin, the captive, was born in the 50th year of his mother's age, and never had slept out of his father's house 'till the age of 16, when he was taken captive, and went to Canada in company with a sister. His sister was very delicate, never had endured any hardship, but performed the journey so well that the Indians would give her something to carry; she would carry it a little way, and then throw it back as far as she could throw it. ● He (John) used to tremble for fear they would kill his sister, but they would laugh, and go back and get it. They acted as though they thought she was a great lady. The captives suffered from hunger, but she had plenty, and gave some to her brother. What her name was or what became of her I cannot tell. [Ruth, and she was redeemed.] He (John) was given to a French Jesuit. The Jesuit tried to persuade him to become a Catholic, but when he found he could not, told him he might go home when he had an opportunity; and when an opportunity presented, furnished him what he needed for the journey, and gave him some money when he parted with him. He was with him two years.

His father and uncle [brother Jonathan?] were killed in the house; he took his father's gun, and his uncle's powder horn, and was going to use them when the Indians took him. The captives were taken to a house, (I do not know what house) and a Frenchman* was brought in and laid on the floor; he was in great distress, and called for water; Mrs. Catlin fed him with water. Some one said to her, "How can you do that for your enemy?" She replied, "If thine enemy hunger, feed him; if he thirst, give him water to drink." The Frenchman was taken and carried away, and the captives marched off. Mrs. Catlin was left. After they were all gone, a little boy came that was hid in the house. Mrs. Catlin said to the boy, "go run and hide." The boy said, "Mrs. Catlin, why don't you go and hide?" She said, "I am a captive; it is not my duty to hide, but you have not been taken, and it is your duty to hide." Who this boy was I do not know. Some thought the kindness shown to the Frenchman was the reason of Mrs. Catlin's being left.

Lucy D. Shearer.

In 1704 the town was built along the whole length of the plateau as to-day. Of its forty-one houses, at least fifteen were within the line of the stockades. About twelve were north, and fourteen south of it. When the night of February 28th closed down, 291 souls were under their rooftrees. Of these, twenty were garrison soldiers, two visitors from Hatfield, and 268 inhabitants. They were of all ages, from Widow Allison of eighty-four years, to John, the youngling of Deacon French's flock, of four weeks. Among them were three negro slaves, one Indian, and three Frenchmen from Canada. In a few hours all but one hundred and twenty-six of the inhabitants were either killed or in the hands of a cruel enemy, on a march over the snow to Canada, three hundred miles away.

By collating the papers before given, one may find a full and particular account of this great catastrophe. We see De Rouville, on his errand of blood, reaching our frontier in such an exhausted condition as to necessitate an ignominious surrender, unless he can surprise his prey. In this he succeeds. We have seen the army leave their lair at Little Hope, steal silently across the north meadows, scale the palisades on the drifted snow, and scatter themselves among the

---

* Probably De Rouville's brother.

houses, when the wearied sentinel has been lulled to sleep. Probably the first to be aroused, he fired his gun and gave the alarum cry, and so hastened the attack before all the houses were invested. If the alarum was heard by the citizens, the fearful war-whoop and the blows of the hatchet on door and shutter must have been heard almost simultaneously. Of the scenes of horror which followed, the picture painted by Mr. Williams of his own experiences will represent those being enacted among his fellow sufferers.

It was in the darkest hour of the night, when he was awakened by the noise of hatchets at his door and windows. Jumping out of bed, he rushed to defend the door, but was too late; it was already broken down, and he saw the dim form of a Macqua chief and his followers crowding through the doorway. Calling upon the two soldiers quartered in his house for help, the brave man sprang for his arms. Failing in his attempt to shoot the leader, he was disarmed and bound. In pitchy darkness the Indians raged through the house. The soldiers leaped from the windows and escaped. The screaming children were dragged from their bed by rough but unseen hands, collected in the ample kitchen and bound, probably with cords brought from Canada for the occasion. The smouldering fire on the hearth was raked open, and the lurid flame from the back-log faintly lighted up the dismal scene. We can imagine the faithful Pathena, resisting in defense of the younger children, for which she was dragged to the door, where all the three were murdered. Had not the pistol of Mr. Williams missed fire, he doubtless would have shared their fate. With fire-brands, or torches, the Indians searched the rooms for plunder, eagerly eating of the food they found and packing up such stuff as they chose to take.* When this was completed, and the prisoners led off, the house was set on fire and burned.

The stout door of Ensign John Sheldon's house resisted the efforts to break it down. It was cut partly through with axes, and bullets fired through the place at random, one of

---

* A silver cup among the plunder came into the possession of the daughter Eunice, who remained in Canada. In 1732 it was by her given to her brother Warham. It is still in the hands of his descendants. It is marked, "Feb. 29, E. W. Obt., 1st March, 1703-4. June 10, 1732, E. W. to W. W." and other inscriptions of a later date.—Letter from Chas. K. Williams of Rutland, Vt., July 6, 1884.

which killed Mrs. Sheldon as she was sitting on a bed in the east room. Entrance was finally effected at the back door, which, according to a family tradition, was left open by a lad who sought safety in flight. Most of the family were captured. Probably the Ensign was not at home. His son, the newly married John, with his wife jumped from the east chamber window. Hannah sprained her ankle and could not escape, but she urged her husband to fly to Hatfield for aid. This he did, binding strips of a woolen blanket about his naked feet as he ran. The tradition says also that the two years old Mercy was taken to the front door and her brains dashed out on the doorstone: and further, that the house, being the largest in the town, was reserved as a depot for captives. Here, then, was the place where Mrs. Catlin relieved the wounded French lieutenant, and secured her own freedom by her practical christianity. It was certainly used as a cover and point of attack on the Stebbins house. It was set on fire, when the last marauders were driven away, but it was saved, and stood until 1849—the widely known "Old Indian House." The scarred and battered door, supported by the original door posts and flanked by great oaken brackets from the front of the house, is now a center of attraction at Memorial Hall.

The house of Benoni Stebbins stood about eight rods southwest of Ensign Sheldon's. It was occupied by Sergt. Stebbins, his wife and five children; David Hoyt, his wife and child; and probably Joseph Catlin with his wife and child, and Benjamin Church, a soldier. There were besides, three other men, and perhaps other women and children. This house being "attaqued later than some," the inmates were aroused, made ready to defend themselves, and the assailants were driven back with loss. It was again beset by a strong force, but the little garrison was a match for that. Again later in the morning nearly the whole army surrounded the house, pouring bullets upon it from every quarter. The fire was bravely returned, and several of the enemy fell before the sharp shooters; among them, a French lieutenant, the second in command of the expedition. Desperate attempts were now made to set the house on fire, which cost the lives of a Macqua chief and several of his men The fury of the assailants increased with their losses, but they were forced to leave the field and take shelter in the Sheldon house and the meetinghouse. From these covers they continued to shower their bullets upon the heroic garrison, which, however, kept them at bay until relieved by the reinforcement. Sergt. Stebbins was killed. Mrs. Hoyt was wounded, and also a soldier, probably Church.

In all the wars of New England, there is not a more gallant act recorded than this defense of an unfortified house, by seven men and a few women, for three hours, against, not only the fury and wiles of an unorganized horde of savages, but also a large force of French soldiers, under officers of the line trained in the wars of France.

The check received here by the enemy, probably tended strongly to stay the tide of devastation, and so saved the south part of the town. The current historical and traditional account, that only two houses in town escaped destruction, must be relegated to that mysterious fertile realm, where so large a portion of accepted history is born and nurtured.

I find no evidence of any attack on the house of Capt. Wells, as stated by Gen. Hoyt; nor is it certain that the enemy penetrated the town beyond the fort. Not one of the slain, and none of the losses by fire or plunder, reported in the Winthrop paper, can be certainly located in that section, and only two of the captives—Sarah Allen and Sarah Mattoon, girls of sixteen. They were doubtless away from home. Nearly all on the list who escaped loss, can be definitely placed south of the fort; while two thirds of those who lost life, or liberty, are known to have been in the fort, or north of it, as was certainly at least five-sixths of the property lost. The Benoni Stebbins house, so heroically preserved from the fury and fagots of the enemy, sad to relate, accidentally took fire and was burned after the valiant garrison had joined the knights of the rescue in the pursuit of the assailants.

De Rouville was aware of the danger from English reinforcements, and all haste was made in removing the prisoners to the rendezvous, and packing up provisions for the homeward march. It was about eight o'clock, and the main body had already withdrawn with the captives, when about thirty men on horse-back arrived from the towns below, which had been alarmed by the light of the burning buildings. Scattered parties of the enemy were still searching for plunder, or wantonly killing the settlers' stock, and a considerable body were yet besieging the Stebbins house. These were quickly driven pell-mell out of the north gate, across the home lots and North Meadows. Capt. Wells, joining the rescuers, with fifteen citizens and five garrison soldiers, took the command, and ordered instant pursuit. Bravely, but rashly and without order, each fighting on his own hook, the pursuers rush on; intent only on avenging their slaughtered friends. As they warm up to the fight, they throw off gloves, coats, hats, waistcoats, jackets and neckcloths. Capt. Wells could not control the headlong chase. *He* had not forgotten the disastrous effects of disorder at Turners Falls. He saw the danger which threatened, and ordered a halt. This was unheeded; the foe was followed recklessly into the inevitable ambuscade. Manly bravery was shown on the retreat, and there was no panic. The pursuers were kept at bay, and their wounded comrades brought off. A stand was made at the palisades, and the bodies of some who fell within gunshot range were protected from plunder.

There is a doubtful tradition, that while our men were gallantly charging over the meadows, De Rouville sent an order to kill all the prisoners, but that the messenger fell before delivering this command. The tradition is accepted by Hoyt, but the circumstance is not mentioned by earlier writers and there is small probability that a messenger from Rouville to the prisoners' guard could have come in range of the pursuers. Had the French army been in real danger, the inhuman deed might have been done. After the escape of Bridgman, Mr. Williams was ordered to tell the captives, that in case another ran away, the rest should be burned.

Having hastily secured the prisoners, and prepared their packs, the invaders began their retreat. The snow had become soft, and the progress of the spoil-encumbered army was slow, until, on the fourth day, it reached the sleds at West river, a distance of thirty miles. All were heavily burdened; beside provisions and plunder, they were obliged to carry their wounded and the young children on their backs. More than half the captives were under eighteen years of age; forty of them not over twelve, and twelve under five. One of the latter, Marah Carter, was murdered before the retreat began; Frank, Mr. Williams's servant, was killed in a drunken frolic the first night; Mrs. Williams his mistress, Hannah Carter, Jr., and a " girl about eleven years of age," according to Mr. Williams, were murdered the next day. No female between the ages of six and twenty-four, is marked on Stephen Williams's list, as having been killed on the march. This girl was probably Jemima Richards. The melting snow, which impeded their march, also secured their retreat unmolested. For lack of snow shoes, the men who soon collected in the desolated town, could only follow in their path. It was impossible to intercept or flank the enemy, or attack in the rear with any hope of rescuing the captives.

The body of Mrs. Williams was recovered, and her grave is still seen in the old graveyard; that of Marah Carter, was doubtless brought in, and consigned to the common grave, in which tradition says, the rest of the victims were buried. This, by the same authority, is located near the southeast corner of the Old Burying Ground. Twenty were slain by the way, "for their manner was, if any loitered to kill them."

Route of the Captives. The night of February 29th, the party camped at Greenfield Meadows, in the swamp east of the old Nims house. The next day they crossed Green river at the foot of Leyden hills, where the monument to Mrs. Eunice Williams marks the spot where she was killed. Thence up the hill in the old Indian path, still to be seen, northeasterly through Leyden, Bernardston, Vernon to the mouth of West river in Brattleboro, where they had left their heavy baggage, dogs, sledges, &c., arriving there, March 2d. Thence up the Connecticut river on the ice. Sunday, March 5th, the army was at the mouth of Williams river, where Mr. Williams preached to the captives, who sang "one of Zion's Songs" to the Indians at their request. The river got its name from this occurrence. March 6th, continuing on the river, they reached the mouth of White river March 8th. Here the party was broken up, the larger part going up White river. The St. Francis, or Abenaki Indians with Stephen Williams, David Hoyt, Jacob Hickson, and perhaps others, continued up the Connecticut. After months of wandering this party struck across to French river, and went down that to Lake Champlain, down the lake, and the Sorel, arriving at Chambly in August, and thence to the Indian fort at St. Francis.

The Caghnawaga Indians, with whom was Mr. Williams, went over the Green Mountain, and struck French river about March 18th. They reached the Sorel, March 29th, and Chambly, April 1st, being a little over a month on the march.

The pathetic story of the dreadful march to Canada, "at least 300 miles," and "the snow up to the knees," by this miserable band of men, women and children, as told by Mr. Williams in the "Redeemed Captive," is accessible to all, and is as familiar as household words to every student of New England history.

The journal of his son Stephen, a boy of ten years, as complementing his father's narrative, is of great interest and value. This was printed by Dr. S. W. Williams, in the Northampton edition of the "Redeemed Captive," in 1853, and again by the P. V. M. Association in 1889, with an appendix and notes by George Sheldon.

One man has been found foolish enough to doubt the truth of these narrations. His efforts to cast a shadow upon the integrity of Mr. Williams, will be as successful as an attempt to shut out the rays of the noonday sun with a wire fence.

Deerfield as a Military Post. We usually speak of the catastrophe of February 29th, 1704, as the "destruction of Deerfield," and rightly, too. For twenty years the persistent settlers had struggled bravely, not only against the inevitable hardships of a new plantation, but against the plague of worms, frost and drought; against war, pestilence, and almost famine. But the end had now come. The ground could be held no longer. They were but twenty-five men, twenty-five women, with seventy-five children, forty-three of whom were under ten years of age. More than half the population, including their loved minister, were being swept over the snow to Popish Canada, or laid underneath it, in one wide grave hard by in their own God's acre. Their cup was more than full; and this sad despairing remnant, giving up all hope, deliberately resolved to abandon their all in this fatal spot; to let the "candlestick of the Lord be removed," and this speck of civilization become once more a waste place in the wilderness, from which they had tried to redeem it, while they sought refuge in the towns below. But fortunately, this broken people were not the arbiters of their own destiny. The policy of the rulers forbade the sacrifice.

Connecticut had usually responded promptly to calls for aid in defending Hampshire county. October, 1703, her General Court had established a Council of War, with authority to send sixty men in case of invasion. That number, and eighty-seven men more, arrived here before the close of March, 1704. A special session of the General Court of Connecticut convened March 15th, when sixty men were raised for permanent service in this county, in scouting and garrison duty. They soon came up under Capt. Benjamin Newbury. A committee came also to confer with Col. Partridge, how they could be employed to the best advantage. It was something more than neighborly kindness which prompted these efforts; it was in accordance with a wise policy of keeping the northern frontier as far as possible from their own borders. It was in pursuance of the same end, that Col. Partridge, on the 2d of March, forbade the inhabitants of our town to desert the place; and establishing here a military station, impressed all the able bodied men as soldiers in the Queen's service. The non-combatants were sent to the lower towns.

Gradually the men of Deerfield rallied from the great shock. By slow degrees, the situation took on a new aspect. Houses were left to shelter them; soldiers were there for their protection; the rich meadow land was still theirs. Their faith in an overruling Providence became once more a controlling power, and the future became more hopeful. Bravely they set about gathering up the broken threads of their lives as best they might.

The house of the town clerk, Thomas French, though ransacked, was not burned, and the town books were preserved. On their time-stained pages bearing record of town action, there is not a single syllable referring to this great catastrophe. Those initiated, can see why the spring meeting was deferred seven weeks; why the list of officers is incomplete; why a new handwriting appears on its pages. To other eyes nothing unusual is revealed. A meeting was held April 20th, when town clerk, selectmen, constable and fence viewers were chosen, and the machinery of a municipal organization so far set in motion The functions of the constable were chiefly military; the fence was a necessity; for with stock running at large no crops could be raised on the Common Field unless this was in repair. Arrangements were made whereby two days out of five were allowed the impressed inhabitants by turns to labor in the fields. In this broken manner a small area of land was cultivated; but every hour thus spent was at the imminent risk of life. The woods were full of lurking Indians watching chances for spoil. Their first success is thus briefly recorded by Stephen Williams in his appendix to the "Redeemed Captive."

"May 11th, 1704, John Allen and his wife were killed at a place called the Bars." A manuscript account says Mrs. Allen was killed "about a mile or two from the place." Edward Allen, the new town clerk, a brother of John, makes this record: "Joh Allyn, ye head of this famyly, was slaine by ye Enemy May ye 11, 1704." He makes no note of the death of Mrs. Allen; by which it appears that her fate was then unknown. Her captors finding her an incumbrance in their hasty retreat, probably, knocked her on the head in the woods, where her body became the prey of wild beasts, the scalp being retained, to grace their triumphant reception at home. Allen was forty-four years old.

The next blow fell upon an outlying hamlet of Northampton, called Pascommuck, containing five families.

Near the close of 1703, complaint was made to De Vaudreuil, by the Penaski Indians, of losses by the English, and aid demanded. The Governor at once sent Sieur de Montigny with five or six Frenchmen to "reassure them," and "engage them to continue the war" with the English. On the triumphant return of De Rouville from Deerfield, Montigny, with about twenty French, and fifty of these Indians, was sent to this valley to avenge their wrongs. May 13th, he surprised Pascommuck, and took all the inhabitants prisoners. As soon as the captives could be secured, and provisions and plunder packed for the journey, De Montigny began his retreat.

When the news of this disaster reached Northampton, Capt. John Taylor led a company of horsemen in pursuit, with a calamitous result, as we shall see. Whether or not the death strokes were actually given by the savages, the ordering of affairs was with Sieur de Montigny, the representative of France, "who," says Vaudreuil, "distinguished himself particularly on that occasion."

The following account is taken from the Recorder's Book for Old Hampshire County, which is relied upon as being an original record, though differing somewhat from the account given by Judd:—

May 12, [13] Pascomok Fort taken by ye French & Indians, being about 72. They took and Captivated ye whole Garrison, being about 37 Persons. The English pursueing of them caused them to nock all the Captives on the head Save 5 or 6. Three, they carried to Canada with them, the others escap'd and about 7 of those knocked on the head Recovered, ye rest died. Capt. John Taylor was killed in the fight, and Sam'l Bartlett wounded.

Those carried to Canada were Esther, wife of Benoni Jones; her niece, Margaret Huggins, eighteen; and Elisha, son of John Searles, eight. The slain were Samuel Janes, forty, with wife Sarah, and children, Obadiah, five, Ebenezer, three, Sarah, one; four children of Benjamin Janes, Hannah, eight, Miriam, four, Nathan, one, and one of unknown name and age; Benoni Jones, about thirty-five, with his children, Ebenezer, six, and Jonathan, one; John Searles, about fifty-eight, with three children, names and ages unknown; Moses Hutchinson, and one child, and Patience Webb, forty-six, or her daughter Patience, seventeen.

About a hundred miles up the valley, near the mouth of Wells river, was a tract of pine woods, called by the Indians Cowass, [a place of pines], and near by, many acres of clear meadows. Here a party of Indians located a camp, and planted the meadows with corn, it being a convenient summer rendezvous, from which to sally out on the frontier. The captives from Pascommuck, and some of those from Deerfield were taken to the place. It was there that in May, 1704, David Hoyt died of starvation. It was not far from there that Stephen Williams found Jacob Hickson, so weak from want of food, that he died before the end of July, at French river, while being taken to Canada. Rumors of the establishment at Cowass reaching the English, about the 6th of June, a scouting party, made up of Caleb Lyman and five Connecticut Indians, was sent up to make an examination. On the 14th they discovered a camp about twenty miles this side of Cowass, which they surprised, and killed six men and one woman, while two others escaped, one mortally wounded.

Making a hurried retreat, they reached home with six scalps in five or six days.

The method of the English scout was exactly the same as that of the enemy. Coming near the Indian settlement, Lyman sent forward a spy, with his head and body covered with green leaves, to make what discovery he could. He found a wigwam not far away, and it was determined to attack it by night. Creeping on all fours, Lyman's party reached the wigwam undiscovered, and deliberately fired on the sleeping inmates. Then dropping their guns, "we surrounded them," says Lyman, "with our clubs and hatchets, and knocked down several we met with."

No provisions were found, but loading the skins, guns and other plunder into the canoes, Lyman retreated down the river about twelve miles, when at daylight he broke up the canoes and took to the woods, knowing that parties of the enemy were between him and home. They had but one meal each in their packs, and lived on "birds, grass and strawberry leaves" until they reached Northampton, June 19th or 20th.

The General Court gave Lyman £21 and the Indians £10. Major Whiting of Connecticut gave the Indians £40. This was repaid him by Massachusetts some time after.

When the Indians at Cowass heard the result of this foray, they deserted the place in alarm, and went off to Canada *via* French river and Lake Champlain. The Lyman scout proved to be a great and unexpected success. Great fears were entertained for their safety, for Lyman had hardly got away into the woods, before news came that an army was on the march from Canada to this valley. On this alarm Major Whiting came up from Connecticut with 342 men to aid in defending the frontier. Within six weeks, two more reports of the same nature followed, and each time, additional soldiers came up. These reports were true, the alarm well grounded, and the preparations timely and effective.

The Governor of Canada, elated by the success of De Rouville, had resolved "to lay desolate all the places on the Connecticut river." To this end he gathered a force of about 700 Indians, and adding 125 French soldiers, with several young and active officers, put the whole under Captain de Beaucours, who set out for this valley soon after the return of Montigny from Pascommuck. There was great rejoicing in Canada on their departure. "This force," says Vaudreuil, "would be competent to attack whatever posts or village they please," and he "regarded as certain, the success of the expedition." The Jesuits, says the captive John Williams, boasted what great things this army would do; "that they could not devise what they should do with us, we should be so many prisoners when the army returned." And yet, adds Mr. Williams, "the great army turned back ashamed." Probably they found our towns too much on the alert for a surprise, and they had no stomach for an open attack. De Vaudreuil, however, in his home report assigns another cause for this disgraceful retreat. He says, "a French soldier, one Peter Newgate, deserted within a day's journey of the enemy; a panic hereupon seized the minds of our Indians to such a degree that it was impossible for Sieur de Beaucours to prevent them retreating."

While this army lay on our frontiers its spies and scouts filled the woods, hovered about the towns, and waylaid the roads. Some of the results are given by Stephen Williams:—

About the middle of July [the 10th,] 1704, a friend indian was killed at Hatfield Mill. His name was Kindness. The enemy had not opportunity to scalp him. On the same week, Thomas Russell, a young man of Hatfield, (being then a soldier at Deerfield) was sent out into ye woods with others as a scout, but he rambling from his company, was kill^d by ye indians.

Some tracks discover^d Deacon Sheldon wth some others went after y^m & came in sight of y^m, & shot at y^m, & y^y at ye english at a great distance, & then y^y past along on ye west side of ye Town, & fir^d y^r guns in a bravado, & went along up to ye Northward, & kill^d Thos Russell July 20, 1704.

July 30, 1704, one Dr. Crossman with two or three more men were riding in the night between Hadley and Springfield & were fir^d upon by the enemy, who wound^d Dr. Crossman in the arm. This is ye only time (that I can learn) that they ever fir^d upon anybody travelling in the night.

About this time, Sergt. John Hawks was fired upon while riding to Hatfield, and wounded in the hand. July 29th, Thomas Battis, who had been sent post to Boston, was killed on his return, east of Hadley. His dispatches were taken to Canada, and were the grounds on which Vaudreuil wrote the French war minister, in the report already quoted.

Though this party broke up, it did not fail, My Lord, to cost the enemy considerable sums; the advices they received of it, having obliged them not only to postpone their meeting the Iroquois nations, but also, to remain a great portion of the summer idle, not knowing where this party might strike.

July 31st, a scout was ambushed near Westfield, and two Connecticut soldiers, William Olmstead and one Benton, killed. Another English scout coming up soon after, killed in turn two of the Indians.

No more depredations in the valley this year are recorded, but the harassing uncertainty spoken of by De Vaudreuil still kept the Connecticut troops here, and parties constantly scouting on the frontiers; it prevented labor in the fields, or any efficient action in getting a living. A strong garrison was kept here, and Benjamin Choate, a Harvard graduate of 1703, was sent here by the General Court to be "chaplain to the Town and Garrison," for six months from November 1st. He was continued here by the same authority until the return of Mr. Williams, on a salary of £40. Part of this was paid by the inhabitants.

The country tax for 1703-4 was £68, 10 s. Thomas Wells, Constable, received a warrant from the Treasurer, directing him to collect and send in that amount. One-half was paid in 1703; the rest was due in May, 1704. October 25th, 1704, the Constable sent a petition to the General Court, asking relief; saying "The town was so far destroyed, that at least one-half that should have paid it, were killed or taken captive." One-half of what was due in May was abated, and Col. Partridge, Preserved Smith, and Capt. Jonathan Wells, made a committee to reassess the balance of £17, 2 s, 6 d.

As a preparation for a winter campaign, the General Court ordered, November 15th, that "5 s be granted to every person who are or shall be furnished according to law with snow shoes and mogginsins." Their necessity had been demonstrated at Deerfield, Feb. 29th, 1704; and two weeks later, 500 pairs had been ordered for frontier use. At that time the price was three shillings, which went up to seven shillings before the war closed.

1705. This year no enemy appeared on our borders. Vaudreuil was crippled by the loss of the "Seine," his annual store ship of supplies, with "two millions of wealth." It was captured by the English in October, 1704. The Bishop of

Canada, with twenty ecclesiastics were on board. It was a severe blow to the enemy. Negotiations for a treaty of neutrality were set on foot this year, pending which, there was less disposition for hostile action. There were several alarms here, however, and much marching of troops, and continuous scouting.

The following petition, found in the Massachusetts Archives, gives a vivid picture of the town at this time:—

To His Excellency, Joseph Dudley, Esq., &c., &c.:
The Petition of the Militia of the Town of Dearefeild Most Humbly showeth—

That after the Bloody Desolation made by the French and Indian Enemy in the s^d town on the last of Feb 1703-4 wee ware unanimously Determined to Desert the town & seek shelter and safty whear we could find it; But the Hon Left Colo Sam[11] Patridge Issued forth a warant whereby we were Impressed into Her Magestys service & Posted as Garrison Souldiers in the s^d town & our hopes of seaving our lives by Quitting our Habitations superseeded by fear of Incurring the Penalty of Deserting Her majstys Service, And have Continued ever since the 2d of March 1703-4 under the said Impress, not being as yet Dismissed so that we are uncapable of Attending to our business to procure a maintenance for ourselves & families as otherwise we might Have done, being obliged to be in actuall duty as souldiers three fifth parts of our time.

And in Confidence that we should Receive the Pay & Subsistence of those in Her Majstys searvis wee went to the neighboring Towns & run in debt for Provisions to sustain ourselves & familis & upon the same Expectations have been Credited by them. we have also thankfully to Acknowledge that the Account for our Pay & subsistence hath been accepted & Passed by your Excellency & Honors to the first of Dec last but understand by Çol Patridge that our pay and subsistence for the time since that, is not alowed, which constrains us further to Acquaint your Excellency & Honors & submit to your favourable Consideration that when the enemy slew & captivated the one half of our town they also plundered & destroyed the greatest Part of our Provision & stock of cattle, that the last Summer the frequent Alarums & continuall Expectations of the Enemy, with our obligations to Attend the Duty of Souldiers Put us by our Labour so much, that our crop of grain on w^h we Depend for our livelihood was inconsiderable, that we were in no wise capable to Discharge the Debts we have already Contracted for Supplying our necessities, If we may not obtain Pay for our searvis & subsistence for the time past. And we expect that as soon as it is known that we are Dismissed the searvice & to have no pay, that our creditors will arest us for what is now due & trust us no more for the future.

We therefore Most Hnmbly pray your Excellency & Honors to take the Premises into your Compassionate Consideration, & grant us wages & subsistance for so long a time as we are continued in the searvis & when we shall be Dismissed such Protection as that we may be enabled to follow our Husbandry, and we shall use our utmost diligence & endeavours to be no farther charge to the Publick. And the Petitioners shall as in Duty Bound ever Pray.

JONATHAN WELLS, in the name & behalf of ye rest.

This petition was received Sept. 6th, 1705, and pay and subsistence was allowed the petitioners up to July 27th, 1705, at which time they were dismissed.

At a town meeting Nov. 24th, 1705,—

Voted yt Capt. Jonathan Weals should have aight pound in money, for his charges and sarvis in geeting our bill past.

It was also agreed and voted yt Capt. Weals should recave his 8 pounds out of ye money yt was obtained by his sarvis and to have deducted out of every man's bill, according to proportion.

Soldiers' Pay.—" In Council, July 12th, 1704. A Muster Roll of the soldiers posted in garrison at Deerfield under the command of Capt. Jonathan Wells, containing an account of Wages for their service from the 28th of Febuary, 1703 to the 27th of June, 1704, amounting to the sum of £199, 10s, 2½d, having been examined by Mr. Commissary General, was presented," and a warrant to the Treasurer made out to Mr. Samuel Porter, to the order of Capt. Wells and company. A bill of £11, 5s, 6d was also allowed "for keeping the Post and scout horses, at the garrison in Deerfield" for the same period.

November 20th, 1704, £397, 18s, 10d was allowed on the Deerfield Muster Roll, on account of "wages for the service & subsistence from the 28th of June to the 20th of October, 1704, and for subsisting the Auxiliary forces sent thither, and other incidental charges."

December 13th, a supplementary account for £26, 10s, 3d, was allowed. The allowance for subsistence, fixed March 22d, 1703-4, was " 1 pound of bread a man a day, allowing one eighth for breakage; Two pieces Pork, each containing two pounds, to 6 men per day, and sometimes two pieces of beef, instead of Pork, each containing 4 pounds to 6 men per day, 3 pts of pease for 6 men per day, 2 quarts of Bear to a man per day."

REDEMPTION OF CAPTIVES.

In the efforts for the recovery and redemption of the captives from Canada, Ensign John Sheldon was a central figure. To his tenderness of heart, to his unflagging faith, his indomitable will, his muscles of iron and nerves of steel, is due in a large measure, the success which followed. His wife and their baby, his brother-in-law, and daughter's husband were slain. Four of his own children, his wife's brother with a large family, were in captivity. His house remained, but his hearthstone was desolate. The house of worship was spared, but the voice of his loved pastor was unheard within its walls. His colleague, Dea. Hoyt, was in captivity, and he alone was left to uphold the shattered church. Dea. Sheldon could give sympathy and Scriptural words of comfort to the bereaved, for he drank daily of the bitterness which flooded their souls; but unfitted for other sacerdotal duties, he mourned sadly for his pastor and friend, and pondered in his heart the possibilities of his redemption. Other public duties also devolved on this man. Ensign Sheldon was second in command of the garrison, and the incessant labors of that summer of fear and disaster, we have already seen. But as the season waned and the blasts of autumn laid bare the thickets which had been the coverts of the enemy, the danger lessened; and when Rev. Benjamin Choate was sent to be their chaplain and spiritual guide, in November, and the deacon was thus relieved of his ecclesiastical duties, he felt his presence less essential, and a grand purpose gradually took form. He resolved to risk his life in a visit to his distressed children and friends in Canada. He could no longer endure the uncertainty hanging over their fate, which constantly haunted him. Had they met a lingering death, on the march, through hardship and privation? or a sudden one by the merciful hatchet? Had their flesh been given to the wild beasts, and their bones left to bleach on some desolate hill, or moulder in some dark morass? How many, and which, of their precious ones were dead? How many of the younglings of the flock were imbibing Popish poison in cruel bondage? These and similar questionings must be answered. Inspiring young John Wells (whose sister had been killed and mother captured) with like resolution, both set out for Boston, to get the necessary leave from the government.

Dec. 13th, 1704, Gov. Dudley informed the Council that "John Sheldon and John Wells of Deerfield, who both had relations in captivity, were now attending him, and very urgent to have liscense to travell thither." On the 19th, he announced that Capt. John Livingstone of Albany, who was acquainted with the route by the lakes, was in town, and was willing to go with Sheldon and Wells for £100 and his expenses. The Council advised his being employed, and the next day the three Johns, with credentials from the Governor, and letters to Marquis de Vaudreuil, took the Bay path for Hatfield, where they were fitted out for the journey by Col. Partridge. Their route was over the Hoosac Mountain to Albany, and thence northwards through the wilderness.

In an historical sketch of Ensign John Sheldon, read before the Pocumtuck Valley Memorial Association, Feb. 27th, 1878, C. Alice Baker says of this journey:—

We need not go back to King Arthur for exploits of chivalry; our colonial history is full of them. This man, long past the daring impulses of youth,—this youth, whose life was all before him—show me two braver knights-errant setting out with loftier purpose, on a more perilous pilgrimage.

Three hundred miles of painful and unaccustomed tramping on snow-shoes in mid-winter, over mountain and morass, through tangled thickets and "snow-clogged forest," where with fell purpose the cruel savage lurked; with gun in hand and pack on back, now wading knee-deep over some rapid stream, now in the teeth of the fierce north wind, toiling over the slippery surface of the frozen lake, now shuffling tediously along in the sodden ice of some half-thawed river, digging away the drifts at night for his camp; wet, lame, half-famished, and chilled to the bone, hardly daring to build a fire,—a bit of dried meat from his pack for a supper, spruce boughs for his bed, crouching there wrapped in his blanket, his head muffled in the hood of his capote, eye and ear alert, his mittened hand grasping the hilt of the knife at his belt; up at daybreak and on again, through storm and sleet, pelted by pitiless rains, or blinded by whirling snow, —what iron will and nerves of steel, sound mind in sound body, to dare and do what this man did!

Slowly and warily, they traversed Lakes George and Champlain, down the Sorel to the St. Lawrence, and thence to Quebec, where the worn travelers arrived without having been molested by the savages. Here the minister and his deacon met. Here the latter heard the welcome news that his children and relatives were still alive, and the sad story of those who fell by the way, among whom was the mother of John Wells, his companion.

The envoys were well received by De Vaudreuil, and encouraged to believe they would be successful in their mission. Mr. Williams, who had been sent down to "Chateauriche"* to prevent his hindering the Jesuits in their efforts to convert the captives to popery, had been allowed to come up to Quebec. Every effort was made to learn about the prisoners and forward measures for their relief. The Jesuits, who had great influence with Vaudreuil, obstructed the envoys in their mission in every possible way, and at their request, Mr. Williams was returned to Chateau Richer, after being at Quebec but three weeks. "One of chief note," probably the intendant, invited Mr. Williams to dinner, where he was tempted with an offer to collect all the prisoners about him, and have a pension "large enough for an honorable maintenance for you and them," if he would be of their religion. The Puritan replied, "Sir, if I thought your religion to be true, I would embrace it freely, * * * but so long as I believe it to be what it is, the offer of the whole world is of no more value to me than a blackberry." His lordship then earnestly requested me, says Mr. Williams, "to come down to the palace to-morrow morning and honor me with your company in my coach to the great church, it being then a saint's day," who replied, "Ask me anything wherein I can serve you with a good conscience, and I am ready to gratify you, but I must ask your excuse here." It was after the Jesuits had given up all hope of any seeming compliance even, to their forms, that he was sent away from Quebec.

The apparently courteous reception of Mr. Sheldon really afforded him little opportunity of communication with the captives, but as his presence in Canada became known, "it gave revival to many," says Mr. Williams, "and raised expectations of a return, * * * and strengthened many who were ready to faint, and gave some check to the designs of the Papists to gain proselytes. But God's time of deliverance was not yet come." The Indians feared an exchange of prisoners, when the French might take away their captives without ransom; so they hustled them into hiding places, and pretended they were absent with hunting parties. March 29th, Mr. Sheldon received a letter from his son's wife enclosing the following note, probably from Mr. James Adams, who had been captured at Wells, by Beaubassin, August 10th, 1703:—

---

* So Mr. Williams writes it, but Miss Baker has no doubt that this place is the present Chateau Richer.

I pray giue my kind loue to Landlord Shelden, and tel Him that i am sorry for all his los. I doe in these few lins showe youe that god has shone yo grat kindness and marcy, In carrying youre Daighter Hanna, and Mary in pertickeler, through so grat a iorney, far beiend my expectation, noing How Lame they war; the Rest of your children are with the Indians, Rememberrance liues near cabect, Hannah also Liues with the frenc, Jn in the same house i doe.

In reply the father sent the letter following, which, with that of Mr. Adams, has been preserved among the Sheldon family manuscript. By this it appears that Mr. Sheldon had before heard of his son Remembrance's whereabouts, but had not been able to get sight of him:—

QUBECK, the 1 of Aperl, 1705.

der child:—this is to let you noe that i reseued youres the 29th of march, which was a comfort to me; this is to let you noe that i am whele blesed be god for it, and i maye tel you i dont here of my child as it the saye is that he is in the wodes a honten; remember my loue to Mr Addams and his wif and iudah writ and all the reste ase if named and my harty desire is that god would in his time opene a dore of deliurans fore you al and the mene while let us wait with patiens one god for it, hoe can bring lite out of darkness and let us cast al oure care one god whoe doeth care for us and can helpe us. Mr williams is sent downe the riuer a gane about 18 or 20 miles i ded ingoy his company about 3 wekes [which] was a comfort to me. he giues his loue to al the captives there. my desire is that Mr Addames and you wod doe al you can with your mistres that my children mite be redemed from the indanes. our post retorned bake agan in 8 days by reson of the badnes of the ise, they goe again the sekcont of this month and i desine to com up to moreal the beginen of May. John wels and Ebenesere warner giues ther loue to al the captiues there, and soe rites your louene father, JOHN SHELDON.

The following fragment of a letter from Mr. Sheldon to his son John at Deerfield, should be read in connection with the above:—

QUBECK, the 2 of aperl, 1705.

dere child:—thes fue lins are to let you noe that i am in good helth at this time, blesed be god for it. i may tel you that we sent away a post the 18 daye of march, and thay ware gone 8 days, and retorned a gane by reson that the ise was soe bad. this may let you noe that i reseued a letere from your wif, the 29 of march, and she wase whel. 1 may let you noe i hant sene none of my children, but I hear thay are gone a honten. [The rest torn off.]

The "post" referred to went across the country to Casco, in accordance with an arrangement with Gov. Dudley. The dispatches and letters were sent by Capt. Samuel Hill, another captive from Wells, and laid before the Council May 15th by Gov. Dudley. The reply of Vaudreuil to Dudley's proposal for an exchange of prisoners, was diplomatic and evasive, and nothing came of it.

Meanwhile the envoys in Canada, by persistent endeavors, and the kindly aid of Capt. De Beauville, brother to the Lord Intendant, secured the release of Hannah Sheldon, and one other of the Ensign's children, Esther Williams and two others. Early in May, the whole party, escorted by Courtemanche and eight French soldiers, set out for home by the way of Albany. Ostensibly this guard was sent as an act of honor and courtesy, but really to observe the condition of the enemy's country. Livingstone and the escort were probably left at Albany, while Capt. Courtemanche and Ensign Sheldon pushed on to Boston, leaving the redeemed captives at Springfield, on the way. They arrived before June 5th, as appears by the General Court records. On that day a committee was ordered to audit the accounts of the "Messengers to Quebec." June 27th, they voted "that an order be made on the Treasurer, payable forthwith to Vaudreuil's Commissioner for the amount," taken up on their letter of credit, by Ensign Sheldon, which was 4000 livres. Courtemanche bought duplicates of the dispatches which Vaudreuil had sent Dudley by Samuel Hill, and another futile attempt was made to arrange an exchange of prisoners.

Courtemanche being taken sick, Capt. Vetch with his brigantine, was engaged to take him home by sea. Capt. Hill was returned by the same conveyance. At the solicitation of the French envoy, William Dudley,[*] son of the Governor, accompanied him to Quebec. The latter bore new proposals to Vaudreuil for an exchange of captives. The vessel reached Quebec in August, and on the petition of Dudley and Vetch, Mr. Williams was allowed to go up and join them. He and his son Stephen were entertained by Courtemanche, at his own house "most nobly," until September 19th, when he was sent back to Chateau Richer, because he hindered an English friar from making converts among the prisoners. Mr. Williams says the priests "were ready to think their time was short for gaining English proselytes and doubled their diligence and wiles."

---

[*] Young Dudley was the orator at the Cambridge commencement, 1705, where "he spoke of Mr. Williams in Captivity." Courtemanche also attended commencement.

When Dudley arrived at Quebec, Vaudreuil was at Montreal busy settling troubles among his Indian allies at the west, and on the 16th and 17th of August he was holding a conference with the Iroquois, who complained that while he had persuaded *them* to be neutral, their kindred in Canada [the Macquas] had been incited to take up the hatchet. The Governor defended his action as best he could, on the ground that it was necessary for them to make common cause with the Abenakis, who had been wronged by the English, and said that he must follow this course so long as the war between France and England continued. To the English envoys he held different language when he came down to Quebec. He professed a great desire for peace, but found excuse for amending and returning the draft of the treaty brought by Dudley. He said the war could "never contribute to the glory of their sovereigns, or the aggrandizement of their States, but merely to the ruin and desolation of some poor families," and the priest at Chateau Richer told Mr. Williams he "abhorred their sending down heathen to commit ravages against the English, saying that it was more like committing murders, than managing a war."

October 12th, Capt. Vetch sailed for Boston with young Dudley, where he arrived November 21st, having done little towards accomplishing the object of their mission, unless, as Ponchartrain, the French minister, suspects, the illness of Courtemanche was a pretense, "assumed as a cover for trade," under an arrangement with Gov. Dudley. This conjecture appears more than probable, by the operations of Vetch the next year.

The vessel, however, brought home eleven captives, only three of whom are known—Stephen Williams, Samuel Williams and Jonathan Hoyt. Nov. 30th, 1705, John Borland was allowed £22 for their passage.

By the same vessel which brought the captive boys, came the following letter and petition, addressed:—

To the Honored Paul Dudley, Esq., her Magesties Attorney Genr'all for the province of the Massachusetts Bay in New England at his house att Boston in New England:

Worthy Sir:—I hope at the receipt of this you will be made right glad at the return of Mr. Dudley, who has merited the thanks & a great reward of his country, for the great service he has done them here. These are humbly to request that favour of you as to draw up

a petition to the General Assembly on my behalf, for the reimbursing Capt. Vetch money he has lent me for paying what I have been forced to expend for my comfort & the necessary relief of my children. j have on the other side drawn up some minutes for you to lay before the Honored Court that i desire you would better form, & give it to my son Samuel to present. in so doing you will abundantly oblige your afflicted friend. i know i need not use arguments to stir up your generous mind to plead the cause of such as are in distress, & therefore forbear them & do humbly offer my best respects to yourself & good lady, wishing you all happiness, & am sir
Your humble servant,
JOHN WILLIAMS.

Quebeck octob 10. 1705

To the Honor'd Generall Court of the province of the Massachusetts Bay in New England:

I have for a long time (well known to yourselves) been in sorrowful state of Captivity under many exercising trials having so many children captivated with myself among the enemies & some of them among the heathen where they were reduced to many straits, so that i have been necessitated to be at considerable expense for their & my own comfort. One of my children came to me from the indians the first of May past without so much as a shirt upon him, & unless i would be unmercifully cruel & have hardened my heart to all unnaturalness i could not avoid charges i have for the honour of my country & the comfort of my children expended £18, 6s, 9d.

These are humbly to request you to make payment of the same to Capt. Samuel Vetch who has been so charitable to give me several things that he saw I had a need of, though he had never seen me before, who has also put me in a capacity to make payment for what i owed for my son's clothing &c. i hope you will be so generous as to reward the service he has performed with such prudence & unfailing industry & so charitable to me, as to make him full payment of the above named sum. our adversaryes upbraid our religion that it falls so short of theirs in charity & good works, whom i have put to silence in assuring them that our charity to all in affliction & good works of every nature far exceeding theirs. i promise myself your charity to me in my affliction and want (having lost what I had at Deerfeild) without any repining will yet give me occasion from my own experiences to refute their calumnyes. your charity herein will also be encouraging me still to keep my post (if God graciously return me) a post lost without any default of mine. wishing you the guidance of God in all your publick affairs & concerns i am

Dudley wisely chose to lay this ingenuous and high-minded appeal before the General Court, in its original form, fresh from the heart of the writer. I find the following record of action endorsed on this petition:—

Nov. 22, 1705, Read in the House of Representatives.
Nov. 27, Read & Resolved, That the Prayer of this Petition be Granted, and the sum of Eighteen Pounds Six Shillings and nine pence be Paid out of the public Treasury to the s^d Capt. Samuel

Vetch, to Imburse him the same sum, which he supplied Mr. Williams the petitioner.
Sent up for concurrence.

THOMAS OAKS, Speaker.

In Council, Nov. 28, 1705.
Read & passed a concurrence.

ISA. ADDINGTON, Sect'y.

SHELDON'S SECOND EXPEDITION TO CANADA.

The Governor and Council could not accept the proposals brought from De Vaudreuil by Vetch, and the whole matter was left to Gov. Dudley, who was to advise with Lord Cornbury, Governor of New York. To forward the business of exchange, Dudley sent forty-seven French prisoners to Port Royal in December, and on the 17th of January, 1705–6, he read to the Council his answer to Vaudreuil, which was "to be dispatched to Quebec by Mr. John Sheldon, attended with a servant or two, and accompanied by two French prisoners of war." Mr. Sheldon left home January 15th and on the 17th he received an outfit from the Commissary General at Boston, costing £4, 11s, 6d, and a bill on Lewis Marchant of Quebec for £2, 10s; and for John Wells, on the same service, 16s, 6d. Joseph Bradley of Haverhill, it seems, got leave to attend the envoy as one of the servants. His wife was now in a second captivity in Canada. January 20th, Sheldon, bearing funds to the military chest in the valley, with Bradley, and the two Frenchmen, left Boston for Hadley, where they arrived the next day, as shown by the following paper:—

Rec'd of Deacon Shelding this Jan'ie 21, 1705, three hundred fortie one pound eight shillings & one penny wch s^d sum he Rec'd of Mr. James Taylor, Treasu'r in Boston, & Brought & delivered to me as aboovs^d, wch I own I have the day of the date aboovs^d Received.
per me,

SAM'LL PARTRIDGE.

John Wells joined the party at Deerfield, and on the 25th of January, 1706, the ambassador plunged once more into the wilderness for a winter journey to Canada. His experience now aided him in battling with the elements, and a truce which had been arranged for five weeks, secured him from Indian hostility, and thus enabled him to push on more rapidly and so arrive before its expiration.

April 28th, 1706, De Vaudreuil writes to Ponchartrain, enclosing Dudley's propositions by Capt. Vetch, and his own reply; with an account of the attempt to arrange a treaty of neutrality. He says:—

This induced Mr. Dudley to send me, a Deputy by land, with a letter, about a month ago, but as it is not sufficiently explicit and as Mr. Dudley according to appearances is seeking only to gain time, the term I had fixed in my answer to these propositions having expired, I permitted several small parties of our Indians to recommence hostilities.

This deputy was Ensign Sheldon, but Mr. Williams says the ensign reached Quebec "the beginning of March." On his arrival he was glad to find Mr. Williams; but in a few days the latter was sent down to Chateau Richer, and Sheldon was left alone to prosecute his mission, which he found difficult and perplexing. Dudley's dispatches were not satisfactory to Vaudreuil. The Jesuits used their all-powerful influence for delay, and redoubled their artful efforts to seduce the young captives to popery. The sturdy envoy persisted in pushing his claims to at least as many captives as would equal the French prisoners which Dudley had sent to Port Royal, in December, 1705; and he so far succeeded, that on the 30th of May, he embarked for Boston with forty-four English captives, on board the French vessel La Marie, chartered at an expense of 3000 livres, for Port Royal and Boston. After considerable delay at Port Royal, he reached his destination August 2d, 1706.

In this company came James Adams of Wells, Hannah, wife of Joseph Bradley,—one of Sheldon's attendants, Ebenezer(?) and Remembrance, sons of Ensign Sheldon, and his daughter Mary, Thomas French, Sen., John Burt, Benjamin Burt, his wife Sarah, and their children, Christopher, born April 4, 1704, while on the march to Canada, and Seaborn, born July 4, 1706, on the home voyage. Mrs. Mary Hinsdale gave birth to son Ebenezer, on the voyage. Both babies were baptized by Samuel Willard, on landing in Boston. The names of the others are unknown, but the greater number were presumably Deerfield captives. August 8th, with light hearts, these began their homeward march.

Mr. Williams not being allowed to see the assembled company of returning captives, wrote them a "Pastoral Letter," dated at Chateau Richer, May 28th, 1706. It was sent on board, "Per Samuel Scammon, Q. D. C. Present with

Care I Pray." This was to be read to his flock on the homeward voyage. He says:—

"Inasmuch as I may neither be permitted to return with you; nor be permitted to come to see you before your return; these come to acquaint you that I am truly desirous of Prosperity for soul and Body. I would bless God who is opening a door of Return for you; and if God be your Front Guard & Rearward, it shall go well with you. * * * Pray for us that are left behind, that God would preserve and recover us, and give us Grace to Glorify His Holy name, tho' He continue, yea increase our Trials. * * * What is it that is most upon your heart in your Return? Is it that you may with all Freedom Glorify God, in bringing forth much Fruit, whilst you are again planted in the Court Yards of our God? How sorrowful is it if your greatest design be to see your Friends so long Separated from you; to Gain Estates, and recover your outward Losses; and to be free again to go and come as you list!"

This is the spirit of the whole address. He urges them to make it a business to glorify God.

"Let God have the Glory of preserving you, and dont ascribe it to your own wisdom; dont think to go shares or partners with God in His Glory; He has done it for the honor of His Name * * * Dont think after your return; that having desired publicly in the congregation of God's people to have thanks returned to God on your behalf; you have done your duty * * * *Thanksliving is the best Thanksgiving.* * * * I wish you a healthy, a safe, a speedy passage to your destined port; if it be the will of God. But above all, I wish you a gracious, truly penitent, Christ prizing, and soul enriching, sanctifying voyage to a better port, when it is the pleasure of God to call you to come home to your Father's house."

Zebadiah Williams, captured in Deerfield Meadows, Oct. 8th, 1703, died in the hospital at Quebec, April 12th, 1706. Mr. Williams says: "He was a very hopeful and pious young man, * * * prayerful to God and studious and painful in reading the Holy Scriptures."

Williams had "recovered one, [Joseph Edgerly] fallen to Popery," and after his death, the French told Mr. Williams, "Zebadiah was gone to hell and damned, for he had appeared to Joseph Edgerly in a flame of fire, and told him he was damned for refusing to embrace the Romish religion, when such pains were used to bring him to the true faith, and being instrumental in drawing him from the Romish communion—forsaking the mass—and was therefore now come to advertise him of his danger." "I told them," says the plainspoken Mr. Williams, "I judged it to be a Popish lie!" and he soberly went about gathering evidence to prove it so; and wrote to Samuel Hill and his brother Ebenezer, at Quebec, "to make discovery of this lying plot, to warn them of their danger." It seems he seriously feared its effect upon the superstitious minds of his flock.

On Sheldon's return he presented his bill of expenses to the Governor:—

An account of what John Sheldon (who was impressed by his Excellency to go to Canada to treat about ye English Captives) hath expended upon the Country's account in Canada for himself and the Captives in General:—

	livres.	sous.
By Taylors work in making clothes,	17	00
To Mr Dubenot (?) [—] cloath for cloathing, for stockins, shoes, a shirt & a hat and a pair of gloves & a neckcloath,	106	11
For a carriall to goe to see the captives at the Mohawk fort,	12	00
For a cannoe and men to goe from Quebec to visit Mr Williams,	06	00
More paid to Mr La Count my landlord at Quebec,	38	00
More paid to the Barbour for me and my men and my blooting,	21	10
More paid for washing,	08	00
More paid my landlord at Montreall,	77	06
More paid for my second visit to the cap's at the Mohawk fort,	4	08
More what I laid out for the captives when i came away from Canada & one of the sallers,	42	10
For John Wells for a hat 16 livres, for silk, 8 livres, for a pair of stockins, 12 livres, for a shirt, 8 livres, 11 sous,	44	11
Joseph Bradley for a shirt,	8	13
Delivered to Mr Williams,	200	00
Laid out for my deaughter Mary, for necessary cloathing,	59	00
More for my darter.	15	00
To the doctor for John Wells and for other things for the captives,	12	00
	689	9
Expended at Port Royal for Pocket expenses, £10-00-00-at 20d pr livre,	120	
	809	

Accompanying the above bill was the following petition:—

Aug. 8, 1706.

To his Excellency, Joseph Dudley &c, &c, &c.

The Petition of John Shelden in behalfe of himself, Joseph Bradley, & John Wells, humbly sheweth

That your Petitioner with the afore mentioned Bradley & Wells were Sent by your Excellency & Council the last winter by Land to Canada to Obtain the Return of the Captives wherein they have so far succeeded, as that on the 2d instant They Arrived here with forty-four of the Captives. Your Petitioner entered upon the said service on the 15th day of Janu'ry last, the said Bradley on the 20th day & the s^d Wells on the 25th day of the same month.

Your Petitioners therefore humbly Pray your Excellency & this Hon'ble Court to Take into your Consideration their service aforsaid and the extraordinary Difficulties, Hazzards and Hardships they have undergone & the time spent therein, and Order Them such Allowance & Consideration for the same as in your wisdom you Shall think meet. And your Petitioners as in duty bound shall ever pray.

JOHN SHELDEN.

Wells and Bradley also petitioned in their own behalf:—

To his excellency &c &c—
The Humble petition of John Wells & Joseph Bradley Showeth that your Petitioners were lately sent by his Excellency to Qubeck with Sheldon and in their journey they were necessitated to be at some Expenses and your Petitioner Wells expended above three pounds ten shillings & Bradley forty sh beside snow shoes and pumps which cost him thirteen shillings and a Dog fifteen & beside there was a gun hired for the Voyage valued at 50 s which s^d gun was broken accidentally in ye discharging

Your petitioners therefore humbly pray that they may be allowed the Disbursements above mentioned and ye money for the gun

JOHN WELLS.
Aug 7, 1706   JOSEPH BRADLY.

Action on these petitions by the General Court:—

Oct. 29, 1706, Granted to John Sheldon 35 pounds; to John Wells 20 pounds & to Joseph Bradley 20 pounds over and above what they had in fitting them out.

The successful mission of Ensign Sheldon having opened the door for the captives' return, the brigantine Hope, Capt. Bonner, was chartered to bring another party of them home. August 9th, an order was issued by the General Court, that the captain of the La Marie be kept under inspection, and that the French prisoners be gathered at once at Cambridge, ready to be sent home when the vessel was ready. These prisoners had probably been scattered among the towns. By the following order, found among the Sheldon manuscript, it appears that two of them were at Deerfield:—

To the Constable at Deerfield.
In her Maj'tys Name You are Required to Impress two Squa Lynes & any other Necessary the two Frenchmen now going to Canada stand in need of. fayle not. 27 August, 1706.
SAM'LL PARTRIDGE, Lt. Colo.

Envoy John Sheldon, ensign and deacon, was constable as well, and as soon as his papers were presented and reports made to the Governor, he hastened home and Aug. 27th, he was fitting out these men to join the other French captives now being gathered at Cambridge for the home voyage.

In June, 1706, the "Superior of the priests" told Mr. Williams he was ragged, but that his obstinacy against the Catholic religion prevented them providing him better clothes. Mr. Williams, always a match for a priest, replied: "It is better going in a ragged coat, than with a ragged conscience." This conversation was doubtless reported by John Sheldon, on his arrival at Boston, and reached the ears of Judge Sewall, a friend of Mr. Williams. An entry in the diary of Sewall Aug. 16th, 1706, shows that he attended a meeting of the Governor and Council when he "spake that a suit of clothes might be made here for Mr. Williams." The garments were doubtless sent to Canada by Capt. Appleton.

The brigantine Hope and La Marie, with Capt. Samuel Appleton as agent, sailed for Quebec with the French prisoners soon after, reaching their port about October 1st. Then came a trying struggle between the French priests and Mr. Williams for the possession of the captive children. "I cannot tell you," says he, "how the clergy and others labored to stop many of the prisoners. To some liberty, to some money and yearly pensions were offered, if they would stay." To some they urged the danger of shipwreck at that late season, and "some younger ones they told 'if they went home they would be damned and burnt in hell forever,' to afright them." To Mr. Williams's son Warham, then seven years old, they promised "an honorable pension from the King," and a "great deal" from his master, "an old man, and the richest in Canada." No means were left untried to prevail upon them to stay "at least till the spring. * * * But God graciously brake the snare, and brought them out."

Who can imagine the anxiety and distress of the good pastor in this critical time? or the intense feeling of relief, when the strain was removed, and the Hope spread her white wings over fifty-seven English captives for the homeward voyage, and his lambs were safe and beyond the reach of the Popish wolves? They sailed October 25th and had a narrow escape from shipwreck shortly after; but arrived safely at Boston on the 21st of November, 1706. On landing they were sent for to go before the General Court, which voted that "20s be allowed each prisoner this day returned from captivity." Capt. Appleton's bill of expenses being £1406, 6s, was allowed December 6th; amongst the items of his bill were £2, 13s, 6d, for five Bibles sent to the captives, and 155 livres paid for the redemption of three captives. This sum was probably to reimburse the French for what they paid the Indians as the price of the captives; Dudley having firmly resolved not to "set up an Algiers trade," purchasing the captives from the Indians, as such a course would surely encourage them to further raids.

December 5th, Mr. Williams preached "at the Boston Lecture," from Luke viii: 39—"Return to thine own house, and show how great things God hath done unto thee." The burden of his sermon was that God should be glorified for all benefits received, and showing that God speedily answered particular prayers, while the captives were in the hands of the savages.

December 6th, the General Court voted Mr. Williams forty pounds on condition that he returned to Deerfield within three weeks and remained a year.

"Dec. 7, I invited the Gov'r," says Sewall in his diary, "to dine at Holmes.' There were the Gov'r, Col. Townsend, Bromfield, Leverett, Williams, Capt. Wells, Sheldon, Hook, Sewall." Townsend, Bromfield, Leverett and the host, were members of the Council. December 20th, Mr. Williams preached "at Mr. Bromfield's," and probably returned to Deerfield directly after, with his children and such townsmen as had not previously gone on. It may be he spent part of the winter in Boston writing and getting out his "Redeemed Captive." Sewall writes:—"Mch 8 [1707] Mr Williams visits us and tells me he goes to Deerfield 14 nights hence next Tuesday. His Narrative is now in the Press."

Of all the fifty-seven captives who returned with Appleton, the names of only Mr. Williams and his children Esther and Warham are known.

THIRD EXPEDITION OF SHELDON TO CANADA.

There being still many English captives in Canada whom Vaudreuil had promised to return in the spring. Dudley proposed to the Council, January 14th, 1707, to have "a Person Ledger at Quebec, to put forward that affair, and that Mr. John Sheldon, who has been twice already, may be employed with a suitable retinue to undertake a journey thither on that service." This plan was adopted: Two men of character and standing, Edward Allen, town clerk of Deerfield, and Deacon Edmund Rice of Sudbury, were selected as a "suitable retinue." Nathaniel Brooks, a Deerfield captive, was added somewhere on the route. It was now a time of active hostilities, and this embassy though ever so wise and prudent, ran great risks. They might at any time be fired upon from some cover before their flag of truce was seen or their character discovered.

They set out April 17th, and arrived at Quebec May 9th without molestation. In a dispatch to Dudley of June 20th, Sheldon says they found the city in a fever of excitement, over news of an expedition fitting out in New England against Canada, and active in preparations to repel it. Their presence was unwelcome and the "Ledger" found a less courteous reception than on his former visits. He was not imprisoned, but was kept under strict surveillance and not allowed to go home lest he report the condition of their defences and military preparations. After about six weeks at Quebec, he was sent up to Montreal. Col. Schuyler writing to Col. Partridge, Aug. 11th, 1707, tells him that his Indian spies, just returned, report that "they see Deacon Sheldon at Montreal, who walked the streets, but was told he was detained, and had not the liberty to go home." We find no details of the negotiations for prisoners, for which there could have been but scant opportunity, in this crisis. Within three weeks after Sheldon's arrival an English army had made an attack on Port Royal. The event of the campaign being determined, the embassy was allowed to depart.

On the 11th of August, Sheldon, bearing dispatches of August 16th, [N. S.,] from Vaudreuil to Dudley, set out from Chambly. He was escorted by five French soldiers under Capt. de Chambly, a brother of Hertel de Rouville. They arrived at Albany August 24th, whence Sheldon wrote the Council a letter, received September 2d, in which he says, "Col. Schuyler had obliged him, with the six Frenchmen, to attend the Lord Cornbury, at New York." This was no hardship for the Frenchmen; and it gave them greater facilities for carrying out their secret instructions. Vaudreuil gave a detailed account of this mission in his dispatches to the home government. In reply, Ponchartrain, the war minister, says:—

His Majesty approves of your haven spoken as you have done to the man named Schalden, [Sheldon] whom that Governor [Dudley] sent to you overland in quest of the English prisoners at Quebec, and even had you imprisoned him, and those of his suite, it would have been no great harm. You did well to send these prisoners to Orange, under the charge of an officer, and a detachment of soldiers, and to recommend that officer to inform himself of what was passing at Orange, and in countries in that direction, in possession of the English.

Leaving New York, Sheldon's party traveled eastward, by Saybrook, New London and Seeconk, reaching Boston September 8th, when Sheldon delivered his dispatches to the Governor, and gave the Council a verbal account of his mission. He soon after went home. In October, he was sent again to Boston as an agent for the town. On the 30th, he presented to the General Court the following petition and bill of expenses:—

To his Excellency & Honors—
The Petition of John Shelden Humbly Sheweth:
That your petitioner, accompanied by Edward Allin & Edmund Rice and Nathaniel Brooks were ordered by your Ex'cy to undertake a Journey to Canada in order to recover the English Captives there. In obedience whereunto y^r Petitioner, with the persons afores^d, began their Journey on the 17th day of April last, and Proceeded to Canada, when your Petitioner faithfully & diligently pursued the s^d Designe to the utmost of his power, & so far succeeded therein, as to bring home with him seven captives, and Returned home again on the 18th of Sept., In which journey y^r Petition^r, with the afors^d Persons, endured much fatigue & hardship & passed through great Danger, & by their absence from their Businesse Sustained considerable Damage;

Your Pet^r therefore, Humbly Praies y^r Excellency & Hon^s to Consider the Premises, & order such Compensation & Allowance to him & those that accompanied him, in the s^d service, as in your Wisdom & Justice shall be thought meet.

And your Pet'r as in Duty bound, shall ever Pray.
Boston, Oct. 30, 1707. JOHN SHELDON.

An Accompt of the Sums of Disbursements of John Shelden in his Journey to Canada, in the Service of the Massachusetts Bay, from Aprill 17th to the 18th of Sep. 1707, viz, with 3 men travelling with him:

	livres.	sous.
Viz't from May 9th to June 25th, expended for our Diet and Washing,	174	13
To expenses for Diet & washing from June 24 to Aug. 9,	142	13
To expenses for a pr of shoes for Edw. Allin,	6	
More for said Allin for tobaccoe,	5	7
Ex for Edm. Rice for a pr shoes,	6	
More for sd Rice for Tobaccoe,	4	1
Expences for Nathanial Brooks for a pr shoes,	6	
More for tobaccoe,	2	15
To an Indian to guide us into the way when bewildered,	6	

SHELDON'S PETITION AND GRANT. 341

	livres.	sous.
Pd to ferryman to going to Oso fort to se the captives.	2	
Pd to the Barher for trimming,	14	
Pd for Diet for Henry Segur, captive,	41	
More paid for sd Segur for stockins & shoes,	9	10
Pd to a man for fetching sd Segur from the Indian town to Mont Roy'l,	3	
Pd for a Bottle Brandy for the voyage,	10	2
Pd for a Deerskin for shoes & 3 pr Indian shoes,	8	10
	443	16

	£.	s.	d.
To further expences at Albany in coming home for ye ffrenchmens' Diete,	00	16	10
To Diet for myself,		2	6
for provision and drink for our voyage from York to Seabrook,		12	6
pd for our ffreight,		8	0
pd to ye fferryman at Seabrook,	00	1	4
pd for a man & horse to N London,		2	0
pd for quarters at Stoningtown,		2	10
pd for Shoeing horses,		2	8
pd for quarters at Seaconk & horse hire,		10	6
pd Pocket expenses,	3	00	00
	5	19	2
pd out of his own particuler stock, viz, To money paid for hire of a man & horse to bring a Captive woman from Albany to Woodbury,	1	19	0
and to money paid for provision for the Captives,		10	6
	2	9	6

To pa for the Redemption of a molatto Captive, taken from Exeter 40 pieces of 8s, 8d, at 17d weight which he is to pay me.

This petition was endorsed on the back:—

In the House of Representatives:
Nov. 1, 1707, In ans. to the Pet. on the other side—
Resolved that the Pet'rs Acc. herewith Presented, viz., Seven Hundred Livres amounting to fifty-eight Pounds sixteen shillings & eight pence allowed out of the Province Treasury.
And for his time & Service in the affair within mentioned, the sum of fifty pounds, of which he is paid thirteen Pounds twelve shil's by a Muletto. And to each the three persons that went with him seventeen Pounds apiece.   JOHN BURRILL, Speaker.

A few days later, the following petition was laid before the General Court:—

To his Excellency Joseph Dudley, Esq., Captaine, Generall & Governor in Chiefe in & over the Province of ye Massachusetts Bay & New Hampshire in New England, the Honrable Council and Representatives in Gen'll corte assembled this 18th day of November 1707:—
The Petition of John Shelding of Derefeild, Humbly Sheweth, that whereas I have been a great sufferer in the Common Calamities that hath befallen us at Derefeild, greatly impaireing my estate & family so that I have been Much Unsettled, & the Rather because so many

of o^r neighbors & of my own children were carried away into Captivity, occationing my self to take three journeys to Canada, to obtain and be helpfull in their Release & Returning home againe, which hath been a Verry Difficult and Hazzardous Undertakeing, which I doubt not but this Hon'ble Corte is very Senceable of. Upon the Considerations afores^d, I am imboldened to ask a Gratuity by Granting me a tract of some of the country's Land undisposed of, within or Nere the County of West Hampshire, in some conveynient place where I can finde it, to ye quantity of five hundred Acres or thereabouts, and the Corte shall Judge Most Meet & Conveynient for me, & least prejudiciall to any other Grant. The Consideration of, & allowance to me as above will very much oblidge Your Humble Servant as in duty Bound for yo'r Excellency & Hon'rs ever to pray.

JOHN SHELDON.

"In consideration of his good services," 300 acres were granted the petitioner Nov. 26th, 1707.

The names of the captives brought home by Mr. Sheldon on this ill-timed mission are unknown, save as gathered from the foregoing petition and bill. Nathaniel Brooks was from Deerfield. His two children were left behind; their mother had been killed on the march. Henry Seger was son of Henry of Newtown. Of the Woodbury woman and the mulatto nothing further appears.

Such facts as have been found relating to the captives from Deerfield who remained in Canada, will be given as a contribution to their history. The list made up by Stephen Williams about 1730, and printed in Prince's edition of the "Redeemed Captive," may be referred to in this connection.

The Carter Children. There is a family tradition that Samuel Carter was drowned while crossing a river in Canada and that he was previously engaged to be married to a Deerfield captive. On the death of their father at Norwalk, Conn., in 1728, he left by will estate worth £500 to John, and £100 to Mercy, on condition they would come to Connecticut and remain ten years. It appears by this will, and by a letter from their brother Ebenezer, the residuary legatee, to his brother John, now preserved in the Carter family, that both John and Mercy were married and had children in Canada.

When Col. Stoddard and John Williams were in Canada in 1714, as commissioners empowered to recover captives, John Carter agreed to go home with them; but his attachment to the country was so strong that he changed his mind, and they were obliged to leave him.

The following papers show that some of this family long years after came to New England to visit their relatives:—

ALBANY, July 6, 1736.

LIFT. EBENEZER CARTER:—This is to let you know that your brother John Carter is come from Canada, in Albany * * * and the people in Albany did advice him to go alone afoot to Norwalck * * * We advice him to go with this man William Hobis (?) for he promise to take your brother along to Norwalck, for Reason we was afraid your brother should Lost himself before he comes to you, for he no not the Road. I desire you to Satisfy Hobis (?) when he has delivered your Brother. * * * Do your best Indeavours to make him sta by you, and to bring him to Repentance. Love your Brother, for love is of God. We wiss you well.

And Remain your Humble Servant,
ROBERT WENDELL.
AHASUERAS WENDELL.

Remember my Love to my wife and shildren and parens and all friends.

The bearers hereof, two of the sons of Mercy Carter, an English woman taken captive at Deerfield, Anno. 1703, and since married to a Cagnawaga Indian being desirous to travel to Norwalk in the Colony of Connecticut to visit the Relations of their mother there, this is to desire such persons in said Colony as may see them on their way thither, to direct them in their road, and afford them Necessary and proper Support; and if any Expect to be paid therefor, to bring in their account to us the Subscribers. WILLIAM PITKIN.

Albany, July the 5th, 1751. JOHN CHESTER.

After the close of the old French War, John Carter again appears in his native land. Capt. Ephraim Williams writes from Fort Massachusetts to Lieutenant Governor Phipps, Sept. 3d, 1751, saying:—

Last night came to the Fort 2 Frenchmen & 1 English captive whose name is John Carter; he was taken when Deerfield was destroyed; he is now married in Canada & has a family there. The Frenchmen's mother is an English captive, taken at the same time. She was old Mr. Thomas French's daughter. They had a pass from the Governor of Canada, and are going to see their relatives as they say, but if the truth were known, I believe they are sent for spies.

Three of Mr. French's daughters remained in Canada. It is not known which of them is referred to above.

Abigail Denio.—She was a daughter of John Stebbins, twenty-six days married to James Denio, or Denieur, one of the "three Frenchmen" of Stephen Williams's list, when captured. Their son Aaron when about ten years old came down with a party of Indians to visit his kin. His grandfather persuaded him to stay, and when the Indians were ready to return, Aaron could not be found. He became a noted tavern keeper in Greenfield, was prominent in public affairs, and a soldier in later wars.

Mary Field, Jr.—She was six years old when taken. She was adopted by a squaw and named Walahowey. She married an Indian, and both came down to visit her relatives. Nothing could induce her to remain, although it is said her husband was willing. She told her brother Pedajah, she would contrive his capture, that he might have the benefit of the Popish religion and a life in Canada. Pedajah believed the attempt was once made, and only frustrated by a skillful device which enabled him to escape from the scene of danger.

Mary Harris.—Robert Eastman, captured at Oswego in 1756, and taken to Canada, says "When at Cahnawaga, I lodged with the French captain's mother, (an English woman named *Mary Harris*, taken captive when a child from Deerfield, in New England), who told me she was my grandmother and was kind."

In the New England Historical and Genealogical Register is the following query:—

In the early days of Ohio, 'White Woman's Creek' was a branch of Muskingum, and a town on it was called 'White Woman's.' Gist, in his journal, under date January, 1751, says: This white woman was taken away from New England, when she was not above ten years old, by the French and Indians. She is now upwards of fifty, has an Indian husband and several children. Her name is *Mary Harris*. Can any one tell whence she was taken or anything about her? C. C. Baldwin, Cleveland, Ohio.

Capt. Joseph Kellogg writes from Suffield, Conn., Dec. 3d, 1744, that,—

Two young men, *Mary Harris'* children, have been with me twice, which have lodged at my house. One of them is a very Intelligable man about thirty years of age, and from them endeavoured to critically examine them about the affairs of Canada.

Kellogg was a fellow captive of Mary Harris.

The woman in each of these papers appears to be *Mary Harris*, the Deerfield captive. All agree substantially as to her age, but at present it seems impossible to reconcile these conflicting accounts, and no attempt at an explanation will be made. I have always thought her a child when taken, but have been unable to learn her parentage or previous history.

THE MYSTERY OF ABIGAIL NIMS.

Joanna Kellogg was eleven years old when taken. She married a chief of the Caghnawaga tribe. Many years after she was induced to visit New England, when every inducement was offered, and artifice and strategem used to prevent her return; but all in vain. She died in her chosen home to all intents a veritable savage.

Abigail Nims, aged three when captured. There was a mystery hanging over her life never fully cleared up. It is not certainly known that she was ever heard from by her friends. In her father's will, a provision was made for her in case of her return. There is no indication that the estate was ever called for by her. If the story, of which a glimpse is given in the Massachusetts Council Records, really relates to Abigail, as seems probable from the evidence, it is a tale which, in its suggestions and possibilities, is brimful of sadness and pathos. All that is known bearing on the matter is given below.

At a meeting of the Council, July 31st, 1714, a letter from Col. Partridge, dated July 28th, was laid before it:—

> Giving an account of an outrage in the County of Hampshire, relating to a girl brought thither by a Macqua, and offered for sale; supposed to be an English captive carryed from Deerfield, it appearing so, by her own relation, and divers circumstances concurring. Advised that a letter be written to the Commissioners of Indian affairs at Albany to acquaint them thereof, that a strict examination and inquiry be made therinto, & that Capt. John Sheldon be desired to undertake the journey to Albany with said letter, and assist in said enquiry. And a letter was accordingly digested, signed and expressed to Col. Partridge, with a letter from Gov. Saltonstal, to Capt. Sheldon to undertake said Journey. Further advised, that a copy of this s^d letter be sent to Gen. Nicholson at Pisquataqua, & that he be desired also to write to the Commissioners about this affair.

"Ensign Sheldon," now a captain, and living at Hartford, accepted the mission, and went to Albany with his son. On his return he reported its results to the Council, which took the following action on the case:—

> In Council, Aug. 22, 1714. Upon reading a letter from the Commissioners of the Indian affairs at Albany, by Capt. John Sheldon, messenger thither to make inquiries concerning a young Maid or Girle, brought thither into Westfield by a Macqua and offered for sale, very probably, supposed to be English, & daughter of one [Godfrey] Nims, late of Deerfield, and carried away captive, the Commisioners insisting upon it that she is an Indian.
> Ordered, that Samuel Partridge, Esq., treat with the Macqua, her

pretended master, & agree with him on the reasonablest terms he can for her release, & then to dispose her to some good family near the sea side, without charge for the present, to prevent her fears; unless Capt. Sheldon will be prevailed with to take her home with him.

Paid John Sheldon for journey to Boston from Northampton, and back to Albany, and back, with his son, £17, 16s, 7d, for time and expenses.

In Council, Sept. 20, 1714. Ordered, that the sum of £25 be paid to Elewacamb, the Albany Indian now attending with letters and papers from thence, who claims the English girl in the hands of the English, and her Relations at Deerfield, and that a warrant be made to the Treasurer accordingly. Also that a coat and shirt be given s^d Indian.

So it seems that Partridge was successful in his mission, and delivered the girl at Deerfield, before the above date. Here the curtain dropped. After this, not the slightest trace of Abigail Nims was found.

The Commissioners at Albany believed she was an Indian. But it would appear that the Council of Massachusetts, Col. Partridge and Capt. Sheldon, as well as her "*relations* in Deerfield," believed she was the Abigail Nims she claimed to be. Which was right? What became of her? Did she, chafing under the ecclesiastical rigor of New England discipline, go back to the easy-going forms of Catholicism in Canada? Was she enticed away by some Canadian priest, anxious for her soul's salvation? Did she receive reproof rather than pitiful care, on her awkwardness in household work? Did she rebel against regular labor in any form? Did she find civilized life uncongenial and irksome, and pining for the primitive freedom of savage customs, steal away into the wilderness for relief?

In the list of captives by Stephen Williams, a fellow captive, Abigail Nims, is marked as one who never came back from Canada. Was the pretended Abigail, spurious?—an Indian girl, in a conspiracy with Elewacamb, to obtain ransom money and to run away at her leisure? Did she remain until the return of Ebenezer Nims and wife? They remained in captivity until Sept. 1, 1714, when they sailed from Canada for home. They must have been able to distinguish an English from an Indian girl. Did they detect the cheat, and send her packing? All speculations are idle. No voice comes in answer to all this questioning. This romance and mystery remain, and probably must remain, a sad, unsolved problem of border history.*

Thankful Stebbins, aged twelve. Hoyt, in Antiquarian Researches, says:—

A gentleman who recently resided in Montreal stated, that at the lake of the Two Mountains, near the mouth of Grand river, he saw a French girl who informed him that her grandmother was Thankful Stebbing, who was one of the captives taken from Deerfield in 1704.

Her father, John Stebbins, who died in 1723, made provision in his will for five children then in Canada, provided they returned and remained in New England. Samuel alone returned. Their ages ranged from four to seventeen.

Elizabeth (Price) Stevens.—She was wife of "Andrew Stevens ye Indian." She married in Montreal, Feb. 3d, 1706, Jean Fourneau, a Frenchman, and never came back.

Eunice Williams, daughter of Rev. John Williams, aged seven.—A full and interesting account of this case can be found in a paper read by Miss C. Alice Baker before the Pocumtuck Valley Memorial Association in 1871. She remained with the Indians until she became practically one of them. Nothing could induce her captors to give her up, either to the English or French. "De Vaudreuil," says Mr. Williams, her father, "labored much for her redemption. He offered an hundred pieces of eight for her and was refused. His lady went over and begged her from them, but all in vain." How shall we account for the tenacity with which the fickle, money-loving savages clung to this child? It was said they "would as soon part with their hearts," as with her. Could it have been from personal attachment? Was it not rather through the influence of the Jesuits, plotting a grand triumph over Mr. Williams? Prolonged and earnest efforts were made for her recovery; but when in 1713 she married Amrusus, a Caghnawaga Indian, they were almost as hope-

---

* Thanks to the untiring research of C. Alice Baker, the life of Abigail Nims in Canada has been recently traced. She was baptized June 15th, 1704, [N. S.] by the name of Mary Elizabeth. She lived with *Ganastarsi*, a squaw, who gave her the name of To-wat-a-go-wach. July 29th, 1715, [N. S.], nine months after her supposed appearance in Deerfield, Abigail was married at the Indian fort to Josiah Rising, a fellow Deerfield captive. They settled at the Lake of the Two Mountains, on a farm still held by their descendants. Here Abigail died Feb. 19th, 1748, [N. S.] leaving eight children. The oldest son became a priest; the youngest daughter, Lady Superior of the Community of the Congregation.

A tree transplanted from the home of Abigail and Josiah is now growing near Memorial Hall, on land that was the home lot of Abigail's father.

less. In 1740, she was prevailed upon to visit her brother Stephen at Longmeadow, with her husband, on the guarantee that she should not be detained. They came to New England again the next year, with two children, and stayed several months, visiting her relatives; a third time in October, 1743, and once again later. The General Court granted the family a large tract of land on condition they would remain, but to no purpose; she, fearing it would endanger her soul. The only other reason ever given, so far as it appears, was, that her father had married a second wife.

The papers below show the wide-spread interest in Eunice and some of the efforts for her recovery:—

Peter Schuyler to Gov. Dudley:—

May it please your Excellency
 Your Excellencys Letters of ye 6th & 10th Currant for Expresse have Received togather with five letters for Monsr Vaudreuil gov^r of Canida which have deliver^d to ye french officer Dayeville who goes from hence y^e [19] Instant & have taken his Receipt for three Letters as you Designed which is here Inclosed as to what your Excellency mentions Relating to Mr Williams his doghter, the squaw nor she is not come her yet nor have I heard anything of her Coming altho I shall be very glad to see them and do assure your Excellency If they come together or be it ye squaw alone I shall use all possible meanes to get the child exchanged Either as your Excellency proposes or what other way the Squaw will be most willing to Comply with In the meantime shall Inform my Selfe by all opportunities whether the said Squaw & Child be coming here or if they be anywhere near by. Your Excellency may depend that whatever I can do for ye obtaining of ye s^d Child shall at no time be wanting. So shall take leave to subscribe my Selfe
          Your Excellency^s
            Most humble & obedient
                      Servant
Albany Dec 19(?) 1712   P SCHUYLER

John Schuyler to Gov. Dudley:—

May it Please
 Yo^r Excellency
 I, thought it my duty imediately (wthout any further Omission) to signify to yor Excellency my return from Mount Real to Albany upon ye 15th of this Instant June with Monsr Bolock [Hertel de Beaulac. C. A. Baker] and three more and nine prisonirs a list of y^r Names is herein enclosed: I sett them forward for New engl^d wth Sam^{ll} Ashly and Daniell Bagg upon ye 10th Instant I have not herein incerted the charges; By reason I cann^t make up the Acc^{ts} till ye Officers return to Canada; I have likewise enclos^d for Yo^r Excellency my Memoriall that touches the concern of ye Rev^d Mr Williams ye Minister at Dearfeild for his Daughter My indefatigueable Pains

therein came to no purpose If y^r Excellency hath the Returns of peace I hope to receive them; and then shall dispatch them away as directed. I found a great fatique in my Journey to and from Canada and waded through many Difficulties in ye way wth the Prisonirs To Dilate thereon would be prolix. I now beg leave to assure your Excellency of my Effection and Zeal to every yor Commands and that in all Sincerity I am May it Please Yo^r Excell^y

Yo^r most obedient humble Servt

Albany June ye 10th 1713

JOHN SCHUYLER

Col. Schuyler's narrative of the culminating event in the eventful life of Eunice Williams is as pathetic as it is dramatic. The actors are all truly representative characters; the scene an epitome of the historic verities of our Colonial life. One may be pardoned if he do not quite agree with the honest Dutchman as to the disinterested efforts of the priests to release Eunice, whom they had baptized Margaret.

A true and perfect Memoriall of my proceedings Jn behalf of Margarett Williams now Captive amongst ye Jndians at the ffort of Caghenewaga Jn Canada, Jnsisting upon here Relief and to persuade her to go home, to her father and Native Countrey, it being upon the instant and earnest desire of her ffather now Minister at Dearfeild in New England.

J arrived from Albany at Mont Reall on ye 15th of Aprill last 1713 Where J understood y^t Monsr de Vaudruille Govern^r and Chief of Canada, was expected then every day from Quebeck, Upon which J thought proper not to mention any thing touching the aforesaid Captive, untill his Excellency should be here himself, and accordingly when he arrived here; J propos'd the matter to him, who gave me all the Encouragem^t J could immagine for her to go home, he also permitted me, to go to her at the ffort, where she was to prepare, if J could persuade her to go home, Moreover his Excellency said that wth all his heart, he would give a hundred Crowns out of his own pockett, if that she might be persuaded to go to her Native Countrey; J observing all this, then was in hopes, J should prevaile with her to go home. Accordingly J went to the ffort of Caghenewaga being accompanied by one of the Kings Officers and a ffrench Jnterpreter likewise another of the Jndian Language, Being upon the 26 Day of May entring at the Jndian ffort, J thought fitt first to apply mySelf to the priests; As J did, Being two in Company, And was informed before that this infant (As J may say) was married to a young Jndian J therefore proposed to know the Reason why this poor Captive should be Married to an Jndian being a Christian Born (tho neerly taken from the Mothers Breast and such like Instances &c) Whereupon the priest Sett forth to me Such good Reasons, wth Witnesses that my Self, or any other person (as J believe) could fairly make Objection against their Marriage; (First s^d he they came to me to Marry them) very often wch J always refus'd wth good words and persuasions to the Contrary, But both continuing in their former resolutions to Such a Degree, that J was constrained to be absent from ye the ffort three Severall times, because not Satisfyed mySelf in their Marriage; Untill last, after Some days past they both came to me, and s^d that they were Joined together, And if he would not marry them they matter'd not, for they were resolved never to leave one the other But live together heathen like; Upon wch J thought proper to Join them in Matrimony and Such like Reasons as aforesaid the priest did plainly Sett forth) and after some further discourse, J desired the priest, to let me see her at his house, ffor J knew not where to find her upon which he sent for her, who p^rsently came with the Jndian She was Married to both together She looking very poor in body, bashfull in the face but proved harder than Steel in her breast, at her first Entrance into the Room, J desired her to sitt down wch she did, J first Spoak to her in English, Upon wch she did not Answ^r me; And J believe She did not understand me, she being very Young when she was taken, And liveing always amongst the Jndians afterwards, J Jmployed my Jndian Languister to talk to her; informing him first by the ffrench Jnterpretor who understood the English Language, What he should tell her, and what Questions he should Ask her, Accordingly he did J understood amost all what he said to her; And found that he Spoak according to my Order but could not gett one word from her. Upon which J advised the priest To Speak to her And if J could not prevail wth her to go home to Stay there, that She might only· go to see her ffather, And directly return hither again, The priest made a long Speech to her and endeavoured to persuade her to go, but after almost half an hours discourse—could not get one word from her; And afterwards when he found She did not Speak, he again Endeavoured to persuade her to go and see her ffather, And J seeing She continued inpersuadable to speak; J promised upon my Word and honour, if she would go only to see her ffather, J would·convey her to New England, and give her Assureance of liberty to return if she pleased—the priest asked her Severall times, for answer upon the my earnest request, And fair offers wch was after long Solicitations (Jaghte oghte) which word being translated into the English Tongue their Signifycation (is) may be not) but the meaning thereof amongst the Jndians is a plaine denyall and these two words were all we could gett from her; in allmost two hours time that we talked with her, Upon this my eyes being almost filled with tears, J said to her mySelf, had I made such proposalls and prayings to the worst of Jndians, J did not doubt but have had a reasonable Answere and consent to what J have s^d. Upon wch her husband seeing that J was so much concerned about her replyed had her ffather not Married againe, She would have gone and Seen him, long Ere this time But gave no further reason and the time growing late and J being very Sorrowfull, that J could not prevail upon nor get one word more from her J took her by the hand and left her in the priests house. JOHN SCHUYLER.

The following letter gives us a parting glimpse of Eunice enjoying a serene old age in her Canada home. It was written by James Dean to her brother Stephen. Dean had spent several months at Caghnawaga and knew Eunice intimately.

The original letter is owned by Edward E. Ayers of Chicago, who kindly loaned it for my examination and use. Two extracts are given:—

* * * "She has two daughters & one grandson which are all the Descendants she has. Both her daughters are married: But one of them has no children. Your sister lives Comfortably & well & considering her advanced age enjoy^d a good state of health when I left the Country. She retains still an affectionate remembrance of her friends in New England: but tells me she never expects to see them again; the fatigues of so long a journey would be too much for her to undergo" * * * "Should have written more particular respecting your sister, but I suppose you either have, or soon will receive a letter from herself, which Mr. Frisbee has brought down, in which she gives a particular account of her family."

Where is this letter?

ANECDOTES RELATING TO THE CAPTIVES.

Penhallow, who died in 1727, gives the following anecdote, in referring to the invasion of Deerfield, February, 1704. It is not found elsewhere. A certain historian (?) has transferred this story to the time of the capture of Fort Massachusetts in 1746:—

Some of the captives then in Canada, knowing the enterprise that was then on foot, sent several letters unto their friends, which the enemy did carefully put into a bag and hang it upon the limb of a tree in the highway; which letters were afterwards found, and satisfaction of those that were then alive among them.

There is a tradition in the Nims family, that when De Rouville's expedition was being planned, some of the leaders made John Nims the offer to save harmless all of his friends, if he would act as their guide. The proposition was joyfully accepted by Nims, with the expectation of being able to escape and give seasonable warning. But when the matter came to the ears of the Governor, he forthwith put a stop to the project, as a dangerous experiment.

Soon after John Sheldon left Canada for home in 1705, four young men, disappointed at not being allowed to return with him, made their escape and reached home about June 8th. Their names were Thomas Baker, John Nims, Martin Kellogg and Joseph Petty. They had no arms, but probably a small stock of provisions, and reached our frontier more dead than alive from hunger and fatigue. They were discovered in Wisdom in an imbecile condition, and seemed guided more by instinct than reason, in making their way towards home. Their appearance when brought in was such as to melt the stoutest heart. Nourishment was given according to the judgment of some old men, who had known what starvation was by experience. But the alternate abject supplication, and impotent wrath, with which the poor fellows begged and fought for "more," was more than some of their friends could bear; and stringent measures were necessary to prevent such a response to these appeals as would have proved fatal to the sufferers, according to the theory of those in charge. Broth, in small quantities, was given at first, and by slow degrees more substantial food, until they were filled. It was a long time before their cravings were satisfied. After having eaten all they could, they still felt as hungry as ever.

I had this account, when ten years old, from my grandmother Sheldon, who was fifteen when John Nims died, and who heard it from his own lips. She was then more than fourscore, and the story came from her trembling lips with a pathos never to be forgotten. I recall another incident: One day when the fugitives seemed at the last extremity, they discovered and killed a great white owl. This was instantly torn in pieces, which were laid in four piles, and fairly divided, one turning his back, and responding to the query, "Who shall have this?" until all had been "touched off." Each took his share, and hardly waiting to pull off the feathers, tore the tough fragments with their teeth, like so many ravenous beasts. Grandmother said, "John Nims always insisted that a wing which fell to him was the sweetest morsel he ever tasted."

As an illustration of the value of tradition this story will be left as printed in the first edition. How the slow tortoise of which Petty partook, as appears in the following letter, obtained the plumage of the grave bird is of no consequence, for the "Providential Great White Owl" will still live, with "Goffe the Guardian Angel" of Hadley. And both will plume themselves and dress their feathers on the pages of so-called historical writers, to the music of the silver toned "Bell of St. Regis." To the courtesy and generosity of William F. Havemyer of New York City, we are able to give the following letter, the original of which is framed in

Memorial Hall. It was procured by him at an auction sale in Philadelphia in 1892:—

Rev^a S^r

Upon your desire, I now present you with a Narrative of my escape from Canada, tho it is now so long Since y^t I may possibly forget some particulars. But the acc^t as near as I can remember is as follows *viz*^{t} About thirteen months after I was taken from Deerfield (w^c you well remember) four of us consulted methods to make our escape. Sometime in May upon y^r great procession day we had Liberty to go in & about ye city of Mont Real & there we happened all to meet together & John Nyms & I informed ye other two of our design to make our escape. This was on a thirsday [May 10] & we agreed y^t ye other three were to come down to where I lived w^c was about 9 miles from ye city & w^t was something remarkable ye guns & Provisions w^c I had designed to bring wth us was in another room from where I Lodged w^c exercised my mind very much how I should come at y^m since I Lodged in another room with ye people of ye house & w^t still oppressed my spirits more was, y^t coming in from work at noon I found a bed & sick person placed in y^t room where ye guns & Provisions were: & I thot now it was impossible to escape but upon my return at night I found ye sick person removed & my bed brought into y^t room w^c much revived me.
on ye Sabbath [May 13] following I was to go to ye city again to conclude further about our escape, & having confirmed all matters I returned at night & found my Landlords son there w^c was designed to Lodge with me w^c again dashed my spirits much for now I thot it impossible for me to Escape from him.

But while I sat pausing w^t to do I remembered y^t I was to set up a sign by ye River for ye other three to know where ye house was & I thot I would go & do y^t w^c w^n I had done upon my return I found my Landlord's son moving off & would not stay tho much persuaded to tarry & altho it was very Dark & he did go; w^c again revived me & about break of day ye other three came & I handed y^m two guns & some Provision & we took a Cannoe & passed ye River by sun rising & tho ye people Lived on ye other side we passed by them undiscovered. This was on monday morning [May 14] & on wednesday about sun two hours high at night we arrived at Chamblee River about 9 miles below ye fort y^{re} we made a raft & went over & ye next day we travelled up against ye fort & stopped to get some Provision killed a calf & dryed it, but friday & Saturday rained so hard y^t we could not travel w^c y^n we judged made against us but in Providence we found it otherwise, for those y^t pursued us were in this time returned. on ye Sabbath following we set out for ye Lake & arrived y^{re} on Wednesday about no [torn] there we found two cannoes w^c we judged our pursuers [torn] ad Left one of these we took & came along with our journey, & came along y^t day & all night & ye next day & at night Left our Cannoe [x pou?] we came along on ye east side of ye Lake untill we came to ye mouth of Misisecou River we went up this river all night for it comes along ye same course as ye east shore of ye Lake & next morning we found a small runn [?] wather w^c Led out of ye River into ye Lake w^c we made use of to waft us into yᵉ Lake again: there is extraordoary good Land on each side of this River all yᵉ way we went as far as we could perceive. this day we travelled on yᵉ Lake till night & Lay by yᵉ Lake, but next morning yᵉ wind was so high against us yᵗ we Left our Cannoe & travelled on yᵉ side of yᵉ Lake yᵗ day: & yᵉ next day being Saturday we struck across for French river falls & arrived there on Sabbath about 9 in yᵉ morning. this we travelled up about 2 or 3 dais & Left it & struck away for yᵉ branches of White River & on yᵉ next Sabbath about 9 in yᵉ morning we came to White River Now our Provision was spent excepting some small matters we had Left to fish withal, & yᵗ day we spent in getting Provision & supplied ourselves for yᵗ night & part of yᵉ next day wᶜ was all yᵉ Provision we had untill we came to Deerfield excepting yᵉ leg of a tortoise & a small hook fish wᶜ we brought along a Little way. yᵉ next night we came to yᵉ mouth of white river & made a fire & designed to Lodge there & we set one to fish for us; but by reason of yᵉ flies he was soon discouraged & as soon as he came up I was going down to yᵉ River to drink & espied an Indian on yᵉ East side of yᵉ Great river coming to drink wᶜ made me stop and hide myself untill he was gone off & for fear of discovery we made off yᵗ night & yᵉ next day our provision being spent sometime & we weak & faint we thot best to make a raft upon wᶜ we came down yᵗ day & yᵉ next night on Connecticutt River & yᵉ next day also we still continued our Course on yᵉ raft & on thursday about 9 or 10 in yᵉ morning we came to yᵉ great falls, there we Let go our raft & went below yᵉ falls & made another & came yᵗ day to yᵉ Lower end of yᵉ great meadows or yᵉ place now called yᵉ Cannoe place there we Lodged yᵗ night & yᵉ next morning we came on our raft to yᵉ meadows where yᵉ fort is now there we Left our raft & came on foot yᵗ day into Deerfield about twilight in yᵉ evening & thus thro the good hand of divine Providence (wᶜ watched over us all yᵉ way) we safely arrived to our own native Land again & were joyfully received & well taken care of by our friends upon wᶜ I cannot but say yᵗ we have reason to praise God four our deliverance, & never forget his be [torn]ts. thus Sʳ I have given you a brief & as exact a relation [torn] can well, since t'is so Long a time passed since, & if it may be of any service I Rejoyce & subscribe my self yours to Command   JOSEPH PETTY

[This letter was addressed to]
"The Revᵈ
  Mr. Stephen Williams
    Att
      Springfield
        Longmeadow
          These."

Ebenezer Nims, seventeen when captured. He was adopted by a squaw, and lived at Lorette; perhaps taken to fill the place of a son killed in the expedition. He came home with Stoddard and Williams in 1714, bringing his wife and son Ebenezer. The Indians of Lorette were so much attached to this family that on hearing they had been taken on board the vessel by force, they came to Quebec in a body to rescue them.

Sarah Hoyt, seventeen. The priests urged her to marry. They pertinaciously insisted upon it as a duty, and had a French officer selected as her mate, thus assuring themselves of a permanent resident, and popish convert. Professing to be convinced of her duty in the matter, Sarah declared one day in public that she would be married, if any of her fellow-captives would have her. Ebenezer Nims, a life-long companion, at once stepped forward and claimed her for his bride. The twain were made one upon the spot. The wily priests had met their match, for it is easy to believe that this was a pre-arranged issue on the part of the lovers.

Ebenezer Carter. A family tradition says, "he was stolen away by merchants trading between Montreal and Albany, and restored to his father." Probably this story originated in the following incident: Feb. 11th, 1707, Col. Schuyler writes from Albany to Capt. Partridge: "Yours of the 11th came to hand by this Indian you sent it by. As to the boy the Indians brought here, he is at my house, in good health, and when his friends come to redeem him, shall be delivered up." Samuel Carter, in a petition to the Connecticut General Court, May 8th, 1707, says his son Ebenezer "was redeemed by paying £24, borrowed money." It is probable that some of the Schuylers had been engaged to redeem Ebenezer from his Indian master in Canada, and that he was the boy referred to in the above letter.

Benjamin Burt and his wife were among the captives. Their first child, Christopher, was born April 14th, 1704, on the march. They were among those recovered by Ens. Sheldon, on his second expedition, and a second child was born to them July 4th, 1706, on the return voyage. It was named Seaborn, and baptized on his arrival in Boston by Rev. Samuel Willard, as already stated.

Jonathan Hoyt, sixteen. The story of his redemption is told by his grandson, Elihu Hoyt, who was nine years old when the captive died. When young Dudley was at Quebec with Capt. Vetch, in 1706, he was attracted one day by the English-looking face of a boy on the street; he spoke to him, learned he was from Deerfield, and that his Indian master was in the city, selling garden truck. He found Hoyt anxious to go home, and told him to go and fetch his master. With a light heart he tripped about the city until his master was found and brought to Dudley. The latter holding out twenty silver dollars, offered them for the boy. The savage could not resist the temptation, and accepted the coin. Hoyt was at once hurried on board the English brigantine. As Dudley expected, the Indian soon repented of his bargain, and came back with the money. But it was too late, and he went away lamenting that he had parted with his favorite boy for a few dumb dollars, that could neither hunt nor fish. His home was at Lorette, where Hoyt had learned the Indian language, which he spoke fluently as long as he lived. In after years his Indian master paid him a visit at Deerfield, and was well received and kindly treated. On parting, "they took an affectionate leave of each other, expecting to meet here no more."

Mary Sheldon, seventeen years old when taken, was adopted by a squaw. After the war her Indian mother often visited her in Northampton. She would never sleep in the house but would go out to Fort Hill to sleep every night. On this hill stood an Indian fort before Philip's War.

Stephen Williams, then ten years old, was taken by an "Eastern Indian," named Wattanamon, who, after two or three weeks, gave the boy to his brother, who took him the next summer to the fort at St. Francis, an Abenaki settlement. But, as this savage "could not comply with their rites and customs, he went to Albany," leaving the captive with his kinsman, Sagamore George, a Pennicook chief, who had settled at St. Francis. The latter was a faithless, avaricious fellow, who, while Stephen was yet in the hands of his second master, had taken money of Mr. Williams for his redemption and appropriated it to his own use. He now set a price of forty crowns upon the boy, which, after a long parley, was paid by Vaudreuil.

What is the explanation of the undisputed fact, that children taken among savages soon became strongly attached to their mode of life? There is plenty of evidence that many of those taken from Deerfield, remained in Canada of their own choice; that many who did return were induced to leave savage for civilized life with great difficulty; and some were hardly restrained from returning to it, after many years. Agassiz, in reply to this query, said he thought it was a reaction from the rigid restraint of Puritanic training. Others say, children always fall naturally into their surroundings, whatever they may be. While the latter view may apply to very young children, and the former to those older, neither appears to cover the whole ground. It would seem that our every-day observation gives evidence, that there is an element, underlying all such considerations, where the explanation may be sought, if not found.

We all know the fascination of *camping out*. Nothing so delights the heart of youth as a wigwam in the woods. Although it be represented by a shawl spread over bushes in the garden, or even over chairs in the parlor, the charm is still there. The same feeling governs those of a larger growth, who find no keener enjoyment than shanty life on the borders of some wild lake, or in the depths of a primeval forest, where they can indulge in the natural sports of fishing and hunting. In the same direction are picnic parties, where all are happy in using fingers instead of forks, green leaves for napkins, and a single cup supplies the wants of many; where ottomans and sofas are found on stumps, logs or stones, and pine needles, or green-sward, are a more enjoyable carpet than the most luxurious product of the loom. And the more highly cultivated the participants, the more keen the zest. In the late rebellion, young men, nurtured the most tenderly, living luxuriously all their days, were never happier than when enduring the rough usage of a soldier's life,—the hard march, the coarse fare and the bivouac under the stars. For such, the artificial life of a high civilization, the etiquette of their accustomed social circle often became henceforth irksome; the cramping influences of their old life were unendurable, and thousands have broken away for broader and more natural surroundings. To-day they are scattered all over the plains and mountains of our great Western wilderness; shepherds, "cow-boys," hunters, miners, enduring almost all the hardships incident to a savage life. Here extremes meet; the most scholarly productions of our universities strike hands with the unlettered trapper, or guide, find a common level, become boon companions, and perhaps bosom friends, and but for their maturer years, would easily lapse into the same condition of barbarism which swallowed up the young Deerfield captives in Canada.

Do not these things all indicate a natural desire for a closer walk with nature? a more primitive life? a deep-seated protest against the results of hot-house cultivation? a tendency, which, when the pressure of centuries is removed, becomes the controlling influence? The same tendency may be observed in flowers, fruits, and domestic animals. Those brought by artificial means to the highest degree of excellence, retrograde the most rapidly. It is only by unceasing cultivation and care, that those are kept from falling back into the condition of the original stock.

CLOSE OF QUEEN ANNE'S WAR.

During the negotiations between Gov. Dudley and De Vaudreuil for an exchange of prisoners and treaty of neutrality, there was a general desire for peace on the part of the English. Dudley evidently did not share this feeling. He was ambitious for the conquest of Canada; and his policy seems to have been, to prolong the correspondence until he could recover the captives in the hands of the enemy, and gain time and opportunity to effect his object. During this same period, Vaudreuil, who had become alarmed for the safety of Canada, and therefore desirous of peace, sent no parties of Indians against our valley. The vigilance of our authorities, however, was not relaxed. A garrison constantly occupied Deerfield, and scouts were kept ranging the woods.

The following orders, found among the Sheldon manuscript, have historic interest and value; showing, as pictures of the times, the power conferred upon military officers over persons and property in public exigencies, and their mode of exercising it:—

To ye Constable of Derefield:
In her Maj'sts name, these Require you to impress such & so many men of the Derefield Inhabitants, or others, as are well acquainted with the woods up the River & ajacent woods, to be pilates for the scouts that are now sending out, & shall be sent out according to direction you shall from tyme to tyme receive from Capt. Jonathan Wells, or from Capt. John Stoddart; & hereof you may not fayle at yo'r Utmost Perrill; dated in Hatfield this 21 June, 1706, In the 5th yeare of Her Maj'sts Reign, Anno domino.

SAM'LL PARTRIDGE, Lt. Colo.

To yᵉ consabel of Dearfield, Greting:

This Require you jn Hear Magj'tis Name forthwith to Impress one Good & abel Hors, bridel & sadel, for Hear Majytis sarvis; Hear of you may not fail. Given under my Hand this 20 fo July, 1706.

JONATHAN WELLS, capt.

In her Maj'tis Name you a Required to Impress two Squa lynes & any other Necessary the two Frenchmen now Goeing to Canada stand in need of; fayle not. 27 August, 1706.

SAM'LL PARTRIDGE, Lt. Colo.

To the Constable of Dearfield:

In Her Majisties name you are hereby required forthwith to impress and deliver to Capt. John Stoddard, pork or any other provisions, & so much as he shall direct to, also, men horses, or anything or things whatsoever he shall think needful; to be imployed in Her Majesties service according as he sᵈ Stoddard shall direct; herof fayle not at your peril: dated at Hatfield, this 25th day of Sept'br, in the fifth year of her Majesties Rn, Anno yᵉ Dom'i, 1706.

SAM'LL PARTRIDGE, Lt. Colo.

The above order was not in Partridge's handwriting. It was endorsed on the back:—

Deerfield, Oct. 11, 1706.

pursuant to the within, this warrant John Sheldin of Dearfield, constable, hath impressed pork and other things, all which were done by my order and direction. JOHN STODDARD, Capt.

When the joyful news reached Deerfield of the return of Mr. Williams to Boston, a town meeting was at once called. By the record of its action the town's relation to the Redeemed Captive seems a little mixed. He is called their pastor, and at the same time measures were adopted for his *resettlement*. There may have been no precedents to govern the case.

At a legall town Meeting in Deerfield November 30, 1706, the town then unanimously made choice of Capt. Jonathan Wells, ens. jno. Shelden and Thomas ffrench, to goe down to yᵉ bay for them, and in thair be half to act and treat with thair pastor the reverand mr. jno. Williams, in regard to his resetl'g with them againe in yᵉ work of yᵉ ministry; as also to take advice and counsel of yᵉ Elders in our County for the management of that work; as also to put up a petition to yᵉ generall court or counsel, for a grant of money for yᵉ encouragement of yᵉ reverant mr. jno. Williams in his resetelment in said work with yᵐ; and in all thes partickulars to act and doe according to yᵉ best of thair discration.

As we have seen, the desired grant was voted by the General Court six days later. A conference with "the Elders" probably showed the fact, that no special "management" was necessary, and Mr. Williams was soon reestablished in his chosen work, and field of labor, without further ceremony, having refused eligible offers of settlements near Boston.

From the day of her great disaster, up to this time, Deerfield had hardly been more than a military post, held by soldiers in the pay of the colony; and little attention had been given to municipal affairs beyond keeping up the meadow fence. The discouraged inhabitants had felt that at any time they might be called upon to desert the place. Now, everything was changed. Their loved minister, who had been so much to them, was again among them. Their courage rose. The town should now be held at all hazard; and the regular routine of town business must be taken up. First of all, Mr. Williams must be provided for.

1707. January 9, 1706-7 Att a Legall Town meeting in Deerfield It was y^n agreed and uoted y^t ye Towne would build a house for Mr. Jno. Williams in Derfield as big as Ens Jno Sheldon's a back room as big as may be thought convenient: It was also uoted y^t Ens Jno Sheldon Sar Thomas ffrench and Edward Alln ware chosen a Comity for carying on said work.

At the March meeting, "Sergt. Eleizar Hawks, and bennony more" were added to this committee, Sheldon and Allen having been in the meantime, as we have seen, called to more important duties for the State.

April 5, It was then agreed and uoted, y^t ye town should pay unto Mr Jno Williams: 20 pounds in money and euery male head of 16 years and upward 1 day work a pese and thos y^t haue tames a day with thair tames: for ye yere.

That all land owners should bear their share of the burdens, a petition was sent to the General Court for leave "to rais all thair town charges upon lands only."

The military defenses had become so weak that the labor necessary to strengthen the lines was more than the settlers could bear, and a call was made upon Col. Partridge for aid. The result of this appeal may be seen in the following paper:—

To his Excellency Joseph Dudley, Esq., Capt. Gen'll Governor in Cheife & the Hon'rd Counsell & Representatives in Gen'll Corte assembled this 28 May, 1707:

Samull Patridge Humbly proposeth Refferring to the Settleing of the Broken State of Derefeild & to their building up in a way of deffence against the Comon enemy, it being absolutely nesessary both to the people and Church of Christ & of absolute advantage to the whole county & youre Especiall care & allowance for ye Encouridgem^t

& strengthening the Rev'ed Mr. John Williams in y⁵ work of Christ there is greatly advantageous to us all, for which myself, in the behalf of us all, do Return our thankfulness to this Corte & Humbly spread before you the Nessessetie of Rebuilding the Forts there so as to take in Mr. Williams his house & several other houses for Inhabitants that are & will repaire there for enlarg'mt & strengthening the place: we propose to Rebuild with 120 Rodd of fortification with square timber which may be done at 20s per Rodd: now the people being in a Broken Condition as afores[d] most of their houses to Rebuild upon the former Ruins are incapacitated to Rebuild the Forts as afores[d] therefore I Humbly intreate this Corte's Consideration of the premises & to grant such allowances as are needfull for the performance of the afore'sd which will much oblidge y⁵ whole people & myself youre unworthy serv't ffor youre Honors ever to pray.

SAM'LL PARTRIDGE.

June 13th, 1707, £30 was "allowed towards that part of the general fortification, that falls to the share of the poor of Deerfield, and such as are returned from captivity."

This appropriation, it will be observed, was for the general stockade. No more is heard of the smaller work of square timber proposed by Col. Partridge.

August 11th, 1707, Col. Schuyler wrote Partridge, that his Indian spies, just returned from Canada, reported a party of twenty-seven French and Indians at the mouth of Otter Creek on the 6th, bound for the New England frontier. The spies were charged by this party not to tell of the expedition. To this they would not agree, as the war party "was going to kill our brethren of New England." Nothing more was heard of these enemies. Probably this discovery sent them back. No Indian made an attack but by surprise; according to their ethics, it would be a disgrace to do it openly.

In this war the English adopted the French tactics, and sent small scouts to harass the frontiers of the enemy. From the following paper a good idea of their methods may be obtained:—

Capt. [John] Stoddard set away from Deerfield the 28th of April with 12 men, & Wednesday was a fortnight after, they tracked Indians upon the French river & they followed them till Saturday Night, at which time they had got to the last carrying place, and was quite discouraged & concluded that they had got so far out of their Reach y[t] y[a] could not overtake y[m] & three of them had a mind to take their cano, which was all they had that was serviceable & go to Chamblee and get a Frenchman, or more if they could, and set away upon the lakes & was driven by a contrary wind upon a point of land; & there they discovered some Indians; & two of y[m] staid at y[e] canno, and the third, namely, John Wells, went to observe their motions & after he had got a little way he saw a person with its back towards him, he being in a plain place so that he could not get away without being discovered, & he was loath to shoot, because he was in hopes of getting more booty, & while he was thus thinking the person rose up & stood a little while & for fear of being discovered he shot & she fell down; he took his hatchet out of his girdle & ran up to it to cut off its head & then he saw it had a white face, which very much startled him, & she spake, saying, "Netop, Netop, my master." He ran to the cano; they set off; the Indians shot off two or three guns which he judged were to alarm one another, and they overtook ye rest of y^{ir} company ye same day just at night & they y^n set away for home & arrived the 30th of May. By the discribing of the person y^t was killed Uncle thinks it was an Eastern captive, Namely, Johannah Ardaway, and Wells saith y^t he thought it was she, as soon as he saw her face.

This manuscript was without signature.

October 17th, 1707, a town meeting was held when,—

It was uoted to send a petistion to ye generall Cort for a grant of money towards ye maintainance of ye reuarant Mr Jno Williams in ye work of ye ministry in Deerfield. it was allso uoted y^t Colonall partrig and ensin Jno Sheldon should be implyed to manage y^t afaire: Att ye same meeting, ye town made choise of Capt Jonathan Weals and ensin jno Sheldon for to git a petition drawn to send to ye genarall Cort and allso impowered them to Sine it in the towns behalf:

In their petition the committee say:—

We, Labouring Still under many Difficulties & Streights, being but a Smal handfull of us & most of us very low in the World, are at Considerable charges among ourselves, in Building a House & providing other Necessarys & Conveniencys for the Resettlement of our Rev'd Pastor, not here to be Named, & Many who Deserted ye Place quickly after ye Desolation, By our Rev. Pastor's return and giveing hopes of Settleing again amongst us has encouraged their Return, with many other who Returned out of Captivity, who Instead of helping in such charges, have rather need of help to build Houses for themselves, & providing other Necessarys for their Subsistance. Our Necessities putting us upon it & being Imboldened by former favors & Incouragements, Wee humbly crave your help for the maintanance & Incouragement of our Worthy Pastor amongst us. You were pleased to do considerable ye last year that way. Our necessities being still very great, we Pray you would consider us in that Regard: We have devolved this our Concern into ye hands of ye Worshipfull Col. Sam'l Partridge, Esq., & Capt. John Shelden, to manage for us, hoping your Honors will consider your Poor Petitioners & for your Honors we shall ever Pray.

JONATHAN WELLS,
JOHN SHELDON,

In behalf of ye whole town of Deerfield.
Deerfield, Oct. 25, 1707.

MUNICIPAL AND MINISTERIAL. 363

Eleven days later twenty pounds were granted for one year in answer to this appeal.

December 23d "the town voted to pay thair town charg in prouition pay as followeth Indian corn, 2 s, otes, 1 s 6 d, peas 4 s per bushel." Voted to give "yᵉ Widow Williams all her reats for this present yere." Her husband, Zebadiah, captured in 1703, had died in the hospital at Quebec, April 12th, 1706.

1708. At a meeting Feb. 1st, three men "were chosen a comittee to Masure all yᵉ common fence in Derefield and to stake it out to yᵉ now present proprietors."

February 9th, "Uoted to forgiv john Allison all his reats for yᵉ present yere except one pound, which he hath already paid in sweeping yᵉ house of god." This is the only instance in which I have found the meetinghouse referred to as a sacred edifice, until many years later.

March 1st, the usual town officers were chosen, and "forty pounds in money for his salery yᵉ yere ensuing" was voted to Mr. Williams, and a tax was laid.

March 25th, it was "uoted yᵗ: Martin Smith and widow Hursts and Robert prises comonfence should be repaired upon yᵉ town charg."

Sept. 23d, Uoted yᵗ all swine yᵗ shall be found upon yᵉ comans after yᵉ 3d day of Ocktober shall be ringed, and any that shall neglect to ring their own swine, *thay* shall be forthwith rung by yᵉ hog ringer.

December 10th, "Uoted to pay for yᵉ glasing of meetinghous this present yere," and the price of grain was fixed as follows: "Corn 2 s, peas 4 s, oats 1–6 or 1 s 6 d—1-3 off for money." Voted to pay Deacon Hawks "Six pounds as or in money for his horse which dyed in yᵉ town Saruis."

Although 1708 was a year of alarm and disaster, the above votes are the only allusion on the town record to anything connected with the war; what I have learned of military operations about this period, has been found chiefly in English and French official reports.

About the first of February, 1708, news was received through Col. Schuyler, that a large force had been fitted out in Canada to begin a march against this region January 15th. Active measures were at once taken for defence. Connecticut was appealed to, and sent up Col. William Whiting with several companies of infantry and dragoons. The first week in February Capt. Benjamin Wright led a war party of English and Indians up the Connecticut. He went as high as Cowass; was gone about nine weeks, and returned without seeing the face of an enemy. Scouts were kept constantly out in other directions. The warning and preparation probably prevented an attack. Small parties hovered about the frontiers, however, all the season, keeping up the alarm, preventing any labor in the field except under strong guards.

July 9th, one of these parties killed and scalped Samuel and Joseph Parsons, sons of Capt. John Parsons, at Northampton. July 26th, the house of Lieut. Abel Wright of Skipmuck (now Chicopee) was surprised. Aaron Parsons and Barijah Hubbard were killed and their bodies mangled; Martha, wife of Lieut. Wright, was mortally wounded. Two grandchildren, Hannah, aged two years, and Henry, seven months, lying in a cradle together, were tomahawked. Hannah survived the blow. Their mother, wife of Henry Wright, was captured and never afterwards heard from.

August 5th, Col. Peter Schuyler writes Gov. Dudley that an army was being assembled at Montreal, and that he was trying to find out their design. The next day he sends news that eight hundred men were on the march for New England. The express bearing this information arrived at Boston on the 10th. The soldiers were put under marching orders, and the woods filled with scouts, to learn the point of attack.

De Vaudreuil had been blamed by the home government for beginning this war with the English colonies. He was now urged to prosecute it more vigorously. Ponchartrain, the war minister, wrote him June 30th, 1707, to send out more parties to harass the English, adding, "If you could go out and attack them yourself, his Majesty would be glad of it;" and, again, that the king "expected to receive news of some expedition against them, and is not satisfied with the inactivity in which you remain, with such numerous forces as you have." In accordance with his directions De Vaudreuil had raised a large army of French and Indians, and put Hertel de Rouville at its head.

De Rouville began his march July 16th. To conceal his destination, part of the force went up the St. Francis river and the rest up the Sorel, to Lake Champlain. The latter were mostly French Mohawks or Macquas, over whom Col. Schuyler had great influence. On the march they met Schuyler's messengers, bearing a secret belt, desiring them not to go to war against the English. The Macquas, pretending to the French that some infectious disease had appeared among them, at once turned back and went home.

A large portion of the Indians with the other part of the army also deserted. The plan of the campaign was, for both branches to unite in an attack on the Maine coast, with force enough to sweep all before it. On the desertion of the Macquas, De Vaudreuil ordered De Rouville to push on with his Frenchmen and St. Francis Indians, and surprise some scattered settlement. Henceforth, the barbarous murder of frontier settlers was to please the King of France, as well as the Abenakis.

August 23d, Dudley received word from Schuyler, that the Indians had turned back, and that there was nothing to fear from the French, who could do nothing without them. On this representation part of the soldiers were dismissed, including a force of five hundred volunteers under officers of their own choice.

Meanwhile, De Rouville had traversed three or four hundred miles of forest, and at daybreak on the 29th of August, he surprised the town of Haverhill, killed about forty of the inhabitants, and took many captives. He began his retreat about sunrise, but was pursued by the survivors, who attacked him, killed his brother, another French officer, and seven men; took a third officer prisoner, and rescued part of the captives. In the north part of the township, Joseph Bradley—the same who accompanied Ensign Sheldon to Canada—hearing the alarm, collected a party and sallied out into the woods. He discovered and secured the medicine chest of the invaders, and their knapsacks, which they had taken off before making the assault. It was feared De Rouville would now turn to the Connecticut Valley, and Aug. 31st, the Council sent orders to Col. Partridge to prepare for their reception. A large force came up from Connecticut, and the military companies made ready to march at a moment's warning. Nothing more was seen of De Rouville, but some of his Indians may have remained upon our frontiers.

About this time a scout of six men from Deerfield fell into an ambush of Indians near Cowass. Martin Kellogg, after shooting one of the enemy, was taken captive a second time. A son of Josiah Barber of Windsor, Conn., after receiving a fatal wound, rallied, and getting on his knees, shot the Indian who had fired upon him. Both were found dead by the Indians, shortly after, lying but a few rods apart. The Indian who told this story of Barber's pluck to Stephen Williams, added, "No *he*, (i. e. Barber) but *his ghost*," did the exploit.

Oct. 13th, Abijah Bartlett was killed at Brookfield, and Joseph and Benjamin Jennings, and John Green, wounded, and John Walcott, a lad of ten, captured.

Oct. 26th, Ebenezer Field of Hatfield, was killed at Bloody Brook, while on his way to this place. With his death, the tragedies of the year closed. There could, however, be no relief from anxiety, watching, warding and scouting. The enemy might strike again at any moment. On receiving the report of this year's operations, the King wrote De Vaudreuil that he was satisfied with his application.

1709. During the winter of 1708-9, there was great alarm in Canada upon a report received by Sieur de Joncaire, through the Mohawks, that an English army was coming over the snow against Montreal. De Vaudreuil, with all the regular soldiers, took post at the threatened point, and all the militia were under orders to march at a moment's warning. De Vaudreuil remained in this posture of defense about a month; meanwhile, fortifications were being made in every direction. Quiet was hardly restored before the scare was repeated. This time the grounds of alarm were real. Gen. Nicholson with fifteen hundred men was moving from Albany toward Lake Champlain. April 27th, De Vaudreuil returned to Montreal, where an army was collected, to repel the invaders. Orders were issued to gather all the inhabitants and movable property from the south of the St. Lawrence within the walls of Montreal and Quebec, and on the north side to drive the cattle and remove the women and children up into the forests northward. The walls of Quebec were strengthened in every possible way, the settlers were called from their farms, and much of the harvest was lost for lack of hands to gather it. De Vaudreuil had "sure news" of an intended attack both by sea and land, and the whole spring and summer was spent in preparations to resist it. On the other hand, the English army halted at Wood Creek, waiting until October for the arrival of the fleet which was expected to assail Quebec, while Nicholson went against Montreal. Three forts were built meantime and hundreds of bateaux and canoes in which to cross the lake.

Scouts from each frontier were sent against the other, seeking prisoners and information of military movements. In this the French had the earliest success.

MEHUMAN HINSDALE'S CAPTIVITY.

April 11th, Mehuman Hinsdale returning from Northampton with an ox team loaded with apple trees, was surprised and captured. His team was not molested and was found near where he was taken, standing quietly in the road. The following account of his capture and experience, taken from a manuscript in the handwriting of Stephen Williams, contains enough of general interest to warrant its publication entire:—

April 11, 1709, Mr Mehuman Hinsdell driving his teem from Northampton loaded with apple trees, without any fear of indians (the leaves not being put forth) was met by two indians about half of a mile from the pine bridge who took him prisoner and cari^d him away into ye west woods. The indians were civil & courteous to him on ye journey. They arriv^d at Shamble within about eleven days & an half after they took Mr. Hinsdell. From Shamble they cari^d Mr. Hinsdell to Oso, where he was oblig^d to run the Gauntlett (as they call it) [i. e. to run from the indians who persue & if th when—This is erased] for near three quarters of a mile, but he ran so briskly as not to receive a blow till he came near the Fort when he was met by an indian, who taking hold of ye line (that was round his neck and hung upon his Back) pull^d him down, and so he was struck by one fellow; after he was got into ye Fort, he was set in ye midst of a company and oblig^d to sing and dance, & while thus employ^d, he was struck a very severe blow upon the naked back, by a youth y^t was of such an age as to think of engaging in some warlike expedition, but this being contrary to their usual custom (he having perform^d ye ceremony of running ye gauntlett) was resented not only by Mr H. ye sufferer, but by ye indians in generall &c. From this Fort Mr H was cari^d to the French Govenour who knew him (for this was ye 2^d time of Mr Hinsdells captivity) and told him he expect^d a full account of news from him, especially about an expidition (which he suspected was on foot). Ye governour told him if he would give him a full account of what news there was in his country, he would treat him with respect, but if he found he did not, he would use him worse than a Devill &c. But Mr H. endeavored as best as he could to avoid giving him an account &c. But when Mr Whiting of Bellerica was brot into the country by yᵉ indians and gave an account of an expidition on foot, Mʳ H. was taken and put into yᵉ dungeon &c. [After a while Genˡˡ Nicholson sent an indian as a spy into yᵗ country who was to endeavor to draw off yᵉ indians from the French, and join with Genˡˡ Nicholson, this plan—this is erased, but gives a clue to the story]. After a while yᵉ indians desired of the Governeur, that they might have Mʳ H. to burn, (pretending they should fight the better if they could burn an Englishman) and he was delivered to the indians, who were plotting to leave yᵉ French & go over to Genˡˡ Nicholson & yᵉ Dutch, and designed to have made use of Mʳ H. to have introduᵈ them. All was kept private from the French, & Mʳ Hinsdell was led away towards Montreal from Qubeck. The indians communicated their design to Mʳ H. who was overjoyᵈ with the account (for he thought of nothing but being sacrificed by them) & encouragᵈ it, but before they were ready to execute yᵗ design, a certain indian fell sick, and in his sickness making confession to a priest, discoverᵈ the plot, and so all was dashᵈ. The fellow yᵗ was the projector of it (being one that had come from Albany, or from some of the five nations to them) had timely notice, so as to escape to Shamble, where he putt a trick upon yᵉ officer of yᵉ Fort, pretending to him that he was sent from the governeur, to make what discovery he could of yᵉ English, upon which yᵉ officer supplyᵈ him with arms, amunition & provision and he had been gone but a little while into the woods before his pursuers (the plot being wholly ript up) came after him, but yet he was gone, so as to escape his pursuers. Mʳ H. was taken from yᵉ indians and again commitᵈ to prison, and the next year Mʳ H. and Mr. Joseph Clesson were sent to France in a man of war—and in France he met with great kindness, particularly from the Ld intendant at Roshelle, and after a while they were shipᵈ at Saint Meloes for London, where they met with great kindness especially from Mr Agent Dummer, who interceedᵈ with the Lords of the Admiralty, who orderᵈ them on board one of the Queens Ships which brought them to Rhode island whence they got home in Safty to their families, after Mʳ Hinsdell had been absent from his family abᵗ three years and a half.

He returned October, 1712. Mr. Hinsdell was the first white man born in Deerfield. His first capture by Indians was February 29th, 1704. He died May 2d, 1736. The above story bears evidence of being from his own dictation.

The following intensely interesting narrative, taken twenty years after the event from the lips of the survivors, by Ebenezer Grant, I printed from the original in an appendix to the "Narrative of the Captivity of Stephen Williams," in 1889. The date given is an error. The scout left Deerfield about April 26th, 1709. Here we find a realistic, matter-of-fact description of one of those tragedies constantly occurring, when scouts from the opposing nations met under the primeval trees, or on the lone waters of the great northern wilderness.

Nowhere have I met with a more enlightening account of the nature of this dangerous service. The reports of these desperate encounters are usually of the briefest; sometimes, it may be, none return to tell the bloody tale.

CAPT. BENJAMIN WRIGHT'S SCOUT.

Rever^d Sir—After Due Regards these May Inform you what Lieut. Childs and Mr Hoit related to me concerning the travails of Capt Write & his Company towards Canada & w^h happened to them about that time it is as follows—

Capt Write & a Small Company of men designing for Canada to destroy ye enemy, in ye Beginning of April 1710, [1709] we then set out from Deerfield in Number Containing 16, and travailed up Connecticut River which is usually Called 120 Miles. There we discovered two Bark Canos, by reason of that our Capt was pleased to Leave 6 of his men to Ly in wait of ye Canos Supposing Some Indians would Come there. And then the Capt, with ye Levt & ye rest of ye men set forward up ye White River taking ye Nor west Branch, following it up to the Head then we Steared to French river & travailing down s^d River till we Came to ye 3^d Falls & y^r we built two Canoes & then set out for the Lake & when we came there the wind was so high y^t we were forced to lye by a Day or two. After that one Evening we espied a fire ye opposite Side. Supposing it to be indian we then forthwith Im bark & Steared our Course towards the fire and while we was upon ye water, there arose a terrible Storm of thunder & Lightning which put out the fire y^t we before espied & thro' Gods Goodness we all got safe to land & Drawing up our Canos upon ye Land turned them up for Shelter till next morning & then we making search for the fire that we afore espied & found it had only been ye woods on fire. After that we set out for Canada in our Canoes on ye west side of the Lake till two hours by sun at night & then the wind arose again which forced us to lye by till next day in ye afternoon & then we set out for Shamble & coming to a point of land near Fortlemote, we espied 2 Canos of Indians in number 8 coming towards us then we paddled to Land & running up ye Bank, by this time those indian Canos was got against us, & then we gave them a Salutation out of the mussel of our guns turned one overboard & we still continued firing caused y^m to Paddle away wth all Speed & left y^t fellow Swimming about & when they had got out of ye reach of our guns both Canos got together, and all got into one, & left ye other wth Considerable plunder in it, & when they was moved off we maned out one of our Canoes and fetched in theirs. And he that was Swimming about we Called to Shore to us, And Levt Childs killed him & some of ye men scalped him. And by Information that we had afterward by the Captives, y^t were then in Canada three were killed at the Same Time. And after that Skirmish, we made the best of our way homeward, & Came to ye French River after Dark, and so proceeded all that night up ye French River till we Come to the Falls, and there we Left our Canos and took our Packs upon our Backs and travailed homewards up ye River, and comeing to a Crook that was in the river; we Left ye river & took y^e

nearest Cutt acrost y^t Elbow and so come to ye river again, which was about nine of ye clock that morning, & there we espied a Canoa coming down ye river with four Indians in it and a Captive-man, which was taken at Exeter, named William Moody. We Immediately fired on them and killed 2 the first shoot & wounded ye 3^d & ye 4th Jumped out & Swam to ye Contrary Shore, then our Capt ordered some of his men to tarry there & fire at him when he got to Shore, and they did So, & afterwards we was Informed y^t he was so wounded, that in a few days after he got to Canada, died. Now the rest of the men followed ye Canoa as it fell Down Stream, and the Capt Called to the Captive to paddle ye Canoe to Land, but he replied he could not because the wounded Indian would not Let him, with that the Capt hollowed to him & bid him knock in him in ye head, with that he took up a hatchet to Do it but ye Indian rising up took hold of ye hatchet & got it away from him and then catched up the Paddle & Laid it on his head & they skuffling together turned over the Canoe and parted in the water, & the Indian Swam to the Contrary Shore. As he got out of the water we pined him to the Bank with seven Bullets. The Captive also Swimming towards us, but being very weak fell down a great pace & Cried out he should Drown before he Could get to Shore, with that Lieut Wells flung down his gun upon ye Bank & run Down & Catched up a pool & held out to him & he catched hold of it & ye Lieut. drew him to Land. And John Strong being upon the Bank heard ye sticks Crack behind him & Looked round & cried out Indians & was Immediately fired upon by them & was wounded in the face & breast with a Charge of Cutt Shoot, but not mortal. With that Lieut Wells sprung up the Bank to get his gun & was mortally shot. Now the men being scattered along upon the Bank but the Capt being with ye captive y^t came to ye shore Immediately examined him how many Indians there was, he made answer 19 being in 5 Canos 2 being down stream from that which we shot upon, And 2 above, having been at Exeter took 4 captives (men), which they there had with them and those 2 canos y^t was passed by was ye Indians y^t made ye first shoot upon us.

And we also received Several Shoots from those y^t were above us, which Landed on ye other side of the River. Now we being under no advantage to defend ourselves we every one made ye best of our way and shirked for our Selves & in a short Time Capt Write & 5 of his men got together, three more yet missing. The next Day came 2 more to us where we hid some of our Provisions & there waiting some hours for the other man. But he came not while we tarried there, whereas Capt. Write thinking best to leave a Suitable quantity of Provisions and other necesseries in Case he ever came it might be of service to him in his journey homeward. It being one John Burt of Northampton. Then seting forward on our Journey homewards & Came to our Canoas that we left on White River then we got into them & came down ye river to ye mouth of it, where we left 6 men formally mentioned in our History. And finding them gone, then we set forward homeward & after we had got home, those six men formally mentioned Informed us w^t they had Litt of 6 Days after we left them. These 6 men espied a Cano of 2 Indians Coming Down the River & called to them not knowing but y^t that they was Scattocooks but they refused to come to them & paddled to the contrary shore. Then they fired wounding one, but they geting to the shore Left ye Canoa & plunder. After that ye men made ye best of their way home And some Time after they were got home was Informed y^t they were Scattecooks.

Now returning to our former Story, having an account of two of those Captives y^t were with ye indians that we Litt of on ye french river, are now returned home, & gave us an account y^t we then killed 4 Indians. And Moody that we had taken from them we Lost again, we being then in such a fright, every one took to his heals, But moody being so weak & feeble was not able to follow, now after this the Indians all gathered together on the other Shore, & Moody seeing them hallowed to them to fetch him over & one came & after they had got him over they Burnt him on the Spot. We was informed also y^t w^n the Indians got to Canada they Burnt one more of these Captives Andrew Gilman by name. Now to say a little more concerning Burt, what became of him, having some Transient stories y^t a mans bones, and a gun was found by some Indians above ye Great Falls npon Connect^t River about 60 miles above Deerfield, which some think was s^d Burt.

The number of Days we was taking this march was 32, and the men's Names are as follows:

Capt Benjn Write of North^ton
Levi^t John Wells, killed, of Deer^d
Henry Write, of Spring^d
Timothy Childs, of Deer^d
Jon^n Hoit, of Deer^d
Jabez Olmstead, Deer^d
John Burt, Lost, North^ton
[John Strong, Northampton, wounded, see above.]
Jose^h Ephraim } Indians of Natick.
Thomas Pagan }

The other 6 men y^t set out wth us y^t we left at ye mouth of White River are as follows:

Eben^r Severance of Deer^d
Math^w Clesson of North^ton [later of Deerfield.]
Thomas McCranne of Spring^d
Joseph Wait of Hatf^d, [son of Benjamin Waite.]
Josp. Root of Hatfield.
The other we cannot at present call by name. [Doubtless John King of Northampton.]

In a petition to the General Court of May 28th, 1709, the survivors say concerning the affair on the lake:—

"We judge we killed 4 of the enemy, & one in special. One we got and scalped him, which scalp we now present."

Col. Partridge, in forwarding this paper, says: "They also declared that they are very certain that they killed 4 as above & that on French River they killed 4 more—8 in all. This they affirm to me."

De Vaudreuil, giving an account of these affairs, in a dispatch to Ponchartrain says, two were killed on the lake, and one on the river, and that four or five of the English party were killed at the latter place. Possibly one or both of the Naticks were lost. Captain Wright was allowed £12, and the others £6 each. Bills for losses were paid as follows:—

Capt. Wright, 1 blanket, 10s, gun case, 1s, 6d, hatchet, 3s 6d snapsack, 2s 6d,   0 17 6

Lt. Wells, 1 gun, 2s 10d, blaneket, 7s, hatchet, 2s 6d, jacket, 6s, shirt, 3s, stockins, 2s, compass, 6s 8d, cap, 2s, 6d,   3 19 8

John Strong, blanket, 7s 6d, snapsack, 2s 6d, hatchet, 2s 6d, gun, 20s,   1 12 6

Thomas McCreeny, snapsack, 2s 6d, cap, 3s, sursingle, 1s 6d, belt, 2s, pouch, 8d, horn, 8d, male strapt, 1s, hatchet, 2s, 6d,   12 10

Timothy Childs, blanket, 7s 6d, hatchet, 3s, 6d, a squaw line, 1s 6d, guncase, 1s 6d, cap, 3s, snapsack, 2s,   18 6

Jabez Omstead, blanket, 10s, snapsack, 2s 6d, hatchet, 2s 6d,   0 15 0

Jon. Hoit, blanket, 7s, 6d, hatchet, 2s 6d,   0 10 0

Lt. John King, blanket, 18d, snapsack, 1s 6d,   19 6

Judd says that William Moody, whose attempted rescue was attended with such disastrous results, was by the Macqua Indians tortured to death and eaten.

On the return to Canada of the Indians whom Capt. Wright had surprised, "feeling piqued," says De Vaudreuil, "they asked me to let them go on an excursion with some fifty of the most active Frenchmen and allow Sieur de Rouville and de la Periere to command. I assented on the spot.". He says the force went to "guerrefiille, [Deerfield] where having prepared an ambush, they caught two alive." It is the same affair to which Hutchinson refers as follows:—

In June, one of the Rouvilles with 180 French and Indians made another attempt on Deerfield to destroy or carry away prisoners; * * * but the enemy was discovered at a distance and beat off, the inhabitants bravely defending themselves.

Penhallow gives the following account of the same event:—

The Town of Deerfield which had suffered so much spoil before by Monsieur Artell [Rouville,] was on June 23d obliged to a new encounter by Monsieur Ravell, his son-in-law, who, with 180 French and Indians, expected to lay all desolate. But the town being alarmed they valliantly resisted with the loss of only one man and another wounded.

No other particulars of this fight are found. Stephen Williams says: "Joseph Clesson and John Arms were taken, June 22d, [these were the two "caught alive,"] and the next day Jonathan Williams was killed and Matthew Clesson mortally wounded; and Lieut. Thomas Taylor and Isaac Mattoon wounded, but recovered."

It is probable that De Rouville was discovered the 22d, and that the brave men of Deerfield went out the next day and drove his crew back into the wilderness. John Arms was wounded in two places before being taken.

Soon after this, the General Court allowed bills for horses killed or wounded, arms, and horse furniture lost, to the heirs of Matthew Clesson, and Jonathan Williams, to Jonathan Hoyt, Daniel Belding, Eleazar Hawks, Edward Allen, John Allen, John Wait and William King. Probably all these men were in the engagement.

On the return of De Rouville and De la Periere to Canada *via* the lakes, with reports of the condition of affairs at Wood Creek, De Vaudreuil sent Sieur de Ramezay, Governor of Montreal, with 1500 French and Indians, up Champlain to surprise the English. They left Chambly about the 17th of July, and being discovered when they had arrived near Crown Point by an advanced guard of Nicholson's army, they retreated after a slight skirmish.

The alarm in Canada now became almost a panic. All possible measures for defense were taken. No more war parties were sent against our frontiers; but one already out killed John Clary and Robert Granger, at Brookfield, on the 8th of August.

Gen. Nicholson, tired of waiting for the fleet, left Wood Creek, September 26th, to consult with the colonial governments as to what measures to take. Shortly after, the whole army retired to Albany, burning their forts and boats as they retreated. The expected ships had gone to Portugal, and all the trouble and expense in preparing for the campaign was thrown away. Rev. John Williams was chaplain in this futile expedition, and received £24, 8s, 6d for his time and expenses. During his absence, "Mr. John Avery and Mr. Aaron Porter" were chaplains by turn at Deerfield, and were paid ten pounds each for the service.

THE RANSOM OF JOHN ARMS.

In the winter of 1709–10, De Vaudreuil, under a pretext of exchanging prisoners, but really, as he writes to France, "to obtain information of what is going on at Orange," sent Sieurs de la Periere and Dupuis, with five men to Albany, as escort for Lieut. Staats, a nephew of Col. Schuyler, and three other Dutch prisoners, to be exchanged for Father de Mareuil, and three other Frenchmen; they also brought "a militia officer of the Boston Government," to exchange for " Sieur de Vercheres, ensign of the Regulars." This "militia officer" was John Arms of Deerfield, captured the June previous. One of the French officers probably came with Arms to Deerfield. The dispatches brought from Canada were forwarded to Boston by Col. Partridge. Gov. Dudley is displeased with these proceedings, and writes to Partridge in February that he believes these officers little better than spies, and directing him to send them back, and Arms with them. He says he is ready to exchange prisoners when the French follow the course agreed upon. The French officers reached Montreal on their return about the "time navigation opened." Arms appears to have been left on parole.

The following papers relating to the affair, and events under consideration, are from the Massachusetts manuscript archives.

Letter to Col. Partridge:—

BOSTON, February, ult [28] 1709–10.

His Excellency has this day communicated in Council your letter to himselfe accompanying those from the magistrates of Albany, with a copy of a letter from Mr. Vaudreuil, Directed to Col. Peter Schuyler, by the hand of his Messengers then attending from Mont Real, on pretence of negotiating an Exchange of Dutch Prisoners, & one Armes of Deerfield, brought thither with them, for some French prisoners at New York, Bouvenire, taken at Haverhill, and Leffeur, two of theirs in our hands the latter proposed to be Exchanged for Armes, with a great demand upon him for his redemption out of the hands of the Indians. It is no hard thing to penetrate into their Intreague, The Designe being to conciliate a new friendship and neutrality with the Albanians as they have lately had; to gain Intelligence of the motions and preparations of the English, and leave this and other Her Mag'tys Colony's to take care for themselves.

Mr. Vaudreuil takes no notice of his Excellency, neglects to write to him, thinking to obtain his Prisoners from hence by the interposition of the Gents of Albany, well knowing how false he has been, and Violated his promises made once and again to return all the English Prisoners, and that long since; upon which the French prisoners on his side were sent home by way of Port Royall. Knowing also his Excellency's Resolution never to set up an Algier trade to purchase the Prisoners out of his hands, and Direction not to have them sent to Albany, but to have them brought in a vessell by water from Canada, or down Kenebeck River to Casco Bay, or Piscataqua, In which Resolution he continues, and it is agreeable to the minds of the Council.

So that Armes must go back with the Messengers, unless he can otherwise obtain his Liberty: You will further Examine him particularly referring to the State of Quebec, and Mont Real, how they are as to provisions and Clothing; what store ships arrived there the last summer, and other shipping, and what are there now; what new Fortifications they rasyd in the Summer past and where.

And by the next post from Albany, you must send for Beuvenire from thence, and write to the mayor and Magistrates to adjust the accompt of the Demand for his Keeping,—which, as is Intimated, is very extravagant, beyond what is usually allowed for Prisoners,—and let him draw upon the Government here for pay'mt, and it shall be done.

In case the Hunting Mohawks attend you, it's thought advisable that Major Stoddard joyne a Sergt & Six Centinels of his best hunters, wth them, who will take care to Observe them, and they will be a good out scout, for which you have, his Ex'l'ys Letter & order wth this.

You may adjust the Post as is proposed from Albany. If the service will be as well performed, & the Charge of the Province be thereby eased, but the Albanians must not think to make a purse from us, and to Exact more than it would be done for by our own people. It being much better that they have ye advantage of what must be necessarily expended. This by the Ord'r of his Ex'lcy, with the advice of the Council, from S'r.

Yo'r very humble servant,
ISA. ADDINGTON, Sect'y.

The letter to Mr. Vaudreuil must be sent to Albany by ye Post & forwarded from thence by an Ind'n wthout charge, or otherwise, by ye French Messingers there now attending.

[Endorsed] Letter to Col. Partridge relating to Mr. Vaudreuil's messengers at Albany, and French Prison'rs.

A few weeks previous, Dudley had written in reference to the ransom of Josiah Littlefield, of Maine: "I always pitty a prisoner in Indian hands, especially when their masters are indigent, in necessity of everything; but no consideration of that nature has yet altered my resolution never to buy a prisoner of an Indian, lest we make a market for our poor women and children in the frontiers." He had also in this case, prevented the goods which Littlefield had himself ordered for his own ransom, from being forwarded to his Indian master.

On learning the decision of the Governor and Council, John Arms at once hurried to Boston, armed with letters from Mr. Williams, his minister, and Col. Partridge, seeking to avert the hard fate of being returned to Canadian captivity. He appeared before the Council March 6th, to plead his cause in person; but his mission was fruitless; the policy of the government was fixed, and he "was dismissed, the Governor and

Council not seeing reason to alter anything of their directions to Col. Partridge by their letters last week."

Notwithstanding this decision, our townsman did not return with the French officers, as we see by the following letter:—

To his Honor Cor'n patrigg Leiuing in Hatfield this present.
DEERFEILD, May ye 27, 1710.

Worthey & Reuerant Sur, thes lins are to inform yourself of ye account of my Charges, Both for my time & expenses sence I came into this contry, ye time that I spent in waiting on ye french Gentlemen at Albany, & in ye marching in ye woods contains ten: 10: weeks, whic

at 12 pence per day is	3 00 00
ye charges for my Dieght & Lodgin was	2 06 00
& my charge for 2 hores jorney to albeny at ten shillings per jorney	1 00 00
	6 06 00

having given yourself an account only for my time, & my diat, & my lodging, & my horses jurny, all amounts to six pounds, six shlens —pray sur, present my humble Duty to his Excelency, & inform him of my Dificult Surcumstances, both in Canada, being ther a wounded prisener, & stript of all my Clothes j could get none out their magasend, but was fourst to by them with my one mony, having credit with a gentleman thar, & allso of my oblagations that I am now under; which I supose that ye french captaine has informed his Exelancy abought, & intreat his Excelency to helpe me in so dificult a Cas as I am under. I shall not ade but Remain your
humble sauruent, JOH. ARMS.

This letter was sent to Gov. Dudley, by Partridge, who writes May 31st, 1710:—

I humbly move in behalf of John Armes, now of Derefeild a prisoner to the Frentch, being taken by the enemy in June was twelve-month, & carried to Canada, & since he came hither hath been at great Charges at Albany, as per account annexed, prays it may be allowed and payd him out of the Treasurie of this Province, as also such other allowances for his Losses of his tyme & cloathing & his wounds &c as this corte may judge meete & just, & for y'r Excellency & Hon's shall ever pray.   SAMUEL PARTRIDGE, in behalf
of John Arms afores'd.

The measures Arms took to secure his freedom have not been discovered. It would seem that he had been captive to the Indians, and that a "French captain" had ransomed him for one hundred livres, which he had obligated himself to repay. Arms was also held as a prisoner of war, and a French officer of the line was asked in exchange. This officer, whose name is given as "Sieur de Vercheres," by De Vaudreuil, and "Le Fever" by Dudley, did not return with the French envoys. A prisoner of the latter name was at Hadley two years later, when he refused to return with a party of exchanged prisoners going from Deerfield to Canada, and declared his intention of becoming a citizen.

Arms was allowed six pounds, six shillings, on his bill of May 27th. He became a cripple from his wounds, and a life pension of six pounds a year was granted him in 1721, to which three pounds, ten shillings was added in 1752.

August 10th, 1710, Connecticut voted to raise scouting parties, not to exceed sixty Indians and four or five English, to range towards the lakes; fitting them out and paying a bounty of ten pounds for each Indian scalp.

Of all the troubles from the enemy this year, not a clue is found on the town records, although the action of three meetings is recorded. There had been some difficulty in regard to rights in the wood land.

Wood Land and Turpentine. In 1686 it was voted "That notwithstanding the wood lands are to be laid out in particular to euery person his proportion, * * * all timber, fire wood, stone, clay, &c., shall be common for euery proprietor's use till such time as the town shall other ways order it."

Soon after, the wood lands were divided according to the number of cow commons held by each proprietor. The advantage of ownership, under these circumstances, is not very apparent, for over and above the right given individuals to take timber, &c., where they chose, the town still retained a general control of the whole. None were allowed the use of pine trees for making turpentine without leave of the town, and privileges of this kind were granted by vote from time to time. It appears that in 1708 parties had been engaged in the business without leave; but the town asserted its authority and voted December 10th, "that thare shall be no more pine trees cut for making of turpentine without the town's liberty."

In March, 1709, the town granted unto Joseph Clesson and Ebe Severance a persel of pine trees for making turpentine liing est of Deerfield est mountain by the great river; ye plas is known by ye name of ye pine nook; it is to be understood y^t y^n are to haue y^m three yere.

The town also agreed and uoted to giue all ye pine trees which jos petty and ye trees y^t Sam'll ffield and the trees Joseph Allicksander cut for turpentine the Last sumer unto Edward Allen, Sam'll ffield and jos Allicksander to each and aighter of them an eaquall sheare. Dan'l Belden, Sam'll Allyn, Nath Brooks refus to giue thair right.

It does not appear what the individual rights of the three last named men were, or what was the result of their protest.

The whole matter continued under the direct control of the town, and the policy of restricted use of the pines was continued until March, 1715; when "the town then voated y^t from this time forward no person whome soveer shall cut a tree for turpentine within ye Bounds of ye township of d'fd."

In connection with the abundant town legislation for the protection of the wood lands, there is also found frequent mention of the woods being "burned over," under the direction of committees chosen for that purpose; but no definite information is to be obtained on that point.

On the whole, patient search concerning the extent and character of the forests here at the first settlement, their condition later under the policy of the town, and the real object of the many town regulations, only develops numerous riddles, which I have been obliged to "give up," no solution being found to the apparent inconsistencies in statement and action.

1711. This year another attempt was made to subdue Canada. Fifteen men of war and forty transports sailed from Boston, July 30th, for Quebec. Ten transports and a thousand men were lost by shipwreck in the St. Lawrence August 21st, and the rest turned back. Another army of 4000 men was collected on the old ground above Albany under Gen. Nicholson, but nothing was accomplished against Canada. Rev. John Williams was chaplain on this expedition. The campaign was a total failure except so far as it kept the enemy away from our frontiers. The only loss in the valley was at Northampton, August 10th or 11th, when Samuel Strong was killed and his father Samuel wounded and taken captive.

December was a cold month; the snow was deep, the rivers and lakes were frozen very hard, and an expedition from Canada was feared. December 27th, Connecticut voted that "a small scout of ten or twelve men be posted about thirty or forty miles above Deerfield upon some eminence for the discovery of the enemy until such time as the approach of spring renders it impractical for them to come in a body."

1712. As additional security, Col. Partridge sent a large force up here January 9th, provided with snow shoes, and prepared for a winter's campaign. Two companies of snowshoe men were sent from the Bay, to be employed by Col. Partridge for the defense of Hampshire county, "particularly by posting some of them in conjunction with such as Col. Partridge shall joyn with them, in some convenient place or places, above the scout now stated 30 miles above Deerfield, to discover the approach of the enemy."

March 12th, Lieut. William Crocker was directed to raise a party of English and Indian volunteers to join the scout that Partridge was fitting out, to send "up to Coaset to meet the Indian enemy hunting in these parts." No further account of this most remarkable winter's campaign has been found. No details of the endurance, bravery and heroism of those men who spent the dead of winter in tramping through the forests and camping on the mountains of Southern Vermont; waiting and watching the approach of the subtle foe, while their lives depended on their ability to outmatch in strategy an enemy with a life-long training in the arts of wood-craft. The number of men engaged is not known, but in the spring, Col. Partridge was allowed seven shillings each for 468 pairs of snow shoes and moccasins furnished to that number of men.

Sometime in April Lieut. Thomas Baker left Deerfield with thirty men on a scout to the north. Ebenezer Grant writes concerning it as follows:—

CAPT. THOMAS BAKER'S* SCOUT.

Another story related to me by Livet Childs Concerning Capt. Baker & his Company, and what happened to them in their march is as follows:

April the Beginning Capt Baker, Lieut Sam[ll] Williams Lieut Martin Kellogg with 28 men set out from Deerfield up Connect River Designing for Cowass on purpose to Destroy a family or two of Indians that they heard was there. But when arrived found no signs of any enemy there. Then afterwards we took our journey for mer-

---

*Capt., then Lieut. Thomas Baker of Northampton. He was born about 1683, he died in 1753. He was one of the captives taken at Deerfield, Feb. 29th, 1704, and one of four who escaped and reached home in June, 1705. In 1714, he led the party which escorted John Stoddard and Rev. John Williams to Canada, as Massachusetts Commissioners to treat for the return of prisoners; while there, occurred the romantic episode of his marriage to Madam Le Beau, *nee* Margaret Otis, which is so fully and so well treated by Miss C. Alice Baker, in her paper before the P. V. M. Association, upon Christina Otis.

rimack & coming upon it at ye head of the west Branch following of it Down one Day, & then finding two Indian Tracks which went down the river we continuing our Course next Day Down ye river after them, towards night finding the Tracks of 4 more & then encampt. The officers next morning thought it best to send forth a Small Company of our men to see what they could Discover And in about two hours they returned again & Informed by what they had Discovered that there was a party of Indians not far off. Then the officers took 3 of there Soaldiers to make further Discovery ordering the rest of the Company to Lye still & be very Carefull & make no rout till they returned and in about 3 hours they returned & Informed their Company that they had discovered some Wigwams. Judging [three?] of them to be Indians with families, with that ye whole Company moved in about half a mile of them, and then finding ye wigmans to be on y^e [bank?] of the river and a swamp Lying upon the back side. And Judging it to be best to Devide ye Company into two parts Livt Williams & Livt Kellogge taking one half & Capt Baker ye other. Agreeing also y^t one part should go round ye Swamp up Stream, and the other part Down Stream. Soon after we parted the Company of Capt Baker espied a straggling Indian Coming directly towards them, with a hatchet Stuck in his Girdle & a Stick on his Shouldier, which we judged was a going to peal Bark. Now we knowing that we should be Discovered was obliged to fire him Down & did so, now many guns being Discharged at him, Alarmed ye other Indians & caused the tother part of the men to come back again. After that word was given out to run to the wigwams. After running a Little way Litting of some Indian dogs which we following lead us to the wigwams upon the river Bank & there finding 12 Indians Jest entred into their Canoes to Cross the river & Espying a number of Squas & Poposes on the other Side running into the woods, but we firing briskly on them that was on ye water, Soon turned the bulk of them out of their Canoas, and the other Jumped out and Swam to the Contrary Shore. So we judged we had killed 8 or 9 and afterwards was informed by Some Easterd Captives y^t we did kill 9. After the skirmish was over, we viewed their habitation & judged that they had lived there two or three years, by the quantity of Furs we found there. The Place where we Litt of these Indians, was where the two Branches of the river come together.* After this we returned to the place where we left our Packs, with a small quantity of plunder and there we packed up and Steared our Course for Dunstable & in —— Time reached it, from thence we travailed to Chensford, And the People being very kind to us. Our Capt with a Waiting-man, went to Boston to Inform his Excellency Gov Dudley of his good service done the Province, ordering the Lieut to take the men and march to Marlborough & there to wait for him & in a little time he Came and ordered us to march homewards, from thence we marched to brookfield which was a very hard Day's travail by reason of some men being very Lame, from thence we marched to Hadley, from thence to Hatfield, from thence to Deer^d w^h we first set from. Finis.

---

* One of them since called Baker's river.

CARTEL FOR EXCHANGE OF PRISONERS AT DEERFIELD. 381

On a scrap of paper in the handwriting of Stephen Williams, is found the following:—

Capt. Baker & my Brother's expedition to Cowass & over the Merrimack, where they killed my old master Wottanammon in April, 1712.

With the scalp of Wottanammon and others, Baker went down the Merrimac and to Boston, arriving May 8th. The General Court voted his company £30 besides their wages, for scalp money.

There had been no general exchange of prisoners since John Sheldon was in Canada. Individual or special exchanges had been made occasionally, perhaps as the one side or the other took that method of gaining intelligence of their enemy.

June 16th, a letter was received from De Vaudreuil respecting an exchange of prisoners of war. He proposes "that our prisoners from Canada be brought into or near Deerfield, and that the French prisoners be sent home from thence." This proposal was satisfactory to Dudley, and Col. Partridge was ordered to collect the prisoners here and dispatch them home. Partridge set about the mission with zeal and energy, and in about four weeks, a party of French captives, with an English escort, left Deerfield under a flag of truce for Canada. The departure had been delayed somewhat by difficulty from an unexpected quarter. Of this the following letter gives a graphic relation:—

HATFIELD, July 1, 1712.

I begg yor Excellencys excuse & tender Resentment.

Off our repeated demur & delay of moveing towards Canada by the Frentchmen & o^r Messengers, which is wholie by the indisposition of the Frentchmen, Especially two of them, who will not be p^rsuaded to go, neither by p^rsuasions, nor force, except they be carried, viz., Cossett & La ffever. the Capt. hath used all means with them, especially Cosset, in so much that I believe if they go into woods together, they will murder one another before they get to Canada. Cosset positively refusing to go, chuseing rather to Remayen a prison^r all his days, as he saith, rather than go with him. The Captaine vehemently mad with him, as he saith, will kill him, & its thought by their violent treatm^t one towards another, that murder had been done if o^r men had not p^evented itt They cannot speak together, but some fall to blows, whoever is p^esent. La ffever has been oposite of goeing all a Long, & now it comes too positively opposes it, except he be forct. Yesterday I went up to Deref^d & two of the Frentchmen ordert him & the Frenchman to attend me in order to their goeing immediately away, Haveing all things ready there but am demured, as afores^d, & knowing the sending of but two with o^r Messeng^es, would not comport with y'r Excellency's design in this motion, I chose rather to delay two or 3 days more to waite for yor further direction. I have with much ado, caused the two Frentchmen that are willing to go, to abide at Deref^d til further order: he, viz., the Capt., proposes that two others of his men be sent immediately to go, saying he knows they will go without trouble if y^rself see meet yet to proceed in this motion, though rather chuses to come back to Boston with hopes to get home by water, but he is stay^d as afores^d. In the enclosed paper he gives ye names of ye men &c.

As to o^r Messengers, severall offer themselves to go, viz., Ltt. Baker, Ltt. Williams, Ltt. Wells & Sergt. Taylor; & for men with either of them, Jonathan Wells, Jno. Nims, (an absolute pilot) Eleazer [Ebenezer?] Warner, Thomas Frentch &c., but insist upon 4 to goe, &c.

We had pitcht upon Ltt. Williams, with the consent of his ffather, who hath the Frentch tongue, Jonath. Wells, Jno. Nims, & Eliezer [Ebenezer?] Warner. but haveing in yor last letter a forbidd to any of Baker's company we pitcht on Lt. Wells, Sergt. Taylor, John Nims & Thos. Frentch, who also hath the Frentch tongue, but think the former most apt for ye designe, &c.

I have had no small fategue in this matter, but ye disappointment hath been on the Frentchman's p^t as aforesaid. I am verry sorry there is no better attendence to y'r Excellencys commands, wch I desire to be sencere in attending, to the utmost of my power at all tymes.

Humbly desiring further directions in this matter, with my Humble service p^esented to yor Excellency, Madam Dudley & whole family. Rendering myself much obliged in obeydience & yor Verry Humble serv't. SAM^ll PARTRIDGE.

P. S. Our scouts can discover verry little appearance of ye enemy at the Lake; doubtless more might be discovered & ye enemy more forct to a retirement.

The following was endorsed on the above letter:—

Co'll. Patridg:—Honn'd Sr, I have all along been much against returning home: to Canada: but am now come to a Resolution that I will not go, except the Governor with yourself, doe compell me to returne; which I hope you will not do; I have an Affection for the people and Countery; and therefore do not intend to lieue it untill thare be a Peace; and then only for to give my Parents a vissitt and Returne againe.

from your humble ser'vt to command: this is La ffeveres words.

Dudley writes Partridge, Sept. 26th, "Cosset stays with you; they have abandoned him as a protestant."

The party for Canada left Deerfield July 10th, with Lieut. Samuel Williams finally at the head. This is shown by the following extract from a letter written July 21st, 1712, by Elisha Williams, at Hatfield, to his cousin Stephen Williams, at Roxbury:—

"Cousin Samuel & 3 others from Deerfield, set out for Canada the last Thursday was a seven-night. No news but that we are not, & have not been molested by the enemy."

The "three others" were Jonathan Wells, John Nims and Eleazer, or Ebenezer Warner. Lieut. Williams reached Boston on his return September 24th, bringing nine English prisoners. He was allowed for his services thirty shillings per week. Lieut. Williams, son of the minister, was but twenty-three years old. In March, 1713, he was chosen town clerk, and died in June following.

The quiet noted by both writers above was soon to be broken. July 13th, twenty Indians in two parties left Canada for our frontiers; twelve under the noted Gray Lock.* The news of this movement reached Col. Schuyler July 28th. He sent a post in hot haste to warn Col. Partridge; but it was too late. Partridge writes the Governor August 4th:—

HATFIELD Aug 4, 1712

May it please yor Excellency

On Wednesday the 30 July past in ye forenoone came too me a Messeng^r enforming of a young man taken by a p^{tie} of the Enemy at Springfield in the afternoone a massenger from Deref^d that o^r western scout from thence was attaqued by the enemy & s^d ther were most of them taken & killed, but upon a more full acc^t there is one man killed & two taken of them, at Night a Messenger from o^r Eastern scouts gave news of the discovery of a p^{tie} of 8 or 9 seen & they made shot at y^m but the enemy soon ran out of reach towards Brookf^d We immeadiately sent a post to Brookf^d to enforme them, who immeadiately sent out to all there work folks abroad & in there way see 6 or 8 Indians—Alarmed the ye said workers & disappointed the Enemy who were about Secretly to way lay them, but run for it—by all this it plainly appears the Enemy are on every hand of us—Laying waite for to accomplish their bloody designes—the same night a post from Albany came with the Enclosed, The lett^r doth not speak of it, but the Missing^{rs} say ye Govr of Canada Looks for a speedy Peace, but will do as much spoyle as he can before it comes.

I have Given Notice to Capt How of the Enemys Appearance here wch may soone come over to y^m

Major Stoddard & myself are Secureing all p^{ts} by scouts & guards as much as we can to p^{r}vent the Sudden surprizes of the Enemy who doubtless will do all the mischeef they can before they go off with my Humble Service p^{r}sented to yor Excellency & whole family Rendering my Self   yor Obeydient & very Humble Ser^{vt}

SAM^{ll} PARTRIDGE.

Yo^r Excellency's directions is at
all tymes advantageous to us

---

* For an account of Gray Lock see History of Northfield.

The "man taken at Springfield" was Benjamin Wright of "Skipmuck," and he was probably killed soon after. He was eighteen years old. The man killed on the western scout was Samuel Andrews of Hartford; the captured men, Benjamin Barrett of Deerfield and Sunderland, and William Sanford, a Connecticut soldier. The party was under the charge of Sergt. Samuel Taylor of Deerfield, who did not keep them under sufficient restraint. They were "very careless & noisy as they traveled," says Stephen Williams. Lieut. Samuel Williams was in Canada when the two captives were brought in. Both were recovered by him, and brought back in September.

This was the last raid on this valley during Queen Anne's War. The messenger who brought Schuyler's dispatch to Partridge July 31st, said the Governor of Canada expected a speedy peace, but would do as much spoil as he could before it came. It was in continuance of this characteristic and infamous method of carrying on the war, that De Vaudreuil, to make the most of the time, sent a large force against the eastern towns in September.

A proclamation for the cessation of hostilities was promulgated at Boston Oct. 29th, 1712, and Queen Anne's War was closed by the Treaty of Utrecht, March 30th, 1713.

In this war Deerfield lost sixty-one killed, nine wounded and one hundred and twelve captured. The valley below lost fifty-eight killed, sixteen wounded and thirteen captured. Total in Hampshire county, one hundred and nineteen killed, twenty-five wounded, one hundred and twenty-five captured.

CHAPTER XII.

INTERVAL OF UNQUIET PEACE.

Within a few months after the Peace of Utrecht, signed March 30th, 1713, it became apparent that Deerfield was no longer to be the forlorn hope of civilization in the Connecticut Valley—the extreme point of that wedge of settlements which was being driven northwards to split the wilderness asunder. February, 1714, the General Court appointed a Committee to superintend the settlement at Swampfield. Four years later it dismissed the Committee with thanks, and gave the plantation a charter and the name of Sunderland. Thus the wedge became thickened hereabouts, and in 1714 Northfield was resettled, and that became the entering edge —the post of danger and honor.

The war cloud had hardly rolled away before the Indians from every quarter, under one pretext or another, were freely mingling with the English. In May, 1714, Upehonedie was here with a party of Iroquois; with a pass from Col. Partridge they went to Boston, and appeared before the Governor and Council to express their friendship for our people. The Eastern Indians were anxious for a new treaty; the Pennicooks came also to make complaint of encroachment on their lands. All along our frontiers the Indian hunters who had been at arms against us came to sell their furs, the product of the last winter's hunt. When under the influence of fire-water these Indians would boast of their murderous exploits during the war, making a merit of them as praiseworthy actions of brave warriors. This would rouse the ire of the English, altercations would follow, and sometimes, according to tradition, a swift and secret revenge. At any rate there must have been great provocation to retaliation on the part of the whites, whose friends had been the victims of their barbarity, and the objects of their boasts, which would have led to reprisals, and brought on a general conflict. There was all the while a profound distrust of the Indians, and little confidence was felt in their professions of amity. Men like Thomas Baker, Joseph and Martin Kellogg, who had been in captivity among them, and understood their habits, were employed to go among them to watch their motions, and interpret the meaning. The government gave watchful heed to the intercourse between the red man and the white and made wholesome regulations in regard to their barter. Nov. 14th, 1715, the Council gave Col. Partridge orders to "direct his inspection and care of trade with Indians coming into Deerfield, and other parts within the county of Hampshire, to prevent their being debauched with rum or other spirits or being defrauded and abused in their trade." Perhaps it was owing to his wise management that no outbreak occurred.

During the whole of this interval of peace continuous efforts were made for the recovery of captives still held by the French and Indians in Canada; and for the release of Eunice Williams, especially, no possible inducement was left untried. A large sum of money was rejected; the personal solicitation of the Governor's wife was disregarded. Two captive Indian children offered in exchange for this white girl were refused, but four captive Englishmen were given up for them instead. Even Father Justinian, a French priest captured at Annapolis Royal, was brought to Boston, and kept a long time, as an exchange for the captive child; but all in vain. Col. John Schuyler, however, still had hopes. He writes Dudley April 6th, 1713, that he is going from Albany with some French gentlemen, and that "agreeable to a promise made to Mr. Williams and for Christian considerations, he will endeavour the recovery of his daughter out of the hands of the Indians and doubts not to prevail." The disheartening result we have seen. [See ante, page 349.]

The sorrowing father of Eunice, however, could not yet give up his daughter. We may safely presume that it was through his means that another party was sent for captives the same year. Nov. 5th, 1713, Capt. John Stoddard and Rev. John Williams received their credentials as Commissioners, and were fitted out for a journey to Canada. They left Northampton for Albany, November 13th, attended by Capt. Thomas Baker, Martin Kellogg, Eleazer Warner and Jonathan Smith, all on horseback. They reached the Hudson

November 16th. Here they were detained ten long weeks on account of warm weather and broken ice. At length on the 22d of January they set forward, having in the meantime secured for a guide Hendrick, a Mohawk chief of the Cahnainghas, who had great influence over the Caghnawagas, with whom Eunice Williams and the other captives lived. The party arrived at Quebec February 16th, and were well received by Gov. de Vaudreuil. He assured them that all captives should have free liberty to go home. The Commissioners set about their business with energy and hopefulness, but they soon found the Governor could not be relied upon for assistance. His doings fell far short of his promises. The wily priests put every possible obstacle in their way, and when complaint was made, De Vaudreuil said he could as "easily change the course of the river as prevent the priest's endeavours." Complications on questions of State coming up, Capt. Baker was sent to Dudley for further instructions. He left April 4th, *via* Albany, taking with him three redeemed captives, and a Frenchman to act as guide, and to take back the canoe.

June 8th and again June 11th the Commissioners sent more dispatches to Dudley. Capt. Baker returned to the Commissioners by the way of Montreal, where he secured one captive, and reached Quebec July 23d. The papers he brought from Gov. Dudley had no effect on men who had determined beforehand to keep as many captives from going home as they could by any means in their power.

After six months of difficult and vexatious negotiations, the Commissioners on the 24th of August, embarked on a vessel sent by Dudley to Quebec, with only twenty-six prisoners, leaving behind more than four times that number. Many of these were children when taken, and had become so attached to savage modes of living, that no persuasions could induce them to give up the free, wild life in the wilderness. The land of their birth was with many wholly blotted out, or remembered only as a dream, and they had become really the children of Nature.

Mr. Williams could not understand—no Puritan of that period could understand—that this reluctance to go back to New England might be other than the work of the devil, operating through the Popish priests. When at home, the word of Mr. Williams was law to young and old, but here, with his own daughter, and the young of his flock living at Caghnawaga, his most earnest prayers and solicitations fell on ears that gave no heed and on hearts that were moved by no emotion. No wonder the broken-hearted minister says he found the captives "rather worse than the Indians." Quite a number who had consented, changed their minds at the last, and refused to go home; among them "five who pretended to embark just before we sailed."

The only known Deerfield captives brought home in Dudley's vessel were Ebenezer Nims and his wife Sarah (Hoyt). They brought away, after fierce opposition by the Indians of Lorette where they lived, their only child, a boy of eighteen months, named for his father. The babe had been baptized by a priest, but in 1737 he was baptized anew by the then minister of Deerfield, Jonathan Ashley, who on that occasion preached two sermons "showing that yᵉ chh of rome is yᵉ mother of harlots spoken of by Saint John & that none of her administrations can be valid." Martin Kellogg came home by land bringing his brother Joseph and perhaps other Deerfield captives.

It was while the Commissioners were in Canada that Elewacamb brought Abigail Nims—or her countefeit—to our frontier, as before related. Probably he feared being obliged to give her up to the English without ransom, in accordance with De Vaudreuil's first declaration, and so fled with her to a more profitable field. [See ante, page 345.]

The Kelloggs were taken into the service of the government on regular pay, and employed as messengers, interpreter and spies. Their sister, redeemed later, was also employed as interpreter. In 1715 Martin Kellogg relates in a petition to the General Court, the "hardships of a long captivity, from which by a dangerous adventure he escaped & has since been in the service," and the Court voted him ten pounds "in consideration of his uncommon bravery and suffering in the public service." Twenty-five pounds had been allowed him in 1712, "to repay his ransom money, expenses and loss of arms."

February 25th, 1717 or 18, Joseph Kellogg, representing to the General Court that he has "several near relatives [two sisters] now in the hands of the French and Indians who have professed the Catholic religion & that he has considerable encouragement to undertake a journey thither to persuade them to return to their country and religion," was given leave by the Council to go to them, with an assurance of a good reward if he succeed. Joseph's efforts were in vain at this time, but his sister Rebecca was brought back by him in 1728.

In addition to the information obtained by the messengers to Canada as to the condition of affairs there, the scattered tribes were also watched. In March, 1716, Lieut. Joseph Clesson led a scouting party to the north and east frontiers. He was absent three weeks. April 17th, Capt. Thomas Baker left here on a five weeks' scout towards Canada. The pay of Clesson's party was £35, 4s, 8d; of Baker's £44, 11s, 6d.

CLOUDS ON THE EASTERN FRONTIER.

In the Treaty of Utrecht, "Acadia" was ceded to the English; but its bounds were undefined. By virtue of this treaty, the English claimed the territory along the coast of Maine from the Kennebec to the St. Johns, as against the French; and as against the Abenakis, under deeds given by their sachems many years before. Both French and Indians disputed this claim. When the English began to build on the lands in question, a party of Abenakis went to Canada, and in an interview with the Governor, explained the situation, and asked him if he would help them,—

In case of a rupture, as they had assisted him at the expense of their blood, on every occasion he had required them. The general assured them that he should never fail them in time of need. But what assistance, Father, will you give us? they asked. My children, answered M. de Vaudreuil, I shall secretly send you some hatchets, some powder and lead. Is this the way, then, the Indians retorted, that a Father aids his children? and was it thus we assisted you? A Father, they added, when he sees a son engaged with an enemy stronger than he, comes forward, extricates his son, and tells the enemy that it is with him he has to do. Well, replied M. de Vaudreuil, I will engage the other Indian tribes to furnish you aid. At these words the deputies retorted with an ironical laugh. Know that we all who inhabit this vast continent, will, whenever we please, as long as we exist, unite to expel all foreigners from it, be they who they may. This declaration much surprised the general, who, to mollify them, protested that rather than abandon them to the mercy of the English, he would himself march to their aid. [Memoir sent from Canada to France in 1720.]

The Abenakis were too shrewd to give credit to this forced declaration, and, on their return, spread dissatisfaction through their country.

The Intendant of Canada wishes "some hair-brained fellow of the Abenakis might make some attack on the English that would light up a war" without French agency, but, he adds, "What *will* become of ourselves if these Indians be worsted, and the English become masters of their villages, some of which are in our midst?" Great alarm was felt in Canada on rumors that the Iroquois and the Abenakis were about to become friends: "From which nothing can come but the ruin of the colony," is the word sent to France by the Governor.

The problem of De Vaudreuil was to prevent this union, keep control of the Abenakis, and foment a war between the latter and the English; aiding them so far as he could without breaking the peace between France and England.

Louis XV. writes De Vaudreuil in May, 1719, that he must "prevent the English from settling on these lands either by means of the Indians, or in any other way that would not, however, bring about any cause of rupture with England."

This was the condition of affairs when the newly-arrived Governor of Massachusetts, Samuel Shute, held a conference with the Eastern Indians on Arrowsick Island, August 9th, 1717, and arranged by treaty a settlement of all the disputes.

The policy of the French required that this friendly conclusion should be disturbed, and the Jesuits were successfully employed to that end. Divisions were created among the Indians; aggressions and reprisals followed. Sebastian Rasle, a Jesuit missionary at Narantsouak, or Norridgewock, was the center of this influence. In 1720, the Sagamore of Norridgewock died, and through the action of the old men, Ouikonioumenet, who was for keeping faith with the English, was chosen his successor. By his party an agreement was made with Governor Shute, May 18th, 1721, that the Indians would pay the English all damages; and hostages were sent to Boston to secure payment, and peace. Another meeting was arranged at which it was hoped *all* the Indians would bind themselves to a peaceful policy. This, Father Rasle determined to prevent. The very same day this agreement was made Father Rasle dispatched a letter to De Vaudreuil, acquainting him with this new turn of affairs. The Governor replied, June 4th, [O. S.,] that the condition of things reported about the Abenakis would,—

Subject them to the English if the utmost care should not be immediately taken to prevent so great a misfortune. * * * Without a moment's delay I set out in order to apply myself to the business at Montreal, and then to St. Francis and Becancour, where I prevailed with the Indians of those villages to vigorously support their brethren of Norridgewock. [De Vaudreuil, relating this affair to the King, writes,] If the Indians of this village should confer alone with the English, those that had remained firm until then, might permit themselves to be gained over by their offers; it became necessary that the well-intentioned Indians should be most numerous at the conference.

Accordingly, he sent seven canoes of Indians from Canada. Father La Chasse, Superior of the Jesuits, was sent at the same time, to visit the other tribes of the Eastern Indians, to induce them to attend the proposed conference. At the desire of the Canada Indians, after some scruples, he also sent M. de Croisil, a French officer of the line. These emissaries easily accomplished their object, the more so as Gov. Shute, in consequence of opposition by the House of Representatives had not yet been able to carry out his agreement with the Abenakis to set up truck houses among them.

July 17th, 1721, [O. S.,] La Chasse, Rasle and De Croisil, with 250 Indians armed and painted, appeared under French colors, at Arrowsick Island, the place appointed for the second conference. Gov. Shute having been informed of the progress of affairs, did not think it worth while to keep the appointment. After remaining on the Island about seven weeks, the Indians called together the leading settlers on the disputed territory, laid down 200 beavers to pay for cattle killed, demanded the four hostages given by Ouikonirournenet, and told the settlers they must leave their lands. These demands were put in writing and read by one of the Jesuits. They were then left to be sent to Gov. Shute, with a demand for a reply in three weeks. An answer was sent, calling the Abenakis traitors, and demanding the surrender of Father Rasle, who was regarded as the author of the revolt and the letter. The *direct* agency of De Vaudreuil was not then known or suspected.

In December, 1721, a force was sent to capture the Jesuit and some of the principal men at Norridgewock. They reached the place January 4th, 1722. Father Rasle received sufficient notice to fly to the woods and so escaped. His books and papers were found and brought off.

In June following, the Abenakis captured a number of English at different places, burned Brunswick, and continued their depredations under the direction of Father Rasle. He as their religious teacher had acquired almost unbounded influence over them, and his political and religious zeal combined to inflame the Abenakis against English and Protestant aggression.

During all this excitement on the Maine coast, diplomatic correspondence was continued between Gov. Shute and De Vaudreuil, messengers going and coming by the way of Albany and the lake. Joseph Kellogg and Thomas Baker were employed in this service. Christina, wife of Capt. Baker, accompanied her husband on one trip in 1722. Her expenses were paid by the Council, but no indications of the object of the journey are found. Probably it was an attempt to recover her children, whom she was forced to leave when she came back with Stoddard and Williams in 1714. If so, she was unsuccessful, for they lived and died in Canada.

CHAPTER XIII.

FATHER RASLE'S WAR.

Under the condition of affairs related in the last chapter there could be no settlement of the dispute except by the arbitrament of the sword; and July 25th, 1722, Gov. Shute formally declared war against the Eastern Indians. He sent three hundred men to the scene of the conflict. De Vaudreuil sent one hundred and sixty Indians from Canada, and the whole frontier was soon ablaze, and many were killed or captured on both sides. Col. Samuel Partridge of Hatfield, then seventy-six years old, was military commander in the Connecticut Valley, with John Stoddard of Northampton as his lieutenant. A company of ninety-two men under Capt. Samuel Barnard of Deerfield, and Lieutenant Joseph Kellogg, was raised for the protection of our town and Northfield. During the summer several houses at both places were made defensible, being surrounded by palisades; scouts constantly ranged the woods; watching and warding in the towns was unremitting; but no enemy appeared on our frontiers this year.

By the papers of Father Rasle, it had been seen how the Abenakis were backed by De Vaudreuil, and it was feared he would induce the Caghnawaga, St. Francis and other Indians to join in the war, and come down upon the valley towns. Special efforts were made through agents sent them, to keep them neutral.

Conference at Albany, May, 1723. Massachusetts and New York were alive to the consequences of a general combination of the tribes in favor of the Abenakis, and both united to prevent it. A sketch of some of the measures taken to avoid a general war will throw light on the obscure subject of the dealings of Englishmen and Indians at this period. It will be seen that in diplomatic transactions the native was quite a match for the white man. Their forms and ceremonies covered deep and far-seeing wisdom. At a Council held at Fort

George, Feb. 20th, 1722-3, a letter of Feb. 4th from Governor Dummer was read, thanks were given to Governor Burnett for the interest shown by his letter of Jan. 28th, and the request made that the Indians be directed to assemble at Albany, May 25th, to meet the Commissioners appointed to treat with the Six Nations within his government. Enclosed were instructions to the Commissioners, William Tailor, Spencer Phipps and John Stoddard, which he thinks conformable to "your letter to Gov. Shute & a vote of your Council."

The Commissioners were instructed to remind the Six Nations of "an absolute promise" their delegates made at Boston to "call off the Merrimack & Scatacook Indians from confederating with the Eastern Indians," and of their giving reasons to expect that the Six Nations would "make war against the East Indians;" to tell them a large bounty is offered for scalps, and that each party of ten shall have two Englishmen go out with them.

May 23d the Massachusetts agents appeared before the "New York Commissioners for Indian Affairs" at Albany and presented their credentials. They reported that "Col. Peter Schuyler the President answered & assured us that they would not be wanting to give us all the assistance which was consented to by the rest of the gentlemen, But the Secretary stood up and said 'as far as was consistent with his Excellency Governor Burnets Instructions,'" and that we must tell Gov. Burnett what we were going to say to the Six Nations. Our Agents then invited the Indian Commissioners to go to their lodgings and "take a glass of wine with us which they accepted." So ends the first day.

May 28th. This day was spent by the Agents and Indians in making presents and flattering speeches to each other.

May 29th. The Indians say "the Present was not common, but that it was extraordinary." They give thanks for it not on account of its real value but for "your sincerity"—but—they are not yet ready for a talk.

May 30th. They, like adept diplomates, make a long and diffuse talk meaning nothing.

The Commissioners declare the cause of the war with the "Abnequois" which, as was well understood was a question of the ownership of certain territory. They refer to the deeds from the Abenakis "which your delegates saw." The

Indians are urged to take up arms against the hostile Indians. "We bring you the hatchet," and we will give you a hundred dollars for every scalp of a male over twelve years old, fifty dollars for prisoners, and for "all others killed in fight fifty dollars;" and, if they come into this little arrangement will fit them out, mend their guns, hatchets, kettles, &c.

May 31st. This day the Indians say this is a great matter and they must deliberate upon it until to-morrow evening.

"June 1st, the Scatacooks and River Indians [Mahicans] came to us according to appointment." There was much formal palaver on both sides, and mutual presents, the Commissioners repeated to them the substance of their speeches to the Six Nations, in urging them to espouse the cause of the English. But that they were not expected to take up arms unless their "fathers" did, in that case they were to join in the war. The presents were "divided between the tribes in our presence."

In their answer the Indians say you call us "brethren" we wish you to call us children and we will call you father as we do the Five Nations. If they go to the war, we shall follow. "Fathers," they say, "we were the first Inhabitants of the Country, and some time after the Arrival of the English, they and we made a covenant which hath never been broken and hope it will endure to future generations." This declaration might apply to the Mahicans whom the Dutch discoverers found on the Hudson, but not to the Scatacooks. This tribe was founded by refugees from New England after Philip's War.

June 3. After four days' deliberation the Six Nations make answer to the propositions of May 30th. In long, rambling talks they vaunt their power over the other Indians, and their friendship for the English. They say we sent delegates to the Eastern parts, and found the place empty; on their return we sent a message to the three tribes of East Indians in Canada to take away the hatchet against the English, and they delivered it up, and by their messengers cast it at our feet. We will wait and see what comes of this measure. If you will call a Peace Conference in Boston, we will go and meet the East Indians there, and will try all we can to quiet "our children" in your presence; meanwhile, we will send another delegation to the East Indians.

June 4th the indignant Commissioners, in reply, ask a reconsideration of this action. *They* have nothing to do with "Peace." They want the Six Nations to give hard blows instead of hard words to "your children," the East Indians.

The reply was that hard words will do. We spoke soft before, now we will go to Boston with your hatchet and the one they sent us. Then we will dig a hole before you and them, and bury these hatchets forever, and tell them if they smite you, they smite us. That will settle the case. We will be surety for them.

The Indians have here gained a point in delaying the matter, and will find new excuses for inaction when necessary.

The disappointed Agents make the best they can of the situation, and tell the Indians they will be welcome at Boston to meet the East Indians. They will pay all expenses and make "suitable provisions for your return to your castle."

The messengers selected to visit the East Indians ask that they may be admitted to some post to meet them under a flag of truce.

So ended the ten days' Conference, a high jollification to the Indians and a heavy bill of expense to the English.

Meanwhile preparations for defense went on. May 14th, Partridge writes William Dummer, now Governor of the colony, "The river is pretty well secured by the forts and men at Northfield and Deerfield, yet Sunderland, Hatfield and Hadley, Northampton, Westfield, and Brookfield and Rutland, are too much exposed to invasion from the East and West. * * * These towns can't stand the strain upon them to watch and ward, scout and fort *without pay*, while their spring work is pressing to be done, they can't get a living." A quarrel of some years' standing between the Executive and House of Representatives had blocked the necessary legislation to make appropriations and raise money enough to garrison these exposed towns.

The Schuylers of New York had long been, and long continued to be, staunch friends of the English of New England. The following tells its own story:—

Gentlemen this Encloses a vote of the Gen[ll] Assembly of this Province desiring that one of you Gentlemen as will best suit with your convenience will please to favor us with a visit that we may confer with you upon the Present Scituation of our Capital affairs re-

specting the Maquois & the Eastern Indians which will also Oblige
Gentlemen Y^r Most Humble Ser^t
Wm Dummer
Boston Aug: 13, 1723.
To the Honble Coll: Peter, & Coll John Skyler

No Indians appeared in the valley until Aug. 13th, when a party of five killed Thomas Holton and Theophilus Merriman at Northfield. The leader was the notorious Gray Lock, a chieftain of one of the Pocumtuck confederate clans, driven off in Philip's War. He had been a noted warrior in Queen Anne's War, was well acquainted with the country, the people and their habits, and his advanced age did not prevent his being an active and dangerous enemy. Turning eastward, the same party surprised Dea. Joseph Stevens and his four sons while at work in the field at Rutland. Two of the boys were killed and two captured. Two of the Indians, after an attempt to surprise Mr. Davis and son, who were haying not far off, accidentally met in the road Rev. Joseph Willard. He was armed and shot one of them, and wounded the other; while in a struggle with the latter, the rest of the party came up and Willard was killed. Mr. Willard, formerly the minister of Sunderland, was now the minister elect for Rutland. The slain Indian was a Huron chief of Lorette. One of the boys captured was the famed Capt. Phineas Stevens, of the later wars.

Aug. 17th, Gov. Dummer wrote Col. Partridge:—

Sir These are to direct you forthwith to impress 18 able bodied effective men well armed out of the Regiment under your Command to be employed as Scouts for the several Towns of Brookfield Sunderland Deerfield & Northfield the first & last to have five men apiece, the other two four men in each, to range the woods on the skirts of Several Towns for their Defence & when the Towns have a sufficient number of men & it be most acceptable to the Inhabitants you may raise those Men out of those towns otherwise not.

Appoint a suitable Person to be one of the twelve (*sic*) as an officer to command the scouts of Sunderland Deerfield & Northfield & one Substantial Person to direct the other four (*sic*) at Brookfield. Give a strict Charge to the Officer That he keep the scouts in Constant & regular duty and that they Meet together as often as may be Convenient.

Boston Aug 17, 1723 .

Capt. Joseph Kellogg was kept at Albany to act with Col. John Schuyler in watching the movements of the Indians.

They write Gov. Dummer, Aug. 4th, 1725 : * * * "Gov.

Longuile's son has been among the Ownuntaugas & that the Onitas had [been?] to Onuntawga to hear what he has to say & no doubt he is employed by Govr de Nonville to practice wth these nations to defeat the present purpose of the Indians." Hearing that a messenger from the Eastern Indians was among the Mohawks, they sent a man to find out what sort of a reception the envoy met with. He reported that the "Abanakke messenger met with a rough answer and was told they must meet them in Boston & there heare what was to be said to em;" they add "one of the Onitas said the Sachems from Ownuntawge were soon coming along."

Conference in Boston. Aug. 22d, a delegation of the Six Nations met the General Court in the Court House. Gov. Dummer made them a formal address of welcome, and hoped they were comfortably quartered in Boston. In their reply they speak of the bad news they have heard of the attack at Rutland, and say "we mourn and lament after the way of our country and wipe away your tears." They express themselves satisfied with their reception, but wish to delay further proceedings until the arrival of Col. Schuyler. Aug. 28th, Schuyler having arrived, the Governor, Council and General Court met the Indians in the Council Chamber. It must have been an interesting and impressive scene. Men were not chosen to office in those days for their skill in manipulating caucuses and conventions. Men of character were there, the pick of the colony, with grave countenance and dignified bearing which harmonized with the velvet and gold and lace of their costumes. The Indians also were doubtless dressed in their best; their gayest feathers, their scarlet-hued blankets, their bright beaded moccasins and hair-fringed leggings made a fitting element in the picturesque whole. Of equal interest was the grave ceremony to follow.

The red man is generally spoken of as the child of freedom; but no galley slave was more firmly bound to his task than was the North American Indian by the customs and traditions of his tribe. He had no will of his own. His costume, his habits, his conduct in war or peace, were all marked out for him by inexorable law. In his occasional torture of prisoners and other barbarities he only followed customs handed down from more barbarous ancestors. Contact with civilization made not a whit of change in his mode of conducting public business. At the Court of the "Grande Monarche" Louis XIV., etiquette was not more strictly enforced than with the tribes in their conferences and treaties with the whites. The latter were obliged to conform as best they could to the ceremonial forms of the savage. Governors and Embassadors gravely smoked the Pipe of Peace around the Council fire; lifted or buried the hatchet, brightened the Covenant chain, sent or received the wampum belts, and gave the inevitable present, for no promise was sacred and no treaty binding which was not ratified by an exchange of gifts. Although Schuyler was a friend and counselor of the Indians he was not their spokesman. After the usual opening address, an Indian orator, probably Kajarsanhondare, of the Five Nations, took the floor. Then followed the childish ceremony of mourning for the dead. The "minister" was Joseph Willard, pastor elect at Rutland, who had been killed by a party under Gray Lock shortly before.

> The speaker made a procession through them, lamenting and bemoaning which continued a long time, being now and then prompted by the tribes. The procession & Lamentation being at an end, their speaker took his seat and after some time the Delegates made another heavy moan.

Then the orator in a long speech giving words to their sorrow at "the bloody news" of the "killing of your minister and the others," and at the conclusion "laid half a belt of wampum on his corpse and the other half on the bodies of the others that have been slain."

Sept. 2d, another meeting was held in the Council Chamber. The Indian orator made a long, formal speech. He gave an account of the discovery of America by the White Men, and the several peoples which came to occupy it. The Spaniards, he said, were of his own color. He talked at length of old treaties, and of love and friendship between themselves and the Strangers.

He calls the Scatacooks and the River Indians "Nephews." In presenting a Belt of wampum, he says,—

> This respects more people who have gone from us and settled in Canada naming Chucknawaugaw and Oso Recolect and other Indians that have not meddled in the war. We the eight Nations have agreed that Col. Schuyler be ordered to draw these nations down to be treated with that so they may be kept in peace with the English. We do not mean that Col. Schuyler should go himself but that he

should send some person on this affair and laid the belt down for Col. Schuyler.

He says they came for a peace Conference, but as things stand they will take hold of the "hatchet which you offer." They leave a Belt to be sent to King George and as soon as they get a reply will take an active part in the war. The English are advised to keep a careful watch against being surprised by the enemy.

Strong hopes had been entertained of inducing the Five Nations to join the English in this war. Agents were sent to meet them at Albany, and a large delegation of them came to Boston August 21st. It was soon found to be the old story of the Mountain in labor. After all the ceremonious talk, the most they would do was to allow some of their young men to go out with the English. Two only volunteered, who were sent to the eastward.

It was foreseen that when the result of these negotiations was known in Canada, war parties would be at once sent out against the valley towns; and Col. Partridge, who was at Boston with the Iroquois, sent his orders to Capt. Abijah Dewey at Westfield;—

BOSTON Aug 30 1723

Cap. Abijah Dewey
I have enclosed a Coppy of the Ord^r of the Lt̲t Governor that you Rally up your troop & march to the Upper Towns Scouting & Repaireing to the places of the Most Danger for the space of fourteen days & then for Capt. Dwight to take a turn at the same term of tyme & so by turns for the space of 8 weeks to provide for yo^{r}selves Arms Ammunition & provision all which to be paid by the publique; send the Enclosed ord^r to Capt Dwite after you have p^{r}rused & attend the whole as nere as you can according to the enclosed ord^r

SAM^{ll} PARTRIDGE Col^{ll}

If there be Need at Wesf^d you must take care at home yet must not Neglect this order

Early in September, the Schuylers sent word of a party of the enemy being at Otter Creek, to which Dummer replies:—

Sept. 13 1723

Gent. I have rec^d you^r Advice in a Lett^r Directed to Co^{ll} Partridge of a party of 50 Indians come over the Lake to attack our Frontiers. I hope the seasonable arrival of this Inteligence will be a means to disappoint the Enemy. I do for my self & in Behalf and at the desire of his Majesties Council of this Province give you Thanks for your Good offices to this Govern^t from Time to Time especially in Advising us so opportunely of the Motions of the Enemy & other matters that so nearly concern this Province; and pray the continuance of yoʳ care & Friendship to us in this respect, and we shall very punctually pay yʳ expenses.

Sept. 20th this letter was supplemented by a vote of thanks in the House.

Soon after this Col. John Schuyler visited the government at Boston; on his return he sent the following letter to the Governor by Capt. Kellogg:—

Honᵇˡ Sir the first day of this Inst. I sent two Mohawks to Canhnawaugo with the belt of Wampum the Nations gave me to invite the Chiefts of those people withalle. The 2ᵈ day of this Inst I sent my son with two others Towards Canada with instructions yᵗ if they met with any news of any parties of Inds designed for New England they would dispatch an express directly and also to enquire respecting Captives & any other news that may be Serviceable

I arrived here in health a short time after I left yoʳ Honʳ I am in expectation this day to rid my hands of a troublesome people to their great satisfaction.

He further says he is waiting news of some Caghnawaga Indians whom he suspects are out upon our frontiers; that was why he sent out his son as above.

Oct. 3d Col. Partridge writes Capt. Dewey at Westfield that Daniel Ashley, just from Albany, reports great fears there that the Indians are preparing for an incursion. Again Oct. 11th he sends the following:—

Sʳ These Give you orders forthwith to Move with yoʳ troop up to Deerfᵈ & when there to divide yoʳ troop & send one half of them with one of yoʳ officers to Northfield to improve yʳ tyme in Scouting & Guarding the people to get in the Remainder of their Harvest as also with some of the people to go out scout Northard & Westard in the woods to make discovery of any approaching Enemy & upon any Discovery of a body of the Enemy forthwith to Alarm the people & by a post inform me I pray God guard pʳserve & be yoʳ Safety

I am yoʳ Humble Serᵛᵗ
SAMˡˡ PARTRIDGE Colˡˡ

Hatfield Oct. 10, 1723

The next day the Governor writes Partridge:—

Sir These are to direct you forthwith to impress men out of the regiment under your command for His Majesty's service on the Frontier of your County as to make up [with] those already in the service (excepting those at Brookfield) forty men to be all under the command of Capt. Joseph Kellogg to be employed according to the orders herewith enclosed wᶜʰ pray deliver to him together with his commission.

Enclosed was Kellogg's commission as Captain with directions to look after the frontiers of Deerfield, Northfield and Sunderland, to keep his men busy and report often. At the same date Lieut. Samuel Wright was commissioned to look out for Brookfield, Leicester, Rutland, Shrewsbury and Worcester.

With all these precautions the harvest of Indian corn was a service of extreme danger. From the covert furnished by the standing crop, the whir of the bullet or hatchet, with the fearful war-whoop might at any moment be expected.

The order of Partridge was too late; the Indians arrived before the notice of their coming.

October 9th, they fell upon a party of men at work at Northfield Meadows, killed Ebenezer Severance, wounded Hezekiah Stratton and Enoch Hall, and took prisoner Samuel Dickinson, who had been before captured at Hatfield. [See ante, p. 260.] Dickinson was redeemed and became a prominent citizen of Deerfield. Severance and Stratton had removed from Deerfield to Northfield not long before. Hall was a soldier in Capt. Barnard's company, from Enfield, Conn.

A company of Connecticut troops came up at this alarm and stayed a few weeks. By vote of the General Court, November 8th, "40 effective men to be levied," in Hampshire county to scout about Deerfield, Northfield and Sunderland. About the last of November came news which gave hopes of peace.

ALBANY 28th Nov. 1723

Col. Partridge

I have yours of 19th Instant & I note the Contents therof the two Indians that have been wth ye belt of Wampum to Cagnawago are come back again. They found ye Cagnawago Indians where gone to your parts butt ye Sachems said they went against their will, & s^d y^y had no ware against New England butt would live peaseably with the English. Their young people having been deluded as viz.

Three Cagnawago Indians who have been at Northfield arr^d here yesterday Sagwenoquas & Cahowasso two chief Cap^{ts} & his brother in Law. They tell mee they had no design to do any harme butt Governor Vaudreuil persuaded them & gave y^m powder & shott & tenn Gunns butt they are very sorry & ashamed that they have gonne & say they will never goe againe all the Indians who have beene upwards of three hundred are come back againe except five Eastern Indians who Returned back to your frontiers. I hope they may doe no harme. The Cagnawagos have sent seven hands of wampum that y^y will come in the Spring to treat heare further about theire friendship.

The Gray Lock has killed yᵉ Minister & yᵉ four brothers of which two are alive & two scalpt the youngest is given to the Cagnowagos. I shall Endeavore yᵉ Interest of New England as much as Lies in my power. pray Lett [me know] how these two French Gentlemen proceed at Boston I agreed with bearer herof for 30 s which I hope you will see paid. I have not to add butt Coˡˡ [Peter] Schuyler & Myne Respect to you. I am Sʳ

         Your Very humble Servᵗ
           JOHN SCHUYLER

Dec. 5th, Capt. Benjamin Wright asks the Governor's leave to raise a company of,—

35 or 40 men to go on the track of this Enemy wʰ came to Northfield as far as Otta Creek, & thence round to White River, & so home by Connecticut River * * * This I humbly judge to be very serviceable to this part of yᵉ Country & Probably might be yᵉ means of Destroying some of yᵉ Enemy * * * & if yʳ Honʳ see meet to give order we think it a piece of good service to mark yᵉ road wᶜʰ yᵉ Enemy went as far as Otter Creek.

John Stoddard, reporting for a Legislative Committee, favored this scheme, which might perhaps also include a visit to the St. Francis Indians. Dec. 17th, Capt. John Ashley, Lieut. John Root, Ens. John Gunn, commissioned officers of Westfield, write the Governor that Hezikiah Phelps is enlisting a company of English Indians to go out against the "Indian Rebels." Nothing came of these movements.

As in previous wars, the English took great pains to conciliate the Five Nations, and induce them to become allies, or remain neutral. Many formal conferences were held with them. Delegations were brought to Boston, others were induced to visit the Abenakis, and the Canada Indians. They were feasted and made much of, and a large sum was expended in presents. The Iroquois were fully aware of their importance, willing to receive the attentions of the English, and promised in certain contingencies to engage in the war, but they could not be held to their promises, while under the influence of the Albany Dutchmen. War to the latter meant serious interruption to their lucrative Indian trade, and they left no stone unturned to prevent their customers from engaging in it.

Some bills of expense attending negotiations with the Five Nations are given from the Council Records:—

1722, Nov. 14th, Joseph Kellogg, in consideration of his services as
 interpreter to ye delegates of ye Five Nations,   £10 0 0
Col. Jn. Schuyler, services attending them eastward,   150 0 0

Lawrence, as interpreter to Delegates,	30	0	0
Dec. 11th, Col. John Stoddard, expenses of delegates on their journey hither,	27	11	5
Samuel Partridge, expenses of delegates at Springfield,	14	9	7
Tilley Merrick, entertainer of delegates at Springfield,	2	18	5
Dec. 18th, Luke Hitchcock, victuals to Clorse, the interpreter,	1	3	1
Nov. 22d, Col. Stoddard, charge of the delegation,	17	11	5
Hendrick, De Witt, and each of the other delegates were in Council Chamber in Boston, when a gun was presented each.			
1723, Jan. 9th, Blue Broadcloth for the delegates,	5	0	0
Feb. 8th, To Wm. Tailor, Josiah Willard and John Stoddard, commissioners to accompany delegates eastward, each £25,	75	0	0
Elisha Danforth, physician,	5	0	0
Obadiah Ayers, chaplain,	5	0	0
Peter Martyn, steward,	3	0	0

There was talk of getting the Iroquois to meet the English at a conference at Albany, March 12th, 1722-3, and it was voted to bear the expense of a message to them, and of subsisting them at Albany during the treaty. Col. Stoddard and Col. Philip Livingstone were appointed Commissioners to perform this duty, and Joseph Kellogg was to attend them as interpreter. This programme was soon changed; July 19th, orders were expressed Kellogg to go to Albany, wait the coming of the delegates from the Five Nations, and conduct them to Boston.

BILLS OF EXPENSE.

Aug. 20, 1723, allowed Wm. Tailor, Col. Stoddard and Spencer Phipps, Commissioners for Indian treaty at Albany,	£597	15	7
Aug. 30, Thomas Wells, accompanying the delegates to Deerfield,	3	11	9
Aug. 30, Timothy Dwight, accompanying delegates and expense,	9	6	
Aug. 30, Jos. Jennings, accompanying delegates to Boston, expense,	3		
Aug. 30, Daniel Ashley, attending delegates and expense to Albany,	10	7	
Aug. 30, Ebenezer Pomroy, attending delegates and expense,	3	8	
Aug. 30, Joseph Kellogg, money advanced for delegates on journey to Boston,	44	4	1
Sept. 29, Joseph Kellogg, for going to Albany and conducting the delegates to Boston,	30		
Sept. 29, Jos. Kellogg, money advanced for the expenses of the delegates on their return home,	50		
Sept. 29, Jos. Kellogg, expenses at Albany,	76	15	1
Sept. 29, Col. John Schuyler, for good services,	100		
Sept. 29, William Tailor, entertainment of delegates at Castle William,	38	0	1
Sept. 29, Addington Davenport and Thos. Fitch, provisions, shirts, house hire, &c.,	483	8	8

FORT DUMMER.

It was uncertain whether the Five Nations could be relied upon to defend our river towns against incursions from Canada, and a defensive post above Northfield was projected. The General Court voted, December 27th, 1723 :—

That It will be of Great Service to all the Western Frontiers, both in this and the Neighboring Government of Conn., to Build a Block House above Northfield, in the most convenient Place on the Lands called the Equivilant Lands, & to post in it forty Able Men, English & Western Indians, to be employed in Scouting at a Good distance up Conn. River, West River, Otter Creek, and sometimes Eastwardly above Great Manadnuck, for the Discovery of the Enemy Coming towards anny of the frontier Towns; and that so Much of the said Equivilant Land, as shall bee necessary for a Block House, bee taken up, with the consent of the owners of said Land; Together with five or six acres of their Interval Land, to be broke up, or plowed, for the present use of Western Indians (In case any of them shall think fit to bring their families), and that His Honor, the Lieut. Gov'r, bee desired to Give his Orders Accordingly.

In Council, Read & Concurred.
Consented to, WM. DUMMER.

1723–4. January 10th, Capt. Kellogg writes Dummer that he has forty men at Northfield and ten at Deerfield, whom he keeps watching, warding and scouting. He asks attention to the forts, that "some care might be taken in y^t they might be made better, for they are exceeding mean."

Meanwhile the fort voted in December was being put up. I find no formal naming of this post. In the official records and correspondence it is uniformly called the "Block House above Northfield" or simply the "Block House." The name of "*Fort Dummer*" is first noticed in a petition to the General Court from Capt. Timothy Dwight, of December 2d, 1724, and this name gradually came to be adopted.

February 3d, 1723–4, Col. Stoddard writes the Lieutenant Governor:—

I have committed the work about the Block House to Lieut. Timothy Dwight; Mr. Dwight will this day go to the place with four carpenters, 12 soldiers with narrow axes & 2 teams. I suppose they will hew all the timber for the fort & housing before they return. I hope the fort and houses will be framed and set up this month * * * I have talked with Capt. Kellogg about a lieut.; he seems to be unwilling to say who he desires, but I discover by his talk that he thinks well of one Joseph Clesson, who is universally esteemed a good soldier; the hazard is whether he will take sufficient authority upon him* * * * I presume your honor intends a second to Mr. Dwight at the Block House; Capt. Kellogg tells me Dwight is desirous that Elisha Searle be with him; he is at present a sergeant under Capt. K.; was put in by request of the Assembly at his return

---

*Clesson was a sergeant in Capt. Barnard's company. He was a son of an Irish settler at Northampton, and seems to have had no "influence" to back him. Later he was a captain, and figured largely in the affairs at Deerfield.

from Canada, where he had long been a prisoner; [ante, p. 319.] he seems to be a discreet and careful man * * * Capt. Pomroy is willing, if your Honors think fit, that his son John Pomroy should be Kellogg's lieut.; he hath a soldier like spirit, & if he will exert himself, is more capable of government than the other mentioned. There is a good understanding between him and Kellogg. Your Honors will judge what is best.

After the above letter was written, one Stebbins arrived from the West, bearing letters from Schuyler. These were dispatched to Boston by Col. Stoddard, who writes:—

I perceive Col. Schuyler is worried by the Indians, & embarrassed by the Dutch, so that he is almost dispirited. He hath all along insisted on it that somebody should be sent to Albany to act with him in the affairs of this government. The Indians by degrees grow cool & are daily dissuaded by the Dutch from undertaking anything for our advantage, & unless they be often solicited, there is hazard that we may, in a great measure, lose the expense we have been at upon them. I somewhat doubt the care Col. Schuyler has taken to encourage the Indians to enlist in the service of the Block House. I did not know but the gov't would send to Albany, as Col. Schuyler desires otherwise I should have sent a man to engage the 20 Indians, who should have sent them out of the reach and influence of the Dutch. We suppose if that number came over hither, it would be the most likely method for our safety, & to engage the Nation in the war; for if they should once taste the sweets of our pay, the Gentlemen from Albany cannot draw them from us. Many of their nation will visit them at the Block House. The enemy will greatly fear them, will conclude in case they kill any of the Macquas the Nation will forthwith revenge it. I wrote in my last letter that I had £8, 17 s, 6 d for the 3 Macquas returned from the Eastward, which is ready for them when soever they called for it. I hoped it would be a means to draw them and others hither * * * I have agreed with Mr. Stebbins that he should have 3 pounds for his journey.

Dummer replies, February 7th, "I have your letters by Stebbins of the 3d; was well pleased with orders about the Block House, but don't see how they can lay foundations and dig cellars until the frost is out." He thinks Dwight should have a chaplain, "More especially in respect to the Mohawks;" asks Stoddard to employ a suitable person, and he will arrange for the compensation; sends him £50 by Stebbins for Kellogg, with orders for the latter to join Schuyler among the Indians, and to engage and pay such as he shall see fit; to give it as advanced wages, or as bounty, as he could do best. Stebbins also brought £500 for Capt. Dwight, at the Block House. The fort was about 180 feet square, built of hewn yellow pine, laid up log-house fashion, and was a perfect defense against existing enemies. It was located on the west bank of the Connecticut in the southeast part of Brattleboro, on what is now the "Brooks farm." Lean-to houses were built against the walls on the inside.

When Stoddard sent in his bill in August, he says:—

We agreed with the Carpenters at Nthfield for five shillings per diem, except Crowfoot to whom I promised six, and they allow that he earned his money by doing so much more work than others

The Soldiers had very hard service lying in the woods & were obliged to work hard early and late, its thought they deserve two shillings p^r diem besides the stated pay, and the Carpenters something more. The horses were wrought very hard, and commonly had nothing to eat but oats; and I believe two shillings a day will not be thought an excess for that service.

There was much fear of a winter incursion from Canada. Sunderland is troubled and writes the Lieutenant Governor:—

S^r— These are to inform your honor of the Difficulties we are under by reason of our being Exposed to ye Enemy: We are a very Small People & might be an Easy Pray to them if they should make an attempt upon us

We understand that ye Last May ye Generall Court Granted us a number of Soldiers, and y^t your honor ordered y^t we should have them from Deerfield & Northfield. But they were never sent to us; and we have had no assistance sence, except (for a little while) from Connecticut, but have been put to great Difficulties in Watching, warding, Guarding and Scouting out ourselves.

Wherefore we humbly request that your Honor would Consider our Difficulties and send us a few Soldiers to Defend us.

Your honors Humble Servants

Sunder Land   EBENEZER BILLINGS
Feb 9–1724   Jo^s CLARY

February 23d, Dummer writes Stoddard:—

I have a letter from Capt. Kellogg about the mean condition of the forts. * * * You will review them and advise and encourage the inhabitants to repair them, and let me know the charge, also the necessity they are under of a further reinforcement of men. If our negotiations with the Mohawks does succeed, I hope they will be sufficiently provided for.

Col. John Schuyler had been employed to enlist Mohawks for the new Block House. He wants help and writes Stoddard to send Capt. Kellogg to go among them, as his son Philip is in Canada.

Dummer writes Stoddard again, giving information and instructions:—

BOSTON Mch 18, 1723–4

S^r I have yours of ye 5 of March & am glad to hear that the Garrisons at Northfield are repaired & that the Block House goes forward so well. If Kellog Succeeds in his negociations I think you'll have little to fear on your frontiers. In the mean time I shall Directly give orders to Capt Wright to add another man to the Ministers garrison at Northfield. I have given orders for one man to be posted there some time sence.

I would have Col. Partridge be easy about the Subsistance of the Detatchment he sent to the frontier, for that money ought, & Doubtless will be paid. I have comunicated what you wrote about the Exchange of Dickinson to a Council I had yesterday, & we shall have a General Council next Thursday, when the affair of Exchanges will be further Considered   I am Sr Your Humble Servt
Wm Dummer

As spring advanced, and 'the ill success of Schuyler and Kellogg among the Mohawks became known, the fears of the inhabitants increased. The condition of affairs here is so well shown by the following papers, that they are given in full.

Letter from Stoddard to Dummer :—

Sir, Capt. Kellogg is returned, & I suppose hath given you an account of his affairs; he tells me he expected 4 or 5 Scautacook Indians to have been at Deerfield some days since, which I hear nothing of & am prone to think the Dutch have dissuaded them; it seems probable the Western Indians will not answer our expectations (at present) in assisting at the Block House, & inasmuch as our dependence is greatly on the scouts to be sent from thence, which cannot be well managed without the number of men allowed; it seems necessary that the complement be made of English, for the Present, & in case the Indians do not within a little time join us, undoubtedly it will be best that a number of good dogs be provided, which I hope may near as well answer our design; for I think it considerable probable that by means of some of our friend Indians, they may be instructed so that they will persue an enemy, & in case they should kill one Indian, it will more effectually prevent them coming, than the killing many in anny other way, & although the 5 Nations will not approve such a method, yet they must be silent, inasmuch as their neglect hath obliged us to that method. The people of Deerfield grow uneasy (now the spring comes on) at their having but 10 men; & those of Northfield say, that it will be in vain for them to pretend to manage any business, in case their number of soldiers be not augmented; & I am fully of their opinion, & if order be not speedily given, recruits will not be had seasonably. If we are thorough in our endeavours for the preservation of those in the frontiers, that will greatly quiet the spirits of the people, & I hope to be a means of the preservation of some lives, & probably will no [t] long continue; for I think there is a general disposition in the French, Dutch and Indians, that the present differences between us and the Eastern Indians be accommodated. I am y^r Hon's Most Humble Serv't,
John Stoddard.

Northampton, March 27, 1724.

To the Hon. Wm. Dummer, Lieut. Gov. & Commander in Chief in & over his province of the Mass. Bay in New England :
May it please Your Honor,
We the Subscribers the Committee & Selectmen of Deerfield in the Province aforesaid, Humbly Showeth;
That the season of the year has now come that our business call for us in the fields, & by reason of the war are much afraid to go about our occupations, expecting daily a descent of the enemy on our Western frontiers, which there seems to be more reason to expect, inasmuch as we have intelligence that Grey Lock hath enticed away several of the Scatacooks, which are so well acquainted with the circumstances of our fields, that they are able to take the greatest advantage against us; & indeed the difficulties of the war lie so hard upon us, that several families, & also several young men have drawn off from us, & several more are going in a little time, to the great discouragement of those who are left behind.
For which reasons, we, your Humble petitioners, humbly pray y^r Honors to consider the circumstances we are under & grant us a sufficiency of men, both to guard our forts, & men in the field, (and we are humbly of opinion that we stand in great need of 30 men) for which your Humble petitioners shall be ever obliged, & as in duty bound shall ever pray.

	THOS. WELLS, MAHUMAN HINSDALE,	} Committee of Militia.
April 6, 1724.	SAMUEL CHILDS, SAMUEL TAYLOR, EBENEZER WELLS,	} Selectmen.

No answer to the above appears. Probably because relief appeared in another quarter, or, at least, a renewed expectation of it. Col. John Schuyler writes to Col. Stoddard, April 10th, that he had,—

Enlisted on the 3d inst. Hendrick and Ezeare, the Indians; if Hendrick meets any of the river or Scatacook Indians in the way, he will as he promises me, take so many Indians with him as he can. Five days ago here arrived two canoes of Cagnawago Indians, who say that (among them is ye Cahowasso) ye Sachem of ye Cagnawagos Scauinecdie and Wondatis will come Hether so soon as they come from Hunting, as soon as I hear by a cano they will send before of there coming I will let you know Immediately, y^t you may send Hendrick and some old Scagcooke Indians, to meet them here. I hope all will be good

Schuyler thinks everything is going on well at last. Hendrick was a Mohawk chief, and there were high hopes from his accession to our forces.

April 16th, Dummer writes Stoddard that he has ordered Partridge to impress thirty men; fifteen from Deerfield and fifteen from Northfield; to take them where they have not been hardly drawn upon, and to "do it with the utmost speed, and remember [Rev.] Mr. Williams' house. * * * Capt. Dwight must let the Mohawks have as much victual as they please; their bellies must by no means be pinched & he need not fear the allowance of his account. * * * Acquaint the Mohawks that I have accounts from home, that the King received their belt of the 6th of March very graciously."

April 20th, Col. Partridge writes Dummer:—

4 or 5 Scatacook Indians are come to Deerfield & are gone to see the fort. They say there will be peace. * * * This I would say, if peace could be settled on good terms, it would be best, though diminutive for us, to make peace with them, yet if the Mohawks who are stirring for a peace would engage for them, I am of opinion it would be the best course that can be taken, for the way we are in.

He says John Graves, who has "many infirmities of age— is 70 years old, and deaf—desires freedom from watching," but is willing to attend to any other duty. A page of details could give no clearer idea of the spirit as well as the severity of the service than this simple item,—a man of three score and ten years, infirm and deaf, asking only to be exempt from night watching.

Partridge thinks if Deerfield, Northfield and Hatfield had not been reinforced, the Indians would not have turned back. He says the "enemy can, and doe sometimes, lye in waite 2 months about the towns, before they kill or take, as some of the former enemys have acknowledged." News was generally received through the Schuylers when any considerable party left Canada, but their destination was not often known, and the time they left home for our frontiers more rarely. This uncertainty necessitated constant watch and ward, in all the towns on the borders.

May 15th, the garrison here was increased by fifteen men, and the same number added to that at Northfield. On the same day at a town meeting it was voted:—

That no person shall from and after the first day of next June move any cart that is not four foot wide between ye naves of ye wheels, upon any of ye highways belonging to ye town, * * * and for each offence forfit five shillings to ye use of ye town to be recovered by bill, plaint, or information, before any of his Majisties Justices within the county.

This seems a very queer regulation in the supposed condition of the roads at that time. May it not have been aimed at carts coming from the towns below, and its object to secure the transportation of army supplies by their own vehicles?

There was a party in the county opposed to the establishment of the Block House; but the reasons for it do not appear. May 16th, Col. Stoddard, writing to Dummer about it, says:—

Mr. Parsons [of Northampton] hath promised to some, that he will do two things; * * * one is that the Block House be demolished, or at least slighted, (although the garrison is truly the best, or most probable means of our security that ever the government afforded us;) the other is to obtain the dismission of the Commissioners of Sewers. [A local quarrel at Northampton.]

About this time there was a great scare in Connecticut. May 18th, one Griswold was captured near Litchfield by two Indians who called themselves Scatacooks. They took him twenty-six miles northward. In the night he escaped, bringing off the guns and ammunition of his captors, with great stories of the Indians, about parties out on our frontiers and that they should take him to Canada in ten days. When near home on his return he saw two more Indians. In great alarm Gov. Saltonstall writes Col. Stoddard, May 20th and May 21st, repeating Griswold's stories and saying that several other parties of Indians had been seen since Griswold's capture. He details his action in sending out scouts, and posting guards about Litchfield and Simsbury. May 23d, Major Talcott writes Partridge he has fifty men ranging the frontiers; has got notice of an intended conference at Albany.

In the matter of securing Indian allies the Schuylers were the chief agents of Massachusetts. Col. John writes to Stoddard and Partridge:—

SAREGTOGUE, May 18, 1724

Hon. Srs This comes by Maskimit the Indian & is chiefly to aquaint you that I have advices that ye Cagnawago, Rondox Scawindees Indians are by the way & I hourly expect y^m here, of which please to aquaint hendrick & Ampamit ye Indians. I would also think propper if you would think fit to send any proper person hether that might hear by word of mouth what they say y^{m}selves. Here are severall of our Mohawks Sachems who also would be glad if you would send anybody hether on s^d acc^t

I pray send ye bearer hereof back again immediately & hope you'll favor mee with a Line by him I have paid him here for his journey. I have not to add So I remaine with much respect

Gentlemen Your honors Sev^t JOHN SCHUYLER.

This movement of the Indians was probably in response to the belt sent in November, 1723. This letter was received in the night of May 21st. At three o'clock in the morning it was dispatched to the Governor by Partridge and Stoddard, who say, " Inasmuch as the consequences of this meeting will greatly affect this government we thought it most necessary to send it forward with all speed 'tis probable that there will be present a great number of the Indians at that meeting (either of the 5 nations, or from Canada) so that the charge of subsisting them will be greatly enhanced, if they should stay long at Albany, waiting in expectation of some gen[tlm] from Boston."

May 22d, the Governor directs Col. Stoddard and Capt. Kellogg to attend the meeting, and act in concert with Schuyler in the matter; to keep him constantly informed of affairs there, and of any movements of the Indians; and he also advised Schuyler of that action. Stoddard had not waited for this order. On receiving Schuyler's letter, he at once hastened to Albany, where he arrived May 24th. Capt. Kellogg, with Capt. Ebenezer Pomroy, left Northampton for Albany, May 25th. A post left Albany May 30th, by which Stoddard writes Dummer that,—

The Gen[lm] now here have had a notable difficulty about sending for the chiefs of the five nations, but on perusal of Col Schuylers Instructions they thought they would justify there sending for them especiall considering the necessity of their being present, for if they sh not be here its probable that the French Indians would not treat at all, and the five nations would be greatly disobliged

If affairs are prudently managed at this treaty 'tis hopeful that the Eastern Indians will be obliged by fair or foul means to forbear further acts of hostility: If not our Indians will be greater than ever. there will be nothing further to be done for several days therefore I propose to return on the beginning of the next week.

The reason Col. Stoddard desired to shirk further responsibility appears in the following letters, which also give an inside view to the matter in hand. They are addressed to Governor Dummer:—

ALBANY May 30 1724

S[r] We came hether on thursday last and found five Indians newly arrived with the Enclosed Message from Cagnawago and Sekohandie which was delivered to the Commissioners of Indian affairs, who sent for us and told us that by some mistake the message was delivered to them that they had not sent for them, neither could they send for the Five Nations without an order from their gov[r] & it is not reason that N. Y. should be at the charge of feeding them wch w^d happen if *they* sent for them. Wherefore examining the treaty made at Boston last year we find that the 5 Nations gave a belt of wampum "to be sent to Canada to draw the French Indians to Albany" & so if the 5 Nations were not here the whole would fall through, we took the liberty of sending for the 5 Nations without waiting to hear from Boston

JOHN SCHUYLER
EBENEZER POMROY
JOSEPH KELLOGG

Knowing the reason why Stoddard would not act with them in this proceeding, they write another letter to Dummer the same day,—

Sr Col Stoddard is here upon the spot and notwithstanding what he has wrote y^r honor about Returning homeward next week we hope he will be persuaded to stay, and if he should [illegible] he thinks the government did not do him justice in finding as much fault with his accpts, or at least with the Commissary accompts last year. Whereas he spent so little Its great pitty he should not be at the Conference for he is more knowing: and as well able to serve the government as almost any in ye government
Excuse our boldness who are your honors
Humble & obedient Serv^ts

The same parties write a third letter the same day to Dummer, saying, "here we Remain Waiting your Honors Orders." These letters were dispatched by post to Boston.

June 5th, Dummer sends to Gov. Burnett of New York a formal notice of the belt the Mohawks left for Col. Schuyler to take to the Canada Indians and informs him that Col. John Schuyler and Col. John Stoddard have been appointed to act for this Province at the coming Conference. He hopes Gov. Burnett will aid in it as he can.

Schuyler and Stoddard report progress to Dudley:—

ALBANY June 19, 1724

On Tuesday last the Chefts of Cagnawago Skehandie, Rondox, Nepinsing Indians came hether. The next morning we had a short Conference with them, Copies of what was s^d is Inclosed.

Yesterday the Commissioners sent for Col Stoddard & Capt Pomroy and read to them the minutes of these Indians answer to a Message formerly sent from the Commissioners, the Substance of which we have enclosed. by which it plainly appears that Govr Vaudrouile designs that, if we have peace, it shall be by his direction. it is likewise apparent to us the Commissioners for Indian affairs do aim at the Hon^r of peace being made by their influence. And we doubt not our Government will think it reasonable that they themselves have some direction in an affair of their own. but it seems a great Pitty that an opportunity of being at Peace should be lost by a Struggle who should have the honor of it. we presume that in case the French Indians should propose to us the delivery of the Hostages [in Boston from the East] that the government will allow us to Assure them (that upon the Eastern Indians submission, and giving sufficient Security for there good behavior) the Hostages will be set at liberty at the same time they restore the English Prisoners.

The Commissioners doe pretend to a readiness to serve our government according to their power, yet they plainly tell us that they have been overlooked by our Government, and that the respect due to them hath not been formaly paid them. They endeavour to make us believe that they have the whole direction of the Six Nations & it seems that they have never [informed?] the Nations with ye Resolve of ye Council of New York, that the five Nations should send such a Number of there young men (to our assistance) as they could conveniently spare, altho they long since had a copy of it, nor with the Order of Govr Burnett agreable to s^d Resolve.

The Canada Indians say that they think that Skonodoah is much discouraged for he has been fifteen days since at Maseeskuk, and that none of the Maseeskuk Indians would go with him. they imagine that he will endeavour in case he Proceeds on his journey, to take a Prisoner and not attempt to kill any Body. Some of them say they should be glad that the first bullet that is shot may go through Skenondoah's Body

Upon hearing of the Parties going to war we gave order to a Maqua Sachem to enlist a greater Number of Indians than our govn^t had ordered, supposing it necessary to take this opportunity to Engage them in our interest, and supposed it might be well (if you^r Hon^{rs} approved of it) to post some of them at Nthfield and release some of the English Soldiers, immagining that if a few more were drawn into our party it would not be in the power of the people here to prevent the Nations engaging in the war with us.

We have heard divers times from Onieata (the Second nation of the Iroquois) that they wait the Coming of the Chiefs of the Upper Nations, which they daily expect, their delaying their Coming will necessarily Enhance the Expense of the government. We think it needful that Govr Burnett be aquainted with the state of our affairs which shall be done from hence (if opportunity present) that our business may not be so embarrased as it hath been.

We has been as particular as we could that you should be the better advantaged to know what further Instructions are necessary for the conduct of Your Humble Sevants
JOHN SCHUYLER
JOHN STODDARD

By the same post Capt. Pomroy writes Col. Partridge, giving some more particulars. "Schonodoah" is evidently an Abenaki, trying to raise a war party in Canada, to which the chiefs here are opposed. He says the chiefs of the four tribes mentioned above came last Tuesday:—

In answer to ye Commissioners of Albany Belt of Wampum: they in ye name and in behalf of ye four tribes aforesaid, have Laid down the hatchet of war aganst New England [one sent from the East?] to ye s^d Commissioners: and they further add y^t Skonanda [seems?] some disgust at quarel with a Sachem: was resolved to go to war against there desire and minds * * * We have further inteligence that fifteen days ago Skonanda was at Masixqouoch and could get none of those Indians to joyn with him and there is but six Indians with him.

Tis good for to be very watchful and Careful in Scouting, especially the Indians if Posable to surprise him. if not to way lay him on his Return Soe his utter Ruin I think is desired almost universally in this City by ye aforesaid tribes of ye Canada Indians & ye five Nations. tis almost universally determined y^t Skononda is a great Coward.

We are waiting ye Coming of ye Six nations & our Com^s have now sent an Express to Boston Informing what ye Canada Indians said to ye Commissions. our Affairs Labor under Difficultys, but we hope for a good Issue, and am your honors Hum^l Ser^t

EBEN^r PUMROY.

Sir Tis concluded that this be immeadiately dispatched to Capt Dwight [at Fort Dummer] that he with ye Indians may take measures accordingly Hendrick you may tell his daughter is well.

Schuyler and Stoddard write again to Dummer :—

June 18, 1724

Col. Stoddard did according to his purpose (which was mentioned in our last) send a letter to Govr Burnett a Copy of which is enclosed

The Chefs of the Tribes (except the Senacas of which we could have no Certain Account) being advised we met with them yesterday and [advised?] as our business, but made no great proficiency therin and on the last night the Senacas Came to Town. We hope we shall be ready to speak to the Canada Indians to-morrow, and shall persue our business as much as the Temper of the Indians will allow.

We have endeavoured to Engage some of the five Nations (of greatest influence) by hopes of private gratuities to appear strenously in our Interest.

We have enlisted Seven Maquas and three Onietas in the Service of our Prov^{ce}. they are waiting the issue of this Conference but we will endeavour to persuade them to go to the Blockhouse forthwith. We hope we shall gain several others, Hendrick tells us that upon hearing the news from Canada their young men grew Angry.

While we were waiting came in the Express from Boston with the Paquet from yor Hon^r, We shall carefully observe the present as well as our former Instructions which we secured by our first Express.

We are your Hon^{rs} most Humble and Obedient Servants

JOHN SCHUYLER
JOHN STODDARD

On the 24th the Deputy Secretary Communicated a Copy of a Resolue of the Council of New York, wherein the Commissioners were directed to afford us there assistance in drawing off the Cagnawago Indians from the Eastern Indians and that they should be present at al Conferences, and see what we propose to say to the Indians before it was delivered, and that nothing should be done that should hurt the trade and Interest of New York J.S.

tis probable that our business with the Nations will be finished before the Express can return hether.

The Dutch burghers of Albany could be safely trusted—without instructions—to look after their trade and other interests regardless of consequences to any body else. The charge of selfishness was often brought against them by the other colonies. The question of war or peace was always considered in its supposed effect on their Indian trade.

De Vaudreuil it seems, could not prevent a treaty with the Caghnawagas, but he could prevent a peace with the Abenakis, and later practically nullify the treaty.

Provision was made by the General Court, June 3d, to "procure a chaplain for the Block House, More especially to Indian natives residing thereabouts in the true christian Religion," he to be a "Person of Gravity, Prudence & Ability." A salary of £100 was allowed.

June 9th, a pressing letter was to be sent to Connecticut asking aid in defending Hampshire county. Gov. Saltonstall replies, June 11th, that he will send soldiers, or, what he thinks better, money, as the men at Deerfield and Northfield are so much better acquainted with Indian hunting.

June 13th, Massachusetts voted to raise ninety-nine more men and to keep up scouting all along the frontier; "that the twenty-five men under the command of a Lieutenant at Deerfield, be employed in scouting round that town, and for securing the people thereof and of Hatfield and Westfield in their harvest."—This must be of hay.

Meanwhile the Commissioners at Albany had been so successful in their mission, that on the 3d of July a treaty was made with the Canada Indians, and a covenant entered into with the Five Nations, by which peace was to be secured. Concerning this agreement, Gov. Burnett of New York writes August 9th, 1724:—

Those Canada Indians solemnly promised not to make war any longer on Boston, and our Five Nations undertook to send Deputys to the Eastern Indians, who are now at war with Boston, to perwuade them to come to a peace; and in case they will not make one, to threaten them permptorily, that they, the said Five Nations, will compel them to it by force of arms.

De Vaudreuil, writing of the same transaction to the War minister at Paris, says: The English "have just renewed their alliance with the Iroquois, and obtained their promise to wage war against the Abenakis." De Vaudreuil makes a merit of having broken up this peaceful prospect, and is commended for it by the Minister and King.

There was no cessation of hostilities during these negotiations. The woods on the frontiers were filled with war parties, though constantly traversed by English scouts. Deserters from the Scatacooks had gone to Canada, and were perfect guides for the marauders. This tribe, located about twenty miles above Albany, was partially made up of Pocumtucks and Nipmucks, driven off in Philip's War, who in times of peace hunted in their old haunts, mingled freely with the English, and were intimately acquainted with their roads and fields, as well as the ravines and swamps where an enemy could skulk in safety.

One good result of the Conference at Albany was the information that came to our men of the Indian raids from Canada. The following letter from Col. Partridge was occasioned by a post from Capt. Pomroy,—

HATF^d June 15 1724

Honorable S^r on the 13 Ins at 10 o'clock at night we were Surpris^d with news from Albany per a letter from Capt Pomeroy which inform of Severall p^{ties} of the Enemy Coming this way & intend an attack on some of the Towns & particularly on Northfield, which news I immediately posted to Deerfield and Northfield & to the fort above Northfield & since to Sund^{rl}^{d} advising them to be on there guard & there Sold^{rs} to scout out the more full account of this news I understand is sent by Col Stoddard by the way of Westf^d to y^{r}self. I am of opinion that Sunderland, Hadly, Hatfield & Northampton should have 5 or 6 men each to be in pay, to scout out in the adjacent woods and fields to discover the approach of the Enemy having no men but the men belonging to sayd Towns & all of them out upon there Occasions to get there Bread & that with the perrill of there lives or beg there bread in a little tyme, but *where* I know not if it comes to that o^r dependance is by tilling the ground

This was sent by Capt. Dwight. Even with the notice and extra precaution it was impossible to prevent a surprise. The assailants had all the advantage of a choice of time and circumstance. Like a flash of lightning they struck and disappeared.

HATFIELD June 20 1724

Honorable S^r
On the 18th Inst at 10 o'clock in the forenoon the Enemy made an assault in Hatfield on some of our men at a mowing Field about 3 miles from Town at Nehe Waits swamp lot where he with severall men & carts were loading hay. They killed Benj Smith son of Jo-

seph Smith & have taken Aaron Wells & Joseph Allis Captives as we judge because all the rest Escaped home & these two are not to be found. They also killed two oxen of one of our Temes & drew of, the men that was there judge there was 8 or 10 of the Enemy. We have sent immediately to Deerf^d & Northf^d & the Fort above Deerf^d immedeately sent out 20 men into the Western Woods & we from hence have sent out 17 men, from hence [sic] with provisions for ten days p^{r}sute of the s^d Enemy or discovery of any p^{ties} of the Enemy: I presume this Enemy will take a Westward course clear out of the Reach of all o^r Upper forces So o^r unguarded Towns are in a evil case & although we have some men of o^r own in Northampton Hadly, Hatfield Sunderland & Westfield yet we have none but what have Occasions abroad in the Fields so that our Towns all the day are so emtred of men that we are very much exposed & the Enemy seem to shape there course upon the lower Towns and our men abroad at their work in a moments tyme may be shot down before anything can be seen who it is that doth it

In my let^r by Capt Dwight of the 13th [15th?] inst I proposed for some Reliefe & gave my Reasons I shall not need to ad expecting every hour y^r Honors directions in the p^{r}meses. I think we may say the Lord of Mercy upon us & doubt not y^r care & consideration of our circumstances the seat of the war seems to be here

with my earnest desire & pray^r for divine Guidance & support to y^r Hono^r & the whole Co^{r}te I am y^r

Afflicted & very Humble Servt
SAMUEL PARTRIDGE

The leader of this party was Gray Lock. With his prisoners, he hurried to the woods westward, where Allis was killed the next day, under circumstances unknown. Partridge sent twenty-one men in pursuit, under Sergts. Joseph Clesson and Joseph Wait. They went up as far as Otter Creek, but met with no enemy. It appears by the following statement of Dr. Hastings that this scout suffered severely:—

To the Hon'ble the Gentlemen of the House of Representatives In General Court Convened:

May it please your Hon^s, I being desired by Sergt Clesson and Sergt Wayte to inform what I know of their Expedition in June last to Otter Creek, Do Inform on my Certain Knowledge that the Expedition being suddenly formed Suitable Nessessaries was wanting for such a Long & hard Journey; Saw most of ye men when they went forth, they were Lusty & in good Plight—Effective men; Saw them when they returned & they were much emaciated & their feet so Swolen & galled that they could scarce Travel on their feet, for some they necessitated to hire horses, some one or more applied to me to dress their feet & were under my care for a week or more in bathing & emplastering before they were anything Tolerably Recruited, in Fine they underwent much, & I believe they were hearty in their desires & faithful in their Indeavours to overtake the Enemy & make Reprisals.

With Leave humbly say its Pitty Such Persons undergoing such Difficulties for y⁰ Country's cause should fail of a suitable Reward.

Excuse me, I pretend not to prescribe to y^r Hon's Wishing the Blessings of Heaven on your persons & on your Consultations for the Good of the People whom you Represent, I crave Leave to subscribe yo'r most humble & ob't Sevt, THOMAS HASTINGS.
Hatfield, May 26, 1725.

As we have seen, a post was dispatched from Albany to Boston June 19th. By the following letter it will be seen he was in Northampton the next day. Remarkable time was made by these riders, considering the roads, or paths, of the day. They must have ridden night and day; dispatches sent from the Connecticut Valley were often received and answered in Boston the next day. Notwithstanding this dangerous and constant service, I recall but a single instance in which the messenger fell into the hands of the enemy.

NORTHAMPTON June 20 1724

Colonoll Partridge

Honored Sir: According to your desire I have procured a man to go to Boston on his Maj'ts Service: viz: Daniel King.

Sir: it is the desire of our people at Northampton: myself and the rest of the Commissioned officers: that your Honor would propose to his Honor the Lieutenant Governor that we may have a Number of men, about eight or ten in each town appointed to be there a scout and also to guard our people when they are obliged to goe in exposed places on their necessary Occasions: And also that we have some stores provided in each Town: Especially of Indian Shoes and Biscake: that when we have extraordinary occasion of a sudden (as of Late) we may have where withall to furnish men Immediately for a march: Pray your Honor not only propose as above but that you wuld urge it so far as may be convenient if your Honor see meet which is all at present from your Humble Sevant

JOSEPH HAWLEY

Sir since I wrote the above Benj Alvord is come from Albany ordered to Boston, and to travel to day. I would advise y^t King go along with Him think it to much boldness for one to travel alone especially upon public service: Have sent your letters to yourself pr farefield thinking you might add something: King is now at Hadly wth Alvord waiting your Honors pleasure

Your Honors Sev JOSEPH HAWLEY

June 22d, 1724, Partridge writes the Governor that messengers "from Springf^d out Farms say they are much molested with trails of Indians. So that they fear to get in there Harvest desiring a p^tie of men to guard them * * * they think a fortnight or 3 weeks tyme they hope will serve there turn."

June 24th, 1724, four Indians scouting from the Block House, discovered the tracks of about forty Indians east of the Connecticut, "going towards Sunderland," as they ascertained by marks on the bushes by the way. Capt. Dwight dispatched the news to Partridge the 25th, and the same was sent by Lieut. John Pomroy, from Northfield, to Capt. Thomas Wells at Deerfield the same day.

HATFIELD June 26 1724

Honorable S^r
Your Honors letter of the 24th just Received this day att noone with directions & a Lett^r to ye Hounerable Gov Saltonstall. yor Hono^{rs} directions in the affair I am immediately prosecuting I hope to effect. However shall with as much speed as may be Give an account of that affair to y^r Honor:

S^r as to y^r Hono^{rs} Letter Referring to o^r towns its true about the Middle of May Last I Rec^d y^r Hono^{rs} order for 30 men to be Raysd & plact 15 at Northf^d & 15 at Deerf^d which accordingly was done this supply made 25 at Deerf^d & but 45 at Northf^d. If y^r Honor Remember 10 of these Northf^d men was carried over to the Fort, when the Fort was first settled with men & then Northf^d had but 30 men & the 15 afors^d made them to 45. So that if Northf^d be reduced to 40 men there is but 5 men a spare for Brookfield & none to relieve Sunderland with who indeed have great need of at Least ten men & this day we are alarmed of the Enemies comeing down the East side the river directly upon Sunderland or Rutland or Brookfield and we are forct to leave o^r villages and sent out of Northampton, Hadly & Hatfield 40 men if possible to secure Sunderland & waylay the Enemie & immediately sent to Brookf^d to Alarm them & directed them to Alarm Brimfield & Rutland & so upon y^m Frontiers. Besides the 29 men that went out in p^{r}suite of the Enemie that came upon Hatfield on the 18th & are not Returned.

As to the 25 men at Deerf^d I am of opinion that they are few Enoff to scout watch and ward Deerf^d & can be no Reliefe Hatfield 13 mile distant & much Less to West^d 30 miles distant & therefore Humbly intreat that my two former lett^{rs} may be considered in behalf of Sunderland Hatf^d Hadly Northampton & Westf^d & some Reliefe be ordered if it be but 5 or 6 men in each town afor^d to Guard o^r people in the townes & at there worke. We must improve the means for Bread or dye & the Lord sanctify this day of trouble & Rebuke & be not a teror to us for there is o^r Hope I pray God Support y^r Hon^r. I am satisfyed y^r Burthen is very great & Render Myself y^r Afflicted & very Humble Servt SAM^{ll} PARTRIDGE

Capt. Wells at once led a party from this town in search of the same invaders. None were found by either party in the pursuits. The Indians at the fort "thought the enemy heard the whites coming up the river, & were discouraged at their numbers and fled." It is more probable they concealed their trail and broke up into small parties to skulk about the settlements. Capt. Wells, who apparently believed they were beyond reach, was rudely undeceived. While returning in careless security, June 27th, Ebenezer Sheldon of Northampton, Thomas Colton, and Jeremiah English, an Indian "who used to be Col. Lambs," riding in advance of the main body, fell into an ambuscade about four miles north of Deerfield, probably at the great spruce swamp near Turners Falls. They were fired upon, their horses shot down and the riders all killed.

The company behind, hearing the guns, rode up with all speed, and came upon the enemy while they were scalping the slain, and firing upon them, wounded several. Upon which the enemy fled into the swamp, and the English dismounting their horses, ran in after them, and tracked them a considerable way by the blood of the wounded, but found none. However, they recovered 10 packs and heard afterwards that 2 died of their wounds, and a third lost the use of his arm.

The saddened scouts returned to Deerfield bearing the mangled remains of their comrades. After an affecting service by Mr. Williams, they were laid to rest in the old burying yard. A moss-grown stone still marks the spot where Ebenezer Sheldon sleeps near the graves of his kindred. There is a tradition in the Sheldon family that Ebenezer was killed by a hatchet thrown by one of the enemy, which stuck in his skull; that he wore silver shoe buckles, which an Indian was trying to get off when interrupted by the fire of Capt. Wells. The buckles were bent in the attempt, but not secured. The hatchet and the buckles were long kept in the Sheldon family in Northampton as mementos of that bloody day. Memorial Hall at Deerfield would be the most fitting place for their preservation.

To add to the general alarm, word came from Zachariah Prescott, a prisoner at Montreal, of a report there that the Abenaki hostages "were dead in Boston prison, which has put the Indians in a great rage; that about 700 are gone or going to all parts of New England, in parties of 10, 12, 15, 20, 25." June 29th, an appea was made to Connecticut by Gov. Dudley for help, and Gov. Saltonstall sent seventy-five men under Capt. Goodrich, thirty-seven under Capt. Butler, with forty-two Indians to report to Col. Partridge at Hatfield for orders. This bad news from Canada was soon confirmed. Stoddard writes:—

ALBANY June 28, 1724
in the Evening

Just now hether came Sam[ll] Dickinson from Canada with two Genl[mn] belonging to this place (Dickinson was taken from No[th]field last Oct[br]) they give an accompt that about fifteen days since the Indian called Graylock with eleven others set out for war towards New England and disegn to go with all speed and that last Tuesday night they passed by another company of thirty Abenaquois near the further end of the lake, they knew before of there going to war, and the same day were advised by a Frenchman where they lay so that we avoided them in the night. They add that there were about forty more that have sung their war songs & are preaparing to goe out.

Dickinson tells us further that about ten of the Cagnawago Indians that were for war and that the Sachems told him that they would stone them out of the fort, he adds that *Denion* a French Man (well known in New England) was in the Army at N[th]field last fall. We have aquainted Co[ll] Partridge with the news; and if we omit anything Needful you will attribute it to our hast. Dickinson just now informs us that Mr love hath written a letter to the Interpretre of the Eastern Indians, that [Dote?] Peter is dead. Another of the Hostages is Sick but well looked after the third is well. this hath greatly insensed the Eastern Indians, and they were for going to war and some of them came to the gov[r] for liberty to goe to war against these parts, being angry at Co[ll] Schuyler assisting us.

In reply to the letter from Dudley asking aid, Gov. Saltonstall writes:—

NEW LONDON July 2 1724

On Monday last I had you[s] of y[e] 29th, by an Express from Colo Partridge The next day I saw two of our Indian Tribes of Mohegan & Niantic They would not be pursuaded to March Eastward, but 20 of them agreed to go into your County of Hampshire, whom I have joined to 30 English under the command of Capt Walter Butler. They will begin to march tomorrow, will be in Hampshire next week about the middle of it, with orders to attend such Directions as you have given to Colo Partridge; or your Chief Commanding Officers there

The Pequots could not go "on account of there corn" until a month later.

As the failure to engage the Five Nations or the Caghnawagas as active allies had been disheartening, so the present success in another direction was cheering. It was held to be necessary to secure Indians to fight Indians, they being better able to cope with the enemy in their own fashion, and to meet wile with wile. No doubt they were more to be feared than the English. It is surprising that more damage was not done by the swarms of Abenakis and their Canadian allies which infested the dense forests surrounding the settlements.

As we have seen, a few Mohawks and Scatacooks had been enlisted by Schuyler and Stoddard at Albany, and stationed at Fort Dummer—not then so named.

The Indians at the Block House were well cared for. June 20th, a Committee of the General Court reported, that pursuant to the promise of Col. Schuyler,—

Two shilling per day be allowed Hendrick and Umpaumet, as they are Sachems, and the first of that Rank that have entered into the service of this province; that none of ye Indians be stinted as to allowance of provisions; that all have the use of their arms gratis, and their guns mended at free cost; that a supply of knives, pipes, tobacco, lead, shot, & flints be sent to the commanding officer at the fort, to be given out to them at his discretion; that 4 barrels of rum be sent to Capt. Jona. Wells, at Deerfield, to be lodged in his hands, and to be delivered to the commanding officer at the Block House as he sees occasion to send for it, that he may be enabled to give out one Gill a Day to each Indian & sòme to his other Men as Occasion may Require.

According to the usual estimate of Indian character these attractions at the fort should have drawn crowds into the service under Capt. Dwight; but it is a singular fact that only about a dozen enlisted. Was the counter influence of the Dutch traders stronger, or did the natives really believe the Abenakis were in the right, and acted up to their convictions? In any event, they rejected an opportunity for animal gratification, the like of which could never have been open to them in all their lives before.

Early on the morning of July 8th, 1724, a party of Indians plundered some houses at the Bars, "of rum, meal, cheese, meat, &c." The houses had been deserted, the occupants having doubtless gone to spend the night within the stockade at the Town Street.

Partridge writing Dummer, July 11th, says:—

We are much distressed by lurking enemies * * * We are confident they are still about us waiting to shed blood, so that we, being in the middle of our harvest, are forced to go 30 or 40 men in a day with their arms & with a guard to accompany & work together * * * The whole country is alarmed & upon their guard everywhere, its hopeful the stress of the enemy will abate.

Writing again July 14th, he says:—

These aquainte yor Hon^r that yor Lett^r pr John Huggins I rec^d last

Night with the proclamations enclosed & shall endeav^r to Suppress such pernicious acting, but am not apprised of any that have done so here, but shall enquire about itt [Proclamation not found—Offence unknown]

We have been Much distressed with the Lurcking Enemy^s that first set on a p^tle of o^r men killed a lusty young man, took 2 men Captive (killed a yoke of oxen in a cart.) the next betwixt Deerfield & Northfield they killed 3 young men—a third time they Revlled Several hoases in a village of Deerfield and they wounded 2 men in Deerfield.

This was July 10th. While a party was at work in North Meadows, they were being watched by a party of Indians on Pine Hill,—probably the same that recruited its commissary department at the Bars. Hiding themselves in a thicket at the south end of the hill near the road, the skulkers waited until nightfall and the return of the laborers to their homes. At the right moment they fired from the ambush, and Lieut. Timothy Childs and Samuel Allen were wounded, but not disabled; all escaped, Childs, says Hoyt, " by dashing through an adjacent pond."

Of this affair we give a vivid account from the lips of one who had a finger in it—to his cost:—

He Being at work with 3 men & 2 boys Northward of the Town, Capt Wells working with a Company of men farther Northward Still with 4 guardsmen, having done his work a Little before me, came by and I Desired him to wait a few minutes and so I would go with him home, now he told me he had a Little piece of [work] to do in harrow meadow, West of the Town Plot. Then I desired him to Le^ve me the guards that he had with him, of which two men tarried, and in a Short Time we finished our work and mounted our horses to go home & came to ye South End of Pine Hill when the Rode Carried us Close to the Hill, there being fired upon by three indians that way Laid the Rode, Myself was wounded in both Shouldiers & in one finger, which was so broken that it was forced to be cutt off which was on my right hand & ye same Shouldier the Bullett going so far thro that it was cutt out on ye other Side, which has very much Disabled my Arm from almost any Service: There being one man behind me at the same Time, Sam^ll Allen by Name, who also was wounded by a Shoot going into his Buttock. My horse being also shoot in ye Neck made him Spring forward, so that he threw us both off, but finding that we had ye use of our Leggs soon made our escape, Calling to the rest of ye men to face about, with y^t they turned and fired upon ye Enemy, With that they ran down where we had fallen of ye horse, and catched up Allen's hat. People being alarmed in the Town came out with great Speed. The Indians running acrost ye hill passed over ye river at Cheapside & soon got to the woods without any Damage. Afterwards our people finding 3 packs supposing them to be the Packs of these same Indians which fired upon us which were in Number three. Finis.

Gov. Dummer writes Capt. Joseph Kellogg about the affairs on the frontier and at Fort Dummer:—

BOSTON, July 25th 1724

Capt Kellogg. I have your L^{tre} of the 20th & am glad you find your garrisons in Good order & the Service so well performed You do well to have great regard to the protection of the people in there Harvest which you must always do in the most impartial manner

I have wrote to Coll° Partridge & Coll° Stoddard that you may exchange your men until you have got a good company. I have an ac^t from Capt Dwight of one George Swan who behaved in a very villianous manner in his Garrison (who would have been shot for it in any Garrison in Eng) & that in your absence Hee was admitted into your Company at Nffield. Let the fellow forthwith be turned out of the Company with disgrace I would you as soon as you can Inlist a Surgeon for the Service of your Company & Capt Dwight & in the meantime I enclose you my warrant to enable you to ffetch a Surgeon when you want one. I shall be glad to see a scalp or two brought downe by some of your scouts. I am y^r H^{ble} Sv^t

Wm DUMMER

An active correspondence was kept up between the governors of Massachusetts and Connecticut concerning the Indians in the service, their officers, their supplies and their movements. Gov. Saltonstall writes July 23d, 1724, to Secretary Willard:—

It fell out unhappily ye Lt Govr is out of town, for tho what you sent me shows w^t wages or Premiums on scalps; yet I cant tell whither such a Small Number as our Pequods wch at ye most will not be above 25 or 30 will be acceptable to him or whether He will like that they should have English officers of there acquaintance from here, w^h they always expect.

They seemed rather inclined to try for a scalps about Menadnuck and the back side of Dunstable & Groton.

My account of scalp money from Col Partridge much exceeds your a^{ct} in many particulars; How the Indians will like y^t when they come to understand I cant tell

I appointed to meet the Pequods on Wednesday next in order to there marching but am obliged to put it off till the Return of the Post the week after that I may know the Lt Gov^{rs} Inclination as low number of Indians & there being joined with English, as also whether He will fit them with arms at Boston, for the Indians have very few. We have had now about a fortnight [40?] English and Indians in Hampshire county for a standing party, but I have heard nothing from them, above a week

July 27th, the Secretary writes that "the Govr is pleased with the offer, wishes them sent out at once. They can go where they suggest until October & will then send them eastward. May choose there own officers if the Govr approve them. He cant arm them for his supplies are exhausted."

By another letter of the 27th, it appears that thirty Pequot Indians,—having I suppose, finished hoeing their corn,—were to be "employed in scouting about Manadnock and other parts between Connecticut & Merrimack Rivers." Orders were sent to Stoddard and Partridge to,—

Dispatch them to Col. Tyng at Dunstable as soon as they come to you. Let them take such a Rout thither through the woods as will be best for the Defence of the Frontier & you must take effectual care that in there coming in to you, & going from you to Col Tyng, the places through which they pass may be notified & apprised of it; that the Indians have some signal, which must also be known by our people to prevent any evil that might otherwise happen.

With our limited knowledge of frontier warfare in those days, it seems that it must have been a difficult thing indeed, to devise any scheme by which friendly and enemy Indians could be distinguished in the woods, in season to prevent the "evil" which the Governor fears. And we must bear in mind that should harm come to one of them by any mistake of the English, the rest would instantly become active enemies.

In this case the people in Middlesex were alarmed and an order was sent to Col. Stoddard by the Governor "that some effectual method may be agreed on to distinguish there Indians or to limit them in there hunting so as that there may be no Danger of the Towns being Alarm'd by them, or there being Surpriz^d & hurt by our scouts." If no method can be devised for the safety and security of both parties, then the Mohegans must be told of their danger, "and that it is absolutely necessary that they desist from Hunting on our Frontiers."

The defensive policy of the English not being successful in preventing incursions of the Indians, it was resolved to carry the war into the enemy's country. An army of two hundred and eighty men, including three Macquas, under Captains Harman, Moulton, Bourn, and Lieut. Bean were sent to the eastward. August 12th, they surprised Norridgewock, destroyed the town, killed thirty or forty men, among whom were six noted warriors and Father Rasle, the chief agent under De Vaudreuil, in fomenting the war. The following

French account of his death is utterly irreconcilable with that of the English. Charlevoix says the attacking force was,—

1100 men, part English, part Indians * * * The noise and tumult gave Father Rasle notice of the danger his converts were in. Not intimidated he went to meet the enemy, in hopes to draw all their attention to himself, and secure his flock at the peril of his own life. He was not disappointed. As soon as he appeared, the English set up a great shout, which was followed by a shower of shot, and he fell down dead near to a cross which he had erected in the midst of the village, seven Indians who accompanied him to shelter him with their own bodies, falling dead round about him * * * The English first fell to pillaging, then burning the wigwams. They spared the church so long as was necessary for their shamefully profaning the sacred vessels, and the adorable body of Jesus Christ, and then set fire to it * * * The Indians returned to their village, where they made it their first care to weep over the body of their holy missionary. They found him shot in a thousand places, scalped, his skull broke to pieces with the blows of hatchets, his mouth and eyes full of mud, the bones of his legs fractured, and all his members mangled in a hundred different ways.

This charge of barbarity in the treatment of the body of Father Rasle is held by some Romanists to be true, and brought by them against the English, to offset, or palliate, the wanton cruelty so often practiced by the French and Indians in their raids against New England. But such an outrage on the body of the missionary was not only contrary to the habits and character of New England people, but there is not a particle of evidence to support the charge of Charlevoix. De Vaudreuil, who must have had all the accessible facts, writing to the home government, Nov. 18th, only three months after the event, says: "All the circumstances attending the affair deserve to be fully narrated; you will permit me not to omit any of them," and then gives the following details of the affair:—

Father Rasle * * * went out of his house on hearing the noise, but the moment he made his appearance the English fired a volley at him by which he was immediately killed. Those of the Indians who possessed not the courage to resist, fled towards the river as soon as they perceived the Father was slain * * * The mass of the village which escaped amounts to 150 persons, among whom there still remain 29 warriors, who were so incensed at the death of their Missionary, and the profanation of the sacred vessels belonging to their church, that they would have pursued the English the day following their defeat, had they not found themselves without arms, powder and clothes.

The next spring, April 24th, 1725, De Vaudreuil and Father de la Chasse, Superior of the Jesuits in Canada, unite in sending to the War minister an account of the same affair. This agrees in every particular with the account given above. In neither is there the slightest hint of any indignity to the body of the fallen missionary. The omission of such a charge against the English can only be accounted for on the ground that there was no foundation for it whatever.

The truth seems to be, that Father Rasle was killed in the heat of the attack, while encouraging his charge in defending themselves; that even his death under these circumstances was against the moral sense of the English commander, and that pretexts were sought to excuse the English soldiers. Capt. Harman did not perhaps know, so well as it is known to-day, that his death was justifiable, on the ground that to him more than to any other the opening and continuance of the war was directly chargeable.

The following is the English version of the event taken from Hutchinson's History of Massachusetts, p. 282. After the Indians had been driven across the river,—

The English then returned to the town, where they found the Jesuit in one of the wigwams, firing upon a few of our men who had not pursued after the enemy. He had an English boy in the wigwam with him about fourteen years of age, who had been taken about six months before. This boy he shot through the thigh and afterwards stabbed in the body, but, by the care of the surgeons he recovered. I find this act of cruelty in the account given by [Capt.] Harman on oath: Moulton had given orders not to kill the Jesuit, but, by his firing from the wigwam, one of our men being wounded, a lieutenant Jaques, stove open the door and shot him through the head. Jaques excused himself to his commanding officer, alledging that Ralle was loading his gun when he entered the wigwam, and declared he would neither give nor take quarter. Moulton allowed that some answer was made by Ralle, which provoked Jaques, but doubted whether it was the same as reported, and always expressed his disapprobation of the action.

August 17th, 1724, Col. Schuyler writes to Stoddard:—

I send you the answer what Jacob and his company brought from Canada * * * Note that the Cagnawagoes and Scawinadees stand strict and honorable by there former Resolution and promise * * * There is now againe fourty Indians Gone Against your Gov^t but I know not where they will make there attempt

Later advices show that somebody is mistaken. Aug. 23d, 1724, Capt. Kellogg writes Stoddard the news that four of his

Macquas brought from Albany about the messengers which the Five Nations sent to carry a Belt to the Caghnawagas—one "to take the hatchet away," the other to invite them to a Conference at Albany. In reply to the first they returned "an Extraordinary Large Belt of Wampum w^c was very much redded & told y^m you our fathers of ye Six Nations say we take the hatchet out of your hands. but these are to aquaint y^t we shall not deliver it up but shall still war against ye English," giving as a reason that the English have taken away their land and keep their Hostages in prison.

They also report a Conference between the Caghnawaga and the Eastern Indians before the governor of Canada.

This last item explains the action of the Caghnawagas in the first. De Vaudreuil never let slip an opportunity of keeping the Indians on the war path towards New England.

Aug. 17th, 1724, Col. Stoddard writes to Dummer:—

> I hoped that the enemy, (who have been very troublesome to us) were drawn off, but we are again informed from Fort Dummer that their scouts have discovered tracks of several Indians coming towards us, but we have had that advantage, that not one party of the enemy has passed the fort without being discovered and seasonable notice given, which hath undoubtedly been a means of preserving many lives. The like discovery we were never able to make in any former war. Several parties of the Enemy have been afraid to return their usual way but by Hooseck, which is near Albany.

Fort Dummer was Stoddard's pet, and did good service; but the notices did not always prevent disaster, nor was this possible, while the subtle enemy had only to lurk and wait until a favorable opportunity offered, when the stroke came like a flash of lightning.

August 25th, Noah Edwards, while going with others from Easthampton to Northampton with a load of hay, was shot and scalped, and Abraham Miller was wounded. The next day a party of the enemy, probably the same that shot Edwards, appeared at Westfield. An Englishman was wounded, and one of the assailants, a Scatacook, was killed by Noah Ashley, who received £100 for his scalp. The chiefs of this tribe said that he had deserted and gone to Canada, and they were not responsible for his conduct.

August 27th, Col. Pynchon writes to Lieut. John Root at Westfield, concerning,—

> The Mischief done at Northampton upon the Rhode Saturday,

nere unto Joseph Bartlett's house, about 4 score Rodds from s^d House toward Northampton, which alarms us to be carefull in o^r going out, & I advise & order that you be very careful in yor goeing out, not to goe, near or further of, from town with less in number than 12 or 15 men to guard & before any work is done to scout the wood Round about the place where the work is done before they goe to work & the Guards to be very Watchfull all the tyme they are out; * * * Also to give notice of this mischief to the Carters and Guards coming from Hartfort.

High hopes had been entertained after the treaty of July 3d, 1724, but no important result followed. The Abenakis were not intimidated by the threats of the Iroquois. Their messengers sent to Canada were told the war should be prosecuted until the English gave up the land and hostages of the Abenakis. Those Mohawks who went eastward pretended, at least, to have been convinced of the justness of the Abenakis' claim. The Iroquois, when upbraided by Gov. Burnett, in a conference at Albany, Sept. 14th, for not keeping their promise, say they only offered "to be mediators for Peace." On being further pressed, and confronted with their language of July 3d, they said they would give the English Commissioners an answer. On the 16th this was given. They tell the English that they had sent messengers three times to the Abenakis, who said they would make peace on the "Return of the Land and the hostages, and the matter respecting peace seems to lye with you. All mankind is not without thinking, and our thoughts are, that the delivering up the Hostages is the likeliest way for Peace. * * * If we should make a war it would not end in a few days as yours doth, but must last till one nation or the other is destroyed, as it hath been heretofore with us." This is plain Indian common sense. They also say they have no answer to the belt sent to the King of England on the subject.

In a speech to them Sept. 19th, Governor Burnett again charges the Iroquois with bad faith. "I find you do not deny your promises, but only you say, wait for King of Great Britian's orders in answer to your Belt. Now this is not a just Pretence. * * * You know very well you have promised that if the Eastern Indians did not accept your last messengers you would take up the Hatchet, and you ought to stand to this." In their reply to the Governor's speech, the next day, the Iroquois with diplomatic silence entirely ignore the

Eastern question; making no reply to this charge. In a conference with the Scatacooks, Sept. 19th, Gov. Burnett accuses them of harboring and furnishing supplies to the hostile Indians, and allowing some of their men to join in the war against New England. They reply, that those who have deserted and gone to Canada are seeking revenge; for two years ago they were "arrested while hunting, and shut up in Boston jail." [They had been mistaken for enemies, and were soon released.] When again urged to join the English against the Abenakis, they finally say, "the Belt they sent King George concerning the war has not been answered, and you are our father, and the Six Nations our Leaders, where they go we shall follow." The truth seems to be, that the Iroquois had no notion of going to war, but confidently expected their threats would frighten the Abenakis into yielding to the English demands. This doubtless would have been the result, but for French encouragement. De Vaudreuil says it "Seriously intimidated them," and "cooled them down considerably," but having more favorable news "he hopes shortly to make them to act with more vigor."

The policy of both the English and French towards the Indians, looked solely to their own respective security or agrandizement, with no regard whatever to the effect on the native tribes. The wonder is, that the Indians were able to match them so ably as they did, in shrewdness and statecraft.

September 2d, the Massachusetts General Court authorized Col. Schuyler "to give the Six Nations one thousand pounds, if they will come into ye war with the Eastern Indians."

September 2d, Timothy Childs of Deerfield was appointed Commissary for Hampshire county and was directed to send £300 in goods to Fort Dummer for the use of the Indians and others in the service there.

September 4th, Capt. Kellogg reports to Gov. Dummer that he continues scouting "as usual up the River & then Eastward, that it might be the best security to the Towns below, but have made no Late Discovery." It was the duty of Lieut. Childs to look after the west side of the river, and Stoddard thought it best that he should be made captain, and command that part of Kellogg's company then at Deerfield and the men at Sunderland. Kellogg says he "is very free

Lieut. Childs shall be set off, in case it don't Hazzard my pay, nor the pay of under officers." Childs was commissioned captain Oct. 7th, 1724, and stationed in Deerfield. The following shows service not elsewhere found:—

DEERFIELD Sept 9, 1724

These may Testifie whome it may concerne that I came in to This Plase with a company of Inglish and Indians for ye Defence of this place and were entertaind by Capt Thomas Wells his order till ye 14th Instant, ye Number of men 43.

This 14th Day of Sep^{tr} 1724   JOHN MASON Capt.

He probably brought the Pequods and Nianticks Partridge speaks of below.

HATFIELD, Oct. 1 1724

Honorable S^r I am to inform yor Hono^r of a very troubelsome summer we have had in getting in o^r Harvests, the Indian Harvest not all gott in yet ye Enemy frequently discovered by their trals lying in waite to shed blood & some they have as I suppose you^r Honou^r hath heard from tyme to tyme so that we have been working with perrill of our lives. 15 20 30 40 in a Company with Guards, the Coniticott Forces have been very helpfull to us in this County & speak off drawing off in a fortnight or 3 weeks time, our Forces expend much of o^r stores of amnition I am forc't to supply them with some for which I have good governo^r Saltonstons engage^{mt} to answer o^r Government for itt of which I shall be ready to give account of it

If the war Continue there will be great need of more amnition be sent up to Hartford now while vessels are goeing, I am sorry we have no better success with the Mohawks but we must put o^r trust in God in vain is the help of Man

with my humble duty, submission & obedience I am yor very humble Servt   SAM^{ll} PARTRIDGE

The following letter shows a new cause for anxiety and caution:—

ALBANY ye 5th of Octo^r 1724

Col Stoddard, Sir This accompanys my Former Letter wrote you by Sekekeko and his companion dated ye 30th Last past You will understand my meaning therein, these Indians went *via* Shagtekoke as they came from hunting above Saretogue they seen a Large path of a number of Inds butt could not directly guise what the number might bee but the path went directly towards N E. as y^y say. And the said Indians of Skagtekoke told y^m y^t ye Onongongus had laid way for y^m in ye Road upon which [illegible] I have consulted by myself and concluded to dispatch ye bearer hereof John Tyson with ye enclosed and these

There is since my last unto you nott ans^d any one from Canada neither Indians or christians. I shall not at p^rsent Enlarge but my due Respects as in my former. I am S^r your Humble Servt

JOHN SCHUYLER

This letter was forwarded to Boston from Northampton, Oct. 12th, with the following letter from Stoddard to the Governor and Council:—

I received your Hon'rs of the 6th. There are now no Indians in the Block House, save two Mohikans [i. e. Mahicans] or River Indians. All the Macquas went to Albany at the last treaty. Since my coming from thence I hear nothing about their young men. I rec'd the enclosed letter by express last Wednesday; our people are pretty much alarmed therewith. I am ready to imagine that it is [Cattanawlet's?] son who is cos'n to Grey Lock, that hath either made or aggravated the story of tracks, to afright the Indians & prevent their bringing the letter, presuming that in it was an account of Grey Lock being out, but I dare not mention such a thing to our people, lest it should make them too secure. This Cattanawlet is a French Indian & was in Deerfield Meadows when our people were wounded & from thence he ran to Scatacook, there married a squaw & is suffered to dwell there.

In the former part of the summer there were 42 Connecticut Indians at Deerfield, Moheags & Nehanticks, as likely men as I have seen. They drew off & near 40 Pequods & Nehanticks supplied their place. The Pequods look pretty well, but the people at Deerfield say they can't compare with the Moheags, not being so active, & unused to the woods; there is some misunderstanding between them & they don't do well together; there are some some likely Indians at Farmington & Hartford. I hear the Moheags incline to come up hither again in the winter. * * * Capt. Wright & others have pretended to make some marches, but their designs have dropped through & I don't expect anything will be done this way before winter; but I cannot be weaned from the expedition proposed to your Hon'rs last winter when Govr Saltonstall was here.

He gives details of the proposed march to Canada. To guard against discovery, and insure a surprise, he would "send two Indians with a belt of wampum to Grey Locks place to invite the Scatakooks to return home, and to the St. Francis to let them know we delight not in blood, but are willing to hearken to any reasonable terms of peace; or it matters not what message."

Capt. Kellogg, at Northfield, could not be depended on to intercept the enemy. He had written Oct. 7th, 1724, "'Tis difficult keeping a scout out constantly, by reason of guarding ye people, who are now busy getting in ye harvest. I have a scout out now, ordered to go 40 miles up ye Great River, and from there to the eastward to Great Monadnock."

The party about whose movements Schuyler warned Stoddard, October 5th, did not appear on our frontiers. Schuyler writes October 24th:—

Since my last to you am assured of the french Indians of Cagnawaga & the Shaweenade have hitherto kept the Treaty here made with you and can have no other design than continuance of the same by them two tribes. Here have been since your departure above 20 Canoes: Two Days ago hendrick and six more Mohawk Indians came here to offer their services to your government, on which condition I have delivered them the following things out of your stores left in my hands: 4 guns, 6 shirts, 30 lbs lead, 3lbs powder, 4 hatchets & 4 cutlashes: 6 knives, some spirits, paint, and one blanket, hope they may be of Service to the government in some way or other. If one or more should happen to be killed in the service. I believe it would animate the others to revenge the cause

Pray make my Respects acceptable to your ffather, mother and all other aquaintance and you[l] oblige S[r] your friend and Humble Sev[t]

JOHN SCHUYLER

Schuyler sends the same to Gov. Dummer by Mr. Trescot "who will be able to give you an account of the proceedings in Canada where he has been a prisoner for some time."

These seven Indians appeared in the Council Chamber at Boston, November 17th, offering their services against the Eastern Indians, and were accepted by the Governor.

November 6th, Stoddard, writing Dummer, says he is supplying the Indians with extra stores, to keep them quiet. Thinks there will be no danger until the last of January, or February, when the enemy may come on snow shoes. November 17th, he writes, "The Block House has been of great service; notice was received from there of every party of the enemy that came by that route, saving many lives by putting people on their guard. I have been obliged to guard the men while gathering crops in the distant fields, or several people must have lost their corn and other fruits." He thinks Grey Lock has gone back. The frontiers were too well guarded for successful forays. And it may be doubted whether any Indians left Canada after the news of the disaster to the Norridgewocks, and the death of Father Rasle August 12th; and there appeared an evident desire for peace.

To test the feelings of the Eastern Indians, Saccamakton, one of the Abenaki hostages from Norridgewock, was sent home on parole for six weeks. Saccamakton was true to his engagements, and it was through him that peace was finally established.

Capt. Thomas Wells of Deerfield had command of a company this year. His muster roll has not been found, but in December, 1724, he was allowed for their pay £162, 4s, 6d, and for subsistence £90, 12 s, 10 d, with £9 for funeral charges for soldiers. To pay off sergeants' commands in Hampshire county, £64, 4 s, 6 d was put into his hands December 21st, and £90, 10 s, 12 d, for subsistence. Capt. Samuel Barnard of Deerfield was stationed at Hadley, with about 100 men. Lieut. Timothy Childs was commissary, and the supplies for Fort Dummer passed through his hands. He was commissioned lieutenant under Capt. Kellogg in October, and stationed in Deerfield. Sergt. Joseph Clesson had a scout under his command, and received in December, £32, 1 s, 6 d, for their wages and subsistence.

Among the expenses of the campaign of 1724, three Macquas, "Christian, his son Christian, and Isaac" were paid 40 s per week for five weeks.

On such muster rolls of Fort Dummer as I have found were Ezerus, Kewakcum and Cosannip, under the Mohawk Sachem Hendrick. Wakumtameeg, Poopornuck, Ponagum, Suckkeecoo, Noonoowannet, Waunoowooseet and Taukaquint, Scatacooks, under Ampaumeet of Hudson River.

When the rivers and lakes were frozen and the snow was the deepest, the enemy were the most to be feared, and parties constantly ranged the woods to prevent a surprisal of the settlements. Capt. Kellogg reports to Gov. Dummer the journals of those sent out by him in the winter of 1724–5. The story is that of the every day duty by soldiers guarding the frontiers, told in the fewest words. We must look through the matter-of-fact language for the underlying heroism and romance, to see the brave hearts, tough fibre and high sense of duty, which carried these men through the cold, the snow, and the danger. We should see them tramping all day through interminable forest, on cumbersome snow shoes, gun in hand, hatchet and bullet pouch at the belt, pack with provisions and blanket on the back; with senses all alert, the strained ear noting every sound, the trained eye peering behind every tree, scanning every thicket, and snuffing the very air for signs of the foe. They would be found camping in the snow where the falling night finds them; eating in silence their scanty supper of salt pork, raw and frozen it may be, with no fire to warm their benumbed bodies, with no song or story to cheer their spirits; cutting with muffled strokes of the hatchet a bed of spruce or hemlock boughs;

with a watchful sentinel standing a little apart, the rest of the wearied men stretching themselves in their blankets to pass the long and dreary night as best they may; shivering under the driving blast, or cased, perchance, in icy armor of frozen rain; fortunate, indeed, if they found themselves in the morning, sheltered under a blanket of soft-falling snow. Harder and more tedious than all this, was lying inactive for days together on the bleak summits of the highest mountains, watching for smoke from the fire of an incautious enemy. Only constitutions of iron could endure these hardships unharmed; and the gravestones of those generations testify to the cost of such service. Kellogg says:—

> The first scout on Nov. 30, 1724, went up on ye west side of Connecticut River & crossing ye West river went up to ye Great Falls, and returned, making no discovery of the enemy. The second scout went up to West river & followed up s^d river 6 miles, & then crossed the woods to ye Great Falls & returned seeing no new signs of ye enemy. The third scout went west from Northfield about 12 miles, then northward crossing West river, and steering east came to the canoe place about 16 or 17 miles above Northfield * * * The fourth struck out northwest about 6 miles, thence north across West river & so to the Great Meadow below ye Great Falls, then crossed the Connecticut river, and came down on the east side. This meadow is about 32 miles from Northfield. The fifth, the men were sent up West river mountain [Wantastiquat] there to lodge on the top, and view morning and evening for smoaks, and from there up to ye Mountain at ye Great Falls, & there also to lodge on ye top, and view morning and evening for smoaks. The sixth went up to West river, which they followed 5 miles, then went north till they came upon Saxton's river, six miles from the mouth of it, which empties itself at ye foot of ye Great Falls; then they came down to the mouth of it, & so returned. In addition we watch & ward 3 forts at Northfield continually, besides what those 10 men do at Deerfield, & ye people are uneasy that we have no more men to keep ye forts than we have.

Some of these scouts penetrate to the lake, and even to the borders of Canada. The employment of Indian scouts, and the permission of the Mohegans and Scatacook Indians, to hunt in our woods, added much to the difficulties of scouting. If by means of smoke, or otherwise, an Indian camp was discovered, the scout must not fall upon the occupants until their spies could discover their character,—a service of peculiar delicacy and danger, requiring the utmost circumspection, knowledge of wood-craft and judgment. A fatal mistake would rouse a whole clan to vengeance. To facilitate recognition, the authorities required these hunting Indians to wear some distinguishing mark on their heads, but the difficulty the scout must find in discovering this sign, under all conditions, is too obvious to need comment.

The successful campaign of Capt. Lovewell in December, and his unfortunate one in April following, are too well known to need detailing here. In their effects on the campaign, one neutralized the other. For a full and interesting account of Lovewell's fight see Gen. Hoyt's Antiquarian Researches, page 216.

Men under Capt. Joseph Kellogg in Northfield & Deerfield in 1724:—

Lieut. John Pomroy, Northampton.
Sergt. Josiah Stebbins, "
Sergt. Waitstill Strong, "
Corp. Jas. Stephenson, Suffield.
Corp. Japhet Chapin, Northfield.
Corp. Benoni Wright, "
Eldad Wright, "
Stephen Belden, "
Jonathan Belden, "
Hezekiah Stratton, "
Eleazer Mattoon, "
Edward Grandy, "
Hezekiah Elmer, "
Benjamin Brooks, Deerfield.
Joshua Wells, "
James Corse, "
Nathaniel Hawks, "
George Swan, "
Nathaniel Brooks, "
John Allen, "
Daniel Severance, "
John King, Northampton.
Orlando Bridgman, "
James Porter, "

Asahel Stebbins, Northampton.
David Smith, Suffield.
Ebenezer Smith, "
Joseph Allen, "
Eb. Williams, Hatfield.
Joseph Burt, "
Samuel Bedortha, Springfield.
Shem Chapin, "
Abraham Elger, servant to Rev. Mr. Doolittle, Northfield.
Jonathan Warriner, Springfield.
Benjamin Bedortha, "
Benjamin Miller, "
Benjamin Munn, "
Daniel King, Westfield.
John Beaman, "
Samuel Vining, Enfield.
John Brown, "
Enoch Hall, Westfield.
Joseph Merchant, Hadley.
George Bates, "
John Seargant, Worcester.
Daniel Shattuck, "
Josiah King, Clerk.

About December 1st, 1724, Dummer received dispatches from De Vaudreuil, through Col. Schuyler, who wrote him by the same post: "Mons. Vaudreuil is very sorry and weary of the war & would willingly see one or two gentlemen empowered by New England governments to endeavour to put an end to that war." Believing this story, with which the wily Frenchman had imposed upon the honest Dutchmen, to be true, the Governor on the 24th of December, appointed William Dudley and Col. Stoddard Commissioners to go to Canada in response to its suggestion. Dudley, Samuel Thaxter, and Thomas Atkinson of New Hampshire were finally sent. They were accompanied by Schuyler, and reached Montreal March 3d, 1725, N. S.

1725. The project of harassing the Canadian frontiers by large war parties was a subject of much correspondence. Feb. 3d, Col. Stoddard in reply to a letter from Gov. Dummer says:—

I retain my former opinion that if our people had gone to Grey Locks fort (which lyeth up a small river which emptieth itself into the Lake near the further end of it) [at Missisquoi bay] and had made spoil upon the Indians, those that should escape would in their rage meditate revenge upon our Commissioners, either in going to or returning from Canada; but an expedition there in the spring, about the time of planting corn, which they wont suppose the Commissioners privy to, may not be attended with like inconvenience; tho' I think ordinarily men are in less danger in the winter & more likely to be successful. Since my last to y^r Honor Lieut Pomroy hath aquainted me that about thirty of Capt Kelloggs best soldiers offer to goe out this winter or rather early in the spring

There hath likewise some of Deerfield men been with me to manifest their desire to go out with a small party in the spring and to ly on some Rivers in [——]

They say there are eight men at Deerfield some of which are men of Estate & have been prisoners with the Indians, and know there maners. They propose to add some from the lower towns but would not have their number exceed twenty.

I am in a great measure a Stranger to the Business of the Commissioners, and so incapable to Judge whither such Enterprises are consistant with there affairs or what the consequences of doing spoil on the enemy at this Juncture may be, but doe assure our people that in case we should be advised that a Truce should be agreed on then all designs against the Enemy must be laid aside. But if your Hon^r think it expedient, I think it probable that parties may be raised amongst us to go to the upper part of St. Francis river, where these Indians plant, or towards the head of Connecticut river, where the Indians hunt, or to the Amanoosuck, which emptieth into the Connecticut River & is the Common road from St. Francis to Amascoggin, & to the East Country, or to Grey Locks fort, and possibly to all of them, provided y^o be allowed to assure the men of such encouragment as they shall Judge reasonable. but they will be slow to go wholly on uncertainties. it will be needful that your mind be known as soon as may be, for it will soon be time to make canoes for such as go by water.

Yesterday two of the Moheage Indians were with me, and say that most of their people are at Springfield and a little below Enfield they Suppose, to be here next week to take directions where they shall hunt. I suppose they may be allowed to hunt on Swift river, Ware river, Pequoquag & about Monadnock, but not to pass Contocook river eastward. I presume your Hon^r will advise the officers at Dunstable and the other neighboring towns although I think their scouts seldom if ever goe so far westward. When I have opportunity I shall learn their disposition about going to war.

I am y^r Hon^{rs} most humb^l Ser^{vt}
JOHN STODDARD.

Joseph Lyman was paid thirty shillings to go post to Boston with this and other letters.

Dummer replies Feb. 8th. He agrees,—

That to send any parties into the French Country at this juncture will very much hazzard the safety of our Commissioners. However I have taken advice of His Maj^{ts} Council upon your proposal of sending twenty men of Deerfield and other Towns to waylay the Indians, and they have voted the encouragment for that small party, *viz*, that they be allowed half a crown per Day each man (they to find themselves with provisions) during there being out upon actual service and for the time necessary for fitting themselves out and that they be entitled to the same Rewards for scalps & prisoners as the volunteers without pay provided you cannot agree with them at any Lower Rates, and I desire you would accordingly encourage there designe. But for any marches into the French Country we must not think of it

Should likewise have Capt Kellogg's men that have offered themselves sent out upon such service as you shall judge most promising of success. The Indians must not come hunting East of Ware & Swift rivers at present, for parties are out about Monadnock scouting, and can't get notice.

The following is given as a specimen of the marching orders issued when scouting parties were sent into the woods. The place, the kind of service and time is usually carefully defined. This was made out in blank by Secretary Willard.

S^r these are to direct you forthwith to prepare for a march along Meremack River up to Winnepesaukee Ponds with the Company under your immediate Command including the men posted at Dracut together with the Comp of Capt Josiah Willard who is hereby ordered to attend your Directions in this Affair & proceed with you on the aforesaid march. Let him therefore be forthwith advertised hereof that he may have his Company in due Readiness You must give orders for the making five or six Canooes of white Pine for the more Convenient Conveyance of your Baggage & setting your People over & along the Rivers & Ponds

Lett the said Canooes be so made as to be as little expensive to the Province as may be in wch you may direct to employ your soldiers at cheapest rate you can. You must begin your March the 25th day of this month if the weather be favorable & the Rivers & Ponds be open enough for such an undertaking If otherwise as soon as you can with Convenience. You must scour all the Country adjoining to the River & the branches thereof Especially the small hunting & fishing Places of the Enemy in those parts, and always have a very careful & vigilent scout on each side the River for discovery: You must take the utmost care that your Marches be performed with the greatest Secrecy & Silence, wch is absolutely necessary for your Success herin: It will be best for you to carry provisions for thirty or forty days

If you have Opportunity of exchanging your men that are not on all acconts so fit for the service for such as are more capable & effective you have my Leave & Order to make such exchanges from Time to Time as such Occasions shall offer which is agreable to my verbal Order to you formerly

Probably this order was made out for Col. Tyng, but for some reason never issued.

As should have been foreseen, the attempt to make a treaty of peace with the Eastern Indians in Canada came to naught. It was the settled policy of the French to keep the Indians up to the fighting point as long as possible, and on his own ground, De Vaudreuil had every needed advantage.

March 16th, the Commissioners held a conference with De Vaudreuil. To their demand of the restitution of the English prisoners taken by the Abenakis, he said he had no control over those in the hands of the Indians, but those ransomed by the French should be given up. At another conference the next day, the Commissioners demanded that the supply of food, ammunition &c., to the Abenakis, should be stopped. The Governor replied, that what had been given them was only the annual present from the French King; that the English were to blame if these things were used against them, as they had provoked the war. De Vaudreuil "is entirely governed by Pere La Chasse the chief of the Jesuits." At another meeting on the 18th, the Commissioners asserted that the lands in dispute had been bought of the Abenakis, and showed deeds from the Indians. The reply was that the Abenakis did not acknowledge these deeds, and declared them forgeries. We told the Governor, they say, "We desire no grace or favor from him but Demand only Justice." If he would not favor a peaceful issue "he must be looked upon by God & man as the instigator of the war, which we could & did prove by his other letters & the hindrance of Peace." His course is vacillating, "one today another tomorrow," don't know how things will come out. "But if the governor had that Stedynes & Sway he ought only to have we should have nothing to doubt." They doubtless give De Vaudreuil more credit for integrity than the result warranted.

April 24th, the Commissioners met deputies of the Abenakis at Montreal. De Vaudreuil says in a letter to France that he was "not in the humor to dispose the Abenakis to a peace," and told them before they spoke to the English "that it was not enough to demand the demolition of the forts on their territory, or the restitution of their land and prisoners, but that the death of Father Rasle, and the burning of their church, ought to make them demand heavy indemnities, without which, they ought not to listen to any proposal for peace or a suspension of hostilities."

It was in accordance with this advice that, at the meeting with the Commissioners, "the chiefs of the Abenakis spoke with such haughtiness and firmness to the English," says De Vaudreuil, "that so far from agreeing together on any point, they separated with dispositions very adverse to peace." The Abenakis claimed all the land so far west as the "River Gownitigon, otherwise called the Long River, [Connecticut] which was formeyly the boundary which separated the lands of the Iroquois from those of the Abenakis," but would give up all to one league west of the Saco. They also demanded suitable presents to atone for the death of Father Rasle and the destruction of their church. The English promised to report at Boston and the mission ended. The Commissioners left Canada, April 26th, N. S., and reached Albany, May 1st, O. S., 1725. The action of De Vaudreuil was approved at home. He is told "nothing better can be done than foment this war." As we return to the events of 1725 it will appear that he was not negligent in that direction.

Lieut. Timothy Childs' bill for a sick soldier at Mr. Williams's:—

Six Weeks attendance by Rev. John Williams' Maid, 4d,	0	1	4
4 pounds Sugar 4s, 1 Pt wine 1s, Spice of Sundry sorts, 2s,	0	7	0
Horse for messenger to Northfield, 13 miles,	0	2	2
Horse for messenger to Hatfield, 13 miles,	0	2	2
Horse for messenger to Northampton, 18 miles,	0	3	0

April 24, 1725.   Allowed.

March 20th, 1725, Schuyler writes Gov. Dummer that he has been sounding the St. Francis Indians, and that it appears they intend to make peace with the English next June.

Dummer writes Stoddard to "send a messenger to conciliate Grey Lock, & to try to get him to come in, & assure him not only of safety & protection, but of kindness & good usage."

April 19th, 1725, Capt. John Ashley writes from Westfield asking for six or eight men to guard the workmen in the fields. He says, "We have no news from our Gent^{ln} that are gone to Canada, neither from Capt Wells, neither from Albany, but only a gentleman sends to us to be careful as he expected the Indenss would be revenged on us for the Inden wee kiled of thars at my farme."

By the following letter from Partridge to the Governor, April 21st, 1725, it appears that there was so little expectation of peace in high quarters, that preparations were being made for another winter campaign. Partridge sent a list " of men that are ffixed with snow shoes & Mogesens on the west side of the river," there were thirty in Hatfield "under Sergt John Waite their leader;" twenty in West Springfield "under Sergt Henry Rogers their Leader." He continues:—

We hear nothing from o^r Gentlemen that went to Canada, nor from Capt Wells & about 65 men that have been out one month or more I pray God we may heare good when it comes, the hand of God is much upon the several Towns upon o^r River in Sore Sickness & many deaths. [In a postscript he adds,] Before sealing this Lett^r I perceive there is news from Canada & in this mynett I Rec'd yor Hon^{rs} Lett^r dated April 2 1725 & shall attend to yor ord^{rs} therein directed

This news came in a letter from Capt. Ashley of Westfield. It had been sent him from Albany by Philip Schuyler, who had dispatches from the Commissioners in Canada. Philip Schuyler writing from Albany, April 8th, says, "Your gentlemen in Canada desired me to let you know that all the enemy Indians was out in order to invade your frontiers, & were gone before their arrival." This was as unexpected as startling. A meeting of the military officers was held at Hatfield and a post was sent Gov. Dummer with Ashley's letter and the dispatch from Canada. Stoddard writes by same post. He says:—

April 21, 1724

Many of o^r Towns are in a poor Condition, as particularly Westfield Nth Hampton Hatfield Sunderland and Hadly, having no soldiers to scout or cover there laborers in there out Fields and in case we employ any men in such service the government refuses to pay them so that many of our people are in a fair way to be ruined, altho they escape the Enemy Col Partridge hath sent a copy of Capt Ashleys letter to Gov Talcott, but I dont expect any good effect of it. Some think it very strange that our Gentlemen [in Canada] should write only two letters one to y^r Hon^r the other to Mr Schuyler unless they are under some restraint We have not heard anything from Capt Wells.

Three days later the result of his expedition and sad ending was known to Stoddard.

March 9th, 1725, Capt. Thos. Wells of Deerfield led a scouting party of sixty-five men out towards the frontiers of Canada. They came back on the Connecticut river in canoes. April 24th, one of these, containing Lieut. Joseph Clesson, Samuel Harman, James Porter, Simeon Pomroy, Thomas Alexander and Noah Ashley, was upset in the rapids at the "French King," near the mouth of Millers river, and the three last named were drowned. The others reached land with great difficulty with the loss of all their arms and effects.

The next news from the Commissioners is contained in the following letter to Dummer:—

ALBANY April 27 1725

Sr The enclos^d I rec'd to be forwarded to New Hampshire from Mr Atkinson who I expect here in 10 or 12 days from Canada wth Mr Dudley. Col Thackster, Capt Kellogg & Jourdain remain at Canada sometime Mr Vaudreuils Sonn goes to Boston wth Col Dudley as a token of Peace this was the last agreement [between?] Vaudreuil & ye Boston gente as I am advised by my sonn who has been always present at all conferences, by a l^{re} of ye 8th Instant

Pray forward the enclosed by the first opportunity as I was desired to do but not by express. In doing wch you^l oblige him who has wrote you in former times 50 L^{trs} from Col. Schuyler my dead brother in law & who now is S^r at your Command & y^{re} very Humble Servt. JOHN COLLINS

Excuse haste

Partridge to Dummer, "Hatfield, 14 May 1725 * * * Although the River is pretty well guarded by the Fort & men at Nfd & Dfd, yet Sund Had Nh Hat Westf^d Rutland & Brookfield are now more exposed" Thinks there is no prospect of peace, and all the people much exposed. It is hard to spend so much time watching and scouting and "all without pay from the publique & carry on their Husbandry affairs, especially when they get there Bread with the perrill of there lives & now & then men snatched away by a Secret undiscoverable enemy til men are shott down."

May 1st, Edward Allen petitions the General Court to be exempt from watching on account of infirmity, and says he is this day 62 years old, and has for forty-six years faithfully performed his duty in that service.

May 22d, Sunderland feels the need of guards and petitions through the selectmen for help. They represent that,—

We being very [poor?] living altogether by husbandry, our lands not being thoroughly subdued & lying scattered & remote from one another, & compassed round on the wilderness side with thick swamps, fit receptacle for the enemy to hide & lurk in to our damage, hath occasioned our maintaining in the last year a considerable time a scout and guard of our own men at our own charge (as yet) for the covering our labors.

SAMUEL GUNN,
ISAAC HUBBARD, } Selectmen.
JOSEPH FIELD,

This season the agressive policy was settled upon by the authorities as the best protection for the frontiers. Dummer suggested to Capt. Benj. Wright to raise a company of volunteers to go against the Indian settlements in Canada. Wright replies, May 29th,—

I am very willing to go & do what I can but ye undertaking being so difficult & ye fitting out so chargable y^t ye men cant possably go upon the encouragement but if there was suitable encouragement, no doubt ye men would go (but ye unhappy loss of men by ye mismanagement of ye officers has very much dispirited people young & old) and it seems to me the most probable place to be obtained & the most serviceable when done is Massesquich, Grey Locks fort.

Partridge writing the Governor the same day advises that Capt. Wright's party be "allowed double pay [5 s] if after 6 or 7 weeks they return with scalps." He fears the enemy are on our borders, and "parties of 30 or 40 go out together to their work." It was probably this caution that saved them from attack, and the planting season passed without molestation. Meanwhile Wright's expedition was settled upon, and Kellogg at Northfield and Dwight at Dummer, were directed "to make up (by volunteers, or by impressment of good men,) his company to 60 or 70 men." The journal of the march is given entire as illustrating this kind of service at first hand. A large discount must be made of the estimated distance. It would be surprising if the miles did not seem very long to these tired men. Wright probably followed one of the usual paths of the enemy in coming against the river towns, and struck the lake at the mouth of French river, about seventy-five miles from the point of his destination. It will be seen that the home march was made with surprising celerity. No visible results followed this expedition beyond defining a line of march for future service.

A true Journal of our March from N Field to Misixcouh bay under yᵉ Command of Benj. Wright, captain, began July 27, Ano Dom, 1725.

July 27. It rained in yᵉ forenoon; about 2 o'clock in yᵉ afternoon I set out from N Field; being fifty nine of us & we came yᵗ night to Pumroys Island, 5 miles above Northfield.

28. We set off from Pumroys Island & came to Fort Dummer & there we mended our canoes & went yᵗ night to Hawleys Island 5 miles above Fort Dummer, in all 10 miles.

29. We departed from Hawleys Island & came to a meadow 2 miles short of yᵉ Great Falls, 18 miles.

30. We set off from yᵉ great meadow & came to yᵉ Great Falls & carried our canoes across & from there we went 10 miles.

31. From there we set off & came within 3 miles of Black river, 17 miles.

August 1. We came to yᵉ 2d falls, 15 miles.

2. We set off from hence & came to the upper end of white river falls 13 miles & ½.

3. From yᵉ upper end of white river falls to paddle Island, 13 miles.

4. Foul weather & we remained on paddle Island all Day.

5. from paddle Island we went up 13 miles & encamped.

6. from thence we came to the third meadow at Cowass, 20 miles yᵗ day.

7. from thence we came to Wells river mouth, 15 miles.

8. We encamped here and hid our provisions & canoes, it being foul weather yᵗ day.

9. foul weather in yᵉ forenoon, in yᵉ afterpart of yᵉ day we marched from the mouth of Wells river N. 5 miles.

10. This day we marched West & by North 10 miles.

11. We marched to yᵉ upper end of yᵉ 2d pond at the head of Wells river upon a N. W. course ten miles. About noon this day we came to yᵉ first pond, 5 miles & then we turned round N. West & travelled 5 miles further in very bad woods.

12. We marched from yᵉ upper end of yᵃ upper pond 3 miles in very bad woods & here encamped by reason of foul weather; here David Allen was taken sick.

13. We lay by to see if Allen would be able to travel.

14. We marched from yᵉ upper end of yᵉ 2d (?) pond W. by N. to French river 9 miles; we crossed yᵉ French river & travelled 1 mile & ½ in all 10 miles & half.

15. Here we encamped all day by reason of foul weather; this day Clerk Hubbard being very lame was sent back & two men with him to the fort at the mouth of Wells river.

16. We marched from our camp 3 miles and came to a branch of yᵉ French river; from thence we marched 6 miles & came to a beaver pond, out of which ran another Branch of said river; from thence we travelled 6 miles & came upon another Branch when we camped, our course being W. N. W. 15

17. We marched from said branch 13 miles & crossed a vast mountain & there we camped that night. 13

18. We marched from our camp a Little & came to a 4th branch of French river & we travelled down sᵈ branch 10 miles & then

struck over ye Mountain 6 miles further & then we camped; our course was W. N. W. 12

19. We marched from thence W. N. W. to the top of a vast high mountain which we called Mount Discovery, where we had a fair prospect of ye lake 4 miles; from whence we went down s^d mountain 2 miles on a N. course & then travelled 6 miles N. W. on a brook; here arose a storm which caused us to take up our lodgings something before night.

20. We followed said brook N. N. W. 9 miles & then ye brook turned N. & we travelled on it 9 miles further & ye brook increased to a considerable river. 18

21. We marched 6 miles N. & then came to where ye river emtyed itself into another very large river coming out from ye east somewhat northerly; we travelled down said river W. 7 miles; then the river turned south & we marched 7 miles further & here we encamped at ye foot of ye falls. 20

22. Here we lay still by reason of rain.

23. Now I gave liberty to some y^t they might return home by reason our provision was almost spent & there appeared 41. The Capt Lt & Ens with 12 men marched over ye river at ye foot of s^d Falls & marched 6 miles S. S. W. & 3 miles W. & y^n came to ye Lake & marched 6 miles down upon ye Lake & this N. W. & y^n N. W. end of ye Lake or bay being at a great distance, & then we turned homeward without making any discovery here of any enemy.

25. We set off from ye Lake to return home & came to ye mouth of Wells river in five days and a half; here we discovered 3 Indians who had waded over ye River just below ye fort which we took to be our own men by reason y^t ye two Indians which were with us & one man more set away early in the morning to hunt; but it proved upon examination that they were enemies, but it was too Late for they were moved off.

29. We set off from ye fort at ye mouth of Wells river & came to Northfield Sept. 2d at Night.

I have given your Honors a true Journal of our marches & submit ye whole to your Honors censure and am your Honors most humble & obedient Sev^t to command. BENJ. WRIGHT.

Sept. 4th, Wright transmits this journal to Gov. Dummer,—

W^h will aquaint your Honour of w^t happened in our journey & how far we went I humbly wait upon your Honours order whether to Dismiss my Company or to prepare for a March again & humbly pray your Honour to let me know your pleasure in this affair I shall speedily send a muster roll & humbly pray it might be made payable to me for I have been at considerable charge to procure Canoes for them & other things wch I shall lose if ye Muster Roll be not be made payable to me. I am your Honours Jn all Respects to Command BENJ^n WRIGHT.

Dummer replies Sept. 13th, 1725:—

S^r I rec'd your Lett^r of the 4th Instant and sh^d have been glad your muster Roll had been sent down, but lest your men sh^d want Money to fit them out for a Second March I have sent you Three

Hundred Pounds by Mr Jo⁸ Lyman which is about Half the wages due on the Roll. You must distribute it to your officers & men in due Proportion as Part of their Wages, that so they may be encouraged to proceed with you again. I am sorry for your Mistake by which you mist those three Indians; I hope you will be more careful for the Time to come not to lose such advantage: & so the principal design off this [chargable?] March. Having fresh tidings of the Designs of yᵉ Enemy, I now desire & direct you with all possible Dispatch to set out with your Company & Proceed on a Second March in Quest of the Enemy; Get what Intelligence you can of the Usual Places of there Passing from Canada to our frontier, that so if possible you may meet them & do some notable Execution upon them: Let no time be lost in this Affair: I leave it to your discression what particular Rout to take in your March. Having a very good Opinion of your Courage & I have the Rather chosen you to go out again that so you may be on your Way to retreive your former Error in Letting those Three Indians escape.

The cost of this expedition was about £600, and had the "three" Indians been caught the governor would consider it money well spent; £200 a head for Indians was a good investment.

The Governor can't get over Wright's bad "error" of mistaking three enemy Indians in the distance for friend Indians, and so losing a chance for attempting to catch them. Not content with meanly thorning Capt. Wright, he returns to the matter in his letter to Col. Stoddard of the same date:—

Sʳ I have yours of the 10ᵗʰ Instant. You have now Enclosed an answer to that from the Albany Commissʳˢ which please to forward by the first Opportunity. it was a very great over sight in Capt Wright not to Secure those Three Indians which would have been a Good effect of that Chargable March however in hopes he will be more Careful of Such a mistake another Time I have now given him an opportunity to Try if he can Retrieve it, The orders for his march goes by this bearer, & whilest he is going into the Enemies Country I desire you¹¹ give orders to Capt Kellogg & to his Lt at Dearfield & to Capt Dwight to Detatch as many men as they can spare under Good Officers to Scout Diligently on the back of the Towns, as you shall Judge best * * * I have wrote again to Gov Tallcot pressing him to give us some Speedy aid in this Juncture, for news I enclose you a copy of a Letter from Mʳ Newman to Col Quincy, which is a Surprising Story to us all & Such Management here & at home as is not to be accounted for.

Capt. Wright with about forty men began another march the first week in October, having been delayed through a "lack of public stores."

The very day that Capt. Wright set out on his first march, a war party of one hundred and fifty Indians fitted out at

Montreal, arrived at Chambly, where the party was to be increased to four hundred and a descent made upon New England. Belated news of this was received here about Aug. 26th, through John Hanson, a returning prisoner. The story of Hanson was confirmed by another messenger a week later, but the warning came too late. Relying upon the movement of Capt. Wright, the people became careless. Col. Stoddard writing Gov. Dummer, says:—

> The people in the towns can't be careful many days together. Upon the rec[t] of your Honors last express, I protested to our officers against our careless way of living, & used all arguments I was capable of to persuade them to order a watch that might be of some significancy in case of the approach of an enemy, but to very little purpose.

It was an exhibition of this feeling, when on the 25th of August, Deacon Samuel Field, Deacon Samuel Childs, Sergt. Joseph Severance, Joshua and John Wells and Thomas Bardwell left town to look after some cattle at Green River Farms, with but a single musket in the party. Crossing North Meadows and the river north of Pine Hill, up through Cheapside until the present town line was crossed, when a cow they were driving ran out of the path. She was followed by Deacon Childs, who soon discovered Indians in ambush and gave the alarm, when they arose.

The following is from an MS. account of the affair by Rev. Stephen Williams about 1730:—

> August 25, 1725, Deacon Sam[ll] Field, Deacon Sam[ll] Child, Sergt Joseph Seavrance, John Wells and Joshua Wells, and Thomas Bardwell, went over Deerf[d] river to go to Green River Farms, and they took a cow with them, designing to put her in a pasture; the indians ambush[d] them, but Deacon Child driving the cow discover[d] them and cry[d] out indians; John Wells discharged his gun at an indian who fell upon his fireing. Deacon Field being at some distance from the company rode towards them, but the company being before separated from one another, retreated towards the mill, and at a considerable distance from the hill they halt[d], y[t] John Wells might load his gun, and then the indians fir[d] upon them, and wound[d] Deacon Sam[ll] Field, the ball passing through the right Hypocondria, cutting off three plaits of the mysenteria; a gut hung out of the wound in length almost two inches, which was cut off even with the Body; the bullet passing between the lowest and the next rib, cutting at its going forth part of the lower rib, his hand being close to his body when y[e] ball came forth, it entered at the root of the heel of y[e] Thumb, cutting the Bone of the fore finger, resting between y[e] fore and 2[d] finger; was cut out, and all the wounds thro'

the blessing of God upon means were heal^d in less than five weeks by Doctor Thomas Hastings, whose death since ye war is a great frown upon us &c.

In the letter below the story is told as reported to Col. Partridge:—

HATFIELD Aug 27, 1725

Honorerable Sr These acquaint y^r Hono^r that o^r Guards according to yor appointment have attended the service in the severall towns till the greatest part of the English Harvest is in without any appearence or disturbance of the Enemy till the Last Night between Deerf^d & Northf^d some of our men goeing out for Cattle discovered a p^{tle} of the Enemy that had killed a mare & a Lott of men made shott upon them & they upon o^r men & wounded one of o^{rs} its thought a dangerous wound, its Certaine now they are now nere in o^r Borders & doubtless intend further Mischiefe before they goe off we have no Ord^r for the mustering men to go out p^{sue} I am very Loth to put men upon such Expeditions & they much indisposed haveing I doubt too little incorridgem^t & allowances for such hard services; if the Enemy abide in Molesting of us now the Harvest is mostly in, may make great disolations by fire as well as Killing off men I am of opinion we might have men from Conitticott if desired it is Certaine Small p^{ties} of the Enemy may do great damages as afore^{sd} I thought meet to acquaint y^r Hon^r with ye p^{r}sent Circumstances praying yor directions. We expect Every hour the Enemy will strik somewhere the good Lord grant divine Guidance to yor Hono^r in all the Weighty & momentous Concerns under yor hand. I am much obliged in Obeydience & yor Hono^s Humble Servt

SAM^{ll} PARTRIDGE

Dummer replies:—

BOSTON Aug 28 1725

S^r I rec'd your Letter Dated yesterday this morning: I am sorry our People made no better use of there Advantages in the first Discovery. However it is a good Providence that you know of the Enemies being about before you feel any great Blow from them: You will take Especial Care that your Frontiers keep Careful Guard & Watch & that they do'nt go out unarmed & Single & when the Enemy Appear they do there duty in Repelling them with Courage & good Conduct: I sent last Thursday to Gov. Talcot to give you some assistance and it will be well if you express to him the Circumstances you are in & pray him to give Dispatch to his Forces: In the mean time I direct you forthwith to Detatch a Comp. of fourty or fifty men either Horse or Foot (as you shall think will be most Serviceable) to scout upon your Borders for a week or ten Days, or until the Connecticut forces come up to you. It is a critical Juncture of our affairs, and I hope your Men will behave themselves handsomely so as that the Enemy may have no Advantage on us. You need not doubt of y^r Troops being allowe^d for there Service

To Col Partridge   Yo^r Servt

The Indians met at Wells river August 30th by Capt. Wright, as noted in his journal, were probably the party which wounded Dea. Field, on their homeward route. This, of course, was not known to the authorities, and the appearance of the enemy, when, according to repeated warning, a large party was to be expected, aroused them to action. Dummer sent to Connecticut for aid, as indicated in the above letter, to protect the towns, while Capt. Kellogg from Northfield and Lieut. Childs from Deerfield filled the woods back of our towns with scouts.

Stoddard writes, Sept. 10th, "I think the scouts from Fort Dummer and Nthfield are constant an vigilant. Those men at Deerfield are very busy and careful, but so few that they are chiefly employed in guarding the labourers I have no dependance on any Assistanc from Connect^{ct} but think it will be of great benefit to continue Capt Wright & his men in pay and in ranging the woods."

Sept. 13th, 1725, Lieut. Childs wrote from Deerfield to Col. Partridge:—

This morning there came a man from a scout sent out by Capt. Dwight, [from Fort Dummer] who informs that there were 6 men in the scout & last Saturday, about 2 o'clock, about 6 or 8 miles west of North River, they sat down to eat, & in a few moments after they sat down, they discovered some Indians on their track, within about 8 rods of them, & they jumped up & ran about 7 or 8 rods & then the Indians made a shot upon them & they turned & shot again upon the Indians & he says he saw two of them fall, & they were forced to scatter. Thomas Bodurtha of Springfield and John Pease of Enfield were killed; Edward Baker of Suffield, John Farrar of Ashford, Nathaniel Chamberlain of Hatfield were taken; Anthony Weirsbury only escaped and returned to the fort.

Of this tragedy in the wilderness, thus briefly told, absolutely nothing more has been found.

The great solitudes stretching hundreds of miles away to Canada were often disturbed by conflicts between the scouts of the opposing forces. Beneath their sombre shades lie hidden unwritten romances without number. Here the price of life was skill in woodcraft, vigilance, strategy, courage, and, above all, nerve and self-possession in the crucial hour. No gladiators were they, with the arena walled by crowded galleries, to witness the death struggle, and cheer the victor. The giant hemlock and primeval fir were about them; the dark morass drank the blood, the beasts of the forest revelled on the flesh of the victims, and their bones were denied even the shelter of an unknown grave. How little can we of this generation realize the deeds of daring, or the severity of the service and sufferings, which were the price of our dearly bought inheritance!

In the same letter quoted above Lieut. Childs writes:—

Last Saturday, near Sunset, Capt. [Thomas] Wells being in his great pasture, heard crackling of sticks & saw the bushes move, within 8 rods of him, and being apprehensive of an enemy, he ran home & took sundry men to the place where they found the tracks of two Indians & followed them through two pieces of corn; which Indians we think came to spy out our circumstances. I was sending out 5 men on a scout this morning, but hearing this news [of the North river tragedy] Justice Wells tho't it not best to send out so small a number, and not being able to enlarge [it] and defend the fort, [and concludes by saying he is waiting further orders].

Partridge sends this letter to Col. Stoddard, who endorsed upon it:—

Since this is the 2d news of the approach of the enemy in our parts I think best to hasten Capt. Wright's men to Deerfield & have sent for him to be in Deerfield to-morrow & we have reason to send out a party to range our western woods & Deerfield theirs. If you have not, send to Conn. this news & all the former news, & if they still will do nothing, we must raise men of our own, & command all our men to be well fixt and in readiness yourself, & not scatter to work but a sessation at present.

If any large body of the enemy did leave Canada for our frontiers, the activity of our officers kept them at a distance.

Sept. 14th, good news and bad news was received at Northampton. The Indian Commissioners at Albany write, Sept. 10th:—

Since our last of the 6th we are assured by one of this place who arrived last night in 13 days from Canada that the 140 Indians * * * encamped near Chambly with a design to go out against your frontiers are actually returned home partly by the pursuations of the people of this place, and partly by there Sachims * * * We are told that one party of 9 & another of 14 Inds are out who design to be sculking about your Western frontiers of the Last Greylock is Leader * * * We hear the Indians are weary of the war and would long since have come to terms of peace & submission if the Govr of Canada & his priests did not encourage & set them on

This letter was to Cols. Stoddard and Partridge. Stoddard writes:—

Noth HAMPTON Sept^{br} 14
at one a clock in the morning

Just now came an Express from Capt Ashly with the Commission's letter of the 10th Instant which he Intends to send by an express early in the Morning, therefore I take the opportunity to enclose the Inteligence from Deerfield which I receiv^d yester evening of which we expect a fuller accont very speedily I cant learn that any of our men were hurt before they parted I sent a letter to Gov. Tallcot in the evening to aquaint him * * * what hapened to our Scout. If Capt Wright could Immediatly March with his company, or a part of them 40: or fifty miles up Connect^{ct} River and then Cross over to Otter Creek he might probably Intercept some of our Skulking Enemy, but having no Publick stores I doubt whither they can be ready Seasonably.

The same Albany post which brought the above letter, brought another from the Commissioners for the governor, from which the following is an extract:—

A messenger 13 days trom Canada arrived here last night, who delivered us 7 hands of wampum, from the part of the Caghnawagas, Rondox and Shawrenadas Indians living in Canada; desiring thereby to speak with you, or some person deputed by you his excellency our governor, & the sachems of the Six Nations, at this city, by the first of October. The Indians are weary of this war, but are vigorously set on by the Governor of Canada and their Priests.

In spite of French interference, however, the end was nigh. Father Rasle, the instigator, had gone to his reward. On his death the Abenakis of the east were discouraged and disposed for peace, and negotiations were begun. They were, however, overborne by the clans in Canada, who, pushed on and backed up by De Vaudreuil, had been high in their demands, and bold in enforcing them. Now the scene changed. Philip de Rigaud, Marquis de Vaudreuil, the mainspring and spur of the war, died at Quebec, Oct. 10th, 1725. He was succeeded as Governor of Canada by Charles Marquis de Beauharnois, whose influence over the Indians, with all the priestly power behind him, was not strong enough longer to enforce the French policy upon the reluctant Abenakis. A treaty of peace was arranged between them and the English without difficulty. Other clans in Canada were kept in a hostile attitude a few months longer, but no more depredations on our frontier are recorded.

Some of the Deerfield men who served in Father Rasle's war are:—

Capt. Samuel Barnard.	Corp. Isaac Mattoon.
Capt. Joseph Kellogg.	Corp. Joseph Severance.
Capt. Timothy Childs.	Samuel Allen.
Lieut. Joseph Clesson.	John Allen.
Sergt. Joseph Atherton.	John Beaman.

Nathaniel Hawks.
Daniel Severance.
Daniel Belding.
Nathaniel Brooks.
Benjamin Brooks.
John Catlin.
James Corse.

John Combs.
Jonas Holmes.
Joshua Wells.
Aaron Denio.
Michael Mitchell.
George Swan.

Since giving an account of Fort Dummer on pages 406-7, I have been furnished through the kindness of Miss I. A. Brackett with a copy of the ground plan of the fort (made in 1749,) the original of which is in the New Hampshire MS. Archives. By this I find my previous printed source of information was incorrect; that the fort was not square, but irregular in form. The north side was 157½ feet; the west, 136 feet; the south, 108 feet; the east—the river side—85 feet. In the west and south sides were gates, not included in the above measurement. At the northeast corner was a house 22 x 21 feet, with "a cannon mounted in it;" at the northwest corner two story house 17½ x 22 with "a cannon mounted in it;" adjoining this on the east was a one story house, 40 x 16½ feet; at the southwest corner was a two story house 34 x 22 feet. Each of these houses projected beyond the walls from four to eleven feet, forming bastions to defend the walls. The fort was built of hewn pine logs and was twenty feet high. The walls of the houses were of the same material. Within the enclosure were six smaller houses; and in the center of the "Perade," was the "Citydale" 14½ feet square. At a later period, but before the Old French War, a stockade had been built around the fort enclosing an acre and a half of the meadow. This continued an important post until the conquest of Canada.

CHAPTER XIV.

MR. WILLIAMS AND THE MEETINGHOUSE OF 1729.

Some account of the early meetinghouses of Deerfield has been given on pages 200-5, 253.

In the meetinghouse built in 1695, long benches, or seats with backs, occupied the place of the modern pew, but, as we have seen, these were carefully graded as to rank. Pews came in gradually. The first were built near the front entrance, and for many years this situation was held to be a place of honor, rivalling, if not exceeding, the neighborhood of the pulpit. From time to time new pews were put up, extending to the right and left of the front door, until met by another series, which began on either side of the pulpit; and the whole wall space was thus occupied by pews. The last gap was filled under the following vote passed March 8th, 1725: "To make ye flank seats in ye meeting house into pews: and to esteem them equal with ye Second Seat in the body, and y^t ye Select men with Jno. Catlin shall be a Com'tee to see it done forthwith." The center or body was still covered with benches. Children were gathered in lots according to age under the watchful eye of the tithing man. The men sat on the north side of the house, and the women on the south, separated by the broad aisle.

The first pew erected was for the minister's family. At a town meeting December 2d, 1709, "Y^e town granted Mr Jno Williams a liberty to bild a pue for his wife and famyly to sit in in one of ye pleses left for a gard Seat:"

"At ye same meeting ye Town granted liberty to Sam^{ll} Williams Jona Weals & Sam^{ll} Barnard to bild a Sate or pue in ye other gard seat place:"

Mr. Williams had been appointed chaplain in the expedition against Canada in June, 1709. In September he was paid £24, 8 s, 8 d for this service. From this money, we may assume, the expense of the pew was paid.

READJUSTMENT OF THE SALARY. 455

During his absence with the army, John Avery and Aaron Porter had supplied his pulpit. They were fresh graduates from Harvard, and probably brought along the new fangled notions about pews.

The spaces thus alotted for this innovation were on either side of the front door, and had been reserved as suitable places, where, under the care of a small guard, the men of the congregation could deposit their loaded guns on entering for worship. This space being now converted to another use, indicates some new method of guarding the meeting-house which does not appear.

March 14th, 1710, the town "empowered the select men to repair all meeting hous seats which want repairing" and votes for repairs were often passed so long as the house stood.

October 20th, 1711, voted sixty pounds for Mr. Williams's salary, to be paid in *money*. No reason for this change is apparent. The next year substantial aid was received from the government.

"June 14, 1712, In Council £32 was allowed Rev. John Williams of Deerfield towards his maintenance, the coming year in the work of the ministry."

1712, John Allison had "20s for sweeping the meeting house," and this was the usual pay for that service.

Dec. 21st, 1714, the Proprietors granted Mr. Williams eighty acres of wood land adjoining his lot at Cheapside, extending along the south bank of the Pocumtuck.

Nov. 12, 1716, Att a Legal Town meeting ye town mad choyce of Cpt Wells and De ffrench & Sam^{ll} Barnard, as a Comity to go and discours with Mr Jno Williams in the Towns behalf in order to make a new bargin with him what he shall have yearly for his salary and how it shall be paid.

Dec. 25, 1717, The Town then agreed that their minister's Rate Should be made for a year and a quarter to terminate on ye last day of february 1717–18.

There seems to have been no settlement of the salary question under the vote of Nov. 12, 1716. It came up again at a meeting March 20th, 1717–18, when,—

The Town made choice of Capt. Jona Wells, lieutt Thomas Wells and Thomas French Senr, as a Comitte to Discourse and agree with the Reuerend Mr John Williams about his sallery for ye year 1718, how much and in what manner it shall be paid.

Dec. 30, 1718, The Town agreed and voted to give unto ye Reverend John Williams Eighty pounds in current money of New England yearly for his Sallery so long as he shall Continue in ye ministry amongst vs in Deerfield, provided he will Relinquish his former Bargain Recorded in ye Town Book Concerning his Sallery: and that he doth Relinquish his former Bargain is evidenced by his setting his hand to this as here it followeth   JOHN WILLIAMS

As time went on, changes in the congregation required, now and then, a new arrangement of seats. Sept. 7th 1721, the selectmen were directed to repair the seats and were authorized,—

To Divide ye seats in ye Gallery into two teer, and to haue ye meeting house seated this fall.

Y^e town Chose Cpt Jonath Wells Judah Wright dea. Thomas French ltt Sam^{ll} Barnard and dea. Hawks, a committee to Seat ye Meeting house. Voted, y^t ye aboue s^d Committee shall Seat all persons aboue ye age of 16 years by these Rules; Namely age estate and qualification.

In 1724, a new departure was taken. The town voted "y^t ye forescore pounds due Mr. Williams shall be Raised in distinct tax by itself." This became henceforth a permanent practice.

May 15, Benj. Mun, Judah Wright and Sam^{ll} Field were chose to seat all *white* persons in our meeting house above ye age of 16 years as they shall think fit, hauing Regard to ye Rules of seating, *viz.*, age, estate, and qualification—and to Remain in their office during ye town's pleasure.

This may have been another new departure. Perhaps, under former votes some ambitious person of the proscribed color had claimed honors in the house of worship, not intended for such as he, and *complexion* now became one of the "qualifications."

January, 1725, voted Mr. Williams sixty loads of wood; the selectmen "to giue gen^{ll} notice to ye inhabitants for getting it."

December 16th, voted to "give him twenty pounds in money in Lieu of said wood."

December 15th, 1727, voted to repair the meetinghouse "to make it something comfortable for a few years. Voted Mr. Williams sallery shall be made up for ninety pounds this year." The winter following proved that the present meetinghouse could *not be* made "something comfortable," and Oct. 25th, 1728, the town voted to build a new one, and,—

That it shall be set up and the out side of s^d house to be Couered, in ye year 1729 at ye Charge of ye town in s^d year.

Voted that s^d house shall be 40 Foots in Breadth and fifty foots in length:

Voted Cpt. Thos Wells John Catlin sen^r, Deacon Sam^{ll} Childs lieut. Timothy Childs and Doct Thos Wells shall be a Com^{tee} to provide work-men and all necessaries for ye building s^d house and to see that it be done seasonably.

The building committee set about their work with zeal and activity. Meanwhile the exact site of the new house became a subject of discussion, with great difference of opinion. A town meeting was called for December 11th, to settle this question. It was then voted to set it,—

On ye highest part of that nole between ye sine post and Deacon Childs his shop ye east side of it to Range with ye front of ye west teer of home lots.

Att ye same Meeting they voted to delay fixing y^u place for ye meeting house till next spring. [But the work of preparation went on. April 28th, 1729, voted,] y^t ye Select Men Shall provide on ye towns charge a Suitable quantity of Drink and Cake to be Spent att ye Raising of ye Meeting house.

All agreed that these essentials must be made ready, although disagreeing as to the place where they should be used. This, however, was soon to be decided. May 19th, the town met and after general debate, it was by vote,—

Concluded to move out and stand at 3 places discorst on, for Seting ye meeting house and that ye bigest number shall haue ye place, upon Tryal they Concluded on ye Middle most of ye three.

This was probably the spot described in the meeting of Dec. 11th, 1728, and on it the fourth house of worship was built. The *original minutes* of this meeting have been found, by which it appears that provision was also made for a meetinghouse bell, the first of which there is any hint, except in fiction. The action relating to the bell is not on the record, but in the original minutes, which are signed by the moderator; it follows the vote last quoted, and it is copied in full:—

We subscribers do promise that we will [give, *erased*] lend to ye town towards pay for ye bell for our Meeting house, as followeth:—

Cpt Thos Wells,	£10	Doct Thos Wells,	£5
Thos French, jun'r,	10	Sam'll Tailor,	2 10
Lt Timothy Childs,	10	Sam'll Bardwell,	2 11
Jno Arms,	5	Ens Jon'th Wells,	5 00

Agreed with Mr. Grant for £43; began May 15; allowance 8 days.

Below this entry is the following, which was also omitted in the record of the meeting on the town book:—

An account of what was promised to be lent unto yᵉ town and by whom:—

Ens Mehuman Hinsdell,	£15	Dea Thos French,	£ 1 10
Ens Jon'th Wells,	5	Cpt Thos Wells,	10 00
Lut Eben'r Smead,	5	Dea Sam'll Childs,	4 00
Dan'll Arms,	10	Eben'r Wells,	5 00
John Arms,	5	Jno Stebbins,	5 00
Dea Sam'll Field,	3	Jon'th Hoyt,	5 00

There is no reason to doubt that the intention of the town to procure a bell at this time was carried out. But its tones never reached the ear of the one who of all others must have been the most interested to hear it.

The preparations for building a meetinghouse were interrupted, and the community thrown into confusion by the sudden death of Mr. Williams. He was struck senseless by apoplexy, June 9th, 1729, and died on the 12th, at the age of sixty-four, after a faithful ministry of forty-three years. The character and standing of our pastor in the colony may be seen by expressions gathered from contemporary writers. It appears that his death was considered not only "a Grievous breach upon Deerfield," but his loss was widely felt and lamented, for with him fell "one of the pillars of the Land."

"In his loss the Public sustained no Little Loss of Strength and Glory." He was one of "those who shone as *Lights* in the world, and taught by *example* as well as Preaching."

"He was an ardent lover of New England, its religious principles, its Ecclesiastical and Civil Rights & Liberties."

"He was charitable, peaceful & benign, full of respect to superiors, condescention to Inferiors, & Civility to all; Candid to the Faults of others; patient under Injuries; of a most forgiving Spirit; and a Hater of Contention."

"His heart was engaged in his work, and he was abundant in his labors, both in season, and out of season, plainly, faithfully & frequently, warning, urging & intreating."

"He was much in prayer & singularly gifted in it," and "his prayers, counsel & example did not a little to the encouragement of his people."

June 17th, 1729, the town voted "to Render unto yᵉ Reverᵈ Mr. Chauncy the thanks of this town for his funeral sermon preached here & to request of him a copy thereof for the press."

This was printed at Boston the same year. A single copy has recently been found; it is an able and appropriate discourse by Rev. Isaac Chauncy of Hadley. After the fashion of the times it is divided and subdivided into forty-two numbered heads. The following extracts are taken from that part devoted to a full estimate of the character of Mr. Williams:—

His Piety. He was one that not only savoier'd of Piety in his Conversation or Ordinary Discourse, but loved the House of God, and the place where God's Honour dwells. His Spiritual Appetite to heavenly things he discover'd not only by his being at the Chief place of Concourse, one of the first of the Inhabitants, but by frequenting those Lectures which were seven, thirteen, eighteen miles distant from him. Yea, he discovered his Piety by making Religion his business by being frequent at his Devotions by his strict Observance of the Sabath, and Fast-days whether Public or Private.

His Zeal. Your Teacher displaid his Zeal against Sin by his impartial administration of Reproofs to Sinners, and of Discipline towards the Scandalous. As he was Patrone of Innocence, so he was a Boanerges when there was Occasion for it—As for those who were upon the Brink of Destruction, and in the Suburbs of Hell, he endeavour'd by the Terrours of the Law to unveil their eyes, and rowse them from their Slumber, that they might escape the Talons of the Infernal Fiend and flee for Refuge, to lay hold on the hope set before them. He worthily attempted to Stem the Tide of Corruption and the Torrent of Iniquity, by linking to it the dangerous consequents of it, and by discovering the Rocks and Shelves that Sinners were in danger of.

His Affections. In his Writings he useth the most loving Compellations, and addresseth himself to those he was concerned for in an Endearing Language. And where he might with Authority, command, then for Loves-sake he rather beseecheth, that he might ingratiate himself with them, and insinuate into their affections—that he might catch them with holy Craft and Guile, and render his Admonitions, Warnings and Exhortations more acceptable.

His Strength. It's true, your Reverend Pastor hath been with you above forty years; but if we consider his activity, and the firmness of his Constitution, they gave a hopeful Prospect of a longer Continuance.

His Love of His Work. I'll instance four things which belong to the Sacred Function *viz.,* Visiting the Sick, Reading good Books, Preaching and Praying, and he delighted in them all. He would not only visit the sick when desired, but he would visit them unsent for; yea, he would (when divers were sick) walk the Circuit almost every day, and visit them all except they were remote from him. He had the spirit and Gift of Prayer, and could accomodate his Expressions to any emergent Occasion. He chearfully laid hold of all opportunities to pour out his Soul before God; for Prayer seemed to be his Element. And that he might not neglect the Businiss of feeding of Souls with the Bread of Life, but promote their Edification by his Ministerial Tallents, he was careful not to entangle himself in with Affairs of this Life, or encumber himself with Secular Cares. He did not content himself with Preaching upon the Lord's Day, but would frequently Preach upon Week-days. His Custom was to Preach a Lecture once a month, and a Sermon the Friday before the Sacrament, and frequently a Sermon either to the Elderly, or to the young people. He preached so often, that his example is scarcely to be parrallel'd.

His Example. In the Conversation of your spiritual Guide, there was a lively Image of those Vertues and Graces, which he recomended to the practice of his Hearers:—

1. He was Public Spirited. How careful was he to inform himself of the Transactions and Affairs of *Europe*, and to understand the State and Circumstaces of the Province, that he might calculate his Prayers accordingly; Religion exalted his Spirit and inspired it with generous and beneficent Affections to the Publick, and those in whom the publick Trust was reposed. And how he was grieved, when he understood that things ran in a wrong Channel, and how was his Spirit rejoyced when publick Affairs were in a flourishing Posture.

2. He was Valiant and Courageous, a man of Fortitude and Resolution. In the Heat of the War, when Deerfield was the Frontier Plantation, he stood his ground and encouraged his Neighbors to do so too. And when the Enemy had taken his Fort and entred his Lodging Room, he attempted to kill some of them, but Providence prevented him. And when at *Canada,* he was threatened with sudden Death by a violent hand if he would not conform to the *Romish* worship, he resolutely resisted the Temptation, and came off a Conqueror. The menaces of Death could not unsettle his noble Resolutions, or tempt him to stain and eclipse his Vertue, or to blur his Evidences for Heaven.

3. He was Patient under Affliction. His Captivity was a Complicated affliction, and his Conduct under it a considerable passage in the Scene of his Life. It was a stumbling block to some that such a Religious Family should meet with so much Adversity. His Loving Consort was Slain, and two pleasant Branches of his family were lop'd off by the Sword of the Wilderness, and Several Others together with himself led into Captivity into a Strange Land and his House plunder'd and burnt to the Ground. Under all his trials, who ever heard him open his mouth in a way of murmuring and repining? Under dismal Aspects of Divine Providence, he encouraged himself in his God, and took Shelter in the Munition of Rocks He readily took upon him his Cross, yielded Passive Obedience, and Glorified God, by ascribing righteousness to him, and acknowledging his Sovereignty and Resignation to the Divine Disposal did hush, quiet and compose his thoughts, lenefie the bitterness of his Sorrows, and fortify his mind: So that he did in patience posses his own Soul.

4. He was Grateful to Benefactors. After his Return from *Canada* Divine Providence took Special care of him and his and rais'd up Relief and Friends for them:—there were Several at *Boston* who were moved with Compassion towards him and his Family, and accordingly were liberal and open-handed towards them. Yea, there was a Publick Collection at *Hartford* to Repair there Losses, and to set them up again. And he did not think it below him to have his Estate repaired in part by Contribution, neither was he ashamed to make an acknowledgment to his bountiful friends:—yea, when he had Liberty of access to the Throne of Grace, he frequently, if not always prefer'd this Petition, Lord reward our Benfactors.

5. He was Hospitable. He having a well furnished Table (for you must note, that his Life was checker'd with Adversity, and Prosperity, as *Job's* was) he cared not to eat his Morsal Alone And having the portion of a full and overflowing Cup, others might be welcome to share in it. How often did he invite persons of other Towns (occasionally there) to rest and repose themselves under his Roof, And his winning carriage was an Inducment to them to accept of the Invitation.

6. He was Charitable to the Poor. He was remarkable for Charity and Benificence to those who wanted Necessaries for the Support of there natural life. He did not rest in verbal Expressions of Kindness, but furnished them with real Supplies and he not only relieved them with his own hand, but stirred up the people to make Contributions, that their might be a Fund or Stock, out of which the Stewards of the Church Alms might Communicate to them, before they were reduced to Extremities.

7. He was in his Carraige obliging to all. Nature and Grace combin'd to plant a blessed Temper in his Breast, So that he had all the Attractiveness of humane Conversation Chearfulness, Sweets of Behavior, proffitable discourse. He behaved himself towards his Superiors with submission, Modesty and Respect, towards his Inferiours, and persons of low Estate with Condescention and affability, towards his Equals with becoming familiarity * * * And it was his Endeavour to live inoffensively towards all men, and to promote peace & unity amongst his Neighbours. In a word Religion inspired him with every social Vertue, which would brighten his character; and his Vertues like glittering Flowers sent forth their grateful Odours.

8. He had a low, modest and Sober Opinion of himself and his own Abilities. And he was not ambitious of Superiority, but was forward to give others the Preemience, beyond what is common in persons of his Rank and Character * * * was not confident in matters of doubtful Disputation, did not judge and censure those, that differed from him in Extrafundamentals.

9. He was temperate in Eating and Drinking. His views and happiness did not centre in sensual Gratifications * * * He was so far from overcharging his heart with Sufeiting and Drunkenness, or indulging his sensual appetite in any excesses, that as to eating, he would frequently at Festival Entertainments rise from the table before others were done; and as to Drinking, he would sometimes deny himself that lawful Liberty of refreshing himself after Preaching, that he might not give the least countenance to the love of strong Drink.

10. He was just in his Dealings. He was careful to wrong none, to give to every one there Due, to be plain and upright in his Dealings with others, to owe no man anything but to love one another. He could make the same Challings that *Samuel* did to the people & come off triumphantly (no doubt) as well as he.

11. He was careful to perform Relative Duties. How Careful was he to fill up every Relation he stood to his Household, with the proper and genuine Duties belonging to it? In the Conjugal Relation he was a Loving Husband, in the Parental Relation he was a tender Father, in the Relation of a Governor of a Family, he trained them up in a Knowledge and Observance of Divine Laws he instill'd Sound and Orthodox Principeles into there Minds, he set good Examples before them and kept them under the Restraints of wholesome Discipline that he might form there Souls to Vertue.

12. He was weaned from the world. I'll mention two instances of his Mortification to the world. One is, when he return'd from Captivity he was importunely invited to settle where his worldly Interests might be more promoted, than if he return'd to Deerfield; and there were plausible Pleas he might have made for his accepting the Invitations, since Deerfield was in a Shatter'd Condition, and reduc'd to a Small Number, and his own family had Suffer'd so much there and might suffer a great deal more, if he return'd. But he consulted not Flesh and Blood, but resolved to return to his Charge and spend the Remainder of his dayes with them; though it interfered with his Secular Interest. The other Instance of his Contempt of the World was in leaving the Quantity of his Salary to the determination of the people, without intermedling with it himself.

Humble yourselves under the mighty Hand of God, that he may exhalt you in due time. A good man, and worthy Minister is fallen in our Israel. There is a great breach made upon the Ecclesiastical Order * * * And as to this Church and Congregation, who are as Sheep without a Shephard, You ought to lament it, that the Crown is fallen from your head: Your Pious Instructer was had in honor for his Works Sake, whilst he lived, and you should Embalm his Memory now he is Dead. Examine the Ground of God's Controversy, and wherefore it is, that God hath been pleased thus to be contending with you. Lament your Unprofitableness under Means and pray that God would not lay to your Charge your Barrenness and Unfruitfulness in his Vinyard * * * Pray that God would sanctify this Providence to you and yours, though he comes as a Spirit of Judgment, and a Spirit of burning, as a Refiners Fire and Fullers Soap: You are under a frown of Heaven, wrestle therefore in Prayer for Comfort and Joy in the Return of God's favour to you.

John Williams, born Dec. 10th, 1664, was the sixth of the thirteen children of Samuel and Theoda (Park) Williams. His father, deacon and shoemaker of Roxbury, who died in 1698, at the age of sixty-five, came from Norwich, England, with Robert *his* father, about 1637. John was educated by William Park, his maternal grandfather. He was graduated from Harvard College in 1683, in his nineteenth year, the second in a class of three; the first being Samuel Danforth, his minister's son, and the third, William Williams, his double cousin, their fathers being brothers who married sisters. Graduates were ranked in the catalogue then, not by merit, but according to station in society; and Danforth, son and grandson of a minister, of course stood first. John came next, we may suppose, by virtue of his father being a deacon,

FAITH IN SPECIAL PROVIDENCES. 463

while the father of William was only a captain, and representative to the General Court.

These three young men were married about the same time, and all entered the ministry the same year. Danforth at Taunton, where, after raising fourteen children, he died in 1727, at the age of sixty-one. William Williams settled in Hatfield, and the early intimacy between the cousins was kept up until the death of John. The latter began preaching here about the middle of June, 1686, and continued " dispensing the blessed word of God" and was ordained, Oct. 17th, 1688, at the age of twenty-four.

From the very first Mr. Williams seems to have had the confidence of the people, and he was prominent in all their affairs, civil and military. He was generally their mouthpiece in communication with the colonial authorities, and was intimate with the leading men in the colony.

In 1709 he was appointed chaplain in the expedition fitting out for Canada. In 1710, and again in 1711, he was selected for the same duty. In 1714 he was appointed commissioner, to go with Col. John Stoddard to Canada, to arrange for the release of captives. For a full account of this important mission, see "Stoddard's Journal." Prince says:—

> Mr. Williams used every May, yearly, to come down to the General Convention of Ministers of the Province of Boston; where he was always very affectionately entertained.
>
> At the convention in May, 1728, (being chosen the year before) he preached a very moving Sermon to the Ministers; when, I remember, he expressed his Joy in the great Advantage we at that Time had above the preceding Ministers in the General Awakenings thro' the Land by the Great Earthquake in October foregoing.

Prince speaks of him again as "a Person of eminent Piety, Humility, Sincerity and Sweetness of Temper." His most prominent characteristics seem to have been faith in God, and in the efficacy of prayer. He was a firm believer in special providences, and often noted common, every-day events as coming in immediate and direct answer to his prayers. His aim was to glorify God for all blessings, and justify his ways, under all circumstances, however adverse. His relations to his people were tender and considerate. With them he cheerfully struggled for the bare necessaries of life during the long years of Indian hostilities. In a letter to Gov.

Dudley, Oct. 21st, 1703, he says, while asking aid for the town,—

> Formerly I was moved by certain knowledge of their poverty and distress to abate them of my salary for several years together, tho' they never asked it of me, & now their children must suffer for want of clothing, or the country consider them, & I abate them what they are to pay me. I never found the people unwilling to do when they had the ability; yea, they have often done above their ability.

This presents a touching glimpse of the condition and relations of the pastor and people.

Several of his manuscript sermons are in the collections at Memorial Hall; but it is almost impossible to decipher them. His published writings are a sermon "preacht at Springfield Lecture, Aug. 25, 1698," on the execution of Sarah Smith,— Boston, 1699. A "Pastoral Letter" to a company of captives when leaving Canada for home, May 30th, 1706. This was printed by Mather before the return of Mr. Williams, and with it a wretched poem of one hundred and forty-four lines, addressed to his son then in Canada; and another of one hundred and four lines of like quality, credited to Mary French but evidently the composition of Mr. Williams. In both piety was abundant, but poetry was conspicuously absent. "The Redeemed Captive," with the annexed sermon, preached at Boston Lecture, December 5th, 1706, was published in March, 1707; and soon after, another sermon, preached before the Governor and General Court, entitled "God in the Camp; or the only way for a People to Engage the Presence of God with their Armies." No other printed works are found until after his death, when abstracts of several of his sermons were published under the title of "A Serious Word to the Posterity of Holy Men, calling upon them to Exault their fathers' God."

"The Redeemed Captive" is a well-known account of his captivity and sufferings in Canada. It has passed through many editions, and was never more sought after than now. It is a work of great historical value to the student of the French and Indian wars; the relation of captor and captive is nowhere else so well shown. At his death Mr. Williams left a library containing one hundred and ninety volumes, and three hundred and forty-nine pamphlets. This library was a rich collection, under the circumstances, but there was no poetry, or so-called fiction. The catalogue of this library is given entire, probably a rare instance of a complete ministerial library of that period.

Inventory of the library of Rev John Williams taken by Capt Thomas Wells, Deacon Samuel Childs and Deacon Samuel Field. Reported at Court Sept 3, 1729.

Bible & Psalm book 15s, Concordance 35s,	£2	10	0
Burket 30s, 3 vols of Henry £3 15, Willards Body &c £2 00,	7	5	0
A Petri 8, Calvin on Isaiah 8, Plutarchs Lives 8,	1	4	0
Burgess' Scripture directory & Spiritual Refinings,	0	18	0
Moreland of Persecution 8, Shepherds Parable 12,	1	0	0
Wilsons Dictionary 10, Vine's Gods Withdrawing 4,	0	14	0
French book 4, St Martyr 4, Squires Exposition 3, Aretius 2,	0	13	0
Moores Warnings 3, Early Piety 4, Le pastoral 4, Heaven Opened 2,	0	13	0
Wadsworths Guide 2-6, Life of Justification 2-6, Taylor's Christs Victory 3,		8	0
Tradition 3, Corbetts Remains 4, Elton's Tryumph 5, Dr Sibbe's Returning 4,		16	0
Strong's Select Sermons 7, Shutes Divine Cordial 2-6, Philips Mourning [?] 2-6,		12	0
Raynolds 3, Treatises 10, J. N. on Joel 4, Stevens on Original Sin 2-6,		16	6
Peter's Repentance 2-6, Sclators Key 1-6, Sharps Divine Comfort 5,		9	0
Silenus' Mr Appleton 4, Ratio Discipline 2, De Launs Plea 2-6,		9	6
Indian Converts 7, Pope's Sure Refuge 2, Hobarts Absence 2-6,		11	6
Gazeteer 3, Flavell on Fear 3, Pastor 6, Pemberton's Sermons 14,	1	0	6
Bervridge on Prayer 2, Prince's Ordination 2, Willards Fountain &c 2,		6	0
Mr Henry's Life 4, Hall's Great Imposture 2-6, Stoddards Sermons 2-6,		9	0
Mathers Heavenly &c 2, A Grey 2, Wms Great Salvation 2-6, Malachi 1,		7	6
Nesscons Popery 1-6, Pastoral desires 1, Divine Warnings 1-6, Gods Existance 1,		5	0
Lylyes Anatomy 9, Woodwards 12 Sermons 2-6, The Redeemed Captive 1-6,		13	0
Foxcrofts Godly &c 2-6, Stoddards Vertue of &c 2, Wms Duty 1-6,		6	0
Taylors Parables 6, A Diswasive Power &c 2-6, Origo Protestantium 3,		11	6
Mathers Solemn &c 1, Maslorat 5, Parei Opera 2 vols 30,	1	16	0
Tirini Comment 4, Clavis Scripture 5, Thomas Aquinas 5,		14	0
Comment Posantre 5, Opera Junii 2 vols 12, Eusebius 6,	1	3	0
John Martyr 8, Roger's 7 Treatisis 6, Top of Praises 2-6,		16	6
French History 1, De Ancilus [?] Div. 2-6, Homilus 2 vols 6,		9	6
Mager's English 4, Gerhards Com's Places £1-16, Tennezi Sacra 2-6,	2	2	9
Poliandri Comment 5, Thesauries Sap 6d, Clarkson on Liturgus 4,		9	6
Two old Homilies 3, Polanies on Hosea 2-6, Cornelius on Romans 1,		6	6
Catechisms ad &c 1, Idea Theologia 1-6, Thesaurus Poeticus 1,		3	6
Book without a title 6d, Walters Practich &c 2, Ad Appium 8d		3	2
The Strait Gait 1-6, Mather of Faith &c 1-6, Ditto the Glory of 1-6,		4	6
Personal Reformation 2, Our Saviour's Legacy 1-6,		3	6
Meditations on the Glory &c 1-6, Sermons by J M 1-3,		2	9
Three Essays 1-3, Szegidinus [?] 6, Philip of Mourning 1, The Arraegum 1-6,		4	3
Sphera & Hedham 9d, Pashions of the Mind 1-6, Comment on Lamentations 1-6,		3	9
Tryal of Romish Clergy farwell Sermons 2, Catechisms and Solomons 2-6,		4	6
Theryer 4, Justinas 1-6, Arithmetick 8d & Desires 8d, Comment in Octa 1-6,		8	4
Catrehesis Religions 1-6, Rolloct in Epist 1, French book 4d, Ezasmic Tonus 8d,		3	6
Communicants Companion 4, Foxcroft on Psalm 119 2-6,		6	6
Psalterium 1-6, Perils of the Times 1-3, Williams' Funeral Sermons 1,		3	9
Froughton 1-6, Joshua's Resolution 1-6, Wadsworth's Invitation 1-6,		4	6

	£	s	d
Hale of Witchcraft 2, Walter on Vain Tho'ts 2, Christianus 1-6,		5	6
Wadsworth on the Judgment 1-6, Lord on Baptism 1,		2	6
Mather on Earthquakes 1, Cotton's 2 Sermons 1,		2	0
Wadsworth on the Sacrament 1-3, Sanctifying 1-3, A disquisition 1,		3	6
Coleman on Mirth 1-6, Works of God 6d, Now or Never by J [I?] M 8d,		2	8
Looking Glass 1-8, The Well ordered family 1, A Call to Delaying &c 1-2,		3	5
Old Psalm book 1, Victorina 8d, French Dictionary 12, Prideaux Counest [?] 2 vols 25,	1	18	8
Bonifacius 2, Dr Mathers Life 8, 349 Pamphlets £5, 22 Catechisms 10,	6	0	0
Sixty of Mr Williams Sermons @ 6d,	1	10	0
Some Sermons of Mr Flavell Concerning Christs Tender Care for his Mother, which were distributed amongst the family.			
	£44	0	3

His real estate was:—

Home lot & buildings, £300; 20 acres at Cheapside, at £23, £460,	£760	
Great Meadow Land 8 acres at £18,	144	
Ten acres at Eagle Brook at £9,	90	
The great pasture at Deerfield River,	100	
Wood land at Cheapside, £20; Islands in Great River, £2,	22	
New Fort & New Field 16 acres at £5 10s,	88	
18 commons, 2 acres, 120 rods, at £3 per common,	54	
Country Farm Land 14 acres, 114 rods at 20s,	14	
3 wood lots lying between Deerfield River & Hatfield bounds,	16	
Total of real estate,	£1288	

The inventory of personal property would fill several pages; it was minute down to the smallest article of household use. Some interesting items are given:—

	£	s	d
The Mulatto boy Meseek,	80	00	
The Black boy Kedar,	80	00	
Two Neck bands at 3s per band,		6	
4 Bands 2s, 4 old bands, 3s, 1 silk muslin handkerchief 1s,		6	
2 pair shoes 14s, 1 pair boots 5s,		19	
Blue china, Curtains and vallants,	6	00	
Blue Linsey Woolsey Curtains & Vallants,		05	
Calico Curtains & Green vallants,	1	13	
Feather bed & bolster in the outward chamber, Feather bed & bolster in study chamber,	1	10	
Bed & bolster in the Hall £4, 10s, do. in the outward room £6,	10	10	
Bedstead, cord & iron rods in study chamb'r,		15	
Do in Hall,		15	
Bedstead & Cord in outward chamber,		5	
Do in outward Room,		—	
5 aprons for the children 1s 8d, 7 clouts 3s 6d, two infants' waistcoats, 1s,		06	
6 alchemy spoons,		2	
An old cane 3s, spectacles & case 3s, Tobacco 2s, 6d,		08	
A gun of the old Queen's Arms 40s,	2	00	
A long fowling piece, Tobacco tongs, &c,		—	
Silver tankard £19, silver cup, buttons & old spoon, 20s, 10 silver spoons, 7–10–0,	27	10	

[Of Pewter ware, there were 12 platters, 25 plates, 7 basins, 3 porringers, 3 tankards & 1 mug. Of wooden ware, 2 wooden platters and 2 knot dishes. Of the live stock, I give:—]

	£	s	d
6 cows £25, yoak of oxen, £14, Dun heifer, £4,	£43	00	
A weak backed cow £3, a sparked heifer £2,	5	00	
A sparked steer,	1	04	

21 sheep at 9s,	£ 9 09
Black horse £16, a one-eyed horse £8, a grey mare £5,	29 00
The old Mare & colt £5, Bay Mare & colt, £6, Bay Mare £3, 10s,	14 10
Grey Mare £5, Brown horse £6, young bay horse £2,	13 00
Legacy from Uncle Smith of Roxbury,	50 00

So we leave the kindly patriarch, thrifty, and humane as he sees the light; walking among his children and his servants, and overlooking his herds with tender care for the weak and maimed. The good man and good minister, pipe in mouth and silver mug at hand, poring over his old Latin tomes, and pounding away at thick-shelled theological nuts. The faithful pastor, serenely guiding his flock beside the dark waters, and pointing out the way to the haven of sweet peace and rest beyond. His body was laid beside that of his murdered wife, in the old graveyard. A third grave was made there when his second wife died, a quarter of a century later. The interesting inscriptions on their gravestones attract general attention.

The New Pastor. Five days after the death of Mr. Williams, a town meeting was held to provide for preaching. Acommittee was chosen :—

> To advise with some of ye neighboring ministers Whoom we shall hire to preach the gospel unto us & make report unto ye town.

July 25, 1729, the town Chose Dea. Sam^{ll} Childs to go in quest of a preacher and to advise first with Hatfield Mr. Williams, & get him to write to his Son Mr. William Williams & to Mr. Warham Williams then to Repair to them for advice who to get to preach to us for a small term of time (who is hereby Directed to act Discressionary upon y^r advice).

Rev. Benjamin Pierpont of New Haven, a graduate of Yale in 1726, was meanwhile supplying the people here with apparent satisfaction. August 25th, the town voted "that Dea. Childs shall be stopt in his journey for the present in search of a minister," and a committee was chosen to hire Mr. Pierpont for three months. November 29th, the people took up their burden again, and voted "to go on and finish ye meetinghouse." They realized that even under their great loss, there must be no halting in the affairs of the settlement.

January 5, 1730, they Voted that the Worthy Mr Benj Pierpont shall have a call to Settle among us to be our Pastor & teacher, by a great majority of votes thirty-six for him & fourteen against him. Voted that Sert Joseph Severance Mr. Ebenezer Sheldon and Doct Thomas Wells shall be a Com'tee to Endeavor to Stay Mr. Benjamin

Pierpont for ye Present and till we can Conveniently have opportunity to agree with him Respecting a Settlement among us & to agree with him for his wages in the meantime.

March 2 they Chose Mr Benjamin Munn, Doct Thomas Wells and Thos French to invite ye Worthy Mr Benj Pierpont to Settle among us in the pastoral office & to propose terms therfor & to Receive his answer & make Report to ye town in a town meeting, of their negotiations.

But there was trouble ahead, a growing element of dissatisfaction in the community. Rev. Mr. Williams of Hatfield, who favored Pierpont's settling here at first, was now busy in trying to prevent it. He gave out hints that he had discovered something wrong in the man, and could not in conscience keep quiet about the matter. The minority of fourteen, whom he had influenced to vote against Pierpont's settlement, had now increased to eighteen, who did at this meeting "actually Enter their disents against ye proceeding Respecting ye Settling Mr. Benj. Pierpont among us in ye pastoral office," and caused their names to be recorded.

Benjamin Pierpont was a man of the highest social rank; and was graduated on that basis, the first in a class of twenty-six. He was born in 1707. His father was James Pierpont of New Haven, for thirty years a leading minister in Connecticut, and his mother, the daughter of Rev. Samuel Hooker. His sister was the wife of the distinguished Jonathan Edwards, with whom he was then living. He was endorsed by the associated ministers of New Haven county, and by Elisha Williams, rector of Yale College, third son of the "Hatfield Mr. Williams," who led the opposition. Pierpont urgently pressed Mr. Williams to bring charges and witnesses, that they might be met. The committee seconded the candidate in this demand. At length Mr. Williams put in writing his opinion that Mr. Pierpont "was not of Prudent, Grave & Sober Conversation," but on the contrary "was vain, apish & jovial, particularly among females." He repeated some idle reports he had heard; one was, that "a girl said she should be as much afraid of him, as she should have been of Mr. Willard of Sunderland;" and "a say of Mr. Hopkins, when asked his advice concerning his settling in Deerfield; that he didn't know but that he might do, when he had sowed his wild oats, and that he knew he had sowed a good many already." So many, it seems, that they sprung up to block his way to our pulpit; and "Hatfield Mr. Williams" carried his point, as it appears by the following:

At a meeting Oct. 9th, 1730, a committee was chosen "to agree with yᵉ Worthy Mr. Benj. Pierpont for his preaching from yᵉ time that he was paid till yᵉ 4th of October inclusive & give him the thanks of yᵉ town for his services." Pierpont, however, left town with a certificate of good character:—

> Yᵉ governing part of yᵉ House-holders, & almost all yᵉ principal men of yᵉ town being moved by the Injuries his Reputation has suffered by this means, have given it under their hands that he was accounted a person of good character during his abode there, and that as to any Reports to the contrary, they never perceived that they were ever looked upon by Sober & Judicious men as worthy to be regarded.

But the young man seems never to have recovered from the blow dealt him by Mr. Williams. He went to the West Indies, where he died within four or five years.

October 28th, Dea. Childs was directed to seek a preacher "out of yᵉ candidates of Harvard College." He soon returned with Mr. John Warren, who gave great satisfaction.

The new meetinghouse was fast approaching completion, and November 20th, a committee was chosen "to sell yᵉ old meetinghouse this night to the highest bidder, reserving only yᵉ benches and liberty to meet in it until next March."

The new house was being finished with benches, and the people were confronted with the grave question, how shall they be occupied? There were evidently two parties, with different views on the matter. It may be the Pierpont discords had not been harmonized. If not, it was the good fortune of Warren, the new minister, to finally bring them into unison.

May 6th, 1731, "yᵉ town conseeded with yᵉ church in yᵉ choice of yᵉ Worthy Mʳ. John Warren for their pastor and teacher by a universal vote," and a committee was chosen to confer with him in the matter. It appears that Warren declined the call. We do not know the reason, neither did the astonished people.

At a town meeting, July 2d, the committee were directed to write,—

Mr. Williams of hatfield & Mr. William Williams of West town, & to Mʳ Warham Williams to desire yᵐ to use their interest with Mr. Warren for us & to enquire into yᵉ cause of his denying our unanimous Request of his being our Minister and send us an account why it is as soon as they can with Mr. Warren's inclinations.

Mr. Warren did not change his mind; and in their extremity a fast was appointed by the church in Deerfield. If our fathers believed the trouble arose from the anger of God, and that He could be placated by their going hungry, or mortifying the flesh in some other form—which was the central idea, adopted from the heathen—they were only like those all about them, only a part of the times in which they lived.

The advice given by the ministers who assembled at the observance of the fast was to try Mr. Warren again with new proposals. This advice was followed, but with no better success; and August 19th, "they chose Dea. Sam'll Childs to go in search of a minister." He probably brought back James Chandler, for October 19th, the town directed Dea. Thos. French, Dea. Childs and John Catlin to hire Mr. Chandler "to preach here some time longer." November 3rd, "they chose y^u Worthy Mr. James Chandler to be their pastor & teacher by a great majority." November 21st, "Voted to send for Mr. Chandler; * * * that Capt. Wells should go for him." Capt. Wells "went for him," but in vain; and December 17th, Dea. Samuel Field was sent into Connecticut after a preacher. His success may be inferred by the vote of Jan. 9th, 1731-2, "to invite ye Worthy Mr. Jonathan Ashley to preach the Gospel here a few Sabaths;" while mindful of their former disappointments, they agreed at the town meeting to send a man "in search of a minister, and they chose Dea. Sam'll Childs to go on s^d business."

February 7, Voted to hire Mr. Ashley two months.

Monday, April 10, 1732, the town chose ye Worthy Mr Jonathan Ashley for there minister by a great majority of votes, therein concurring with ye church vote:

Justice Wells Dea^n Field, Dea^n Childs, Mr. Eben^r Hinsdel & Capt Wells were chosen a committee [to acquaint Mr. Ashley of this action,] and make to him in order to his taking office here, ye propositions as was last mad to Mr. John Waren. * * * Thomas French, Jr., did Actually enter his dessent against the vote.

Thursday, August 3, Hauing receiued Mr. Ashley's answer they Voted y^t it should be lodged with Dea Saml Childs & y^n made choice of Dea^n Field Dea^n Childs and Thos French, Ju^n, a Com'tee to draw up ye agreement with Mr. Ashley in form agreeing with the former proposals w^h he hath accepted * * * and present the same to ye town.

Propositions made to Mr. Ashley, and accepted, and under which he was ordained Nov. 8th, 1732:—

1st That when he ye s^d Mr. Jonathan Ashley shall take office and ye pastoral Care and Charge of this Church and Congregation we promise and agree y^t for his Settlement he Shall haue p^d by this town three hundred pounds in bills of publick credit s^d bills to be Equivalent to Silver at eighteen shillings ye ounce which is to be understood that one once of Silver shall pay eighteen Shillings of s^d Sum; which £300 ye town promiseth to giv ye s^d Mr. Ashley within three years after his inauguration, one hundred pounds in each year or if he wants it sooner in case of his buying or building then to pay him one hundred and fifty pounds in each of ye two first years.

2^d This town promiseth to giue him, ye s^d Mr. Ashley ten acres of land as convenient as may be found for a pasture

3ly. This town promiseth to giue him ye s^d Mr. Ashley one hundred and thirty pounds yearly in bills or Silver as aboue expressed in y^e £300 Settlement

4thly. This town promiseth to giue to him ye s^d Mr. Jonathan Ashley ye use and improuement of ye towns house lot yearly to be continued as ye Sallery

5th. This town promiseth to find him ye s^d Mr. Ashley his firewood yearly

6ly. This town promiseth that he ye s^d Mr. Ashley shall haue ye liberty of ye Commons for his creatures to Run on yearly, as other proprietors haue and to get timber Stone Clay or ye like for his own proper use—provided Allways and it is to be understood by both parties, anything herin contained to the contrary notwithstanding that he ye s^d Mr. Jonathan Ashley shall in time convenient after his inauguration signe a Relinquishment of all ye lands in this town Sequestered to ye Ministry, except ye house lot aboue Mentioned ye use of which might otherwise accrue to him by virtue of his being our pastor

This contract seems explicit enough, but never-ending trouble grew out of its provisions.

The meetinghouse of 1729 when finally completed was a structure far exceeding in elegance the country meetinghouse of to-day. It stood on the training field, its front ranging with the west side of the street, its northeast corner fifteen rods and nineteen links, from the southeast corner of the present brick meetinghouse. It was forty by fifty feet, with a pitch roof, from the center of which rose the steeple, surmounted by a brass cock and ball, which Jonathan Hoyt was directed to purchase, " at a price not exceeding £20." The bell rope hung down in the center of the broad aisle in front of the pulpit. There were three doors, one in the front and one at each end.

The front entrance was an elaborate affair. The door was double and finely panelled. The surrounding work was of complex character, but highly ornamental, the top being a handsome pediment formed of two long-armed volutes, meeting in the center, where, in a niche thus formed, was placed a sort of urn-shaped ball. There were thirteen windows in front; the lower tier capped with sharp triangular pediments; the upper tier close up under the eaves. The windows on the back side corresponded with those in the front, except that a very large one with round top was built in the rear of the pulpit, some ten feet from the ground. The interior was finished in fine style, and "the timbers coloured." The galleries, built on three sides, were supported by turned oak pillars with gracefully carved capitals, specimens of which may still be seen in use, in a porch at the Willard house. The front of each gallery was handsomely panelled. The square pews when finally finished were also of panel work and ornamented with a row of balusters about ten inches high running around the top, including the panelled doors. The seats were stationary, not hung on hinges according to the fashion of the times.

The pulpit was on the west side opposite the front door, set well up on the wall, and reached by seven steps, and through a door at its north end. It was about ten feet by four, with a semi-cylinder shaped projection in front, for the reading desk. The front and ends were of fine panel work, running up and down, with a heavy cornice at the top. This and the top of the desk were covered with a green baize cushion, from the outer edge of which hung a heavy fringe. The interior of the pulpit was lined throughout with green baize, the stuff being woven in wales, as was that of the cushions on the seat and desk. The lining was held in place by a great array of brass nails.

The semi-circular desk did not extend to the deacons' seat below, but, tapering from the pulpit floor, it was finished off as a richly-carved cornucopia, the point turning up to the left. The whole was painted a dark olive-green. At the rear of the pulpit was a large ornamental window, draped with curtains of the same baize, the voluminous folds of which were caught back and held by huge curtain pins at the sides.

The sounding board, also painted dark green, hung upon iron rods directly over the desk. It was circular or octagon-

ARRANGEMENT OF INTERIOR. 473

al, the edge ornamented by a handsome cornice some eight inches wide. The under surface was divided into fan-shaped panels by bars which radiated from an elaborately carved star in the center.

The deacons' seat was in front of the pulpit facing the broad aisle. Upon its panelled front, hung upon hinges the long wide board, which when swung up and fastened, served for a communion table. This pew was entered by a door at the north end.

On the floor at the right of the pulpit were three wall pews, and on the left, two. There were two pews on either side of the three doors. These occupied all the wall space under the gallery, except in the southeast and northeast corners, in which were stairs, respectively, to the women's and men's gallery. The body of the house seems to have been at first occupied by benches, probably those reserved when the old meetinghouse was sold. These were gradually crowded out by pews.

There appears to have been a good deal of friction and trouble in deciding how these pews and seats should be occupied. Votes passed at one town meeting would be reconsidered at the next, or at an adjournment of the same. The difficulties doubtless grew out of the matter of "*seating*" the worshipers, or, as it was termed, "seating the meetinghouse," which was a subject of annual debate in the town meeting.

In 1744, under leave of the town, a clock was placed on the spire by individual enterprise, "to be taken care of by the Selectmen." It was put up by Obadiah Frary, a grandson of Samson, our second settler. The hands of this clock and part of the works are still preserved in Memorial Hall.

In 1746, Voted that Elijah Williams be allowed a Liberty to make three Pues out of ye Two on ye South side of ye East Door of the meeting house on his own charge & that ye Reurd Mr. Ashley shall have his Choise of the three pues, and then the said Williams to have the next choice for himself and mother [the widow of Rev. John Williams] he to have the pue no Longer than he shall stay in Town, and no Liberty to alienate the same.

Voted that Messrs Eben'r Wells John Nims John Arms & Daniel Arms be allowed a Liberty to make Three Pues on ye North Side of ye East Door and that on the same terms that Capt. Williams hath the Pue on ye South side of ye Door Ens. Wells and John Nims having ye first Choice of one of ye Three pues & then John & Dan^{ll} Arms, to have ye Second choice.

In 1748, four pews were built in the body in front of the six last described. In 1754, at a special meeting it was voted to build six more, which must have covered the rest of the floor. This vote was not carried out in full, for in 1787 the seating committee were directed "to see that pews where the *short seats* are be erected at the cost of the town."

The steeple or spire appears to have been insufficiently supported; it sagged, and spread the walls of the building. Ever after 1748, it was a subject of discussion in the town meeting, and committee after committee were chosen to examine it with skilled workmen and repair it. At length in 1767, after several plans had been voted and reconsidered in previous years, the town,—

Voted to Erect a Steeple at the North End of the Meeting house, to be in proportion to the body of the house, in the same proportion as the Steeple of Northfield Meeting house is to the body of that house, & that Lt. David Field & Mr. Joseph Barnard be the Committee to see the same effected, which Committee hereby engage to do the same for the sum of one Hundred Pounds Lawful Money.

The charges for removing the old spire were:—

233 feet of boards at	£0	6	2
2,000 shingles,	1	13	10
2,000 4d nails,	0	8	0
150 10d nails,	0	1	6
3 days' work,	1	12	0
For taking down the spire, Samuel Conable was paid,	1	10	0
Joseph Barnard paid,	0	3	7
David Hoyt, "for a quart of rhum, and 2 Mugs ½ of flip,"	0	2	10

The new steeple was built from the ground, against the center of the house over the north door. It was square, with an entrance on the east side. The bell deck was open, with eight pillars, which supported a tall, graceful spire, surmounted by the old cock and ball. This had been sent to Boston for renovation as it appears by the following bill, dated March 2d, 1768:—

Dr. Mr. David Field to Thomas Drowne:
Gold, & guilding a Weather Cock, Ball & diamond, rectifying Bruises, and fixing new Globe Eyes; for Deerfield Meeting House, £2, 12s.

John Field was paid for "carting weather cock, ball, &c., from Boston," 3 s 10 d.

The old rooster kept his perch until the steeple was pulled down in 1824, when the writer witnessed his plunge to the ground and assisted in helping him to his feet. After another

NEW SPIRE AND NEW PORCH.   475

journey to Boston for repairs, he was placed on the spire of the new brick meetinghouse.

Capt. Jonas Locke was the architect and builder of the first steeple. Other carpenters who worked on the building were Thomas and Abraham Billing, Nathan Oaks, Joseph Chamberlain, Samuel Dwelly, Francis Munn, David Harrington and Benjamin Munn, Jr.

There is a tradition, which I cannot now verify, that one of the workmen engaged in building this steeple fell to the ground and was nearly killed. No one recalls the man's name.

The committee to build the steeple were also directed to build a porch over the south door. This was a very elaborate structure; in form, the half of a dome-capped cylinder, two stories high and about twenty feet in diameter. Bills for more than £50 expended on the porch are found; among them that of David Harrington for seventy-eight days' labor in summer, at 3s 4d, and twenty-nine and one-half days in winter, at 3s; and of Capt. Locke and others for thirty days more. Ens. Childs furnished crooked plank for porch rafters; Joseph Wheeler shaved two and a half thousand shingles to cover it, and David Hoyt, Landlord of the Old Indian House, supplied "two quarts of rum and eight mugs of flip at the raising."

In the porch, stairs were made to the second floor, from which a door opened into the women's gallery, and in the steeple at the north end, were stairs to the men's gallery. Pews were built, both below and above, in the corners where the stairs had been originally placed. Another committee, consisting of Joseph Stebbins, John Nims, Seth Catlin, Jonathan Arms and Thomas Dickinson, had charge of general repairs to the main building. They covered it with new clapboards, and put in new window frames and sashes. The bill of work for the latter may interest mechanics.

David Armses accompt:—

The town of Deerfield, Dr. July, 1769.

To carting bords from Cheap Side to the Meeting House for the Meeting house sashes,	0	2	0	0
to making 644 lights of sashes,	6	8	9	2
to spreading, turning & haking sash timber five weeks,	0	6	0	0
to cutting thirteen hundred pieces of tin,	0	4	0	0
To two days of work making 50 wate of putte,	0	6	8	0
to fifteen days' work and a half fitting in Sashes, Washing, Seting, Puting and Tining meeting house glasse,	2	8	11	0

By direction of the town, the house was "coloured; yᵉ Body Dark stone Colour; yᵉ Window frames white; yᵘ Doors a Chocolate." The bell was raised and hung in the new belfry by Capt. Locke at a cost of five and a half days' work, 16 s; fifty double ten spikes, 1 s 10 d, and one quart of rum, 1 s 9 d; 19 s 7 d in all. John Regular and Isaac Marshall were assistants. Obadiah Frary was paid for putting up the clock and painting the dial £2 12 s, and for fourteen days' board at 8 d a day, 9 s 4 d; for horse-keeping at 4 d a day, 4 s 8 d.

The town voted *not* to put a "Wire or Rod & Points above the weather cock of the Meeting house for the preservation of the same from lightning." This was about fifteen years after the invention of the lightning-rod by Franklin.

The meetinghouse now stood forth to all appearance an entirely new building—no! the old roof with its great patch where the steeple had been taken off was an eye-sore, and marred the effect. Measures must be taken to restore harmony. The purse-strings of the town had been loosened little by little, as one item of improvement after another had been called for by those most interested; but they were now tied in a hard knot, and an extra twist put in. "No more taxes," said the majority, but "if any generously disposed persons are willing to shingle the meetinghouse at their own expense they have free, full and ample liberty." The challenge was accepted. A subscription paper was drawn up, and the undersigned:—

For promoting so laudable purpose, promise to give the several sums affixed to our names in Cash, Wheat, or Rye, and have the same ready, if in Grain at the time the shingles are delivered in Deerfield; if in cash, when the shingling of the meeting house is completed.

Elijah Williams, in Grain,	$20	Sam'll Childs, in wheat,	8
Thomas Williams, in Grain,	20	Daniel Arms, in Rye,	15
David Field,	24	Joseph Barnard, Jr.,	8
Joseph Barnard,	24	Jonathan Hoit,	10
David Hoyt,	12	Ebenezer Wells,	10
Salah Barnard,	10	Asahel Wright, in Rye,	10
Joseph Stebbins,	24	Joseph Mitchel,	4
Thomas Dickinson,	24	Seth Catlin, in Wheat,	8
Zadock Hawks,	8	Nathaniel Dickinson,	24
John Nims,	4	John Hawks,	12
Eldad Bardwell,	4	Simeon Stebbins,	4
John Sheldon, 500 shingles,		John Amsden,	12
John Bardwell,	6	John Russell,	6
Jonathan Arms,	12	John Hensdel,	9
David Sexton,	10		

PEWS BUILT IN THE GALLERY. 477

Timber for the shingles was given by E[lijah?] Arms; the cost of making and laying and other expense is found below:—

Joseph Wheeler, making 16 M. shingles at 10s 8d,	£8 10 8
Looking out and clearing road two days by David Hoyt and Joseph Barnard,	6 0
Carting the shingles, five loads at 6s,	1 10 0
Laying the shingles, twenty-eight days,	4 18 5
Board of workmen 16 days at 8d,	10 8
Joseph Barnard for 5½ M. shingle nails at 4d,	1 2 0
Saving old nails by Eb. Wells, Dea. Childs, Lieut. Field, Maj. Barnard, Maj. Williams, David Sexton and John Hinsdale,	12 8
Jona. Arms bill "for straiting shingle nails,"	3 8

Sixteen thousand five hundred common shingles would not cover the old part of the roof, and those shaved out by Wheeler were probably "puncheons."

No changes appear to have been made in the interior of the house except to take down the stairs to the galleries, and fill the vacant spaces with pews above and below. The arrangement of seats or pews in the gallery at first does not appear; but as early as 1739, the "pue over the woman's stairs" is mentioned. In the warrant for the March meeting of 1789 was an article to see if the town would build any pews in the gallery, or allow others to do so; but there is no record of action on it. The warrant for the March meeting of 1793 contained the same article, and leave was granted for pews to be built under the direction of the selectmen, on condition that four pews shall be built in each gallery, and that the town may take them at any time on paying the cost. It does not appear whether this offer was accepted or not. In 1803 the selectmen were made a committee "to lease the back part of the north and south galleries for the purpose of erecting pews." This action was to allow the trustees of Deerfield Academy to "build pews for the accommodation of scholars." They built a long pew in the southwest corner for the girls, and one in the northwest for the boys. Other pews were occupied by students at a later date.

In 1791, the selectmen were directed to procure shutters for the lower windows and the pulpit window, and £40 was raised to paint the house. It is remembered by the old folks as being yellow, when taken down in 1824.

At length it dawned upon the people that a milder temperature in winter would be conducive to both health and com-

Seating the Meeting House—Copy of Plan reported to the town about 1777-8.

Sam'l Field, Doc.[Eb.]Barnard, Sam'l Barnard, John Williams. **16**	Amasa Smith, Jona. Holt, 2d, Obed Hawks. **18**	Eber. Wells, Zadock Hawks, Thomas Arms. **10**	Sam'l Barnard, Maj.[S.] Barnard, Eldad Bardwell. **4**	FRONT DOOR.	William Arms, Elijah Arms, Jona. Holt.	Madam Ashley, Wido. Williams, Esq.[Jona.] Ashley. **5**	Doct.[Elihu] Ashley, Aaron Arms, Sam'l Childs, 2d. **11**	Amzi Childs, John Sheldon, Jr., Wido.[H.]Russell, John Clap, Eliakim Arms. **17**
Clement Hoyt, Joseph Clesson, David Holt, Jr. **24**	John Kendell, Joseph Wise, Aaron Pratt, Solomon Newton, Simeon Burt, Edward Joiner. **28**		Daniel Sexton, Mathew Clesson, Isaac Parker, Justin Hitchcock, Wido Herbert. **20**		Elijah Smith, Moses Chandler, Thomas Wells, Augustus Wells, Wido. Munn, Lt. Taylor, Wido.[Lucy] Tyler. **21**	Phineas Munn, Lt.[Elihu] McCall, William Felton, Ebenezer Burt, Francis Munn. **29**	Waitstill Hawks, John Sexton, Zeb. Graves, Elisha Nims, Elias Stone. **25**
Nathan Robbins, Edward Joiner, Eber Allis, Seth Arms, Ariel Nims. **30**								Wm. Anderson, John Anderson, John Stebbins, Amos Alexander, Joseph Sweet. **31**

Meetinghouse Seating Plan

North Door; through Steeple.

South Door; through Porch.

Pew 26
Cap. Ol.r Shattuck,
Elihu Murry,
Itbamar Burt,
Nath'l Frary, Jr.

Pew 27
Phineas Arms,
Eliphas Arms,
Rem. Grandy,
Thos. Mighills.

Pew 8
Levi Newton,
David Sexton,
Lt. Seth Catlin,
Jono. Arms.

Pew 9
Lt. John Bardwell,
Moses Stebbins,
Col. [Jos.] Stebbins,
Lt. Joseph Barnard,
Wido. Snead.

Benches.

Pew 23
Lt. Thos. Bardwell,
Lt. David Stebbins,
Sam'l Childs, 3d,
Wido. R. Childs.

Benches.

Pew 14
Nathan Catlin,
Seth Hawks,
Asa Hawks.

Pew 2
Joseph Stebbins,
Daniel Arms,
Capt. [Nath.] Frary.

Pew 3
Caleb Allen,
Paul Hawks,
Eunice Allen,
Sam'l Harding.

Pew 15
John Sheldon,
Jeremiah Nims,
David Hoit,
Wido. [Abigail] Nims.

Pew 6
Sam'l Dwelley,
Simeon Harvey,
Capt. [Abner] Mitchell,
Gideon Dickinson,
Capt. Jonas Locke,
Sam'l Tennant.

Pew 7
Jos. Mitchell,
Jos. Snead,
John Amsden,
Moses Nims,
Wido. Rhoda Childs,
" Sarah Shattuck.

Pew 22
Thos. Faxon,
Jno. Bull,
Justin Bull,
John Hinsdale,
Alpheus Newton.

Pew 1
Col. [John] Hawks,
Col. [David] Field,
Ens. [Joseph] Barnard,
Madam [Abigail] Silliman,
Capt. Thomas Dickinson.

Mrs. Childs,
Mrs. Wright,
Des. Noah Wright.

Deacon [Samuel] Childs,
" [Asahel] Wright.

PULPIT.

Pew 13
Maj. [David] Dickinson,
Eliphalet "
Capt. [T.] W. "
Oliver Field, "
Elihu "

Pew 13
[south side marker]

Ground Plot of the Pews Above Stairs in the Meeting House.

[Accepted by the town, Feb. 4th, 1796.]

					Anny Luddin
					Lina Sanderson
					Lydia Eustiss
					Kentfield
					Jewett
					Sally Locke
					Patience Denio
					Faithy Ball
					Hannah Ball
					Nash
					Wright

			Patty Hitchcock	Fanny Cooley
			Spidde Stebbins	Anny Joyner
			Susanah Arms	Ennice Childs
		Dorothy Catlin	Sophia Cooley	Roxana Nims
		Fanny Granger	Filana Cooley	Abigail Nims
		Polly Arms	Patsy Hawks	Fanny Harvey
	Solo Ashley	Ester Childs	Orrey Harvey	Hannah Pain
	Elijah Williams	Betsie Amsden	Thankful Hawks	Smith
	Elijah Rufsell	Hannah Barnard	Nancy Catlin	Smith
Joseph Sanderson Jr	Zenas Hawks	Eunice Barnard	Lucy McCall	Clapp
Reuben Sanderson	Richard Catlin	Lyddia Ames	Louis Sanderson	
Calvin Sexton	Lem'll Russell	Suhmit Childs	Experience Barnard	
Amzi Childs Jr	Will'm Sheldon	Jude Allen		
Benj Walker	David Wait	Sally Hawks		
Seth Clapp	Jonathan Cobb			
Elijah Newton				
Luther Newton				
Eliel Allen				
Silas Hawks				
Levi Sanderson				
Graves				

	David Childs
	Qnartus Hawks
	Dan'l Arms
	Sam'll Childs 2d
	Henry Barnard
	Denis Stebbins
	Thos Ashley
	Jonth Dickinson
	George Herbert
	James Willies
	Parle Holt

Charles Pierce
Will'm Logan
James Logan
Reuben Field
Asaph Allen
Othniel Hannur
Oliver Moreton
Levi Luddin
David Butler
Benjamin Nash
Elias Joyner
Thos Childs
Moses Newton
Jonth Wright
Waitsfill Hawks Jr
Israel Childs
John Saxton
Stephen Morton
Elijah Dwolly
R McKene
Ebn'r Barnard 3d
Elihu Barnard
Clark
John Leifolt seated at the upper end of the fore seat in the upper tier

THE FORE SEATS ARE LEFT FOR THE ACCOMODATION OF SINGERS IN THE GALLERY.

fort, and Dec. 5th, 1808, measures were taken to have the meetinghouse warmed, and a large, square, box stove was procured for that purpose. The worshipers may have been moved to this action by the appearance among them that season of a delicate exotic, in the person of Mrs. Susan Barker Willard, the bride of the new minister. Or, possibly, the toning down of the theological temperature, which occurred in the church about this time, may have made this innovation necessary. The stove was placed in front of the deacon's seat, the pipe ran thence north to the gallery, and followed that on the north, east and south sides of the house, and so out through a port-hole in one of the west windows; for there was no chimney.

As early as 1799, considerable repairs became necessary on the steeple, and after much money had been spent in trying year after year to make the house "something comfortable," on the 23d of February, 1823, the end came in a vote "Not to repair the old Meeting house," but to build a new one. In accordance with these votes the old house was demolished and the present brick house built in 1824.

The Meetinghouse bell. An account of the method taken to procure the first bell has been given. March 5th, 1733, the town voted that "the Bell be rung at nine of ye clock at night, night by night." This custom was kept up until about 1850. It was also rung at noon during the summer months. This bell responded to all calls upon it for more than fifty years, but at last it gave out. In 1773, a committee was chosen to write to Quartus Pomroy, the noted cow-bell maker of Northampton, to take a view of it, "and if he can mend it, to agree with him to do it, and if he thinks it must be sent *home* to be new cast, or run, the s^d committee are hereby empowered to send the same to England, or to get it run in this Country, if practicable, as soon as may be, and also to make such additions of metal as shall make the new Bell Weigh Five Hundred Weight." After about forty years' service this bell was replaced by one to weigh eight hundred pounds.

The action for dignifying the seats and seating the worshipers in the third meetinghouse was given on page 205. When the fourth house was finished in 1730, seaters were chosen in town meeting, to dignify the seats and pews, and report a detailed scheme, to be acted upon at a subsequent meeting. The proceedings of this committee did not give general satisfaction. There seems to have been two parties of nearly equal numbers, with different views in regard to the vexed question of dignifying the seats, and which diverged more widely in establishing the relative social position of the occupants. Some radical plans were urged, but the conservative element finally prevailed.

> At a town meeting Monday, Nov. 23, 1730:
> Voted to seat men and their wives in ye pues.
> Voted to leave it with ye seaters to dignifie the pews and seats.
> Voted to seat without having regard to qualifications:
> Voted to seat by ye rules of age & estate.
> Voted that a pound Rateable estate as in ye list shall be accounpted equal with a year's age
> Voted to seat by the rules of age, estate & qualifications.

After all these contradictory votes, the people stopped to take breath and get a fresh start, and then:—

> Voted that ye aboue written votes made on this adjournment shall be void & of non effect.
> Voted to seat men and their wifes together in ye peues
> Voted that ye Seaters which shall be Chose to Seat ye Meeting house shall be a Com^{tee} to Dignifie ye Seats & peus & present their work to ye town, in a town Meeting to put a Santion before they begin to Seat.
> Voted that s^d seaters shall seat y^o Meeting house by ye Rules of Age, Estate & quallifications.

The seaters chosen were Eleizer Hawks, Thomas French, Jr., Jonathan Hoyt, John Catlin, Jr., and William Arms, Jr. These young men appear to be of the party which attempted the rash innovations above noted, and were beaten. They refused the sop thus thrown them, and others were chosen November 27th, at an adjourned meeting. December 7th, "the town accepted of ye Dignifieing of ye peus & seats as then presented in a map." This map has not been found. So far as it appears the people remained quietly for a few years in the positions assigned them by this committee.

> Dec. 20, 1737, voted that ye Seaters farther make some necessary alterations in Seating ye Meeting house as they Shall see meet According to ye rules given them.
> 1738 Timothy Childs, Benjamin Munn, Thos. French, Samuel Childs and John Catlin 2d were chosen *standing* seaters.

January, 1739, efforts were made to have more pews built or the old ones altered; but without success, and the seaters were instructed to "adhere to yᵉ Instructions which have been already given." The opposition, however, gained one point.

Voted that Messrs Samuel Field John Catlin and Thomas Wells 2d shall be a Com'tee to Determine how many Persons their shall be Seeted in Each Pue & to make return thereof to yᵉ Seaters.

With this double-barrelled authority quiet prevailed for two years; but in May, 1741,—

Voted that there shall be some alteration in the seating of people in yᵉ Meeting House & that yᵉ womens pue in yᵉ Galery shall be Seated with men.

It was in this pew, perhaps, certainly it was about this time, that Joseph Barnard sold to Samuel Barnard, Joseph Stebbins and Remembrance Sheldon each a "right in a pue over the woman's stairs." The price paid was seventeen, twenty and fifteen shillings respectively. There is found no precedent or subsequent action, showing, or hinting at exclusive private ownership in any pew or seat in this meetinghouse, and this anomalous transaction stands wholly unexplained. The erection of four new pews in 1748 disturbed the balance of ecclesiastical dignity among the worshipers, and the town made choice of a committee "to new dignify the Seats & Pues in the Meeting house, & to Seat persons accordingly." A movement to sell the pews made at this time was not sustained. It does not appear how the galleries had been occupied previous to 1750. That year the seaters had "Liberty of appropriating yᵉ whole of yᵉ Front Gallery for yᵉ use of Seating Men, in order for the better accommodation of Women below."

In 1753, the secession of quite a large part of the congregation to the church just formed in the Greenfield District, left matters in a somewhat chaotic condition, and the pressure in all grades, except the highest, towards seats of higher dignity thus left vacant, made new legislation necessary. These seats could not be left unoccupied, and in a general forward movement to close up the ranks, people might be placed in seats of higher "dignity" than they were entitled to by their "qualifications." Would not this have a tendency to give these people an exaggerated idea of their importance? and might not their consequent assumption be troublesome to "their betters"?

Here was a dilemma truly. But, as in every great crisis in the affairs of men and nations, a genius equal to the occasion appeared upon the stage. In fitting season he easily procured a popular vote in town meeting, "that the Dignification of the Seats in the meeting house be Intirely set aside." This was an astonishing change indeed! Hereafter democratic ideas and usages must prevail, and all be equal before the Lord in His holy service. Each worshiper could select his or her seat on entering, without let or hindrance from constable or tithingman. Not quite! Wait a little. The inspiration of our genius is not yet exhausted. The master-stroke took form in a vote,—

To new Regulate the Seting of the meeting house, having regard to the Age, Estate and other Qualifications of people in Determining who shall have the most Convenient seat, &c., and so on through the whole house. [A committee was chosen to carry out this vote] according to the best of their judgment, that is, ye Best or Most Convenient Seat to ye first man; ye second to ye next, and to place as many in a pue as they may judge may conveniently sit in it & ye Necessity of Seating may Require.

This arrangement furnished a sliding scale of dignity for the seats, to be settled by demand and supply, and self-adjusting. The seats were to be dignified by the occupants, and not the people by the seats. The "upper crust" retained all it had before, and the dilemma had disappeared forever. The committee were directed to reserve seats for Col. Ebenezer Hinsdale and Mrs. Abigail Wells, and this direction was repeated at other meetings.

Dec. 6th, 1762, a committee was chosen to new seat the meetinghouse, according to age, estate and qualifications. Nothing was said of Col. Hinsdale or Mrs. Wells. For some reason the seaters were dissatisfied, and a new town meeting was called for December 20th,—

To know whether the town will make any alteration in any of the seats of the meeting house agreeable to the representations of the Seaters; if not, the Seaters Desire a Dismission from that business, or otherwise give them some further directions; and in *particular* respecting allowing seats to *non-residents*.

Voted that Col^o Ebenezer Hinsdale and Mrs. Abigail Wells be allowed Seats in the Meeting house.

Col. Hinsdale was brought up in Deerfield, and his wife was daughter of Rev. John Williams. He had a home lot, house and place of business here, and another at Hinsdale, N. H.—a town named for him—and where he usually resided. Mrs. Wells was wife of Jonathan Wells of Road Town; her mother was a Deerfield woman. The Colonel and Mrs. Wells were both members of the church here, and their family ties were mainly with Deerfield people. It is a curious condition of affairs, when all this agitation and this town meeting was on the question whether two seats of presumably high grade should be left in reserve for the occupancy of these two non-residents, when they attended meeting here only occasionally. The seaters carried their point at this meeting, but at the next meeting, March 7th, 1763, a new committee was chosen as "Standing Seaters, to seat the meeting house from time to time as they shall think needful. Nothing more is heard of seating non-residents. In the warrant for the December meeting in 1769, was an article,—

To see if ye town will direct their committee for Seating the Meeting house not to seat ye fore seat in ye front gallery & ye fore seat in ye lower tier of ye womans side gallery, but leave ye same for singers.

There is no record of any action on this article, but the movers in the matter did not give it up. Dec. 3d, 1770, it was,—

Voted to leave and not Seat the two fore seats in ye front gallery & ye two fore seats in ye lower tier in ye womans gallery for ye use of singers.

[In 1785, the town was] desirous that persons should qualify themselves in the best manner that may be for singing in the Meetings for public Worship, and that the choice of tunes on these occasions shall be left with those who shall conduct that part of the Public Worship.

April, 1787, the seaters were directed to build pews "where the short seats now are, in the Body of the Meeting House." These short seats were directly opposite the north and south entrances. They seem to have been in the least desirable localities and were the last places filled with pews. See annexed plan. The seaters did not attend to this direction, but at the meeting of December 3d, a new committee was chosen, who promptly put up the pews, and January 7th, 1788, they reported a plan of seating, which is still preserved, on which these pews appear completed, and furnished with occupants.

Unsuccessful movements had been made from time to

time to have the pews leased or sold. In May, 1791, the town "Voted to lease the pews in the Meeting House, and that the money arising therefrom be appropriated to pay the Minister's tax. Voted that the term for which said pews be leased be *ninety-nine years.*"

In March, 1800, another attempt was made to lease or sell the pews, but without success. The matter was followed up at a meeting in May, and a committee was chosen to prepare a plan for leasing or selling. In a report made March 11th, 1801, the committee recommend a lease of the pews on the lower floor to the highest bidder, for six years. But the opposition was now in the ascendency, and voted to reconsider the vote under which the committee was chosen, and to discharge the committee.

March, 1802, "Voted to Sell the Pews in the Meeting House." Eleven men had their protest against this action recorded. Then a vote passed "to sell for six years." In December the committee was directed "*not* to sell the pews."

In the gallery, before 1787, eight pews were built against the wall across the east side. The four southerly pews were seated with young women; those on the north side with young men. A high, close partition separated the sexes. About eight or ten were seated in each pew, except those in the corners, which were about twice as long east and west, and furnished corresponding accommodation. In 1803 the trustees of Deerfield Academy were allowed to build pews in the southwest and northwest corners for students; the girls sat on the south side and the boys on the north. The space between these and the pews on the east side was occupied by the miscellaneous crowd not entitled to the honor of being seated—boys and girls too old to sit in the pews with their parents, hired men and women, apprentices, &c. A special provision was doubtless made for negroes.

The pews in the meeting house were never leased or sold, and the system of seating, which is being considered—that last relic of aristocratic English inheritance—survived until it went down forever with the old meetinghouse in 1824.

The accompanying plan was reported about 1780. The numbers indicate the rank or dignity of the pew.

CHAPTER XV.

THE PROPRIETORS OF POCUMTUCK. AGRARIAN RULES. GRANT OF 1712. TOWN LINES. CONWAY AND SHELBURNE LAID OUT.

The tenure on which the first settlers held their land has been already pointed out, and also the origin of the term cow-common; but a brief review may be convenient. For the two thousand acres which Dedham gave up for the Indian settlement under Eliot, at Natick, the General Court, in 1663, gave Dedham eight thousand acres, to be located in the wilderness. The right of the Colony to this wilderness will not be here discussed. After due explorations, the grant was laid out at Pocumtuck in 1665. Seven hundred and fifty acres were given the party which located and surveyed the land. The remainder was held in common by the land holders of Dedham, but was divided (on paper) into five hundred and twenty-two shares called cow-commons. This was in accordance with the rule still applying to all undivided territory in Dedham. These shares changed hands in the market until, in 1670, they were all in the hands of thirty-one parties, organized under the title of "The Proprietors of the 8000 acres at Pocumtuck."

The actual settlers here became land owners by virtue of the purchase of shares, or else by grants of commonage made them as inducements to join the little colony. The number of cow-commons was in this way increased to five hundred and fifty-seven, but in 1673 a large proportion of them were still held by non-residents. But it was to the "Inhabitants of Pocumtuck," the actual settlers on the spot, that the General Court gave the "seven miles square" in 1673. This grant was "such an addition of land to ye eight thousand acres formerly granted there to Dedham, as that ye whole be to ye contents of seven miles square." By some unknown process of mensuration our thrifty progenitors seem to have extended this " addition " so as to cover a territory lying along the Connecticut from Whately to Northfield, of about seventy square miles, including the Dedham Grant. In 1674 the owners of the latter and the grantees of the former consolidated their respective interests in the whole tract, forming a new association entitled the "Proprietors of Pocumtuck." This body held in fee the whole seventy square miles, excepting the town plat, and the meadow land already set off to individuals, and to it was assigned the,—

"*Additional Grant*" *of 1712*. While the war was still raging, a movement was made to enlarge our territory. No action of the town is recorded. The petition of Mr. Williams is not found, and the following is the only account or history of the transaction discovered:—

May 28: 1712 In Council
Upon Reading a petition of Mr John Williams Minister of Deerfield in Behalf of the s^d Town of Deerfield praying y^t ye Bounds of ye s^d Town may extend Westward from Connecticut River as Northampton and Hatfield Doe *viz* nine miles from ye River into ye Western woods: Also that ye two Islands in ye River afores^d Right against ye Town plat may be granted to the Petitioner and his heirs forever (provided no former grant Intervene) Containing between thirty and forty acres in them both Ordered That ye prayer of ye said petitioner be Granted

Concurred by ye House of Representatives
Consented to J. Dudley

The thrifty Agent, it will be seen, looked out for himself as well as for the town. The islands granted him, it has been generally supposed, lay above the mouth of the Pocumtuck river, where small islands still remain. But by the "Town Plat" is usually meant the "Old Street." No islands are found "right against" that. Mr. Williams sold one undivided half of his grant to John Sheldon. No transfer of this purchase, or anything relating to the other half, is found on record. It is probable that these islands were two of those named in the deed of Mashalisk to Pynchon in 1672, and that they have been swept away by the river.

Nov. 24th, 1715, the town chose Capt. Jona. Wells, Lieut. Samuel Barnard and John Arms a committee "to discourse and agree with Northfield Committee concerning the bounds between each of these towns," and were authorized "to Joyn with Northfield Committy to prefer a petition to the Generall Court in order to the confermation of w^t these two Commities shall agree upon concerning there town bounds aforesaid."

No result of this conference is found. Probably there was no agreement where the line should run. But the matter reached the General Court and was settled in another way, as we see below:—

June 11 1717 Upon Reading a Petition of Thomas Wells, Representative of ye Town of Derefield, setting forth that the General Court in ye year 1673 Granted to said Town an addition of a Tract of land that was to be laid out at the north end of the said Town, and to contain the quantity of Seven Miles Square, wch Land was accordingly laid out & the Bound Marks still to be seen. But upon Searching the Records they cannot find any Entry thereof; Praying that it may now be allowed & confirmed & be of Record to prevent future Trouble.

Wells was directed to make a plan of the tract by the old bounds and present it to the Court at its next session. Pursuant to the above order, a plan was presented to the House, Oct. 29, 1717, which was accepted. But the Council non-concurred. Nov. 9th, a committe of Conference was appointed of five from the House, and three from the Council. Nov. 19th this committee reported to the Council,—

That having maturely considered the Evidences and Pleas therabout, are humbly of opinion, that the Bounds of the Seven Miles Square granted to Deerfield, Shall be and Remain According to Platt now exhibited to this Great and General Court; Provided the line run from the north end of said Tract to the Great River be an East line.

The report was adopted. The objectors were doubtless Northfield people, but the particular points in the controversy do not appear. The grant thus accepted and confirmed, covered essentially the territories now occupied by the towns of Greenfield and Gill. The bounds of the Additional Grant of 1712,—

Begin at a large chestnut tree at the Country farm so-called which is the North West corner of the 7 Miles Square, already confirmed & runs thence West 1670 perch to two large white oak trees standing close together, thence South 19° West 3800 perch to a great hemlock tree with stones heaped about it, thence East 1670 perch to the South West corner of the 7 Mile Square, thence North 19° East 3860 perch to the chestnut tree.

The west line of this grant was thus made parallel to that of the Seven Mile grant. The latter is still known as it was then, as the "Seven Mile Line," and can still be traced from Whately to Colrain.

The Ashfield Line. In 1736 a township was granted Capt. Ephraim Hunt and his company for services in the Canada campaign of 1690. It was to be laid out adjoining Deerfield on the west. A controversy soon arose between the Proprietors of Pocumtuck and the Proprietors of "Huntstown" respecting the boundary line between them. This was settled only after appeals to the General Court and the Judiciary.

In 1736 the town made provision for "Surveying ye River on ye East side of the Town" as a basis for establishing the Seven Mile Line, as all agreed that the west line of the Additional Grant should be parallel to this, as this must be parallel to the river. A plan of the whole township was made based on this survey.

May 30 1737, Thomas Wells Esq of Deerfield is chose & appointed in ye name & in behalf of s^d Town to appear in ye Great & General Court of this Province, then and there to do any & all things that shall be conducive to get a plat of s^d Township confirmed.

The legislature was then in session and Esquire Wells was soon before it with his petition:—

June 29 1737. In the House of Representatives, Ordered, that Col. Chandler, Col. Almy, & Capt Hobson, with such as shall be joined by the Hon^l Board be a Com^{tee} to take the plat of the township of Deerfield under consideration, and the papers Accompanying the same, Relating to the lines or boundaries of said Town, that they carefully examine the said plat & consider the said papers & make Report thereon, so far as may relate to the true west line of said Town for the Courts further consideration & order in adjusting the same agreable to the Additional Grant.

The Council added William Dudley and Joseph Wild to this committee. Probably Wells's plan was not found to be sufficiently accurate or comprehensive to base final action upon, at any rate another town meeting was called.

July 22d, 1737, Thomas Wells, Ebenezer Smead and Elijah Williams were made a committee to "Survey the Township of Deerfield, & get an accurate plan of s^d Township to lay before the General Court as soon as may be."

The plan was made, and laid before the General Court, but by some means never understood by the people of Deerfield, the plan disappeared while awaiting legislative action. The whole matter seems to have then dropped until the Proprietors of Pocumtuck became alarmed by the proceedings of the Huntstown settlers and took the matter into their own hands.

Feb. 2d, 1741, at a Proprietors meeting Thomas Wells was again called to the front and "Appointed to procure a Plan of the Township forthwith," and a committee was chosen "to run the west side of the town & see the same well marked."

The plan made under the above vote was probably the one presented to the General Court by Elijah Williams, the representative from Deerfield, in July following. With this plan he offered this memorial in behalf of the town.

Some years ago, a plat of s^d Township was presented to this Court for Confirmation, but so it was, that either said plat was taken from the files, or was mislaid so that it could never be found to this Day & the s^d Town have at great charge and trouble procured another plan of s^d Town & the s^d Town labors under many inconveniences for want of having the bounds of s^d Town confirmed & established:

Therefore your Memorialist Humbly prays that a consideration of the s^d affair may be had and the plat now presented passed upon by this Court & your petitioner as in Duty bound shall ever pray.

ELIJAH WILLIAMS.

This memorial was referred to a committee consisting of Samuel Jackson, Joseph Blanchard, and Adam Cushing. They reported favorably, and the plan was confirmed. Nov. 2d at a meeting of the Proprietors:—

Voted that Missrs Elijah Williams, Thomas Wells Esq, & John Catlin, the second, be a Comitee or agents for the proprietors to sue or prosecute any person or persons, who have, or shall hereafter trespass on the Lands of ye proprietors, by any way or means whatsoever, on the west side, or else where in our propriety, who are also hereby empowered to Substitute one or more attorneys to manage or carry on any actions of trespass for the proprietors as s^d Com'ttee shall see fit.

Voted that Missrs Elijah Williams, John Hawks and John Catlin 2^{ond} be a Com'tee to provide a Survey^r to run the line on the west side of ye Town & see the same well marked.

Voted that Missrs Elijah Williams, Thomas Wells 2^{ond} and David Field be a Com'tee to go and fence and clear a peace of Land for the proprietors on the West side of the Mill Brook joining near the south line the Township. * * * and empowered if they think it will be for the benefit of the proprietors to lease out ye afors^d land to any person who will appear to take the same for five years, & the proprietors hereby oblige themselves to defend & save said Com'tee or those to whom they may let said land, free from any cost or charges that may arise by reason of their or his being anyway molested or Disturbed by any person or persons whatsoever in their or his Improvment or possession as afores^d.

All this action is aimed at the Huntstown people. They had run their east line, and were pitching their tents on land claimed as being within the bounds of the Additional Grant. The ground to be cleared and fenced was doubtless on the disputed territory. The evidence as to the merits of the controversy is scanty. Both parties were agreed that the west line of the Pocumtuck grants should be nine miles from the river; and they also agreed that the starting point from which to measure the nine miles should be the place where the line between Deerfield and Hatfield struck Connecticut river. [*Whately* was *not* then.] The disagreements appear to be, the *course* from the starting point, and the *course* from its western terminus, to the northward. Hunt's party claimed that the line from the river should be measured on the Hatfield line nine miles. One line is marked on an old plan, probably used in this case, as running " North 87° 23' East." The Deerfield men would run from the river at right angles to it, which would carry them about two or three hundred rods farther west. From this western terminus, when once fixed, both agreed that the line northward should be straight, and parallel to the river, which was the east bound of the town.

The battle was thus necessarily fought upon this river line. The difficulty was, the river was *crooked*. To average this, and form a base from which to lay off its west line, the Proprietors ran a line from the agreed southeast corner, northward through the mouth of Fall river, which gave a course of north 17° 45' east. The other party starting at the same point, would run north 20° 50' east, crossing the Connecticut a mile and a half east of Fall river; and run their east line parallel to that, nine miles westward. This would cut off above nine square miles claimed under the Pocumtuck grants. The evidence tends to show that the Hunt party failed in this attempt, but succeeded as to the south line of measurement from the river. But the end was not yet.

In March, 1742, Maj. Adam Cushing, in behalf of the Proprietors of Huntstown, petitioned the General Court, that a committee be appointed to settle the line, claiming:—

I. That when they went to lay out their Grant, Deerfield people refused to go and show them their west line 'Minding that we should so lay out the Grant so as to leave a gore between said towns to be swallowed up unknown to the Province' * * * We searched and found the Grant made to Deerfield in the petition of Rev. John Wil-

THE COURTS MUST SETTLE THE QUESTION. 493

liams in 1712 which extended nine miles West. We began at the river and ran on the Hatfield and Deerfield line 9 miles, then ran parallel to the river 7 miles for our East bounds.

The answer to this by Elijah Williams is that so far from refusing to show the line, a messenger was sent in the night to Northampton to get a copy of the survey, but the papers could not be found: and that three pounds value of provisions were furnished to the Proprietors, by the town, to their surveyors, while searching for the West line. If a gore *was* left one town would be as likely to swallow it up as the other.

2^{ondly} When the Proprietors settled a site for the Meeting House, it was near the easterly bounds so as to be near our Deerfield neighbors & now we are clearing & settling on lands Deerfield claims by virtue of their plan, which was confirmed this year & they will not enter upon the land so we can sue them nor sue us but by way of banter tell us to clear as fast as we can, that hereafter they shall get it from us, whereby many of us are discouraged & drawing off. Further I beg leave to observe that the critick that they lay hold of is, that to run 9 miles at right angles is about west north west instead of running west according to Hatfield and Northampton do, which is the occasion of their falling upon our grant and we desire the line settled so that we can be certain of clearing our own lands.

Williams answered, This question of ownership can only be settled at common law & it is trifling with the great and General Court to bring personal banter, and jesting of particular persons before it. In regard to a committee to look up the bounds he says, a committee was appointed last year, but we do not object to another if they will bear the expense and not Deerfield.

Commissioners cant settle the line. The Gen Court has made the Grants and if a dispute arises the law must settle it. Last year Samuel Jackson Joseph Blanchard and Maj Cushing [the present petitioner] were appointed, (upon my memorial respecting Deerfield plat being confirmed, which is herewith presented) who reported they were of opinion that the plat contained the just quantity of the grant, and is laid out with most conveniency, so as not to prejudice the Town, or adjoining lands, and most conformable to the grants to Deerfield, and that it should be accepted and confirmed.

March 25th, 1742, the General Court ordered that the Selectmen of Deerfield be notified to appear on the first Tuesday of May next, and show cause, if any they have, why the petition should not be granted. "In council June 2, 1742, Deerfield not having timely notice, the case is postponed to Thursday the 24th, if the Court be then attending, if not to the first Thursday of the next setting, and notice to be given Deerfield."

A town meeting was called June 19th, 1742, and "Thomas Wells and Samuel Barnard Esqs, & Mr Elijah Williams chose a committee to make answer to the Gen. Court." At the final hearing it appeared that Huntstown people had encroached on Deerfield 5362 acres.

It does not appear why their grant was not extended westward and relocated; but instead, an equivalent of eight thousand acres was granted them "to lie northward on Deerfield bounds to Boston Townships No. 1 & No. 2."— Charlemont and Colrain—This grant was held to include the falls in the Deerfield river at Shelburne Falls, and March 1st, 1743, the General Court "ordered that the salmon Fishing Falls in Deerfield River, so called, be reserved for the use of the public, with twenty acres around them for conveniency of fishing."

Even this, however, does not appear to be the conclusion of the whole matter. In 1763, Conway was laid out to the several owners of commons. Soon after by a judicial decision it was found the west tier of lots was encroaching on Huntstown. From the data accessible it would appear that a diagonal piece, averaging about 100 rods wide, was cut off, and annexed to that town. To compensate the thirteen losers by this change, an equivalent of 1259 acres undivided land was given them by the Proprietors of Pocumtuck, and laid out to them on both sides of the river, at Hoosac. The farm of 371 acres thus awarded Consider Arms is still held, or was recently, by his descendants. Other changes in the bounds of the town will be noticed in a subsequent chapter.

The status of the Proprietors of Pocumtuck was never changed. Its meetings were held and records kept, for one hundred and thirty-five years and until the entire property was disposed of by grant, division or sale. All titles to land in Conway, Shelburne, Greenfield, or Gill, are derived from this body; and all in Deerfield, with the exception above noted. On the union of interests in 1674, the "Town" and the "Proprietors" became identical; but with the influx of new settlers, their authority and functions grew to be separate. Until about 1718, however, the jurisdiction of both seem to have been concurrent in several particulars. Each legislated in regard to laying of roads, the control of the water power, the regulation of the wood lands, the running of town lines, the granting of land to settlers and the care of fences to protect the Common Field. The "Town" chose town officers, established schools, controlled ecclesiastical affairs, raised

STATUS OF TOWN AND PROPRIETORS. 495

money by taxation, ordered its expenditure, fixed the time for closing and opening the Common Field, established the price of provision, and of labor, and regulated municipal affairs generally. The "Proprietors" were owners of the soil. Although small grants of land were often voted by the Town for convenience of parties, or for service performed, no grant was valid until ratified by the Proprietors. With a clerk, assessors, and treasurer of their own, the Proprietors raised money by taxation—always so much to the cow-common—and expended it by vote, at will. It shows the intimate relations of the two bodies, that their records were kept in the same book, and for many years the Proprietors' meetings were called by the selectmen of the town; the Proprietors' clerk, under their direction, posting the warrant on the "sign post" five days before the date of the meeting. But beyond that, after 1718, the two bodies had little or nothing in common. During the wars and the struggle of the infant colony for existence, transfers of land were carelessly made, with lines loosely defined, bounds indefinite, and landmarks temporary and uncertain. Evidence of ownership was not carefully preserved, and there came to be a conflict of claims, and confusion of titles. On the Peace of Ryswick, some advance was made in an attempt to remedy the evil.

Aug. 31st, 1699, seven men were chosen "to Settle the lines between Neighbour & Neighbour whose bounds are not evident,"—the agreement of any four to be binding. Again, at the close of Queen Anne's War, when the settlers were able to cultivate the soil in comparative security, special pains were taken to define the lines of divisions and establish individual ownership.

Dec. 21st, 1714, a committee was chosen to "Settle Green River Lands as neere as they can wth ye towne plat and ye other Lands to ye former laying out and make Return what they have done, to ye clerk of ye proprietors."

Provision was made for landless men. In 1714 it was voted "that any of ye inhabitants of this town whomsoever shall haue Liberty to improue Lands on ye West hills for ye space of 6 years in Such places where ye Com^{tee} shall Lay it out, not exceeding 6 acres in a place."

Down to 1718, the following divisions had been apportioned

to the holders of cow-commons, and were held in fee by individuals.

I. The Town Plat, in 1671.

II. The First Division of Plow Land, 1671.

III. The Second Division of Plow Land, 1671.

IV. The mowing land. This was laid out about the time with the above in two Divisions; no record of the transaction is found, but a fragment of the original plan has been recently discovered. These Divisions lay on both sides of the river, west of the Town Plat and First Division of Plow Land.

V. The First Division of Wood Land south of Long Hill. This covered the territory between the road to Hatfield by the Bars Long Hill and the Sugar Loaf range. Turnip Yard lies within this Division, as do the houses and lots on the east side of Bloody Brook street, north of the Lathrop monument.

VI. The Second Division of Wood Land at Long Hill. This lay west of the Hatfield road and extended westward to the Seven Mile Line. Mill river and nearly all Bloody Brook are built on this Division, which extended south nearly to the present Whately line. Both Divisions were drawn in 1688.

VII. The East Mountain Division of Wood Land. This took both ranges, from the river at Cheapside, and ran three and a half miles south.

In all these tracts the lines of divsiion ran easterly and westerly. The same is true of all later divisions, with the exception of the First and Second Divisions "North of Cheapside and East of Green River." Those were "choice" or "pitch lots;" and there the law of irregularity fairly ran riot, in their forms, especially the lots in the second drawing. Some of the recorded plans suggest a pile of carpenter's tools thrown down at random; others might fairly represent a collection of modern agricultural machines grouped for close storage.

In 1712, on the petition of Rev. John Williams, the west bounds of the town were carried west from the Connecticut nine miles into the woods, and it added about sixty-two square miles to our township, covering essentially the territory now occupied by Conway and Shelburne. This grant, the "seven square mile grant," and the Cheapside and Great

River additions, are soon after for the first time spread upon the town records, and there arose doubtless much discussion as to whom this land belonged. There seems to have been an attempt by the *Town* about this time to absorb the *Proprietors* and take all the landed territory into its own hands.

Since 1698, town business had been transacted each year, "at a Legal Town Meeting in Deerfield;" but March 3d, 1717-18, "a Legal Meeting of the Inhabitants of Pocumtuck" was called. At this meeting town officers were chosen, the usual municipal business of the annual March meeting transacted and Samuel Barnard was chosen Proprietors' clerk. Then followed votes which implied a full control, not only of the Additional Grant, but of all the undivided land in the township, and action was taken to divide the whole among the "Inhabitants of Pocumtuck." Minute arrangements were made for the disposition of the lands at Green River and for the examination and establishment of all titles and claims to ownership in the township.

March 20th, 1718, a meeting of the Proprietors was held. There is frequent allusion to the meeting of the Inhabitants, on the 3d, as an "illegal meeting," but the matters canvassed there, were fully gone into, and most of the votes repeated, and the relation of the land owners to the commonage was defined. A committee was chosen to,—

> Consider ye Sircamstances of those men who haue not in y^r purchases of Land Bought ye Common Rights, provided that Eury of ye aboue s^d inhabitants do giue Suffitiant Security * * * that if they shall at any time herafter purchace the Common Rights that belong to their s^d home lots or medow lands that they will draw for s^d Common Rights no more than to make this grant up equal to other Common Rights provided also that if upon examination of ye deed of s^d meadow and home lot lands it appear that Common Rights be excluded such deed or inhahitant shall haue no benefit by this vote * * * Capt. Jonathan Wells, Dea^n Thomas french Mehuman Hinsdel were chosen tor a Com^{tee} to view each proprietors deeds & to pass Judgment on them as to ye legal power of Draft in the undivided lands and so find out what each proprietor can draw according to the Rules agreed to and voted by ye proprietors.

This vote probably brought harmony to the Town; as those who had home lots or meadow land without commonage would now share equally with the others in the undivided lands. An elaborate examination of titles was made and the ownership traced back to the original cow-commons.

Five years later the committee laid before the Proprietors a minute report of the exact proportion each held in the common land. This report became the basis of all future divisions.

At a meeting of the Proprietors May 8th, 1723, the report of the committee chosen in 1718 to find out,—

The rights and interests by commons in the 8000 acres formerly granted to Dedham [was made,] and having Considered the List of Commons or Common Rights of each Inhabitant as Presented to Them by the Committee, which was accepted by the Proprietors with some amendments and is as followeth, viz.:

Names.	Commons.	Acres.	Rods.
Joseph Atherton,	5	7	80
Edward Allen, Jr.,	5	7	80
Jn. Allen & Edw'd Allen, Sen.,	17	7	81
John Arms,	17	1	0
Daniel Arms,	13	12	80
John Amsden,	3	0	0
William Arms,	11	11	80
Samuel Bardwell,	7	12	0
Daniel Belden,	11	4	0
Hannah Beamon,	6	0	0
Daniel Beamon,	6	0	0
John Beamon,	2	0	0
Capt. Samuel Bernard,	44	5	91
William Belden,	3	0	0
Joseph Brooks,	3	0	0
Ebenezer Brooks,	8	3	40
Nathaniel Brooks,	3	0	0
Samuel Childs,	6	9	120
John Catlin's Heirs,	15	12	60
John Catlin, Joseph's Heirs,	3	0	0
Timothy Childs,	13	3	88
Samuel Dickinson,	12	5	20
Thomas French, Sen.,	9	7	144
Thomas French, Jun.,	3	0	0
Samuel Field,	3	0	0
Nathaniel Frary,	10	0	0
Mehuman Hinsdel,	103	6	11
Dec'n Eliezer Hawks,	28	4	60
Jonathan Hoit,	13	10	100
David Hoit's Heirs,	7	0	0
David Hoit yᵉ 2d's Heirs,	7	0	70
Benjamin Hastings,	3	10	64
Jonah Holms,	2	0	0
Benjamin Mun,	15	0	156
Isaac Mattoon,	3	0	0
William Mitchel,	2	0	0
Michael Mitchel, Jun.,	2	0	0
John Nyms,	13	1	131
Ebenezer Nyms,	3	0	0
Moses Nash,	3	0	0
John Shelden Second's Heirs,	16	2	0
Ebenezer Shelden,	9	0	0
Samuel Smeed,	3	0	0
Ebenezer Smeed,	25	0	89
John Smeed's Heirs,	5	12	100
Joseph Severance,	12	8	1
John Stebbins, Jr.,	23	1	50
Joseph Stebbins,	2	0	0

	Commons.	Acres.	Rods.
Samuel Taylor,	15	0	120
James Tute,	2	0	0
Lieut. Thomas Wells,	46	9	12
Ebenezer Wells,	9	7	60
Jona Wells, Esq., & Jona Wells, Jun.,	27	12	28
Thomas Wells, Jun.,	8	2	130
Joshua Wells,	2	0	0
Mr. John Williams,	18	2	120
Zebediah Williams' Heirs,	3	0	0
Judah Wright,	3	0	0
James Cors, [added later]	2	0	0

Under the practice of the Proprietors, in granting land to encourage settlers, and in payment of services, the number of cow-commons had increased from five hundred and twenty-three to the six hundred and eighty-seven represented in this list. This increase indicates a corresponding decrease of value in each right. Although this list gives the exact proportion of each in the undivided land, it does not necessarily indicate the amount already held in severalty. It probably does this substantially.

At the above meeting of the "Inhabitants of Pocumtuck" on March 3d, 1718, the following action was taken respecting the Green River settlement, and it was confirmed by the Proprietors, March 20th:—

Whereas there hath been formerly several grants of land unto particular persons upon ye Green River, and no place mentioned where it shall be laid out, we do therefore propose that Jeremiah Hull, Samuel Smead, William Brooks, Joseph Goddard, Robert Goddard, John Severance, John Allyn, Edward Allyn, Benoni Moore, Joseph Petty, Peter Evans, Michael Mitchell, Ebenezer Severance, Martin Kellogg and Zebediah Williams Shall have their grants laid out beginning at or near ye brook called Brooks Brook, runing from ye Green River westwardly to ye swamp, and so in breadth to make up their compliment, that a Committee be chosen to lay out s^d grants, and ye Rest of ye grants shall be laid out above and below ye abovs^d Brook, as near as the Committee can to ye place where ye abovs^d men pretend it should be, and ye afors^d Committee shall view and lay out a suitable quantity of ye lands adjacent to ye above alotments for Commonage, and y^t ye aboves^d Grantees shall have their proportion of it with the rest of the proprietors according to the quantity of their abovs^d grants of s^d commonage, always provided that ye abovs^d Grantees Doe Relinquish and throw up, and quit claim, to all former grants of land to them from ye Town upon s^d Green River; further we propose that they themselves or some meet persons on their Behalf (whome the Towns men shall accept) shall within two years after ye Date herof, Build each man a Mansion house upon their house lots upon ye spot called the Town plat, and that they shall live upon s^d lands 3 years after they have Built thereon, but if ye wars shall drive them off before s^d term be up they shall have five years after s^d wars to make good their title.

Provided also, that ye abovs^d Grantees Doe (together with these men that shall have lands laid out on ye west side of Green River) from time to time forever make and maintain a sufficient fence which shall prevent all creatures from passing to ye west side of ye Green River."

[At the Proprietors' meeting, March 20, 1718,] It was granted that those men that have had grants of Lands upon the Green River shall out of the lands that shall be laid out or set apart for Commonage near to s^d grants on Green River: draw for a twenty-acre right equal with four Common rights in the eight thousand acres and so proportionally to a greater grant.

The house and meadow lots each had six cow-commons, and each drew ninety-one acres of adjoining common land. On this basis the "Proprietors of the Commonfield" in Greenfield were organized. They will be noticed hereafter.

March 26th, 1719, Samuel Smead recites in a petition to the Proprietors that he had forfeited a home lot and twenty acres granted him in 1686, and that he is "not very well able to perform" the conditions of the renewal of 1718, and asks the Proprietors to "Consider my Sircumstances and grant me twenty acres of land and home lot without any other condition than that I make and maintain fence as others do."

This petition was granted; and on the same condition Isaac Mattoon, Thomas Wells and Samuel Childs were each granted twenty acres on Green river "without any commodities," and Thomas Wells, another twenty-acre tract, and a home lot for "sarvis in getting your bounds confirmed," on condition he build, and live three years, on his house lot.

May 19th, 1719, voted that the "Proprietors' measurers should lay out a high way up the Green River to the Country farms."

May 9th, 1720, "The Proprietors agreed and voted that parcel of Land lying upon Green River, already laid out, and that which shall be judged suitable for improvement be brought into a Common field and fenced according to each man's propriety." The owners of this tract of land became a distinct organization, with its own officers, and raised money on its own rate list by rights or shares. Their book of records was recently, and probably is still, in existence, containing entries down to a recent period.

At the same May meeting a committee was chosen "to sell

to Joseph Atherton a tract or tracts of land on Green River, to yᵉ value of fifty pounds and to receive yᵉ money for the propriety."

During Father Rasle's War nothing more was done towards settling Greenfield, but March 27th, 1727, the committee appointed in 1718, reported in relation to the lands on Green River,—

Yᵗ yᵉ sᵈ Lots be Settled and Returned after the following method: William Brooks yᵉ first lot, bounded on Quintin Stockwell south, [the lot granted him in 1683, for boarding Mr. Mather, the minister] abutting on yᵉ west Line of yᵉ township as Returned upon the Gen. Court Records, to wit: of yᵉ contents of seven mile square [the seven-mile line] extending easterly 128 Rods.

			acres.	width.	length.
1.	William Brooks,		20	25	128
2.	Jno. Severance, abutting on sd line west,		10	12½	128
3.	Jeremiah Hull,	Same	10	12½	128
4.	Robard Goddard,	"	10	12½	128
5.	Joseph Goddard,	"	10	12½	128
6.	Jno. Allen,	"	10	12½	128
7.	Edward Allen,	"	10	12½	128
8.	Benoni Moore, abutting on Green River East running Westerly 128 rods,		15	18¾	128
9.	Joseph Petty,	Same	15	18¾	128
10.	Peter Evans,	"	15	18¾	128
11.	Michael Mitchell,	"	15	18¾	128
12.	Samuel Smead,	"	20	25	128

Northward of Samuel Smead, twenty-acre lots were laid out successively to Isaac Mattoon, Thomas Wells and Samuel Childs, each lot being twenty-six rods, eleven feet wide, and running from Green River one hundred and twenty rods west. By a subsequent vote the holders of the lots from one to seven in the Upper Division, then called "Brooks Plain," were allowed to extend their lots westward, over the seven-mile line, probably to take in all the flat land to the foot of the Shelburne mountain.

1.	In ye Lower Division ye first Lot to Jno Severance, bounded on land of Joseph Atherton, north, abutting on Green River east, Running westerly 100 rods			10	16	100
2.	Jeremiah Hull,	Running westerly 100 rods		10	16	100
3.	Robard Goddard,	"	"	10	16	100
4.	Joseph Goddard,	"	"	10	16	100
5.	Jno Allen,	"	"	10	16	100
6.	Edward Allen,	"	"	10	16	100
7.	Ebenezer Severance,	"	111½	30	43	111½
8.	Martin Kellogg,	"	96	30	50	96
9.	Zebadiah Williams,	"	92½	30	52	92½
10.	Benony Moore,	"	80	15	31	80
11.	Joseph Petty,	"	"	15	31	80
12.	Peter Evans,	"	"	15	31	80
13.	Michael Mitchell,	"	"	15	31	80

Y^e List of names with ye buts and bounds of their Lots, together with ye number and order of s^d lots as set forth in ye above written List shall be entered on Record for Standing buts & bounds to s^d Lots.

The numbers of the Upper Division began at "Brooks' Brook," on a twenty-acre lot granted Quintin Stockwell in 1683, and ran north. Below Stockwell lay the land bought of the Proprietors in 1719 by Joseph Atherton, and from his lot the numbering of the Lower Division began and ran southward.

At a meeting of the Proprietors, May 7th, 1723, it was voted to "Lay out to the Proprietors a tract of Land lying upon Green River, bounded north on the Country Farms, westerly on the Ridge of hill west of Green River, Running Eastward so far as the Land is Platted, and bound south against a Pine tree at the North east corner of Samuel Childs' Land." Lots were cast for drawing. The lines were to run east and west. The tract laid out under the vote was about four hundred and fifty rods north and south by two hundred in width, and contained five hundred and fifty acres. The lots varied in width from one rod one foot and five inches, to sixty-four rods, and in area, from one acre and ninety rods, to eighty-three acres and seventy-one rods. No. 1 was at the north end of the plot. The report of the committee which laid out the land was acted upon March 21st, 1726.

At this date, the following parties each held by grant a home lot on Green River street, now Main street, Greenfield, and twenty acres in the Meadows: Edward and John Allen, heirs of William Brooks, (three sons, Ebenezer, Nathaniel and Joseph,) Joseph and Robert Goddard, Jeremiah Hull's heirs, Peter Plympton's heirs, John Severance, Samuel Smead, Ebenezer Wells, Thomas Wells.

Others holding meadow lots, without accompanying home lots, were Samuel Childs, Isaac Mattoon and Thomas Wells, each twenty acres; Peter Evans, Martin Kellogg, Michael Mitchell, Benoni Moore, Joseph Petty and heirs of Zebediah Williams, each held thirty acres. David Hoyt held a home lot, and Joseph Atherton a large tract in the meadow by purchase.

March 29th, 1736, voted to divide "part or the whole of the undivided land north of Cheapside and east of Green River" at the rate of eight acres to the common. A new method for division was adopted, which was by *choice pitch*. There were fifty-nine Proprietors. Lots were cast for precedence. He that drew No. 1 had the right to take his pitch or allotment —not to exceed ten commons in a body—in any place within the division he might choose. No. 2 had the second choice, and so on to No. 59. Then a double corner was turned, and No. 59 had the first pitch in a second division, No. 58 the second, and so on. Each proprietor had one day in which to select his lot or lots in each division. No. 1 began April 22d, No. 2, April 23d, and so on, excepting Sundays, for fifty-nine days. "If by reason of wet weather, any one shall be prevented from Laying out his land on his own Day, voted that his putting in a pitch in wrighting to the Com'tee shall secure it to him." A committee of twenty was chosen to lay out the choice lots. An accurate survey and plan of each lot, signed by at least three of them, was necessary to give a title, the plan and description to be spread upon the Proprietors' book of records. These plans are an interesting study. While in the early chosen lots right angles are not uncommon, in the second division it was sometimes necessary to box the compass several times to get angles enough to outline the pitch.

A tax of sixpence on a common was laid to defray the expenses of the Proprietors. Assessors, a collector and a committee on accounts were chosen. A committee of six was chosen to lay out what highways they think necessary before any allotments be made. But one road was returned for record. That began "at Green River Street at yᵉ west side of Samuel Dickinson's Lot running along by said lot, and is laid out ten rods wide." It ran northerly, crossed Mill Brook Falls at four hundred and sixteen rods, struck the "Edge of yᵉHill," at 1046 rods, ran eighty-eight rods by the "Edge of yᵉ Hill," thence "North 33° east through yᵉ bounds."

In pitching lots there was wide scattering. Jonathan Wells, No. 1, pitched his eighty-acre lot adjoining Samuel Dickinson's home lot. Judah Wright, No. 2, pitched his forty acres in "Grave Brook Swamp." Mehuman Hinsdale, No. 3, eighty acres on Green River, bounded north on the "Country Farm Lots." Samuel Barnard, No. 4, eighty acres "on Connecticut River, in the first intervale above Millers

Falls." Nos. 8 and 9 were laid out on Woodward's Brook. Nos. 12 and 13 were laid out on the Connecticut River "in ye Nook of ye Falls." As several of the Proprietors had more than ten cow-commons, there were in all ninety-three lots laid out. Edward Allen drew No. 91 in the first draft, and of course was No. 3 in the second draft. He pitched both lots, containing one hundred and thirty-seven acres, together, "joining to the country farm, and encompassing ye Otter Pond." This was the farm on which the Gill branch of the Allen family settled.

The surveyors who laid out the choice lots were Elijah Williams, John Catlin, Thomas Wells and Timothy Childs.

It must have been in the northeast part of Gill that Joseph Severance and John Arms secured by an arrangement with the Proprietors in 1723, a large tract, bounded "On the Great River East'ly, on ye road to Northfield West'ly, on a Brook at ye North end of fall hill North'ly, and so Extending one Mile and one-half Southwardly."

Joseph Brooks had taken possession of a lot of land without warrant, "near the head of Millers Falls in Deerfield," and for several years attempts were made by the Proprietors, with the aid of "the best Councell they can get," to eject him. He was finally dispossessed of the land about 1739. Several parties were prosecuted by the Proprietors about this time for cutting wood and timber on the commons.

Shelburne Laid Out. In 1742, the north half of the "Additional Grant," now Shelburne, was divided "to each proprietor according to his Interest by Commons in s^d Land." The tract was laid out into eight tiers of lots, each two hundred rods wide, except the seventh, which was two hundred and twenty-eight; and cut into two divisions by a ten-rod road east and west across the middle. A six-rod road was laid on the north side, and another along the seven-mile line. Parallel to the latter, roads ten rods wide were laid between 2d and 3d, the 4th and 5th, the 6th and 7th, and one of six rods between the 7th and 8th tiers; so that every lot should front on a road east or west. Thirteen acres were allowed to a common, in each division, and proprietors might divide their commons into as many parts as they chose. The number of lots settled upon in each division was eighty. The numbering in each case began at the southeast corner and ran across the tiers from left to right and right to left throughout, the last number being at the southwest corner of each division. At the south end of the fifth tier, in the north division, a lot of one hundred acres was reserved for the Proprietors; and one of one hundred and fifteen acres, made up of contributions by individuals, was allotted Rev. Jonathan Ashley, the minister, in the south division. This drew No. 5, and the land is probably the same now held by his descendant, at the "Old World." The extension over the seven-mile line westward of the grants on Green River, and "the Division at the Country farm" made trouble and extra work for the committee of eleven who had the matter in charge. A tax of "eighteen pence old Tenor" was laid on each common to defray expenses.

Petty's Plain, Wisdom Hills and Hoosac. In 1743 another division of land was made. The tract divided covers Petty's Plain and Wisdom above the meadows, and Hoosac to the Long Hill wood lots, and is described on the records as "all the ungranted and undivided Land lying between the Division of Land up the Long Hill on the South, and the west line of the Seven Miles Square on the West, and the Divided and Granted lands on the Green River on yᵉ North, and on the Divided and Granted land, and on yᵉ Country Road on yᵉ East." A committee of nine was chosen to survey the tract, lay out all grants that had been made in it, and devise a plan for division. They reported Oct. 7th, 1743, that they "had taken a survey of yᵉ Lands and drawne the plans, and find the whole contents to be 5569 acres, including the Grants that are made in said lands, and are of opinion that there may be seven and one quarter acres laid out to each common, and that it would be best to lay it out in two Divisions. That part of the land lying south of Deerfield River to be laid in two tear of lots running east and west, the first tear to begin at the South end of the plan and Extend itself from the Country Road Two Hundred and Eighty Rods west, and then run north by the needle to Deerfield River. The Land over the river to be divided into two tear of lots until it comes to the south side of Petties Plain, and then be divided into three tear, until it come to the Green River land, and from there one tear until it come to the North end of the Land to be divided. The West tear on the North side of Deerfield River, as also the middle tear to be 200 rods in length, easterly and westerly, and on the South side of the river, what Remains after the first tear is taken off." Three and a quarter acres were laid to the common in the first division, and four in the second.

Owing to the difficulty of having straight roads, none were laid out, but privilege of crossing each other's lots was reserved. The first division began "at the South East Corner of the Land by the Long Hill Lots [on wood lot of Thomas French] by the Country Road, and so take that tear of lots that is next the meadow, until that tear comes to the South End of the Middle tear on Petties Plain, and then take the middle tear until that be ended, then to begin at the South End of the East tear on Petties Plain, and proceed to the North End thereof." The second division began at the Green River lands and ran along the seven-mile line to the Long Hill wood lots. These tracts were afterwards known in records and deeds as the "First" and "Second Divisions of Inner Commons." The lines of division between the lots north of Deerfield River, all ran "West, nineteen degrees north."

As being of interest to holders of land on the tract, the result of the drawing will be given. The numbering began at the south end of the first division and the north end of the second. The first column of figures in the table below shows the numbering of lots in the first division, the second the acres, omitting fractions, the third the numbering of the lots in the second division, the fourth, the acreage:—

Nos.	Proprietors.	Acres.	Nos.	Acres.
1	Samuel Bardwell,	43	12	56
2	Judah Wright,	13	45	17
3	Samuel Hinsdale,	112	13	138
4	Ebenezer Williams,	10	5	12
5	Joseph Severance,	41	48	50
6	Ebenezer Smead,	81	28	100
7	William Arms,	39	41	47
8	Thomas French,	50	42	62
9	Samuel Dickinson,	40	43	50
10	John Nims,	49	3	60
11	John Arms,	55	46	68
12	Samuel Smead, }	9	36 }	12
13	Sarah Smead, }		37 }	
14	Mary Wells,	30	19	37
15	Daniel Arms,	75	7	94
16	Thomas Wells, 2d,	97	31	120
17	Daniel Belden,	22	32	27
18	Joseph Atherton,	18	50	22

Nos.	Proprietors.	Acres.	Nos.	Acres.
19	John Catlin,	32	53	36
20	Michael Mitchell,	6	54	8
21	John Hinsdale,	112	33	138
22	John Stebbins,	75	11	93
23	Warham Williams,	14	17	15
24	Timothy Childs, }	43	20 }	9
25	Stephen Williams, }	7	21 }	35
26	Joseph Clesson,	7	18	8
27	Jacob Warner,	13	38	16
28	Ebenezer Wells,	31	56	38
29	Jonathan Wells, Esq., & Jonathan Wells, 2d,	91	44	112
30	John Sheldon,	33	16	40
31	Elijah Williams,	34	27	42
32	Othniel }		8 }	
33	John } Taylor,	37	9 }	45
34	Jonathan }		10 }	
35	Joshua Wells.	7	39	8
36	Ebenezer Sheldon,	41	23	51
37	Ebenezer Nims,	14	29	17
38	Obadiah & Nathaniel Frary,	33	47	40
39	Benjamin Munn,	49	30	60
40	Samuel Field,	10	55	12
41	John Catlin, 2d,	33	35	40
42	John Amsden's heirs,	10	6	12
43	Edward Allen,	27 }	22 }	51
44	Samuel Allen,	19 }		
45	Aaron Deniour,	7	2	8
46	Capt. Thomas Wells, Esq.,	151	34	187
47	Capt. Samuel Barnard,	146	49	178
48	James Corse,	7	51	8
49	Jonathan Hoit,	52	40	64
50	Dea. Samuel Childs,	26	4	35
51	Eleaser }		24 }	
52	Nathaniel } Hawks,	93	25 }	113
53	John }		26 }	
54	Ebenezer Hinsdale,	137	15 & 52	155
55	Thomas Bardwell,	9	1	11
56	Samuel Belden,	18	14	23

March 19th, 1747, the Proprietors voted to lease for five years the undivided land east of Sugar Loaf, to be sowed with wheat or rye.

Dec. 12th, 1748, four men were added to the "Standing Committee." The functions of this body are nowhere defined. They probably had a general oversight of the Proprietors' affairs, and transacted much business not on record. One case appears: In 1749, the heirs of "Mary Howard, alias Mary Judson," an original proprietor in the Dedham Grant, presented a claim to the undivided land belonging to her eleven cow-commons. The Standing Committee heard the evidence, and found the claim just, and it was allowed. Soon after a committee was chosen to "Search and Collect any Papers that belong to the Propriety, & Lodge them in ye Clerk's Office;" and another committee chosen to run the seven-mile line.

March 19th, 1749, a committee to examine the state of the treasury, reported that they found "in the Treasurer's hands thirty-nine bushells three quarts & ½ a pint of wheat & a Bond payable June 1, 1750, for £119 8s, Old Tenor."

April 30th, 1750, a committee chosen to run the lines of the twenty-acre lots on Green River report that the dividing lines should run "East 21° 30′ South," although they had been thought to "Run East but 20° South."

Town Sheep Pasture. Dec. 14th, 1753 "Voted that all ye Proprietors' Land Lying East of ye Country Road to Hatfield, south of Nathan Frary's Land be Sequestered for ye use of ye Town as a sheep pasture, for ten years; Reserving all timber on it not necessary for fencing it." A shepherd to have charge of the flock, was chosen by the town, but paid by the owners of the sheep, *pro rata.*

This pasture was an extensive tract of land about the Sugar Loaf range, and according to the custom in Old England, a *turnip yard* was established in connection. This enclosure became a permanent land mark, and when school districts were established by the town, the territory thereabout was named the Turnip Yard District. A sickly sentimentality, from which intelligent people are now happily revolting, has endeavored to change this characteristic and historic designation of Turnip Yard to the stale and commonplace name of Hillside. Some of our foreign population change the *i* in the first syllable to *e*, and many ungodly natives are strongly tempted to do the same. If a *descriptive*, topographical name *must* be given, Hillridge, or Ridgepole, would be more appropriate to the locality.

Conway. Dec. 10th, 1750, "Voted to divide ye South half of ye West Additional Grant"—now Conway—and a committee was chosen to "take a view" of the tract, and run and mark lines two hundred rods apart, "to run South 19° West."

Dec. 14th, 1753, John Blackmer was granted ten acres "including a place for a mill just before the crotch of South River," provided he can prove a right to as much as one common. Agents were chosen to prosecute trespassers on the commons, but proprietors were allowed to cut as much timber as they would for their own use in building or fencing.

April 21st, 1760, a committee was chosen to run the nine-

FINALLY DIVIDED. 509

mile line, and establish the Ashfield bounds, the line against Hatfield, and mark the south line of Shelburne grants.

Ten years had now elapsed since the vote to divide the Conway land, and now, June 16th, measures were taken to lay it out to individuals. It was to be cut into seven tiers of 200 rods, each parallel to the nine-mile line, and an eighth tier, taking what was left to the seven-mile line, with four intersecting roads. The next day lots were cast for the draft. But the last French War was still raging, and nothing further appears to have been done towards effecting a settlement. The proprietors, most of whom lived in Deerfield, had land enough and to spare, and many of them sold out to speculators, or men desirous of settling on the territory. In 1763, the whole tract was in the hands of forty parties or estates, and more than one-half of this was held by seven men.

On the conquest of Canada the times were ripe for a change. The giant oak, the towering pine, the sombre hemlock, which had for long ages held sway over the hills and valleys of Conway, were now to be crowded off by the slender, pushing grass, and the shining grain. In 1763, the territory was surveyed and alloted to the owners in severalty. The plan of 1760 was dropped, and it was laid in seven tiers, parallel to the nine-mile line; six of them, 240 rods deep; the seventh, lying on the seven-mile line, 150 rods. Thirty acres were laid to the common, and only five commons were to be laid in a body, except to accommodate small fractions. Probably no lot was smaller than seventy-five acres. One hundred acres were reserved near the center for the "Minister's Lot." With these arrangements, there were drawn one hundred and forty-one lots. Of these, one hundred and two were 150-acre lots. The following table gives the ownership, the number of the lots drawn and the acreage, the latter only approximately accurate:—

Owner.	Commons.	Acres.	Rods.	Nos. of the lots.	Acreage.
Allen, Samuel	2	10	40	15	87
Arms, Consider	58	10	37	10-11-20-23-47-48-52 56-90-100-118-134	1767
" Thomas & Jona	4	2	156	125	128
" William	9	11	80	45-123	295
Atherton, Joseph's heirs	5	7	80	83	167
Baker, Noah	49	13	24	2-46-51-70-71-101 107-108-133-137	1495
Bardwell, Thomas	4	10	12	8	142
Barnard, Joseph	5	0	0	29	150

Owner.	Commons.	Acres.	Rods.	Nos. of the lots.	Acreage.
Barnard, Samuel's heirs	44	5	91	21-24-42-67-72-81 97-129-135	1337
Belding, Samuel	5	8	120	119	167
Burt, David,	18	0	0	53-92-94-98	540
Catlin, Joseph & Seth	51	2	18	64-68-80-99-103-110-111 117-122-138	1535
Childs, Asa & David	3	11	154	85	115
Clesson, Mathews's heirs,	9	7	116	37-113	287
Dickinson, Samuel,s heirs	19	5	52	77-102-121-126	580
Dwelley, Samuel	44	1	104	2-25-26-41-54-95 112-127-136	1323
Field, David	6	10	5	58	204
Frary, Nathl. & Obadiah	10	0	0	63-116	300
French, Thomas	45	9	10	2-13-19-22-34-43-82-86	1370
Grout, Hilkiah		8			18
Hawks, Nathaniel's heirs	2	10	73	132	82
" Simeon	2				60
" Eleazer	9	5	153	65-139	284
" Col. John	11	3	58	9-35	338
Hinsdale, Abigail	13	8	11	5-36-131	39
" Ebenezer's heirs	42	3	31	16-55-62-87-88-91 114-124-128	1208
" Hannah	8	6	120	57-66	255
" John	9			79-93	270
" Samuel	34	6	91	7-17-33-50-104-109-130	1035
Mitchel, Joseph	4			27	120
Nims, Ebenezer's heirs	4	2	16	60	125
" John's heirs	15	1	31	6-12-32	453
Severance, Joseph	3			69	90
Smead, Joseph	30	8	9	40-49-73-76-106-140	918
Southworth, Elisha	18			18-61-75-84	540
Stebbins, Moses	23	1	150	28-31-44-59-115	694
Wells, Jonathan (Hatfield)	9	7	60	38-39	285
" Mary	5	1	36	30	153
" Thomas 2d's heirs	3	3	16	74	100
Williams, Elijah	23	12	46	14-78-89-105-120	715
" Warham	3	10	20	96	105

The "Minister's Lot" lay between Nos. 77 and 78.

The next recorded meeting of the Proprietors was held Jan. 21st, 1782, when agents were chosen to divide or sell at vendue so much as they think best of the "Common & Undivided Land in the township of Deerfield, and townships or districts of Greenfield, Conway and Shelburne." The results of this commission are not found, but in 1788 considerable land was still held in common. In 1794, a gore "lying between the East Mountain Division on the north, the Connecticut river on the east, the Long Hill Division on the south, and on the road from Deerfield to Hatfield by the Bars on the west, 180 acres" was divided to nine parties. Nov. 19th, 1799, this action was ratified by the Proprietors and ordered to be put on record by the clerk. How and when the affairs of this corporation were finally wound up does not appear.

The first act recorded in the volume before me was dated

Aug. 19th, 1699, and with the action of this meeting of Nov. 19th, 1799, closes the century of records contained in "*The Book of Records Belonging to the Proprietors of Pacumtuck alias Deerfield.*"

CHAPTER XVI.

LAND GRANTS—FORT DUMMER—CORSE'S JOURNAL—INDIAN CONFERENCES—THE LAST INDIAN.

With their release from harassing military service, our hardy yeomanry returned to the tillage of their farms with telling effect. To men accustomed to long tramps in the wilderness, often in the depth of winter, with provision and blanket at the back, hatchet and bullet pouch at the belt, and heavy matchlock in hand, spending weeks and making hundreds of miles at a trip, it was mere pastime to handle the hoe, the scythe and the sickle. Agriculture prospered under their sturdy and willing hands and a season of plenty prevailed.

Land Grants. During the interval of peace which followed Father Rasle's War, emigration from the older towns into the wilderness was rapid and constant. The large families of the period furnished plenty of material for new colonies. "The three brothers who came over" in so many family traditions, are often found in this emigration from the old settlements to new ones.

There was little difficulty in getting possession of the virgin soil. The government encouraged new plantations, and on the slightest pretext, granted land with a bountiful hand to such as would· occupy it. To soldiers who had been wounded or captured, and to the heirs of those killed in the wars; to those who had done or suffered anything unusual in any department of public service, recompense was made by drafts on the unfailing Land Bank.

Townships of six or seven miles square were granted corporations, or military companies, almost for the asking. Three were granted Boston, on her representation of paying heavy colony taxes. These were located at Charlemont, Colrain and Pittsfield, and were called Boston Townships Nos. 1, 2 and 3. Fall Town, or Bernardston, was granted to the survivors and heirs of those under Capt. Turner at the Falls fight,

1676; Hunt's Town (Ashfield) to those under Capt. Ephraim Hunt in the Canada expedition of 1690; Warwick to the company of Capt. Andrew Gardner in the same army. It was called Gardner Canada.

On the petition of Jonathan Wells, and others who came to the rescue of Deerfield people, Feb. 29th, 1704, they were granted a "township of land ten miles square on the west side of Connecticut River in the county of Hampshire." It was to be laid out in sixty-three lots, "one of which was reserved for the first-settled minister, one for the ministry, and one for the school." Within three years, a house "18 feet square and 7 foot stud" must be built on each of the other lots, and six acres brought under cultivation; a meetinghouse built and minister settled. What advantages the petitioners derived from this grant does not appear. A portion of it was laid out by Nathaniel Kellogg, and a return made to the General Court as follows, Sept. 20th, 1736:—

A plat of 11,038 acres of Land Lying west of Hatfield & bounded east on Hatfield & all the other bounds on unappropriated lands. Beginning at a hemlock tree on Hatfield North west corner, from which we run West 10° North 868 perches to a stake & stones, thence north 10° West 1920 (?) perch, thence East 10° 868 perch; thence north 10° east 1920 (?) perch to where we began.

The north line crossed a "large brook" about 150 rods from the place of beginning. Shutesbury, called "Wells Town" and "Road Town," was granted Thomas Wells and others for clearing a road from Lancaster to Sunderland; New Salem to a company in Old Salem. Eighteen square miles was added to Sunderland. Many townships were granted in other counties. Nearly all these grants were made about 1731-5, as also were those named below.

Col. John Stoddard had 1000 acres in 1734, for public service. People connected with Deerfield history who had grants at this period were:—

The heirs of Rev. John Williams, seven hundred acres adjoining Northampton on the south and west. Maj. Elijah Williams, one-half the two hundred and fifty acres of land reserved in 1673 for the Country Farm. For the other half he was to pay £6 5s in "Bills of Credit, Last Issue." This was a vicarious reward; being "on account of his brother Samuel's services in the Indian War." Samuel had been dead nearly thirty years. The widow of the Joseph Bradley who went to Canada with Ensign Sheldon, two hundred and fifty acres. Ebenezer Sheldon and his sister Mary (Sheldon) Clapp, children of Ensign John, three hundred acres, on their representation that,—

In their long captivity in Canada, they contracted an acquaintance with the Caghnawaga Indians, who now put them to an extraordinary charge to entertain them when they come to Deerfield.

[Capt. Timothy Childs, three hundred acres,] which Lyeth west of the Township of Deerfield, beginning at a white oak tree about ten rods north of the Great Falls in the river called the Deerfield River, from which it runs E. 19° South, 140 rods, thence N. 19° East 342 rods 14 feet and 2 inches. Thence West 19° N. 148 rods. Thence S. 19° West and closed; which land was surveyed July 10, 1740. Elijah Williams, surveyor, John Hawks & John Sheldon, chainman.

Can anyone locate the following reservation "for the conveniency of" fishermen? By the General Court, March 1st, 1743, "Ordered that the Salmon Fishing Falls in Deerfield River, so-called, be reserved for the use of the public, with 20 acres around them for the conveniency of fishing."

Other grantees were John Sheldon, Joseph Clesson and Mehuman Hinsdale, three hundred acres each. Robert Cooper, Samuel Dickinson, Aaron Denio, Samuel Field, Joseph Kellogg, Benoni Moore, Joseph Petty, John Smead and Joseph Severance had two hundred acres each, and the heirs of Robert Bardwell one hundred acres.

The following had shares in the township of Keene: John Nims, William Smead, John Hawks and Seth Heaton.

In "No. 4," Charlestown, these were original proprietors: Jonathan Wells, Dr. Thomas Wells, Samuel Barnard, David Field, Samuel Field, Joseph Clesson, Joseph Severance, Ebenezer Sheldon, David Hoyt, John Catlin, Benjamin Munn, John Nims, John Hinsdale, Thomas Wells, Daniel Belding, Ebenezer Nims, Benjamin Dickinson, Samuel Dickinson, Samuel Mitchell. Each share would give three or four hundred acres. All the above were Deerfield men.

Fort Dummer. This station was kept up as a military post, and a *Truck House* established, where business was carried on by Capt. Joseph Kellogg as Truck Master, under the direction of the Governor and Council. The policy of the colonies was to encourage the Indians to go there to barter the proceeds of their hunting, and to furnish them goods at a lower rate than the same could be had at the French trading posts in Canada. The object was to cultivate friendly relations with the tribes on the west and north, and detach them from the French interest. Some houses were put up for the use of the Indians, and a small garrison was kept, principally to keep order among the members of the various tribes which were expected to resort thither.

Three Caghnawaga chiefs were there with commission and pay from our government, viz:—

Colonel Ontosogo, with salary of £15.
Lieut-Col. Thyhauselkou, £10.
Major Cohneighau, £10
There were also three chiefs of the Scatacooks:—
Captain Masseguan, £10.
Captain Nannatoohau, £6.
Lieut. Massamah, £6.

Ebenezer Hinsdale of Deerfield was acting as chaplain in 1731. Dec. 11th, 1733, Hinsdale was ordained at Boston as Missionary to the Indians, under the auspices of the Edinburgh Society for the propagation of Christian knowledge, and stationed at this fort. He remained chaplain here until 1740. Edward Billings, afterwards minister of Greenfield, succeeded him, and he was followed by Dudley Woodbridge.

Chaplain and Missionary Hinsdale was much interested in the natives, but punctilious in his method of dealing with them. On one occasion a party of squaws having some crude notions of the efficacy of the rite, brought their children to him for baptism. The missionary had scruples about sending these young heathen to heaven in an irregular way. The mothers not being church members, in good and regular standing, he could not clearly see his way to baptize their children; so he sent them away for a season, while he wrote to some ecclesiastical authority in Boston for direction. There are no records to show whether these savages reached the happy hunting ground without his aid, or whether they went to the other place for want of it.

If this little incident, showing such narrow bigotry and lack of sympathy with the natives, be the measure of the tact and zeal of the Protestant missionaries, we need not wonder at their small success in attracting the natives to the Englishman's religion, or standard. Any Roman priest would have gone through fire and water for the opportunity which this especially ordained missionary to the heathen thus passed by.

The following letter gives the details of the transaction noted above:—

To His Excellency Jonath^n Belcher Esq ed^t the other Honour^{ble} & Revd Commissioners for Propagating The Gospel Among The Heathen

May it Please Your Excellency ed^t others The Honour^{ble} and Revd Commissioners

It was Some Considerable Time after I Came hither before I Saw any of the Indians they being All out at y^r Hunting, but since y^r has been Some Number here yet but few compared w^b what had been here heretofore, and wth those y^t have been here I have Endeavor'd As much As In me Lies to Ingratiate myself w^h by manifesting An Ernest Concern to y^m for y^r Wealfare, & as I have had Oportunity I have Endeavoured w^n I think they will be most ready to hear, to Introduce some Discourse on Divine things, & many times they will hearken w^h Diligince & Consent to what I say One Came Into my Studdy & Sat w^h me Sometime & I having ye holy Bible in my hand took occasion from thence to tell him of ye Excellencies of ye Book, from whence it came & ye End it was Sent Into ye World for he would Consent y^t it might be sent for a Rule to ye white people but not for y^m & argued it from y^r never hearing of it before ye English Came among y^m & from y^r not being able to read it. I told him ye Almighty offered it to some first & y^n to others and y^t Many In ye world besides y^m ware Intirely Ignorant of it, & y^t now he was pleased to offer it to y^m & as to ye reading of it, We ware all of us tought one of another & y^t I was now sent to teach and instruct y^m In it & y^t I should be Glad to teach him if he would Learn, he Gave me some slight Encouragement y^t he would learn In ye Spring. Some time after this I perceived they had a mind to have a Child Baptiz'd y^t was wth y^m I purposed to Discourse w^t y^m about it, but before I had oportunity to my Surprise y^r came a number of y^m on ye Sabbath between metings to offer ye Child to Baptism but ye Capt: by whom they must speak being Suspicious of y^r Design absented himselfe y^t they might take a more convenient opportunity to Discourse w^t me, In ye Evening after ye Sabbath ye Grand parents of ye child ware sent to treat wth me Concerning it I told y^m y^t y^r ware Certain Qualifications necessary In those y^t offered y^r Infants to baptism & first of all it was necessary they should be Instructed In ye principles of Religion y^t they might be Qualified to receive ye Ordinance y^{m}selves & w^n they ware so I told y^m y^r Infants should have ye Seale administred y^m as readily as to ours I told y^m further I was sent to teach & Instruct y^m and was allwaise ready to Do it & should be Glad they would Come to me they Seamed to be well pleased & satisfied at what I had said to y^m & they gave me Incouragement y^t ye mother of ye Child Should live near & come to me this Winter to be Instructed, but she is this week Gone into ye Woods w^t ye others to y^r Hunt Contrary to my Expectation But my Expectations are now rais'd wth respect to some Children now in ye Woods, ye mother of y^m has ye Character of a woman more free from vice y^n

yᵉ Generality of yᵐ & manifests a Concerne for yᵉ vices she sees In her husband & told (as I am Informed) of Going to Canady next spring for yᵉ sake of Having her Children Instructed. This Week she came out of yᵉ woods for provisions and Gave me a Desired opportunity to offer my Service to Instruct yᵐ In yᵉ principles of religion & to read & write. She is now returned to her Children In yᵉ woods & Gives me some Incouragement she will bring yᵐ to me in Spring. In yᵉ meantime & at all Times I shall Endeavour to pursue my Instructions & Strive If Possible I may be an Instrument of bring (*sic*) at Least some of yᵐ to yᵉ true Knowledge of God In Christ Jesus & Intreat Your Prayers yᵗ Gods Blessing may be Granted upon yᵉ Labours of your | Most Obedient Humble Servᵗ,

EBENEZER HINSDELL.

Fort Dummer January yᵉ 26th
Anno Dom. 1732–3.

The free intercourse between these parties so recently in barbaric warfare, with all its advantages, was not without serious danger to both. The savages when in drink, would boast of their exploits against our frontiers and detail their barbarities. The friends of their victims, according to tradition, did not always restrain their resentment, and some of these boasters mysteriously disappeared, and were never again heard of. The rights of the Indians were strictly guarded by law but the law did not always have popular respect or support.

The following letter from Col. Partridge to the Governor, dated June 19th, 1727, points out some of the dealings, dangers and consequences of this condition of affairs:—

I thought it meete to inform yoʳ Honoʳ that considerable numbʳˢ of Indians from their hunting come in at Deerfᵈ, Northfield & the Fortt; the English Trade with them; and it sᵈ some of oᵘ men goe Out and carry them strong liquoʳˢ & make the Indians Drunk & get their fures for a small matter so that when they get out of their Drink & see that their furrs are gone, they are mad, & care not what Mischief they do a Ready way to bring on Outrages & Murders if not the Warr againe. I Humbly am of Opinion, that it is needful either to prohibit trading wᵗʰ them, or to Regulate their tradeing as yʳ Honʳˢ the counsell or Corᵗᵉ may judge mete. We have some disorderly spirited men, in particular one Daniel Sevarns, that declares openly, that he will kill yᵉ Indian that scalpt his ffather. I have given him warning that if he should do such a thing in tyme of Peace he must come upon Trial for his life, & if I understand he persists in such a Resolution, I shall send for him & send him to geole, these things may be of ill consequence, if men be suffered in them.

Daniel Severance was continued there as a garrison soldier for several years, doubtless in a subdued frame of mind.

Journal of James Corse of Deerfield. Monday, the 27th of April, 1730, at about 12 of the clock, we left Fort Dummer & traveled that day 3 miles & lay down that night by West river, which is three miles distant from Fort Dummer.

No ta bene. I traveled with 12 Canada Mohawks that drank to great excess at the Fort & killed a Scatacook Indian in their drunken condition, that came to smoke with them.

Tuesday we traveled upon the great river about ten miles.

Wednesday we kept the same course upon the great river,—traveled about ten miles & eat a drownded Buck that night.

Thursday traveled upon the great river within two miles of the great Falls, in said river, there we went upon land to the Black river above the great Falls went up that river & lodged about a mile & a half from the mouth of Black river, which day's travel we judged was about ten miles.

Friday we crossed Black river at the Falls, afterwards traveled through the woods N. N. W., then cross Black river again about 7 miles above our first crossing, then traveled the same course & pitched our tent on the Homeward side of Black river.

Saturday we crossed Black river, left a great mountain on our right hand & another on the left, kept a north west course till we pitch our tent after 11 miles of travel by a brook which we call a branch of Black river.

Sabbath day. Soon after we began our day's work an old squaw, pregnant, that traveled with us, stoped alone & was delivered of a child & by Monday noon overtook us with a living child upon her back.

We traveled to Black river at the three islands between which & a larg pound we passed the river, enter a mountain that afforded a prospect of the place of Fort Dummer. Soon after we enter a descending Country & travel until we arrive at Arther [Otter] creek in a descending land on this day's travel which is 20 miles; we came upon several brooks which run a north west course at the north end of said mountain. From Black river to Arthers Creek we judge is 25 miles.

Monday, made canoes.

Tuesday, Hindered traveling by rain.

Wednesday, We go in our canoes upon Arther creek till we meet two great Falls in said river. Said river is very black and deep & surrounded with very good land to the extremity of our prospect. This day's travel is 30 miles.

Thursday, we sail 40 miles in Arthers Creek. We meet with great Falls & a little below them with two other great falls and about 10 miles below the said falls we meet with two other pretty large falls. We conveyed our canoes by these falls & came to the Lake. This day we sailed 35 miles.

Corse had a passport from Gov. Dummer, with the Province seal, dated April 13th, 1730, and probably had pecuniary aid in his outfit.

On his return to Deerfield, Corse sent a petition to the

PREPARING FOR ANOTHER WAR. 519

General Court asking the "consideration of the court for his charges he has been at in a journey to Canada, in order to Redeem his sister, who was captivated by the Indians when Deerfield was taken; and for services by him done the Province on his Journey thither." February 20th, the Court "voted that the further sum of ten pounds be allowed and paid to the Petitioner James Corse for the service therein mentioned."

Elizabeth Corse, sister of James, was in Canada in 1716, and I do not find that she ever returned.

At the near prospect of another French war Corse felt encouraged to ask further compensation, and sent the following memorial:—

Memorial of James Corse of Deerfield Humbly Shoeth :
That your Memorialist in the year 1730 at his own expense & charge went to Canada in order for the recovery of his sister out of Captivity where she had a long time been & was encouraged by Mr. Dummer the Commander in chief that he should have some reward from the Public provided he should go in the Indian road from fort Dummer to otter creek which the government were then about to employ some person in order to find out.

Now your Memorialist begs leave to represent that he did go in the Indian road from said fort to otter creek & kept a Journal of his travels & has since his return communicated said Journal to the Gen. Court of this Province in which there is a full description of said road & by which the same may be easily found when in time of war its probable will be of service to the Public & your Memorialist being at £50 cost & charge in & about said affair.

Your Memorialist prays your Excellency's & Honors to take the premises into your wise consideration & grant him some suitable reward for his pains & cost & services & your Memorialist as in duty bound shall ever pray. JAMES CORSE.
Deerfield, May 21, 1743.

In March, 1744, the Court voted him three pounds "as an encouragement to him to serve the government as a pilot if need be." Corse finally settled in Greenfield, where he was quite famous as a hunter of wolves and other wild "varmint." He died in 1783 at the age of 90.

CONFERENCE WITH THE CAGHNAWAGA AND OTHER TRIBES AT DEERFIELD IN 1735.

To keep up friendly relations between the Colony and the Western Indians, a conference was planned for the renewal of the treaty made at Albany in 1724. A large committee was appointed from the members of the General Court to attend Gov. Belcher on the occasion, and July 3d, 1735, this committee was enlarged by the addition of ten members of the Council. The time and place for the meeting was fixed for the last week in August, at Deerfield. Monday, August 25th, Gov. Belcher and his imposing suite rode into town, where the Indians were waiting to meet him. He was followed, doubtless, by his commissary carts and two mounted field pieces.*

The only evidence tending to show that the Iroquois were represented at this meeting is found in a letter from John Schuyler to Gov. Belcher dated at Albany, Aug. 10th, 1735. He says,—

> This day the Delegates of the 6 Nations are moving from hence towards New England as prudently fitted & instructed as I am capable of. I doubt not but that they will ans^r the expectations of the govern^{nt} of the Massachusetts, tho 'tis likely there may be more in number of the delegates than by y^r gov^{nt} is expected it is that wch I could not avoid
>
> If at any time I am Capable of serving y^r Govrn^t in anything of this or other affair I am sincerely ready to do it. If anything is thro^{gh} inadvertancy overlooked & y^r Excel^y not advised of it I refer y^r Excel^y to Mr. Kellogg who is knowing to the whole business, wch wth my Humb^e rega^{ds} to y^r Excellency & Lady is the pressent needful from y^r most Humb^{le} Servt JOHN SCHUYLER

In conferences between the English and Indians a journal was always kept, in which was recorded in full all the speeches, propositions and replies of each party, both at their public meetings and private interviews. Nothing of the kind relating to this conference can be found. Our eminent historian, Gen. Hoyt, in his "Antiquarian Researches," speaks of a treaty with the Caghnawagas in 1735, but he did not know it was held in his native town, and even on the acres of an ancestor. If he had heard the traditions of the fact, he discredited them, and says the treaty was at Fort Dummer, and what is very singular, he was so certain of this, that disbelieving the statement of an Indian chief, whom he was quoting, that the conference was "at Deerfield," he garbled the quotation, to make him say that it was "at Fort Dum-

---

* It is to be hoped that Gov. Belcher here found relief for his needs as indicated below. Some time before he had written Col. John Stoddard:—"I am told there is a Small Root, about as big as a Knitting Needle found at Deerfield, that gives good Ease in the Gravel. If you'cou'd procure me some of it, I should take it kindly." [Samuel A. Green, M. D.]

mer." According to a tradition which Harriet N. Hitchcock had from Charles Hitchcock, her father, the Council Fire was built on the home lot of Landlord Jonathan Hoyt, the place where J. H. Stebbins now lives. Jonathan, when a lad of sixteen, had been carried off in 1704, from this very lot. He lived in captivity among the Caghnawagas, learned their language, and may have been interpreter on this occasion. The same tradition has preserved a single Indian word, which was repeated so often on the occasion as to be remembered—"Squawottuck," meaning "*more rum.*" This word probably indicates a prominent part of the proceedings.

Although no records of this conference have been found, one may safely picture some of its prominent features, from the journal of other meetings of the kind, and the slender threads of tradition. The whole week was spent in settling the public affairs, and feasting the Indians. We can imagine the Governor and his suite in cocked hats, scarlet coats laced with gold, with ample ruffles at wrist and bosom, wearing great powdered wigs and silver-mounted swords, all seated in imposing array in a semi-circle on rude benches, each according to his rank. The dusky warriors, crowned with eagle plumes, and decked with all their finery, seated by tribes on the ground opposite, complete the circle; with the Council Fire blazing in the centre; the soldiers under arms on one side, the inhabitants, curious spectators, grouped on the other; the formal speeches by Gov. Belcher; the dignified bearing of Ontosoga, the Caghnawaga orator, as he rises to deliver his address, and to thank the governor for his presence and his words, to say these shall be deeply pondered and an answer given the next day. The Indian rarely responded to any proposition until he had slept upon it. At the next meeting Ontosoga, reciting the words of Belcher, answers them point by point, in formal language, laying down a beaver skin, or some other present, at the conclusion of each topic. Presents were exchanged,—blankets, shirts, knives, ammunition and rum on one side, and wampum and peltry on the other. The Pipe of Peace, from which each takes a whiff, passes slowly round the circle; all drink to the health of King George, and then to the governor and to each other; the platoon fire of musketry and roar of artillery closing each day's conference. The immediate results of this conference were satisfactory to both parties. The Indians went home loaded with substantial presents and the assurance of peaceful measures. The English fancied they had secured firm allies in case of a rupture with France.

But although this treaty was ratified in a conference at Fort Dummer, two years later, and although Ontosoga and two other chiefs of the Caghnawagas were given commissions in the garrison there, the first breath of war found many of the Caghnawagas on the side of the French.

As I have said, no record of this conference at Deerfield has been found, but we are indebted to Miss Baker for two important papers relating to it, which she has lately discovered in the MS. Archives at Quebec.

Rumors had reached Canada that the English were about to make a settlement and build a fort on Otter Creek. Probably this rumor was not unfounded. As early as 1730, Gov. Dummer had sent James Corse to explore a route over the Green mountains to that stream. A post on Otter Creek would be a great protection against inroads from Canada to the Connecticut valley. It would also be a serious menace to Fort Frederick, a post the French had established at Crown Point. The Canadian authorities were alive to the importance of defeating the project, and the Maquas at Caghnawaga were used as an instrument to that end. Ontosoga, or Ontansoogoe, their leading chieftain, was sent to the conference at Deerfield, charged with a speech written by the Intendant of Canada and committed to memory, to be fired off at Gov. Belcher. It is safe to say that the Indian speeches at the New York and New England conferences were generally prepared in Canada. The evidence in this case is absolute.

How far the attitude of the Maquas served to check the project for a settlement on Otter Creek nowhere appears, but I hear nothing about it of a later date.

The two papers spoken of above follow, as translated by Miss Baker:—

1735 12th October
Letter from M de Beauharnois to the Minister

My Lord You will see by the words subjoined, that I have had a journey to Deerfield, and to Orange also, made by trustworthy people; and the speech I have had made to them in reply to a belt which they of Deerfield sent this winter *sous terre* to our chief of the Sault which has astonished them not a little. There is reason to think that the English and Dutch will not dare to make the least Settlement on the Otter River where I have had a watch all summer. The last I sent there returned but a short time since. I shall take the same precautions next spring * * * I am with very profound respect my Lord * * *

Your very humble and obedient servant, BEAUHARNOIS.

Words which Ontasoga and some other Iroquois of the Sault Saint Louis went on behalf of the village of the Sault Saint Louis to carry to the English at Deerfield:

My brothers, There is a rumor in my Village, which I do not hear with pleasure, and of the truth of which I come here expressly to be informed, perhaps it is the evil spirit, the Enemy of the peace of mankind and of the repose we are enjoying on our mats, that is speaking this bad news, and that means by it to embroil the land.

Listen my brothers, I am going to speak to you more clearly and to tell you what brings me here to you to-day. I have learned in my village that you my English brother, are preparing to make a settlement and a fort in the Otter River, on my lands, on that of my Father Onnontingo five leagues from *Pointe a la Chevelure* [Crown Point].

You cannot do this without becoming guilty of that which each of us ought to fear,—that is without disturbing the Tree of peace which has been planted throughout all this country. You know, my brother, that it was agreed that if any one should be so rash as to wish to cut off the smallest of its roots, all the rest would unite against him to bring him back to his duty.

You are then accused of being the first to think of breaking this treaty made in the presence of all nations, and that the first wrong claim which you will make is to build a fort on land which does not belong to you, and on a river where I go hunting every year.

My brother, my mind and heart are well disposed. I don't like quarrelling. I am delighted with the peace which we have long enjoyed and I dread to see it ended. That is why I beg you to abandon immediately the design which it is said you have formed, supposing that you *have* actually resolved upon it.

The first news which I have received of this, made me rise promptly from my mat to come and declare to you that I would never suffer such an enterprise. I shall not wait until the Frenchman my Father starts to come to put a stop to your temerity. As soon as I learn that you are at work and building I shall come with all my people to destroy all your work. I warn you seriously.

So take care what you do, if you do not want our hatchets to be blood-stained. Strive with us on the contrary for peace; and if there are among you any who are restless and uneasy, warn them while there is yet time.

This is my sentiment and that of all my village. This is what I had to say to you *here*.

Another embassy was sent at the same time to Albany. The story of the projected enterprise was told there. The sharp Dutch traders were doubtless delighted with this opportunity of currying favor with their old customers. They say, "We promise you my brothers that we will never allow the English to establish themselves on Otter Creek." [No! not if we know ourselves, and the laws of trade!] Several belts were given the envoys, and "The Dutch Council has also added to all these belts a great Calmat" to be carried to all the Maqua villages.

The speeches of Gov. Belcher and Ontosoga were not the only attractions of this eventful week at Deerfield. Beside the conference with the Indians, Belcher had another object in coming to Deerfield. Arrangements had been made by the American agents of the English "Society for the Propagation of the Gospel in Foreign Parts," of whom Gov. Belcher was the head, to ordain Mr. John Sergeant as minister and missionary to the Housatonic Indians. These Indians left home in a body for Deerfield, August 18th. Mr. Sergeant joined them here on the 29th. The ordination services were on Sunday, Aug. 31st. The sermon was by Rev. Nathaniel Appleton of Cambridge. Rev. William Williams of Hatfield made an address to the governor as the representative of the English corporation, and to Mr. Sergeant. Rev. Stephen Williams of Longmeadow, through an interpreter, spoke to the Housatonics, who rose in a body. The ministers and elders of this and neighboring towns gave the fellowship.

The interior of the meetinghouse must have presented a novel and interesting spectacle. The array of ministers in the pulpit and deacons' seat, with their white bands and black coats; the governor of the colony and the large committee, in elegant attire, occupying the seats of highest dignity; the Housatonic Indians, in half-civilized costume, seated in a group; Ontosoga and his fellow delegates, in blanket and feathers, grave and stolid spectators of the solemn scene; the adult population of the town, and many drawn hither by the attractions of the day, crowding the galleries to overflowing; the children peering in at the open doors and windows, their eyes round with wonder at the remarkable congregation within. It was indeed the most notable gathering Deerfield had ever seen, and the hospitalities of the people must have been strained to the utmost.

Some of the bills of expense attending this conference have been found. Ebenezer Pomroy, Thomas Ingersoll and Joseph

Bartlett were allowed charges in connection with the Housatonics. The bill of Francis Foxcraft, presented in 1738, shows that the council were in attendance "18 days, at 15 s per day," being "£13, 10s each, or £4, 10s, New Tenor." The total expense, including presents to the Indians, so far as it appears, was £7020, 17s, 11d.

CONFERENCE AT FORT DUMMER 1737.

Province of the Massachusetts Bay Fort Dummer, 1737

Pursuant to an order from his Excellency the Govenour to us the Subscribers directed appointing us to Confer with Ontaussoogoe and some other Delegates of the Cagnawaga Tribe of Indians we come to Fort Dummer aforesaid where we arrived on the fifth of October Anno Dom 1737

We acquainted the said Delegates that his Excell^ey the Governour having been Inform'd that they were come to Fort Dummer to Treat about some Publick Affairs, he had there upon ordered and Appointed us on behalf of the Government of the said Province to Confer with them of such matters as were given them in Charge and that we shou'd be ready to hear what they had to say when they were prepared to speak. The usual Ceremonies being over they withdrew.

Oct^b 6. Being met in the morning, Ontaussoogoe said to us as follows viz^et Brother the Broadway Two Years past I was at Deerfield, the matter then delivered to us by you was, that the old covenant of Peace and unity between our Brother the Broadway and us might be continued

We now return in Answer for our three Tribes, That our desire is that it might remain firm and unshaken and do from our heart promise that the Covenant shall not be broken on our parts, but if ever there shou'd be any breach it shall begin on yours and the God of Heaven who now sees us and knows what we are doing be witness of our sincerity, then laid down a belt of Wampum.

Ontaussoogoe then said Again, We your Brethren of the Three Tribes have learnt by heresay That our Brother the Broadway has lost his wife Such losses ought to be made up & we did not know whether the Gov. wou'd be capable of a Treaty under his Affliction, but find that he is and are thankful for it—Then gave a belt of Wampum to quiet the Gov^rs mind and remove his grief for the Loss of his wife and added I rowl myself in the dust for the Loss of our great men. Ontaussoogoe said again We do in the name of our Three Tribes salute the Govr and all the Gentlemen belonging to him, Tho' at a great distance and strangers yet something acquainted. This was their desire and our design when we came from home thus to salute you with this belt, wishing you happiness and prosperity; laid it down and said they had done speaking.

We then said to them we wou'd take what they had delivered into Consideration and return answer thereto in the afternoon. We then drank King George's health to them. They also drink'd King George's health and the Governour's to us. In the afternoon being met, we said to Them You have in Strong Terms assured us that the Covenant of friendship renewed two years agoe at Deerfield between this Government and the Cagnawaga Tribe shall always remain firm and unshaken and we do in the Name and behalf of the Government assure you that they will Cultivate the friendship they have Contracted with your Tribe and that nothing in our own hearts nor the Instigation of others shall ever prevail upon us to break our solemn Engagement to you, but we shall always hold ourselves under the strongest Obligations to a punctual observance of what we have promised & we then gave a Belt of Wampum.

You have in your speech made to us this day Condoled the Death of the Governour's Lady Her Death was the Cause of much Grief to him we doubt not but your sympathising with him will tend to abate and lighten his sorrow; We take this occasion to express our concern for the Death of your friend, and to Comfort your hearts under your afflictions, we then gave three Black Blankets instead of a belt.

We kindly Accept the Salutation of your People and esteem it a Token of their respect and friendship. And we do in the name of the Government return the like salutation to your old men and young both to your Councellors and to your men of war, to all of them we wish prosperity and happiness forever. Then we gave a belt of wampum.

Ontaussoogoe, said Gent[n] I return thanks, You have rehearsed all that has been said this day. Are glad your hearts are disposed as we find they are to friendship and desire that they always may, and declare that ours ever will and thank God for it and wishing well to all We then drink'd the Gov's health.

The speeches being ended we then in the name of the Government gave a Present to them of the value of seventy Pounds ten shillings

JOHN STODDARD
EBENEZER PORTER
THO[s] WELLS
JOSEPH KELLOGG
IS[r] WILLIAMS

At the breaking up of the meeting, "We then drank King George's health to them. They also drank King George's health and the Governor's health to us." Notwithstanding all the amity and fair promises, it was not long before a son of Ontosoga was leading a war party against our frontiers.

The Last of His Race. There can be little doubt that the Bars was a favorite resort, if not the headquarters, of the Pocumtuck clans—the lords of the Connecticut valley. It is at the Bars that is found the last trace of their peaceful footsteps, and it was at the Bars where the last hostile blow was struck within the borders of Deerfield. The following paper is from the Massachusetts MS. archives. The Allens referred to lived at the Bars.

Edward Allen's acc't for keeping an Indian belonging to yᵉ five Nations above Albany, who has been Long Confined with fever Sores at Deerfield:

Oct. 4, 1732, To building a wigwam or place to keep him in,	£0 12
To 19 Loads of wood at 4s.	3 16
To Cutting of ye wood & Tending of his fire,	3 16
To diet and tendance 28 weeks, at 10s per week,	14 0
	£22 4

Deerfield, May 20, 1733.   EDWARD ALLEN.

From the Council Records we learn that:—

Mch. 24, 1735, Samuel Allen was allowed £8 18s for taking care of, and burying a poor wounded Indian.

June 4, 1737, Samuel Allen was allowed £10 3s 4d for boarding a poor lame Indian, and his mother, one year ending in May last.

The closing word in this extract is significant and noticeable, as being literally the "last" word on the Colony Records, referring in any way to Indian occupation on our soil. The "last hostile blow," referred to above, was struck by a party of French Indians, August 25th, 1746; and fell upon this same Samuel Allen while at work with his children in a hayfield hard by the old homestead. He was cut down while bravely confronting the rush of savages, that his children might escape by flight.

In the old burying yard, a slate-stone slab, "with uncouth sculpture decked," marks the spot where he was laid to rest; and although his mortal frame has mouldered into dust, his voice still preaches the gospel of peace, in the following quaint epitaph:—

> Listen to me ye, mortal men, Beware
> That you engage no more in direful
> War; By means of War my Soul from
> Earth has fled, My body's Lodg'd in
> Mansions of the Dead.

A tradition handed down in the Allen family of the Bars is easily connected with the last item from the Council Record, given above. Near the Allen mansion stood a wigwam —it may have been the one built by Samuel Allen for the sick Mohawk—in which lived a squaw with her only child, a sickly son. They were kindly cared for by their Christian neighbors, and many nourishing dainties were furnished the failing invalid, the child of the forest. But he died and was buried. The place selected for sepulture,—still called "Squaw Hill,"—was on a high bluff overlooking the broad meadows in the fair valley of the Pocumtuck, with the misty hills of Berkshire and Southern Vermont in the distance.

On rumors of a war with France, which would surely bring Indian hostilities to this valley, the mother dug up the remains of her son, cleaned and dried his bones, and with the precious relics securely tied in a pack upon her shoulders, she—the last of her people—turned her slow steps towards the setting sun.

The subdued sadness which must mingle with the thoughts that linger around this spot, as the vanishing point of the native race, is overborne and sunk in the rush of feeling, when we associate this place with the untimely loss of Deerfield's most distinguished son. The old brown mansion, in which the squaw kept her best blanket, moccasins and wampum, still standing on the Allen homestead, where it has braved the storms of more than seven-score winters, had become in these later years the studio of George Fuller. Opposite stands the house where he was born, and where his life struggle went on, his great power unseen and unfelt. Each day he saw the slant rays of the morning sun light up the broad front of the old house across the way; and at nightfall, when he played his boyish games on the almost unbroken green stretching between, he saw its dark bulk, with its huge chimney, loom up against the western sky. It was in this house that his deepest aspirations took on form and color. It was here, in the quiet atmosphere and surroundings of the Bars, that his masterpieces were conceived and brought forth, and not in the stirring, busy metropolis of New England.

The Pocumtuck chieftain may never again return to this classic ground, and he himself is but a faded memory; but his favorite haunt will be forever immortalized by the name and fame of George Fuller.

HISTORY OF DEERFIELD.

CHAPTER XVII.

THE OLD FRENCH WAR.

Hostilities between England and Spain had been raging for years, when the question of the Austrian Succession arose, and convulsed the greater part of Europe in its complications. To France this appeared an excellent opportunity to humble her old enemy. and she backed the claims of Charles Edward, the Young Pretender, to the throne of England. March 15th, 1744, she declared war against England, and soon after sent an army of invasion across the channel.

Swift messengers had meanwhile been sent over the sea. May 13th, 1744, before news of war had reached New England, an army from Louisburg surprised and captured Canso. Succor was sent from Boston, by William Shirley, now Governor of Massachusetts, just in season to save Annapolis from the same fate. England declared war against France, March 29th, but the news of war only reached Boston, May 20th or 22d. Somehow,—probably by the way of Albany and Canada,—our town had become aware of the coming hostilities, and a town meeting was promptly called to prepare for the struggle. This was held May 21st, only eight days after the fall of Canso, and fully as early as Boston had news of the war.

Our fathers knew too well that this European quarrel meant for them a bloody and cruel war on our exposed frontier, and they at once made preparations to defend their families and homes against savage attacks. At the meeting May 21st, 1744 :—

Voted to build Mounts at one house in Green River and at four Houses in the Town, viz. at Mr. Ashley's house at Capt. Wells house at Capt Williams house and the Com'tee to determine at what house at the South end Mounts shall be built at and that Edward Allen James Corse & Aaron Deniur see to building the Mounts at Green River & John Sheldon John Nims 2d & Sam[ll] Hinsdell see to y[e] building yᵉ Mounts at Mr. Ashley's, and that Capt Wells Joˢ Severance & Daniel Belding see to the building those at Capt Wells's and that John Catlin Thoˢ French & Ebenezer Barnard see to building those at Capt Williams' & John Hawks Danˡˡ Arms & Timᵒ Childs build those at yᵉ South End.

Voted to build two Mounts at Wapping & that Judah Wright Eleazer Hawks & Samˡˡ Childs 2d be employed to see the same built.

John Nims added to yᵉ Comittee for forts in the room of T. French & Jonᵗ Hoit and Samˡˡ Bardwell added to yᵉ Com'ttee for Mr. Ashley's fort & Jnᵒ Hinsdell at yᵉ South Fort.

" Mounts " were primarily square towers with a strong post at each corner, built for watch boxes. I find them from fourteen to forty feet high, according to location. The top story, about eight or ten feet square, was usually planked and made a bullet-proof sentry box.

The places fixed upon for these defences were the lot where Jonathan Ashley now lives, that where Charles Jones lives, and that on which Dickinson Academy stands; and the committees chosen to build them were in each case those living nearest, and naturally the most interested in having the work done.

Probably no defensive works of any kind were then in existence. At a town meeting in March, 1733, apparently called for no other purpose, it was voted that " John Catlin, Thomas French, Thos. Wells & Benj. Hastings be a comittee to dispose of yᵉ Three Forts for the Town's benefit." Six years of peace had lulled the inhabitants into a sense of security; or, it may be, the works were going to decay, and this action was to save some of the material. Perhaps their locations were bad, but there is no clue to their situation. For ten years not a word appears on the record relating to fortifications.

It seems by the votes of May 21st, 1744, given above, that at least two mounts were to be put up at each station. While sentinels on their tops could warn the people of approaching danger, and could repel slight attacks, in the day-time, these mounts could have been of little service in a night assault. Something more in connection with them was evidently contemplated. Votes at subsequent meetings throw some light upon the matter, but there is no definite statement defining these defenses.

From all given data it appears that the selected houses, with a rectangular piece of ground, were first enclosed with a high, close board fence, the house forming one angle. The mounts were erected at the two other diagonally opposite corners; the sentry-boxes projecting so far beyond the fence that the occupants could deliver a flanking fire to the right and left to protect the walls. These board fences had no value as defenses, save to deceive an enemy and keep him at a distance. At leisure these shells were lined with stockades, when the structure became bullet-proof, and could be defended by a small force against any number of Indians.

When the mounts were provided for in May, it seems to have been expected that the adjoining householders would, from self-interest, unite in completing the palisades. November 23d, the town voted to pay "no more for yᵉ Garrisons than what yᵉ town have already voted, *viz* the building the Mounts."

Something was done under this system, but not what the public safety required, and a new policy was adopted. Feb. 11th, 1745, the town,—

> Voted that yᵉ Town will pay for what hath been already Expended for the fortifying the houses heretofore voted to have Mounts erected at them & that yᵉ Com'ttees for building said Mounts be Directed to Inclose said Houses with bords and line the same with timber as soon as conveniently may be.

March 4th, 1745, the Committee was directed "not to proceed to line the Forts till further order from yᵉ town." The vacillating course of the town was doubtless caused by reports from Canada that the Indians would or would not engage in the war.

Either from indifference or inability, the convenient season, so far as the fort at Greenfield was concerned, had not been found in nineteen months; and Dec. 10th, 1745, the town directed the—

> Com'ttee for Building the Fort at Green River be Directed to line the Fort at Green River on the East side of it & so far on the North side of it as till the House will Defend it & so at each side of the South Gate & also at each side of the Well, to be lined with Stockades: to be paid by the Town, provided there be nothing from the province Granted to them for forting, nor any alteration of the Grant that is already made to the town for forting.

One week later the town voted "Samuel Allen and the Rest of the Inhabitants at the Bars leave to draw from the town treasury their proportionable parts," of all money expended

THE OLD FRENCH WAR.

in "building all the forts in yᵉ Town, Green River & Wapping * * * provided they Build Mounts and fortifie themselves at yᵉ Bars, and not elce."

Had the people at the Bars been able to carry out this suggestion, perhaps the swift destruction which overtook them the next year, could have been averted. Leaving the subject of fortifications, we now return to the progress of affairs which called for their construction.

It is not my intention in this chapter to follow the operations of the armies in the field through the different campaigns. These are fully given in general history; and the particulars of the events in this region have been put forth in the History of Northfield and by Drake in his "Five Years French and Indian War." So that only those affairs will be noticed in which Deerfield, or Deerfield people, are concerned.

Our town was no longer a frontier town. Small settlements had been established at Charlemont, Colrain, Fall-Town and Vernon, since the last war, and along up east of the Connecticut river as high as No. 4, now Charlestown, N. H. But the Indians who had traded at Fort Dummer, as well as those under pay there,—those who had mingled with the whites in the most friendly manner, and knew the situation of every farm-house and field,—promptly returned to their tribes at the first breath of war, and the settlers knew they would soon return in hostile parties, or as guides for others.

The usual route of the invaders from Canada to the Connecticut Valley, was up the Sorel river to Lake Champlain, and thence by several passes over the Green Mountains. One was up the Winooski and down the White; another up the Otter Creek, and down the Black, Williams or West rivers, according to destination. A third was from the upper end of the lake, up Wood Creek, Paulet and Indian rivers to the Hoosick Valley and over the mountain to the valley of the Pocumtuck.

To cut off these avenues of hostile approach, the Colonial authorities in the summer of 1744 directed the establishment of a cordon of forts to run from Fort Dummer over the mountain to the New York line. Before the close of the French wars the following defensive works were practically in this cordon: Fort Dummer, Forts Sartwell and Bridgman in Vernon; the forts of Lieut. Ebenezer Sheldon, Elisha Sheldon, and of John Burke in Bernardston; South Fort, McDowell's Fort, Forts Lucas and Morrison in Colrain; Forts Taylor, Rice and Hawks in Charlemont. Fort Massachusetts at Adams, Fort Shirley in Heath and Fort Pelham in Rowe, were built by the Province in 1744, but the two last named were abandoned before the last French war. The others were generally picketed dwellings provided with mounts, but at times of greatest danger were garrisoned by Colonial troops, or militia in the Province pay.

John Stoddard—the same who was a soldier in the house of Rev. John Williams on the night of Feb. 29th, 1704—now colonel of the Hampshire regiment, was put by Gov. Shirley in command of the line of forts, and intrusted with the defense of the western frontier. Israel Williams of Hatfield was second in command, and Capt. Elijah Williams, son of Rev. John, had charge of the scouting parties from Deerfield, to cover the frontier on the north and west. June 5th, 1744, Capt. Williams returned from a consultation with Gov. Shirley at Boston. As illustrating the condition of affairs here, and the means taken to defend our homes, beyond the erection of defensive works, some notes will be given of the operations of a single week, soon after his return.

Saturday, June 8th, Capt. Williams sent out a scout to Hoosac Mountain. They returned on Tuesday with a report of having seen the trail of about forty Indians, at the head of the west branch of North river, which they followed as long as they dared. Another scout was sent out Monday, the 10th. They discovered the tracks of three parties of the enemy between North river and Green river, and sent one of their number to report to Capt. Williams, while the rest followed the trails toward the southeast, to make further discovery. On this news, Capt. Williams dispatched a post to Maj. Williams at Hatfield, who commanded in the absence of Col. Stoddard who was attending an Indian conference at Albany.

Thursday, the 13th, another scout was sent out, which returned Saturday, and reported having seen on the Deerfield river, about eight miles above Rice's settlement at Charlemont, a place where three men had made a fire and camped, and saw two coats made Indian fashion hanging up to dry. Thursday the watch at the south part of the town saw an Indian, and at Green river another was seen on the 15th. Moccasin tracks were discovered in the morning, but the Indians were not.

Saturday, June 15th, Stoddard writes Maj. Williams, by an express from Albany, that he has news which leads him to believe a large party from Canada is out against our frontier, thus confirming the reports of the scouts. Stoddard says he saw the day before a son of Ontosoga, who had come down with a party of fourteen to say that the Caghnawagas will not meddle in the war, and that the priests and the Governor of Canada knew and approved this course. Stoddard believes this to be only a French trick to keep the English quiet, which the event proved true. Stoddard said further that twenty-five Scatacooks from Fort Dummer had just arrived and report seeing signs of our scouts, and were "concerned lest they should meet them and took a different course from what they usually did."

Monday, the 17th, Capt. Williams went to Hatfield to consult Maj. Williams and make up dispatches for Gov. Shirley.

This severe and dangerous service of scouting was performed by the inhabitants, no succor having yet arrived, and it was doubtless owing to their faithfulness and vigilance that no damage was done this year within our borders.

The expense of "forting and scouting" was heavy, and at a town meeting, Sept. 25th, 1744, Capt. Williams was chosen a committee to represent to the General Court that the town was not able to bear the burden, and to ask an allowance for what had been expended. It was at this same meeting that measures were taken to have a town clock placed on the steeple of the meetinghouse. The significance of this act at this time is not apparent.

At a meeting, November 23d, the town bravely shouldered all its burdens, and voted to raise by tax money enough to pay all debts, and "£20 additional for a town stock." At the same time measures were taken for relief. "Mr. Ashley and Deacon Childs" were desired to use their influence with the Representatives in the towns below, that they might report our distressed condition to the General Court, and "use their interest at Court to get an allowance for the Charge & Cost the Town have been at for building Garrisons to fortifie and Defend themselves, & thereby their neighbors, and to use their Interest y^t we may have some Soldiers sent us to secure &

defend us from yᵉ Enemy who may reasonably be expected here before spring, we being so near Crown point." It was well known that a French fort named "St. Frederick" had been built at Crown Point, and that parties of the Caghnawagas, if not other Canada Indians, were established there.

Some provision was made "for those drove in by the wars" by allowing them to "have hogs, pens and gardens" in the street. Houses were provided "for James Tute & Davidson families." For Tute a house was built "in the street in the side of the hill in front of Lieut. Hoit's lot that was Sheldon's," the place now occupied by the steps to the Unitarian meetinghouse.

Capt. Elijah Williams was acting as under commissary, and during the last week in July and the month of August, 1744, he dispatched to Fort Shirley twenty-one men with horses, bearing 1520 pounds of pork, 1052 pounds of biscuit, twelve bushels of peas, twenty-eight gallons of rum, two brass kettles, chalk lines and chalk, grindstone, gouge, auger, frow, adz, steelyards, dividers, spade, broad hoe and stub hoe. The latter may be the one found in that vicinity a few years ago, and now in Memorial Hall.

Dec. 3d, 1744, Joseph Kellogg, Indian Interpreter, writes Gov. Shirley news from Canada. The Mary Harris spoken of was a fellow captive from Deerfield, Feb. 29th, 1704:—

Two young men Mary Harrises children have been with me twice, which have lodged at my house one of them is a very Intellegable man about thirty years of age and from them indeavored to critically examine them about the affairs of Canada

The Canada Govʳ was doing his best to make the Cagnawagas & others take up the hatchet He went about killing five oxen & giving a great feast, Hung the war kettle & got the younger braves to sing the war songs &c.

One party came down the Lake but a Maqua of Cagnawaga meeting them told them he would turn over there canoes if they went on &ç they turned back

Undoksogo sends Complements to the governor & would have been down with his young men but for Sickness, will be down this winter by the middle of it if he gets well

Some of the young Scatacooks have gone to Canada to live with Graylock at his fort at Masoeekoyueag where they have a French Priest

Specimens of the military and civil action have been given. An ecclesiastical touch will make the picture of the times more complete. Mr. Ashley, the minister, considered the distressed condition of the land as being due to "God's anger at the sins of the nation;" and the only remedy, the repentance of the people. He speaks of this as,—

> A time of General Distress and Calamity, when God is pouring out His Judgments on Mankind, and so is speaking to this people in his anger this day.
>
> God speaks in anger by the Judgments he executes; the Judgments of God are his voice, and you should always attend to hear what God says to us then. God doth as truly speak to us in his Judgments, as if he should utter a voice from heaven and tell us that he is greatly offended with us; when he sends war and pestilence, he is speaking to man in his anger, and is speaking to the people in his anger this day—with the majesty and anger of a God—the terrible voice of an angry God.
>
> The voice of the ministry is the voice of God, when they stir up to repentance. The voice of God in anger speaks through the minister in this case.
>
> It is an unsuitable time to seek honor, riches, or preferment, when God sends his sore Judgment of war upon us. Who will think of riches or advancement to honor when in danger of his life being taken away by the sword? God is offended with us, for his Judgments are not answered if we are not weaned from these things by the calamities he sends upon us. It shows we are incorridgable & ripe for destruction.
>
> I know our days are determined in this world by God; our bounds are set, and they can't be lengthened nor shortened; but yet it is our duty to use means appointed for the lengthening out of our lives, and to defend ourselves against such as seek to take them away. If it is unlawful for others to take our lives away, it is our Duty to hinder them.

The preacher takes a pessimistic view of affairs, and compares the condition of the nation to that of Jerusalem at its worst estate. He laments with Jeremiah, and predicts sad things, unless saved by repentance:—

> Y^r enemies shall come upon you from the north with bow & spear; y^y shall be cruel & merciless; y^r hands shall wax feeble & anguish shall take hold on you. You shall not be able to go forth into the fields, for ye sword & fear shall be on every side, & the spoiler shall come suddenly upon us,—when men shall be pursued out of their houses, their fields taken out of their hands, & y^r wives ravished & they themselves shall fall in Battle.

He then proceeds to "Confess the sins of the Nation" in the following vigorous fashion. Perhaps he hedged just a little in the free use of the query:—

> Does not England send forth her wickedness like a fountain?
> Did ever the sins of Jerusalem exceed those of England?
> Were *their* sins ever more numerous or continued?

Does not *their* cry come up before God?

Was ever a nation more given to uncleanliness, intemperance and pride?

Don't the allowed & known houses erected for uncleanliness show how dreadfully the nation is sunk in wickedness?

All tables are full of vomit!

Swearing & taking God's name in vain are continued as a fountain!

The Sabbath neglected & all religious duties trampled upon.

And is not the ear of the nation as undisturbed as ever that of the Jews was? & is not the word of the Lord a reproach? Don't men despise it as a thing of naught, and are not such reproached who show any respect for it? The Bible is rejected by the nation as much as God's word was by the Jews. And is the nation less [illegible] than the Jews were?

And are not ministers in the nation corrupt?

And don't multitudes of them preach falsehoods & heal ye hurt of wounded sinners selfishly?

Don't they refuse to enquire for the good old way & dispise those Doctrines which our forefathers believed?

Here we learn what is our Duty, how loud a call we have to do it this day; & it is to mourn & weep for the sins and miseries of ye nation! We have a loud call this day to turn our rejoicing into mourning, to cry to God for mercy & pardon. It becomes us this day to confess the sins of the nation to God & entreat him to pardon & spare it for his name's sake. God is greatly angry with us & threatens sore destruction upon us, & if we repent not we may expect he will give our houses & fields & wives unto others. God's anger will consume the nation if repentance prevail not. Does it not begin to burn already? & when it will end God only knows.

It does not appear how far the people agreed with their minister, as to the cause of the trouble, or the proposed remedy, or what steps were taken to appease the wrath and avert the threatenings of God; but as we have seen active steps were taken to defend themselves against the rage of their earthly enemies, it seems they did not rely solely on spiritual means for relief.

But it was not alone the "Sins of the Nation" which disturbed the pious pastor; there were matters nearer home, touching him personally, where "repentance" and works meet thereunto, would have gone far towards calming his perturbed spirit, if not softening "the terrible voice of an angry God." Unfortunately, Mr. Ashley's character was not a lovable one, and his unpopularity seems to have blinded his flock to a sense of justice towards him. His complaint that he was unfairly treated in the payment of his salary seems well founded. This was to be paid in "Bills of Public

Credit, Equivelent to Silver at Eighteen Shillings y⁵ ounce." To this fluctuating currency, it often became necessary to adjust the salary; and it is to be feared that this was sometimes done on that wave which best suited the interests of the tax payers. About this time they had voted to pay his salary "in Bills Equivelent to Silver at 30 shillings the ounce," which called forth the following letter:—

To the Inhabitants of Deerfield.

Gentlemen

I am informed you are to meet this day; I send my Desire to you to do Something with respect to my Salary which has not been fixed for Last May. I shall be contented if you will fix it at 34ˢ per ounce, and Lower than that I shall not be easy with, for I am certain Silver has been Sold Last May for 35 & 36 the ounce and in the month of July & August it amounted to 38 & 40 and now remains near about 38. the General Court has fixed it as I am informed at 30, which they do by bills of Exchange; but their price of Silver is no more a Rule for me than the price of provisions in old England is for us here—

this is a troublesome way for me to haue my Salary to fix every year paper money is so fluctuating I should be glad you would pay me my Salary in Silver as you may See you haue obliged yourselues to do if you look into your agreement with me. And I will giue you one Shilling in the ounce for your trouble. I dont See why my Salary Should be kept at 20 or 30 pounds below what I can Sell the Silver for which you are obliged to giue me, there are none of you will Sell me the necessaries of Life below what yʸ will fetch

I am your friend & Serveant

Decem. 9. 1745   J. ASHLEY

In response to this appeal, the town chose a committee to make examination and compute the necessary expenses of a family the size of Mr. Ashley's. Beside the matter directly in hand, their report throws a good deal of side light on the life of the times. Mr. Ashley had a boy of eleven, girls of eight and six, and a baby. No account seems to have been made of his slaves, Jenny and her boy Cato.

Computation of the Expenses of a family consisting of a man a woman 4 children & a maid:—

	£	s	d
Wheat 40 bushels at 22s 6d,	45	0	0
Beef 500 lbs at 12d,	25	0	0
pork 17 score & ½ at 18d,	26	5	0
Mutton & veal,	10	0	0
fish,	3	0	0
Indian Corn 12 bushels at 11s 8d,	7	0	0
Malt 11 Bushels,	11	0	0
Cyder 12 Barrels,	18	0	0
Rum wine metheglin &c,	20	0	0
Sugar 100 lbs,	25	0	0

MR. ASHLEY'S APPEAL. 539

	£	s	d
Tea Cocolate & Rice &c,	12	0	0
Butter 200 lbs at 3s 6d,	35	0	0
Milk 2 quarts per day,	35	0	0
apples,	4	0	0
Turnips,	2	0	0
Spices raisins &c,	6	0	0
Salt,	4	0	0
peese,	1	0	0
Chees 60 lbs at 3s,	9	0	0
Tallow 27 lbs at 3s,	4	1	0
Clothing for the family,	125	0	0
Doctors Bill,	20	0	0
Pocket Expenses,	10	0	0
Blacksmiths bill,	5	0	0
Keeping a horse,	15	0	0
pipes & tobacco,	4	0	0
Books,	15	0	0
paper ink & quils,	2	0	0
Schooling the girls,	7	0	0
Maids work,	47	0	0
Mans help,	10	0	0
House repairing & wear of household goods,	25	0	0
	587	6	0

The following may well be given in this connection:—

Gentlemen & Bretheren

I am sensible there is Scarce any thing so disafects a people to y^r minister as to ask for more Salary. I would therefore Assure you I do not ask you to give me more than you your selves proposed as necessary some years past.

And I intreat you to Consider what it was this people gave your former pastor in yor infancy £80 lawfull money stated upon provisions if I remember right wheat 3 s pork 3 d a pound.

When I Settled the Salary you gave me was vastly Better than what I have now for the support of a family ——

When money come to be fixed by an act of the Gouernment things had so unexpectedly altered that my salary was but £48 3 s or thereabouts.

you then Choose a Committee to Compute the expenses of a family consisting of 7 persons.

the Computation y^y made amounted to 587 O. T. wheat y^y Set at 22 s 6 d beef 12 d pork 18 d which computation I desire you to review: I desire you would Consider how much less you giue me than that— In a word I cannot with what you giue me & all my other incomes support my family without consuming what little I haue, or running in debt:

I ask nothing extraordinary for the Support of my family: I am Commanded to be giuen to Hospitality and the occasion therefor increases: and it would not be for your credit y^t I should shut up my doors and refuse entertainment

I ask nothing more than a reasonable Support so long as you are pleased I shall be your minister & when you choose to be freed from my ministry you may retract it I am gentlemen your Servant in the Gospel   JONATHAN ASHLEY

Deerfield Decem. 1. 1760   To the inhabitants of Deerfield

1745. This was a memorable year in the history of Massachusetts and New England. The spirit and prowess of her sons were shown in the expedition which captured Louisbourg, that "Gibraltar of America," which surrendered to Pepperell June 15th. England and France were alike astonished at this brilliant success, and the attention of both was at once turned to the New World. Both determined to send strong forces across the sea the next year; England, to follow up this success and expel the French from Canada; France, with the determination to recover Louisbourg and ravage the whole Atlantic coast. The fates' decreed that the efforts of both should be abortive.

No Indian depredations within our township this year are known. At Putney, July 5th, William Phipps was killed after killing one and mortally wounding another of the enemy. The 10th, Josiah Fisher was killed at Keene. October 11th, Nehemiah Howe was captured at Great Meadows, Putney, a short distance from the fort. Two Indians were fatally shot while dragging him away. On the retreat, about three miles up the river, a canoe in which were David Rugg, a Deerfield man, and Robert Baker, was discovered coming down the Connecticut, near the eastern bank. It was fired upon by twenty or thirty of the enemy. Rugg was killed, but Baker escaped to the shore. The Indians swam over and brought in the canoe with the body of Rugg. His scalp was taken and his otherwise unmutilated body was left naked in the canoe. Rugg left a wife and children in Deerfield. Howe, Rugg and Baker were soldiers stationed in the fort at Great Meadows. The party went up on the west bank of the Connecticut, thence up Black river and over to Fort Frederick, at Crown Point. They entered the fort in triumph, bearing aloft on a pole the scalp of Rugg, upon the inner side of which they had made the likeness of a face with red paint.

News of Howe's capture reached here the same day, and at three o'clock, a party of twenty-nine men, of whom Dea. Noah Wright was one, set off on horseback for Putney. They reached Fort Dummer at ten, where they found eleven Northfield men. Sunday morning, the forty men set out and reached Great Meadows at two o'clock. Col. Josiah Willard, who commanded at Fort Dummer, had preceded them, and had just left the fort at Great Meadows in pursuit of the enemy, leaving orders for the reinforcements to follow. The party soon overtook Col. Willard, who had fifty-four men with him. The Deerfield men reached the scene of the disaster only an hour or two after Col. Willard, although the latter had twenty-five miles the start and many hours earlier notice. The united force followed the trail until about sunset, when they reached a point where the enemy scattered, and Willard encamped for the night. He marched for No. 4 the next morning, and striking signs of the enemy, prepared for the fight, but no Indians were found. Tuesday morning they all set out for home by the way of Ashuelot and Northfield. The Deerfield men reached home Wednesday night. No other depredations in the Connecticut valley are recorded for this year.

1746. This was a disastrous year all along our frontiers. Beauharnois, Governor of Canada, apparently in a spirit of revenge for the loss of Louisbourg, sent out, all through the spring and summer, three or four war parties a week, to harass isolated families and small settlements on the English borders, and called it making war on England. These parties were in number from three to twenty, and on their return with miserable women and children as captives, or the bloody scalps of their husbands or fathers, a full record of their exploits was made for transmission to France, for the delectation of "His Most Christian Majesty," the King of France.

Not content with using the Abenaki and Canada Indians, Beauharnois invited the savages from the far western lakes to come and share the blood and plunder. In but a single instance did he order an attack on a military post or an armed force.

During the spring and summer, skulking parties of the enemy killed, wounded or captured sixteen persons at No. 4; at Northfield, and on the Ashuelot above, ten; at Vernon, four. An attempt to surprise Sheldon's fort at Fall Town, May 9th, was defeated by three men and a few women. John Burke, afterwards Maj. Burke of the Rangers, was wounded in this affair. At Colrain, May 10th, Matthew Clark was killed while making a stand to enable his wife and daughter to escape, but both were wounded. David Morrison was captured July 28th, a little more than a gun-shot distance from Morrison's fort.

May 9th, John Hawks of Deerfield and John Mighills were out a short distance from Fort Massachusetts. Mighills was mounted, and Hawks got up behind to cross Hoosac river. He was in the act of dismounting, when two Indians appeared; one fired upon them, wounding both. Mighills escaped to the fort, but Hawks fell to the ground, with a shot in his left arm. Both Indians dropped their guns, and rushed towards him for his scalp; but Hawks was not ready to part with that useful appendage. He had inherited, along with his name, the quick wit and steady nerve his grandfather displayed in the fight on Hatfield Meadows. He rallied instantly, and resting his gun on his wounded arm, covered the approaching foe. Both dodged; one down a bank, the other behind a tree, from which shelter neither dared venture to reach the loaded gun which one Indian had dropped in an exposed place. Hawks kept them both at bay until they called for quarter, as it afterwards appeared, which the wounded man unfortunately did not understand. Finding, after a while, that Hawks had the best of the game, both ran off in different directions. The spirit shown by Hawks on this occasion earned him the confidence of his officers and the respect of his enemies, and neither had cause to change their sentiments at his next appearance before the public.

June 11th, Gershom Hawks and Elisha Nims, two young men from Deerfield, posted at Fort Massachusetts, were sent to do some work about sixty rods from the fort, with Benjamin Taintor as guard. They fell into an ambuscade. Nims was killed, Hawks wounded and Taintor captured. On the account book of Joseph Barnard I find the Province charged "for my horse to Hoosock after Gershom Hawks, wounded."

By the following it would seem that the assailants did not get off scot-free:—

Deerfield Oct. 16, 1747.
These may certify that James Rider & Salah Barnard both of Deerfield were at Fort Massachusetts in June 1746 presently after ye attack there & saw the scalp taken off from ye Indian there found
To the Truth of which they made Solemn Oath

June 2d, 1746, Gov. Shirley issued a proclamation for raising troops for the invasion of Canada. Capt. Ephraim Williams, afterwards colonel, the founder of Williams College, had been in command at Fort Massachusetts. In 1746, he

CAPTURE OF FORT MASSACHUSETTS. 543

was in the army which made the futile attempt to invade Canada, and left a small garrison at the fort under John Hawks, now Sergeant. Nothing new will be added to the many accounts of the capture of this fort; but as the "Hero of Fort Massachusetts" was one of our citizens, it seems fitting to insert a brief account of the affair.

Pierre Francois Rigaud de Vaudreuil, a brother of Governor Vaudreuil, so often mentioned, left Canada August 3d with 440 French and 300 French Mohawks and Abenakis. His route was up the lake to Fort Frederick, where he was joined by Lieut. DeMuy as second in command, thence up the lake, up Wood Creek, and over the divide to the Hoosac Valley; his destination Fort Massachusetts. August 18th, the main body encamped on the Hoosac river, four miles below Fort Massachusetts.

An advance guard had been skulking about the fort, and a party had been several days before stationed in ambush on the road to Deerfield, to cut off reinforcements. Signs of the enemy had been discovered by scouts, and on the 16th Hawks sent a party of fourteen men to Deerfield for ammunition and supplies. With this party was Dr. Thomas Williams, surgeon to the line of forts. They passed within a few feet of the enemy in ambush, but were not molested, the object of that party being to prevent the increase, but not the depletion of the garrison. Nor did they wish to raise an alarm. Sergt. Hawks had but twenty-one men under him, of whom eleven were on the sick list with dysentery. Several of them were new recruits, but each of them proved true as steel, and their names should be recorded here:—

Sergt. John Hawks, Deerfield,
Chaplain John Norton, Fall Town,
John Aldrich, Mendon, killed,
Jonathan Bridgman, Sunderland, killed,
Nathaniel Eams, Marlboro',
Phineas Forbush, Westboro',
Samuel Goodman, Hadley,
Nathaniel Hitchcock, Springfield,
Thomas Knowlton, wounded,
Samuel Lovett, Mendon,
John Perry, Fall Town,
Amos Pratt, Shrewsbury,
Josiah Reed, Rehoboth,
Joseph Scott, Hatfield,
Moses Scott, Fall Town,
Stephen Scott, Sunderland,
Jacob Shepherd, Westboro',
Benjamin Simons, Ware River,
John Smead, Athol,
John Smead, Jr., Athol,
Daniel Smead, Athol,
David Warren, Marlboro'.

Adding to the numbers, and perhaps to the strength of the garrison, were Mary, (Allis) wife of John Smead, with three young children, Elihu, Simon and Mary. Miriam, wife of

Moses Scott, with children, Ebenezer and Moses;* and Rebecca, wife of John Perry—thirty souls in all. These inmates of the fort were now called upon to confront in a deadly assault 750 fighting men—more than thirty against one.

On the morning of August 19th, De Vaudreuil left his camp, and at about half-past eight o'clock he appeared before Fort Massachusetts. He advanced his colors, which his standard bearer displayed from behind a tree at a distance of thirty rods, when the whole horde rushed towards the fort from every side, with hideous shouts and showers of bullets. Hawks was on the alert, and stationed his men, sick and well, each at his post. He watched the surging mass in silence until it was within twenty rods, and every sharp-shooter had covered his man, then sent a deadly volley, which stopped the advance and sent the assailants to cover. From behind logs and stumps the firing was kept up, and returned as chance offered a mark. The chief of the St. Francis Indians exposed himself while urging his warriors forward, when a bullet from the gun of Sergt. Hawks left the tribe without a leader. All day long this assault continued, the enemy creeping nearer and nearer whenever shelter could be gained. Bullets becoming scarce, Hawks set his non-combatants to molding more, when he found to his dismay that the supply of lead was nearly exhausted. Thereafter not an ounce of lead was allowed to leave a musket unless it was pretty sure to be a messenger of death. During the day De Vaudreuil joined his standard bearer, but having been observed by one of the besieged, he was soon sent back by a shot in his right arm.

After twelve hours of incessant firing, the main body retired to their camp. A night assault with an attempt to burn the fort was expected. Every vessel was filled with water and every possible preparation was made to resist the storm, but not one man suggested the white flag of surrender. At daylight the next morning the firing began again and was continued until twelve o'clock, when De Vaudreuil stepped forward with a flag and called for a parley. Hawks and Norton went out to meet him. He promised good quarter if they

---

* There is a tradition in Bernardston, that this family was captured in that town.

would surrender, and Hawks told him he would give an answer in two hours.

After prayer, a consultation was held. One man had been killed and two wounded, but the men still believed that, although there were but eight men in health, they could repel another assault. When it was found out, however, that only three rounds of ammunition per man remained, further defense became impossible, and at three o'clock the heroic garrison surrendered upon honorable terms. The accounts of De Vaudreuil's loss vary from forty to seventy men killed and wounded.

The prisoners were kindly treated; the wounded, the disabled and the children were carried on the return march. On the evening of the second day Mrs. Smead gave birth to a daughter. The baby was baptized the next morning by the chaplain, and named Captivity. The mother and child were henceforth carried upon an extemporized litter by French soldiers.

August 22d, the affair of Fort Massachusetts being unknown, ten men left Deerfield for Colrain. They were fired upon from an ambush, and Constance Bliss of Hebron, a soldier from Connecticut, was killed and scalped. The rest fled, presumably to the Colrain forts. In their flight they left some rum, with which the Indians became drunk. When they awoke from their drunken frolic, the next morning, they found themselves very near one of the forts in Colrain, but they escaped thence undiscovered.

The Bars Fight. The Indians who killed Bliss belonged to a party of sixty which left De Vaudreuil after the surrender of Fort Massachusetts. According to the best information attainable, they were dissatisfied with the small number of prisoners, and came over the Hoosac by the Indian Path, and down the valley of the Deerfield, to secure captives to grace their triumphant return to Crown Point and sell to the French in Canada. Sunday, August 24th, they observed some partly made hay in Stebbins Meadow, near the foot of Stillwater. Judging that the workmen would return to the place, the next day they formed an ambush in the thicket, at the foot of a hill hard by, and waited a favorable opportunity to accomplish their object. The hay belonged to the Allens and Amsdens.

Monday morning, August 25th, the hay-makers went to their fate. As far as known the party were Samuel Allen, aged 44; his children—Eunice, 13, Caleb, 9, and Samuel, 8; Oliver Amsden, 18, and Simeon, 9, orphan sons of John Amsden.

The Allen and Amsden families lived at the Bars, on the table land just south, but had deserted their homes to lodge in the forts, at Wapping, or at the Street. Two soldiers seem to have been sent out with them as a guard,—John Saddler, a townsman, and Adonijah Gillett from Colchester, Conn. With the party was Eleazer Hawks, brother-in-law to Allen, who, being out of health, was on a fowling excursion. He was the unconscious marplot of the occasion.

The news of the assault on Fort Massachusetts had not yet been received by the commander here, and presumably he was ignorant of the attack at Colrain, or a larger guard would have been sent out and a more vigilant watch kept. Capt. Holson (or Hopkins, by another account), a Connecticut man, was stationed here with a party of Connecticut soldiers, who were the "standing guard."

The hay-makers went to work in the very jaws of the enemy, with no examination of the thicket, and, so far as appears, no precautions against surprise. Had not prisoners, instead of scalps, been their object, the Indians might have killed the whole party at a single volley. They were waiting, however, for a favorable moment for stealing between the men and their guns, when the whole party would become an easy prey. Their action was precipitated by Hawks, who, going into the copse in search of partridges, stumbled upon the ambush. He was shot, the war-whoop given and a rush made for their victims.

The astounded men did the best they could. They urged the children to fly to the fort, while they tried to check the pursuit by a fighting retreat to the mill. They were so hard pressed, however, they could not reach it, but took shelter under the bank of the river near it, on the flank of the line of pursuit. Here they made a stand, hoping to divert the attention of the enemy from the fleeing children. The odds were too great. Allen shot the foremost Indian, but he and Gillett were soon overpowered and killed. Saddler, amid a shower of bullets, dashed through the water to a thicket on an island in their rear, and so escaped across the river. Meanwhile part of the assailants had been busy with the children. Oliver Amsden fell early in the attack. He was scalped and his head severed from his body. His brother Simeon was overtaken and killed after a brave defense, his hands and arms being cut in pieces by the knives of his captors. Caleb Allen escaped by dodging about and hiding in a field of corn. Samuel was caught by a young Scatacook Indian, his pursuer, and after a sharp resistance with teeth, nails and feet, was secured unhurt as a prisoner, and carried to St. Francis. Eunice was the last to be overtaken, but finally an Indian split her skull with his hatchet and left her for dead, not stopping, however, in his haste, to secure her scalp. Eunice survived the blow for seventy-two years, but she never fully recovered.

But a few moments were occupied by the Indians in the bloody work, when they made a hasty retreat with their captive boy up the river and reached De Vaudreuil at Crown Point about noon, August 31st, with the scalps of the five killed at the Bars and that of Constance Bliss. The following concise account of the tragedy is given by Dea. Noah Wright, who was doubtless on the spot at the first alarm:—

Aug. 25, 1746. In the southwest corner of Deerfield Meadows a number of Indians came upon our men at work, killed and scalped Samuel Allen, Eleazer Hawks, and one of Capt. Holson's soldiers named Jillet, and two of the Widow Amsden's children, taken captive, one boy of Samuel Allen's and chopped a hatchet into the brains of one of his girls. They are in hopes she will recover. One man killed one of the Indians, who got one gun from them, and lost three guns by them.

Rev. Mr. Doolittle of Northfield criticises the military officers here for their neglect of discipline, saying "Had there not been a continual firing in the Town from Day to Day, the People would have took the Alarm, and might have been upon the enemy before ever they could have got out of the meadow." This must refer to other parties working in the meadows. It could not apply to the garrison two miles away.

When the alarm reached the town there was vigorous action by her citizens. Lieut. Jonathan Hoyt with one party followed the trail of the marauders up the river, and it was probably Lieut. Joseph Clesson who led another party across the hills to intercept them at Charlemont. Neither party had any success.

From the Massachusetts MS. archives we get the names of a few men who went to the rescue. It seems that Othniel Taylor rode so hard as to kill his mare, for which £6 was allowed him by the Province. In relation to this affair:—

Jona. Hoit testifies & says that when the Indians on the 25th of August last attacked & killed sundry persons in the south part of the town of Deerfield, on the alarm in the town sundry persons were sent out to relieve those in distress &c, and as I was going to the field aforesaid, I came up with Othniel Taylor, on horseback, & ordered him to put on faster. He told me his horse was about beat out. I ordered him to whip on as fast as he could to the mill & I myself continued the pursuit after the enemy, & when I returned I saw the mare that said Taylor rode lie dead near the mill, & I determine she was killed by riding as aforesaid.

Deerfield, Oct. 2, 1746. JONA. HOYT.

[Joseph Barnard certified that when he] came up to Taylor, near the mill, and when 1 was dismounting my horse, said Taylor spake & said he had killed his mare, & as I turned about I saw her fall on the ground, & when I returned from pursuing the Indians, I saw her lie dead on the spot & determine she was killed by riding in pursuit of the Indians.

The only other contemporaneous account of this affair, beside those noticed, is the following effusion from the lips of "Luce Bijah." She was a bright negress, wife of Abijah Prince, "servant" of Ebenezer Wells and a member of the church in 1744. She has an interesting history, to be given by and by:—

> August, 'twas the twenty-fifth,
> Seventeen hundred forty-six,
> The Indians did in ambush lay,
> Some very valient men to slay,
> The names of whom I'll not leave out:
> Samuel Allen like a hero fout,
> And though he was so brave and bold,
> His face no more shall we behold.
>
> Eleazer Hawks was killed outright,
> Before he had time to fight,—
> Before he did the Indians see,
> Was shot and killed immediately.
>
> Oliver Amsden he was slain,
> Which caused his friends much grief and pain.
> Simeon Amsden they found dead
> Not many rods distant from his head.
>
> Adonijah Gillett, we do hear,
> Did lose his life which was so dear.
> John Sadler fled across the water,
> And thus escaped the dreadful slaughter.
>
> Eunice Allen see the Indians coming,
> And hopes to save herself by running;

> And had not her petticoats stopped her,
> The awful creatures had not catched her,
> Nor tommy hawked her on the head,
> And left her on the ground for dead.
> Young Samuel Allen, Oh, lack-a-day!
> Was taken and carried to Canada.

The mill spoken of in the narrative belonged to Samuel Dickinson, and was known later as Locks' mill; it stood on the bank of the Deerfield river, a little north of the spot where the ruins of the "John DeWolf house" now stand. It was at the outlet of a brook, which, coming from the south, divided Stebbins Meadow into two parts. Its bed is now to be seen, but its waters were cut off in 1796, when the canal was dug which supplied power to Stebbins's mill and other works at the Mill village.

The place where Allen and Gillett fell is believed to be against Locke's Island, a few rods above the mill. There is a tradition in the Allen family, that Samuel Allen stopped in the open field, exposing himself to certain destruction, that he might check the onset of the foe, and give one moment more for his children to escape. This tradition will be stoutly maintained by some of his descendants, but it has no historical support, and the probabilities do not favor it, if Samuel Allen was as prudent and collected as he was brave. His object would be more effectually accomplished under the partial shelter of the ravine, on the bank of which there used to be a stone, said to mark the spot where he fell.

A post sent from Deerfield to Fort Massachusetts returned August 30th, and brought the first news of its capture. Probably he turned back at once on coming in sight of the ruins, for the letter which Chaplain Norton nailed on to the well crotch does not appear here until September 11th.

Beside plundering some houses and killing cattle at Northampton about this time, nothing more is heard of the enemy this year in the Connecticut Valley. The reason may have been that parties of Mohawks had begun to make forays on the Canadian frontiers. To encourage these inroads the General Court of Massachusetts offered them these bounties: £40 for male prisoners over twelve years, and £38 for their scalps. For women and boys under twelve made captive, £20; for their scalps, £19. It does not appear by this schedule that the desire to secure captives was particularly urgent, or that many of the redskins were likely to be brought in alive from Canada.

The Mohawks did very effective service against the French and their allies, and created a general alarm in Canada, thus seriously interrupting operations against our frontiers.

1747. Three companies of the valley soldiers had been organized as "Snow Shoe Men." The northern company was commanded by Elijah Williams, with John Catlin as lieutenant—both Deerfield men. March 3d, Maj. Israel Williams sent Capt. Williams ten pairs of moccasins. March 6th, Col. William Williams delivered him fifty pairs more, and the same day, Moses Nims of Deerfield handed over to him sixty pairs of snow shoes, which he had made for this company. With this equipment these men could traverse on the deep, soft snow, the otherwise impassable woods.

During the winter No. 4 had been deserted, and the settlements at Winchester, Hinsdale and Keene were left tenantless. These towns had been settled under the authority of Massachusetts, but on establishing the north line of the state they had fallen into New Hampshire. The Massachusetts soldiers were withdrawn and New Hampshire had refused to provide for their defense. Fort Dummer, however, was not wholly deserted.

It was seen on all hands, that the maintenance of these posts north of the line were essential to the safety of Massachusetts towns; and on the opening of spring forty men were sent to Fort Dummer under Lieut. Dudley Bradstreet, Capt. Phineas Stevens with thirty men, was sent to No. 4, and all the block houses and other defenses on the northern frontiers were reinforced. Fort Massachusetts was rebuilt under the direction of Col. William Williams, then living here.

Meanwhile large parties were being fitted out in Canada and sent against us. March 30th, Shattuck's fort in Hinsdale was surprised, and partially burned the night following. But the brave inmates were not overcome, and the assailants withdrew the next morning, burning on their retreat the deserted settlements at Winchester, Hinsdale and Keene. On the alarm reaching this town, Joseph Severance rode post to Northampton to give the alarm. Lieut. Jona. Hoyt at once led a party to the spot. They were Matthew Clesson

Ebenezer Hinsdale, David Field, Asa Childs, Daniel Nash, Jonathan Severance, Gideon Bardwell, David Hoyt, Samuel Belding and Joseph Barnard. They hastened to Northfield and joined the force of Capt. Benjamin Melvin in a pursuit as far as Great Meadows, where there was an ineffectual skirmish. This party was paid by the Province for two days' service, at 2 s 6 d per day.

A characteristic bill:—

Province of the Massachusetts Bay } To Joseph Severance of Deerfield   Dr

August [30] 1746 To myself & Horse Riding Post from Deerfield to Hatfield when Massachusetts Fort was Burnt. This Acc't was passed once but burnt with the Town House before paid   0 7 6

Dec. 1746. To myself & Horse Riding Post from Deerfield to Northampton when the smoaks were Discovered   0 10 0

Mch 31, 1747 To myself & Horse Going Post from Deerfield to Northampton when Shattucks Fort was Burnt   0 10 0

May 1747. To my horse going part of the Way to Mass Fort to bring in a Soldier Taken Sick on the Road Two days the Horse   0 7 6

   1 15 0

Deerfield July 27. The above are Justly Charged by me Joseph Severance
Hampshire S S
Deerfield July 27, 1749. The above Subscriber Joseph Severance appeared & made oath to ye above Acct. being Justly Charged & yt he as yet hath Received no consideration for the Service before me

This was "Examined & allowed by the Committee J. Osbonne" } Thos Wells Justis peac

April 7th, No. 4 was attacked by a large force under Chevalier Jean Baptiste Boucher de Niverville, a French officer of the line. For unknown reasons this man's name is always given by English historians as Mons. Debeline. The fort was gallantly and successfully defended by Capt. Stevens. For a full and graphic account of this defense see Hoyt's Antiquarian Researches. After a three days' siege, Niverville drew off his forces and steered for Northfield. There they formed an ambuscade at Pochague Hill, where they killed Nathaniel Dickinson and Ashael Burt, April 15th, and then returned to Canada.

Early in the season a large force of "Canada men" was employed under Col. William Williams, in rebuilding Fort Massachusetts. When nearly complete, a detachment of one hundred men was sent to Albany, to bring out stores in wagons. Indian spies observing this movement, ran to Crown Point with the news of this good opportunity to capture the fort, there being but a small party left therein. Six hundred Indians at once left Fort Frederick; on reaching Hoosick, one-half made for Fort Massachusetts, while the rest marched to waylay the train from Albany. Had they been a day sooner the results might have been sadly different. The party sent to intercept the train struck the road in its rear. They were alarmed at the signs of the carts and men and dispatched their swiftest runner to warn the other party at the fort, to look out for themselves, as a large army was marching from Albany. It so happened that the runner reached them just as they were creeping up to attack the fort, on the morning of May 25th. It also happened that the pioneers of the Albany train, that had been sent forward to repair the road, came up at the same moment. They discovered and fired upon the advancing party, and thus alarmed the workmen in the fort, who presently sallied out, and the Indians soon fled.

July 15th, Eliakim Sheldon, aged nineteen, who had removed two years before with his father, Lieut. Ebenzer Sheldon, from Deerfield to Fall Town, was shot while hoeing corn. He reached Sheldon's fort but died the night following. July 22d, John Mills of Colrain, while going home from South Fort, was fired upon and killed.

M. Rigaud de Vaudreuil had collected a force of ten or twelve hundred men, all but two hundred Indians, and gone up the lake to Crown Point and South Bay. Rumors of this movement reached here in July. Capt. Thomas Wells at once dispatched a scout to watch their motions. It consisted of John Nims, Jr., Samuel Stebbins, James Corse and Gideon Bardwell. They returned in safety.

A report had reached Gov. Shirley that Vaudreuil's party were fortifying somewhere about the head of Wood Creek, and by his order Col. William Williams organized a party under Lieut. Matthew Clesson, which left here August 4th, to scout up Black river and over the mountain and find out what the enemy were doing. With Clesson, were Moses Harvey of Sunderland, Aaron Terry of Springfield, Aaron Belding of Northfield, and Martin Severance of Deerfield. This delicate and dangerous service was satisfactorily performed, and the party returned after an absence of twenty-two days. Clesson received for the service, £8 5s, and each of the others £5 5s.

October 16th, a French partisan officer was wounded at

Winchester, of which a further account will be given presently. From there his party went southward, and on the 19th, between Northfield and Montague, they killed and scalped John Smead, one of the heroes of Fort Massachusetts. He had returned from Canada only about two months before. His wife and two oldest sons, and the babe Captivity, had died in Canada of ship fever, which prevailed among the prisoners; the surviving children returned with him.

October 22d, a party of thirty-five French and Indians from Fort Frederick, under Ensign de Lery, captured Jonathan Sawtelle, and burned Fort Bridgman, which they found deserted.

CHAPTER XVIII.

RAIMBAULT OR SIMBLIN—THE PLAIN FACTS OF A ROMANTIC STORY. HAWKS'S JOURNAL. MELVIN'S SCOUT. HOBBS'S FIGHT. TAYLOR'S SURPRISE. AARON BELDEN KILLED. LIST OF SOLDIERS.

Although at this period France had adopted the New Style, in this narrative, all dates will be given in Old Style, unless otherwise noted. To correct the date of events occurring in Canada, eleven days must be added to those here given.

Oct. 16th, 1747, Col. Josiah Willard, Capt. Ebenezer Alexander, and one Dr. Hall left Fort Dummer on horseback for Northfield. Just within the borders of Winchester, Capt. Alexander, who was foremost, saw a man in French uniform in the road before him. The latter spied the captain at the same time and dodged behind a tree, but not in season to prevent a bullet from Alexander's gun striking him in the breast. The wounded man came forward to surrender. He was a cadet in command of forty Indians who had left Canada for this valley, September 16th, and was then guarding their packs, while they had gone to kill some cattle in the neighborhood. As he approached the English he fainted and fell; they, supposing him to be dying, and knowing that the report of the gun would bring an unknown number of the enemy to the rendezvous, prudently hurried on to Northfield. It does not appear that this adventure was pushed any further, which argues a very demoralized condition of affairs among the people at Northfield. When the marauders heard the report of Alexander's musket, they returned to find their leader wounded; and after carrying him a short distance, the cowards basely deserted him as an incumbrance, for fear of pursuit, and hurried homewards.

News of the return of this party reached Quebec, Nov. 3d. They reported finding their commander, Sieur Simblin, in a dying condition; that he only lived long enough to tell them he had been "shot by a party of twenty horsemen." But the poor wounded Frenchman, although deserted by both enemies and friends, did not die. He made a fight for life, bound up his wounds, lived on what the woods afforded. Oct. 20th, four days after the event, he appeared at Northfield, and made a signal of surrender to the first man he saw, who, oddly enough, chanced to be Capt. Alexander himself. The prisoner was kindly received and put under the care of Rev. Benjamin Doolittle, who, like most of the clergy of the period, had a good knowledge of medicine and surgery.

Nov. 14th, Chevalier de Longueuil, with forty Canadian Indians, surprised twelve men near No. 4, killing Nathaniel Gould and Thomas Goodale, wounding Oliver Avery, and taking John Anderson captive. Longueuil learned from the prisoner that the French officer was alive and had been sent to Boston. This news was reported to the Governor at Quebec, Dec. 3d. By this it appears that the young man was so far cured of his wound in four weeks, as to be able to take a journey of one hundred miles.

The captive was well treated by Gov. Shirley, and the Marquis de la Galissoniere, in a letter to him, by Sergt. Hawks, makes an acknowledgment for this courtesy. It is said the prisoner made quite a sensation among the women in Boston. His commission to lead the expedition in which he was so unfortunate, taken from his person by Capt. Alexander, is still in the hands of his descendants. The following is a literal translation.

Orders Sire Raimbault, cadet in the troops, to go at the head of forty savages, upon the cities of the government of Orange in order to there make war upon our enemies of whatever nations are armed as warriors, upon him enjoining to prevent as much as he can the savages from using their tortures customary against the prisoners which they shall make. BONBERTHELAT.
Montreal the 27, [16, O. S.] September, 1747

In this paper the officer is called Raimbault and in all English accounts of this affair he is called by this name, or variations of it, as Rambout, Rainbou, or Rainboe. There is no room to doubt the identity of the person, but this confusion of names has been a stumbling-block to historians of the period. O'Callaghan speaks of the French account of Simblin, and the English account of Raimbault, but "cannot determine what connection there is between the two." Drake thinks his true name was Simblin, but that "he passed himself off with the English under under the assumed name" of Raimbault; but he does not attempt to account for that name being in his commission. The historians of Northfield could see no way to solve the conundrum, and gave it up.

Further research has established the fact, that the name of this young cadet was Pierre Raimbault St. Blein. He was grandson to M. Raimbault, Governor-General of Montreal. He had two brothers, Sieur Duverger de St. Blein and Cadet Groschene St. Blein, both active partisan officers and both led parties of Indians against the English. Sieur Louis Simblin, another leader of savages against our frontier, may have been the father of the wounded captive.

St. Blein was a person of some consequence, and he did not long remain a prisoner. He negotiated an exchange with Gov. Shirley, by which he should be given up for Nathan Blake, who had been captured from Keene, and young Samuel Allen, taken at the Bars. Shirley appointed Sergt. John Hawks, the hero of Fort Massachusetts, with Matthew Clesson and Samuel Taylor as assistants, to take the prisoner to Canada and bring back Blake and Allen. The story of this journey is well told by John S. Lee, D. D., of Canton, N. Y., in a paper read before the Pocumtuck Valley Memorial Association in 1882, which can be found in the archives of the association, and my narrative shall be a bare recital of facts.

Shirley intended that the party should go by the way of Albany, but on account of the weakness of St. Blein a shorter route was taken. The four men being fitted out with stores for the journey, by Col. Wm. Williams, sub-commissary here, left Deerfield, Tuesday, Feb. 8th, 1747-8, on snow shoes, with provision on their backs. They set their faces northward, and reached No. 4 Feb. 10th. The next day they set out to cross the Green Mountains to the lake. All was then wilderness. The towns named are those of to-day. The first day's march was up Black river to Cavendish, where they lodged upon an eminence, now known as Hawks Mountain. According to tradition, a party from No. 4 escorted them on this day's march, one of whom was a young man named John Stark, later the hero of Bennington, but then unknown to fame. This tradition is not verified by any recorded facts. On the contrary, Mr. Doolittle in his journal says that when "the

French prisoner" was at No. 4, some of the garrison told him that "they would gladly accompany him part of the way, but they had neither *Indian Shoes or Snow Shoes*." He adds "Thus poorly have Garrisons been stored; whilst many Hundred Pair of Snow Shoes lie on Spoil some where or other, which the Province has paid for." Information of this kind would not be lost on St. Blein. It might be expected, as a matter of course, that he would notify the Canadian authorities of this destitution, which rendered the garrison almost helpless outside the walls of the fort. Accordingly, on the very day of Hawks's arrival at Montreal, Galissoniere, who had been there about three weeks, sent out a French cadet with seventeen Indians to our frontiers. March 15th, as eight men were getting wood about sixty rods from the fort, at No. 4, the enemy came upon them. The snow was deep and soft, and without snow-shoes the workmen could only get back by the beaten path. The Indians got into this, and intercepted their retreat, killed Charles Stevens, wounded Nathaniel Andros and captured Eleazer Priest. Having no fear of pursuit they went leisurely away, arriving at Montreal, March 29th, with one scalp and one prisoner.

Pursuing his journey, Sergt. Hawks crossed the watershed, in Mount Holly, Feb. 12th, and soon struck a branch of Otter Creek, which he followed to the main stream and down that through Clarendon, Rutland, Pittsford to Brandon, thence westward to the lake opposite Ticonderoga, and down Lake Champlain and the Sorel, reaching Montreal Feb. 27th. It does not appear that any of the enemy were encountered on the way. The envoys were unarmed, but their white flag would have been a sure protection, *provided* it was seen in season. Hawks stopped on the way, between Montreal and Quebec, to visit the home of the prisoner, who was received with great rejoicing, and the escort most hospitably entertained.

Feb. 27th, Count de la Galissoniere, Governor of Canada, makes this record:—

Sieur Simblin, military cadet, who was wounded at the close of October last within four leagues of the fort of Nortfields, and taken to Boston, arrived at Montreal in company with three Englishmen sent with him by Mr. Shirley. We have them well treated and closely watched. They ask to take back with them two prisoners, men of family, who are here. We shall see to their departure, if it be proper to release these two men.

In the Hawks family there is a tradition that it was only by the most strenuous efforts that their ancestor achieved the release of Blake; and similar traditions are current in the Allen family respecting Samuel Allen. The French account of the exchange is given below:—

April 13, 1748, the General [Galissoniere] sends back from Montreal the three persons who came with a cartel on the 27th of February. They were conducted to the frontier by Sieur de Simblin, whom they had brought back. We found no difficulty in surrendering to them the two prisoners whom they have asked of us on arriving.

It is said that young Samuel Allen at first refused to speak to Hawks, who was his uncle, and with whom he had been well acquainted, and that it was only by force that he was brought away. He lived to be an old man, always maintaining his preference for the Indian mode of life.

It was the middle of April, by our reckoning, and the snow may have lain deep in the Canada woods, when our adventurers, with the redeemed captives, plunged into the wilderness on their return to Deerfield. Here we lose sight of them for eleven days, when they emerge from these shades. Hawks shall tell the rest of the story in his own words.

Some years ago, while mousing amongst the MS. archives of the state, I came across a paper without signature or date, but indexed as of 1725. I was interested enough to copy it, expecting the key to it would turn up sometime. It proved to be a fragment of the journal which Sergt. Hawks kept on this very march. From Gen. Hoyt's account of Hawks's journey, I am confident he had seen the first part of this journal. *This* part he certainly had not seen. The question is, where is the first part now?

Fragment of John Hawks's Journal—Apr. 25, traveled about 2 m. S-east & then So. till we come to the crotch of the river where is their common road from C. Point to No. 4 and other places. They had informed us that there were but 12 Inds out on our frontier, & when we were come to this path they found the signs of them returning with one captive. [Doubtless Sieur Bonut with 3 French and 13 Indians, who reached Montreal April 17 with Daniel Sargeant, taken near Fort Dummer, March 29th. Other parties were out in other directions, but the scene of operations for every party was fixed at Montreal. Bonut was sent out Feb. 24.] Our guard told us there was no danger & that they need not come to No. 4, as they had proposed, provided these Indians were not returned, & therefore they told us they w^d travel to the hight of land by black river & w^d bid us farewell. We kept on our way & a little before night we saw the track of an Ind just come before us in our path; traveled this day 30 miles camped on the west side of the mountain between black river and otter creek.

Apr. 26. Set out in the mor'g, our guard accompanied us 9 miles to the top of the mountain, when we parted with them, but notwithstanding they assured us there were no Inds out, yet they cautioned us not to keep the plain road. After we had took our leave of them, they set out on their journey while we were tying our packs. They had not been gone many minutes before Mr. Rainbout, turning back, Hallowed to us, to make haste away from that place, & not to go in the com'on road, which, with some other things, made us suppose we were attended with more Indians, who designed mischief to us after our guard had left us.

Many of the Gent. in Montreal advised us to bring guns with us, & not come unarmed; the Gov. gave liberty we should purchase some guns & said it was not safe to come without.

We immediately set out on our journey, turning another course from what we had traveled, that if we were pursued they might not know where to follow us. We traveled about 6 miles south, crossed a small river that runs into Black river; tra'ld this day 15 miles; camped near the head of W^{ms} river; we made no fire lest we should be discovered.

Apr. 27. Set out in the morning early, traveled S. E. by south, crossed several branches of W^{ms} river & came to the river; we traveled south down the river 9 miles, traveled this day 19 [?] miles.

28. Trav'ld down the riv. S. E. to Con. river; this river comes into Con. river about 2 miles above the Great Falls; tr'ld to the foot of the Falls. Tl'd this day 14 miles; got to the foot of the falls about sunset, where we made a raft, finished it about 10 o'clock in the night & then set sail down the river.

29. About 9 o'lk in the morni'g we arrived at ft Dummer, refreshed ourselves, set out on our raft for Northfield, where we Lodged.

April 30. Set out for Deerfield on horses accompanied by many of our friends from North. Half way from North. met Col. Williams with near 20 of our friends from Dfd. We delivered our little traveler to his mother & had the pleasure of seeing a poor, disconsolate mother made joyful beyond expression by the reception of her son from a miserable captivity.

From the moment Sergt. Hawks received the parting charge of Sieur St. Blein, a heavy responsibility weighed upon him, and for several days the strain must have been intense. His task was to cover his trail and baffle his pursuers. He knew that every red winterberry crushed under foot, every bit of bark disturbed on a fallen and rotting log, every, upturned leaf, every dry branch snapped off as they passed, every bruise on the tender sapling, every bent or broken shoot or twig, was to these children of the woods like a guide-board directing the traveler on a broad highway. His familiarity with Indian wiles, and his knowledge of woodcraft gained in his captivity, now stood him in hand. With all his ingenuity and his resources in play, with all his senses on the alert, with the watchful eye and cautious tread, Hawks threaded the valleys, crossed the streams, followed their beds, doubling upon his trail, snatching a little sleep in some deep ravine during the darkest hours. So, he guided his charge in safety. The burst of sentiment in his matter-of-fact journal, when, at length, surrounded by a strong force of friends from home, testifies to the reaction, when this great nervous tension was relaxed, and he "had the pleasure of seeing a poor, disconsolate mother made joyful beyond expression by the reception of her son from a miserable captivity," and the happy and successful issue of his mission.

St. Blein left Hawks's party April 26th, and returned to Canada. May 21st, writes Galissoniere, "15 Abenaquis have been fitted out for a war party. They are commanded by Sieur Simblin the Elder, who has only just returned from escorting the English cartels." "Sieur Duplessis Fabert, ensign of foot, with 15 Canadians & 33 Indians" was also sent out from Montreal by the Governor the same day. June 25th, the Governor records, "The three different war parties, commanded by Sieurs Duplessis Fabert, Simblin and Laplante, are returned to Montreal. These parties, having united, made an attack on Northfield, brought in 6 English prisoners and 5 scalps."

They had ambushed fourteen men who were going from Hinsdale's fort to Fort Dummer, June 16th. [See Temple and Sheldon's History of Northfield, page 226.] This ambush was laid within one or two miles of where St. Blein was wounded, and was doubtless arranged by him.

Hawks had but a few days of rest before he was again called into service. May 9th, Noah Pixley was killed at Southampton by a party of the enemy. The same day Sergt. Hawks, with Matthew Clesson as his right hand man, went out in pursuit of the marauders. We can imagine the spirit with which Hawks engaged in this expedition. St. Blein had told him at the parting of their ways, that no party of Indians were out in this region, and he had reason to believe that these were the fellows that dogged his steps from Canada. The Deerfield men under him were "Jona. Wells, Azariah [Jeremiah?] Nims, John Cofferin[?], Asa Childs, Jona. Hoyt, Thomas Arms, Phineas Nash, David Childs, Asahel Wright, Thomas Nims, John Saddler, and Cæsar, servant to Mr. Timothy Childs."

The tables were now turned. Hawks was not now a skulking fugitive. With a strong force at his back he plunged boldly into the woods, and soon struck the trail of the enemy going westward, and gave a hot chase; but he failed to come up with them, and turned back after reaching the Dutch settlements at Hoosick.

1748. During the spring and summer, inroads on the Connecticut Valley were incessant. The enemy came in large parties, and were generally successful in surprising the English; and many were killed, wounded and captured. None of the enemy penetrated as far as our town, but Deerfield men were active in the service; though none were killed this year, unless Asahel Graves, who was killed above Northfield, July 14th, was a son of Abraham of Deerfield.

Capt. Melvin's Scout. May 13th, Capt. Eleazer Melvin, with eighteen men, left Fort Dummer for a scout westward. He reached the lake at a point nearly opposite Fort Frederick, May 25th, when he discovered a party of Indians in canoes. He fired three volleys at one canoe, which was within range. It was probably a company of thirty Indians which had left Canada May 1st, for our frontiers, under the command of Sieur Monet. Upon this mishap they went back again, reporting the loss of one killed and one wounded. The firing was in plain view of the fort, three cannon were discharged to give the alarm and one hundred and fifty men started out in pursuit. Melvin at once made a hurried retreat through the drowned lands and over the mountains to the head of West river. Here, in the town of Londonderry, on the morning of May 31st, he made a halt on the bank of a small river. Having baffled his pursuers he felt himself safe. The men's packs were unslung, and some of them began shooting salmon in the stream for breakfast.

While so engaged, in careless security, a party of two

Frenchmen and nine Indians, under "Sieur Louis Simblin" (St. Blein?) who had struck their trail and followed it, or who had been attracted by their guns, was cautiously creeping through the underbrush towards them. When within a few rods, they poured a deadly volley upon the amazed English, killing John Howard, Isaac Taylor, John Dodd, Daniel Mann and Samuel Severance, and wounding Joseph Petty. The members of each party were now equal, but the English were surprised and demoralized, and after a slight resistance they scattered and fled for Fort Dummer. The victors, satisfied with the result, did not attempt a pursuit, but hasted away homeward with the five scalps and entered Montreal in triumph June 8th.

Petty, the wounded man, soon gave out, and was left at a spring by his companions, who made him a bed and shelter from boughs, left him a cup of water and told him to live if he could until help reached him. Capt. Phineas Stevens led a company to the scene of the disaster and found the five slain soldiers, but failed to find Petty. On his return to Northfield, his townsmen determined to know the fate of Petty. June 5th, sixteen men sallied out and were gone four days. They found his dead body and buried it. Joseph Petty was a son of Joseph and Sarah of Deerfield, who were captured Feb. 29th, 1704; Joseph escaped, [See ante.] his wife was redeemed. They removed to Northfield.

It was probably in view of the disaster to Capt. Melvin's scout that a fast was appointed at Northfield for June 16th. Our minister, Mr. Ashley, preached the sermon on this occasion. It may have been in the midst of this solemn service that the "great gun" at Fort Dummer announced to the startled congregation a new cause for alarm, and a loud call for help. The occasion was the attack on a party going from Ashuelot to Fort Dummer, already noticed. Capt. Ebenezer Alexander with fifteen men at once set out from Northfield in response to the call. They found that a party of fourteen men, marching from Ashuelot to Fort Dummer, had fallen into an ambush of the enemy; that Joseph Richardson, John Frost, Jonathan French and William Bickford were killed, and six others captured. These were taken to Canada, where they arrived June 25th.

The enemy were Raimbault St. Blein, Sieur Duplessis Fa-

DEATH OF COLONEL JOHN STODDARD. 563

bert and Sieur La Plante, who had combined their forces, doubtless under the direction of St. Blein, who had been wounded within a mile or two of this place.

Rev. Mr. Ashley wrote an account of the affair to Col. Stoddard at Boston, and to Col. Partridge at Hatfield. His letters were dispatched by Lieut. Sheldon the same day. It is not likely that Stoddard was ever troubled at the bad news, since he died at Boston June 19th. Eleazer Porter, lieutenant-colonel, succeeded to the command in the valley. It was said, and generally felt, that Col. Porter "had no genius for war," and Maj. Israel Williams was not satisfied with the state of affairs. He writes to Boston: "When the person can be found to make up the great break upon us, in the death of Col. Stoddard, I know not. God has pleased to take him who was in a great measure our wisdom, strength and glory. We are now like sheep without a shepherd. Every one will do about as he pleases, till some person have general command." Porter resigned and Maj. Williams was put in command, November 16th.

Capt. Hobbs's Fight. June 26th, Capt. Humphrey Hobbs, while leading forty men from No. 4 to Fort Shirley, was attacked by a large body of the enemy. After a contest of four hours, the Indians withdrew. Ebenezer Mitchell, son of William of our town, Samuel Gunn and Eli Scott were killed; Samuel Graves, Daniel McKenney, Nathan Walker and Ralph Rice were wounded. For a graphic account of this affair see Hoyt's "Antiquarian Researches."

Thomas Taylor Surprised. July 14th, Sergt. Thomas Taylor with sixteen men was ambushed above Fort Hinsdale. Asahel Graves, probably son of Abraham of Deerfield, and Henry Church were killed on the spot. Robert Cooper, formerly of Deerfield, was wounded. Taylor and ten others were captured. Two of them, James Rose and James Billings, being wounded and unable to travel, were soon killed. Temple and Sheldon's History of Northfield gives a minute account of this affair.

July 23d, Aaron Belding was killed in Northfield Street. August 7th, Capt. Ephraim Williams writes Maj. Israel Williams, from Fort Massachusetts, that he,—

Was afraid the party sent to Deerfield for provisions would be waylaid, but to my great joy, yesterday at 2 p. m. Lt. Severance and

Hawley arrived safe at the fort and made no discovery of the enemy, but in less than two hours after they arrived, the dogs began to bark & ran back on their track; we all then determined that the enemy had followed them in. This morning at daylight, being out at the gate observing the motions of the dogs, determined there was an ambush about 40 rods from the fort, between the fort & where we cross the river to Deerfield. Concluded to go out & attack them there, the nature of the ground being favorable; but before we could get ready, one of the Indians fired at our dogs, which I suppose would have seized him immediately had he not. Upon that went a volley of 12 or 15 guns at some men who had gone out unbeknown to me, who returned the fire and stood their ground. We made a rally with 85 men in order to save those that were out & must in a few minutes have fallen into their hands. Engaged the enemy about 10 minutes & drove them off the ground, upon which about 50 men (about 10 rods off) arose on our right wing & partly between us & the fort & fired upon us, upon which we were obliged to retreat; fought upon a retreat until we got into the fort, when they attacked us immediately upon our shutting the gates. Upon this I ordered the men to their posts, (it being our turn now). I played away with our cannon and small arms for an hour & ¾ by the glass & then they retreated.

As to the killed and wounded of the enemy is uncertain. We see them carry off but two, just as the fight was over. This is certain, a great many of the men fired 4, 5 or 6 rounds apiece in fair sight & at no greater distance than 15 rods, a great many not over 7 rods. Lt. Hawley was shot in the leg; Samuel Abbot shot below his naval, the shot cut out of his buttock. [He lived but a day or two.] Ezekiel Wells shot in the hip, the bullet lodged in his groin * * * All behaved like men, not one flinched.

The assailants were forty-six Canadians and ninety Indians, who left Canada July 6th, under Chevalier Jean Baptiste Boucher de Niverville. He is the same officer who made the unsuccessful assault at No. 4. Chevalier Niverville on his return found, at Fort Frederick, letters from the Governors of Massachusetts and New York to the Governor of Canada, dated August 1st, 1748, [O. S.] with a copy of the King of England's proclamation for a cessation of hostilities. These he took charge of and delivered on his arrival home August 16th. He reported that his men fought but indifferently in the attack, "so that there were killed only 5 Englishmen," and that he had two Indians wounded.

August 19th, Galissonniere sends back word that he has "ordered all hostilities to cease, and so far as depends on him, will put a stop to all hostilities on the part of our Indians." The war between France and England had now virtually closed. A treaty of peace was signed at Aix la Chapelle,

CLOSE OF OLD FRENCH WAR. 565

Oct. 7th, 1748. But the Indians made occasional incursions until the treaty with the Eastern Indians at Falmouth was signed, Oct. 17th, 1749.

A large number of Deerfield men served on the frontiers during the war. Many of them held important positions. Lieut. John Catlin was second in command at Fort Massachusetts, and was in charge of Fort Shirley, with Joseph Allen and Adonijah Atherton as under officers, and thirty-eight men. Lieut. Samuel Childs commanded at Fort Pelham, with John Foster as sergeant and Samuel Barnard as clerk; his other Deerfield men were Josiah Burnham, Ezekiel Foster, Joshua Wells, Jacob Foster and Joshua Hawks; twenty-two other men were on his roll.

Capt. Ephraim Williams was sub-commissary for the western forts; Col. William Williams, with Col. Josiah Willard of Fort Dummer for the northern forts, and this town was a place of great activity during the whole war. It was the rendezvous of the Connecticut troops sent up on special occasions. Some of the billeting charges show that the soldiers were quartered on the inhabitants and their bills paid by the Province.

One bill by David Field, dated June, 1748, is for soldiers under Capt. Elijah Williams. He charges for "meals of vituals" 1 s 9 d, and, 1 s 2 d each meal. For "lodging," uniformly, 6 d. The usual liquor charges are "$\frac{1}{2}$ point of rhum, 1 s 8 d."

Samuel Bardwell's account shows that he entertained Nanniad Curtis, Ealy Scott, and Zebediah Ealis of the same company, John Pease and John Beaman of Capt. Kent's company; Aleheuale [Elihu Yale?] John Winchell and Darius Pinney of Capt. Pettibone's company; William Daget, Robbard Robbens, Joseph Ealey and Timothy Pike of Col. Williams's company.

Considerable difficulty was experienced in furnishing supplies for the swarm of soldiers which it was necessary to keep on the western frontiers, and the commissaries had a perplexing task. Col. William Williams had his headquarters in his store, which stood on the lot where the Everett House was burned; Capt. Elijah Williams at his store just opposite, on the corner of his home lot, the historic lot now occupied by the Dickinson Academy, known to the older generation as the "Ware Corner." Three original papers, preserved in the Sheldon family, are given as being of historical value and interest:—

HAMPSHIRE SS., DEERFIELD, June 12, 1748.
To the Constable or Constables of the town of Deerfield aforesaid, or either of them, greeting: In His Majesties Name you are hereby Required fourth with to Impress fifteen Eable horses & make Returns of this Warrant & your doings thereon to me.
THOS. WELLS, Justice peace.

In this case success does not seem to have followed his endeavor, and a higher authority was appealed to:—

HATFIELD, June 14, 1747.
I received your verbal message, that the horses could not be obtained. I now send you a Warrant to Impress them, which you must give to ye Constable & have the business done forthwith. Tell your Sister Childs not to deliver any Provisions to any Scouts or parties of men without my Express order in Writing. Attend my former directions in writing.   I am y^r Sevt.,
ISR. WILLIAMS.

Don't let it be known you have a warrant. See to it that ye Constable does his business without delay. It will be best you accompany him.
[Addressed]   On His Majest's Service, to
              Mr. John Sheldon
                at Deerfield

p^r Capt. Pettibone.

Warrant to Impress Wheat:—

HAMPSHIRE ss. To the Constable of Deerfield in said County or either of them, Greeting:

Whereas application has been made to me, the subscriber, one of his Majest's Justices of the Peace, by Maj. Josiah Willard, setting forth: That he is under absolute necessity of about one hundred and thirty bushels of wheat in order to supply the Garrison at No. 4, with bread, without which the said Garrison must be deserted for want of Provision, contrary to the design and order of the Government, and that sundry Persons in the Town of Deerfield are Posses'd of Considerable Quantitys of wheat, who refuse to part with the Same for the use aforesaid. These are therefore in his Majestys name to require you immediately to Impress one hundred and thirty bushels of wheat in the Town of Deerfield, for the use and purposes aforesaid, and the same deliver to Maj. Willard aforesaid, for which he must pay a reasonable price, by you to be paid to the Person or Persons or from whom you shall Impress the wheat; for all which this shall be your sufficient Warrant.

Hereof fail not at your Peril. Dated at Deerfield this 23 day of Sept. in the twenty-second year of his Majesty's Reign, Anno Dom. 1748.   Is. WILLIAMS, Just. Pac.

[Endorsed]   Major Willard left £5 10 s with me.
JOHN SHELDON.

MEN SERVING IN THE OLD FRENCH WAR.

In October, 1748, Willard and Williams resign their office of commissaries on account of the difficulty of supplying the forts, but they seem to have continued in the service on increased pay.

The following list of names of men serving in this war is gathered from the account book of the commissary for this period. It will prove of interest to the genealogist if to no others. They are not all Deerfield men:—

Allen, Edward
Allen, Joseph
Allen, John
Allis, Zebediah
Amsden, Isaac
Arms, Daniel
Atherton, Adonijah
Atherton, Shubel
Avery, Oliver
Baker, Thomas
Bardwell, Ebenezer
Barnârd, John
Barrett, Benjamin
Bebe, Simeo
Brooks, Moses
Brooks, Nathaniel
Brooks, Samuel
Brown, Andrew
Burke, John
Button, John
Carey, Richard
Catlin, John
Chamberlain, John
Childs, Asa
Childs, Samuel
Coats, Charles
Cole, David
Cook, Jonathan
Crocker, John
Crosby, David
Crossman, Thomas
Daniel, Ichabod
Day, Timothy
Denio, Aaron, Jr.
Ellis, Reuben
Elmer, Edward
Elmer, Hezekiah
Ely, Joel
Ely, Nathaniel
Evans, Jonathan
Fenton, William
Ford, Jonathan
Foster, John
Frost, John
Georgaw, Simon
Georgaw, Noah
George, Thomas
Gillett, Adonijah
Goff, William
Graves, Aaron
Graves, Bela
Graves, Ebenezer
Graves, Elisha
Graves, Samuel,
Green, Barrilla
Guage, John
Guage, Nathaniel
Guild, Benjamin
Hale, Moses
Harmon, John
Harvey, Moses
Harvey, Peter
Hascal, John
Haven, Ebenezer
Hawks, David
Hawks, Eleazer
Hawks, Gershom
Hawks, John
Henderson, John
Houston, Seth
Houston, William
Hubbard, Isaac
Huntley, Elijah
Huntley, Jonathan
Kellogg, Ephraim
Knights, Benjamin
Knights, Simeon
Lamb, Thomas
Lamberton, James
Lincoln, Josiah
Lock, James
Loveredge, Joseph
Lovering, Joseph
Marshall, Benjamin
McKenney, Daniel
Meacham, Ebenezer
Mitchell, Joseph
Moore, Philip
Morse, John
Munn, John
Murray, Daniel, died Dec. 1748
Nash, Daniel
Nevers, Phineas
Nims, Elisha
Osborn, William
Pafker, Abraham
Parsons, David
Peck, Abraham
Pitts, Joseph
Porter, James
Prince, Abijah
Quangued, George
Rankin, Reuben
Rider, James
Rose, Richard
Sawyer, Jesse
Sedawdy [Indian]
Severance, Joseph
Sextnn, Gershom
Smead, Ebenezer
Smead, William
Somerville, Robert
Stebbins, Asahel
Stiles, Amos
Stoddard, James
Swan, William
Symons, Joseph
Taylor, James
Taylor, Moses
Taylor, Othniel
Taylor, Thomas
Tawney, Joseph
Town, Edward
Walker, Daniel
Ware, James
Wells, Ebenezer, Jr.
Wells, Samuel
Wells, Simeon
Wheelock, David
Whipple, David
Wickwise, James
Wight, Nathaniel
Woolworth, Reuben

The following who served for short terms are found on "A muster roll of the company in His Majesty's Service under the command of Thos. Wells, Captain, *viz.*, began the 23d of April, 1746:"—

AARON BELDING KILLED. LIST OF SOLDIERS.

Elijah Williams, Capt.	Elea'r Patterson, Sent.	Dan'll Danilson, Sent.
Jon Hoit, Lt.	Dan'll Arms, Jr. "	Jno. Taylor, "
Jos. Clesson, Capt.	Jon'th Wells, "	Sam'll Taylor, "
David Field, Sergt.	Phinehas Nash, "	Timo. Childs, "
Mathew Clesson, "	Jno. Nims, "	Thos. Williams, "
Nath'l Hawks, "	Sam'll Bardwell,Jr. "	Aaron Scott, "
Jos. Barnard, Clerk,	Eldad Bardwell, "	Aaron Denior, "
Rubin Bardwell, Sent.	Jon'th Catlin, "	Jos. Stebbins, "
Jon'th Severance, "	Moses Nims, "	James Couch, "
Sam'll Stebbins, "	Josh. Hawks, "	James Corse, "
Isaac Foster, "	Asael Wright, "	Benj'n Mun, Jr. "
David Hoit, "	Sam'll Allen, "	Josh. (?) Wells, "
Eliz Wells, "	Thos. Phillips, "	Jon'th Hoit, Jr. "
Jos. Smead, "	Richard Ellis, "	Dan'll Graves, "
George Howland, "	Jno. Amsden, "	Eber Atherton, "
Eben'r Arms, "	Jno. Sadler, "	Jno. Sheldon, "
David Wright, "	Abner Barnard, "	Benj'n Hastings, "
Amasa Nims, "	Samuel Gunn, "	

I have never met with any reference to a military hospital in the Connecticut valley. Probably the sick and wounded soldiers were cared for in private families. Representative bills for such service are given below. Ezekiel Wells' was wounded at Fort Massachusetts, Aug. 2d, 1748.

Province of the Massachusetts Bay Debtor to William Arms for Extraordinary Charges of Bedding, firing candles, tendance &c for Ezekiell Wells Whilst Sick and Wounded at his house from Nov 6, to January 17, 10 weeks and 2 days at 10s per week   N T £5 0 0

HAMPSHEAR SS DEERFIELD March 27 1748-9
William Arms appeared and made oath to the truth of the above account and that he had not received any reward for the same before me   THOS WELLS Just peace
Deerfield March 27 1749 Alow^d by the Com^r

Province of the Massachusetts Bay } To Samuél Bardwell of Deerfield   Dr 1749

	£	s	d
To Nursing & Attendance of Sam'l Trumble one of Cap't Phinehas Stevens's men In his Long & very Grevious Sickness from Apr'l ye 8th to August 30th Twenty Weeks & four Days at 1s pr Day	7	4	0
To Twenty one pounds of Butter @ 1s per lb	1	1	0
To Twenty Six pounds of Suger @ 1s 3d	1	12	6
To Six pounds of Candles @ 1s 2d	0	7	0
To Fire Wood 30s	1	10	0
To Damage Done my Beding 30s	1	10	0
Totall New Tenor	£13	4	6

The above acct Is Justly Charged Errors Excepted by me
                                    SAMUEL BARDWELL

HAMPSH^r sc^t Nov: 25th 1749
Mr. Sam^{ll} Bardwell made oath That the abov Acct Is a Just & True Acct: & That he has Never Received any Consideration of the Province or any other theirfor   before me THO^s WELLS
                                                            Just peace
Read and alow^d by ye Com^{tee}
to be p^d Col HINSDAL   J OSBORNE

HOME HOSPITALS. 569

		Deerfield Nov 5th 1748			
Province of the Massachusetts Bay	To Sarah Wells	Dr			
		£	s	d	
To Nursing & Attendance Jonathan Stone whilst Sick & In the Province Service *vizt* 3 weeks at 7s 6d pr week		1	2	6
To Sundry Necessaries *vizt* Sugar 1lb 2s 6d. Candles 2s Butter 1 lb 2s Wood ¼ Load 12s 6d			19	
Damage done Bed & Beding 5s			5	
		£2	6	6
Aug 30 1749 To Nursing & Attendance on Samuel Trumble whilst Sick *vizt* Six Weeks at 7s 6d pr week		2	5	
To Sundry Necessaries *vizt* Candles lb i 2s Sugar lb iv 5s Butter & Lard lb 12 12s Wood ⅔ of Load 7s 6d		1	6	6
Damage done Bed & Beding 10s			10	
		4	1	6
	Brot Down	2	6	6
	N. Tenor	6	8	
	L. M.	3	8	3
True amt Error Excepted	SARAH WELLS			

HAMPSHIRE ss DEERFIELD Mar. 12. 1749
Then Sarah Wells Subscriber to ye above Amt personally appearing made Solemn oath to ye Truth of the same & that she had rec^d no Consideration for any Part thereof   Co^m Wm Williams
                                                                                Just^s Pac^e

Alow^d by the Com^{tee} J Osborne

CHAPTER XIX.

MUNICIPAL AND JUDICIAL AFFAIRS, 1714–1774. GREEN RIVER AFFAIRS. SEQUESTERED LAND. MILLS. GAME. SURGEONS. FERRY. SUGAR LOAF. CONWAY SET OFF; SHELBURNE SET OFF; BLOODY BROOK WANTS TO BE. HIGHWAYS. PRICES.

At the close of Father Rasle's War the settlers at Green River made a permanent lodgment. Some of them lived in houses on what is now West Main street; others settled on farms which fell to them in the division of commons, two, three or four miles distant. Schools were founded for this part of the town as early as 1732, and money was granted for preaching when communication was difficult. Specimens of town legislation on these matters will be given:—

April 12, 1736, voted to have a school Master in ye Town & a School Dame at Green River which shall be paid p^r scholar four pense p^r week.

Jany 15, 1739, Upon hearing ye Petition of the Inhabitants of Green River with respect to y^r being Sett off for a Separate Parish &c as may be seen at large by y^r petition on file, &c The Question was put whether the prayer of ye Petition be Granted and it past in the negative

Mch 30, 1740, Voted *not* to build a school house at Green River. Voted that ye Town will hire a room or House at Green River for a School house there proportionable part of ye year y^t ye School is to be there. Voted that the Selectmen shall be a com'ttee to determine when and how long ye School shall be at Green River & so at Town.

Nov. 22, 1742, Voted that ye Selectmen are Directed to provide a School Master also to get some person to preach at Green River for this winter or so long as they shall think best.

What seemed "best" to the selectmen probably fell short of what was desired by the ambitious people north of the river; at any rate, a movement was soon on foot to be set off from the old town with the name of Cheapside.

At a Meeting March 7, 1743, the Question being put whether the petition of the Inhabitants of Green River so called with respect to their being set off as a precint should be granted & it past in the negative.

FIRST APPEARANCE OF THE CHEAPSIDE QUESTION. 571

November 15th the same petition was again presented. The bounds asked for were these:—

North on ye North bounds of ye Town East on Connecticutt River South on Deerfield River to extend up s^d River to Sheldons brook so called & y^n to run West by ye needle till it comes to ye West line of ye seven miles square & then to extend northwardly by s^d line, till it comes to ye north bounds of ye Town.

The Question being put after the matter had been fully Debated whether they should be set off as aforesaid and it *unanimously* passed in the negative.

The Question was put whether the matter of Green River being set off as a Precinct should be left to Com^{tee} to consider of some proper bounds to sett off s^d Inhabitants by and it passed in the negative.

Upon hearing the Request of Green River Inhabitants &c and the matter being fully Debated the Question was put whether the Town will set off said Inhabitants as a *Town* with the following bounds, *viz.:* North by the North bounds of the Town East by Conneticot River South by the Eight Thousand acre line so called, & a line West by the needle from the Northwest Corner of s^d eight thousand acres so far as to ye west side of the seven miles square & West by the west additional Grant made to ye Town and it passed in the affirmative.

It seems that the people of Greenfield were not ready to cut loose and set up housekeeping for themselves unless they could take along the name and territory of Cheapside. Here we find the elements of a strife, carried on with great bitterness for more than a hundred years. At the same meeting there was voted to Green River to provide preaching, "forty shillings Old Tennor a sabath, for three months." One point was thus gained; the money allowed for preaching was to be expended at their own will instead of at the will of the selectmen.

At the annual spring meeting in 1744, a committee was chosen to "fix the boundaries of the Green River homelots and deliver them to the town clerk." A committee was also chosen,—

To Consider what may be thout Reasonable to allow Green River towards maintaining Preaching & Schooling this year * * * & were Impowered to look into Green River affairs respecting the schooling & preaching for ye last year & Make their Return to the Town that they may make their vote upon it accordingly.

Green River people were found to have been faithful stewards, and the committee reported accordingly, recommending that henceforth thirty pounds a year be allowed them, to be expended in preaching or on schools, as they should elect. The question of secession seems to have been abandoned during the war which was now upon the country. The usual appropriations were made for preaching and schools.

In 1749, "voted that the sum of thirty shillings, Old Tenor, be granted to the School Dames at Green River for their services per week in the summer past." By this it appears that more than one school was kept; but no schoolhouse appears to have been built. This year the selectmen defined and put on record a plan of "Green River Street." This is the present Main street of to-day.

Dec. 18, 1750, Voted to allow the People of Green River a School master two months, provided they can procure a suitable room to keep the school in.

Dec. 9, 1751, Voted that a School be kept at Green River 3 months in the winter season this year & y^t ye school be omitted 3 months in ye Town, in ye summer, [thus robbing Peter to pay Paul,—and to provide preaching on their side of] ye river at such seasons as it is difficult for them to attend the Publick Worship in Town.

A schoolhouse was probably built this year, for at the spring meeting in 1752, it was "Voted to allow the people living at the Farms the Liberty of the School House on Sabeth Days, they finding their own wood."

All concessions to the demands of the Green River people seem to have made them more determined to become a separate political organization. The population of Greenfield at this date is not known, but in 1755, three years later, it was one hundred and ninety-two souls. At a meeting,—

Jan'y 3, 1753, In answer to the Petition of Green River People this day presented to this Town Requesting that they may be set off as a Separate District or a District Precinct by such meets and bounds as may be thoat proper for them & us &c Voted that the Town are willing & do consent that they should be set off Into a Seperate District or Precinct, provided their bounds and limits be as follows, *viz.*: To begin at the northeasterly corner of the Township on Connecticut River and to proceed Southerly on s^d River until they come to the Line of the Eight Thousand acres & then proceed Westwardly on said Line to the end of it & Continueing s^d Line to the West end of the first Tier of Lots west of the seven mile line and from thence to proceed Northerly taking in said lots to the north end of our bounds & then to go East on the Town Line untill they come to the first mentioned boundary on Connecticut River.

The petitioners do not appear to have been satisfied with this action and sent another petition to the meeting held

March 5th, 1753. This paper is not found. The reply to it is, "Green River Petition being heard and Considered, voted to dismiss the same."

Still strenuous that the Deerfield river should be their south bound, the petitioners caused a town meeting to be called for April 2d, when it was,—

Voted that Col° Oliver Partridge Doct° Samuel Mather and Lieut Ebenezer Hunt be Desired to Consider and Determine where the Dividing line shall be between the Town and the proposed District on the north side of Deerfield River; and also to Consider and Determine where the Meeting house shall be placed in said District & also to consider and determine whether the aloted and Divided lands in s^d District shall be subject to a tax towards building a Meetinghouse and Settling a Minister, and if they think it proper it should be taxed then what Tax it shall pay p^r acre, p^r annum and for how many years, and also to Determine what part of the Publick tax they shall have laid on them, and also what part of the Sequestered land they shall be entitled to and for what term. In all these things to act and Determine as if there had been no votes of the Town Previous to this with Regard to said Land or District with respect to the Boundaries.

Voted that the said Committee shall be paid for their Trouble by the Town if the Committee shall bring their South Line further South Than the Town have voted it already, and if they do not then the Inhabitants of Green River are to pay them.

Voted that Mr Aaron Denio be Desired to notifie the Gentlemen of their being chose and to get them to do the business they are chose for.

Voted that Messers Elijah Williams Aaron Denio Capt John Catlin & Ebenezer Wells the second be a Committee in behalf of the Town to wait on the Committee before chose and to let them know what is expected they will take into consideration and to acquaint them with the Lands as far as they are able.

Williams and Catlin represented the town, the others Green River.

At an adjourned meeting, the commissioners to whom these large powers had been mutually intrusted reported:—

Whereas the Town of Deerfield at their Town Meeting April ye 2d, 1753 voted that we the Subscribers should be Desired to Consider and Determine where the Dividing Line shall be between the Town and the proposed District on the north side of Deerfield River. Also to Consider and Determine whether the unimproved lands lying in said District that are Divided and aloted shall be subject to a tax for building a Meeting house and settling a Minister, and if so how much p^r acre & for what term of time, also to Determine where the Meeting house shall be placed in said proposed District, and what part of the Country Tax shall be paid by said District & also what proportion of the Sequestered land the said District shall be Intitled to &c In Complyance therewith we met at the Town of Deerfield upon the ninth day of said April and on the next Day we proceeded to view the Lands proposed for a District being attended by a Committee of said Town two whereof belongeth to the old Town and two to the proposed District after we had made a thoro view of lands by passing thro the same in various places we heard the alligations of the Committee on both sides upon articles above mentioned and having maturely considered the same do adjudge and Determine it to be Reasonable that the said District be set off in the manner following, *viz.*

That a line be run as far northward as the line known by the name of the Eight Thousand acre line to run from Connecticut River West to the west end of the first tier of Lots which lie west of the seven mile line so called, thence North 19° east to ye north side of ye Town bounds, thence East on the Town line to the Connecticut River, thence as the River Runs to the first Bounds

We further judge it Reasonable that the lands lying in a certain meadow or Intervale which lies north of Deerfield River known by the name of Cheapside which belongs to Timothy Childs Jr and David Wells who Dwell in Said proposed District should pay taxes to said District when set off

We are further of opinion that it is Reasonable that a tax of one penny farthing p^r acre Lawful money be levied upon the unimproved cleared lands in s^d District so soon as the frame of a Meeting house be erected in said District and a further tax of one penny p^r acre upon said unimproved lands so soon as a minister is settled in said District to be Imployed for building the Meeting House and settling a minister

We have also fixed the place for erecting a Meeting House at a place called Traps plain where we have fixed a white oak stake. We further Judge it Reasonable the same proportion of the Country tax laid on the town of Deerfield hereafter, be paid by the said District when set off as was laid upon the Inhabitants and Ratable Estates in the limits of said Districts for the last Tax, and that the said District have the Improvement of one-half of the Sequestered lands in said Town of Deerfield lying north of Deerfield River.

OLIVER PARTRIDGE.
SAM^{ll} MATHER.
EBENEZER HUNT.

Deerfield, April ye 12th, 1753.

June 9th, 1753, the district was incorporated with the name of Greenfield, by an act of the Legislature, agreeable to the provisions of the above award, excepting, that the provision for sharing the rents of the Sequestered lands should only continue "untill there shall be another District or Parish made out of the town of Deerfield;" and further, that the right to tax the Cheapside lands of Childs and Wells should continue no longer than they were owned by persons living in Greenfield.

Dec. 10th, 1753, the town chose a committee of five to,—

Come into some Measures to Divide the Sequestered land north of Deerfield river with the Minister or people of Greenfield & to act and do whatever shall be necessary to be Done in order to accomplish and Settle the Improvements of said Sequestered Land.

Feb. 15th, 1754, the town voted to give Greenfield the rents of the sequestered land in the same proportion as they pay the Province tax:—

Provided the said District will accept of the same, and that they do by their vote at a meeting called for that purpose, or by a committee by them chose for that purpose, give the town of Deerfield a Discharge from all demands that they have in and to the said Rents for the year passed, which the Town votes as a *free Gift*, and not as anything they are by law enjoyned to.

Voted to Referr the further consideration of the report of the committee for Dividing the Improvement of the Sequestered land &c with the Inhabitants of Greenfield to next March Meeting.

By the last two votes there seems to have been a hitch in the proceedings somewhere, which does not otherwise appear. Although according to the vote the cost of making the award should have been paid by Greenfield, at this meeting it was voted to divide it "in equal halves."

Committees to lease the Sequestered lands continued to be chosen in town meetings as before the incorporation of Greenfield, and the land was amicably occupied in common until 1767, when Conway being set off as a district, Greenfield, according to the terms of her charter, had no more rights to the income of these lands. In spite of this provision, however, Greenfield continued to claim what she had held for fourteen years, and backed her claims by forcibly taking away the crops in 1768 and 1769. In August, 1768, Lieut. Seth Catlin, as agent for the town of Deerfield, began a suit at law against Jonathan Severance and others for trespass, under the advice of "Gentlemen versed in the Law." Catlin won the case in the Superior Court, after the usual law's delay, and Greenfield settled the affair by paying £40 lawful money.

Greenfield then appealed to the General Court for such a change in her charter as would make it in accordance with the award of the commissioners in 1753. She met with no success, although the committee to whom the matter was referred reported a bill under which Greenfield should share the income of the Sequestered lands in common with Deerfield, Conway and Shelburne, the latter town having been set off in 1768. This did not pass, and the matter rested with the decision of the Superior [then the highest] Court that the Sequestered lands could not be divided with any seceding bodies, but must remain with the party for whom it was sequestered for the use of the ministry in.1686. The lands are still held by trustees for the "First Congregational Parish in Deerfield," to which they descended under this decision.

The peace which followed the treaty at Aix La Chapelle was little more than an armed truce in Europe, and, so far as the prosperity of the colonies went, little better than open war with the Indians here. The farmers had no assurance when planting that their crops would not be reaped in terror and blood; and cultivation of the soil was kept down to the bare necessities of life, as much as in time of declared war. The poverty of our townsmen was such, that to avoid the expense of a representative, the town in 1751 voted not to send one. In those days "Representation and Taxation" went literally together. Being called to account by the General Court for slighting their precept to send a representative, the town by its selectmen sent a statement which well shows the condition of affairs here in this unquiet interval of peace. The letter is given below:—

To the Hon[ble] House of Representatives in Gen. Court Assembled May 29 1751—
We the Subscribers Selectmen of the Town of Deerfield and at the request of s[d] Town on our and there behalf
Humbly Desire
In excuse for not sending any Person this year to Represent us in the Great & General Court; To offer the following reasons—
That we have been great Sufferers in the last War, in being Drove from our improvements so that we have been obliged to go into the lower Towns & some to Connecticut for our Bread Corn And altho in years Past we Used to furnish the Market with some Droves of Hoggs, yet for the six years past we have been obliged to buy pork of our Neighbors and have had befor the War, more fat Cattle in our Stalls in May, than has been fatted in Town any year since the War Commenced, and what few we fatted the last Year take the Town together did not fetch what they cost in the Fall, by which our Time, Hay & Provender was entirely lost to us. That through Difficulty we have Repaired our Fences that were not Burnt & made Such new as were; and at the Desire of Many & particularly some Gentlemen in Boston; have laid ourselves out to our utmost by Clearing, Fitting & Sowing some Hundred acres of Wheat; for an

Experiment whether we Cannot raise as good as the Other Governments. In doing of which we have unavoidably expended what little Money we had, which will in no poor Degree be evidenced by the Acc^{ts} of the Committee Appointed to give Certificates [to] such as had any Money to Exchange for the Dollars

The uncertainty of Success in this our Attempt (should the Seasons prove favorable) by reason of our Remoteness from market, The scarcity of Money Amongst us and the Apprehension of an Heavier Tax this year so influenced the Town, that we had not a vote for a Representative and Caused us to Hope should this our State be laid before Your Honours, you would not lay a fine upon us (who are scarce 100 families) for not Complying with the Precept sent us in all which is submitted to Your Hon^{rs} Wise Consideration by your Hon^{rs} obedient Humble Servants   EBENEZ: HINSDALE
Wm WILLIAMS
DAVID FIELD
JONAth HOIT

The petition was endorsed "To be considered with other cases," but no action was found on the premises. The "fiat money" of this period was so depreciated that the price for a day's work was fixed at 15 s in summer and 10 s in winter; and £800 were voted for Mr. Ashley's salary, for the £300 due in the same bills by the terms of the settlement. In 1751, Capt. Catlin was chosen to,—

Fence the Burying Yard with a Good five railed fence, with a good Gate to enter s^d Yard, and to purchase a Pall for the use of the Town, not to exceed the price of £5-8-8, Lawful Money * * * but if any Person or Persons will add to s^d sum so as to purchase a velvet Pall he may procure that.

Judicial Affairs. Our Justices of the Peace for this period were Jonathan Wells, 1715,—I give earliest dates of official action noticed—Thomas Wells, 1734; Elijah Williams, 1744; Ebenezer Hinsdale, 1747; William Williams, 1750; Thomas Williams, 1754; Jonathan Ashley, Jr., 1770.

In 1737, the town voted *not* to join Northampton, Hatfield, Westfield, Hawley, Sunderland and Northfield in paying for one-half of a court house to be built at Northampton. In 1763, our representative was,—

Desired to oppose in the Gen'l Court a Division of this County according to the present plan for dividing the same, or any other Division that may be proposed by a North & South line.

March 5, 1770, Voted that the Town have no objections respecting the alteration of the Inferior Courts being held in the County of Hampshire, saving it would be more agreeable to have the August & November Terms held at Northampton & the March & May Terms held at Springfield.

This is very modestly put, but it shows that our little commonwealth claimed the right to have a voice in judicial, as well as in ecclesiastical, civil and military affairs.

Mills. From 1701 to 1709, nothing is found about corn mills on the records. It may be that during Queen Anne's War the meal was home-made by means of wooden mortars and sieves. March, 1709, the town "Voted that Joseph Parsons of Springfield should com and perform his former bargain in building a grist mill for ye town of Deerfield." [See ante, page 269.]

Dec. 2d, the town granted Parsons leave "to build a grist mill upon Deerfield River, at a place called Sutliefs Falls." It does not appear whether he availed himself of this privilege; but his bargain with the town was canceled January 6th, 1713-14, and three days later the town "granted to Capt. Wells ye Green River stream to set a corn mill upon;" and to encourage him he is given £50, to be paid "by Michaelmas next." The town reserved the right to set a saw-mill on the same stream. At a meeting April 23d, 1715,—

The town then agreed y^t there should be a mill set upon Green River about 60 or 100 rods above the other mil.

At ye same Meeting the Town voted y^t they would build a dam for Capt Jonathan Wells on ye place above mentioned & s^d Capt. Wells stands obliged as in ye former bargain & ye Town shall have all ye old dam.

A committee was chosen to build the dam and £60 raised to pay the expense. Wells is to have for grinding "1-12 part of Indian corn, 1-14 part of rye & provender, 1-16 of wheat & 1-18 of barley malt." He is to have the stream so long as he shall keep a mill there in good condition to do the town's grinding. In default of this, the property reverts to the town, "except in case of extraordinary providence:" and "s^d Jonathan Wells or his heirs shall not be Rated for s^d Mill for ye defraying any Town charges." I suppose the present grist mill stands on the site of that built by Jonathan Wells, and here for one hundred and seventy years much of the "town's grinding" has been done. March 8th, 1714,—

The Town Granted Ed Allyn: Ben More Jno Smead Jno Nims Saml Childs Jno Allin; Saml Field; Ebn Smead; viz.: ye stream y^t formerly ye Saw Mill was set upon provided no former grant Intervene: on the other hand these persons above s^d are to get s^d mill fit for work by this time Twelve month:

It is not certain where this stream was. Before 1766, Adonijah Taylor had a mill on Roaring Brook at the place now called Sanderson Glen. In 1771, there was a mill called Taylor's mill, standing on the small "Roaring Brook" a few rods south of Cheapside bridge.

A traditionary story has it that a mill was built here by a young man who, when it was completed, sent for his father to come and see this great effort of his genius. The old gentleman looked it over with a quizzical smile that troubled the son, but said nothing. "What's the matter, daddy?" asked the son at length, "don't you think my *dam* is safe?" "Wal--yis—tolerbul safe," replied the sire, glancing at the scanty supply of motive power, "it would be *par*fectly safe in case of a *flood*, but I was wonderin' what in the world you'd do in case of a *fire*."

Deer. Through greed or wantonness, deer were slaughtered in season and out of season. As buckskin was an article of prime necessity, not only for breeches, but for snow-shoes, military accoutrements, and a dozen other things, the Legislature passed laws for the protection of deer. An officer, called a deerreeve, was chosen in each town, whose duty it was to see these laws enforced. These regulations were often supplemented by town legislation, when votes like the following were passed:—

Mr. Joseph Clesson was chosen to inspect and see y^t y^r is no Deer killed from ye 10th of December to the first of August, & to Complain of all breaches of ye Laws made for ye preservation and Increase of Deer y^t shall come to his knowledge.

During the soft snows of winter, deer became an easy prey to hunters on snow-shoes; and the time of the protection was extended, to cover the season when the doe was rearing her young, and until the fawn became able to take care of itself.

Surgeons. As a general thing, the practicing physicians of this period were not versed in the science of surgery. The following vote, which carries its own interpretation, was passed at a time when Dr. Thomas Wells was here, where he had been in practice for a dozen years or more. Mch. 27th, 1739,—

Voted that Mr John Catlin be appointed to go to Hatfield and meet the Comtt^{ees} of Northampton, Hadley & Hatfield, and there in behalf of this Town to act and determine what to give Dr. Porter for his encouragement to settle as a bone setter in this part of yᵉ Country; that is to say, whether to give fourteen Pounds, or what part soever thereof shall be by him accounted to be our proportion with yᵉ rest of yᵉ towns, considering yᵉ circumstances of yᵉ town with regard to their distance from him; and what he shall agree for, the Town will and do hereby order to be raised for him in a rate on the Town, to be raised according as yᵉ Law Directs for yᵉ raising of Town taxes.

The man referred to was probably Hezekiah Porter, from Farmington, Ct., who settled in Northampton about this time.

The Scow. There were two roads to Greenfield in use; one was down the lane by the old burying yard across the Pocumtuck at the old ford, by Old River and Little Hope to the Green River farms. The other was from the north end of the street across Great Plain east of Pine Hill, crossing the river to the Sequestered lands, and through Cheapside. The river at this point was not fordable and a "scow" for teams, and a canoe for foot men, were kept here at the expense of the town. The main need of this ferry was to allow convenient access to the town lands at the mouth of Green river; and first and last the town expended a good deal of money upon it. By means of sudden freshets and the carelessness of men, the boats were often carried away, to be utterly lost, or recovered from below at some expense. Stringent legislation and strong chains "to seize them withall" were provided for their safe keeping.

In 1714, a scow was built and put under the charge of the selectmen, and they agreed with the "Proprietors of Cheapside" to take the care of it six years in view of the extra benefit they had from its use.

In 1720, voted "to make a new scow provided the Mill Men, the Cheapside and Green River Men" will be responsible for its safe keeping, "it being delivered to them with sufficient chain of seizure to seize it withall." Perhaps no party would take the responsibility, for in 1722 a committee was chosen to treat with Joseph Parsons about building a bridge.

In 1726, a canoe was built to be used with the scow.

In 1727, voted to build a bridge "at the first turn of the river below the road at Cheapside."

In 1727, voted not to build the bridge, but to build a scow and two canoes, and to procure "an anker, alias grappling, to seize the scow."

In 1731, a new scow was built, and "on account of great

loss of vessels," stringent provisions were made against their being taken from their harbors without authority.

In 1733, John Catlin was awarded damages for want of the scow when he last hired the Sequestered lands.

In 1736, another scow and a canoe were built, and soon after the committee in charge was directed to prosecute at law any one who put them in the water after they were taken out in the fall.

Mch. 2d, 1747, the selectmen were authorized to procure two canoes for the town, and Jona. Hoyt, David Field and Aaron Denio were "fully Impowered in the fall of the year at such time as they shall think proper to secure the scow and canoes that belong to the Town in such manner & place as they shall think convenient & that they be Impowered to prosecute any person or persons who shall remove said vessels from the place where they put them without there Liberty so to do." A similar vote was passed in 1754 and again in 1755.

Thus far the fleet kept on the river was principally for the accommodation of those who hired the Sequestered lands, and those having land at Cheapside Meadows. The tide of emigration was now setting northward and the scow was called upon to officiate as a ferry-boat, but nothing is heard about tolls.

In 1754, a committee was chosen to report the cost of a bridge to "accommodate travellers." No report is found, or any further action about a bridge until after the Revolution.

In 1758, the matter of a regular ferry was agitated, and by order of the Court of General Sessions the town was directed, about this time, "to keep and maintain a ferry over Deerfield River, between Deerfield and Greenfield," and in 1761 a lot of land was bought of David White, "west of the County Road, between s^d Road and Pine Hill & Samuel Bardwells lot." This was the "Old Ferry Lot," held by the town until it was exchanged for a gravel pit a few years ago. On this lot a house was built for the use of the ferry-man, "18x20 feet, with a stone cellar under or near one side of it as the Committee we chose shall think best & all at ye Town Cost." An old schoolhouse was utilized in the construction. A bunch of house lilies still marks the site of this house, at the northeast corner of Pine Hill.

The ferry appears to have been run at the town charge, and the scow used also for the convenience of farmers. In 1764 it was,—

> Voted that Lt David Field Messrs Joseph Stebbins & John Sheldon be a Com^tee to take care of the Scow & to give liberty to Persons to use the Same up or down the River from the Road at Cheapside as they shall think reasonable—except on Mondays Fridays & Saturdays

Why travelers were specially favored these three days does not appear, but this action is given as a feature of the times. As nothing later about the ferry appears on the records, it is presumed it became a private enterprise. Moses Chandler was ferry-man here as early as 1771, and during the Revolution; his son, Dr. Amariah Chandler, so long minister of Greenfield, was probably born in the old ferry house, Oct. 27th, 1782. Moses Chandler kept a store here in connection with the ferry business. Some of his stock in trade was procured in Albany—"which reminds me of a little story." It belongs to the Revolutionary period, but being on the spot, the season will be forced a little, to give it place here, although it will lack its natural surroundings:

Chandler was suspected of Tory proclivities—and justly, too, if tradition can be relied upon. It is said among his descendants, that many a Tory found shelter in the garret of the ferry-house, while going up and down on treasonable errands, and that a gable window facing the side hill was a ready means of escape to the woods on Pine Hill. Something of this kind doubtless reached the ears of the "Committee of Safety," and a delegation was sent to examine the premises for evidence of treason. They were abundantly rewarded. A search revealed mysterious documents written in *cypher*, which was proof enough of a conspiracy against the dawning liberties of the new nation.

The culprit was seized, and with the evidence of his guilt was hurried before the Committee of Safety for trial. But to the intense chagrin of the zealous Whig officers, and to the hilarious delight of the Tory spectators, an examination showed that this "damnable proof of treason," this mysterious correspondence with the enemy, was none other than invoiced bills of goods bought at Albany, and made out in *low Dutch*.

There is another story connected with this ferry that may as well be told now that the subject is up. Of course, as the framework is wanting, it could be better appreciated at the time of it than now. But it is given at a venture:

It was in May, 1780, that a constitution for the new state was laid before the people for their examination and action in town meeting—and the subject was uppermost in the minds of all Whig politicians. It so happened that at this time there was lying on the bank of the river at the ferry—where it had been landed from a boat, and was waiting transportation—a *smoke-jack*, which Esq. John Williams had just bought to place in his house, the one now known as the Wilson house. A smoke-jack was a new thing in this region, and a traveler naturally made inquiry as to what the strange looking object might be; Mrs. Chandler, who had no more sympathy for the Whigs than her husband, venting her wit and her spleen at one breath, replied: "Oh, that's the new *Constitution* that everybody is talking about now days."

Sugar Loaf People. Nov. 29th, 1758, Thomas French petitions the General Court that his property may be exempted from taxation for ministerial purposes in Deerfield, as he lives within one mile of Sunderland, and goes there to meeting. He is ordered to notify the town of a hearing on the matter "the second Friday of the next Setting of the Court." Nothing more is heard of this matter; but in 1761 others join him in a similar petition.

Thomas French, John Hooker and Elijah Billing of Deerfield, Joseph Sanderson, Nathaniel Sawtelle and Philip Smith of Hatfield, represent that they all live within one mile of Sunderland meetinghouse; that they attend meeting there and send their children to school at Sunderland; and ask that they be taxed to support public worship and schools in Sunderland and exempted elsewhere. The petitioners were ordered to serve the towns of Deerfield and Hatfield with a copy of their petition and give notice of a hearing on it, "on the second Tuesday of the next setting of the Court." No sequel to this has been found.

Conway set off. The action of the Proprietors of Pocumtuck on this matter has been given, [ante, page 508.] We now take up the municipal action. March 2d, 1767, the people of "South West" appeared in town meeting with a petition to be set off into a separate district. About this time a large sum of money was being expended by the town in repairing the meetinghouse. From its location, the people of Conway could get little comparative benefit from the taxes they would be called upon to pay in footing the bills. The same amount expended at home would give a much more satisfactory return. This consideration probably hastened the inevitable act of a separation.

This petition probably contains nearly a full list of the voters in South West at this time. It is addressed:—

To the Inhabitants of the Town of Deerfield in the County of Hampshire qualified by Law to vote in Town Meetings

We the Subscribers inhabitants and owners of lands within that tract of land in the s^d Township of Deerfield called the South West Division, for too many reasons herin to be mentioned, humbly request of you that you would by a vote give your full Consent and declare yourselves willing that the s^d South West Division should be sett off from ye s^d Township of Deerfield and made into a distinct Township or District and that the inhabitants therof should be incorporated and vested with all the Power and Priviliges which Towns or Districts within this Province are by Law vested withal, if the Genl Court of ye s^d Province upon application to them made shall judge the Same Expedient

Deerfield Jany 12 1767

Thomas French,	Alexander Oliver,	Simeon [Jones?],
Moses Daniels,	Silas Ransom,	Elijah Wells,
David Parker,	Jonas Twitchell,	James Gilmore,
James Oliver,	Nath. Field,	James Gilmore, Jr.,
Robert Hamilton,	Robert Oliver,	John Rand,
Samuel Wells,	Elias Dickinson,	Will'm Smith,
Josiah Boyden,	David Whitney,	Abra. (?) Marble,
John Thwing,	Israel Rice,	Mathew Graves,
Cyrus Rice,	Will Warren,	Nathaniel Marble,
Joel Baker,	Jearamiah How,	Joseph Cutler,
Daniel Davidson,	James Dickinson,	John Merrit,
Ebenezer Allis,	Benj'm Pulsipher	[Abel Marinan?].
Stephen Davidson,	John Boyden,	

At the town meeting March 2d, 1767, a committee of nine was chosen to "Confer together & draw up a proper vote for the Setting off the South West part of Deerfield into a Separate District and lay the same befor the Town for its Acceptance." The meeting was adjourned one day for a mature consideration of the proposition, when it was:—

Voted that the Prayer of the Petitioners be granted upon the following Conditions, *viz.*: That the Inhabitants afores^d be set off with their Lands into a town or separate District by the following Meets & Bounds, *viz.* East upon the seven Mile Line, so called, untill it comes to Deerfield River; West upon Ashfield Bounds, or the west line of Deerfield; South upon Hatfield Bounds; North, partly upon Deerfield River, untill it comes to the Northwest Division so called, & thence by s^d Northwest Division untill it comes to the west line of the Town.

Provided also that they pay the same proportion of the Yearly Province & County Tax laid upon Deerfield, as the Polls & Estates of the Inhabitants of s^d South West were set at & Assessed in the last list & Tax.

With this consent, the Conway people at once applied to the Legislature, and on June 17th, 1767, Gov. Francis Bernard signed the act which gave Conway a separate municipal existence.

Shelburne Set Off. The "North West" was not slow to follow the example of "South West." Perhaps the mother town attempted to quiet the inhabitants by voting them, Dec. 7th, 1767, "6 pounds towards hiring preaching there when it was the most difficult for them to come into the town; provided they have preaching there between this time and May next." Whether this offer of six pounds was sufficient inducement for the Shelburne people to raise the rest of the necessary funds to secure a preacher for five months, does not appear. Probably they did, and concluded from the winter's experience, that it would be more comfortable to have a minister of their own. At the next March meeting they petitioned to be set off into a separate district, the seven-mile line to be the east bound. Their petition "being read & the Question being put whether the town would set off the s^d Inhabitants * * * by such meets & bounds as set forth in the Petition, & it passed in the negative." Evidently the bounds were not satisfactory. At a meeting May 9th, 1768, another petition was preferred. In this, they ask,—

That they will set the Hool of the North west division except part of a kang that is Sett off to Greenfield. [Those signing the petition were]:—

John Taylor,	Benj'n Hosley.	Philip Jordon,
John Wells,	James Taft,	David Boyd,
Ebenezer Fisk,	Thomas Wells,	Mary Rider,
Stephen Kellogg,	Daniel Nims,	Martin Severance,
Samuel Poole,	Lawrence Kemp,	John Heaton,
Jacob Poole,	Asa Childs,	Joshua Gray.
Ebenezer Heart,	Watson Freeman,	

[After debate] on ye Petition the Question was put whether the Town would set off the above s^d Inhabitants in any shape, & it passed in the affirmative.

Then the Question was put whether the Town would set off the aforementioned Inhabitants agreable to there petition.

Then the Question was put whether ye Town would set off the before mentioned Inhabitants with the Lands that lie upon the South side of Deerfield River, & it was voted in the affirmative.

Then the Question was put whether the Town would set off the Inhabitants with ye Land to ye South side of Mr. John Taylor's lot, & it passed in ye affirmative.

A charter was granted by the General Court, June 1st, 1768. The bounds fixed were:—

Beginning at the north westerly corner of the district of Greenfield; from thence, southerly upon the west line of said Greenfield, to the south line of said Greenfield; thence, east, upon the said south line of said Greenfield, until it comes to a line in said Deerfield, called the Seven-mile Line; thence, southerly, upon the said Seven-mile Line, to the south side of the lot on which John Taylor now lives; thence, westerly, upon the south line of said lot, to the west end of said lot; thence, southerly, upon a line parraled with the said Seven-mile Line, until it comes to the south side of the third lot from said Taylor's lot; thence upon a line extended westerly, the same point of Compass with the said south line of the said third lot from the said Taylor's lot, until it meets with the north line of Conway; thence, upon the north line of the said Conway, to the north west Corner therof; thence, upon the west or westerly line of the said town of Deerfield, to the north west corner of said Deerfield; thence, upon the north line of the said Deerfield, to the first mentioned bounds.

The first district meeting was held Oct. 31st, 1768. The officers chosen were John Taylor, moderator; John Wells, clerk; John Taylor, John Wells and Robert Wilson, selectmen; Ebenezer Fisk, constable; Samuel Hunter, deerreeve. All but Wilson were from Deerfield.

Other Deerfield men who settled in Shelburne about this time were John Allen, Asa Childs, Moses Hawks, Lawrence Kemp, Archibald Lawson, Daniel Nims, Reuben Nims, Daniel Rider, Obed Taylor and Thomas Wells.

Bloody Brook Wants to be Set Off. The setting-off fever became catching, and in 1768 the following was presented to the town:—

The petition of the Inhabitants of the South part of Deerfield Humbly showeth:

Whereas we your Petitioners Considering the Great distance we live from the place appointed for public worship as also the badness of the Roads in certains Seasons of the year which renders it very difficult even for those that have Horses to attend upon the public Duties of the Sabeth & quite Impossible for those who have not

As also the Desire we have of Setting up maintaining and regulating schools among us for the instruction of children and youth in a better manner than it is possible we should under our present Sircumstances

These Gen'l Men & Sundry other reasons moues us at this time as in duty bound to lay before you this our Humble Petition begging that out of your Great Goodness you would not only free us our lands and all other rateable estate that we own in this part of the Town from all public charges that may heareafter arise in the Town but also Grant that the whole of the Land lying between Conway East Line & Coneticut River Begining at Hatfield line & extending North three miles may be devoted to be taxt according to Law & Custom for the aboue mentioned purposes that thereby with the addition of those parts of the town of Hatfield known by the Names of Cantur burey & the Streights we may be enabled to Settle the Ordinances of the Gospel among us and defray all other charges that will arise in s^d District either of a Civil or Eclieiastical nature So begs your Humble Petitioners and in duty bound shall ever pray:—

Samuel Graves,	Elijah Arms,	William Anderson,	Eber Allis,
Nath'l Parker,	David Arms,	Zebediah Graves,	Nath'l Parker, Jr.,
John Allis,	Thomas Arms,	Thomas Chamberlain,	Jos. Sanderson.
Nathan Frary,	Eliakim Arms,		
Sam'l Barnard,	Samuel Dwelle,	Abel Allis,	

After an adjournment of the meeting where this petition was presented, and due consideration, the request was refused.

In 1769 a schoolhouse was built at Bloody Brook, the town paying £6 towards its cost. Samuel Barnard was schoolmaster there in the winter of 1767 and Nathan Frary in 1769. In 1767-9, Rebecca Childs kept the summer school. The people of this district were allowed to select their own teachers, but sometimes it was required that the teacher should be approbated by the selectmen.

Roads. In 1715, a road was laid "from Deerfield river to the place where the corn-mill is to be set as it may be most convenient for the mill and country road."

1719, a committee was directed "to stake out ye hieway in Ens. Jonathan Wells his lot, at Cheapside, from Deerfield river to ye farther or north end of it."

1738, voted to make a road up to Petty's Plain.

1741, voted to build a road to Colrain.

The proprietors of the East Mountain wood lots laid a road running north and south through the whole range which can generally be traced to-day in "woods roads." It ran just west of the "Narrows," and near this point it was met by a road from Memorial Lane, up the hill eastward. The proprietors' road from this point north gradually neared the Traprock

Ridge, and crossed it in a gap at Flag Pond. It continued east of north through Sheldon's woods and the Dooley farm to Sheldon's Fields and Deerfield river. At the gap in the ridge a road turned eastward by the Keet farm to Wells's ferry—now Rice's—and Montague.

A road from the north end of the street struck the proprietors' road somewhere. In 1748, Rev. Mr. Ashley represented that in this road the cows going to the east woods were obliged to travel daily four hundred rods further than need be. He offered to lay a new road in exchange for the land occupied by the old one. His offer was accepted and a road was opened, which ran up the hill north of the Boyden lot, by the present railroad culverts and east to the proprietors' road. Much trouble grew out of this arrangement between Mr. Ashley and the owners of the land over which the old road passed, and in 1754, the *ante-bellum* condition of affairs was restored and the present road as far as the Flag Pond was apparently established as a private way.

But the end was not yet. After an apparent truce during the Last French War, the trouble again broke out, but the last that is heard of it is, when in 1763 a committee was chosen "to take a proper Course of Law for opening the Town Road at the north end of the Town to the Country Road that goes to Wells's Ferry," and to employ an attorney or attorneys to effect the same.

1749, Bars street was laid out eight rods wide.

1752, a committee was chosen "to look out and mark a Rhode to Charlemont, also to Hunt's town, & to clear the Roads of logs & bushes fit for a Riding Rhode."

1757, the surveyor was instructed to "repair & mend the path from ye South end of y^u Town by y^u outside of ye common Field fence to Wapping," so as to be a feasible horse road but not to expend over ten days' work upon it.

Voted "y^t ye Road from Hatfield bounds to ye Bars Street be six rods wide and from thence to y^u gate at ye Bars to be the whole width of ye Bars Street and from ye Bars gate to y^u South end of ye Town to be two rods wide.

1764, voted to accept of the Road laid out by the Selectmen from the Country Road to Pine Noock."

1766, "voted to accept of the Road laid out by the selectmen from Muddy Brook to Taylor's Mill."

This settled a contention of years' standing in regard to its location; but in 1769, Mr. Frary was allowed to set up three gates on this road where it passed through his land. "Brooks's ferry," "Oakes's ferry" and "Farrand's ferry," are mentioned about this time, as well as Wells's ferry.

"Jan. 7, 1771, a committee was chosen to take care of ye County road to Eagle Brook to prevent the river from wearing away the road for the future & to purchase land to accommodate the road." The highway at this time followed the road which now runs by the houses of Rufus R. Williams and Patrick Burke, westwardly to a point more than half way to the present new channel of the Deerfield river, and thence south across Log Meadow near Martin's Falls to the Bars gate, skirting the river and Stebbins Meadow as now.

The above committee reported that they had expended £5, 9s, 10d in procuring timber for building a wharf and in buying land. Some of the items of the bill were 1s each to Samuel Childs, Daniel Arms and Jeremiah Nims "for looking timber." Daniel Arms was paid for fifteen loads of timber 18s, and for two hands and a team three days drawing timber 24s. Samuel Childs had the same charge, and Seth Catlin for one hand and team three days, 18s 6d and John Hinsdale for fourteen rods of land from his home lot, 19s.

Hinsdale's home lot of three acres, fronting south on the road, lay far beyond the present high bank westward, probably quite beyond the present "old bed" of the river.

It appears by the vote that there had been previous trouble at this point, and the wharfing did not put an end to it. The river continued its annual eastward migration for almost a century later, and until it cut for itself a new channel through Old Fort Meadow. The older voters will remember the yearly agitation of the matter in town meeting and the expense of keeping this road on *terra firma.*

May 13, 1774, Voted that the town will build a House at the end of the Lane near the burying Yard for a Tradesman to dwell & work at his Trade in, s^d Tradesman to keep a Ferry near Harrar Meadow Bridge; s^d House to be of the contents of Thirty two feet in length, eighteen in breadth, one story high.

It does not appear how long a ferry was kept up here, but in 1780 the ferry house was devoted to the use of the poor of the town.

Prices of Labor, Produce, &c. During the period under consideration, prices varied so widely that no standard of value to compare with the present can be fixed. This is due to some extent to good and bad seasons—more largely perhaps to the French and Indian Wars—but the widest fluctuations are directly chargeable to the changing value of the Government "Bills of Credit," of "Old Tenor," of "New Tenor," of the "Last Issue," of the "Middle Issue," and so on, which well-nigh brought financial ruin upon the people. I use such material as the original manuscripts at hand furnish.

In giving the price of labor, I have generally followed the pay fixed by the town for work on the highway in summer, when near home. When obliged to "lay out" on the long roads to Charlemont, Colrain and Huntstown, a sixpence a day was usually added. The fall and winter work was generally a shilling less than summer.

The period given covers the time of "Old Tenor" "Middle Tenor" and "New Tenor" currency, which was at an end in 1752.

1737	£	s	d
Labor per day,		3	0
Wheat per bu.,		15	0
Rye per bu.,		14	0
Indian corn, bu.,		5	6
Oats, bu.,		4	0
Salt per bu.,		10	0
Ploughing per acre,		8	0
Threshing & fanning wheat, bu.,		2	6
Fanning & chessing,			8
Beaver per lb.,		7	6
Bucking & weaving duck per piece,	3	10	0
1742-3			
Labor per day,		6	6
Wheat per bu.,		14	0
Oats per bu.,		4	0
Rye per bu.,		12	0
Flax per lb.,		2	0
Tobacco per lb.,		1	6
Potatoes, bu.,		8	0
Rattlesnake balls,		4	0
Black wolf skin,	8	0	0
Bear skin,		6	0
1751			
Labor,		20	0
Pork, lb.,		1	8
Flax seed, bu.,		30	0
Rum, gal.,		35	0
Cider, bbl.,		35	0
Sheet of paper,		2	0
Silver dollar,		25	0

1737	£	s	d
Weaving linen cloth per yd.,		1	4
Weaving Stript cloth per yd.,		1	8
Weaving Lindsey Woolsey,		1	2
Hemp per lb.,			5
Flax per lb.,		1	3
Barrel cider,		17	0
Scyth,		20	0
Deerskin,		75	0
Sheepskin,		2	0
Team to draw boards from Bernardston per day,		9	0
1742-3			
Bear meat, lb.,			2
Venison, lb.,			3
1748, labor,		15	0
1749-50, labor,		20	0
1748, Feb., wheat, bu.,		40	0
1748, April, wheat, bu.,		45	0
Flax seed, bu.,		18	0
Salmon, lb.,		1	0
Turnips, bu.,		10	0
1751			
Coon skin,		10	0
Martin,		20	0
Beaver,		48	0
Fisher,		55	0
Fox,		20	0
Mink,		5	0

WHAT THINGS COST.

1752	£	s	d
Silver dollar,		45	0
Wheat & Pease, bu.,		25	0
Rye & Barley,		18	0
Corn,		12	0
1757			
Labor,		2	0
Wheat, bu.,		4	0
Rye, "		2	3
Barley, "		2	8
Corn, "		2	5
Pease, "		3	0
Oats, "		1	4
Flax, lb.,			6
Pork, "			2½
Beef, "			2
Venison, "		1	0
Bear's meat, "			6
Bear cub meat, "			5
1762-6			
Labor,		3	0
French rye, bu.,		4	0
Barley malt,		3	0
Flax seed, bu.,		6	4
Dozen shad,		1	0
Barrell cider,		7	0
Beef, lb.,			3
Salmon, "			2½
Venison, "		1	0
Bear, "			6
Bear cub, "			5
Fawn skin,		4	0
Fisher, "		5	8
Fox, "		5	8
Red Fox, "		3	4
Wolf, "		2	8
Sable, "		2	8
Mink, "		1	6
Fat oxen,	8	0	0
Cow hide,	3	0	0
Horse to fat for week exclusive of provender,		4	0
Horse on hay,		2	6
Horse 60 miles,		8	0

1752	£	s	d
Oats, bu.,		9	0
Beef, lb.,		1	4
Pork, lb.,		1	6
1757			
Tobacco, lb.,		4	0
A fat horse,	12		
Hair for a wig,		40	0
Wig for Capt. Burke,		26	6
Pair pistols,		44	0
Coon skin,		1	3
Martin,		3	0
Fisher,		7	6
Otter,		9	0
Red Fox,		3	0
Grey Fox,		2	5
Wild Turkey,		2	8
1762			
Clapboards per M.,		60	0
Boards,		28	0
Shingle, per M.,		13	4
Making Indian shoes,			8
Making Indian stockings,		1	8
Making leather vest,		8	6
Making leather breeches,		6	6
Making clapboards per M.,		30	0
Board per week,		5	3 pence far.
Meal of victuals,		6	0
Mess of oats,		3	2
½ mug of flip,		3	2
A button of flip,		2	0
Gill rum,		4	2
Gill cherry,		5	1
A dram,		2	2
Dram bitters,		2	1
Mug cider,			3
½ mug cold grog,		5	0
½ mug cold toddy,		4	2
½ mug egg punch,		8	0
Egg rum,		1	2

In November, 1768, Joseph Barnard sent Silas Hamilton to Albany to buy furs. He was gone four and a half days, and brought back on his horse one hundred and two pounds of beaver and twenty-four raccoon skins, which cost at Albany £39, 18s, York money. His time, horse and expenses were £2, 6s, 3d, a total of £42, 4s, 3d, "which was in lawful money," £31 13s, 2d. Hamilton agreed to make up this stock into hats on the following terms:—

"*Viz* I engage to work up yᵉ Best of yᵉ Bever into hats, I to finde Linings & trimmings Coloring stuff &c. at 8s per hat the Beverit hats at 7s 4d each." Barnard sold "Bever Hats" at 30s each and "Castor Hats" at 18s.

In 1760 Ensign Barnard paid David Harrington for making a "Case of Draws" £2.

1760. Duck was woven in Deerfield and sold in Salem for "£12 0. 0. per bolt." It cost 6s for transportation.

1756. John Crosby, Jr., charged Esq. Williams:—

	£	s	d
To a wig for your Lady,	9	0	0
To a new top to your brown wig,	1	0	0
To a fan for ye tale of your brigadier wig,	0	15	0
To 20 times shaving,	2	0	0

These prices were in Old Tenor, which had been supplanted by "Lawful Money" in 1751; a few conservatives still clinging to the old way. 1763 Nathaniel Dickinson paid workmen 12s per M for sawing boards.

1770 Jonas Locke decides that Francis Munn should have 12s for making the town a bier, he finding the stuff.

It may be of interest to know what books were in demand by our ancestors. In 1758 Elijah Williams bought a lot in Boston for Deerfield market. A few will be named:—

	s	d
9 Marshall on Sanctification at	5	1
5 Dodridge' Rise & Progress &c. at	4	
7 do on fine paper, at	5	1
2 Praceptors 2 Vols, at	21	9
3 Centaurs at	5	1
12 Oxford Testaments with clasps 3 Bibles & 4 Apochrypha with clasps Circle of Service 7 Vols Red at	17	5
6 Gazetteers at	6	1
10 Baileys Dictionary at	10	4
4 Salmons Gram at	11	6

For lighter reading he had:—

The Bucaniers of America, Ansons voige, Lives of Peter the Great, Duke of Marlboro and Marshall Saxon, and Polite Tales.

Under the general laws of settlement, many forms were necessary to save the town unnecessary expense in aiding the poor. Hundreds of persons were officially "warned out of Town," to depart in so many days under a penalty; many of these became permanent and influential residents. No one was allowed to receive a stranger into his house without due notice to the town officers, giving age, sex, occupation and last residence.

Action similar to the following, to prevent people from becoming town charges, is often recorded:—

Feb. 6, 1758, Voted that the Selectmen be directed to warn the two children of Margaret Choulton out of Town Immediately. [In Aug. 1756, she had given birth to three living sons at the fort of Lieut. Ebenezer Sheldon at Fall Town.]

Voted that Lut Field and Samuel Hinsdale be desired & authorized to take due measures in ye Law to free ye Town from the charge of supporting Margaret Choller & her children & to endeavor to bring ye s^d charge on ye Master of s^d Margaret, or otherwise, as they shall think best or advise.

1766. Voted that the Selectmen be desired to prosecute all Persons who have or shall receive Strangers into their houses as Inmates or Boarders, & who shall not or have not Entered the Caution, as the Law directs.

CHAPTER XX.

HOMESTEADS ON THE OLD STREET.

Not all the lines bounding the house-lots as drawn May 14th, 1671, can be definitely defined. They were not laid out uniformly, as will be seen. The size of these lots was in proportion to the number of cow-commons held by each Dedham proprietor, and varied widely. A few remain unchanged as they were drawn; others have been divided, and still others combined. The lines bounding some few lots have been easily traced, and others with great difficulty. The results given, however, may be relied upon as substantially correct. Omitting many minor additions and subtractions, the attempt has been made, at the cost of much time and labor, to trace the successive ownership of these lots from the original draft to the present generation. Not always with success, for many transfers were informal and even verbal. Some of these are only discovered through quit claim deeds given many years later by the heirs of the grantor to the heirs of the grantee. Many deeds were never recorded, and are lost; and probably some have been overlooked on the records. Therefore, in spite of all research, gaps in the line of ownership often occur, which in the earlier transactions can never be filled. Much, however, has been recovered interesting to those whose ancestors were here born, and whose lives were identified with these homes and acres, where their part on the stage of history was acted, and whence they were carried to their last resting places on the bank of the Pocumtuck, or the hill overlooking its beautiful valley.

A list of the houselots drawn by the Committee this 14–3, 71: [May 14, 1671.]

	No. Lot	Cow Com.	Sheep Com.	Acres	Roods	Rods
Rob't Ware, Nat'l Fisher,	1	15	00	5	¼	7½
Eleazer Lusher, Gent.,	2	9	1	3		39¾
Timothy Dwight's farm,	3					
John Allin, Gent.,	4	16	0	5	½	24
John Hubbard,	5	3	0	1		9½

DRAWING HOUSE-LOTS.

	No. Lot	Cow Com.	Sheep Com.	Acres	Roods	Rods
Timo. Dwight,	6	12	0	4		38
Anthony Fisher, Jr., [farm]	7					
Ensign Phillips,	8	16	0	5	½	24
Saml. Hensdell,	9	16	0	5	½	24
Peter Wooderd,	10	20	0	7		10
Samson Frary,	11	9	3	3	¼	22½
Capt. Pynchon,	12	16	4	5	¾	29¼
John Stebbins,	13	20	0	7		10
Capt. Pynchon,	14	18	0	6	¼	17
John Fuller,	15	9	3½	3	¼	28
Peter Wooderd,	16	20		7		10½
Mary Hayward,	17	11	0	3	¾	21½
John ffarrington,	18	18	2	6	½	
Ed Richards's farm,	19					
Church Lott,	20	8	0	2	¾	12
Leift. Fisher's farm,	21					
Seargt. Avery,	22	13	1	4	½	25¾
Thomas Mason,	23	13	1	4	½	25¾
John Bacon,	24	7	3	2	½	29½
Seargt. Thomas Fuller,	25	20	0	7		10
Saml Daniell,	26	12	0	4		38
Deacon Chicerins,	27	8	3	2	¾	12
John Haward,	28	8	0	2	¾	12
Peter Wooderd,	29	20	0	7		10
Isaac Bullard,	30	11	1	3	¾	33
Rob Hensdell,	31	8	0	2	¾	12
Nathl Coleborne,	32	11	1	3	¾	33
Ensine Phillips,	33	16	0	5	½	24
Left. Fisher,	34	6	[1	2		33]
Saml Hensdell,	35	16	0	5	½	20
Saml Hensdell,	36	14	3½	5		30½
Mrs. Bunker,	37	17	3	6		34½
Ensigne Phillips,	38	16	0	5	½	24
John Baker,	39	13	2	4	½	38
John Gaye,	40	11	2	3	¾	24½
Ensign Daniel Fisher,	41	13	0	4	½	[14½]
Thomas Paine,	42	6	0	2		19
Capt. Pynchon,	43	20	0	7		10
[Total,		515	35]			

When homesteads were passed for several generations from father to son, the successive owners are not generally given.

The numbering of the lots began at the north end of the street on the west side, and ended at the north end on the east side. The "farm" lots were the tracts granted the surveyors who laid out the grant. The claim of the surveyors to house-lots by virtue of their acreage seems to have been partially allowed in the above draft and report, but in point of fact it was sometimes resisted in the actual laying out of the lots. Conflicting claims consequently arose, which created some confusion. The final mode of adjustment does not always appear. In some cases the claims of the "Farmers," as they were called, were bought out by those interested.

The settlers here generally belonged to that class which should be ranked the highest in all civilized society, as being the most essential—the producers. For the first century, manufacturing, trading, and the learned professions, were generally, and perhaps always, combined with the cultivation of the soil. To this prime industry the energies of the community were devoted, as being the real source of subsistence. Other occupations, as convenience suggested or necessity compelled, came in gradually, until at length almost every branch of the handicraft of the period was represented in the Old Town Street; and for generations this was the business center of a large surrounding territory. To this fact the old account books preserved in Memorial Hall bear abundant testimony.

The location of these various industries is given, when known, as a matter of interest. This interest would be largely increased if the time when they were carried on could be more definitely fixed. The same is true regarding the old houses, whose age can only be approximately given, as a rule, and often only guessed at. But it may be safely stated as a fact that more than one-half of the houses on the Old Street were built in the last century, and the average age of these is probably more than one hundred and thirty years. They were built by workmen who put their consciences, as well as their muscles and ten-inch oak timber, into their frames. The modern houses—the mushroom ten-penny nail and hemlock scantling affairs—will stand small chance, even with the six-score years in their favor, in a struggle with these old veterans for the survival of the strongest. *Time* seems to have no effect on *them*. They can only be conquered by fire.

In the following sketches the first name after each number is that of the party who drew that lot in the division of the Town Plat, May 14th, 1671. The statistical notes which follow will be of the briefest character.

House Lot No. 1.—Robert Ware and Nathaniel Fisher. The lot ran west to Broughton's Pond. Ware had the north part, which in 1686 was owned by John Broughton. Here Thomas Broughton, his brother, and all his family, were murdered by Indians in 1693. House and lot were inventoried at £20. In 1694 James Brown bought the place and sold it in 1697 to John Severance for "a mare at £3, & new cart wheels at £2." No conveyance from Severance is found. Fisher's half was held by Richard Weller, and by his son John, who died about 1686, when it was inventoried at £25. John Weller, Jr., succeeded his father, and sold it in 1694 to Godfrey Nims. John, son of Godfrey, held this part, and probably the whole, in 1719. It remained in the Nims family until 1774, when Abner Nims sold it to Thomas W. Dickinson for £90. His son Richard was a large manufacturer of brooms here, 1830-37. House, broom shop, two barns and many outbuildings were burned in 1843. It was sold by Richard Dickinson to Elbert Amidon for $1000, who built the present house in 1867.

No. 2.—Eleazer Lusher. He sold to John Pynchon, who in 1683 sold it to Lieut. Thomas Wells for £50. It was here that the murderous assault was made upon Widow Wells and her children in 1693. [See page 230.] In 1720 Lieut. Thomas Wells sells to Thomas Wells, cordwainer, for £50. In 1721 Wells sells to Moses Nash, and Nash to John Wells in 1726, who probably built a house on it. June 28, 1733, John Wells sold the place for £250 to Rev. Jonathan Ashley, who had been settled here as the minister the year before. Through his son Elihu, doctor and farmer, and his grandson, Thomas W., farmer, it has come to Jonathan Ashley, the present owner. Parson Ashley's house was stockaded during the French and Indian wars. This house was removed to the rear of the barns, and replaced by a new one in 1869.

No. 3.—"Farm lot," drawn by Timothy Dwight. This was the 150 acres he received for services in laying out the "8000 acre grant." Rev. John Russell of Hadley bought this farm and gave it to his son Samuel, who in 1707 sold it to Wm. Arms and Nathaniel Dickinson. Thirty-three acres meadow land were laid out in the Neck and Pogue's Hole as part of this farm. This was accounted and taxed as 11 cow commons and a corresponding home lot was claimed by the Russells. Arms and Dickinson sold their title to John Sheldon, as below, but they had also bought out the claims of those holding under John Allyn, and no lot was actually laid out for No. 3.

No. 4.—John Allen, Gent., [minister of Dedham.] He died in 1672 and it was held by his son, Daniel Allyn of Boston. The lot appears to have been bought by Rev. William Williams of Hatfield, who in 1691 sold it to Hannah, widow of Samuel Porter. In 1701 she sold to Wm. Arms, and he in Feb., 1702-3, a part of it to Ebenezer Brooks. The north part, probably through Timothy Dwight, whose farm drew No. 3, was claimed by Rev. John Russell of Hadley, whose son Samuel sold all his claims to Wm. Arms and Nathaniel Dickinson in 1707. The house of Brooks was burned Feb. 29th, 1704, and he probably gave up the property, as, on the 22d of March, 1708, Wm. Arms and Nathaniel Dickinson, in whom the title was then vested, sold the whole to Ens. John Sheldon. For one hundred and seventy-seven years this lot has been handed down from father to son. From Ensign John to son John, who died in 1713, to *his* son John, who died in 1793, to *his* son John, who died in 1806, to *his* son Seth, who died in 1860, to *his* son George, the present scribe. The house was built before 1743. A school was kept here about 1790. Through the hands of four clergymen it came to the Sheldons, who have all been farmers.

No. 5.—John Hubbard. Held in 1700 by Thomas Wells; by Ebenezer Brooks, 1708-15, when he sells to John Beaman, Thomas Bardwell and Thomas French. The latter sells out to Beaman in 1725, and Beaman in 1732 sold the whole lot to Jonathan Hoyt for £286. About 1783 David Dickinson bought the lot and built the house now standing. In 1832 his daughter Charissa sold to Asa Stebbins, who gave it to his son Henry on his marriage, and it is now held by his heirs. The house is about 100 years old.

No. 6.—Timothy Dwight. He sold to Nathaniel Sutlief, who was killed with Capt. Turner in 1676. The sale was confirmed by Dwight's heirs to Nathaniel Sutlief, Jr., in 1700. He sold it a year or two later to David Hoyt, who was here captured with all his family in 1704. Here his son Jonathan kept tavern for many years after his return from captivity, and it was on this lot that Gov. Belcher held a conference with the Caghnawaga and other tribes of Indians in 1735. [See ante, page 519.] Lieut. Hoyt and wife died in 1779-80. It was occupied by Simeon and Bridget Burt awhile, but the Hoyt heirs soon after, sold to David Dickinson, whose daughter Charissa sold to Asa Stebbins in 1832. With No. 5 it went to Henry Stebbins, who built the house upon it for his son John H., in 1858. It was later bought by Stephen

Day of Rowe. It is now (1894) owned by J. Amelia Stebbins.

No. 7.—Anthony Fisher's farm. This was sold soon after it was granted, to Gov. Leverett, who in 1667 sold it to John Pynchon. Thomas Wells bought it of Pynchon, May 7th, 1683; but the deed was not given until July 4th, 1692, and then to his heirs. Joseph Selden lived here, 1683-9. This farm of one hundred and fifty acres included thirty-three acres of meadow land, and an eleven cow common home lot was claimed with it. March 6th, 1688-9, Joseph Morton sold it to Thomas Wells and Samuel Barnard, and with it the house where he lived "in the great fort." The deeds given show conflicting claims; how they were settled does not appear. Thomas Wells probably bought out all claimants. Lieut. Thomas Wells succeeded his father. At *his* death in 1750 he left it by will to Capt. Thomas Dickinson, his nephew. It was held by his son Eliphalet, and grandson George Dickinson. The latter in 1835 sold it to the trustees of Deerfield Academy, who sold it to Ephraim Hines in 1845. In 1847 Hines sold to Charles Jones. Elihu Brown bought of Jones the north half the same year and sold it in 1848 to Rev. John F. Moors. Moors built the house now standing there at that time, and in 1861 sold out to Rev. Daniel Hovey. A. W. Ball purchased the place of Hovey in 1865, and is its present owner.

No. 8.—Henry Phillips. Francis Barnard was the next known owner, and his son Joseph Barnard, the Proprietors' Recorder and first Town Clerk, lived here as early as 1685. Joseph was shot by Indians at Indian Bridge in 1695. From different heirs of his estate the lot was bought in 1701-9 by Lieut. Thomas Wells. At his death in 1750 it passed by will to Capt. Thomas Dickinson, his nephew. Held by his son Eliphalet and grandson George. It was upon this lot that the Morus Multicaulis speculation struck hard in the winter of 1835. An excavation through three feet of frozen ground was made and a hot house built for the propagation of the tree. Considerable capital was invested in the undertaking by George Dickinson and his partner, John G. Williams. They were too late. The multicaulis fever had abated—the bubble burst. Their assets were represented by a hole in the ground and a good many square feet of glass. This lot had been incorporated with No. 7 and with that went to Deerfield Academy, Hines and Jones. The latter settled on No. 8, where he is still living in the house built or extensively repaired by Capt. Thomas Dickinson about 1752. Capt. Dickinson had a store south of the house before the Revolution—certainly in 1770-5.

No. 9.—Samuel Hinsdale drew this on the rights of Timothy Dwight, by some unknown arrangement. Hinsdale was killed with Lothrop at Bloody Brook in 1675. His heirs, in 1685, sold to the heirs of his brother, Experience Hinsdale, who was killed with Capt. Turner in 1676, and it was occupied by John Evans, who married the widow of Experience. In 1715 Daniel Belding bought out the Hinsdale heirs. In 1729 Belding gives it to his son Daniel. Daniel sold it March 5th, 1744, to Dr. Thomas Williams—our second male physician—who came to Deerfield about 1740. He was ancestor of the later generations of the Deerfield Williams family. From father to son this lot of four and a half acres came down through Solomon, Ralph and Solomon, who sold it in 1860 to Israel Billings, whose heirs now hold it. The house may have been built about 1740-50, and was originally gambrel roofed. The doctor's office was in the garret. Here, in a narrow closet, hung the human skeleton which his daughter Cynthia, when a young miss, went up and rattled in the dark at midnight, on a wager, walking backward both ways. This was considered—as indeed it was, in that age of ghosts and witches—a very bold thing to do. Until within a few years the house was painted a deep yellow.

No. 10.—Peter Woodward. He sold to William Bartholomew, a carpenter, who occupied it at the breaking out of Philip's War. He did not return at the resettlement, and sold it in 1685 to Daniel Belding. Here, in 1696, Belding's family were overwhelmed by the disaster, narrated in *ante*, page 254. In 1729 Belding gave it to his son Samuel. Samuel's heirs sell to Joseph Stebbins in 1761. About 1772 Stebbins built the present mansion, and gave the lot to his son Joseph. He was succeeded by *his* son Baxter, who was a large manufacturer of brooms. It is now held by the heirs of his son James. The broom shop was moved to No. 11.

No. 11.—Samson Frary. This lot was not early built upon. It was sold by Nathan Frary, son of Samson, in 1719, to Mahuman Hinsdale. Daniel Belding held it in 1723, with No. 10. His son Samuel in 1744 held both lots, and *his* heirs in 1761 sold to Joseph Stebbins. From his son Baxter it passed to Asa and Henry Stebbins, who sold it in 1854 to Luther B. Lincoln. Lincoln sold in 1866 to Joshua G. Pratt. Chester Damon bought of Pratt in 1870, and sold in 1875 to Geo. A. Arms, the present owner. The dwelling upon the lot, built by Baxter Stebbins in 1830, was burned in 1888. Broom making and shoe making have been carried on here and several stores kept, by Philo Munn and others. The old "Ware store" was moved to this lot in 1879, and destroyed by fire in 1881. There is now a commodious hotel upon the lot— completed in 1885—by Geo. A. Arms.

No. 12.—John Pynchon. This lot was drawn on the sixteen cow commons which Pynchon bought of Joshua Fisher in 1665. John Hawks occupied it before Philip's War, and soon after he made a bargain with Pynchon to buy the lot. He settled on it in 1683 or 4, and lived here until after 1687, but as he did not fulfill the conditions of the bargain Pynchon sold it to John Sheldon soon after that date. Sheldon here built the dwelling which has gone into history as the famous "Old Indian House." The events which gave it this prominence were detailed in the chapter on Queen Anne's War. The exact date of purchase or building is not found. Sheldon soon added one and a half acres to the south side from No. 13. The south line then ran through the site of the brick meetinghouse. In 1698 he bargained with the town for about one-fourth of an acre out of the training field, that he might build his house within the stockade. A minute description of this house was given on page 276. Here Ensign Sheldon kept a tavern before 1704, and perhaps after. In 1723—John, his oldest son, being dead—he gave the place to his second son, Ebenezer. By him the lot was sold in 1744 to Jonathan Hoyt, whose son David had married the daughter of Ebenezer the year before. In 1762, and perhaps earlier, David was keeping tavern here, and during the earlier part of the Revolutionary war the Tories had their headquarters at his house. The Whigs had theirs at Sexton's tavern, at the opposite end of the common. Hoyt was also a "maker of wigs and foretops." Col. Elihu Hoyt, his son, succeeded him in 1813. Capt. Henry K., son of Elihu, was the next owner. In 1848 he took down the "Old Indian House" and built the one now standing on its site, which is now held by Mrs. Laura [Bradford] Wells. Somewhere, well up to the line of the street, Justin Bull had a "shop"; his business is unknown. At the east end of the lot on the side of the hill next the Street, the town built a house for James Tute in 1744. West of this on the knoll stood a small building used by Gen. Epaphras Hoyt, son of David, for a post-office, office of the Register of Deeds, before Franklin county was organized, and for the High Sheriff's office afterwards. This building was subsequently moved to lot No. 18. In 1824 the knoll where it stood was bought by subscription for the site of the new meetinghouse. It was graded down and the present brick meetinghouse put up that year. The triangular piece of level land on the northeast corner of the lot, the "Cocked Hat," was sold to Edward Hitchcock in 1839, and by him in 1840 to Nathaniel Hitchcock and Sophia Arms. In 1841 they sold the south part to Arthur W. Hoyt. In 1842 Hoyt sold out to the Town Street school district, which put up the structure now standing there. On the abolition of the district system it was bought by the town and sold in 1874 to Dexter Childs and others. By them it was named "Grange Hall," and the upper story was occupied by the Patrons of Husbandry while settling the laws of trade and the financial affairs of the country, to their own satisfaction. The lower floor is now occupied by Miss C. L. Ray for a variety store. The Deerfield Reading Association held weekly meetings here for thirty years, and until their library was given to the trustees of the Dickinson Academy. About 1838 Joshua G. Pratt moved on to the north part of the "Cocked Hat," a building put up by Alvah Hawks for a broom shop, built an ell, and fitted it up for a dwelling and shoe shop for his own use. The dwelling has since been occupied by the Pratt family. The shop has been occupied by Joshua G. Pratt and Lemuel H. Russell for shoemaking, Nathaniel Hitchcock for harness making, Samuel Willard for shoemaking and shoe store, J. G. Pratt for eating saloon, shoe store and groceries. Henry Dickinson, tailor, also found lodgment in this building. About 1857 it came into the hands of Martha G. Pratt, its present owner. The shop was occupied by the late James C. Pratt for a grocery and shoe store, and now [1894] for a postoffice and express office by the owner, she having been postmaster since 1870.

No. 13.—John Stebbins. His son Benoni attempted a settlement here in 1677, but was captured by the Indians. He returned and built there at the Permanent Settlement the house which was so heroically defended Feb. 29th, 1704. In 1721 John Borland of London took it on execution against the widow of Benoni. Half of it was claimed and recovered by John, brother of Benoni, and in 1724 the whole came into the hands of "Thomas Wells, cordwainer." In 1737 Wells is called doctor and he practiced medicine until his death in 1744. So far as known he was the first of the profession in town. Ebenezer, his son, who succeeded, was followed by his sons, Ebenezer and Samuel—by Augustus, son of Samuel, and Samuel F., son of Augustus. It is now held by the heirs of Samuel F. The house may have been built about 1725-30. The first or second Ebenezer kept a store on the premises. This house was burned in 1891.

The committee appointed to lay out the town Street in 1670 were instructed to indicate a place for the "meetinghouse, minister's & church officers' lots." There is no record to that effect, but it may be presumed that the two lots which fall between Nos. 13 and 14 were reserved at that time, one for the minister and one for the church. The first was voted to Mr. John Williams in 1686, and a house for him was built here by the town. This house was burned and himself and family were captured, Feb. 29th, 1704. In 1707 the town built him another house. He was succeeded by his son, Maj. Elijah, and grandson, "Esq. John." The latter sold it in 1789 to Consider Dickinson, whose widow, Esther, at her death in 1875, left it with a large amount of other property to the town for a free Academy and Library. Buildings for these purposes were put up on the site of the old house, which was removed about a dozen rods westerly, where it now stands. The Training Field, in front of this lot and No. 13, was laid out twenty rods wide from the east line of the Street. Authorized encroachments have been made upon this from time to time. When "Esq. John" Williams sold the historic house lot of his grandfather, a store standing on its southeast corner was reserved, with the land under it. This building, originally a cider mill, had been moved to this lot, fitted up and occupied by Maj. Elijah, his father, for a store, from 1741, except two or three years, to his death in 1771. During the French and Indian wars this was the center of military operations for northern Hampshire. Here sub-Commissary Maj. Williams fitted out numerous scouting parties for the frontiers, and many companies have hence set their faces westward to join the armies on the lakes, destined for the conquest of Canada, their powder horns, bullet pouches and knapsacks well filled from its stock. The road to Albany ran down Hitchcock's Lane and across the river at Old Fort. The writer remembers the guideboard, nailed to the old corner store with its finger pointing down the lane, directing the traveler "To ALBANY." "John & Eunice Williams" succeeded their father in trade until the marriage of Eunice, when "Williams & Upham" continued in trade here until 1785. John Williams was chosen Register of Deeds for northern Hampshire in 1787 and had his office in the old corner store. Here, as Justices of the Peace, both John and his father Elijah held their courts, and the amount of litigation which came before them would astonish the present peaceful community, as the dockets and files of cases now in Memorial Hall bear witness. Elijah Williams, better known to the older people as "Uncle Josh," succeeded "Esq. John" as Register, and bought the corner store about 1796. He also carried on his trade of saddler here. In 1800 "Uncle Josh" sold out to "Esq. John," who in 1802 was commissioned postmaster. In 1801 Orlando Ware, a new comer, bought the place. He also was postmaster for a short time and continued in trade here until 1831, when he was succeeded by his son Edwin. After the death of Edwin in 1870, the business was carried on by his daughter Fanny, until failing health compelled her to retire in 1874. This corner was the literary as well as the business center of this region. The "Social Library," established here before 1800, had a marked influence on the character of the generation following. It was a large and valuable collection of books; the remnant, of about eight hundred volumes, was given to the library of the Pocumtuck Valley Memorial Association in 1879, by those to whom the shares had descended. In 1875 Miss Ware sold out to Geo. A. Arms, and he, the same year, to George Sheldon, by whom the mercantile history of the old corner was wound up in 1876. Oct.,

THE COMMON. 605

1875, the P. V. M. Association bought this corner to secure a site for a Memorial Hall. This was accomplished Dec. 15th, 1877, by an equitable arrangement with the Trustees of Dickinson Academy, under which the corner was restored to the original Parson Williams home lot, and the Association came in possession of its present quarters. In 1878 the Trustees sold the building to George Sheldon, who sold to Geo. A. Arms, by whom it was removed to lot No. 11, where, in 1881, after being occupied as a dwelling and store, its history and being were ended in flames, after a service of one hundred and forty or fifty years.

Standing in the highway, at the southeast corner of Parson Williams's lot, was a small house built—with the permission of the town—by John Hawks, for himself and son John. This was burned in 1704, and of its nine occupants six were "smothered in a cellar" under it.

Within the palisades, or the "Great Fort," as it was called, were several small houses, some built by the town for the poor and others for themselves, which were occupied in time of unusual danger. In 1689, upon the alarm occasioned by the burning of Schenectady, the town voted to provide "habitations within the fortifications" for such as were not able to do it for themselves. John Sheldon, Benoni Stebbins and Edward Allen were chosen "to appoint where every person's house or cellar shall stand, with ye bigness y^a shall be, y^t is, such houses or cellars as are to be built by ye town." It nowhere appears exactly what these "cellars" were. A tradition tells of a "sort of a side hill house," where Benjamin Munn lived Feb. 29th, 1704, which was so covered with snow as to escape discovery. Three of these "old houses nearest ye old meetinghouse," were pulled down when the new meetinghouse was built, in 1729.

"Tradesmen's" shops were also scattered about within the lines of the stockade.

The third meetinghouse, built in 1695, and the fourth, in 1729, stood on our "common;" the latter covering the site of the Soldiers' Monument, the one previous a few rods northeast of it. A brick schoolhouse was built a few rods south of the monument in 1813. It had two school rooms on the ground floor and a hall above. This hall was used for lyceums, lectures, &c., and for town meetings after the meetinghouse was taken down in 1824. It was partially burned and demolished in 1841.

The next lot south of Hitchcock Lane was, in 1686, sequestered for the use of the ministry. In 1759 the town petitioned the Legislature for leave to sell the property to "tradesmen." The petitioners say "the soil of s^d lot is poor and Baren & for want of manure is rendered of but little proffit to the minister * * * Have good opportunity to dispose of s^d lot in such manner as would be greatly to their advantage & the sum of money would be more proffitable than that of the land is." Mr. Ashley adds his consent, provided the profits be secured to him during his ministry. Under a Legislative enabling act it was divided into nine parcels in 1760, beside the old graveyard at the west end, and all but one sold.

No. I. The southeast corner was sold to David Sexton, who built the present house and occupied it as a tavern. It was held in succession by David Sexton, Jr., 1800; Rufus Sexton, 1803; James Reed, 1813, who enlarged the building towards the west; Ebenezer H. Williams, 1825; Isabella H. Bryant, 1852; A. W. Hoyt, 1854; George F. Gale, M. D., 1854; R. N. Porter, M. D., 1856; Robert Childs, 1860. The house was the headquarters of the Whigs during the Revolution. The Reed extension was occupied by him as a tailor shop, and in 1829, by —— ——, a tailor. In 1831 the "Franklin Freeman," a weekly anti-Masonic newspaper, edited by Gen. Epaphras Hoyt, was published there by Currier & Fogg. Later the postoffice was established there, under "Dr. Charles" Williams.

II. The northeast corner was reserved. It has never been sold and now lies open, in front of No. III, south of the training field, or common.

III. Three-fourths of an acre was sold in 1760 to John Partridge Bull, gunsmith. Dr. William Stoddard Williams bought of him in 1794 and enlarged the present house. It is now owned by the heirs of his son Ephraim.

IV. Half an acre was sold in 1760 to Silas Hamilton, feltmaker. He sold it with shop, to John Sexton, cordwainer, in 1768. Sexton was followed by Isaac Parker, watchmaker and jeweler, about 1780. In 1804 Dr. Williams bought out Parker, and Nos. III and IV have since been one lot.

V. Sold in 1760 to Elizabeth Amsden, weaver. Her shop was burnt about 1768. It was owned by John Amsden in

1773. After this it was owned by Justin Bull, blacksmith, and by John Williams, who in 1778 sold it to Justin Hitchcock, hatter, for 115 bushels of wheat. From his son Henry, a saddler, it passed to his grandson, Nathaniel, its present owner. The house was built in 1779.

VI. Sold in 1760 to David Sexton. In 1791 he sold the lot, with house and shop, to his son David, shoemaker. David Hoyt bought of him in 1794 and sold to his son Epaphras in 1801. The latter sold to Charles Hitchcock in 1815. His son, Justin B., built a new house on the west half in 1858. The old house, still standing, built about 1760-70, was sold in 1889, with the east half, to Annie C. Putnam of Boston, who now occupies it as a studio.

VII. Three-fourths of an acre was also bought by David Sexton in 1760. His son, Ebenezer, shoemaker, sold it in 1802 to Wm. Russell, carpenter. Russell moved the building then standing on the place and it now forms the rear part of the house on No. 14. Later he built a shop here and employed a Mr. Graves in making coffins for the market, the first ready-made article to be found in this region. This was frowned upon as a scandalous innovation and was not successful. Graves was followed in this shop by one Death, a wheelright. Russell sold in 1850 to Luther B. Lincoln, who built the present house and established here a school for boys. In 1853 it was bought by Mrs. Eleanor M. Whitman, who sold to Sarah A. Lawrence in 1870. It was bought of Mrs. Lawrence by Orange D. Hunter, in 1880. On this lot was the town pound, which was sold to Mr. Russell.

VIII. Three-fourths of an acre, sold in 1760 to Silas Hamilton, feltmaker. John Sexton, cordwainer, bought it of him in 1768, and sold it in 1801 to Isaac Parker. Dr. Williams bought it of the latter in 1804. It has since been held as above by the descendants of Dr. Williams.

IX. Sold in 1760 to John P. Bull. Sold by Bull to Dr. Williams in 1794, and now held as above. Probably neither of the two last lots was ever occupied by buildings. West of this is the graveyard, beyond which stood the ferry house, built in 1774.

No. 14. John Pynchon. In 1671 Pynchon bargained with James Osborn for this lot, and in 1673 he sold it to John Earle. It does not appear whether it was occupied by either.

Probably both bargains fell through and the land referred to in the extract below is this lot. Dec. 31st, 1674, Pynchon agreed with Nathaniel Foote of Hatfield to build him a,—

House at Pacumtuck on my land there, of 29 f long, 21 f brd, 10 f stud, he to doe all ye carpentry work from felling to finishing: all y^t is to be done by carpenters for closing and finishing all; he likewise to do all ye carting, for all wch worke well, substantial & workmanlike done & ye house wholly finished, excepting nails, stone work & chimney—only that ye mantletrees for ye chimney he is to find:

I am to allow him £30, whereof £3 I am to pay in to G. Meekins for Bord & sawing he is to have of him & ye rest I am to pay him in ri, wt & porke; ye porke at £3 5s. p^r barrel dl'd at Hartford, not above 3 or 4 barels in porke, ye rest in corne as afores^d, or goods, or pay, to his content, as soon as ye worke is done, or p^t beforehand: ye worke to be done by April come 12 mo. Heretoe he sets his hand this 31 Dec. 1674: NATHANELL FFOOTT:

Dec. 8th, 1674, Pynchon made a bargain with Joseph Leonard to build a house of the same size in Suffield, so we may assume this to be the standard house of the period. He pays Leonard £25, 2 gals. rum, and the use of his "sawmill to saw out the bords, joice, braces and rafters."

Samuel Hinsdale appears to have been the next owner of this lot and to have been here in 1675. He was killed with Lothrop, and in 1677, on the petition of his widow, the Court gave her this lot for her own. She married the same year, John Root, who was killed here by Indians, Sept. 19th, 1677, while preparing a home for his new wife on this lot. After his death it was again confirmed to her. This lot has been divided into three homesteads. The north part was occupied by Mehuman Hinsdale in 1704, whence himself and wife were carried to Canada and where their only child was killed. They came back here when redeemed. He died in 1736 and his widow lived here with her second husband, George Beal. Her sons, Col. Ebenezer and Samuel, who kept tavern, and *his* son John, who followed the same business, succeeded. Calvin Dickinson sold it in 1798 to Mrs. Abigail Norton, *nee* Hinsdale, who sold the place in 1802 to Asa Stebbins. In 1806 Stebbins sold to Wm. Russell, by whom the house was greatly enlarged. It is now held by his heirs. South of the house, on the spot where the stand-pipe of the aqueduct company mystifies the stranger, stood a house occupied by one Gillet, which early in this century became the cabinet shop of Wm. Emmons.

Part II. Owned as early as 1698 by John Richards. His house was burned and a daughter captured here in 1704. According to a family tradition, Benjamin Munn, his step-son, was living on the lot at this time in a sort of side-hill cave, which was so covered with snow as to escape the observation of the enemy. However that may be, he with wife and baby, escaped the horrors of the night unharmed. Richards rebuilt the house and in 1709 sold out to Benjamin Munn. There is a tradition that another house was burned on this place in the night-time, and that a cat awakened the sleeping occupants, Benjamin Munn and wife, "by running across their faces, just in time for them to escape, and that the cat *was never seen afterwards*." Benjamin Munn, Jr., the carpenter, succeeded his father, and Joel, *his* son, sold the place to Peter Gates in 1780. Gates sold out to John Williams, who lived here until his death. By his will, on the death of his widow in 1832 it passed to the Trustees of Deerfield Academy. They sold it in 1848 to Col. John Wilson, and it is now held by his heirs. A weaver's shop was on the place when held by the Munns. Col. Wilson here made plows and cultivators of his own invention. By a deed of Oct. 9th, 1756, it appears that Oliver Partridge sold this lot to Elijah Williams. This transaction I cannot explain.

Part III. Nathaniel Brooks lived here as early as 1700. The whole family was captured and the house burned in 1704. He only returned. His brother Joseph sold it in 1713 to Samuel Porter. It was owned from 1756 to 1767 by Samuel Dickinson. His daughter Hannah, wife of Col. William Williams of Deerfield and Pittsfield, sold it May 3d, 1791 to Solomon Williams, for £115, who, May 30th, 1791, sold it to John Williams. Hezekiah W. Strong bought it of John Williams in 1798, and the next year sold to Jonathan Arms. Augustus Lyman bought of Arms in 1803, and probably about that time he built the house now standing. In 1816 Lyman sold the place to Ephraim Williams—"Uncle Bob"—reserving the southeast corner, on which stood his blacksmith shop. The heirs of Williams sold to Dr. Stephen W. Williams—"Dr. Steb"—in 1839. Oct. 5th, 1857, he sold to John Birge; from him it went to Miss Theoda Dickinson, who sold it to Dr. R. N. Porter, by whose heirs it is now occupied. A blacksmith shop was built here about 1800, by

Augustus Lyman, and business carried on by himself, Elisha Wells, A. F. Wells, Reuben Nims, George Smith and others. It has been discontinued about forty years. Henry C. Mason has now a carpenter's shop on the lot.

No. 15. John Fuller. Owned in 1686 by heirs of Barnabas Hinsdale, who was killed with Lothrop at Bloody Brook. They sold to Samuel Carter in 1707. He sold, probably about 1718, to Timothy Childs, and he to John Russell, Aug. 1st, 1767, subject to a mortgage to Samuel Hopkins. Russell died in 1775. His widow, Hannah (Sheldon,) bought up this claim in 1787. Augustus Lyman bought of her in 1794, for £230, and sold in 1798 to Solomon Williams, and the latter to his brother Elijah—"Uncle Josh"—in 1800. The place is now held by J. W. Champney, whose wife is a granddaughter of Elijah Williams. The house was probably built by Timothy Childs. In 1825 a strip was sold from the north side to Elisha Wells. He sold to Benjamin Ray, who, in 1835, built the present house and a wagon shop about 1830. This estate is now held by his heirs. Upon this place John Russell set up a tailor's shop in 1765, and later combined with it store and tavern keeping. His account books of this period are in Memorial Hall. Here his son, Maj. John Russell, probably set up his trade of watchmaker. "Uncle Josh" brought here in 1805 his saddler's business. He also did a large business in making worsted covered pocketbooks. His shop was afterwards used for book-binding and jeweler's business. Still later, Ebenezer Saxton here made boots and shoes. The spot is now graced by the art and literature of James W. and Elizabeth W. Champney.

No. 16. Peter Woodward. In 1686 Peter Tufts sold it to Jonathan Wells, who built the stockade which protected it against the enemy in 1704. His son Samuel kept tavern on the north half many years and sold out in 1768 to Joseph Barnard. Ebenezer, son of Joseph, practiced medicine here—1772–1790. His heirs sell to Thomas Wells in 1792. Wells built the house which was moved from here and now stands beside the railroad bridge on Memorial Lane. In 1818 Wells sold to Oliver Cooley, from whom it passed in 1826 to Pliny Arms and Seth Nims. A. W. Hoyt bought it in 1840 and sold it in 1851 to Mrs. Jane (Ware) Keith. In 1857 it went to Josiah Fogg, who built the present house in 1868. It is now (1895) held by his heirs.

Part II. The south half was held by Jonathan Wells, Jr., who died in 1735. Bought as above, in 1768, by Joseph Barnard, who gives it in 1785 to his son Joseph. In 1792 Joseph sells to Stephen Barnard, who in 1798 sells to Elijah Williams, and he the same year to Solomon Williams. In 1799 H. W. Strong buys it of Solomon and sells it in 1802 to David Wells. Ebenezer Saxton, cordwainer, buys of Wells in 1807, and here worked at his trade. He sells in 1822 to Dr. Stephen W. Williams. Dr. Joseph Goodhue buys one-half soon after. Stephen Higginson bought of their heirs in 1853, and in 1885 his heirs sold to Henry C. Mason. Mason sold to Horatio Hoyt and he to Henry S. Childs, its present owner, in 1886.

No. 17. Mary [Judson] Hayward. She was widow of Samuel Judson and the property went to the children of Judson by a former wife. Robert Price was living here in 1686, but he probably did not pay for it, as in 1693 the daughters of Judson sold it to John Baker. Samuel Baker, son of John, sold it in 1700 to Eleazer Hawks, but no deed was given until 1710. His son, Col. John, succeeded him, buying out all the heirs in 1754. John Williams bought it May 5th, 1784, of Col. Hawks, and sold June 4th, 1787, to David Hoyt. It has since been held by *his* son Horatio and now by Horatio, Jr., and co-heirs. The old house was built in 1803. The house on the south side of the lot was built by Horatio, Jr., its owner, in 1868. In 1816 Rodolphus Dickinson and John Wilson established a printing and publishing house here, in a building erected for their use. Book agents are no new evil under the sun. From this house they were sent unto the uttermost parts of New England and New York, carrying their productions unto a market, even for a seventh edition, in one case. In the same building Elijah Booth, John Bryant and Chas. Howard engaged quite extensively in bookbinding. Here Harry Catlin kept a grocery store and began the business of cabinet making. He removed this occupation, building and all, to his father's homestead, where we shall note its further travels.

No. 18. John Farrington. In 1683 his son Eleazer of Boston sells it to Isaac Sheldon, Sen. Eleazer Hawks held it in 1704, and tradition says he built the present house in 1712. Sept., 1713, the town voted "y^t Deacon hawks shall make Brick in the street." Whether this was mandatory or permissive does not appear. Probably it was leave to make brick for his chimney. Originally the house had a big chimney in the center, as was usual in the older dwellings. About eighty years ago it was repaired and left in its present form by Elijah Russell. The heirs and assigns of Nathaniel Hawks, son of Eleazer, sold the place about 1788-90, to Hannah, widow of John Russell. In 1815 Lemuel and Elijah, her sons, sell to Epaphras Hoyt. His son, Arthur W., sells in 1847 to John M. Forbes. Elisha Wells bought of him in 1848 and sold in 1850 to Rev. Preserved Smith. Christopher A. Stebbins, the present owner, bought of Smith in 1862. The building moved here from the site of the brick meetinghouse, as noted under No. 12, was used by Gen. Hoyt for a postoffice, and the Registry of Deeds, until the formation of Franklin county in 1811. Later it was occupied by Thomas Bardwell for a shoe shop, and afterwards by Stephen Allen, until about 1828. It was finally removed down on the Wapping road, where it now stands, converted into a dwelling by Timothy Gay.

No. 19 was Edward Richards's farm.

No. 20. "The Church Lott." This was the most southerly draft on the west side of the street. The lot for the church, as we have seen, was really located on Meetinghouse Hill, and it would seem as if Richards claimed and held a house-lot here by virtue of his 150-acre farm grant. It is found at an early date in the hands of John Richards, probably a son of Edward of Dedham. In 1705 John Richards sold it to John and Benjamin Munn, calling it No. 20. It was probably owned by William Arms as early as 1724, and certainly in 1749. In 1762 Arms sold John Hinsdale two acres and a half on the west end of the lot. This was long ago washed off by the river. Elijah Arms, son of William, settled just west of his father, and in 1768 one acre and a quarter there was given him by William. The house of William Arms on the corner was burned in 1768, and Rebecca, his wife, perished in the fire, being caught, according to tradition, by an avalanche of grain from an upper floor, while she was trying to save some flax. In 1773 Phineas Munn, surveyor, held the lot and sold it in 1781 to John Williams. July 12th, 1791, Williams sold the corner to Abigail Norton. David Saxton bought it of her the same year. His son Rufus bought it in 1798. It passed from his heirs in 1861 to Abigail Bigelow. Mrs. B.

sold to Elisha Wells, April 12th, 1887. Wells sold the same year to Mary W. Lincoln, who thoroughly repaired the house. It was burned Dec., 1890. In 1890 Miss Lincoln sold a building lot west of the house to Charles Barnard.

In 1788 John Williams sold to Francis Munn a small tract west of the corner lot sold Mrs. Norton. Here Munn built a house and shop, where he made fanning mills. His heirs in 1820 sold to David Wright, who built the house now occupied by Rufus R. Williams.

In 1797 Williams sold another tract still farther west to Ithamar Burt, who had on it a dwelling, a tailor's shop and store in 1806. In 1813 Jonathan Arms and Augustus Lyman sold this place to Thomas Bardwell, shoemaker, who built the house burned here in 1885. Patrick Burke, who now owns the place, built the house now standing, in 1885. Still westward lived Elijah Arms, on land mostly washed away by the encroachments of the river. He removed to Mill River about 1770. It has since been the home of Israel Wells, of Israel Marcy who died in 1823, and Amos Temple who died in 1831. Moses Smith had a small lot on the southwest corner in 1796. A number of other families have had more or less footing on No. 20.

West of No. 20 was a lot belonging to Mehuman Hinsdale, which in a division of his estate in 1745 is thus described: "A Houselot Containing about 9 acres bounded on ye County road South, on John Hawks North, Deerfield river West, on ye Rear of ye Houselots East," [as late as 1775 John Hinsdale sold Joel Munn, "43 rods, with the buildings thereon," on the southeast corner of this lot.] This was set off to John Hinsdale, and at the same time a lot of three-fourths of an acre, between the Hatfield road and Eagle brook, "Bounded on Deerfield river or highway West, on Daniel Arms East, on ye County Road North, on Eagle Brook South." Men now living have seen the remains of the well of this place, over on the island. The bed of the river in 1670 was probably about as far west as the present channel, which was formed by the river cutting through the meadows in 1869. The Hatfield road originally ran along the south side of No. 20 and Hinsdale's 9-acre lot, to the river, and followed its bank across the present Log Meadow, by Martin's Falls to Stebbins Meadow and the Bars, and up Bars Long Hill.

At the east side of the street, at the south end, the road to the mountain originally ran east across what was later the Arms lot, a little north of where it now is. In the triangle thus formed south of this road, the town granted Edward and John Allen a homelot of six acres, in 1685. John Field sold this to Thomas Wells in 1705. In 1753 it was sold by Samuel Childs to Selah Barnard. In 1768 it was sold by Barnard to Samuel Childs. His grandson Samuel, "Brigadier Childs," died here in 1808, and his heirs in 1811 sold to Jonathan Arms, for his son, J. Lyman Arms. It was sold to Orlando Ware in 1824. Nathaniel Hitchcock bought of Ware in 1836 and sold to Edwin Ware in 186–. In 1872 it was bought by Geo. A. Arms, who still holds it. The road was changed to its present location at an early date and in 1728 a heater piece at the west end of this lot was sold to Daniel Arms and it is now a part of the old Fisher lot. East of this a lot was sold later to Ralph Arms, who built upon it about 1816. It was bought of his heirs in 18— by Rufus Rice, and from him it passed to Almon C. Williams, its present owner. Some of the Childs family were weavers and had a weaving shop on the place. Across the road, south, a cider mill and distillery were located and operated by Christopher T. Arms and Orlando Ware. The cider mill was sold to Horatio Hoyt in 1827. The house near by, on the " Hutchins lot," now owned by G. A. Arms, was a shoe shop moved from No. 36. Geo. W. Shaw has a blacksmith shop on the corner of this lot. The house owned by John Burns was built by Frank Russell and Alvin Goodnough.

No. 21. Joshua Fisher's farm. Fisher also appears to have a homelot by virtue of his farm grant. This fell into the hands of Jonathan Hunt, who in 1691 wills it to his son Thomas. William Arms bought it of Thomas Hunt in 1698. It was divided into three homelots, for his three sons. By bargain, subsequently, the center lot was divided and joined to the others. The south part was held by Daniel, his son Daniel and grandson Aaron, whose son Christopher T. sold it in 1828 to Phineas Warren. Arthur W. Hoyt bought of him in 1836 and sold it in 1841 to Geo. A. Arms, son of Christopher T., who now holds it. The central third of this lot was sold by C. T. Arms about 1820, to Harry Catlin, who built the house burned there in 1871. From Catlin it passed to Hepzibah Dennison, widow of Lemuel Russell, who gave it to her daughter-in-law, Mrs. Leonora Russell. Geo. A. Arms bought it of her and restored it to the original lot. He made it over to R. C. Arms, the present owner, in 1872. The north third was sold by John Arms, grandson of William, to Joseph Barnard in 1763. He gave it to his son Joseph in 1769. It has since been held by *his* sons, Theodore and William, and it is now held by the heirs of William.

No. 22. Sergt. [William?] Avery. Held in 1696, and probably much earlier, by Philip Mattoon, and by his heirs as late as 1714. It was owned by John Catlin, who died in 1758. His son Seth succeeded and kept a tavern on the place for many years. It was a great resort for Tories in the Revolution. Richard, son of Seth, held the place until 1819, when it passed to Quartus Wells. From Joel B., his son, it passed to George M., his grandson, whose heirs now hold it. House burned in 1882. New house built in 1885. At the east end of the lot, on "Bijah's Brook," once stood a fulling mill.

No. 23. Thomas Mason. Owned by Daniel Weld, who wills it to his son Daniel in 1699. The latter sold in 1709 to Samuel Smead, with house. Smead sold in 1714 to Samuel Dickinson. His daughter, Hannah Williams, sold it for £150 to Consider Dickinson in 1788, who sells the next year to Quartus Wells for £175. In 1853 his heirs sold to Elisha Wells. House burned here in 1853 and the present one built in 1857, by Elisha Wells and John Hare. It is now owned by Mr. Wells. Rhoda B. and Catherine W., daughters of Quartus Wells, did a large millinery business here half a century ago.

No. 24. John Bacon. It was held by John Plympton in 1672. His son Peter sold it in 1705 to John Wells. Owned in 1712 by Jonathan Wells; in 1714 by Samuel Childs. In 1729 John Bacon quit-claimed the place to Mahuman Hinsdale, but it does not appear that Hinsdale ever made good any claim on it. Samuel Childs sold it to Samuel Childs, Jr., Dec. 5th, 1753. In 1778 it was owned by Nathan Catlin and his son John. Here they made pewter buttons and established a ropewalk, where they supplied the demand for cart ropes, bed lines and halters. Samuel and John, sons of John, were engaged in trade here, and in teaming to Boston in canvas covered wagons. These wagons, so common on all the main roads leading to Boston fifty years ago, disappeared upon the advent of railroads and were last heard of as "prairie schooners," in the far west. Here their brother Harry continued cabinet making in the building removed from No. 17, and was succeeded by Franklin Russell. About 1833 this building started on another journey and it will be met once more upon its travels. About 1800 Solomon Ashley had a shop on this lot for cutting gravestones. The old Catlin house was torn down and a new one built about 1815. That was burned in 1872. The present one was built soon after. In 1874 the heirs of John Catlin sold the place, and Cyrus Brown is now the owner.

No. 25. Thomas Fuller. William Smead bought of him in 1671 and in 1674 he sold the north part to Godfrey Nims. In 1701 Nims sold to Ebenezer, son of William Smead. He died in 1753, leaving it to his son Joseph, who held it until 1765, when it was bought by Simeon Harvey. In 1793 he sold to Samuel Wells. David Saxton, Jr., shoemaker, bought it of Wells in 1794. In 1798 he sold the south half to Rufus Saxton, and the north half in 1799 to Ebenezer Saxton, shoemaker. Benoni Grover, tailor, bought this of him in 1800, and in 1801 sold to David Wells, who bought the south half the same year. In 1811 David Wells sold the whole to Dr. William S. Williams, for his son Thomas. Thomas sold the south half to Elizabeth R. Whitmore in 1842. It was occupied by her father, Thomas Whitmore, cartwright. She sold to Stephen Higginson in 1865. Stephen W. Williams, brother of Thomas, sold the north half in 1853 to Chas. Hawks, who in 1859 sold to Pliny Read. In 1865 Higginson bought of him. His heirs sold the whole to the Northampton & New Haven railroad in 1884. On the northwest corner of this lot stood the blacksmith shop of Simeon Harvey, facing its rival across the street. Here John Birge, hatter, plied his trade about the time of the Revolution. And here was the "South end" schoolhouse 1795-1800.

No. 26. Samuel Daniels, who lived here before Philip's war. Held later by Samuel Northam, carpenter. In 1696 he sold to John Catlin. In 1703 George Stileman of Hadley came in possession through a suit at law, and sold it in 1705, with house and barn thereon, to William Arms, a great speculator in real estate. Thomas Wells sold it in 1717 to Ebenezer

Wells, who here kept tavern. His house was burned and he probably built the one now there. David Wells, son of Ebenezer, sold the place in 1801 to Hezekiah W. Strong, who had a law office here, probably in the north chamber, which was reached by outside stairs on the east side. Ebenezer Barnard kept a store and the postoffice here in 1804. There was also a tailor's shop here not far from that date. South of the house stood a store building, which was moved to the east end of the lot and made into a dwelling for Arad Munn, about 1810. This has since been owned by his son Philo, Osborn Hutchins, Cyrus Brown, Charles H. Sturtevant and William P. Saxton. About 1805 Strong sold out to Orlando Ware, trader. Ware was for many years a large munufacturer of cider in the building lately standing east of the barn on Memorial Lane. Eastward, where the Canal railroad has plowed across the road, stood the wagon shop of Benjamin Ray. It was removed and is now occupied as a woodshed by his daughters on No. 15. Still eastward stood the residence of John Saxton. On the Saxton lot stands—after four removes—the Harry Catlin cabinet shop, fitted up for a dwelling by William H. Saxton and now owned by John Murphy. East of this, on the northeast corner of the lot, were the shoe shop and residence of Joel Saxton. Both have disappeared. Just round the corner was the house of Arad Munn, cartwright, spoken of above. His shop stood across the road east, the site now covered by the Connecticut River railroad. This shop was removed by Nathaniel Hitchcock and now does duty as a barn on the "Hutchins lot." The house now standing on the southeast corner of the lot was built by Edwin Ware for himself in 1842.

No. 27. John Chickering. Sold by his heirs to Peter Tuffts, who sold to Jonathan Wells in 1686. In 1715 Wells was holding three-quarters of an acre on the southwest corner of this lot, but there seems to be a sale of the whole lot in the deed by which, in 1692, the administrators of Benjamin Barrett sell to Godfrey Nims, cordwainer. Nims's house was burned Jan. 4th, 1693-4, and a step-son, Jeremiah Hull, was burned in it. All this lot, except the present dooryard on the southeast corner, has been sold in small parcels and occupied—by the Orthodox meetinghouse in 1837; by the Town house in 1846; by Memorial Hall, which was built for

HOMESTEADS ON THE OLD STREET.

Deerfield Academy in 1798; by Joel Saxton and others for a shoe shop, 1805; for a dwelling by David Wells, which was sold by his heirs to the present owner, Patrick Kennedy, in 1840; by Baxter Stebbins for a brickyard, about 1835; by Isaac Ball, cooper, for a dwelling at the extreme east. A malt house probably stood near the site of the Town house, and a schoolhouse on that of the meetinghouse. There is a tradition that the malt house was burned. Close to the sidewalk in front of the town house stood, in 1836, Harry Catlin's cabinet shop, then used by Hiram McKee for a wagon shop. About 1842 the old cabinet shop took another journey, eastward, to the brickyard, and once more, across the road south, where, after four removes, it became the dwelling of Wm. H. Saxton, as before noted.

No. 28. John Howard. Later owned by his son Thomas and by Benjamin Hastings, carpenter, in 1686. He sold it, Nov. 21st, 1694, to Godfrey Nims. The house burned the previous January on No. 27, as noted above, was rebuilt on this lot about 1695, and was burned Feb. 29th, 1704, and three children of Nims perished in it. The present house was probably built about 1710 and repaired by substituting the present hip roof for the old pitch roof, three-quarters of a century later. This lot has been occupied by John and Ebenezer, sons of Godfrey; Jeremiah, son of John; Seth, son of Jeremiah; Edwin, son of Seth, and Eunice, daughter of Edwin. Sold 1894 to Sylvanus Miller. The postoffice was kept here from about 1816 to the death of Dea. Seth Nims in 1831.

No. 29. Peter Woodward. He quit-claimed this lot to Nathaniel Frary, son of Samson, in 1719. This has been cut into three homesteads.

I. The south part, held by Samson Frary, 1685. There is testimony that Daniel Wells held it in 1698, which cannot be reconciled to the fact that it continued in the Frary family and that the heirs of Nathaniel Frary, son of Samson, sold it in 1752 to Joseph Barnard. David Arms held it in 1761 and sold in 1763 to Salah Barnard for £175. The north part of the present house was standing in 1698 and escaped the conflagration of Feb. 29th, 1704. The south part was built by Salah Barnard, and the whole occupied for a tavern before the Revolution. Erastus, son of Salah, followed in the same business in 1796–1815. The south half of it was sold by

FRARY HOUSE. 619

Salah Barnard's heirs to E. H. Williams in 1811, who sold soon after to Augustus Lyman, who sold to Seth Nims in 1816. The southwest front was used as a store and a small building was put up in front of this to be used in connection, about 1812. This was occupied by Cooley & Dickinson, Lyman & Dickinson, Oliver Cooley & Son, Cooley & Nims, Edwin Nims, and others. Pliny Arms moved the little addition to the rear, to serve as a kitchen. About 1839 there was a wagon shop in the rear of the house. Lyman sold the south part of the house to Eunice Arms in 1828; held by Pliny Arms, her son, until his death in 1859. Elisha Wells owned the north part of this house in 1828 and sold to John Forbes in 1834, who sells it back in 1835, and Wells sells it the same year to Consider Dickinson. In 1868 Richard Dickinson sells the whole to Samuel P. Billings, and he in 1876 to John Kelliher. C. Alice Baker, a descendant of Samson Frary, bought it of his heirs May 24th, 1890, and it has been thoroughly restored. It is the oldest house in the town.

II. Samson Frary in 1685; in 1719 it was held by his son Nathaniel. In 1752 Col. William Williams owned it and kept a store in connection with his business as Commissary in the last French War. In 1757 Henry Bromfield sold the lot to Maj. Elijah Williams. Salah Barnard held it in 1789 and in 1800 his son Ebenezer sold it to Justin Ely. Hezekiah W. Strong bought of Ely in 1804 and sold to John Bement for $2100 in 1805. In 1808 or 9 Bement sells to Oliver Cooley, innholder. Cooley adds 30 feet in width to his lot from the heirs of Amasa Smith on the north. Seth Nims buys out Cooley in 1816. The tavern was kept in 1818-19 by Augustus Lyman. Seth Nims followed—1820-27. Ebenezer H. Williams bought the place in 1826. Williams leased the tavern to Col. Thomas Gilbert, 1828-30; to Edward Russell, 1831; Alvin Lawrence, 1833; Col. David Wright, 1834, and perhaps others, and sold it in 1835 to Oliver Davenport. Alvin Lawrence bought out Davenport in 1838 and his heirs sold to Justin and L. W. Lawrence in 1840. They sell in 1844 to D. N. Carpenter, who the same year sold to Alexander H. Newcomb. David Hoyt buys of Newcomb in 1846 and sells in 1853 to the Pocumtuck Hotel Company. This company moved the old building to the rear and put up a new one on a larger scale. The landlords under this company were Wm.

C. Perry, A. D. Phillips, Ball & Messenger, Hezekiah Broughton, A. D. Phillips and Chas. O. Phillips. The Hotel Company sold in 1866 to Chas. O. Phillips and he in 1867 to Smith R. and Henry M. Phillips. The house was burned in 1877, with the old one, which had been occupied for a postoffice. In 1880 H. M. Phillips sold to a list of subscribers, who gave it to E. J. & G. F. Everett. They put up a fine large house, which in 1883 met the fate of the former.

The south room of the old tavern was occupied for a store in 1824, when the scribe recalls buying filberts there. The door was cut in halves and the boys could peek over the lower half before entering. Capt. Elijah Williams kept store and had a law office here in 1830. In a room in the rear of this was Perkins's marble shop, and under it a meat market, about the same time. Later Philo Munn occupied it as a shoe shop, and the library of the Deerfield Reading Association here for awhile found lodgment.

III. Samson Frary, 1685. This part contained four acres and was sold in 1685 to John Catlin. Here he and his son Jonathan were killed while defending his house in 1704, but it was taken and burned. His son John was captured. He came back and built a house here about 1715. He was a housewright and was always spoken of by tradition as "Master Catlin." Amasa Smith, hatter, bought out the rights of the several heirs of Catlin, 1775-90, and probably some of them earlier. In 1775 he had leave of the town to set up a hatter's shop in the street in front of this house. This shop was moved on to the north part of the lot, occupied by a jeweler, and later became the hatter's shop of Seth Nims, and finally the rear part of Smith's house. Smith's heirs, in 1814, sold a strip 30 feet wide from the south side, and in 1820 sold the remainder to William Russell, for his son Thomas, who lived here until his death in June, 1826. Mr. Russell built a shop on the north side of this lot, where Moses Graves made coffins and another man cut gravestones. In 1831 Hiram McKee occupied this shop and advertised in the Deerfield newspaper as a "maker of chaises and waggons." Later William Barnard occupied it for a paint shop. About 1843 Philo Munn moved it to the place he now occupies, where it was destroyed by fire in 1870. Russell gave the place by will to his granddaughter, Mrs. Hannah P. (Russell) Long.

In 1854 she sold to the Pocumtuck Hotel Company. Arthur W. Hoyt bought the place in 185-, took down the old Catlin house and built the one now standing there. He sold out in 1864 to Virgil M. Howard, who in 1870 sells to Loren Hayden, of whom it was bought in 1873 by Mrs. Elizabeth Chapin, who sold it in 1893 to Clarence A. Hoyt.

No. 30. Isaac Bullard. Quintin Stockwell was here in 1673. His house was doubtless one of those fortified in Philip's War and here Mr. Mather, the minister, boarded. In 1685 Stockwell sold to John French; his son, Thomas French, lived here in 1704, when his whole family were killed or captured. He was a blacksmith and his shop stood in front of his house, on the street. His son Thomas followed him and in 1758 sold to Jonathan Arms, of the same trade. A strip was set off to Augustus Lyman from the south side of this lot, on which Arms had a store. In 1829 Lyman sold this strip to John G. Williams. The old store was moved toward Cheapside, set up on the old Trask road and made a dwelling house for Stephen B. Hale. "John G." put up a brick building here and kept a store for many years, sometimes alone and sometimes with his brother, Charles Williams. "Dr. Charles" was also postmaster. Store and postoffice were continued here until the place was sold to Arthur W. Hoyt, who pulled down the building. It is now the north part of the Chapin lot. In 1840 the assignees of Pliny Arms sold Charles Williams the north part of No. 30. In 1848 Luther B. Lincoln buys him out. The next year Lincoln sells it to the trustees of the Orthodox Parsonage Fund, who took down the old French house and built the one now there, which is used as a parsonage.

No. 31. Robert Hinsdale. This was held in 1673 by Joseph Gillett, who was killed at Bloody Brook in 1675. In 1692 it was claimed by Peter Woodward, and Joseph Gillett, Jr., "was obliged to redeem it." In 1694 he sold to Samuel Carter, who also seems to have had some trouble about the title, for Dec. 23d, 1700, Timothy Dwight of Dedham sold it to Mahuman Hinsdale. Carter apparently held it, however, and it has since then been incorporated with the next lot north.

No. 32. Nathaniel Colbourne. Held by Joseph Gillett and his son Joseph, as in No. 31. Sold with the latter in 1694 to Samuel Carter. It is then described as "Sometime two town lots, 16½ by 72 rods, with a house on it." Carter's whole family was killed or captured in 1704, he only escaping. Dec. 8th, 1705, Carter sold to Samuel Allen, grandfather of the famous Col. Ethan Allen. Joseph, the father of Ethan, was born here in 1708. In 1711 Samuel Barnard bought of Allen. In 1723 he bought of Thomas French a strip on the southwest corner, ten rods long and one rod wide, running east and west on the south line. Samuel Barnard died in Salem in 1762, leaving by will, this lot, with a large amount of other land, to Joseph, oldest son of his brother Ebenezer, the whole being entailed on Samuel, son of Joseph, then 15 years old, and his heirs male forever. In 1768 Joseph built the house now standing. On the death of Joseph in 1785 his son Samuel— "Lawyer Sam"—succeeded him; but the entail could not hold under the Constitution of Massachusetts, and went no farther. "Lawyer Sam" sold the place in 1794 to Ebenezer H. Williams and removed the next year to Vermont. In 1807 the house was rented to Hosea Hildreth, then Preceptor of Deerfield Academy, and here, on the 28th of June, his son Richard, the historian, was born. In 1811 Williams sold the place to Rev. Samuel Willard for $3333. Dr. Willard died here in 1859. Here lived his son-in-law, Luther B. Lincoln, Principal of Deerfield Academy, and Samuel Willard, Jr. It was sold by his heirs in 1885 to Annie C. Putnam and Madeline Y. Wynne. A juvenile library was established here through the influence of Dr. Willard in 1827. For some dozen years before his death, "Dr. Charles" kept the postoffice on the southwest corner of this lot, in a small building which was moved to Bloody Brook in 1873.

No. 33. Henry Phillips. In 1685 John Parsons sells this to John Catlin. In 1694 it was held by Thomas Allison and by him sold to Rev. John Williams in 1711. Samuel Taylor bought it of Williams in 1714 and here kept tavern until his death, Mch. 5th, 1733-4. His son Samuel continued the business until his removal to Charlemont in 1754, when he sold it to Joseph Stebbins, cordwainer. The house was burned, Nov., 1799, and one Widow Cook perished in the flames. A schoolhouse was built on the southwest corner in 1788. The fire engine house stood on the same site in 1837. Philo Munn moved a building from No. 29 on to the same site for a shoe shop and variety store in 1843. This was burned in 1870, and he built the one he now occupies on the same spot.

No. 34. Joshua Fisher. In 1671 the town of Dedham voted him leave to sell this lot to Nathaniel Sutlief. Sutlief was killed with Capt. Turner in 1676. James Brown held it in 1685, Samuel Hinsdale in 1690, David Hoyt before 1704, and Jonathan, son of David, in 1714. In 1731 the administrator of Joshua Fisher quit-claims to Mahuman Hinsdale. Hinsdale, it appears, had a habit of buying up all sorts of claims to rights in cow commons and houselots, and thereby first and last made the proprietors and individual owners a good deal of trouble. David Field owned this lot in 1754, and in 1785 made it over to Joseph Stebbins and Jonathan Hoyt. In 1807 Hoyt sells his half to Asa Stebbins, who had the other half and No. 33 from his father Joseph. Asa built the brick house now standing in 1799. Both lots thus united are now [1894] held by J. E. Lamb as one. Joseph Stebbins was cordwainer, also tanner and currier, and did a large business here in both these trades.

No. 35. Samuel Hinsdale. The administrator of Hinsdale deeds this to the heirs of John Allen in 1866. This was probably the residence of John Allen, and sold to him by Samuel Hinsdale before the death of both at Bloody Brook in 1675. John Stebbins held it in 1690. Here his family were captured in 1704. David Field owned it 1754-85. He built and occupied a store standing flush with the street, part on this lot and part on No. 34. During the Revolution this was a favorite resort for the Sons of Liberty and a tall liberty pole was set up in front of it. Sunday, Aug. 7th, 1774, Col. Israel Williams of Hatfield, a rank Tory, was in Deerfield and attending meeting, where he doubtless heard from Parson Ashley a good Tory sermon. On his way to the house of the preacher he spied this liberty pole and declared "*Such a Pole was a Profanation of the Ordinance.*" We do not learn that it was taken in Sundays in consequence of this judgment. In this store Col. Field was followed by his son Oliver. It was later occupied by Ebenezer Wells, silversmith, and David Bliss, trader. In 1794 E. Williams was here selling "European & Indian goods;" later Ebenezer Saxton and Lyman Frink, shoemakers, and "Aunt Orry" Russell, a tailoress; it was also her residence for thirty or forty years. Her sister, Mrs. Fanny Merrill, occupied another part of the same building until her death in 1861. This store and dwelling was torn down in 1880. The homelot was held in 1772-4 by Simeon Stebbins and later by Oliver Field, who sells the store to Joseph Stebbins and the lot to William Hyslop in 1787. The latter sold in 1795 to William Hyslop Abercrombie, and he in 1797 to David Sheldon. The north part was held by his son David, and the south part by Joseph A. Ashley. The house was built by David Field, the chimney by John Locke. Mrs. Silvia Munn remembered it as being painted red.

No. 36. Samuel Hinsdale. Held in 1675 by Joshua Carter, who was killed at Bloody Brook; by his heirs in 1691, and by Samuel Porter in 1699. Martin Kellogg lived here in 1704, when all his family save his wife were killed or captured. In 1710 Kellogg sold to Joseph Severance, tailor. Severance was living here in 1756. In 1772 it was in the hands of Zadock Hawks, tanner and currier. A large business was carried on by Zadock and his sons Zur and Zenas. Zenas had the south part of the lot and built the house now standing there in 1805. He had a shoe shop back of his house. After Hawks gave up the shoe business the shop was occupied by Lyman Frink, Henry Russell and Philo Munn. It was finally moved to the south end, and placed on the Wapping road by Clark Hutchins, and fitted up for a dwelling. It is now owned by Geo. A. Arms.

The north half of No. 36 fell to Zur Hawks. His son Alvah did a heavy business making brooms. His broom shop was moved about 1837 to No. 11, and soon after to No. 12, and is now owned by Martha G. Pratt and occupied for a postoffice and dwelling. The place was bought in 1839 by Seth Sheldon for his son William, and it is now held by *his* heirs. The house was an old one in 1825, when the front was thoroughly repaired and the rear rebuilt.

No. 37. Mrs. Bunker. Held by Peter Tuffts in 1684 and sold by him in 1687 to Simon Beaman. On this lot stood, in 1694, the first known schoolhouse. Widow Hannah Beaman, the school dame, sold the lot in 1722 to Thomas Bardwell. Through his son John and grandson Henry it came to the hands of Mrs. Catharine E. [Bardwell] Allen. It is now held in the Allen family. On the northwest corner a store was kept by Thomas Bardwell and his son John.

No. 38. Henry Phillips. In 1683 Henry White sells this to Wm. Clarke. Jonathan Wells, Jr., and William Belding own the place in 1710, when Wells sells out to Belding. In 1723-4 John Stebbins and his son John sell to Ensign Jonathan Wells. It is next found in the hands of the Clesson family, but no conveyance can be found. Capt. Joseph Clesson and his sons, Lieut. Matthew and Joseph, lived on this lot in a house which stood on the site of the Unitarian parsonage. This was torn down and what was intended for the rear part of a new one built near the north line in 1814. Abigail, the widow of Capt. Joseph, sold the lot in 1818 to Eliphalet Dickinson, who gave it to his son William. In 1851 his heirs sold to Josiah Fogg. Fogg sold in 1853 to David Hoyt and in 1871 Hoyt's heirs sold to Alfred A. Upson. V. M. Howard bought of Upson in 1872 and built the present house that year. It is now owned by his heirs. The one built by the Clessons in 1814 is now a dwelling house at the east end of No. 43, on the Cheapside road. In 1861 Hoyt sold the southeast corner to Elbert Amidon, who built the house now standing. Amidon sold to Charles D. Gale in 1867, and Gale to the trustees of the Ministerial Fund and Sequestered Land, who still hold it as part of the fund for the benefit of the First Congregational Parish.

No. 39. John Baker. Wm. Pixley owner in 1675-84. Solomon Stoddard had it in 1710 and sold in 1713 to Joseph Atherton, Ebenezer Field, Edward Allen and Samuel Bardwell. In 1714 Bardwell bought out his partners. He probably built the house now standing in place of one burned on this site in 1771, where he kept tavern. His son Eldad succeeded him in this business, as did Eldad, Jr. The heirs of the latter sold to Joseph Stebbins in 1799. Joseph conveyed it to his son Dennis, whose assignees sold to Henry Stebbins and he to Louisa, Lucy and Mary Stebbins, who now hold it. Dennis Stebbins was an extensive manufacturer of brooms. His shop was used as a schoolhouse in 1842 and soon after moved to lot No. 1, where it was occupied as a dwelling. It was taken down by Elbert Amidon when he built in 1867.

No. 40. John Gay. Samuel Hinsdale was owner in 1675. His son, Mahuman Hinsdale, held it in 1713 and combined it soon after with the next two lots.

No. 41. Daniel Fisher. John Stebbins bought of Fisher about 1688. His sons, John and Benoni Stebbins, sell to Joseph Gillett in 1690. Timothy Nash held it after 1699 and his son Moses sold it in 1709 to Mahuman Hinsdale. In 1723 the heirs of Fisher confirm to the heirs of John Stebbins the sale of 1688. The deed had probably been lost, or perhaps never given.

No. 42. Thomas Payne. Held in 1673 by Nathaniel Sutlief and in 1675 by Samuel Hinsdale. In 1719 it was owned by Mahuman Hinsdale, since that time Nos. 40, 41 and 42 have been incorporated in one and have the same history. Col. Ebenezer, son of Mahuman Hinsdale, followed his father and held it to his death in 1763. He had a store here for many years and in 1756 tailoring was carried on here also. His heirs sold the place to Elihu Field in 1773. In 1785 Joseph Stebbins and Jonathan Hoyt had it of the Fields, and sold in 1788 to Rev. John Taylor. Andrew Bardwell bought of Taylor in 1809 and sold to Ebenezer H. Williams in 1816. The house, then an old one, was about that time remodeled to its present form. Williams sold to his sister, Lydia Williams in 1834, and she in 1850 to Charles D. Gale. In 1852 Asa Stebbins bought it of Gale for his son, Francis W. The latter sells to Erastus Cowles, the present owner, in 1876.

No. 43. John Pynchon. He sold to Joshua Carter in 1669 twenty cow commons, with this homelot, at 20s a common, to be paid in pork at 56s a barrel. Carter was killed with Capt. Lothrop, probably before the title was perfected. Samuel Hinsdale had it in 1675. In 1714 it is called "Lieut. Wells's lot," but in 1718 Samuel Hinsdale, son of Samuel, sells it to Mahuman Hinsdale, his uncle. Samuel, son of Mahuman, succeeded his father in 1738, and in 1771 sold to Jonathan Ashley, Jr. April 20th, 1786, Joseph Stebbins bought of Ashley, who was then of Shelburne, and sold to William Dennison in 1801., Asa Stebbins bought it of the latter in 1804. In 1824 he built the present brick house for his son Asa. Edward W., his son, succeeded him and it is now owned by his widow, Lydia A. Stebbins.

The next house round the corner was built by Asa Stebbins for his son Edward W., in 1849, and willed to Lydia A., wife of Edward. She sold in 1866 to Francis W. Stebbins, who now owns it. At an early date some of the Hinsdales had a tannery on the upper part of this lot. The house now standing near the east end, as before noticed, was moved from No. 38, where it was built by the Clessons in 1814. The

Boyden lot was originally part of No. 43. It was bought of Samuel Hinsdale in 1758 by Zadock Hawks, who may have begun his business of tanning here. Held in 1801 by Solomon Ashley, who made pottery and cut gravestones. It was owned in 1820 by Ambrose Boyden, shoemaker, and is still held by his heirs.

A house stood at the "north end" facing the street southward, which was occupied by the widow of Asa Childs, a noted doctor. This house was burned long ago, and the writer has found cart irons, chains, &c., in the old cellar hole.

CHAPTER XXI.

THE LAST FRENCH WAR.

The ink with which the treaty of Aix la Chappelle was signed was hardly dry before it became evident to close observers, that the design of the French was to keep the peace only so long as their interests required. France never for a moment ceased encroaching on territory claimed by the English, nor for a moment forgot her settled policy of aiding and abetting the border Indians in making forays on the English frontiers.

At Aix la Chapelle the question of the boundaries between France and England in this continent was left to be settled by a joint commission. This commission met at Paris in 1750. In a protracted conference England gained—nothing. France gained what she needed—time. For two years England was amused with arguments concerning the ownership of the insignificant island of St. Lucca, while France was steadily pushing her Indian traders and forts along Ontario and Erie, and down the Ohio, thus connecting her settlements on the St. Lawrence with those on the Mississippi, thus shutting up the English within the narrow limits of the Atlantic coast, and securing for France the whole vast continent stretching away to the Pacific.

Even while the commission was in session there had been friction and even bloodshed in Acadia, to which the attention of the English, so far as this continent was concerned, had been almost exclusively directed; but at length they became aware of the far-sighted policy of the French, found the toils tightening around them, and saw the necessity of preparing for another struggle with the French and Indians. Fort Massachusetts had been rebuilt in 1747-8. The following bill shows that it was now being put into a better condition for defense.

1751, Province of Massachusetts to Ephraim Williams, Dr.
June, to erecting a Watch Box 40 feet high & 28 foot square.

NOTE OF PREPARATION.

To Cash paid a Carpenter 10 days at 4s,	£2 0 0	
" " " 2 laborers 10 days at 2s,	2 0 0	
" 15 Jacks at 3s,	2 5 0	
" Cash paid freight of 3, 4 pounders with Carriages to them from Boston to New York,	2 0 0	
To ditto from N. York to Albany,	1 10 0	
To ditto from Albany to the Landing place at Bandeihidey,	9 0	
To transporting them 36 miles to Fort Mass.,	2 0 6	

Lawful Money, £12 4 6

Boston, Jany 18 1752   E. E.   EPHRAIM WILLIAMS.
  Accepted Jany 22, 1752.

[Williams is also allowed for:—]

Sundries for the Sick—1 firkin Butter, ½ bbl. New England Rum, 1 peck oat meal ½ bbl. Rice, ½ bbl. Sugar, 10 lbs. Currants, 10 lbs. Rasins, also for cash paid Maj. Pomroy for mending the Soldiers guns posted at fort Mass.

Aug. 21st, Joseph Pynchon, Josiah Dwight, and John Ashley, a committee appointed by the General Court to visit the Mohawks, were in Deerfield buying "Calico," and "Garlick," for presents to the Indians; making a bill at the store of Col. William Williams, of £4, 5 s, 3½d.

The following bill is given in total ignorance of its subject matter, in the hope that it may prove a clue to matters of historic interest:—

  1751, Province of Massachusetts to Ephraim Williams, Dr.
For provisions and other subsistance supplied the French Protestants after the provision was expended that the Commissary General supplied them with.

Dec. To Cash paid for provisions for them at Hatfield,	£0 7 2	
To ditto at Deerfield,	1 15 0	
To ditto at Charlemont,	0 10 6	
To Billiting them at the fort and provisions till their return to Boston, 76 days for 1 man,	4 13 8	

Lawful Money,   £7 6 11
Boston, Jany 7, 1752.
           Errors Excepted,   EPH WILLIAMS, JR.
Allowed Jany 25, 1752.

The object of sending these "French Protestants" on a winter trip from Boston to Fort Massachusetts is left for conjecture. Could it have anything to do with mounting or managing the new armament of the fort?

In 1753, Dinwiddie, Governor of Virginia, sent young George Washington over the Alleghanies to find out what the French were about on the Ohio. He was flatly told that the territory belonged to France, that it was occupied by orders from the king, and would be held against all comers.

1754. In the summer of this year Dinwiddie again sent Washington over the mountains, this time with a Major's commission, and a small force to drive off the invaders. After some success the Major was obliged to surrender his command to a large force of the French. On the first scent of blood the border Indians put on the war paint and the whole frontier was in danger from their incursions.

In June, William Shirley, Governor of Massachusetts, issued orders for the towns to lay in a stock of ammunition and prepare for their own defense. In August he put Col. Israel Williams in command of all the forces raised or to be raised for the defense of Hampshire county, and the line of forts on the northern frontier was strengthened under the direction of Elijah Williams of Deerfield, who, on the 27th of September was commissioned major. Deerfield was made the depot for military stores for the northwest frontiers, Maj. Elijah Williams appointed Commissary, and a company of soldiers put under him for their defense. This company appear to be from Connecticut and under the command of Ensign John May. Shirley sends a lieutenant's commission to Sergeant John Hawks, "whom," he says, "I have a good knowlidge and opinion of," and Col. Israel Williams put him in command of the forts at Colrain with twenty men. Lieut. Hawks made his headquarters at Fort Morrison, the most northerly defense there. Forts Pelham and Shirley were considered badly located, and were deserted and dismantled, "the swivel guns there to be taken care of by the governor."

Sept. 6–9 Col. Israel Williams writes Secretary Willard that,—

> The people of the new settlements have generally withdrawn; some few have shut themselves up in poor forts and palisaded houses * * * What Fall-town people could not get into Lieut. Sheldon's fort are withdrawn * * * Some remain at Charlemont & are picketing a house & some of the inhabitants remain * * * Pitsfeld deserted * * * 6 Indians seen at Southampton yesterday [8th.] [He writes Shirley, Sept. 12:] It is open war with us & a dark and distressing scene opening. A merciless miscreant enemy invading us in every quarter.

A particular description of the defense at Charlemont, alluded to by Col. Williams, will give a good idea of the "forts" of the period.

Othniel Taylor had a house 38 x 16 feet, his brother Jonathan one 26 feet square, both presumably one story, and of logs. These were moved to a suitable position and left 60 feet apart, facing each other east and west, the south ends being on a line. A palisade ran from house to house, enclosing a parade between them, 60 x 38 feet, containing a well. This was the citadel. Another palisade, 140 x 80 feet, enclosed the whole, the outer line being about 25 feet from the houses. On the southeast corner of Jonathan Taylor's house was a mount, or watch box, 15 feet high and 5½ square. One-half of its width projected beyond the house south and east, thus flanking two sides of the citadel. Probably a mount was subsequently built at the northeast corner of Othniel Taylor's house to defend the north and west sides, but none appears on the plan. This was at East Charlemont. At the west part of the town, Gershom and Seth Hawks made the same arrangement. Garrison soldiers for both were furnished by the Province.

At Colrain, Hugh Morrison picketed his house and built a watch box 23 feet high. Fifty feet square were added to the South fort, and still the people say they "have not garrisons enough for half the people," although Fort Lucas and McDowell's forts were open to them.

Corporal Preserved Clapp of East Hadley, [Amherst] was sent with ten men to Huntstown, [Ashfield] but there was no fort there. The corporal from the college town says they "garded the inHabitance vn til We had a De-smishon from them." Maj. Ephraim Williams was stationed at Fort Massachusetts, and all the frontier towns were provided for by the Province. "38 pair of Indian shoes for the scouts at Fort Massachusetts, and ye line of forts, at 4s 4d, and a deer skin to mend them at 8s 10d," were charged to the Commissary General. Col. William Williams had left Deerfield and was now at Blandford, with forty-seven men, serving with a captain's pay.

The alarm had been precipitated by the capture at No. 4, Aug. 30th, of Ebenezer Farnsworth, Peter Labaree, James Johnson, his wife and three children, and Miriam Willard, a fifteen-year-old sister of Mrs. Johnson. A fourth child was added to the list of captives the next morning, while the party was at the present town of Reading, Vt. A stone with the following inscription marks the site of this camp:—

> This is near the spot
> Where the Indians encamped the
> Night after they took Mr. Johnson
> Family, Mr. Labaree & Mr. Farnsworth,
> Aug. 30, 1754, and Mrs.
> Johnson was delivered of her child
> Half a mile up this Brook.
> When trouble's near the Lord is kind,
> He hears the captive's Cry;
> He can subdue the Savage mind
> And learn it sympathy.

The child was named Elizabeth Captive Johnson. The Indians, eleven in number, were of the St. Francis tribe.

1755. This was a year of great activity and great disaster in the colonies. Plans were laid by Gov. Shirley, who was Commander-in-chief in America, to push the French in every quarter. Expeditions were planned against Du Quesne, Niagara, Crown Point and Acadia. All but the latter failed. Details will be given only where Deerfield people are concerned. The western frontier garrisons were continued essentially as in 1754. Maj. Williams remained Commissary and Deerfield the center of operations. Powder and lead were carted here from Boston, as appears by his account book.

Gov. Shirley began operations early. Feb. 10th he sent directions to have Capt. Ephraim Williams and Capt. Phineas Stevens each raise a company for his regiment, and to march with them to Col. Lydias's farm and build a fort for the protection of stores to be gathered there for the Crown Point expedition. This farm, I suppose, was on the Hudson, at the "great carrying place," the site of Fort Edward. From this place they were to cut a road to the upper end of Lake George, where Fort William Henry was afterwards built.

Shirley offered to make Williams the "Captain Lieutenant" of his own company, and, to "engage him heartily, will give him the perquisites of the company." The Colonel, Lieut. Colonel, and perhaps the Major, had each his own company, and presumably in addition to the regular pay, a captain's pay and the "perquisites"; the "Captain Lieutenant" doing the work and getting the honor of a captain, with the pay of a Lieutenant. The men to be enlisted for Shirley's crack regiment must be "not under 18 or over 35, sound men, not under five feet four inches in their stockings, & no Roman Catholic." The bounty was £10, but they may give

£15 rather than fail, "but the £5 must be a gift from you" which will be "allowed by the governor."

Feb. 10th, Maj. Elijah Williams sent Ensign Joseph Barnard to Boston for £530, which he had expended in repairing the line of forts. The Major was the active member of a committee appointed for that purpose. March 5th, the Major charges Lieut. John Hawks "five quarts of rum for Daniel Ward, a Sick Soldier, and one quart for his Lame Leg."

March 7th, Capt. Ephraim Williams writes Shirley that he cannot enlist the best men unless they can be assured that they shall not be called south, and that he or Stevens shall command them, "agreeable to the former arrangement." He has heard that "your first lieut. is coming over," which will prevent his obtaining the promised position, for he will *not* take an inferior commission and is not anxious for the one offered—not he. March 11th, Shirley replies that the rumors are true, and that he cannot do what he promised; is sorry and will do what he can for him "in the other service to the Northward." Here was the parting of the ways for Capt. Williams. One would have taken him to a French prison, through Oswego; the other led to a bloody grave at Lake George.

March 15th, Commissary Williams charges the Province for "15 lbs. powder & 30½ lbs. lead & 3 doz. flints, del'd Lt. Hawks for Morrison's fort." March 18th, he charged for the same amount delivered each to Othniel Taylor, for Taylor's fort; to Andrew Lucas, [for Fort Lucas?]; to Joshua Hawks, for Hawks's fort; to John Burke, for Burke's fort. Among other supplies given out during the winter were nine gallons of rum to Lieut. Hawks for Colrain; 19 gallons to Lieut. Burke, for Sheldon's fort; 20 gallons to Ensign May for Rice's fort, Charlemont.

March 29th, Shirley writes Col. Israel Williams that he is going to meet Gen. Braddock, and wants his aid in selecting officers for a regiment to go north. He says, "it will be a great pleasure to have Maj. Ephraim Williams engage as one, and I can't be content without having the officers of one regiment from your parts, and Maj. Hawley is going up to settle the affair with you." After a hot contention among the "Lords of the valley," in which Hawley was offensively prominent, the matter of the staff officers, was settled, according to the roster given below, with their monthly wages:—

Colonel Ephraim Williams, Deerfield and Hatfield,	£12	16	0
Lieut. Colonel, Seth Pomeroy, Northampton,	10	13	4
Major, Noah Ashley, Westfield,	9	1	4
Surgeon, Thomas Williams, Deerfield,	10	0	0
Surgeon's Mate, Perez Marsh, Hadley,	5	6	8
Chaplain, Stephen Williams, Longmeadow,	6	8	4
Commissioner of Hospitals, Eleazer Burt,	5	0	4
Adjutant, Philip Richardson,	2	2	8
Armorer, John P. Bull, Deerfield,	2	0	0

The wages of the line officers at this time were, for a captain, £4, 16s; lieutenant, £3, 4s; ensign, £2, 2s, 8d; sergeant, £1, 14s, 1d; corporal, £1, 9s, 10d; clerk, £1, 14s, 1d; drum major, £1, 14s, 1d; drummer, £1, 9s, 10d; private, £1, 6s, 8d.

There was doubtless a fair proportion of other Deerfield men in this regiment, but the number is not ascertained. At this time, Deerfield was also largely represented by both officers and men in the line of forts.

May 31st, Col. Williams had orders to march his regiment to Albany. As the colonial troops concentrated there for the invasion of Canada, the frontiers of New England were left open, and the Indians swarmed in on all sides. Ebenezer Hinsdale, whom we have met as the chaplain at Fort Dummer, the builder and owner of Fort Hinsdale, and who is now a colonel, says that he is,—

> Moved with indignation to think that a few barbarous wretches should make such havoc on our Frontier as to kill and captivate our people, kill our cattle and fire their guns in hearing with great audacity, as we hear they Daily Do at No. 4 and other places and none to Repell or Silence them.

The indignant colonel is now sick at Deerfield and Madam Hinsdale is with him at their house on the lot where E. C. Cowles now lives. Here both were safe. But their principal estate was at the "Cellars," or Fort Hinsdale, where their crops and cattle were daily exposed to Indian depredations, or neglect from fear of the enemy; and when the colonel became convalescent, his brave wife, a daughter of the "Redeemed Captive," determined to go and take charge of their affairs at this post of danger. June 5th, the Colonel writes to Col. Israel Williams, that he is better, and "able to ride when set on a horse;" that his wife has gone to his fort, "not being easy to stay away these difficult times." He wants

"Lieut. Clesson and Deacon Sheldon sent out on a scalping encouragement, they being well acquainted with the Indian descents upon us, both by West and Black rivers." He offers to advance money to fit them out, and take his pay from the bounty they get on the scalps they may harvest. One of them might perchance be that of his brother-in-law Amrusus, who not long before had been seen in the valley.

June 11th, Moses Rice, the first settler of Charlemont, with his son Artemas and grandson Asa and a lad named Titus King, went on to the meadows to hoe his corn. After placing their guns against some logs at one end of the rows of corn, Moses, with his grandson to ride horse, went to harrowing, while the others used their hoes. Phineas Arms of Deerfield, a garrison soldier who had gone out as a guard, walked, musket in hand, back and forth across the cornfield, scanning the coverts and peering into the ravines at either end. Meanwhile from the hill above a party of Indians were watching all these movements and taking in the situation of affairs. Stealing down a ravine on the border of the hill they lay hid until the workmen were at the farthest from their guns, and at the right moment they rose and fired. Arms was struck in the head and fell dead and Moses Rice was badly wounded. The two boys were captured, while Artemas Rice ran for his life and escaped to Taylor's fort. Moses was taken a short distance and killed, but the boys were carried to Canada. From Taylor's fort the sad news was dispatched to Deerfield, and twenty-five men from there reached Taylor's that night, and in the morning of the 12th went to the scene of the disaster. Nothing could be done but speak words of comfort to the bereaved and bury the dead, who were laid side by side on a fair slope overlooking the Pocumtuck river.

Phineas Arms was son of William of Deerfield, born at the "South End" in 1731. According to a tradition he had been impressed to go on the Crown Point expedition—doubtless in Col. Williams's regiment—but through friends at court he had been transferred to the less dangerous post at Charlemont, where his cousin was living as the wife of Sergt. Othniel Taylor. The bullet which reached Arms's brain is now in Memorial Hall. It was found in his skull while putting in the foundations for a monument which Orlando B. Potter, a descendant of Moses Rice, was about to erect over the graves of Rice and Arms. This monument was dedicated by the Pocumtuck Valley Memorial Association, Aug. 2d, 1871.

On getting the news of the attack at Charlemont, Shirley ordered the garrisons in the forts to scout constantly, and authorized large scalping parties to fit out for a thirty days' scout.

June 21st, news was received that a large party had left Crown Point for this region. Joseph Dwight writes from Stockbridge that tracks had been found about there. "One track, prodideously large, 11½ inches by actual measurement." This track would not be more than an average now, and the query is, was the Indian foot a very small one, or were the feet of the English so much smaller then than now that this track of 11½ inches was a noticeable one?

June 27th, an attack was made at Bridgman's fort in Hinsdale. Caleb Howe was killed and Benjamin Gaffield drowned in trying to escape across Connecticut river; Jemima, wife of Howe, with seven children; Eunice, wife of Gaffield; and Submit, wife of Hilkiah Grout, with her three children, were captured and taken to Canada. Mrs. Howe is known as the "Fair Captive," a prominent character in romantic history. Mrs. Grout was daughter of Nathaniel Hawks of Deerfield, whence the family had removed to Hinsdale about 1751. Three days later the Indians made an attack on Keene, in which an aunt of Mrs. Grout, Thankful, daughter of Eleazer Hawks, was involved. By the bravery of Capt. Wm. Symes the enemy were driven off, after taking Benjamin Twitchell captive and killing many cattle. Seth Field writes from Northfield to Maj. Williams at Deerfield that "the enemy are thick about No. 4—Great Meadows—Walpole and Hinsdale."

July 5th, Maj. Williams writes to Col. Israel Williams that the scouts report making frequent discovery of signs of the Indians about Fall Town, Colrain and Charlemont, and that Indians are seen every day about Fort Massachusetts. He hears,—

From Albany last evening, by John Arms and others, that Col. Lydius informs that there are large numbers of Indians out, some say 300, some 4 or 500, and that one party of these Design for Deerfield, &c., all which accounts together with the account I sent you a few days ago from Mr. Field, has so alarmed the people that there are always some of them applying to me to seek and send them some relief, but, as it is not in my power, should be glad if you would give orders that there should be a long scout from these parts up West river, even to the head of it, or to the height of land, where I doubt not the enemy lie secure. I have no dependence on any persons going out on the scalping act, unless you so far encourage it as to appoint a set of officers equal to the service, which I hope you will. We have so few men for gards at Deerfield and Greenfield and other places that the inhabitants are discouraged & think that they shall lose almost all the crops they have on the ground. What to do, or say to them I know not—hope Sir you have some directions from the governor before he left the Province to raise succors in such a time of distress as it is now in the Poor Distressed Frontiers. Please Sir to let me know by Ens. Childs what I shall say to the people. These in the utmost haste, from, Sir, your assured frend & Servent, ELIJAH WILLIAMS.

[July 8th, Col. Williams, who must have other than the above official news from Deerfield, writes to Maj. Williams:—]

I am sorry the people of Deerfield are deaf to the notices of their danger * * * I am not disposed to judge those of my neighbors who differ in sentiment from me; nor to determine the causes, whether from pique, or conceit, or weak understanding. Yet as I have the care of the frontiers committed to me in a twofold capacity I shall endeavor the safety of the whole & to persue such measures as I shall apprehend will contribute thereto—I look upon it as reasonable that the minister & his family should be cared for better than his people are disposed to, or than he may expect from his neighborhood. I therefore direct you to post 3 of the Soldiers at his house until further order, which I esteem as serving the whole—

I have been exceeding loath to do anything whereby any of mankind should have the least color to say, I had a particular regard to my friends. [Mr. Ashley's wife was his sister.]—But considering that Gent as the minister of Deerfield, his situation in the Town, & the peculiar circumstances of his family—these I say determined me to give the above order without a motion from him, or any one else. Those people who will collect themselves & act the prudent & necessary part for their protection and safety, I am determined shall be watched and guarded, if others being now sufficiently warned tho they are constrained to do something for their neighbors' safety, go without. To suppose our enemies intend nothing further by all their efforts is to believe just as some did a few weeks past, the effect of which has proved fatal to 'em.

I am, Sir, your assured friend & Servant, Is WILLIAMS.

About July 4th, a small party of men from Fort Massachusetts "fired upon some Indians & killed one as they supposed & after a weeks pains found him & got his scalp." July 11th, Capt. Isaac Wyman, from Fort Massachusetts writes Col. Williams about an Indian scalp "found about a mile from where he was shot down." He enclosed the following names as of parties having an interest in the affair: "Ens. Barnard, Sergt. Taylor, Clerk Chapin, John Wells,

Gad Corse, Elijah Sheldon, Benj. King, Enoch Chapin, Paul Rice, Seth Hudson, Jabes Warren, Gideon Warren, Isaac Searl."

The following, without date, is taken from a fly leaf in an account book of Ensign Joseph Barnard. No reference to this exploit is found elsewhere:—

> Last night at ten, being upon the watch, I discovered Six men who appeared to be in the Indian habit. After I had cocked my gun and got ready to fire, I cald Stand, three Several times, upon which they made of. I fired after them & cald to arms, at which shot I had the good fortune to strike two of them so that they could not Budge of [apace?] But fell into my hands presently.

July 22d, Col. Hinsdale had an express from his wife at Hinsdale, detailing how four men, guarded by three soldiers, at about 60 rods from the fort getting pickets, were set upon by a party which got between them and the fort. John Hardiclay, a soldier, and John Alexander, a citizen, were killed, and Jonathan Colby captured. She says in a P. S.:—

> Hardiclay was found dead upon the spot, with both his breasts cut off, and his heart laid open. One of the inhabitants was found within 60 rods of the fort and both scalped. We fired several larrums and the great gun at Fort Dummer was shot. Thirty men from Northfield came to our assistance and helped to bury the dead. They followed the Indians, found Colby's track, who was barefoot. They found no blood, which gives us reason to hope that Colby is well. The rest escaped to the fort. ABIGAIL HINSDALE.

It was probably the same party that a day or two later killed Daniel Twitchell and John Flint at Walpole. One of the two was cut open, his heart slashed in pieces and laid on his breast.

July 22d, news was received of the death of Braddock at Fort Du Quesne, on the 9th, when his army was defeated and a remnant only saved by the bravery and skill of Washington. The frontiers were drained of men to keep up the army of invasion at Albany. The garrisons were employed in constant scouting, very little could be done in guarding people at their labor, and the greater part of the harvest was lost.

July 29th, Col. Williams writes Lt. Gov. Phips that,—

> The people are much distressed and much grain must be lost for want of guards—I expect many will venture hard to save their corn, not knowing to support without it, without which multitudes will be

ruined—The people conduct with caution and prudence—of late—as I ever knew them—They are sufficiently fortified & are at great expense in hiring guards. No mischief has happened since the disaster at Charlemont—tho they have made frequent attempts—I fear they will be too cunning for us.

Aug. 2d, Maj. Elijah Williams writes that Lieut. Clesson was ready to go out on a scalping expedition and was awaiting orders.

Aug. 4th, while a party of Greenfield people were out at work with a guard, Samuel Wells tied his horse and left his coat at some distance from the others. This was observed by lurking Indians who were preparing an ambush to catch him when he came for his horse, but they were discovered by the guard. Such constant and extreme vigilance was the price of life or liberty.

Col. Hinsdale, who had gone to relieve his wife of the charge of Fort Hinsdale, writes that the Indians are all round them, killing cattle, &c., and "was so bold here last week as to return our watchword in the night, 'Sharp—all is well.' A good harvest but the crop must be lost unless a guard is sent."

Aug. 5th, John Catlin, in a letter from Fort Massachusetts, says the scouts have cleared the coast about there—says he has learned that "one of the skulks, who killed Phips at the Great Meadow rec'd his death wound and died at Crown Point." [See *ante*, p. 540.]

Aug. 7th, Capt. Nathan Willard is here *en route* for Boston, after help. Maj. Williams writes by him to Phips, showing the real need of more soldiers. He gives the situation of the people at the north and says,—

The Inhabitants of Gf'd are in great distress & are daily obliged to find guards themselves, beside the soldiers that are allowed them —who are all but two out every day on the guard; only two left to keep the garrisons   *   *   *   I am informed by Colrain people that the Indians have been about ye South fort & have called out to ye watch one or two nights, w^h looks to be very strange conduct in an enemy   *   *   *   We at Deerfield being reduced by so many of our peoples being gone into the Service of the Province that we have but about 70 men left in the town & how we shall be able to to get hay to keep our stock and seed our ground I know not—Hope the Province will afford us some relief.

These in haste, Capt. Willard being in waiting. From your assured friend & Sevt,   ELIJAH WILLIAMS.

Aug. 8th, Lieut. Matthew Clesson had his scout of fifteen

men at Morrison's fort and "sent for Mr. McDowell to pray with them before they went out." He led them to the head waters of Deerfield river and over to the head of West riv-river, found tracks of Indians and lay some days in ambush, but came back *via* Forts Dummer, Hinsdale and Sheldon, reaching Deerfield the 22d, without seeing an Indian. McDowell's house had been picketed and a garrison placed there.

Aug. 20th, Acting Governor Phips writes Col. Williams:—

I think it very necessary that ministers on our frontier should be protected, which has been in all times of danger the care of the governor * * * You will give such orders as may be necessary for the succor of Mr. McDowell & his family, at Colrain. This is a good place for scouting parties to go out & come in.

Meanwhile the armies assembled at Albany and above had done little. Shirley's expedition to Niagara had failed. William Johnson, commander of the Crown Point expedition, built a fort at the great carrying place called Fort Edward, and in August he pushed on and established a camp at the upper end of Lake George, fourteen miles northwest of Fort Edward.

Meanwhile a French army under Baron de Dieskau was marching from Canada up the Sorel and Lake Champlain.

Sept. 7th, Dieskau landed at South Bay, about twenty miles north of Fort Edward and sixteen miles northeast of Johnson's Camp, and marched for Fort Edward, with Johnson lying on his right flank. When within four or five miles of the fort he was deceived by false intelligence and turned at a right angle and marched towards Johnson's Camp.

Johnson had early news of the march of his enemy, but instead of hurrying out to strike him on the flank he contented himself with sending an express to Fort Edward with notice of the danger. At midnight Johnson had news that Dieskau was near Fort Edward. It seems here was an opportunity of falling on his rear and crushing him between two fires. Instead of that nothing was done until the morning of Sept. 8th, when he sent Col. Ephraim Williams with his regiment and the Mohawk Sachem Hendrick with two hundred Indians, "to intercept the French in their retreat, either as victors or defeated in their attempt." As we have seen, Dieskau had turned from Fort Edward and the two bodies were approaching each other. Dieskau got the first information of this state of affairs and laid an ambush, into which Williams marched. Williams and Hendrick were killed, with many of their men; the rest fled until they were met by a succoring party, when the fight was renewed. Flushed with his success, Dieskau pushed his enemy back towards Johnson's camp, upon which he made an assault. After four hours' fighting his army was driven off and he fell, a wounded prisoner, into the hands of Johnson. Dieskau's wounds were dressed by Dr. Thomas Williams and he lived until 1767, but his wounds never fully healed. Many men from this valley were killed with Col. Williams and his march is known hereabouts as "The Bloody Morning Scout."

Upon the news of the French invasion, new troops were raised, and Sept. 16th, Maj. Elijah Williams reported that he had enlisted from his command Samuel Smith, Daniel Kellogg, John Eastman, John Clary, Joseph Lyman, Jr., Jona. Bissell, Elisha Hubbard and Charles Wright, and had impressed David Smith, Nathaniel Coleman, Ebenezer Marsh, Jr., Jona. Warner, John Miller and Peter Smith. He writes to Col. Israel Williams, Sept. 21st, that "Beside the ammunition for Crown Point there arrived at Sunderland and will be here to-morrow, 200 hatchets, 200 worms & wires, 200 blankets, 100 tin kettles, 300 knapsacks and bullet bags. The men in Col. Worthington's Reg. can be supplied here if they wish."

None of the troops from the valley marched to relieve Fort Edward, as far as known. Col. Worthington wrote that from the news he heard he "thought the army would be defeated before succor could reach them, and so did not" make the attempt. His prophecy did not prove exactly true, but with the battle of Lake George, Sept. 8th, active operations ceased on both sides for the year 1755.

Many sick or wounded soldiers from the army or the forts were in charge of Dr. Israel Ashley, at Westfield. On a bill against the Province for this year we find the names of David King, Amos Risley, Joseph Barber; Herbert Miller, son of Jonathan, from whom he "cut out his bullet;" "John Badcock, a wounded soldier;" Lt. Clark from Crown Point, Lt. Hale and son, Daniel Granger, Francis Poland, Eph. Noble, Capt. Fellows, Enoch Johnson, Ebenezer Lamb, Danl. Jaquith, Israel Adams and father; Eph. Farnsworth, who died on his hands; Ebenezer Holt, Thomas Johnson, John Hersey, Benj. Thirston, Ebenezer Miller, David King, Lt. Gibbs, Thomas Wilder, Wm. Lane, Richard Woodbury, Wm. Crooks, Ebenezer Morgan; Lt. Saml. Renolds, "came down on a horse litter;" Isaac Wilkins; "Coffee Peacock, Capt. Bullard's negro;" Peter Harmon, James Poor, Benj. Hudson, Solomon Smith. One item was a charge, Aug. 20th, 1755, for "a visit to Poontusuch 40 mild" to see Sergt. Wright, Jabez Hyde and others.

1756. Petitions for aid were early sent to the Governor from Charlemont, Colrain, Northfield, Hinsdale and No. 4, with general and particular representations of distress and fear of the enemy, and that without guards the cultivation of their fields would be at the instant peril of their lives, and their homes must be abandoned. Plucky Lieut. Ebenezer Sheldon of Fall Town sends a petition of a different character. He is not blindly ignorant; he has been for years a captive among the Indians. He says his,—

Is the only garrison in the place. The enemy were here several times last Summer & Repulsed. His son was killed. He has expended £300, O. T., in rebuilding and picketing his fort, which is a place of security for himself and neighbors. This your petitioner has done, being determined not to flee before the enemy if he can *possibly* help it. But his circumstances are such that he is unable to bear so great a charge.

He asks pecuniary aid in the matter of repairing the fort.

March 23d, Col. Williams puts Lieut. John Hawks in command of the line of forts from Northfield to Hoosac mountain. He is instructed that "the duty of his men posted at Charlemont, Fall-town & Colrain is marching," although the men in South Fort, Lucas's, and the ministers' fort in Colrain, may guard the people at labor when marching service does not demand them, "provided they will work together in companies & submit to your direction in that article."

The duty of the garrisons at Greenfield and Northfield he says are to guard the laborers, "provided they desire it & will work together as you judge reasonable, to afford them a guard. Put the men in Greenfield in Corse's garrison there to watch and ward." The *people* at Greenfield, Colrain and Northfield are expected also to watch and ward. His sergeants were directed "to keep an exact journal of their daily

GARRISON DUTY.

service and performances by their men, & transmit the same to you every 14 days, or oftener if need be." These, with a journal of his own service Hawks was to send to Col. Williams "as often as I require it." "I expect you and the officers to attend to your duty at your respective posts & govern the men well, but the men have reasonable furlows, which I hereby empower you to grant 'em."

Hawks's headquarters were at Morrison's. The other men of his command were:—

Sergt. Oliver Avery and 5 men at South fort.
Sergt. John Taylor and 5 men at McDowell's fort.
Corp. Abner Peck and 5 men at Fort Lucas.
Sergt. Joseph Allen and 12 men at Northfield.
Sergt. James Rider and 8 men at Greenfield.
Sergt. Othniel Taylor and 11 men at Taylor's fort, Charlemont.
Sergt. Gershom Hawks and 11 men at Hawks's fort, Charlemont.
Sergt. Ebenezer Sheldon, Jr., and 7 men at Sheldon's fort, Fall-town.
Sergt. Remembrance Sheldon and 7 men at Burke's fort, Fall-town.

March 27th, Col. Williams writes Shirley that,—

Huntstown people quitted their place last summer for want of protection, but several families returned and lived there thro' the winter & others will join them if they can have help. Encouraged by what they heard from you by their messenger they have begun to fortifie & in a few days will have a garrison completed—Before the war they had fitted a large area of land for tillage & raised considerable provisions. That is gone & they know not where to look for their bread, or what method to take for their support, & unless something can be done for them they must again leave the place—With a guard of 10 or 12 men they think they may work upon their land with tolerable safety.

Williams recommends putting part of the men under pay to guard the rest. July 8th, he is directed to send a guard to Huntstown.

April 19th, Othniel Taylor reports: "Two of the scouts from Colrain to Charlemont saw two Indians by a log house, one of them very much painted with red * * * It was a rainy day & his gun was wet or he mit have done the execution of one of them * * * Will Morris has gone with Rogers."—But a fragment of this report remains.

June 7th, Seth Field sends Maj. Williams an express from Northfield with news of the capture of Josiah Fisher and family at the Bow. The Major suggests to Col. Williams the sending a scout up West river, above the crotch, to intercept them; "the woman being weakly & the children small they can't travel fast." For fear the Indians would kill the captives, nothing was done. Col. Hinsdale writes to his brother in Deerfield the same day that he sent out a party to discover the marauders, who found two canoes hid at the mouth of West river, and five horses killed and an ox with three bullets in it. The same day Capt. Wyman sends word of trouble at Fort Massachusetts. Benjamin King and Wm. Meacham were shot within half a mile of the fort. He sent out Ensign Salah Barnard after the enemy, but he could not overtake them.

June 19th, Col. Hinsdale sends news that Lieut. Moses Willard was that day killed at No. 4, and his son Moses wounded by a spear thrown at him. Five Indians were seen.

July 2d, as a party of men were engaged in haying over at New Fort, the watch discovered and fired upon an Indian who was lurking in the bushes. John Catlin, writing to Col. Williams about the affair, says, "had they all gone to work we have reason to think more or less of them must have fallen a prey into their hands."

July 9th, Othniel Taylor reports that "this day at 4 o'clock John Stewart went out about 40 rods from the fort to get some bark, heard a noise 5 or 6 rods from him & saw an Indian making towards him. He shot at him & made for the fort.—A party went out & saw the blood where he fell & a bullet which he dropped out of his mouth."

July 13th, news arrives that Sergt. Chidester and his son James were killed at Hoosac and Capt. Elisha Chapin captured. Lieut. Barnard went out with a party to bury the dead and found where one hundred of the enemy had laid in ambush between the fort and the town. Two days after this affair Frenchmen with laced hats were seen near Fort Massachusetts.

July 20th, John Catlin was made Captain at Hoosac, in place of Chapin; Salah Barnard lieutenant, and Jonathan Hunt, ensign. Of the two first, Col. Williams writes to the

Governor, "I have had a large experience of their courage and good conduct, both in the last and present war."

Aug. 21st, Seth Field of Northfield sends a post to Major Williams here of an attack on two men at Northfield. Maj. Williams expressed the news to Lieut. Hawks at Colrain and Hawks sends the following letter—which tells its own story —to Charlemont, the same day:—

COLRAIN, Aug. 2, 1756.

Sir:—I just now by express from Maj. Williams that at Northfield, informing that is Zeb. Stebbing & Ruben Wright ware Returning from labour sun about half an hour high at night a little below Stebbinses Island ye Indians lay in the Path that they come till within 6 or 7 rods of them they fired at them. Shot Ruben Right through the arm but did not brake the bone tha Both rode back about 60 or 70 rods & stoped the Indians son came up and fird a second gun at them they still Rhode back a little way and stoppd tho tha had but one gun tha saw but 3 or 4 Indians in a minute an Indian come up in the Path after them—Stebbins took Wrights gun shot at him he fell down & cried out then the men made off as fast as they could

I remain Yours to Serve

JOHN HAWKS

P. S. Y^e Col Williams gave orders that Warner [or Warren] mit go to Hawks or your fort if he inclined—Send word to Hawks' as soon as you can—I have no more nus only Cholter [?] has brought forth three living sons. To Sergt Othniel Taylor. J. H.

Aug. 23d, Shubal Atherton, Nathaniel Brooks, Benjamin Hastings, Daniel Graves and his son John Graves, went up to the Country Farms to harvest grain. They had no guard and placed their guns together against a stack of flax when they began their labor. A party of Indians on an adjacent hill saw this condition of affairs and creeping down got between the men and their arms. They then rose and fired upon them. None of the men were hit and they all ran for their lives. Hastings and John Graves dashed through Green river, ran across Irish Plain, westward, and came out at the Arms place in safety. Atherton plunged down a ravine near the river and lay still. He was seen and shot where he lay. Daniel Graves and Brooks were captured. Brooks was carried to Canada, where he was heard from in 1758, but not afterwards. Graves, fifty-eight years old, was lame, and not being able to travel fast enough, was killed near the foot of Leyden Glen. His son Daniel had been killed the year before on the "Bloody Morning Scout."

Atherton was thirty-six years old. Married at twenty-one,

he had been the father of eleven children, the youngest now seven weeks old. His father had been wounded while serving in the troop as trumpeter. His grandfather was Rev. Hope Atherton, chaplain under Turner at the Falls fight in 1676. Some particulars of this calamity, which it is thought have never been published, may be found in the following extract from a letter of Major Elijah Williams to Col. Israel Williams, dated at Deerfield, August 23d, 1756. Hoyt erroneously gives the date of this affair as Aug. 12th:—

I immediately went to the place with as many men as could be soon rallied, when we came there we found Greenfield people who had got there before us gone on the track after the enemy, except one or two who informed us what course they steered, & that they judged they had one or two captives with them. We went in search of one man, who, allowing two to be taken was still missing: after some time we found Shubal Atherton killed & scalped—I judge he jumped down a steep pitch amongst the brush & lay there til he was found and killed for he was shot in his breast & out of his back near his waistband & his breast shot full of powder * * * A lad of Joshua Wells was going to his labor near where the men were & in open sight of them, says when he came to his work he saw the Indians a Drawing off & that they had two men with white shirts &c —but that he did not then think so much of Indians as to leave his work til people from Greenfield meadows got up—he thinks there were 7 or 8—but by what signs I could discover I judged there was not more than six.

Sept. 6th, Capt. John Catlin returns a list of men he had "impressed for his majesties Service," doubtless for the army under Lord Loudon, near Albany. These men were the real bone and muscle of Deerfield and could not well be spared in her straitened circumstances. Greenfield and Northfield were drained in the same manner of their best material for Loudon's army. They were:—

Sergt. John Sheldon, Sergt. Joseph Smeed, Sergt. David Hoyt, Corp. Nathan Frary; Centinals—Seth Catlin, Samuel Dickinson, Joseph Mitchell, John Hinsdale, John Hawks, Jr., David Childs, Caleb Allen, Eliakim Arms, Samuel Belden, Moses Nims, Augustus Wells, Jona. Catlin, Soloman Newton, Samuel Hinsdale, Justin Bull, Benjamin Munn, Jr.

Being thus deprived of her living defenders, Deerfield took measures for other modes of defense. At a town meeting, Oct. 13th, 1756:—"Voted that there shall be forts built at the charge of ye Town." A committee of nine men was chosen "to Consider & Determine in what way & manner to carry on yᵉ forting to Report next Thursday at 5 o'clock afternoon," to which time the meeting adjourned.

After hearing the report of the committee, "Voted that their shall be five Garrisons built in yᵉ Town & one at Wapping each to have two mounts & to be boarded around & lined with pallasadoes as high as a man's head." A committee of 15 was chosen "to provide materials & see yᵉ work effected as soon as may be, [a committee also chosen] to prepare a petition to send to yᵉ Genˡ Court setting forth yᵉ Distressed Condition of this Town & humbly pray for Relief."

March 14th, 1757, the Bloody Brook people present a petition to the town which tells its own story:—

Wheras your Petitioners are Settled Remote from the Town, and being Determined to Abide by our Possessions if possible, where we have already been at Considerable Charge to provide for our Security and Defence, and Expect it will be Expedient to make Still further Provisions; and proposing if Necessitated to Leave our Inheritance, not to Repair to the Town of Deerfield, but Elsewhere: We Apprehend we Shall have no benefit or advantage by the Fortifications proposed to be erected in said Town of Deerfield [after this threat they proceed] we humbly Pray, Gentlemen, Fathers, and Bretheren, that you would Consider our Circumstances, and free us from bearing any proportion of the Charge of Erecting said Fortifications: who by reason of our beginning new Settlements, together with the great Disadvantages arrising from the war, are very unable to Bear the Burden thereof, and in Duty Bound Shall Ever Pray
Your Dutiful Children
NATHAN FRARY   THOMAS FRENCH JR
NATHˡ PARKER   THOMAS ARMS
SAMUEL BARNARD

The response to this petition may be found in the vote below. The late scare was over. "Mch 14th 1757 Voted that yᵉ Comᵗᵉᵉ chosen to Fortify yᵉ Town &c be Directed to Desist from any further proceedings about sᵈ Garrisons till further order." It does not appear that "further orders" were ever received. It became evident soon after, that the government had determined that, at whatever cost, Canada should be conquered; and with the fall of Canada, all danger from Indian incursions would be at an end.

But the end was not yet. A year of disaster was now to follow. This, however, only made this determination stronger, and the necessity of subduing Canada more apparent.

Gov. Shirley had succeeded Gen. Braddock in 1756, as Commander-in-chief of the English forces in America. He had planned a vigorous campaign early this year against Niagara and Crown Point and was collecting a strong force near Albany; but he was superseded by the Earl of Loudon. Loudon delayed coming, to engage some German officers of note, and sent General Abercrombie to take command, who arrived at Albany June 25th. He did little but wait for Loudon, who joined him July 29th. While Loudon was celebrating his arrival at Albany, Montcalm on the 12th of August, captured Oswego, with twelve hundred men and a large amount of stores, shipping, &c. This was a serious loss to the English, and the season passed without further movement on either side.

The men impressed from Greenfield for this campaign were: Isaac Foster, Moses Bascom, Asher Corse, Elijah Wells, Agrippa Wells, George Frost, Joseph King, John Foster, Lemuel Smead and Seth Denio.

Oct. 5th, Benjamin Hastings and others petition the government for aid. They have nothing but picketed houses to fly to in times of danger, and they want fortifications built, and to be exempt from general taxes. "Have but 42 men who can be called inhabitants * * * 192 Souls in all * * * but 8 soldiers to guard us, and alarms often call us off our work."

Montcalm writes home, Sept. 22d, that "I will as much as lies in my power, keep up small parties to scatter consternation and the miseries of the war throughout the enemy's country." His success in this laudable undertaking must have been gratifying.

These extracts have been given as the best exposition of the condition of affairs during this war. The man of thought, and even he of the dullest imagination, can picture the daily life of the pioneer far better from such notes than it can be painted by the readiest pen. The parting each morning—which may be the last—as the husbandman, taking his life in his hand, goes forth to sow or to reap, that those dependent on him may have bread. A slow death for them by starvation, or the risk of a swift one by the bullet or tomahawk for him, was the only alternative; for from the bosom of mother earth only could their sustenance be drawn. We picture the heavy hours of torturing anxiety to the wife and mother, till night brought the loved ones home; the incessant warding by day and watching by night; their narrow mental as well as physical horizon—away from the world of thought, with the interminable forest with its real dangers and shadowy horrors shutting them in on every side. We hear with them the startling hoof beats under the galloping post, disturbing the midnight stillness or the quiet of the day, as he rides to the corner store, the headquarters of Maj. Williams. We see the people hurrying to learn the tidings he brings— the quick barring of door and shutter by those who remain at home—the asking with white lips whose husband, father or son is this time the victim.

But amid all the harrassing distress of this dark period the men and women were not the subjects of abject, helpless fear. They were brave and determined and held their own by sheer force of character—and we must not forget that they were the fathers and mothers of those who fought at Bunker Hill, Saratoga and Yorktown.

1757. This year a large army was in the field under Lord Loudon. Twelve hundred men went against Louisburg, but came back without striking a blow. Gen. Webb commanded seven thousand men collected at Forts Edward and William Henry, but his every movement was attended with disaster. The chief event of this year was the surrender of Fort William Henry by Col. Munroe, the barbarous butchery of the prisoners, and the consequent alarm in New England. The line of forts on our borders continued under the command of Col. Israel Williams. He placed the four in Colrain under Lieut. John Hawks and Sergt. John Taylor; Sergt. Remembrance Sheldon and sixteen men at Fall Town; Sergt. John Brown and fifteen men at Greenfield; Sergt. Ebenezer Belding and nine men at Huntstown; Sergt. Hilkiah Grout and fourteen men at Northfield; Sergts. Samuel and Othniel Taylor and Gershom Hawks with fifty-one men at Charlemont.

April 20th, a party of seventy French and Indians burnt the mill at No. 4 and captured Dea. Thomas Adams, Samson Colefax, the miller, David Farnsworth, George Robbins and Asa Spafford, who were taken to Canada. Lieut. Hawks dispatched two men on horseback to Fort Massachusetts with the news. The horses were to be left at a certain place on the Hoosac mountain and the men to "go on foot not in the road." In June, Hawks says, one of these horses, worth £8, was killed by the Indians. He was allowed £6 for the loss.

May 10th, Col. Williams received orders from the Council to put the frontiers in a posture of defense and prepare for an invasion. The alarm may have been caused by the activity of the French on Lake Champlain and Lake George. "M. de Pegaud de Vaudreuil, brother of the Governor," left Canada for Fort William Henry with fifteen hundred French and Indians. The fort was defended, but all the shipping, houses and stores beyond the range of its guns were destroyed.

May 23d, Lieut. Hawks writes Col. Williams from Colrain:—

> Have according to your orders stationed men in all the 3 forts & at the South fort there is no inhabitants gone in to live or lodge. I am forced to send some out of the fort to board. I went to Lt. Magee & Ens. Stuart to know what they wanted soldiers for when the inhabitants lived and lodged ½ a mile distant each way from the fort—They dont think any will go into the fort until further mischief—Sergt Avery chose to go to Hawks instead of Lucas's—Paul King I have put in Camels place who went to Cold Spring to get his gun & failed to return.

By this letter it appears that the South fort built by the Province was situated like a schoolhouse, in the center of the district, and that the garrison, like the schoolmarm, boarded round—a unique military post. It was probably little more than a stockaded enclosure to which the adjacent inhabitants could flee in case of an alarm. Rev. Mr. McDowell writes Col. Williams that Archibald Lawson, being "more contiguous to the South fort," wants to be shifted there—that Lieut. Hawks is willing, "& I am willing he should leave my fort provided no ruffian or otherwise known disorderly person be sent in his room."

John Taylor writes the following letter—doubtless from Morrison's fort—to Sergt. Othniel Taylor at Charlemont:—

COLRAIN June ye 6 1757

> Pursuant to Lieut Hawks orders you are required forthwith to send to Huntstown y^t ye Indians are Discovered very thick between North River and Deerfield River that they be upon their guard.
>
> from your affectionate and Loving Brother   JOHN TAYLOR.

The writer was also directed by Hawks to take twelve men and scout four or five days above the head waters of the Deerfield river. In spite of this and other precautions, a party of the enemy came to Charlemont about the 12th, who murdered one Wheeler and killed a horse belonging to Lieut. Hawks. June 14th, Indians were discovered at "Chestnut Plain" and seen to "run above 3 or 4 rods," but nothing further was heard of them.

June 24th, Lieut. Hawks gets word by a dispatch from Fort Massachusetts of an attack on Saratoga, and that three parties of the enemy had been seen starting this way. Maj. Elijah Williams gets the news here from Hawks at ten p. m. of the same day. Scouts were sent out to discover the invaders. Those from Colrain found nothing. Those from Charlemont found many traces of the enemy, who returned without doing harm.

June 28th, Capt. Burke writes from Fort Edward that Caleb Newton was killed and Ezekiel Smith was wounded in a recent skirmish. Both were of his company.

In the great disaster of this year, the capture of Fort William Henry, called by the French, Fort George, many men from this section were involved. The fort was held by Col. George Munroe with twenty-five hundred men. It was besieged by Montcalm August 3d, and on the 9th it surrendered upon honorable terms. The French troops were to escort the garrison towards Fort Edward, under the terms of the capitulation; but no sooner had the English marched out of the entrenchments than the savages fell upon the officers and soldiers and robbed them of all their baggage, and soon began to butcher the sick, the women and children, and many soldiers shared the same fate. Hundreds of the English were slain and mangled with barbarian ferocity. The guard of French soldiers looked passively on or made but slight and ineffectual efforts to stop the inhuman carnage. The gallant career of Montcalm, and his heroic death on the plains of Abraham, cannot wipe out the foul blot on his escutcheon which was left there by the blood shed on this occasion.

The French attempted to excuse themselves on the ground that the English had given rum to the Indians to make friends with them. De Bougainville says,—

> Some of their soldiers, in spite of all the warning that had been given them, had given them some rum to drink, and who in the world could restrain 2000 Indians of 32 different nations, when they have drank liquor? The disorder was commenced by the Abenakis.

Montcalm, in a letter to Gen. Webb, August 14th, tells the

same story, with variations. He says the Indians were given rum, and that the Abenakis began it. "You know," he says,—

What it is to restrain 3000 Indians of 33 different nations, & I had but too many apprehensions, which I did not conceal from the commandant of the fort in my summons. I consider myself lucky that the *disorder* was not attended with consequences as unfortunate as I had reason to fear.

Then in the name of good faith and humanity why did he not take measures to prevent this horrible "disorder?" For an account of this affair in detail, read the Travels of Jona. Carver, one of the sufferers. How many Deerfield people were under Col. Munroe cannot be ascertained. Some of them were Lieut. Salah Barnard, Consider Arms, Elijah Sheldon, John Hinsdale, Samuel Taylor, Reuben Petty, Jonathan Oakes, Joseph Denio. Lieut. Salah Barnard was seized by two Indians; each grasped one of his hands and dragged him towards the woods to strip and murder him. Barnard was an athletic man, and while the three were in this relative position, they reached a steep descent. Just at the moment the Indians began to descend, Barnard braced himself back, gathered all his strength, and swung the heads of the Indians together with such force as to stun them both. He made his escape and finally reached Fort Edward.

The readers of "The Last of the Mahicans," may take the assurance that the writer did not overdraw the bloody scenes of this faithless and cowardly massacre.

The alarm caused by the fall of Fort William Henry was general on the frontiers. The capture of Fort Edward and the invasion of New York or New England was expected to follow. As soon as Gen. Webb at Fort Edward was informed of the advance of the French army he sent out for reinforcements, and Aug. 8th "Sir William Pepperèll, Major General of His Majesty's forces and Lt. General of the Province of Massachusetts." was ordered to Springfield by Gov. Pownell to collect the forces raised for the defense of the country and to reinforce Gen. Webb. In case Webb was defeated he was to succeed to the whole command. A draft of one-fourth part of each regiment in the Province except three was ordered; the levies to be sent to Springfield. August 10th, Sir William was ordered to dispatch every available man to the seat of war, and he forwarded the regiments of Col. Worthington and Col. Williams of this county and Col. Ruggles of Worcester county. The same day, Col. Oliver Partridge, who succeeded Col. Israel Williams in this quarter, writes Pownell that he has news of one hundred and fifty Indians coming down the river, and that he has ordered two companies to march to Deerfield and wait events.

August 11th, Col. Partridge gets news from Albany of the fall of Fort William Henry, and official letters to this Province reached Pepperell at Springfield, August 12th, at midnight, with the same sad news. The previous alarm now became almost a panic.

August 13th, Col. Chandler's Worcester regiment reached Springfield. The same day Pownell sends Sir William orders to prepare for the threatened invasion. He is instructed:—

> If the enemy should approach the frontier, you will order all waggons west of the Connecticut River to have their wheels knocked off, and to drive the said country of horses, to order in all provisions that can be brought off & what cannot to destroy. You will receive this as my orders not to be executed but in such case of necessity & then not to fail to do it.

August 12th, Capt. Christie, A. D. Q. M. G., writes Pepperell from Albany that he does not think the enemy will come farther, but go back. He was right, for after dismantling and destroying the fort, Montcalm on the 15th marched back to Ticonderoga. Williams and Ruggles led their regiments as far as Kinderhook, when, hearing of the fall of William Henry and the expected invasion of Montcalm, instead of pressing on to support Gen. Webb, they turned round and marched home. Gov. Pownell was "amazed to hear that the regiments had not reached Albany on the 11th." And no wonder. The world has yet to learn the cause of what appears to be an unmanly retreat by Williams and Ruggles.

Pownell had ordered " one-fourth part of the militia and all the horse" to put themselves under the command of Sir William at Springfield.

August 15th, Sir William in a letter to Pownell, says he thinks the danger is past; he does not think the enemy will appear and that the militia need not come. He thinks the danger less here than at the East, and that he ought to go there. In a postscript he adds: "I have advised Capt. Christie of your zeal in forwarding the militia for their relief."

August 17th, the governor replies, asking him to thank the troops that turned "In iorm out for me," and to use his judgment about the disposition of the returning troops. August 24th, the scare was all over and Pepperell was in Boston and the stores collected for the troops were put on the market and sold.

September 13th, a company raised here on the alarm, with John Catlin, captain, Salah Barnard, lieutenant, Jonathan Hunt, ensign, Seth Catlin, drummer, and forty-nine men, marched from Deerfield to take charge of the defenses at West Hoosac. Catlin arrived on the 17th and reports the fort in a rotting condition, shot going through the timber of the mounts at fifteen rods. He returned December 1st, leaving Sergt. Seth Hudson in command.

Lieut. Hawks continued in command at Colrain until he had a major's commission in the regiment of Col. Williams.

There were no more attacks or alarms on the frontiers this season, but the winter was a gloomy one. The campaign had been one of disaster. The French were gaining in strength and the future looked dark indeed.

Deerfield men on the descriptive rolls of Lord Loudon this year or the winter following, are:—

Alexander, Joseph	Denio, Joseph	Nims, Reuben
Allen, Caleb	Dickinson, Samuel	Pease, Abner
Amsden, Asahel	Frost, George	Pease, Noadiah
Arms, Consider	Hawks, Asa	Petty, Reuben
Arms, Eliakim	Hawks, Moses	Rose, Seth
Bardwell, Medad	Hawks, Paul	Sheldon, Elisha
Birge, John	Hinsdale, John	Stebbins, Simon
Burt, Ebenezer	Kentfield, Solomon	Taylor, Samuel
Carver, Jonathan, [the traveler]	King, Joseph	Victory, John [born in Venice]
Catlin, Seth	Mitchell, Abner	Wells, Elisha
Davidson, Barnabas	Munn, Benjamin	
	Munn, Phineas	

1758. After three campaigns, disgraceful and disheartening to the English, William Pitt took the helm in the management of colonial affairs in England, and troops were raised in the colonies with a fresh ardor for the operations of this year. February 11th, Capt. Ebenezer Larnard with forty-six men spent a day here on his return from the camp. Samuel Wells furnished them one hundred and forty-seven meals at 5d. Deerfield, taking heart, now appears to feel secure from invasion, for at the town meeting, March 6th, it was voted:—

That Lt. Field, Samuel Hinsdell and John Sheldon be a committee to sell & Dispose of ye Timber provided for Building Garrisons in ye Town & also to Dispose of ye Remains of ye Old Garrisons within this town that They Judge unfit for use for the most they will fetch.

The line of forts was put under Capt. John Catlin. Under him were Sergt. Gershom Hawks and nine men at Hawks's, Charlemont; Corp. Joseph Denio and seven men at Rice's, Charlemont; Sergt. Othniel Taylor and eleven men at Taylor's, Charlemont; Sergt. Remembrance Sheldon and eleven men at Burke's, Fall Town; Sergt. Amasa Sheldon and eight men at Sheldon's, Fall Town; Sergt. Moses Wright and nine men at Huntstown; Sergt. Jacob Abbott and nine men at North fort, Colrain; Sergt. James Stewart and nine men at South fort, Colrain; Sergt. Chas. Wright and fifteen men at Greenfield; Sergt. Josiah Foster and ten men at Northfield.

Indian inroads began early. March 6th, Capt. Fairbanks Moore and his son were killed at Brattleboro, and the wife and four children of the latter taken captive.

March 21st, a party of Indians appeared at Colrain, wounded two men and burned a house and barn of Capt. Morrison. The following contemporary account of this affair by Rev. Jonathan Ashley is the most authentic to be found. It is written on the margin of a sermon which he preached March 26th :—

March 21st, about 50 Indians came to Morrison's Fort, wounded John Morrison and John Henry, killed several cattle and sheep, and after they had roasted, and fed themselves, came and fired at the fort and went off and lodged within a mile and a half of ye fort.

Ashley was not satisfied with the conduct of the people on this occasion, and in his next sermon he belabors them heartily, over the shoulders of poor Scriptural Ephraim. The text was from Hosea 7:11—"*Ephraim also is like a silly dove without heart.*" He is indignant that "no attempt was made to pursue and overtake" the marauders. He berates them for,—

Trying to make themselves great, and how contrary the effect * * * How their enemies were afflicting and distressing of them but they were no better y^n doves to defend themselves, to save themselves from approaching ruin. [It is well enough to be harmless as the dove, but] it shows the miserable state of a people when y^y are like ye dove in silliness; to be without a heart to understand, and a heart to prepare measures for safety is a shame and shows such a people most contemptible and miserable * * * The silly dove has not a heart to defend herself against any bird ot prey that seeks her life, flies from the least danger, and has no resolution to withstand any and suffers itself to be made an easy prey; and how natural to turn that over to ourselves and consider how much like silly doves and silly Ephraims we are, and perhaps these words were never truer of Ephraim than y^y are of us at the present day. We are about as easily put to flight by our enemies as a company of timorous doves. We are without a heart to take counsel. What are all your counsels better than the hoarse croakings of doves?

It would be interesting and instructive to know the comments made by the hearers on this sharp arraignment, but none are found. It is not unlikely that the following order grew out of the excitement it raised.

HATF'D, Ap'l 4, '58.

Lt. Hawks complains that his scoutsmen are destitute of Indian shoes, without which they can't perform their duty. The safety of ye Frontiers, the lives of ye men greatly depend upon their being well equipped. This necessary Provision is what ye Government have been always at ye expense for and what is your business as a Commissary to provide and til now supposed you had orders accordingly.

I hereby direct that you without delay get a sufficient number for that service and deliver them to Lt. Hawks, taking his receipt therefor, depending upon your Care in this matter.

I am y^r Hum'l Sev't,   Is. WILLIAMS.

MAJ. ELIJAH WILLIAMS.

[Endorsed.]   Deerfield, April 7, 1758.

Rec'd Deersleather for mogosons to the value of twenty-nine shillings and four pense.   JOHN HAWKS.

Hawks served in the Lake George campaign as major, commanding a company in the regiment of Col. Williams. Some Deerfield people under him were:—

Caleb Allen,	Nathaniel Davidson,	Phineas Nevers,
Asahel Amsden,	Nathaniel Dickinson,	Reuben Nims,
Richard Carey,	Hilkiah Grout,	Abraham Pease,
Jonathan Catlin,	Asa Hawks,	Samuel Stebbins,
Seth Catlin,	Moses Hawks,	Simeon Stebbins,
Moses Chandler,	Paul Hawks,	John Victory.
Barnabas Davidson,	Phineas Munn,	

The following is inserted as giving some idea of the service of scouts.

COLRAIN, May the 18, 1758.

S^r I have ordered the scout from this place to go once in a week to Deerfield River about 8 miles above the province Line, and fall town Scout to strike the North River 6 miles above us, and direct you to send your Scout once a week to Deerfield River at the province line. we have no news, but all well.

I am your sevent,   JOHN CATLIN.

[Addressed] To Sergt. Othniel Taylor, Charlemont, on his Magestys service.

COLRAIN, May the 30, 1758.

Sr Last Sunday night I rec'd an account from Sergt. Hawks that his Scout had made Some discovery of an Enemy not far from pelham fort. These are therefore to direct you to taek one man from your fort with you and go to Rice's, and taek two men there to Hawks' and taek Samuel Morrison with one man, five in whole, and go to the place where they took their start, and make a thourer Search, and if you make no discovery then carry the Scout as hy up as the province Line, and make return to me. Your Sevnt,

JOHN CATLIN.

To Sergt. Othniel Taylor, att Cherlymount.

May 27th, Capt. Salah Barnard marched his company from Deerfield to join his regiment in the army of invasion. They served through the whole campaign, returning in November. Thomas Alexander of Northfield was his ensign.

June 25th, three Deerfield men, Martin Severance, Matthew Severance and Agrippa Wells, with William Clark of Colrain, serving in Rogers's Rangers, were taken prisoners in a skirmish at Sabbath Day Point.

July 8th, Gen. James Abercrombie, who had succeeded Lord Loudon, led an army of seven thousand men against Ticonderoga, and was repulsed with a loss of nineteen hundred killed and wounded.

July 26th, Louisbourg surrendered to General Amherst, with all its stores, a large amount of shipping and three thousand men.

August 27th, Fort Frontignac, on the north side of Lake Ontario, with a large amount of cannon, ammunition and provisions, was taken by Gen. Bradstreet, which crippled the operations of the French at the westward. They were further weakened by the loss of Fort Du Quesne, which was occupied by Gen. James Forbes, Nov. 24th, the French garrison retiring upon his approach. This post was then named Pittsburg, which name it still bears. Secretary Pitt well deserved the honor of this name, for under the first year of his administration the power of France in North America received a shock from which it never recovered.

The only Indian visitation on our frontier not noticed was at No. 4, August 25th, when Asahel Stebbins was killed and his wife Lydia [Harwood] and Isaac Parker were captured.

September 24th, Capt. John Catlin of Deerfield died in the service at Burke's fort.

Maj.-Gen. Jeffrey Amherst succeeded Abercrombie to the command in America, and Pitt wrote him Dec. 29th in reference to future operations, "That you do immediately concert the properest measures for pushing the operations of the campaign with the utmost vigor early in the year by the invasion of Canada."

1759. In the campaigns of this year, so memorable in the colonial history of this country, Deerfield men took their full share. March 16th, Col. Williams was ordered to enlist or impress two hundred men from his regiment to join the army of Amherst at the Lake; and May 10th, one hundred more to go to No. 4, under Capt. Elijah Smith, to relieve Capt. Cruikshank, that he might join Amherst, and serve in the invading army. There was great enthusiasm this year in forwarding the campaign. The people felt sure that Pitt was in earnest, and they had great confidence in Amherst, his chosen leader. It was generally expected that the dark cloud, that shadow of death, which had for three quarters of a century hung over the northern frontier, was soon to be finally dispelled; and this faith was not in vain.

The last Indian raid on the frontiers of Massachusetts was that described in the following fragment of a letter from Sergt. John Taylor at Colrain, "To Maj. Elijah Williams, or Ensign Jos. Barnard at Deerfield:—"

COLRAIN, March ye 21, 1759.

Sir:—These are to inform that yesterday as Jos. McKoun & his wife were coming from Daniel Donitsons & had got so far as where Morrison's house was burned this day year, they was fired upon by the enemy about sunset. I have been down this morning on the spot and find no Blood Shed, but see where they led off Both the above mentioned; they had their little child with them.

I believe they are gone home. I think their number small, for there was about 10 or 12 came. * * * [Torn off.]

Hoyt gives the name of the above man as John McConn; and Rev. Stephen Williams as Joseph McEwers. Dr. Holland, who tells the story with a large amount of rigmarole, calls the name Joseph McConn or McCowen. In McClellan's sketch of Colrain I do not find the affair mentioned at all. Deerfield was bare of men, but when the news of this raid reached Northampton, Maj. Joseph Hawley came up with a party as far as Greenfield, but went no farther.

Gen. Amherst collected his army above Albany and moved

down Lake George against Ticonderoga, where he arrived July 21st. He felt so certain of a successful and speedy issue that on the 24th he wrote to the officer commanding at No. 4, that Ticonderoga "must soon surrender, and there is no occasion for your services where you are," and directed him to march at once for Albany. "I send one sergt and 3 rangers; keep one for a guide, the others will go to Fort Dummer." Amherst was not over confident, for July 27th, he took possession of the fort. It had been evacuated the night before by the French army, which made the best of its way towards Montreal.

September 18th, Quebec fell into the hands of the army, taken to its walls by Gen. James Wolfe. September 12th, a battle had been fought on the plains of Abraham, close by the city, in which the French were defeated. Montcalm, the French commander, and Gen. Wolfe were both killed on the field.

The glad news of the surrender of Quebec soon reached the frontiers. Everybody felt that the end of the French dominion and Indian devastation was nigh. October 8th, Col. Williams writes Pownell that he has dismissed all the garrisons but those at Fort Massachusetts and Hoosac. He says there are some swivels and stores to be cared for.

The following named men served in the regiment of Col. Israel Williams this year: Lieut.-Col., Oliver Partridge; Maj., Elijah Williams; 2d, Maj., Joseph Hawley; Captains, Joseph Barnard of Deerfield, (promoted from ensign), Seth Field, Joshua Lyman and Phineas Wright of Northfield; Benjamin Hastings and Timothy Childs of Greenfield; Jona. Dickinson and Zaccheus Crocker of Roadtown; Ebenezer Sheldon, Jr., of Falltown; Joseph Root and John Clapp of Montague.

Capt. Samuel Wells had command of the line of forts after John Hawks left for the army, June 4th. Capt. Hawks served in the regiment of Col. Ruggles, and was promoted to be major. Salah Barnard served as captain; Seth Catlin was his 2d lieutenant and Benj. Munn, sergeant. Other Deerfield men known to be in his company were:—

Samuel Allen,	Elijah Mitchell,	Ebenezer Tolman,
Eprhaim Ayers,	Noah Parker,	Ichabod Warner,
Jesse Billings,	Solomon Rugg,	David Watkins,
Thomas Billings,	Solomon Sawtelle,	Benjamin Wilson.
Barnabas Davidson,	John Simons,	

Sergt. Samuel Barnard, Obed Dinsmore and Abner Mitchell served under Capt. Elijah Smith. Consider Arms served under Capt. John Burke.

The Destruction of St. Francis.—No event of the war made so profound an impression on the Indians as the destruction of their settlement at St. Francis in Canada. This had long been the headquarters and point of departure for numerous expeditions against our frontiers, and the village was filled with spoil and trophies of the returning warriors. With the determination to break up this nest, Gen. Amherst issued the following order:—

CAMP AT CROWN POINT, Sept. 13, 1759.

You will this night set out with a detachment as ordered yesterday, *viz.:* of two hundred men, which you will take under your command, and proceed to Missisquay bay, from thence you will march and attack the enemy's settlements on the south side of the river St. Lawrence, in such a manner as you shall judge most effectual to disgrace the enemy, and for the success and honor of his Majesty's Arms.

Remember the barbarities that have been committed by the enemy's Indian scoundrels, on every occasion where they had opportunity of showing their infamous cruelties on the King's subject, which they have done without mercy. Take your revenge, but do not forget that though these villians have dastardly and permiscuously murdered the women and children of all ages, it is my orders that no women or children are killed or hurt.

When you have executed your intended service, you will return with your detachment to camp, or join me wherever the army may be. Yours, &c., JEFF. AMHERST.

To Maj. Rogers.

Rogers went down the lake in boats one hundred miles to Missisquoy Bay. Here he hid his boats and left two men to watch them, and on the 20th, pursued his march across the wilderness towards St. Francis. Two days later the two rangers overtook him with the news that the boats had been discovered and that four hundred men were on his trail. Rogers at once sent a party through the woods to Amherst, asking that provision be sent up the Connecticut river from No. 4 to meet him at Coos, and he began a forced march towards the doomed village, where he arrived on the evening of October 4th. The unsuspecting Indians were having a dance, which was kept up until four o'clock in the morning. Rogers having made his dispositions, at early dawn the English fell upon the sleeping Indians. In the darkness and confusion it was impossible to distinguish age or sex, and after daylight revealed several hundred English scalps flying from poles in the air, there was little disposition to heed the humane order of Amherst, and the slaughter was general. The village was burned, and Rogers began a retreat up the St. Francis river, towards the head waters of the Connecticut, in the greatest haste. Small parties attacked his rear, with some success, but after he had entrapped one party in an ambush, he had no more trouble from the French or Indians.

His battle now was with hunger. His provisions became exhausted about October 15th, and the command was broken up into small parties to find their way to Coos as best they could. As requested, Amherst had sent a supply by Lieut. Stevens, but the half-starved detachment with Rogers reached the rendezvous only to find that Stevens had abandoned the spot and carried off the provisions. His fires were still burning, and Rogers fired guns to bring him back. These were heard by Stevens, but only hurried his retreat. This cowardly and unexplained conduct of Stevens cost the lives of many men, who perished in the woods of fatigue and starvation. The whole loss of Rogers was about fifty men.

Probably no more acceptable service can be rendered to those interested in this campaign than to give what remains of the journal or orderly book of Samuel Merriman of Northfield, who was an officer in the regiment of Gen. Timothy Ruggles. It is fragmentary, and appears to be in two parts; one official entries, the other his own observations, but I have arranged both under consecutive dates. The original is to be seen in Memorial Hall. It was given by his descendants in Northfield.

Merriman was at Albany at the date of the first entry:—

May ye 27, 1759, Won hilandder whipt 300 Lashes.
May ye 29, Won Rodilander shot.
May ye 30, Won Rodilander whipt; we left Albany June ye 1, then we a rived att fort Edard June ye 6.
June ye 9, 1759, Recued ye 1 Lett at fort Edwad from Sister Marey, Dated May ye 21, 1769.
June ye 9, Then I mounted Main Garde in ye camp at fort Edard ye proole falmouth for ye Night.
June ye 14, we Leaft fort Edard & ariued at half way broock & made 3 gard Battrys.
June ye 17, 1759, this Day here came in a flag of truth; what they came for we no not at present.

P. S.—ye general told them that it is not a time of a year to exchange prisoners but giue them orders march of quick, for he told them that he Determined to paye them a uisit uary sun.

Camps Half way Broock June ye 21, 1759.

After orders a worcking party from ye Loques Consisting to tow Capt 6 subbs 8 sargt 2оо men to praid to Morer morning at 6 a'clock to be puntuel at ye time with out any excuse & to worch where ye Inscorat shall think proper, also a couering party consisting of wone cap, 3 subbs 4 sargents 100 rancks & file to gard at ye same time. Cornal Ingerson picket to atend unloding prouisian, If euer their be brought, if not their are to cot * * * at Busheses to couer ye prouisition according to ye Commissionenars Directtion, a couering party of 1 subb 1 sagt.

Halfway Broock, June ye 22 Day, 1759, friday, paroll Richman, Lut Corl Ingerson [Ingersol?] ofeser for ye Day to morrow, all Reports to be made att this— Capt Galord capt omphres of ye connetecotes are a meddately to strike thair tents & to [take] poosesion of ye stockades, capt Galord on ye Right of ye gate to command ye noreste triangle; Capt umphres on ye Left of ye gate to command ye souwest triangle; tha are to mount the gard with 1 corpt.& 6 men to a gard.

Whosoeuer is found Macking Disorder in ye Campes or Stockades after ye Retret, Beeing either by singing, swaring or any Noiss by which ye gard may be Disturbed & ye sentry not able to Distinguis any aproch of ye Enemy, if any shold be lurking—

Camps at Halfway Broocks, June 30, 1759, perole Richmond, Lt Col Engerson field offeser for ye Day. All gards to be moanted as yesterday—al worcking partys for to morrow consisting 1 cap, 2 subbs 2 sergt 150 Ranck & file.

ye connecticut Regement at 1 o'clock after noon to be under arms. al after Date ye agetent to exersise them in platoones, forming them two Deep, these orders Respecting exercising is to be continued after this Day from ye hour of 7 to nine in ye fore Noon & from 4 in ye after Noon until 6 o'clock. NA PAYSON.

Regtl orders that euery offeser commanding companys to giue in a Return of thire companys—setting forth whare as thire men—that euer was in theire companys as Well as those on Duty to be given to morrow morning by 7 o'clock & to be signed By ye Commanding offeser of each company on ye spot. it is expected that thay are made uary cuate as thay will be kept to examine otherse by.

for Nights pickets Lt Joseph Engersol cap. page Lut Wilder Lut Martin for ye Reduble to morrow.

Campts Halfway Broock July 2, 1759, paroule Colchester—all gards to be as mounted as youshal. after these orders are pubbleish heir is to be No fire within ye campes or within ye Lines of this encamptments after ye tattue is beet. whatever parson is found gilty of Disobaying these orders all former orders is to be strickly obayed, a Return to be giuen in to ye Agetent of all those men which ware in ye artilry seruis Last camppane. N. PAYSON.

This Day was killed 7 garses Blues & 1 wounded & 5 tacken at fort henry. theay was out a giting barck without thair armes.

July 4, Campts halfway Broock, 1759—after Proule Shonsbury—

Maj [John] Hawk field offeser for yᵉ Day a sub & 12 men from yᵉ Laynees to cot & burn all yᵉ Leaues & Brucsh that are with in yᵉ Loynes of Sentrys, a worcking party is to be preaded emeadately Consisting 1 cap 2 subbes 3 seart 50 priuates without armes.
N. PAYSON.

all gards to be mounted as ushal. as their seames to be sum Neglect of [one?] exersise it is expected for yᵉ futur that it will be more puntil for yᵉ futer. N. PAYSON.

General orders—it is vary Nitoriously tru that profane cosing & swaring praules in ye campt; it is vary far from yᵉ cristian solgers Deuty; it is not only vary Displasing to God armeyes, but dishonorable before men. it is theire fore Required & it will be expected that for yᵉ futer yᵉ odus sound of cosing & swaring is to be turned in to a prefoun silence. ifter yᵉ publish of these orders if any is found gilty of Bracking after these orders, theay may expect to suffer punishment, & all former orders to be observed. N. PAYSON.

Camps halfway Broock 5 Day 1759.

Rigimental orderss—prole Dubling.

All yᵉ gards to Be mounted as ushul—all axes & spades to haue yᵉ Noumber exactly Right was Left for yᵉ youse of this campts; if wanted after thay may haue them aplyed to yᵉ Quater master. who euer is found to secure one & it Bee None twill Be luct upon as imbastlen of yᵉ kings stores & must answer it accordingly.

Lut Col Englson field offeser for yᵉ Day he is to See yᵉ picket praided & giue them orders is going yᵉ rouns, as for some Night it hath been Neglected. all former orders to be obayed.

Camps at halfe way Broock, July yᵉ 8, 1759.

Prole Wulf—Majer Hawkes field offeser of yᵉ Day—all yᵉ gards to be Mounted as ushal. yᵉ offeser of yᵉ Quarter garde are to taek speshel care as that None of yᵉ oxen Belonging to yᵉ king which will be brought in to Night & put under thair care; if any should get out of yᵉ Sentry they must expect to be anserble for their Neglect—

No solger is upon any uow what soeuer Dow sleep or set Down when on Sentry; if any are or should be found Disobaying these orders for yᵉ futer—all those found sleeping will be sent to yᵉ prouow for trial & those seting will be seuerely punished—these orders to be Read his Night to each offeser of yᵉ Gard at 10 o'clock that it may giuen in Chargue Not only to all yᵉ solgers that are on duty this night but to continue from offeser to offeser when they are Reliued —all former orders to be obeaid. N. PAYSON.

Thare was a man killed by falling a tree on him.

July yᵉ 9 thare was 2 men killed by falling trees on him.

Campts Half way Broock, July 9, 1759.

Prole portsmouth—L Col Engsa—field offeser for yᵉ Day—all gards to be mounted as ushul; all yᵉ troops are to hold them in Redness to March att yᵉ shortest wornind at this campts. all former orders to Bee obaid. N. PAYSON.

Campt Half way Broock, July 10, 1759—Monday—Prole Southlinny [?] Majer Hawkes fieldoffeser for yᵉ Day. all yᵉ men of Deuty are to see emeadly heir armes are clean & set out in yᵉ sun; yᵉ pickate are also to turn out & praid ther armes & thay are Like-wise to set their armes clean & in good order. N. PAYSON.

Campts att Halfe way Broock July 11, 1759—Prole Sutbury—Lt Coll Ingersons field offeser for yᵉ day. All yᵉ tropes att this place excepte yᵉ garsion & Capt Shepardes companey to haue 3 days prouision 2 D of fresh & 1 of salt; one Hundred ax men from Lounes & fifty men from Coll Engersol yᵉ picket to couer them; they are to be praided at 2 o'clock P. M.

Campt at Half brock July 11 [12?] 1759.

a cort marchal to seet this Day at 9 o'clock to trie prisoners that shall be brought before them—capt Whittlese presedend & L Hambleton, Lut how, Lut tripp.

All former orders to Bee O Bayed.   N. PAYSON.

July yᵉ 14, 1759, this Day we left Halfe way Brock & came to Lackgorge. [Lake George.]

CAMPT LACKGEORGE, July 15, 1759—Sunday. This day we had a sarmon preetch yᵉ tex was in Jeremier yᵉ fortieth schapter & tenth vars. This was the first sarmon or publick prais that I haue Heard sense I left Olbany.

July yᵉ 18, CAMPTS ATT LACK gEORGE.

this day came a flag of truth to exchange prisoners; what Return they had Wee No Not. Wee Did not entertan them But Wone Night & sent them a way the Nex Day vary early in yᵉ morning.

CAMP LACK GEORGE, July 18, 1759.

this day our men went tow Loding artilery & prouision in yᵉ Battoe.

CAMPT LAKE GEORGE yᵉ 17, 1759, Proul Sopus—for yᵉ Day tomorror Col fetch field offeser—for yᵉ picket this Night, Regleres Magas Campbel prouuenshels Lt Col hunt—Majer Shipp to morer Night Regler Lut Darby—Prouenishales Lut Col Solislain—Majer Hawkes genrˡ gard to moreow—2 Battalons—Ruggles yᵉ prounshales will Resau 3 Days fresh prouision to morrow morning Beginning at 5 o'clock with whiting, foling Ruggles Wilard Louel Sciler woster fich & babcock, which compleat them to yᵉ 22 Inclusiue—yᵉ Batt of Ruggles wilard Louel & Babcok will each Discharg their defisiant arms & Resieue their amanition, flintes & Bayonets this day at 12 a clock by a plying to Mager ord commanding offeser of yᵉ Royal artiliry a cording to yᵉ Return sent in this Day.

It is Repted that yᵉ men are more puntil in turning out at Rolcaeling at Sun Set, which has Ben greatly Neglected Notwith standing a former orders of a commishoned ofeser attending which will not be Repeted again.

July 21, this Day Wee Set Sale for bogus & we sald as far as yᵉ second Narrows by yᵉ great smooth rock; we lay tossing in y₀ Lack all Night & slept None all Night & vary early yᵉ Nex morning wee saled about yᵉ Lacke till we found yᵉ Rigment & march to yᵉ Landing Run a shore with out any Interaption & march to yᵉ mills & Rogers met with a bout forty Engins & french; he killed fore french & tock 2 prisoners.

July 22, yᵉ fire continered from 9 in the morning till Darck & toock ten priseners.

July 23, our army marched up tow yᵉ frentch Brest worcks with out any molestason & went to trenchen upon yᵉ Enamies ground with in forty Rodes of yᵉ french fort their march in tow Rigments into yᵉ Intrenchments yᵉ enemies continued their fire vary smart— thee Enemi saled out vpon our intrenchmentes they killed one ensine & wound 14 teen & then yᵉ enemy Retired to their fort.

One year before Gen. Abercrombie had lost nineteen hundred men on this very ground in a rash attempt to carry the fort by storm. This costly lesson had not been lost upon Amherst, as we see by the next entry.

July yᵉ 25, 1759. Nothing extrodnary happend this Day only wone helander Col [Roger Townsend] & wone priuate killed with a canon ball. No firering upon our side, thee enemies fire is vary hauey. yᵉ armi hath entrench within 30 Rodes of yᵉ french fort our English went to yᵉ fort & fired at yᵉ sentry upon yᵉ wale. Some of our men went into yᵉ french garden & fetch a armfull ful of cabage to gen¹ & he gaue them tow dolares &c.

July yᵉ 26, 1759, this day yᵉ enemies fired vary smart til eleuen a clock at Night, then yᵉ enemy sot yᵉ Magazen on fire & blew up yᵉ fort & went abord theire botoe &c our English neuer fired won canon att yᵉ enemie till they im bark, then yᵉ fire was vary hot & toock 20 prisners—soe the sege was ouer a gainst ticontorogue, with grate Reioyceing. this Night Mr Rogers persued yᵉ enemie & came so close upon them they was a bligue to Run to Shore & Left their Batoe—So Mr Rogers tuck perssion of thayr batoe with a hundred bareles of powder & wone batoe Loded with french cotes & consideral Dele of other plunder.

July 27, this Day our armie was imployed about puting out yᵉ fire in yᵉ fort & hewing timber for tow sloops. yᵉ enemy fired 600-80 [680?] guns one Day.

July 28, r759, Nothing extrod hapend this Day.

July yᵉ 30, 1759. This day I was calld to yᵉ general Cort Marshal to be examened for kill a Desarter & was aqueted. Col. grant presedent of yᵉ Cort Marshel.

CAMPTS TICONDAROGUE, august yᵉ 2, 1759,—tuesday—this Day wee had a scout of men come in to yᵉ camp & Informed ous that they had Ben to grown poynt and toock posestion of yᵉ forte & for a token that they had Benn to yᵉ forte yᵉ Lut said he went & wrote his name on yᵉ flag stafe & broat some cowcombers & aples from there. So yᵉ gineral sent of this night Majr Rojers with fifteen 1500 men to take posesion of sᵈ garison.

Aug. 3, 1759, this Day there is a Reguler to be hanged for Desearshon & was exceactuted this Day.

agust yᵉ 4, 1759, Satterday, this Day some of our army set out upon yᵉ march to Canaday.

August yᵉ 5, 1759, this Day we Set Sale for Crown poynt at 5 cloch & ariued at Crown poynt at 8 oclocke; we a riued Safe with out any Interrupison.

MONDAY, CROWNPOINT, august 6, 1759.

Nothing extrodnary Hapened this Day.

Tuesday, august yᵉ 7, 1759, crownpoynt this Day I eate a Dinner of green peas in Crownpoynt.

Campts Crown poynt, august yᵉ 12, this Day I receiued tow Letters from home to my Rcioycing at yͤ well fare from their—won from my Son dated July 13, thee other letter Dated July 16.

CAMP AT CROWN POYNT, PROWL AMBAY.

This day I Mounted yͤ Quarter gards 1 Ensine of yͤ gard one sart tow corp'l 29 men.

Crownpoynt, Sept 29, 1759, proal Kensington—for to morrow—Col Montgomry for yͤ pickate this night, regulars, Magʳ hambleton; prouenchales Lt Col Saltonson for yͤ workes to morer royal helanders. magʳ John Whitney of yͤ Rhodesland Rigt has Reciud a commisshon of a Lt Col of sᵈ Rigt & capt Ebanazer Whiting has Reseiud a commisshon as Magʳ & they are to be obayd as shuch.

There are few entries for two months. Amherst was busy in repairing the fort and building a fleet for further operations. The diary begins again:—

Campt crownpoint, October 7, 1759. This day our men are imployed Loding grate gones & artillry stores.

Campt crownpoynt, Oct 8-9-10, for these seural days our men haue been Imployed a bout fixing sales for their battoes & whale botes.

Oct yͤ 11, 1759, this day our genral Set Sale with yͤ fleet to Saint John jest at son set with fiue thousandes & fiue hndred men. they are gone with a brigteen which mounts 20 gones thee briggs name Comberland; yͤ sloope montes 160 gones; yͤ Read Doe [Rideau] mountes 6 twelve pounders & won large mortar, & two arke which mounted 1-24 pounder each & some morters & seuerl boets & three Rogaleys which mounted won 18 pounder each & some morters besides some 6 & 8 pounders & pritey many swifles.

Campst Crownpoint, October yͤ 23, 1759—after genˡ orders yͤ offesers & men for yͤ work for yͤ Day are to praid to morrow morning; Col Ruggls is to a Quant yͤ offesers of yͤ prounshals troops th by a vote of yͤ assemble of that prouence of the 6 of October which yͤ governor have transmitted to the genr'l that Not with standing yͤ time for which yͤ troops for yᵈ present expedition a ganst Canaday Dose expire on yͤ first Day of November Nex, if thiar saruice should be found nesary beyond that time, thare pay shall be continnued to yͤ first of Desember Nex. Col Skiler is to a Quant yͤ offesers & priuate men of yͤ garsey troops, that yͤ goueirner in form yͤ genˡ that there is prouision made to yͤ 15 of Nouember & that if thair saruis is Required be yound that time thay will be payd to yͤ Day of their Return. All yͤ offesers & men of yͤ aboue troopes are to be inform of this by Respecttiue offersers & to be assured that the genˡ will Not keep them a Day longer in yͤ field than what is absolute Nasasry for yͤ safty and presvation of his majistys faithful subgietes in a merica & to put out of yͤ power of yͤ enemi to make any more inuasion of yͤ inhabitance which will be a fectible don by cecuiong yͤ fort at crownpoint.

Amherst did not penetrate Cañada; the season and the elements were against him, and he brought his army back to Crown Point, where he went into winter quarters October

21st, and the dispatches above noted were promulgated. He began at once to prepare for the next year's campaign. That he might open a more direct communication with New England he projected a road over the Green Mountains to connect Crown Point with No. 4. This is the work referred to in the following entries in Sergt. Merriman's journal:—

Campt crownpoint, October 26, 1759, friday this day we set out to clean a rode to No. 4. we crost the Lake about Sun set & then campt.

Satterday the 27, camp east side of ye Lak upon Mager Hawks Rode; this day we sot out to clear ye Rode & cleard as far as 2 mile Brook & we campt. Nothing extraordinary haped this Day.

Sabath October ye 28, 1756, this Day we cleard 4 miles & then campt.

Monday October 29, 1759 this day we marched 2 miles & then came to a stream & made a brigue ouer & then marched 2 miles further & then came to a Nother large stream & there we campt &c.

Tuesday October ye 30, 1759, We maid ye great brigue & march 3 miles & then camp.

October ye 31, 1759, then march 2 miles & then we eat diner.

So ends the journal for 1759, and so ended Maj. Hawks's road from the lake eastward. The next season it was met by one from No. 4, westward. Probably Merriman was engaged on that. Certainly he was with the army of invasion and "in at the death," as appears by the following from his journal:—

Camptes Islenox, august 25, [1760]. Wee opened our Batryes a gainst our Enemy & continuing our fire vary smart—

Camps Islenox augst ye 28, this day the enemy left this place & we toock possession of the same without much Lose—

Campt Isilanox august, this day wee left this plase & Set Sale for sant Johns & sald in about a mile & a half of Sant Johns & by bracke of Daye we campt in sit of this plase & when we was Discouered the Enemy set the fort on fire & made the best of their way of & we Landed & then we coockt some uicttles & then we persued ye enemy; we ouer toock ye Enemy & they fired upon the front of our army & killed 2 & wounded 1 or tow of our men. we goat ye ground & drove them into their brest work & perciuing ye enemy tow numrous for our scout wee turned back to Sant Johns & then wee met our army & in camp here.

Campst att Sants Johns, September ye 1, 1760, this Day we Set Sale for Sant tarnerres & their we met with no Resistance.

September 2, 1760, ye Rengers went down to Shamblee & when we came in site of ye fort we sent a small cout to tack som prisenders & was succeeded & they inform us they would not surrender the fort without fireing two cannon at them. So we returned back to to sant tanerres.

Camp Shamblee, Sept ye 4, this Day we came to this place & Laid

Sheed 12 clock & toock possion of yᵉ fort at son set & toock their armies.

Campt Shamble Sunday 7 day, this Day we set out for Mount Rial; we trauel with in about three miles of Lapprany & there we in campt & ——

September yᵉ 8 we came to Mount Riel & as we came in site with our armie, the enemy capetilateed & gaue up the Sity.

The object of the campaign of 1760 was the capture of Montreal, the last stronghold of the French in the country, and three armies were sent against the doomed city. Amherst, the commander-in-chief, led one by the way of the Mohawk river, Lake Ontario and down the St. Lawrence. He reached Montreal island September 6th. Gen. Murry, with an army from Quebec, went up the St. Lawrence and reached the lower end of the island September 7th. Col. Howland led the third army down Lake Champlain and St. Johns river and, as we have seen, struck the St. Lawrence opposite the island September 8th. This was probably the most remarkable conjunction of independent armies in the annals of the world, each marching and fighting its way for hundreds of miles, and all arriving at the destined point within the space of three days.

September 8th, Vaudreuil surrendered Montreal to Amherst, and the whole of Canada was at last in the hands of the English.

With this surrender the power of France in Canada passed away forever, and with it all danger of Indian incursion. Without the encouragement of French priests, the aid of French government and the lead of French officers, the Indian was henceforth powerless for evil. He had not been battling in defense of his own rights or to revenge his own wrongs. He was only the blind instrument of Romish zeal and French greed of dominion. No one versed in the history of the times will for one moment doubt the truth of this statement.

Many Deerfield men served in this closing campaign. John Hawks was commissioned major in Ruggles's regiment February 10th and made lieutenant colonel July 10th. Seth Catlin, who went out as lieutenant, was appointed quartermaster in the same regiment. Other men were Capt. Salah Barnard, who came back a major; Sergt. Phineas Munn, Samuel Allen, Jesse Billings, Lebeus Childs, Barnabas Davidson, Elisha

Hinsdale, Joseph King, Reuben Nims, Nathaniel Parker, Ebenezer Tolman, Samuel Shattuck, each of whom served from March 1st to December, 1760.

The final treaty of peace was signed at Paris, Feb. 10th, 1763.

Great credit has been given William Penn for buying of the native owners, the land on which he located his settlements; and historians have contrasted his proceedings with those of the founders of New England, to the discredit of the latter, and have declared that the early wars in which they were engaged, and the peaceful relations between the Indians and the Quakers, could be traced directly to their respective treatment of the aborigines in that matter; entirely overlooking the bloody wars in which hundreds of Pennsylvania settlers were butchered by the Indians.

To be sure, these statements are not true; but the assertions are so often and so confidently made, that people generally suppose there must be *some* foundations for them in fact. But Gov. Winslow, in May, 1676, declared in writing, that until the breaking out of Philip's War, the English did not possess one foot of land in the colony that had not been fairly bought of the Indian owners. This was sixteen years after the settlement of our town. Deeds in Memorial Hall at Deerfield, executed in 1666-7, prove that Dedham had bought of those claiming to be the owners, every acre she occupied at Pocumtuck under the Legislative grant of Oct. 11th 1665. Again it is a fact to be borne in mind, but generally overlooked, that the Eight Thousand-acre Grant was not a conveyance of the fee in the soil, but only of the right to buy the land of the native owners. For it was the law of the land that no white man could buy any territory of the Indian, or even take it from him as a *gift*, without leave of the authorities, under a penalty of £5 per acre. And it is patent to every student of our colonial history, that the rights of the Indians were carefully guarded, in good faith, by the practice of the civil courts, as well as by legislation. But here, then as always and everywhere in the court of war, the soil remained with the party having the strongest battalions.

If Chauk, sachem of Pocumtuck;—if Masseamet, alias Milkenaway;—if Grinneackchue, Kunckkeasacod, and their brother Ahimunquat, alias Mequannitchall;—if Mashshalisk, the old woman, and Wuttawwalunksin, her son, and Ackaumbowet, her kinsman, were the actual owners of certain lands at Pocumtuck, called Scowockcooke, Tomholissick, Masquomcossick, Nayyocossick, Wequnuckcaug, Pacommegon, Allinnackcoock, Taukkanackcoss, Manteleleck, Manepaccossick, Pemawachuwatunck, and other tracts, with kindred names, then our ancestors became the true and lawful owners of them all by fair bargain and sale. But, says the critic, the price paid was next to *nothing*; the Indian was practically cheated out of his heritage by the more knowing Dedhamite. Was he? Let us see. In estimating the value of the land, we must roll back the years to the period of the sale, and look upon the transaction in the light of contemporaneous evidence. By this it appears that Dedham paid more than the *market value* of the land in hard cash, in addition to giving up to Eliot's Indians, at Natick, one acre for every four they got at Pocumtuck. The proof of this is,—to repeat a statement made in Chap. I,—that before the place was settled, a block of four hundred and fifty acres of selected land at Pocumtuck, was publicly offered for sale, at two pence per acre in advance of the average price paid for the whole tract; to be paid for, "2-5 in corn, and 3-5 in cattle." No buyers appeared on these terms, although one-third of the lot was of the best meadow land in the town of Deerfield. This seems a fair criterion of the value of real estate to the English at that period.

While it is probably true that the Indian did not fully realize the ultimate result of his sale, he did know as well as his white brother that a change in the ownership of land meant a change of occupants. Thus much he had learned in his wars of conquest.

We have before given the transactions relating to the occupation of the territory by the Pocumtucks, their expulsion by the Mohawks, the grant by the General Court, and the purchase by the grantees, as they appeared on the face. But a peep under the surface will be necessary to a clearer understanding of the supposed rights or wrongs in the case. The critic says the Dedhamites drove a sharp bargain with the ignorant savage. If he will look at the matter a little more carefully, perhaps he will discover that the few remaining Pocumtucks were original Yankees, quite a match for the unsophisticated Englishmen, in this particular real estate transaction. No evidence is found, except in one case, that the parties who received pay for the land sold were ever the *owners* of it. We have evidence that, if they ever did own the land, it had passed years before to the Mohawks, by the right of conquest, according to Indian custom and practice. So the grantors certainly sold what did not belong to them. Again, had the title still remained with them, as they claimed, the land had, under the circumstances, no real or nominal value to them; they could neither regain it by conquest, nor occupy it as it lay. In the hands of the English, however, it would be of real value to them, for they had shrewdly reserved the right of hunting, fishing, and gathering wild fruits. These rights they might hope to utilize under the protection of the new owners. If taking possession under these deeds should involve the English in a war with the Mohawks, in whom the fee was really vested, so much the better. So long as the whites could hold their own, their enemy would be the losers, and the English be the avengers of their blood. These are the simple facts in the case, and who shall say that the Indian did not fully comprehend and act upon them? After all, and back of all, there lie the fundamental questions:

What right had the civilized man to be here at all? What rights have savages in the face of civilization? The casuist has the field.

It will not do to say of the early wars that the Indian was a patriot warrior, fighting to recover land unjustly taken from him by the English, as many writers urge. In no case, can the origin of Indian hostilities in New England be traced to any claimed infringement by the whites on territory of the natives, with a single exception of the Eastern war of 1723. Even then it has been clearly shown that the hostile Abenakis, in this case, were only puppets in the hands of the Canadian governor De Vaudreuil, who moved them at will through his agents, Father La Chase and Father Rasle. [See ante, page 391.]

In the dastardly attack at Deerfield, Feb. 29th, 1704, it was not—as sentimental writers have often professed to believe—a desperate attempt on the part of the Pocumtuck tribes to get possession of their favorite haunts and the graves of their ancestors. Not a Pocumtuck, nor the son of a Pocumtuck, wagged a finger in the affair. The expedition was purely a stroke of French policy, and not the slightest attempt was made to hold the captured town for the Indians. The assaults of the red man on the white, when not prompted by the French, were the natural outgrowth of his taste for a state of warfare and the glory to be thereby gained—a relish *not yet extinct*—and an insatiate desire for scalps to adorn his wigwam, and plunder to make the hard life of its inmates more easy.

One of the great questions of the day is the "*Indian Question,*" and much is being done to arouse the people to a sense of its importance. Agents are sent all over the land to enlist sympathy in behalf of the gentle savage. It is fashionable to ignore his deviltries, or apologize for them, and to dwell at length upon his wrongs. Orators go about abusing our ancestors for their alleged abuse of the Indian, forgetting the enthusiastic and persistent efforts of our fathers to civilize and Christianize the race, and that at a time when public opinion on both sides of the sea was *unanimous* in favor of the undertaking, and also failing to chronicle the almost utter failure to make upon their subjects any permanent impression for good.

Mrs. Rowlandson, a captive among the hostiles in Philip's War, says of Eliot's "Praying Indians" among them, "they were the *worst wolves* in the whole bloody crew."

This is not a new subject. To our ancestors for several generations the "Indian Question" was the great question of their lives. To its importance they were fully alive,—that is, if they were left alive at all. It needed no member of Congress to arouse the people. The Indians themselves did that most effectually, and the enlistment was not of sympathy for the marauding savage, but of soldiers to succor the scattered settlers and to protect, so far as possible, their wives and children from the butcheries of the inhuman barbarians.

ImTheStory.com

Personalized Classic Books in many genre's

Unique gift for kids, partners, friends, colleagues

Customize:
- Character Names
- Upload your own front/back cover images (optional)
- Inscribe a personal message/dedication on the inside page (optional)

Customize many titles Including
- Alice in Wonderland
- Romeo and Juliet
- The Wizard of Oz
- A Christmas Carol
- Dracula
- Dr. Jekyll & Mr. Hyde
- And more...

CPSIA information can be obtained
at www.ICGtesting.com
Printed in the USA
BVOW06s1247080517
483260BV00028B/382/P

HARDPRESS
Classics Series

In this collection we are offering thousands of classic and hard to find books. This series spans a vast array of subjects – so you are bound to find something of interest to enjoy reading and learning about.

Subjects:

Architecture
Art
Biography & Autobiography
Body, Mind &Spirit
Children & Young Adult
Drams
Education
Fiction
History
Language Arts & Disciplines
Law
Literary Collections
Music
Poetry
Psychology
Science
...and many more.